AF559628

INDIAN GOVERNMENT AND POLITICS

(Third Revised Edition)

Dr. S. S. Awasthy

Department of Political Science

PGDAV College, University of Delhi, New Delhi

HAR-ANAND

PUBLICATIONS PVT LTD

Revised Edition, 2013

Reprint, 2024

Published by Ashok Gosain and Ashish Gosain for
HAR-ANAND PUBLICATIONS PVT LTD
E-49/3, Okhla Industrial Area, Phase-II, New Delhi-110020
Tel: 41603490
E-mail: info@haranandbooks.com/haranand@rediffmail.com
Shop online at: www.haranandbooks.com

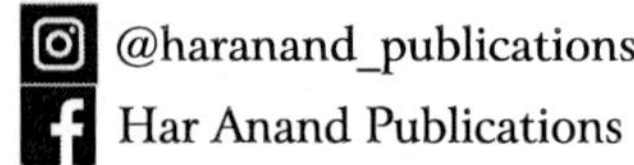

Printed in India

Preface

This book has been written keeping in view the requirements of the undergraduate students of Delhi University. It is very difficult for any book on Indian Government and Politics to be totally updated a for it is not only an explosive subject but also a very—fast changing one. However, we have endeavoured to cover these developments till date. It is hoped that the present work would help both the students as well as the teachers of our discipline. I am thankful to scholars who have been duly acknowledged in the text. For the rest, I express my gratitude for having learnt from them through their scholarly attempts. I also take this opportunity to thank many of my colleagues and friends without whose support this effort would not have seen the light of day. Among them, Dr. N.D. Arora, B.S. Bagla, Dr. Sunder Raman, Dr. S.N. Talwar, Kusum Lata Chadha, Dr. R.M. Bhardwaj, Dr. Kusum Kaushik and Maindar Singh, Advocate, Supreme Court, deserve special thanks for their invaluable suggestions and cooperation. I thank O.P. Grover, Librarian, PGDAV College, New Delhi and his entire staff who have always extended their hearty support whenever needed. The library staff of Nehru Memorial Museum Library, Teen Murti Bhawan, was equally courteous and ever-obliging. I acknowledge their cooperation. I also wish to thank my parents, wife, daughter Ayushi and little son Vaibhav who always had the complaint of being neglected at the cost of this book. I also thank Narendra Kumar, Ashok Gosain and Ashish Gosain for their cooperation and for publishing this book.

S.S. AWASTHY

Preface to the Third Revised Edition

Over the years Indian politics has been undergoing a period of tremendous transitions—creating, developing and nurturing the varied human emotions of joy and sorrow, love and hatred, hope and despair. Lately, there is a sense of desperation, frustration and all hopes seem to be lost in the hazy horizon of politics. Terrorism has become a major menace, a dreaded disease in our body politic, afflicting the lives of millions of people.

Besides, we have gigantic problems, of corruption and criminalisation of politics, which need to be addressed nationally and above narrow political considerations, as they are eating into the vitals of this country. As a result, the country seems to be drifting into chaos and increasingly losing its historical and cultural moorings. We need concerted efforts to pull back India from its present crisis. But this is not a crisis of stability, for, in my view, Indian social, economic and even political infrastructure is strong enough to withstand such instability. Over the years, I also discern a growing maturity among the political players of India and hence I find nothing remorseful about it. But terrorism, corruption and criminalisation of politics alarm me because, if not dealt judiciously they have a potential of developing into a nexus which will attack our democratic roots. And let us face it, we have no option to democracy. Democracy is the fabric of our diversified political culture which clubs us into our single national identity of being Indians. Undoubtedly, Indian nationalism is very potent as it has strong historical and cultural roots which continue to strengthen us, even in the hours of crisis. But we cannot take things for granted. As a student of Indian Government and politics, I have always been optimistic as I have an unshaken faith in my country, but definitely we need to march forward beyond words which have lost meaning in the present context of empty promises and high rhetoric. The crisis that India faces today, is the crisis of living peacefully, fearlessly and safely. The common man's fundamental right to life is under threat from many known and unknown elements, including the state. It is this crisis which is to be addressed not only by the policy— makers and the political and social activists of India, but also by the people of India who, on November 26, 1949 adopted, enacted and gave to themselves the Constitution of India which, fortunately, has withstood the onslaughts of all chaos and confusions created after its adoption. But the problem is the vast ignorance prevalent among the people regarding the Indian Constitution which definitely is bliss for those shortsighted and self-centred criminals who venture into politics to gain legitimacy and create an atmosphere which can only breed crime and violence. If, somehow, this book goes far beyond the academic community to the people of India, my labour will achieve its end.

It is always a matter of great satisfaction and pride for an author when his work is welcomed and appreciated by the academic community. This work, first published in 1999, was an instant success and found its due place among the writings on Indian Government and Politics. I am happy to present this second revised edition to the discerning readers. In fact any book on Indian Politics needs to be updated ever so often because of its immensely dynamic and ever-changing subject.

I take this opportunity to thank my colleagues Dr N.D. Arora, Dr Sunder Raman, Dr Kusum Kaushik, Dr Kusumlata Chaddha, and Shri B.S. Bagla and friends who have helped in their respective ways in preparing this edition. Finally, I put on record my gratitude and appreciation to Narendra Kumar, in particular, who, being an acknowledged author, has always been very kind to me. I also express my sincere thanks to Ashok Gosain and Ashish Gosain for bringing out this book so expeditiously and so elegantly.

S.S. AWASTHY

Contents

and again stressed the need for rapid socio-economic transformation of Indian society.

Let us now examine the state of affairs in Indian polity, economy and society on the eve of Indian Independence.

Indian Polity in 1947

India inherited a fragmented political system where national unity was not achieved. A variety of factors were responsible for political problems which were threatening the very existence of India as a nation. There were apprehensions that India would not remain one, but would break up into many countries. The Indian communists, in particular, had developed a multi-national theory of India which meant India was composed of many nationalities who could form their own nation-states. On the basis of this theory, they had supported the creation of Pakistan. Nehru had expressed surprise at the "....attitude of the Indian communists who wanted to create a dozen or perhaps more divisions of India." Some of the aspects of Indian polity were as follows:

1. *Law and Order Problem*

The British decision to grant independence on 15th August 1947 was a hasty one. Further, the independence was achieved at the cost of partition of the country into two countries—India and Pakistan. This partition was done on the basis of a two-nation theory, which declared Hindus and Muslims as two nations and, therefore, entitled to two separate states. The Muslim majority areas in East and West were carved out of India to become an independent state of Pakistan. However, in both states, there was a considerable number of Hindu and Muslim minorities. The sudden decision to grant freedom to India and Pakistan created panic among the minorities. The Hindus left their homes in Pakistan for India. Similarly, a considerable number of Muslims decided to move to Pakistan. There was no official arrangements for these migrations, nor any planning on the part of the two governments. With the result, that people were left to make their own arrangements for the purpose. The problem became more grave as the British decided to withdraw their troops from India. The Indian army was ill-equipped and ineffective in controlling the situation. The communal riots had already plagued the Indian sub-continent from 16 August 1946 with the Muslim League's call of direct action, which rendered about 4000 people dead, 15,000 injured and 1,00,000 homeless. Very soon entire Bengal was burning with communal frenzy. The trouble spread to Bihar, Bombay and UP. Early 1947 saw the breakdown of law and order in Punjab due to communal violence. On the midnight of 15th August 1947, fresh riots broke out again in Amritsar in India and Lahore in Pakistan. Very soon the entire nation was affected.

More than a million were butchered in the partition that followed the Indian independence. The exact number of those killed still remains a mystery. History provides no similar instance of such a large quantity of migration in such a small time. About eleven and a half million were rendered refugees and came to India. They further aggravated the law and order situation, and the major task before free India was their swift rehabilitation.

By withdrawing the British troops—if the British intention was to exhibit to the world that only they could maintain law and order in the communally—infected India—they had succeeded at least temporarily. The new rulers of India could not control the situation. The communally inclined police was hardly expected to do the same and the Indian army rendered ineffective in the face of swift developments that followed the partition.

In fact, law and order had completely collapsed in most parts of northern India. The authors of *Freedom at Midnight* have this to say about the plight of refuges coming from Pakistan: "The human debris left behind by those columns (of refugees) was terrible. The forty five miles of roadside from Lahore to Amritsar, along which so many passed, became a long, open graveyard. Before going down it, Capt. Atkins would always sprinkle a handkerchief with after-shave lotion and tie it around his face to temper the terrible smell. 'Each yard of the way', he remembered, `there was a body, some butchered, some dead of cholera. The vultures had become so bloated by their feasts they could no longer fly, and the wild dogs so demanding in their taste they ate only the livers of the corpses littering the road." Within a month of India's independence, even Delhi seemed to be out of control of the new rulers. Ultimately, under the leadership of Lord Mountbatten, an emergency committee was formed, which brought some semblance of law and order in the country.

The contribution of Gandhi in this gigantic task cannot be under-estimated Mountbatten referred to him as 'One man Boundary Force.' On 15th August 1947, Bengal was peaceful only due to his efforts. Mountbatten said "In the Punjab we have 55,000 soldiers and large scale rioting on our hands. In Bengal our force consists of one party of the Sikhs. Tara Singh openly declared that Sikhs would live under a united India. However, if India was to be partitioned, he demanded a separate Sikh state with the right to federate with India or Pakistan.

Apart from the religious minorities, we had linguistic minorities as well. Different linguistic groups were demanding separate states for themselves. Congress had also accepted the redrawing of the Indian map according to languages before independence. Its 1946 Election Manifesto explicitly recognised the need for reorganisation of states on linguistic lines. But now after the partition, Congress leaders took altogether a different view. For them it was a divisive threat to the national unity. In 1948, Dar Commission was appointed to look into the demand for separate provinces of Andhra Pradesh, Kerala, Karnataka and Maharashtra. It rejected the concept of linguistic states as detrimental to the growth of Indian nationalism. Dar Commission's report attracted widespread criticism from the different parts of the country. However, Congress was adamant. Its own committee, which included Nehru, Patel and P. Sitaramayya as members, was oblivious to the demand for creation of states on linguistic lines. The report of the committee stated,

".... We feel that the present is not an opportune time for the formation of new provinces. It would unmistakably retard the process of consolidation of our gains, dislocate our administrative, economic and financial structure, let loose, while we are still in a formative state, forces of disruption and disintegration, and seriously interfere with the progressive solution of our economic and political difficulties...." They left this question for the future `if public sentiment is insistent and overwhelming.' Later on, of course, they had to accept such demands and 1956 saw the redrawing of India's political map on linguistic lines.

4. *Democracy—Still in its infancy*

Indian political leadership was committed to democratic ideals and aspirations. They had experienced it in British rule and had a training under Dyarchy introduced by 1919 Act and limited provincial autonomy under 1935 Act. However, the franchise was highly limited. The constituent Assembly of India had been elected by 14.2 per cent of the Indian population. Now, the free India was committed to universal adult franchise where the large population had no experience of democracy. The political culture, we inherited, was basically an authoritarian culture. Thus the task before the leaders of free India was gigantic: to inculcate the spirit of tolerance which India of 1947 was lacking, and to create an atmosphere where democratic political institutions could acquire legitimacy among the people. Nehru was confident about the democratic experiment being a success despite ignorance, illiteracy and poverty. But there were many who were ready to accept his views only with a pinch of salt.

5. *1947—An era of Change and Continuity*

In India, politically two significant changes took place in 1947. Firstly, the transfer of power from British to Indians hands. India acquired the status of Dominion within British Commonwealth of Nations. Indian people became sovereign in the casting of their destiny.

Second was the change at the level of ideology of the administration. The British administration aimed at the sustenance of British rule and was primarily concerned with maintenance of law and order with a view to exploit India economically. The sustenance of British rule was achieved by a policy of divide and rule. For the purpose, the differences between different ethnic groups were not only further accentuated, but new hostile groups were also created and encouraged to inhibit the development of an all-Indian nationalism. The British hardly took any steps for the emancipation of India. Besides exploiting India, they viewed this country in the context of their worldwide interests in expanding and maintaining the British empire on which the sun never used to set. The contribution of the British-Indian army in the First and Second World Wars, the British conquest of China and their expeditions to Afghanistan can never be under-estimated.

However, all this changed in 1947. The free India was to become a democratic welfare state in which the differences between different groups could not be exploited; rather they were to be conciliated with the overall objective of achieving national unity. No longer would India be a colony to serve the interests of the imperial power. Now the objective of polity and administration would be the welfare of the people of India and to achieve the status of a prosperous country. In other words, independence created a revolution, raising expectations among the masses as well as the political leaders, as the major impediment to the development was no longer there.

Yet there was a lot of continuity, which India inherited from the British Raj as Brown puts it, "The institution of government, the structure of society and the fundamental beliefs of most Indians did not change just because the Union Jack was lowered." The changes that took place were in the highest echelons of government and the bureaucracy. The Indians replaced the Britishers. The Communist Party of India took this to another extreme by saying that it was transfer of power from the foreign bourgeois to native bourgeois. Therefore it rebelled against the Nehru government, the latter reacted ferociously, and with venegance, and succeeded in putting down the rebellion.

The factors of continuity were many which contributed substantially to achieving a peaceful and united India from the chaos and confusion of partition which had threatened the very survival of this country. First, came the institutional structure that India inherited. Undoubtedly, the vast Indian masses were naive about the democratic working of the government, yet 14.2 per cent of her population had exercised its right to vote in various elections to provincial and imperial legislative assemblies. The political leadership had acquired enough skill and expertise in running the parliamentary institutions during the British regime. Lutyens had already built a new capital of India—New Delhi—with vast and dignified government offices and structures manned by Indians. This was in sharp contrast to Pakistan, which had to construct its new capital city. Secondly, we inherited a strong bureaucracy which was the steel frame of the British empire. After the First World War, which had left about 6,80,000 English people dead, English recruitment to the Indian Civil Service became increasingly difficult and a large number of Indians joined the civil services. Although the bureaucracy was to be divided between India and Pakistan on religious basis and a certain number of Muslim bureaucrats left to Pakistan, yet the number in India's bureaucracy in 1947 was about three million. With these able, trained and experienced bureaucrats, India was able to recover from chaos of partition.

Nehru, before 1947, had stressed the creation of a new order without Indian bureaucracy. During the entire freedom movement, Congress had despised the bureaucracy and its Indian members as elite, Indian in colour but British in mind. But now the leadership, after assuming power, recognised it as a source of stability. The bureaucracy remains even today the steel frame of the Indian political system. Patel paid a befitting tribute in 1949 at the Constituent Assembly debate. He said, "I have worked with them during these difficult periods. They are patriotic, loyal, sincere, and able. Remove them and I see nothing but a picture of chaos all over the country."

Thirdly, the Indian Army was another positive factor. The Indian army inherited the apolitical traditions of British Raj. Even at the time of heightened communal flames, and political and civilian chaos, it maintained its apolitical and secular character. Hindus and Muslims—all were one in giving highest praise for the role of the Indian army during the communal disturbances. India's democratic experiment owes its success, to a great extent, to the apolitical nature of the Indian army. This is in contrast to the Pakistani army which always remained communal and political. Hence democracy in Pakistan always remained unstable.

Fourthly, India of 1947 inherited a well-organised, huge, political organisation with a broad mass base—the Indian National Congress. During the long period of struggle for swaraj, Congress was able to entrench itself sufficiently in this vast country. To inflame the spirit of swaraj in the entire nation, Congress organisations had extended to every city, district and even small villages, thereby becoming a vanguard of national unity. Because of the Congress Party, India had no problem in taking over the reins of power from the British. Brown rightly says:

"Congress was itself responsible for this fundamental continuity in the institutions of government and consultation—not just by its stance in the Constituent Assembly, but because of its pre-independence role. By cooperating in the provincial institutions through which the British devolved power, by mobilising men unversed in the politics appropriate to such arenas and encouraging and educating a widening social range of supporters to value them, it lowered foreign imports on to an indigenous social structure. By helping the reformed structures to strike deep social roots and ensuring that they responded to the needs of local people it made them effective and durable." It was the Congress Party under the able and secular leadership of Nehru and Patel who could assimilate the various divergent tendencies and formulate the Indian Constitution which was secular and acceptable to all the different segments of Indian people.

Indian Economy on the Eve of Independence

The economic scene, on the eve of independence, was full of both positive as well as negative indicators. This situation was a result of several long-term processes, which had been in operation during the

British political dominance. Prior to the advent of British East India Company, India had experienced military invasions as well as political subjugation at the hands of invaders from Central Asian warlords. However, the subjugation to those invaders was significantly different in one respect: invaders decided to settled down here and rule. The British were different in the sense that they had no intention of settling down here. Their objective was to control India's trade with the rest of the world, extract maximum possible riches from here and use the same for the advancement of their own economy back home.

1. The Agriculture

The advent of the British affected several aspects of the Indian economy. Agriculture was affected in at least two ways—

(a) Britishers introduced a new system of revenue collection. This system came to be known as Zamindari system.

(b) There took place, virtually, a forced commercialisation of agriculture.

(a) *The Zamindari System:* Beginning with Permanent Settlement of Bengal in late 18th century, this system of revenue collection was later on extended to the entire Gangetic plains. Under the system, a number of villages were together designated as one revenue estate and revenue collection rights were handed over to the highest bidder in open auction. This successful bidder was allowed to retain one share of the bid amount for his own use and expenses, the rest was to be deposited with the treasury of the company. This amount was deemed to have been fixed permanently. Therefore, it was given the name of Permanent Settlement.

This system was good in one sense. The rulers knew how much revenue was to be collected every year. The revenue receipts were also sought to be insulated against fluctuations, which used to arise on account of changes in the spread and intensity of monsoon. However it was, and later turned out to be, a highly exploitative system which did not permit any development in agriculture, nor allowed any possibilities of rise in the share of the state on account of possible rise in the productivity. These revenue–collectors gradually promoted themselves in the social hierarchy. Now they would not collect land revenue on their own. They hired a chain of subordinates to assist in this task. Increase in accumulation in their hands led to their further progress up the social ladder, and consequent lengthening of the chain of middlemen in the revenue collection system. Contractors called *Zamindars* moved from *Thekedars* to *Rai Sahib* to *Rai Bahadurs* to *Raja Sahibs.* Their munimjis gradually progressed to Tehsildars and ultimately *Dewan Sahibs/Bahadur.* Naturally each one had to have a longer hierarchy of subordinates to preside over—*Naib Dewan, Naib Tehsildar, Karinda* and *Gumashta* followed by the *lathait.* It was but natural that, to maintain this long list of functionaries with their hangers—on in a typical feudalistic setting, that fixed proportion of original auction amount proved to be grossly inadequate. Thus began the process of extraction of tributes from the peasantry, For construction of a new bungalow for a *Zamindar* or even his preferred concubines, an additional levy was imposed in the name of *Kothiana.* In addition, able-bodied persons were directed to report at the construction site and contribute their labour. If there was a marriage in the family of the *Zamindar,* the peasant had to pay *Shadiana.* In early twentieth century the advent of the motor car led to imposition of a *Carana.* Anyone who tried to escape this kind of extortion was rounded up and then made to pay *Harzana* and *Zurmana* as well. When these additional levies were extracted, the common farmer was not permitted to erect ordinary fences around the farmsteads. The reason: if *Zamindar* or any of his hangers—on came to hunt (hares) then those fences would have been a nuisance. So the crops grown at the mercy of the monsoon gods remained at the mercy of beasts as well.

Zamindars seldom visited their estates. They had only one-way relationship with the peasantry: extraction and extortion. If despite such situations, some farmer was adventurous enough to bring about some improvement in the field, he was always sure of only one reward from the rulers: that piece of land would be taken away from that adventurous peasant and handed over to someone who happened to be close to the charmed circles of *Gumashtas* and *Karindas.* So this revenue—collection mechanism, on the one hand ensured that every possible penny of agricultural surplus would be siphoned off from the countryside and, on the other hand, if still somebody dared to take some initiative for improving the productivity, he would be meted out adequate punishment for the same! Therefore, it was simply impossible to increase agricultural production in the areas controlled by *Zamindars.*

(b) *The forced Commercialisation:* The British did not wish to receive land revenue in kind. They wanted hard cash. This led to a significant change in the nature of economic relations in the countryside. The traditional Indian village community was virtually a self-sufficient economic unit. Its different constituents—like farmers, carpenters, cobblers, blacksmiths etc. were bound by tradition and rendered reciprocal services to each other. In a way the dominant mode of exchange in the village community was barter. Even land revenue was paid in kind. However, insistence of the British on cash payments forced the farmers to sell off a significant proportion of their gross produce at the harvest time. This enormously expanded the role and power of village trader-cum-moneylenders. Earlier on, the trader acted as a link between a village and the rest of the economy. He made available things like salt and spices in exchange for grain to the villagers. Grain thus collected was sold in the nearby towns and things needed by the village community were procured from there. However, cash revenue payments made the peasants sell a disproportionately large portion of their product to the trader at harvest time to fulfil the dictates of *zamindars.* As a result, the agricultural prices came to be determined by the amount of cash available in the hands of the village *baniya.* This near—distress sale of the crop ensured that cultivators would not be able to meet their day-to-day needs even during the normal harvest years. They had to borrow from the traders to survive until the next harvest. In case the rains failed their dependence on the trader's mercy became really critical. Wherever small *zamindars* themselves, or any member of their revenue-collection machinery, also happened to be the village money lender, the plight of farmers became all the more serious. The ordinary *Mahajan* would usually not dispossess the peasant of his land but the *Zamindar* could go to that extent as well. Thus a land-owning peasant could be reduced to the ranks of a landless, unskilled labourer. So we can say that peasantry, in general, was steeped in poverty and indebtedness at the time of independence.

The commercialisation of agriculture was a deliberate, well-conceived policy of the British keeping in view their industrial interests. The industries in England needed raw materials like cotton, jute, sugarcane, groundnuts etc. from India. These commercial crops were encouraged by the British by offering higher prices. Therefore, the peasants shifted from food crops to those commercial crops and started buying foodstuffs from the market. This led to a sharp decline in the production of food crops.

We had two other systems of land tenure or revenue collection in the country. In parts of Punjab and North-west the *Mahalwari* system prevailed under which the entire village was regarded as one revenue unit and payment of revenue to the state was the responsibility of the *Gram Sabha.* Individual farmers had no interaction with the state. The right to cultivate was inheritable, but no farmer had an absolute right to alienate the land cultivated by him, as land was owned by *Gram Sabha* collectively. In the Deccan plateau prevailed the third system of tenure—*Ryotwari.* Under this system, the individual farmer was responsible for land revenue payment directly to the state. However in both these systems also, the peasant's lot was no better.

The poverty of the peasants was the consequence of a variety of factors. Primarily it was because Indian agriculture was put under immense pressure by British colonialism. The destruction of the Indian handicrafts had increased unemployment in rural areas. India had to pay for the extravagant and lavish cost of British administration; the costly imperial wars in Burma and Afghanistan and of course, the Home changes. The major taxes imposed by the British were land revenue, excise, salt tax, stamps and opium. Apart from opium, all the taxes fell on rural areas. The impoverishment of Indian agriculture was completed by the frequently occurring famine, drought and epidemics, which were due more to British policies than nature's might.

Possession of land was in a few hands. *Zamindars* controlled almost the entire northern plain of the country. In South India, the narrow belts of Eastern and Western Ghats were agriculturally most promising areas and were controlled by big landowners called *Ryots.* This way all the agricultural lands in the country were monopolised by big landowners who never cultivated even a single square inch. All the agricultural operation were taken up by small farmers who paid rent to these *Zamindars* and *Ryots.* Both *Zamindari* and *Ryotwari* system were similar in their means and methods of extraction of all possible surplus. After meeting the demands of these overlords, farmers were left with hardly any means of making improvements in the productivity of the soil. It was felt that unless ownership of agricultural lands was handed over to actual cultivators it would not be possible to bring about any large increase in agricultural production. There was a great need felt for a comprehensive programme of land reforms.

2. *Peasant movements on the eve of Independence*

The British oppression, exploitation and neglect of peasantry led to general dissatisfaction among the peasants in the countryside. They did not remain quiet and revolted against the British but the

influences. When the British sought to push machine-made yarn in the Indian countryside, the rural weavers were more than eager to accept it and to agree to weave clothes for the yarn suppliers.

This first phase of decline in traditional handicrafts in the country is also known as the phase of de-industrialisation of India. However, very soon (1840s) new kinds of industrial activities started taking place in the country. In 1842, Britishers set up the first cotton *ginning and pressing mills* in the country. They had introduced long- staple Egyptian cotton in Saurashtra and Vidarbha regions a couple of years ago. They were trying to develop India as an alternative source of supply of cotton for British textile mills. But very soon *Marwaris* and *Parsis* sensed the possibilities of profits in this activity. By 1850, all the ginning and pressing mills on the western coast were owned by these two communities. They had set up the mills on their own in large numbers and also purchased those which were initially set up by Britishers. In 1856, the first integrated cotton textile mill was set up at Nagpur by a Parsi businessman. (Jamshedji Nasarwan Tata—Empress Mills). Thereafter, more and more Indian businessman came forward and cotton textile mills were set up in various parts of the country. Sholapur, Bombay, Ahmedabad, Kanpur and Calcutta became major centres. Gradually, the industry spread to other parts of the country as well. By 1870, Indian cotton textile mills were improving the quality of the cloth. By the turn of the century, textile mills in the country had started manufacturing fine and superfine (100x110 and above) cloth. By 1920, Indian textiles were dominating all the markets to the east of Suez Canal—they had ousted textile mills of Lancashire and Manchester from these markets.

The jute textile industry became significant only during the British period, and through the efforts of the British, as they needed jute bags and hessian cloth to package the goods to take out of India. In terms of employment and production, this industry was just a shade behind cotton textiles. However, it was virtually confined to the neighbourhood of Calcutta port. Partitioning of the country in a way destroyed this industry because over 90% of the jute growing area was made into East Pakistan while almost the same proportion (90%) of the mills were located around Calcutta and they became dependent on whims of Pakistani authorities for the critical raw material.

Sugar industry also made rapid strides during the British period. Britishers developed new markets for Indian sugar worldwide. Traditional Khandsari units expanded their scale of operation and evolved into modern mills manufacturing white crystalline sugar for exports.

Though one open-hearth, traditional, steel-making unit had been operating in Bhadravati in Mysore state, yet the beginning of modern iron and steel industry can be traced to setting up of Tata Iron and Steel Works in the first decade of this century. They were closely followed by Martin Burns of UK who set up Indian Iron and Steel company at a short distance away, after a couple of years. During World War I, Britishers realised that to maintain the control of a large colony like India, they had to make it self-sufficient in the matter of arms and ammunition. Thus was laid the foundation of heavy chemicals and engineering industries in the country.

Just after World War I, when war-devastated European industries were struggling to resume their activities, Indian industrialists were able to dominate the market all around. They also procured machinery from European suppliers at very favourable prices. This way, inter-war years were marked by hectic industrial activity in the country. World War II saw mobilisation of newly emerging industrial complexes for the war efforts of the Allied Forces.

So, on the eve of independence, we find India to be one of the ten most industrialised countries in the world. It had a large engineering industry capable of manufacturing vehicles for civil and defence use, fabricating sea-going ships, locomotives and rolling stock for the Railways, composite textile mills and sugar mills etc. However, this industrial superstructure did have one important weakness as well. With the exception of cotton textile, most of the industries did not cater to the common man. Consumers were, by and large, dependent on imports from European countries for items of day-to-day use. It seems rather surprising that an engineering industry, manufacturing railway engines, could not make bicycle spokes in the country, or an industry, that was exporting textile and sugar mills in the face of international competition, found it difficult to manufacture an ordinary sewing needle to stitch a button on to a shirt. Incidentally, even the buttons were imported. To sum up, we can say that India inherited an economy which had a typical colonial pattern of economic development. Despite rapid strides in the industrial sector, it remained lopsided in development.

A very important factor in 1947 was that India was mostly dependent upon imports for machine tools and machinery. There was no capital goods and machine industry which is necessary for a rapid industrial development. Even the replacements for worn-out capital goods had to be imported.

Another symbol of low economic development on the eve of independence was the rural-urban division. About 72% of the total workforce was involved in agricultural activity, organised industry employed only about 2%, less than 11% of the workforce was engaged in other types of industry. In 1951, nearly 82.3% of the population was rural and 17.3% urban. From 1901 to 1951 the population had increased by 40% but the number of persons employed in processing and manufacturing industries fell from 10.3 millions to 8.8 millions, while in 1901, 63.7% Indians were engaged in agriculture, the number rose to 70% by 1941. Despite such a large number of the workforce engaged in agriculture, it generated just 59% of the national income which shows the backwardness of agriculture. There were few major urban centres while the major parts of the country was dominated by the pro-capitalist sector. Even with the small industrial sector, a strong monopolistic tendency was clearly visible. India also had one of the lowest per capita incomes in the world. It was just Rs. 246.9 per person per annum.

5. *Unemployment*

India was also witnessing, in 1947, a big challenge in terms of employment opportunities which were very meagre. This was largely due to colonial economy. The partition of the country further aggravated this problem because firstly, it added around one crore to ranks of the unemployed. The eastern part of Bengal was carved out and made East Pakistan. Around 90% of the jute mills in the country were centred around the port of Calcutta but 90% of the jute-cultivating area went to East Pakistan. Overnight, the jute industry in India became dependent on raw materials from the not so-friendly regime in Pakistan. As a result there was a large scale closure of jute mills after partition, rendering thousands of workers unemployed. It is to be remembered that before independence, jute textile was the second largest industry in the country, both in terms of volume output as well as direct employment. The effect of partition was disastrous to the jute industry.

At the time of independence, the agricultural sector was the main provider of employment opportunities. One could not estimate the impact and extent of unemployment very precisely. However, one just cannot miss the fact that disguised unemployment in the sector was extremely high. Low productivity and absence of irrigation inhibited the potentiality of this sector in creating more employment facilities. The partition also gave the best canal system to Pakistan.

The expansion of the industrial sector was expected to increase the source of non-agricultural employment in the country and wean away the labour force from then traditional occupation. However, limited spread of the industrial sector as well as unsettled economic and political conditions and social turmoil of those years hardly facilitated any massive investment in the industrial sector. Thus, on the whole, the employment scene in the country was very depressing and no immediate, short-term solution, was visible on the horizon.

To sum up, we can say that India inherited an economy which had a typical colonial pattern of economic development. Despite rapid strides in the industrial sector, it remained lopsided in development. Its agriculture was in shambles and it was a gigantic task to undertake rapid industrial and agricultural development with a view to bring about a rapid economic revolution.

Indian Society on the Eve of Independence

The Cultural Unity

For a foreigner, the cultural diversity of India was baffling. The Indian society presented a picture of divergent, often conflicting trends. On the eve of independence, the vast country exhibited diversity in terms of geography, culture, caste, creed, race, language, religion and even gender. Yet the success of a strong national movement had created a unity of purpose, and people as a whole had aspirations for a better future in free India. However, what the foreigners could not understand was the underlying cultural unity of India. Many common traits, traditions, beliefs and practices— which were the result of sharing a common culture—could be seen throughout the country. The concept of *Vasudhaiva Kutumbakam* ensured the accommodation and assimilation of different kinds of people into one Indian culture that gave maximum freedom to its constituents and at the same time maintaining unity as a whole.

India is one of the oldest countries in the world. Right from the ancient times, the inhabitants of this country never regarded India as a mere geographical expression. To them India was a spiritual entity. J. Ramsay MacDonald, in his introduction to the *Fundamental Unity of India* by Dr. Radha Kumud Mookerji, observes that, to an Indian, the country is 'in his consciousness which actually is his 'greater self'. He further says, "One of the commonest prayers for a Hindu requires him to recall and worship the image of his mother country as the land of seven sacred rivers, the Ganga, Yamuna,

Godavari, Sarasvati, Narmada, Sindhu and Kaveri, which between them, cover its entire area. Another prayer calls up its image as the land of seven sacred cities, *Ayodhya, Mathura, Maya (Hardwar), Kashi, Kanchi (Kanjeeveram), Avantika (Ujjain) and Duaravati (Dwarka),* representing important regions of India. The spirit of these prayers is further sustained by the peculiar Hindu institution of pilgrimage. It expects the Hindu to visit, in his lifetime, the holy places associated with his faith. Each of the principal Hindu faiths or sects has its own list of holy places, *Vaishnava, Saiva, or Sakta,* and these are distributed throughout the length and breadth of India, and not confined to a single province. Thus, the different sects are at one in enjoining upon their respective votaries a pilgrimage to the different and distant parts of India, and thereby fostering in them a live sense of what constitutes their common country.

In the same spirit, Sankara established *four Mathas* (religious schools) at the four extreme points of the country viz. *Jyotirmatha* in the north (near Badri-Kedar on the Himalayas), *Saradamatha* at Dwarka in the West, *Govardhana-matha* at Puri in the east, and *Sringeri-matha* in Mysore. Sectarianism has thus been used as an aid to nationalism in Hindu culture. In some of the sacred texts, like the *Bhagavata Purana* or *Manu-Smriti,* are found passages of patriotic fervour describing Bharatavarsha as the land fashioned by the gods themselves (*devanismitamsthanam*), who even wish to be born in it as heaven on earth for the spiritual stimulus of its environment." This cultural unity was a major positive factor that ensured the survival of India as a country, despite the initial turbulence in 1947 due to partition and its aftermath.

Yet the fact remains that the Indian society was suffering from too many evils which necessitated social change. We have already discussed the sectarian differences between Hindus and Muslims which culminated into the partition of the country and creation of Pakistan. However, it was clear in 1947 that the partition could not solve the communal problem as a sizeable number of Muslims preferred to remain in India and communal riots had taken place in various parts of the country. Besides communalism, Indian society was plagued by many social problems. One of them was the caste system and its bye-product, untouchability.

1. *Caste System and Untouchability*

Caste is a unique Indian phenomenon, unparalleled in the rest of the world. According to Robert W. Stein, "Caste is of the warp and woof of Indian civilization, and Indian civilization is of the warp and woof of the caste." So entrenched is it in the Indian system that, although essentially a Hindu system, it is found in all the major religions in India.

Originally, Indian society was stratified on the basis of *Chaturvarna.* The society was divided into four social groups with a view to achieving harmonious development. The first group consisted of *Brahmans* who were supposed to pursue spiritual and intellectual quests and act as philosopher and guide to the entire society. *Kshatriyas* were the warriors for the defence and protection of the people. The third group was *Vaisyas* or the business class, who were to engage in trade and commerce with a view to bring about general prosperity in society. *Sudras* were the fourth group, who were to do menial work. The first three were known as Dvijas or twice born and were the higher class. Then there was a section of people outside the *chaturvarna* known as outcaste. Later on, this system of stratification became more and more complicated and society came to be fragmented into a large number of groups based on caste. Caste is defined as a system in which the individual's rank and its accompanying rights and obligations is ascribed on the basis of birth into a particular group. The worst aspect of the caste system, as it developed over time was the system of untouchability. The theory of pollution being communicated by certain lower castes to the members of higher castes placed severe restrictions on the extent of social intercourse. With the arrival of Turk-Afghan rulers, such rigidity in social interaction became more and more manifest. The evils of the caste system, especially in terms of untouchability, were recognised and criticised by various social reformers right from Buddha, Chaitanya, Kabir, Guru Nanak to Raja Ram Mohan Roy, Swami Vivekanand and Mahatma Gandhi. Even the *Upanishads* refuse to accept it. Swami Vivekanand declared, "The caste system is opposed to the religion of *Vedanta.*" During the British times, due to a variety of factors, notable among them the development of liberalism (the introduction of western system of education and modern means of transport, especially the railways, and the rise and development of the national movement), created an awareness against the caste stratification of society. Due to these developments, some liberalisation did take place. Yet in 1947, caste remained a force to be reckoned with in Indian society. Despite the efforts to do away with the evil of untouchability—especially by Gandhi and Ambedkar—untouchability was widely practised and the real task of its abolition was yet to begin.

2. *Status of Women*

Another social evil was the backward status of women. Traditional Indian literature held women in high esteem. Manu had said, "where the female relatives live in grief, the whole family soon perishes, but where they are happy, the family prospers ever." He also declared, "where women are honoured, the gods are pleased but where they are not, no sacred rite yields any reward."

Yagnavalkya said, "Women are the embodiment of all divine virtues on earth, *Som* has bestowed all his purity on them, *Gandharva* has given them sweetness of speech and *fire* has showered all his brilliance to make them the most attractive." The *Ramayana* and *Mahabharata* give full credit to women. However the same epics also paint women as just the opposite. Ramayana at one place says: "The faces of women are like flowers; their words are like the drops of honey but their hearts are like sharp razors; no one can know their interior." The *Mahabharata* also declares, "There is nothing that is more sinful than women. Woman is the root of all evils. There is no creature more sinful than woman. She is a burning fire. She is the illusion that *Daitya Maya* created."

Women in this period suffered from many disabilities. There were barbarous customs like burning of a widows on the funeral pyre of her husband, female infanticide, denial of right to remarry for widows, child marriage, the *devadasi* system etc. They were also denied a share in property. Irrespective of their caste and religion, their plight remained the same. After the British conquest of India, Raja Ram Mohan Roy pioneered the movement to emancipate women from their plight. His protest began with the anti-sati movement. In 1829, as a consequence of his pleadings, the British administration abolished the Sati system. Subsequently, female infanticides was also declared a crime, punishable under law. In 1929, child marriage, the root of many evils, was also abolished. As a result of efforts of Ishwar Chandra Vidyasagar, in 1856, remarriage of widows was made legal. Dr. Muthulakshmi Reddi and other social reformers launched a vigorous movement against the evil practice of the devadasis. In 1925 with a view to check the practice, a law was made. Under the penal code, trafficking in minor women was made a criminal offence. Successively, more enactments, such as the Hindu Law of Inheritance 1929, and the Hindu Women's Right to Property Act 1937 were passed to secure the rightful position of women in the society. Gandhi, who also stood for the amelioration of the plight Indian women, declared that the India of his dreams would be a country where, '...women will enjoy the same rights as men.' As a result of his efforts, millions of women joined the freedom struggle and fought along with the men as equals.

However, these efforts touched only the periphery of the giant problem. Still the male domination of society was a fact. Women were suffering immense social oppression within the four walls of the family. Polygamy prevailed. Women did not even enjoy the right to divorce. They were also the victims of illiteracy and ignorance.

Still, the positive factor was an awareness to emancipate women from social evils. All the political leaders were committed to this great task. A symbolic gesture was undertaken by Mrs. Hansa Mehta, a member of the Constituent Assembly, on the eve of independence at midnight, when she presented the National Flag on behalf of the women of India.

3. *Illiteracy and Ignorance*

Another index of social backwardness was illiteracy which was prevalent on a massive scale. As per the literacy figure in 1951, a mere 23.54 per cent men and 7.62 per cent female were literate. In rural areas, the figures were 19.02 per cent and 4.87 per cent and in urban areas 45.05 per cent and 12.34 per cent for men and women respectively. There were only 13,590 middle schools and 7,288 high schools in the country. Besides, there was no scientific and technical education being imparted in India.

4. *Westernization*

Another aspect of the social conditions in 1947 was the contradiction between the Indian intelligentsia and the general masses. The English—speaking Indians had adopted the English values and attitudes. They imitated the western style of living and became westernized. Although anti-imperialists, yet culturally they were closer to Englishmen than Indians. The national movement had definitely given them an opportunity to interact with the masses, yet they lived in their own world, far away from the masses. Many of them had also developed contempt for the rural masses. The Indian political leadership, which was essentially a British product, remained western in outlook.

5. *Rise of the Nuclear Family*

As a result of western influence and new economic openings, the pattern of social relationship was crumbling. In 1920, the

Government had passed Gains of Learning Act whereby the earnings of a person as a result of his individual efforts would wholly belong to him. This was a significant development on the social front. The joint family system was on the decline and nuclear families were on the rise. This was creating new social problems in Indian society.

6. *Regional Imbalances*

Another feature of Indian society was its regional imbalances. The country as a whole had not developed. Some areas had developed while others remained underdeveloped. The worst form of imbalances could be seen in the different standards of living in cities and villages.

Conclusion

Thus, to conclude, one can say that many divergent social economic and political tendencies were working in India on the eve of the Indian independence. There were certain positive as well as negative factors. The positive factors helped in overcoming immediate political problems and assured India a place as a stable country, while the negative factors posed a formidable challenge to new Indian rulers, as their solution needed a considerable amount of planning and rational thinking. By their very nature, their solution would be a long term process. Fortunately, the Indian leadership was aware of these problems and they were committed. Nehru rightly said, "That future is not one of ease or resting, but of incessant striving so that we might fulfil the pledges we have so often taken.... The service of India means the service of the millions who suffer... . The ambition of the greatest man of our generation has been to wipe every tear from every eye. That may be beyond us but so long as there are tears and sufferings, so long our work will not be over."

CHAPTER II

The Constituent Assembly and its Perception of Future Indian Polity

The Constituent Assembly was formed for the specific purpose of making the Constitution of India. The first session of the Constituent Assembly was held on December 9, 1946 and it finally passed the Constitution on November 26, 1949. During these three historic years of its operation, India witnessed many changes including the partition of the country into India and Pakistan, and the independence on 15th August 1947. The real work of the Constituent Assembly started on 29th August 1947, when a Drafting Committee was appointed to prepare a Draft Constitution. Dr. B.R. Ambedkar was appointed its Chairman. Other members were N. Gopalaswamy Ayyengar, Sir Alladi Krishnaswamy Iyer, K.M. Munshi, Saiyid Mohammed Saadulla, N. Madhava Rau and D.P. Khaitan. The Draft-Constitution was to be based on the decisions made by the Constituent Assembly, and its various Committees, plus the texts prepared by B.N. Rau, who was the Constitutional Adviser to the Constituent Assembly. The Drafting Committee submitted the Draft Constitution which had 315 Articles and 13 Schedules on February 2, 1948 to the Constituent Assembly. Over 7,000 amendments were proposed, of which 2,473 were discussed and debated and finally, the Constitution was passed which had 395 Articles and 8 Schedules. Though the Constitution was approved on 26th November 1949 and some of the provisions came into effect immediately, 26th January 1950 was fixed as the formal date, in the memory of 26th January 1930, when the Congressmen had taken the oath of *purna swaraj* (complete independence) at the bank of the river Ravi. Dr. Rajendra Prasad objected to it because he thought it was an inauspicious day. Nehru refused to accept the objection by saying that, "National programme cannot be fixed according to astrology, and if people want it, let them elect astrologers to govern the country. And if they believe in astrology out of ignorance, let us combat it."

Historical Background

In 1922, Mahatma Gandhi, while visualising the future political arrangement, had said, "Let us see clearly what Swaraj together with the British connection means. It means undoubtedly India's ability to declare her independence if she wishes. Swaraj therefore, will not be a free gift of the British Parliament. It will be a declaration of India's full self expression. That it will be expressed through an act of Parliament is true. But it will be merely a courteous ratification of the declared wish of the people of India..." In 1924, Motilal Nehru, as the leader of the Swaraj Party, demanded the summoning of a representative Round Table Conference to recommend, with due regard to the protection of the rights and interests of important minorities, the scheme of a Constitution for India. In 1929, the objective of India's freedom struggle became the complete independence from British Rule. After three Round Table Conferences in 1932, the British Government had drawn up a White Paper which was based upon the deliberations of the Round Table Conferences. The Congress rejected the White Paper and formally raised the demand for a Constituent Assembly. It declared, "The only satisfactory alternative to the White Paper is a Constitution drawn up by a Constituent Assembly elected on the basis of adult suffrage or as near it as possible with the power if necessary, to the important minorities to have their representatives elected exclusively by the electors belonging to such Minorities."

The Government of India Act 1935 failed to satisfy the political aspirations of the Indian people. The Congress again demanded a Constitution made by the Indians. In its Resolution in 1936, the Congress rejected the Government of India Act 1935 which, "in no way represents the will of the nation, is designed to facilitate and perpetuate the domination and exploitation of the people of India ..., the Congress reiterates its rejection of the new Constitution in its entirety." The Resolution also declared, "... that no Constitution imposed by outside authority and no Constitution which curtails the sovereignty of the people of India and does not recognise their right to shape and control fully their political and economic future can be accepted. In the opinion of the Congress such a Constitution must be based on the independence of India as a nation and it can only be framed by a Constituent Assembly elected on adult franchise or a franchise which approximates to it as nearly as possible. The Congress therefore reiterates and stresses the demand for a Constituent Assembly in the name of the Indian people ...." In 1937, the Working Committee of the Congress again demanded a Constituent Assembly thus: "The objective of the Congress is *Purna Swaraj* or complete independence and to that end, all its activities are directed. The Congress stands for a genuine democratic state in India where political power has been transferred to the people as a whole and the Government is under their effective control. Such a state can only be created by the Indian people themselves, and the Congress has therefore insisted on a Constituent Assembly, elected by adult franchise, to determine the Constitution of the country. The Constituent Assembly can only come into existence when the Indian people have developed sufficient power and sanctions to shape their destiny without external interference." A little earlier, in December 1936, Nehru again said, "with the effort to fight the Act (Government of India Act, 1935), and as a corollary to it, we have to stress our positive demand for a Constituent Assembly elected under franchise." In 1938, Nehru repeated the demand for a Constituent Assembly: "The National Congress stands for independence and democratic state. It has proposed that the Constitution of free India must be framed, without interference, by a Constituent Assembly elected on the basis of adult franchise." The demand for the Constituent Assembly was resisted by the British government and the Muslim League as well. The Muslim League and the British Government in India opposed the Congress move for a Constituent Assembly, the reasons in each case were different. The Muslim League feared a future Hindu majority government while the British rejected an immediate and responsible government coming from the demand of the Constituent Assembly.

The outbreak of the Second World War resulted in the change of British policy towards India as it needed India's, more particularly Congress' support. In 1940, the British Government accepted in principle that the Constitution of India would be framed by the Indians themselves. Sir Stafford Cripps, a member of the British Cabinet, was sent to India to declare (under Cripps Proposals, 1942) that the Constitution of India be framed by an elected Constituent Assembly of the Indians. It also made it clear that the Constitution so framed might not be binding on the unwilling provinces. However, the Muslim League wanted the division of the country and the creation of Pakistan. It demanded the creation of two Constituent Assemblies, one for India and the other for Pakistan, which was not acceptable to the Congress. There were also certain other proposals which Congress did not like. Ultimately the Cripps proposals failed.

By 1946, it was clear that a general agreement between the Congress and the Muslim League was impossible. The Cabinet Mission in 1946, had detailed discussions with the leaders of the two political parties. It rejected the Muslim League's proposal for the creation of the separate state of Pakistan. In order "to bring about a stable and practicable form of Constitution for all India, it recommended a Constitution which was to be a 'Union of India' of British India and Indian states in which residuary powers were to be vested in the states and the Central Government was to look after foreign affairs, defence and communications." It also suggested that "The Union should have an Executive and a Legislative constituted from British India and States representatives. Any question raising a major communal issue in the Legislature, should require for its decisions a majority of the representatives present and voting of each of the two major communities as well as a majority of all the members present and voting." The Cabinet Mission also wanted the Constitution of India to be made by the Indians themselves. Under the Cabinet Mission's scheme, the elections to the Constituent Assembly took place, although both the Congress as well as the League had serious reservations regarding the various proposals of the Cabinet Mission. The opening session of the Constituent Assembly took place on December 9, 1946. But the Muslim League, while failing to have a substantial number of members as elected, boycotted the Constituent Assembly. When the partition of the country remained the only alternative, the Constituent Assembly was also partitioned and those who came from regions which formed the Pakistans, became members of the Pakistan Constituent Assembly. The perception of the constitution-makers also underwent a major change. Earlier, for the sake of the unity of the country, and effective cooperation from the Muslim League in the formation of India's Constitution, they had agreed for a weak centre. Now they wanted to have a strong central government in which the powers of the states were to be considerably reduced.

The Constituent Assembly: Was it Truly Representative of the Indian People?

Even, during the period, when the Constituent Assembly was deliberating, it was pointed out that the Constituent Assembly was imposed on the Indian people and that it did not represent them. The socialists and the communists were not there. Similarly the Hindu Mahasabha and the other Hindu communal groups were also not represented. According to Seth Damodar Swarup, a member of the

Constituent Assembly, the Constituent Assembly represented "at best" 14 per cent of the Indian masses. Doubts were also raised regarding the legal status of the Constituent Assembly.

There is no doubt that the Congress had secured an overwhelming majority in the Assembly and its leaders were in full command. But the fact remains that, as a result of its leadership during the freedom struggle, the Congress had developed as an umbrella organisation representing the various sections and ideologies of the Indian population. It is also true that the members were not directly elected by the Indian people, but then they were really the men of the masses and, as such, their true representatives. The Congress also saw to it that all the minority communities were represented in the Assembly and also in its major committees. It is also a fact that Nehru, Patel, Prasad and Azad dominated the Constituent Assembly. They constituted what Austin calls an oligarchy within the Assembly. But then Austin rightly says, "Democratic decision making by the members of the Congress Assembly Party and the oligarchy's refusal to arrogate to itself all wisdom and authority helped to make possible a generally acceptable Constitution." The decisions were made by consensus with due regard to accommodation of different shades of views and interests. The Congress domination of the Constituent Assembly also turned out to be a positive aspect. Dr. Ambedkar paid a tribute to the Congress when he said, "The task of the Drafting Committee would have been a very difficult one if this Constituent Assembly had been merely a motley crowd ... in which each member or each group was a law unto itself. There would have been nothing but chaos. This possibility of chaos was reduced to nil by the existence of Congress Party inside the Assembly which brought into its proceedings a sense of order and discipline. It is because of the discipline of the Congress Party that the Drafting Committee was able to pilot the Constitution in the Assembly with the sure knowledge as to the fate of each article and each amendment. The Congress Party is, therefore, entitled to all the credit for the smooth sailing of the Draft Constitution in the Assembly."

The Constituent Assembly: Perception

On 13th December 1946, Jawahar Lal Nehru moved the "Objectives Resolution" which reflected the perception of the framers of the Constitution. It contained the following:

(1) This Constituent Assembly declare its firm and solemn resolve to proclaim India as an Independent Sovereign Republic and to draw up for her future governance a Constitution;

(2) WHEREIN the territories that now comprise British India, the territories that now form the Indian States, and such other parts of India as are outside British India and the States as well as such other territories as are willing to be constituted into the Independent Sovereign India, shall be a Union of them all; and
(3) WHEREIN the said territories, whether with their present boundaries or with such others as may be determined by the Constituent Assembly and thereafter according to the laws of the Constitution, shall possess and retain the status, of autonomous units, together with residuary powers, and exercise all powers and functions of Government and administration, save and except such powers and functions as are vested in or arranged to the Union, or as are inherent or implied in the Union or resulting therefrom; and
(4) WHEREIN all power and authority of the Sovereign Independent India, its constituent parts and organs of Government are derived from the people; and
(5) WHEREIN shall be guaranteed and secured to all the people of India justice social, economic and political; equality of status, of opportunity, before the law; freedom of thought, expression, belief, faith, worship, vocation, association and action subject to law and public morality; and
(6) WHEREIN adequate safeguards shall be provided for minorites, backward and tribal areas, and depressed and other backward classes; and
(7) WHEREIN shall be maintained the integrity of the territory of the Republic and its sovereign rights on land, sea and air according to justice and the law of the civilized nations; and
(8) The ancient land attain its rightful and honoured place in the world and make its full and willing contribution to the promotion of world peace and the welfare of mankind.

While moving the Objectives Resolution, Nehru compared it with the American Declaration of Independence and said, "We say that it is our firm and solemn resolve to have an Independent Sovereign Republic ... We stand for democracy ... We have given the content of democracy in this Resolution and ... of economic democracy ... We have laid down not theoretical words and formulae, but rather the content of things we desire. We adhere to certain fundamental propositions which are laid down in this Declaration ... Nobody challenges them ...." The Objectives Resolution was passed unanimously on January 22, 1947 by the Constituent Assembly.

Thus the Objectives Resolution envisaged a Union of India of willing provinces with a substantial amount of autonomy. It declared that the Indian people were supreme and all powers of the government were derived from them. The Objectives Resolution also contained a brief list of social, economic and political rights. It assured the minorities, tribals, backward classes, depressed and other backward classes of their rightful status in the new Indian polity. The integrity and sovereignty of India was stressed and the country was committed to the cause of promotion of world peace and the welfare of mankind.

This Objectives Resolution was adopted keeping in mind the unity of the country and the expectation that the Muslim League, which was firm on partition of the country, might join the Constituent Assembly. Very soon it became clear that expectation would not materialise as partition became imminent. As a result of the new development some of the contents of the Objectives Resolution became irrelevant. While the social, economic and political contents were not disturbed, the Constituent Assembly decided to make the Central Government in this country as strong as possible.

The perception of the framers of the Constitution was further reflected from the Preamble of the Indian Constitution which declared India to be a sovereign, democratic Republic with the objective of securing social, economic and political justice, liberty of thought, expression, belief, faith and worship; equality of status and opportunity. It also declared to promote fraternity among the people with the avowed purposes of assuring the dignity of the individual and the unity of the country.

Now let us study these various aspects in some detail.

1. *Unity of India*

Ralph Herbert Retylaff says, "The preservation and fostering of national unity was a primary concern of the framers of the Indian Constitution, and the specific task which confronted them was the creation of constitution provisions which would accommodate the diversities inherent in the problems of communalism, provincialism and linguism while unmistakably setting forth the primacy of the national interest."

Most of the members of the Constituent Assembly were actively involved in the freedom struggle. However, the freedom that was achieved was at the cost of the partition of the country. They had to accept it as there was no other alternative. On their own, they had tried to avoid partition by providing a loose federation but all was in vain.

Now, they were committed, once the partition was made, to the unity of the remaining parts of the country. Undoubtedly they were aware of different kinds of diversities of India in terms of caste, religion, region, language, geography etc. But they stood for, what Nehru called, unity in diversity. As discussed in the first chapter, there were many people both inside and outside India who questioned the very existence of India as a nation and predicted its dismemberment. The members of the Constituent Assembly were determined to avoid any such possibility. Therefore they made adequate arrangements in the Constitution to secure unity of the country. They even avoided the term "federation" and instead declared India to be "Union of States." (Article 1) There were many members who wanted to use "federation" in place of union and accordingly, amendments to the Draft Constitution were moved, but they were not accepted. The citizens of India were given a detailed list of fundamental rights but, at the same time, restrictions were imposed for the sake of unity. The Union government was given wide powers, correspondingly weakening the State Governments. The state structures that were created further strengthened the unity. Single citizenship, the constitutional set up for the States, the election system, all India services, the emergency powers of the President and the like were incorporated into the Constitution to secure the unity of the country. The Directive Principles of State Policy clearly desired a common civil code for all the citizens.

The state of Jammu and Kashmir was to be governed by Article 370 which provided her a special status. But no state was given the right to secede. Dr. Ambedkar called the Indian federation as a flexible Constitution. He emphasised the clear distinction between the Indian Constitution and other federal Constitutions. He said, "... the Draft Constitution can be both unitary as well as federal according to the requirements of time and circumstances. In normal times it is framed to work as a federal system. But in times of war, it is so designed as to make it work as though it was a unitary system." Explaining the reason as to why 'union' instead of 'federation' was used, Dr. Ambedkar said, "But what is important is that the use of the word 'Union' is deliberate .... I can tell you why the Drafting Committee has used it. The Drafting Committee wanted to make it clear that though India was to be a federation, the federation was not the result of an agreement by the States to join in a federation, and that the federation not being the result of an agreement, no state has the right to secede from it. The federation is a union because it is indestructible. Though the country and the people may be divided into different states for convenience of administration, the country is one integral whole, its people a single people living under a single *imperium*, derived from a single source. The Americans had to wage a civil war to establish that the states have no right of secession and that their federation was indestructible. The Drafting Committee thought that it was better to make it clear at the outset rather than to leave it to speculation or to dispute." Thus the term union was the symbol of unity of this country and the federal structure had to be subservient to the cause of Indian unity.

Some members of the Constituent Assembly demanded greater provincial autonomy. K.M. Munshi warned such members "to remember one supreme fact in Indian history that the glorious days of India were only the days, whether under the Mauryas or the Mughals, when there was a strong central authority in the country, and the most tragic days were those when the central authority was dismembered by the provinces trying to resist it. We do not want to repeat that fatal mistake."

2. *Democracy*

The framers of the Indian Constitution were also committed to democratic ideals. They had a considerable amount of training under the limited democratic institution introduced by the British. Further, they shared the liberal ideas of the British school. Therefore there was no reluctance on the part of the Constituent Assembly to have a Parliamentary system of government in which the executive is accountable to the legislative. The Constituent Assembly also adopted the universal adult franchise which in fact was a revolutionary step considering that only 14.2 per cent of India's population had exercised the right to vote in the democratic institutions during the British Raj. Universal adult franchise meant extension of the electorate from 35 million to 170 million.

Alladi Krishna Swami Ayyer asserted the introduction of universal adult franchise in unequivocal terms: "If democracy is to be broadbased and the system of government that is to function is to have the ultimate sanction of the people as a whole, in a country where the large mass of the people are illiterate and the people owning property are so few, the introduction of any property or educational qualifications for the exercise of the franchise would be a negation of the principles of democracy ... It cannot after all be assumed that a person with a poor elementary education and with a knowledge of the three R's is in a better position to exercise the franchise than a labourer, a cultivator or a tenant who may be expected to know what his interests are and to choose his representatives. Possibly a large scale universal suffrage may also have the effect of rooting out corruption that may turn out to be incidental to democratic election." He was confident that universal adult franchise would bring enlightenment and promote the well-being, the standards of life, comfort and decent living of the common man. R.K. Sidhra, a member of the Constituent Assembly, while welcoming the introduction of universal adult franchise said, "The adult franchise is the greatest risk which the Constituent Assembly has taken. I may tell the House it is the greatest risk for this reason that 85 per cent of our population is illiterate and it is even now doubted whether the adult franchise will be successful .... We have taken the risk rightly." An important aspect was Part III of the Constitution which provided following seven fundamental rights to the Indian citizen.

1. Right to equality.
2. Right to freedom.
3. Right against exploitation.
4. Right to freedom of religion.
5. Cultural and educational rights.
6. Right to Property (eliminated by the 44th Constitutional Amendment Act, 1978).
7. Right to Constitutional remedies.

M.V. Pylee rightly says that the fundamental rights in the Constitution are a formidable bulwark of individual liberty, a code of conduct and a steady and sustaining basis of Indian democracy. Besides the office of Election Commission was provided to ensure free and fair elections.

3. *Socio-Economic Justice*

Another important perception of the Constituent Assembly was its concern for the widespread socio-economic disparities that existed in the Indian society. The society had almost stagnated owing to the dominant caste and communal factors. The untouchables were denied the essentials of any human existence. Despite the fact that a considerable number of women took active role in the freedom struggle, women in general were under the pressure of numerous social inequalities. The common man in the country was largely illiterate and ignorant. The health scenerio was no better. The widespread extreme poverty was another evil. The members of the Constituent Assembly were aware of these socio-economic facts and wanted an India which was devoid of such problems. Acharya Kriplani declared that, "democracy is inconsistent with caste system that is social autocracy. We must do away with castes and classes. Otherwise we cannot swear by democracy." T. Prakasam, another member of the Constituent Assembly said, "One great service that this Constitution has done is by way of removing untouchability and making Harijans and Scheduled Castes feel that they are brought on equal footing with the rest of the population." The framers provided adequate measures in the Constitution for the advancement of people in social and economic fields. Here they were influenced by the concepts of ancient Hindu polity. Kautilya's *Arthashastra* declared that "the king shall provide, the dying, the infirm, the afflicted and the helpless with maintenance, he shall also provide subsistence to helpless expectant mothers and also to the children they give birth to." In the modern world, they also had the example of Irish Constitution which provided for Directive Principles of Social Policy, following which Part IV of the Indian Constitution was called the Directive Principles of State Policy. The draft report of the Constitution said that "The Principles of Policy set forth in the Part are intended for the guidance of the State. While these principles shall not be cognizable by any court, they are nevertheless fundamental in the governance of the country and their application in the making of laws shall be the duty of the state." B. Das said, "I think it is the primary duty of Government to remove hunger and render social justice to every citizen and to secure social security." V.D. Tripathy said, "The first basic principle of our Constitution should be that the poor man should have full right to rise to the highest station in life. He should have the facilities to do so, not out of somebody's compassion, but his own strength in the assistance of society." Nehru in his famous "tryst with destiny" speech said, "The service of India means the service of the millions who suffer. It means the ending of poverty and ignorance and disease and inequality of opportunity." The Preamble of the Constitution explicitly declared "Justice—social, economic and political" as one of the objectives for which the Constitution was made.

4. *Secularism*

Another vision of the Constituent Assembly was to have a secular polity. The communal problem had already led to the division of the country and caused unparalleled agonies to the people of the subcontinent. The framers of the Constitution explicitly made it clear that the state shall not recognise any religion as the state religion. The state was also prohibited from discriminating on religious grounds. The people were given the right to practise and profess their religion. However, the framers were also conscious of various social and religious customs of the country unsuitable to modern society. There were child marriages, polygamy, unequal laws of inheritance, untouchability etc. which were practised in the name of religion and their eradication was favoured by all the members of the Constituent Assembly. Therefore it was prescribed that the freedom of conscience and the right to freely profess, practise and propagate religion would not prevent the state from making any law providing for social welfare and reform. Thus secularism is a positive concept in which the state is neither anti-religious, nor there is a separation of religion from the State. The State treats all religions on equal footing, at the same time reforming and readjusting the religions as per the changing needs of the time.

In the Constituent Assembly, certain members, like Loknath Mishra, wanted India to be declared a Hindu State. He declared that if you accept religion, you must accept Hinduism as it is practised by an overwhelming majority of the people of India. However, the consensus was in favour of a Secular State. H.V. Kamath said, "We have certainly declared that India would be a Secular State, but to my mind a Secular State is neither a Godless State nor an irreligious State nor anti-religious State." According to Lakshmikanta Maitre, "by Secular State, as I understand, it is meant that state is not going to make any discrimination whatsoever on the ground of religion or community against any person professing any particular form of religious faith .... The state is not going to establish, patronise or endow any particular religion to the exclusion of, or in preference to, others and that no citizen in the state will have any preferential treatment or will be discriminated against simply on the ground that he professed a particular form of religion." To M. Anantsayanam Ayyengar secularism meant that "the state or the Government cannot aid one religion or give preference to one religion as against another."

Dr. Ambedkar, while rejecting the plea to secure representatives of minorities in the formation of Union Council of Ministers, said, "There is nothing wrong in proposing that the method of choosing the cabinet should be such that it should permit members of the minorities to be included in the cabinet ... I do not think it is possible to make any statutory provision for the inclusion of members of particular communities in the cabinet. That, I think, would not be possible, in view of the fact that our Constitution, as proposed, contains the principle of collective responsibility, and there is no use foisting upon the Prime Minister a colleague simply because he happens to be the member of a particular minority community, but who does not agree with the fundamentals of the policy which the Prime Minister and his party have committed themselves to." Similarly a system of proportional representative to various communities for legislature was also rejected. Only Scheduled Castes were given reservation. Nehru assured full protection to the minorities and considered it a matter of honour for the Government and the majority community to look after minorities. He, however, said, "The one thing that should be obvious to all of us is this— that there is no group in India, no party, no religious community, which can prosper if India does not prosper. If India goes down, we go down, all of us, whether we have a few seats more or less, whether we get a slight advantage or we do not. But if it is well with India, if India lives as a vital force, then it is well with all of us, to whatever community or religion we might belong." Pandit Govind Ballabh Pant tried to be more realistic when he said, "The question of minorities cannot possibly be overrated .... So far, the minorities have been incited and have been influenced in a manner which has hampered the growth of cohesion and unity. But now it is necessary that a new chapter should start and we should all realise our responsibility. Unless the minorities are fully satisfied we cannot make any progress; we cannot even maintain peace in an undisturbed manner. So, all that can possibly be done, should be done." Dr. Ambedkar made it clear that the rights of the minorities should be absolute. For this we should not "wait and see what rights the minorities are given by the Pakistan Assembly before we determine the rights we want to give to the minorities in the Hindustan area." The minorities were given adequate representation in the Constituent Assembly.*

5. *World Peace and Internationalism*

The members of the Constituent Assembly inherited the Indian political tradition which advocated truth, non-violence,

*More on Secularism See chapter XXIII.

internationalism, peaceful settlement of disputes and justice. India's commitment to internationalism was best echoed by Nehru who, in January 1947, said in the Constituent Assembly: "The only possible real objective that we, in common with other nations, can have, is of cooperating in building up some kind of world structure, call it one world, call it what you may." The fathers of the Constitution specially declared their international objectives in Article 51 of the Constitution, which says that "The State shall endeavour to:

(a) promote peace and security;
(b) maintain just and honourable relations between nations;
(c) foster respect for international law and treaty obligations in the dealings of organised people with one another; and
(d) encourage settlement of international dispute by arbitration."

Nehru also made India's commitment to the United Nations very clear by saying, "The United Nations, inspite of its failings and weaknesses, is something that is good. It should be encouraged, and supported in every way, and should be allowed to develop into some kind of world government or world order."

There were many members in the Constituent Assembly who wanted India to withdraw from the Commonwealth as it was supposed to be the symbol of India's subjugation to the British. Nehru had advocated realism when he said, "We join the Commonwealth, obviously because we think it is beneficial to us and to certain causes in the world that we wish to advance." As a result of Nehru's efforts, the Commonwealth had become a symbol of a free connection and India accepted the king as the symbol of the free association of its independent member nations and, as such, the Head of the Commonwealth. The Constituent Assembly confirmed Nehru's decision in May 1949. Nehru made it very clear that "we approach the World in a friendly way, we want to make friends with all countries ... "The Indian Foreign Policy based on non-alignment had, by this time, become a reality which found general acceptance in the Constituent Assembly. R.V. Dhulekar said, "We pray for international peace. We have always believed in it, and I am proud of it when I say that India has never invaded any country outside its own boundaries .... Like Alexander the Great, no king of India marched on another land. Like Nadirshah or Mahmud Ghazni or Mohammed Ghori, no king of India stepped out of the country for any conquest on territory .... Therefore, when we lay it down that international peace is our ultimate aim, I may say that the whole world must believe us."

On the eve of Indian independence, at the midnight, Nehru moved a resolution in the Constituent Assembly in which all the members took the following pledge, "I ... do dedicate myself in all humility to the service of India and her people to the end that this ancient land attain her rightful place in the world and make her full and willing contribution to the promotion of world peace and the welfare of mankind."

To conclude, one can say that the vision of the Constituent Assembly was a strongly united, democratic, secular India where the welfare of the people found the pivotal position, irrespective of their caste, creed, religion or any such considerations. It also gave due regard to Internationalism and world peace.

References

Austin, Granville, *The Indian Constitution; Cornerstone of a Nation*, 1972, Bombay, Oxford University Press.

Kashyap Subash (Ed.), *Perspectives on the Constitution*, 1993, Delhi, Shipra Publication.

Rao, B. Shiva, *The Framing of India's Constitution*, 1968, Nasik Government of India Press.

Basu D.D., *Introduction to the Constitution of India*, 1992, Prentice-Hall of India Pvt. Ltd, New Delhi.

Pylee M.V., *India's Constitution*, 1974, Bombay, Asia Publishing House.

Rau, Sir Benegal, *India's Constitution in the Making*. 1963, Madras, Allied Publishers Pvt Ltd.

Retylaff, Ralph Herbert, *The Constituent Assembly and Problem of Indian Unity*, 1960, a thesis available in Microfilm in Nehru Memorial Museum and Library.

Constituent Assembly Debates.

CHAPTER III

Preamble

A Constitution, generally, provides for a preamble which deals with the purpose and objectives of the framers of the Constitution. The US Constitution says that the purpose of the Constitution is to "establish justice, ensure domestic tranquillity, provide for the common defence, promote the general welfare and secure the blessings of liberty to ourselves and our posterity." The framers of the Indian Constitution also wanted to lay down their broad objectives in the Preamble. Therefore, the Preamble was included in the Constitution. It reads as follows:

WE, THE PEOPLE OF INDIA, having solemnly resolved to constitute India into a SOVEREIGN SOCIALIST SECULAR DEMOCRATIC REPUBLIC and to secure to all its citizens. JUSTICE—social, economic and political,

LIBERTY of thought, expression, belief, faith and worship;

EQUALITY of status and opportunity; and to promote among them all,

FRATERNITY assuming the dignity of the individual and unity and integrity of the Nation;

In our Constituent Assembly this twenty-sixth day of November, 1949, do HEREBY ADOPT, ENACT AND GIVE TO OURSELVES THIS CONSTITUTION.

The Preamble was based on the Objectives Resolution drafted by Jawahar Lal Nehru and moved by him in the Constituent Assembly on December 13, 1946. It was finally drafted by the Drafting Committee of the Constituent Assembly. The Forty Second Amendment, in 1976, made certain modifications. Instead of "Sovereign Democratic Republic," India was declared as "Sovereign *Socialist Secular* Democratic Republic" and "Fraternity assuring the dignity of the individual and the unity of the Nation" was substituted by "Fraternity assuring the dignity of the individual and the unity and integrity of the Nation.

A careful study of the Preamble reveals four basic points. They are as follows:

I. Source of the Constitution.
II. Nature of Indian Political System.
III. The objectives of the Constitution.
IV. Date of the adoption of the Constitution.

I. Source of the Constitution

The first and the last words of the Preamble i.e. 'We, The PEOPLE OF INDIA... IN OUR CONSTITUENT ASSEMBLY ... do HEREBY ADOPT, ENACT 'AND GIVE TO OURSELVES THIS CONSTITUTION.' clearly reveal that the source of the Constitution is the people of India. The people have formulated their Constitution through the Constituent Assembly which represented them. However, the critics point out that this is not true. The Constituent Assembly, it is argued, was not directly elected by the people. It was constituted under the Cabinet Mission plan on limited franchise. In the Constituent Assembly itself, this fact was pointed out. Purnima Banerji proposed an amendment to recast the opening part of the Preamble to be read as follows, "We on behalf of the people of India from whom is derived all power and authority of independent India." This amendment was proposed to make it unambiguous that ultimately the sovereignty rested in the people of India. The original plan of Cabinet Mission had provided for the approval of the Constitution made by the Constituent Assembly by the British Parliament. But after the transfer of power by the British to India on August 15, 1947, this was made redundant because Indians had become the masters of their destiny. There were also critics who pointed out that the Constitution was imposed on the Indian people by the Congress Party and no referendum was taken on the Constitution, thus people's approval was not sought. All this may be true, but it is equally true that the successful implementation and continuation of the Constitution for more than a half century clearly reveal that the Constitution had the people's sanction. The First General Election of 1951-52, based on universal adult franchise, can be taken as the referendum because some of the political parties declared the intention of formulation of a new Constitution and scrapping the existing one, if they came to power. They were all defeated in the polls and the members of the Constituent Assembly and the Congress Party, which was the brain behind the Constitution, was elected. As the time passed on, even those parties which wanted to change the Constitution also accepted it. All this shows that the real authors of the Indian Constitution were the Indian people. Dr. Ambedkar rightly pointed out in the Constituent Assembly, "I say that this Preamble embodies what is the desire of every member of the House, that this Constitution should have its roots, its authority, its sovereignty from the people that it has."

II. Nature of the Indian Political System

The Preamble also discusses the nature of the Indian political system. The Indian polity is a sovereign, socialist, secular, democratic republic. The original Preamble contained sovereign democratic Republic, terms like "socialist" and "secular" were inserted by the Constitution (Forty-second Amendment) Act of 1976.

1. After the implementation of the Constitution on 26th January 1950, India became sovereign. It was no longer a dominion. Sovereignty means the absence of external and internal limitation on the state. It means that we Indians are the supreme power in deciding our destiny. During the framing of the Constitution, and even afterwards, it was said that India's continued membership of the Commonwealth constituted a limitation on India's sovereignty. However, this is not true because Commonwealth is an association of free countries as per the Declaration adopted in 1949. India remained a member of the Commonwealth because of her own pragmatic reasons. Similarly India is a member of United Nations which in no way constitutes a limitation on her sovereignty.

According to K.C. Markandan, the term sovereign includes or implies:

(a) That India was framing a Constitution on her own initiative without any outside assistance or interference.
(b) That the source of authority and power is vested in the people of India.
(c) That the Constituent Assembly was free to determine for the governance of the country any Constitution that it deemed proper for the fulfilment of the hopes and aspirations of the people of India.
(d) That the Constitution so framed would be the supreme law of the land, and as such, it commended reverence and faithful compliance to the various provisions enshrined in it.

2. The Constitution also declares India to be a socialist polity. This was done through the 42nd Constitutional Amendment. However, this was also discussed in the Constituent Assembly. Nehru, while moving the Objectives Resolution, said, "Others might take objection to this Resolution on the ground that we have not said that it should be a Socialist State. Well, I stand for socialism and, I hope India will stand for socialism and that India will go towards the Constitution of the Socialist State and I do believe that the whole world will have to go that way. What form of socialism again is another matter for your consideration. But the main thing is that in such Resolution if, in accordance with my own desire, I had put in, that we want a socialist state we would have put in something which may be agreeable to many and may not be agreeable to some and we want this Resolution not to be controversial in regard to such matters. Therefore, we have laid down, not theoretical word and formulae but rather the content of the thing we desire. This is important and I take it there can be no dispute about it." M.R. Masani agreed with Nehru when he said, "It (Objectives Resolution) does not provide for socialism. It would be wrong to provide for such a thing, because this House has no mandate to go in for far-reaching changes in the country. These changes can be brought about by a properly constituted Parliament when it comes into existence with the mandate of the people. All that we can do as an Assembly here, is to frame a Constitution which will allow these far-reaching changes which are necessary to be made and I submit Sir, that this Resolution goes as far as it can in satisfying the most ardent socialist amongst us." However there were members like K.T. Shah who wanted the term "socialism" to be mentioned in the Preamble. Dr. Ambedkar, while rejecting this demand, said "... The Constitution ... is merely a mechanism for the purpose of regulating the work of the various organs of the State ... What should be the policy of the State, how the society should be organised in its social and economic side are matters which must be decided by the people themselves, according to time and circumstances. It cannot be laid down in the Constitution itself, because that is destroying democracy altogether. If you state in the Constitution that the social organisation of the State shall take a particular form, you are in my judgement taking away the liberty of the people to decide what should be the social organisation in which they wish to live. It is perfectly possible today, for the majority of the people to hold that the socialist organisation of society is better than the capitalist organisation

of society. But it would be perfectly possible for thinking people to devise some other form of social organisation which might be better than the social organisation of today or tomorrow. I do not see, therefore, why the Constitution should tie down the people to live in a particular form and not leave it to the people themselves to decide it for themselves." He also felt that insertion of socialism was superfluous as the directive principles of State policy already contained the objective of socialism. He asked ... "If these directive principles ... are not socialistic in their direction and in their content, I fail to understand what more socialism can be." The original Preamble did not contain the term 'socialist'. In 1976, it was included because of political reasons. Dinesh Chandra Goswami, in the Parliament, said that this had become necessary "because the highest court of the land has completely forgotten the content and they have always interpreted the Constitution in favour of the vested interests and individual rights."

As an ideology, socialism has many shades. In general, it means a social system based on public ownership of property as against the concept of private property and eradication of exploitation. K.T. Shah, in the Constituent Assembly, rightly defined it as ... "a state in which equal justice and equal opportunity for everybody is assured, in which everyone is expected to contribute by his labour, by his intelligence, and by his work all that he can to the maximum capacity, and everyone would be assured of getting all that he needs and all that he wants for maintaining a decent civilised standard of existence."

3. Secularism is another aspect of Indian polity which was included by the 42nd Constitutional Amendment. It may be worth mentioning that the Constituent Assembly also discussed secularism to be included in the Preamble. Prof. K.T. Shah had moved an amendment to the effect which was however rejected by Dr. Ambedkar as unnecessary. The 42nd Constitutional Amendment had tried to define "Secular Republic" as a "Republic in which there is equal respect for all religions." But this was not carried on due to the opposition of Rajya Sabha. Secularism in India contains both negative as well as positive connotations. In its negative connotation, it denotes absence of religious discrimination by the State. Positively it means right to freedom of religion. All the Indian citizens are 'equally entitled to freedom of conscience and the right to freely profess, practise and propagate religion. Citizens are also free to manage their religious affairs. Secularism, however, should not mean right to conversion.

4. The Preamble declares India to be a democratic country. Democracy means a government by the people, for the people and of the people. It means accountability of the government to the governed. The Indian Constitution provides for universal adult franchise. We have adopted the Parliamentary form of government in which the people elect their government after every five years under an independent Election Commission. The citizens have been given fundamental rights which are regarded sacrosanct and are enforceable by the courts. However the term democracy has been used in a comprehensive manner which includes not only political democracy but social and economic democracy as well. Dr. Ambedkar pointed out this aspect when he said, "On 26th January 1950, we are going to enter into a life of contradiction. In politics, we will have equality and in social and economic rights we will have inequality. In politics we will be recognising the principle of one man and one vote, one value. In our social and economic rights we shall by reason of our social and economic structure, continue to deny one man one value ... We must remove this contradiction at the earliest possible moment or else those who suffer from inequality will blow up the structure of political democracy which this Assembly has so laboriously built up." Sadly this contradiction still remains.

5. Lastly, the Preamble declares India to be a Republic. It means that the head of the State is elected. The President of India who is the head of the State is elected by an electoral college consisting of elected representative in the Parliament and the lower houses of the State Assemblies. Republic is in sharp contrast to a monarchy where the head of the state is hereditarily crowned, as in Great Britain.

III. The Objectives of the Constitution

The Preamble also contains the vision of the framers of the Constitution, the kind of polity they wanted to have in India. The framers were the true leaders of the Indian masses and, as such, were aware of socio-economic backwardness of the country. They wanted their total elimination and therefore they set up the objectives for which the Indian polity, particularly the prospective rulers, should strive for. These objectives are as follows:

(i) *Justice—Social, Economic and Political*

As Sir Alladi Krishna Swamy Ayyar pointed out in the Constituent Assembly, "The expression `Justice—social, economic and political,' while not committing this country and the Assembly to any particular form of polity coming under any specific designation, is intended to emphasise the fundamental aim of every democratic state in the present day." However, Justice is one of the most controversial concepts in Political Science which may mean different things to different people. In the Indian context it means the introduction of a welfare state where the individual interests are to be safeguarded and also regulated, keeping in view the over-all development of the society as a whole. This justice has three ingredients—social, economic and political. Social justice means the abolition of all kinds of discrimination which prohibit the healthy development of an individual as a member of the society. It means end of untouchability. It means amelioration of backward castes and classes, tribals and women. It means the fruits of development must be accessible to each and every citizen of India. It means absence of privileges being extended to a small group of people. Nehru declared in the Constituent Assembly, "The first task of the Assembly is to free India through a new Constitution, to feed the starving people to clothe the naked masses and to give every Indian the fullest opportunity to develop himself according to his capacity." He wanted the Constitution to serve as an instrument for socio-economic revolution. Hence economic justice is a corollary to social justice. Economic justice implies the fulfilment of minimum economic requirement of food, cloth and shelter to all. It means equal pay for equal work and everybody should have a right to decent employment. There should not be large inequalities in terms of income and prosperity in the society. There should not be any exploitation of man by man (such as beggar and bonded labour and all other similar terms of forced labour) and India's grinding poverty should be ended as soon as possible. For the purpose, the economically weaker sections may be given extra benefits in terms of reservation in jobs. But economic justice does not mean expropriation of the rich.

For the general development of the society, and for the sake of deprived people, some limitations may be imposed on the right to ownership of property. But poverty is to be abolished by the multiplication of national wealth, by opening new avenues of economic development and improving the existing ones. Finally, economic justice also implies distributive justice which means inexpensive, ready and easily accessible justice to all including the most deprived ones. Political justice means the right to participation in the political life of the country, without any distinction based on caste, creed, religion, education and sex etc. It means universal adult franchise, where every eligible citizen will have a right to vote and a right to get elected if accepted by the people. Political justice also means ensuring adequate representation to the minorities and the backward castes. A careful study of the Constitution and its implementation reveal that political justice has been ensured to different sections of the population. However, social and economic justice are still to be achieved.

(ii) *Liberty of Thought, Expression, Belief, Faith and Worship*

Liberty is the most important content of democracy, for without liberty no democracy can function. Hence liberty (of thought, expression, belief, faith and worship) finds its due place in the Preamble. The Indian Constitution provides for both kinds of liberties—the negative and the positive one. The citizens have been guaranteed right to freedom against the state and other private individuals. At the same time, restrictions have been placed on fundamental rights in order to achieve a harmonious development of the polity in which the weaker sections can also exercise their liberties. That is why the concept of liberty in the Preamble has not been absolute but qualified as liberty of thought, expression, belief, faith and worship. Liberty is to be viewed from the point of view of justice and, for the sake of justice, liberty may be curtailed. This argument was responsible for the abolition of right to property as a fundamental right in the 42nd Constitutional Amendment.

(iii) *Equality of Status and Opportunity*

Equality of status and oppotunity means that state should treat all its citizens equally without any discrimination based on religion, race, caste, sex or place of birth. The public offices and employment should be extended to all without any distinction. It also means absence of special privileges to any section of the population. Articles 14 to 18 deal with the concept of equality in detail. Article 14 states that "The state shall not deny to any person equality before the law or the equal protection of the laws within the territory of India." Article 15 prohibits the state from discriminating against the citizens on grounds of religion, race, caste, sex or place of birth. Article 16 gives equality of opportunity in matters of public employment. However, backward classes, scheduled castes and scheduled tribes have been given protective discrimination. Article 17 abolishes untouchability which has been a curse on Indian society. Finally, Article 18 abolishes all kinds of titles, except academic and military. The citizens have also been prohibited from accepting any title from any foreign state. Article 326 provides for political equality *i.e.*

universal adult franchise. Article 325 says that the people will have a right to vote without any prohibitions based on religion, race, caste or sex. The Directive Principles of State Policy direct the state to secure equal pay for equal work to both the sexes.

(iv) *Fraternity Assuring the Dignity of the Individual and the Unity and Integrity of the Nation*

Fraternity means brotherhood. Common citizenship and the rights of citizens to move freely throughout the country, to reside and settle in any part of India, are some of the provisions which are designed to promote fraternity. The fundamental duties (included in the Constitution by the 42nd Constitutional Amendment) also ensure fraternity. Article 51-A(e) says that it shall be the duty of every citizen of India "to promote harmony and the spirit of common brotherhood amongst all the people of India transcending religious, linguistic and regional or sectional diversities ..." However, this fraternity has to assure the dignity of the individual and unity and integrity of the nation. The fundamental rights and directive principles ensure the dignity of individual. Article 51A(e) protects the dignity of women where it confers a fundamental duty on every citizen "... to renounce practices derogatory to the dignity of women." Further, this fraternity should also ensure the unity and integrity (the term integrity was also inserted in the Preamble in 1976) of the country. If the country remains, all of us remain; if the country is doomed, it means all of us also perish. Communalism, separatism and regionalism are some of the dangers that eat away the vitals of fraternity based on unity and integrity of the nation.

IV. Date of the Adoption of the Constitution

Lastly, the Preamble contains the date on which the Constitution was adopted by the Constituent Assembly. This was 26th November, 1949. A majority of articles of the Constitution came into operation on that date. Formally, it was implemented on 26th January, 1950.

SIGNIFICANCE OF THE PREAMBLE

The Preamble of the Constitution is the vision of the Constituent Assembly. It reflects the dream of the framers of the Constitution as to what kind of India they wanted. As it reflects the aspirations of the framers it at once becomes the philosophy and soul of the Constitution. The rest of the Constitution is the elucidation of the objectives and ideals contained in the Preamble. In the *Keshavananda Bharti* case, Chief Justice Sikri rightly observed, "It seems to me that the Preamble of any Constitution is of extreme importance and the Constitution should be read and interpreted in the light of the grand and noble vision expressed in the Preamble." However the judiciary's approach to the Preamble has not been uniform. Before the *Keshvananda Bharti* case judgement in 1973, the Supreme Court held the view that the Preamble was not a part of the Constitution and it could not be a source of any implied power.

In *Re Berubari Union and Exchange of Enclaves* case it held that although the Preamble is a key to the mind of framers of the Constitution and shows the general purposes for which they made its several provisions, it does not form part of the Constitution. In *Sajjan Singh Vs. State of Rajasthan*, Justice Hidayatullah said, "...Our Preamble is more akin in nature to the American Declaration of Independence than to the Preamble to the Constitution of United States. It does not make any grant of power but it gives a direction and purpose to the Constitution which is reflected in Parts III and IV." In Golaknath case also, the court held that the Preamble can in no way prohibit or limit the power to amend the Constitution contained in *Article 368*. But with the *Keshavananda Bharti* case, a new era began in which the court held that the Preamble was a part of the Constitution. In different judgements it has held almost the entire features mentioned in the Preamble as constituting the essential features of the basic structure of the Constitution. Thus, in the changed context, the Preamble has acquired legal and constitutional significance.

References

Austin, G., *The Indian Constitution: Cornerstone of a Nation*, 1972, Bombay, Oxford University Press.

Basu, D.D., *Introduction to the Constitution of India*, 1992, New Delhi, Prentice-Hall of India.

Bhandari, M.K., *Basic Structure of the Indian Constitution*, 1993, New Delhi, Deep and Deep Publications.

Markandan, K.C., *The Preamble*, 1986 New Delhi, National Publishing House.

Menon, V.K.W., *India Since Independence—From the Preamble to the Present*, 1972, New Delhi, S. Chand & Co..

Pylee, M.V., *India's Constitution*, 1974, Bombay, Asia Publishing House.

Rao, B. Shiva, *The Framing of India's Constitution*, 1968, New Delhi, The Indian Institute of Public Administration.

Siwach, J.R., *Dynamics of Indian Government and Politics*, 1990, New Delhi, Sterling Publishers Pvt. Ltd.

CHAPTER IV

Idea of Justice I—Fundamental Rights

What is Justice?

Derived from the Latin word *jus* and also included *justus* and *justitia* and connected with the word *jungere,* again a Latin word, Justice means what Professor Barker says, "Primarily a joining of or fitting, a bond or a tie" gliding into a sense of binding or obliging. Defining the word, 'jus', Professor Barker remarks that in its original form, it means something what is fitting and therefore, also binding. Elaborating the etymological meaning, he says that the word 'jus' conveys the idea of a valid custom to which any citizen can appeal, and which is recognised and can be enforced by a human authority." Professor Barker gives justice a legal connotation. According to him justice would mean "a body of binding or obliging values which ... the courts recognize as binding, and not only recognize but also enforce." But justice is not merely a relationship between man and man (as about law and as in courts) but it is also a relationship between value and value. Therefore Barker concludes " ... the function of justice may be said to be that of adjusting, joining or fitting the different political values. Justice is the reconciler and the synthesis of political values: it is their union in an adjusted and integrated whole."

Justice has numerous *dimensions* which include legal, political, social and economic.

The legal dimension of justice assumes (a) that law is the declared will of the state; (b) that it includes both the customary and statutory law; (c) that it is issued by a defined authority and is enforced and imposed by the court; (d) that if violated, it is accompanied by a corresponding punishment; (e) that it is limited by the provisions of the constitution or the conventions; (f) that the constitution is its supreme form, regulating the activities of the government and prescribing the rights and duties of the people.

The political dimension of justice is an extension of the legal dimension. Its features include (a) establishment of a democratic order without any discrimination, (b) political equality; (c) one person-one vote; (d) rule of law and not rule by people's whims; (e) enactment of constitutional provisions: (f) free press and democratic rights; (g) free and fair elections.

The social dimension of justice reflects a just society. Its peculiarities would include (a) elimination of all kinds of discrimination; (b) abolition of privileges based on birth, race, caste, creed or sex; (c) social roles to be determined by the capacity; (d) social mobility to be an alternative to rigid stratification; (e) equality of each with each and of each with all; (f) universal brotherhood.

The economic dimension of justice attempts to discover justice in the economic structure of the society. Its features are (a) establishment of a social order as the principle of mutual cooperation; (b) attainment of maximum production achieved through voluntary and independent economic enterprises; (c) equitable distribution of commodities so produced; (d) abolition of exploitation of man by man; (e) social security in the event of accident, illness and old-age; (f) prohibition of concentration of material resources in the hands of a few. These days we also talk about socio-economic justice which means (i) a just and harmonious social order; (ii) right to work; and (iii) right to property to be matched with the end of exploitation of man by man.

The Indian Constitution provides for various dimensions of justice. However, legal and political justice have been provided in Part III of the Constitution which deals with the Fundamental Rights while Part IV of the Constitution deals with social and economic dimensions of justice. This chapter deals with the Fundamental Rights of the Indian citizens.

Nature of Fundamental Rights

(i) *Fundamental Rights have been elaborately stated*

Each and every right has been discussed in detail, so that there is no confusion. No other Constitution in the world deals with fundamental rights in such detail. Part III of the Constitution which deals with fundamental rights, has as many as 27 articles. Then there are clauses and sub-clauses attached to almost every article.

(ii) *The Indian Constitution does not accept the doctrine of natural Rights*

Natural rights were defined by Justice Mathew in the *Keshavananda* Bharti case as "... those rights which are appropriate to man as a national and moral being and which are necessary for a good life. Although called 'rights,' they are not per se enforceable in Courts unless recognised by private law of the State." The fundamental rights, under the Indian Constitution, are the gift of the Constitution. They are natural rights in so far as they help develop human personality and are in tune with man's nature. They are not natural rights in so far as they are not given to the individual by nature.

(iii) *Fundamental Rights are restricted*

The fundamental rights, as such, are not available to everyone in the country. The members of the armed forces, for example, do not enjoy these rights, not because they are not citizens of the country, but because their duties, and performance of such duties do not permit them to exercise the fundamental rights.

(iv) *Fundamental Rights are not absolute*

The fundamental rights are clearly defined in their scope and limitations. They are not declared in absolute terms and are subjected to certain prescribed restrictions such as the unity of the nation, public interest, public order and public security. For example, the right to freedom of speech and expression is subjected to the reasonable restrictions imposed by law in the interest of the sovereignty and integrity of India, security of the state, friendly relations with foreign states, public order, decency or morality, or in relation to contempt of court, defamation or incitement to an offence. Similarly, the right to movement has been restricted in tribal areas. In educational institutions, the general right of admission may be restricted for the benefit of educationally backward classes. Religious freedom is limited by the requirements of public order, morality and health of the people. Similarly, the fundamental rights do not extend to the laws specified in the Ninth Schedule of the Constitution. In fact, the list of restrictions on the fundamental rights is very exhaustive inviting the criticism that the Constitution gives the fundamental rights through one hand and takes away through another. But the restriction has to be reasonable and the courts have the authority to decide the reasonableness of the restrictions. If the restriction is not reasonable, the court can declare such law or action of the executive as ultra vires.

(v) The Constitution provides for both negative as well as positive Rights

The fundamental rights limit the state action. The state has been forbidden from doing certain things. It has to respect the freedom and liberties of the people and not deprive them of their rights. *Article 14* clearly state: "The state shall not deny to any person equality before the law or the equal protection of the laws within the territory of India." Certain Fundamental Rights are positive in the sense that they permit a citizen to enjoy certain freedom. For example *Article 19* gives right to freedom.

(*vi*) *In conferring Fundamental Rights, the Constitution makes a distinction between the citizens and persons*

Some of the rights like equality before law (*Article 14*) or protection of personal life and liberty (*Article 21*) are available to all persons whether citizens or not. However, protection from discrimination on grounds only of religion race, caste, sex and place of birth (*Article 15*) or equality of opportunity in employment (*Article 16*) are given only to the citizens.

(vii) *Some of the Rights are available against the State*

Some of the rights are available against the state such as *Article 14* described above. There are certain rights against individuals also. For example, individuals have been prohibited from practising untouchability or trafficking in human beings or forced labour.

(viii) *Fundamental Rights are Justiciable*

They are pious and sacrosanct in so far as they are guaranteed and protected by the courts. In case of their violation, the individual may approach High Court or Supreme Court for the redress, which acts as the guardian of the Constitution through *Article 32* which Dr. B.R. Ambedkar described as "the very soul of the Constitution and very heart of it." *In Fertilizer Corporation Kamgar Union Vs. Union of India* case, the Supreme Court held that the jurisdiction conferred on the Supreme Court by *Article 32* is an integral part of the basic structure of the Constitution. *Article 13 (2)* specifically states that "The State shall not make any law which takes away or abridges the rights conferred by this Part and any law made in contravention of this clause shall, to the extent of the contravention, be void."

(ix) *The Parliament has the power to amend the Fundamental Rights*

This part needs a little historical analysis because we have a long tradition of conflict between the Parliament and the judiciary on this issue. In *Shankari Prasad* case, the Supreme Court held that the Parliament had the right to amend or abridge fundamental rights. However in *Golaknath* case, the court held that Parliament had no such power. The 24th Amendment to the Constitution (1971) restored this power to the Parliament. This issue again came up before the Supreme Court in *Keshavananda Bharti* case in 1973, in which constitutionality of 24th, 25th and 29th Constitutional Amendments were challenged. In its judgement, the Supreme Court came out with the doctrine of basic structure which meant, as Sikri, C.J. explained, "every provision of the Constitution can be amended provided the basic foundation and structure of the Constitution remains the same." This means certain part of the Constitution cannot be amended by the Parliament. In *Minerva Mills* case, Chandrachud C.J. declared, "... The Constitution is a precious heritage, therefore you cannot destroy its identity." The Court has not disclosed the detailed list of basic structures of the Constitution, but many of the fundamental rights have been declared as basic structures. This means that Parliament's, right to amend or abridge has been highly curtailed by the various decisions of the Supreme Court.

(x) *Fundamental Rights are not the only Rights available to the Indian citizens*

There are other constitutional rights as well. For example *Article 300-A* is a constitutional right which says that "No person shall be deprived of his property save by authority of law. "Right to citizenship for all the persons from within the territory of India or right to vote irrespective of religion, race, caste or sex are other examples of constitutional rights. The difference between fundamental rights and other constitutional rights is that while violation of fundamental rights needs immediate redressal through *Article 32* (Right to Constitutional Remedies which itself is a fundamental right), the other constitutional rights are enforced by ordinary legal processes.

(xi) *Fundamental Rights can be suspended during national emergency*

During emergency the President may, by order, declare that the right to move the court for the enforcement of certain mentioned fundamental rights as conferred by Part III may be suspended. However *Article 21* and *22* cannot be suspended. The emergency has been imposed three times and in all the emergencies, some of the fundamental rights were suspended.

Fundamental Rights—Contents

The Indian Constitution provides for six fundamental rights which are as follows:

(i) Right to Equality—*Articles 14* to *18*
(ii) Right to Freedom—*Articles 19* to *22*
(iii) Right against Exploitation—*Articles 23* and *24*.
(iv) Right to Freedom of Religion—*Articles 25* to *28*.
(v) Cultural and Educational Rights—*Articles 29* and *30*.
(vi) Right to Constitutional Remedies—*Article 32*.

Now we shall study all these fundamental rights in detail.

(i) *Right to Equality*

Article 14 of the Constitution guarantees right to equality to all the persons in India. It says, "The state shall not deny to any person equality before the law or equal protection of laws within the territory of India." The *equality before law* is an English concept which means absence of special privileges in favour of any person. It means law should be equally administered. Equality before the law is a basic tenet of rule of law which means that there should not be any discrimination on any ground whatsoever. This law is to be applied equally to both rich as well as poor. It means all persons should be punished equally in case of similar offence and that no person is above the law.

Equal protection of law is an American doctrine. It means equal laws. i.e. the law would be applied equally in like situations. It implies that there should not be any discrimination between one person and the other. It forbids discrimination, prohibits victimization: legislative and executive, and protects all persons against unwarranted discriminatory laws.

However, the Constitution of India does not advocate absolute equality. The state may classify persons for the purposes of legislation. But this classification should be on reasonable ground and it should not be arbitrary. This classification should be founded on intelligible differentia which distinguishes between those who are grouped together from others and this differentia should have a rational basis to the object sought to be achieved by law. Thus, for speedy trial, special courts may be formed for certain specific offences. For some areas, special laws may be passed and in certain situations, certain persons may be granted immunity.

Article 15 prohibits discrimination on grounds of religion, race, sex or place of birth. It declares, "The state shall not discriminate against any citizen on grounds only of religion, race, caste, sex, place of birth or any of them." This discrimination is prohibited with regard to (a) access to shops, public restaurants, hotels and places of public entertainment, or (b) the use of wells, tanks, bathing ghats, roads and places of public resort maintained wholly or partly out of state funds or dedicated to the use of the general public.

The Constitution provides for two exceptions in this regard. Firstly, the state may make special provisions for women and children. Secondly, the state may also make special provisions for socially or educationally backward classes of citizens or for the Scheduled Castes and the Scheduled Tribes.

Article 16 relates to the equality of opportunity for all citizens in matters of public employment. The state has been prohibited from discriminating on grounds only of religion, race, caste, sex, descent, place of birth, residence or any of them in public employment. However, reservations in public services may be made in favour of any backward class of citizens which, in the opinion of the state, is not adequately represented in the services under the state. The Supreme Court has ruled that ordinarily, not more than 50 percent seats should be reserved.

Article 17 removes a blot in the Indian society and that is untouchability. It declares, "Untouchability is abolished and its practice in any form is forbidden. The enforcement of any disability arising out of untouchability shall be an offence punishable in accordance with law." In 1955, the Parliament passed the untouchability (offences) Act which prescribed punishment for practising untouchability. In 1976, the Untouchability (offences) Act of 1955 was amended and renamed as the "Protection of Civil Rights Act, 1955" In this Act civil right has been defined as any right accruing to a person by reason of abolition of untouchability. The Act of 1976 provides for a maximum of six months' imprisonment for any person who practises untouchability. Its scope has also been widened since.

Article 18 is another step towards achieving social equality. It prohibits, the state on the one hand from conferring any title (the British used to confer like Sir) except for military and academic distinction. On the other hand, the citizens have also been debarred from accepting any title from any foreign state. Those persons who are not citizens of India, but who hold any office of profit or trust under the State cannot accept any title from any foreign state without the consent of the Indian President. Further any person, holding any office of profit or trust under the state, cannot accept any present, emolument, or office of any kind from or under any foreign state without the consent of the Indian President. The President may award Param Vir Chakra, Mahavir Chakra, Vir Chakra and Ashok Chakra for military distinctions. Similarly, Bharat Ratna, Padma Vibushan, Padma Bhushan and Padma Sri are awarded by the President for excellence in the social field.

(ii) *Right to Freedom*

Article 19 of the Indian Constitution guarantees the following six kinds of freedom to every citizen of India:

(a) Freedom of Speech and Expression
(b) Freedom of Assembly
(c) Freedom to form Associations and Unions
(d) Freedom of Movement
(e) Freedom of Residence and Settlement
(f) Freedom of Profession, Occupation, Trade or Business

(a) *Freedom of Speech and Expression:* Freedom of speech and expression is very necessary because through it the individual is able to obtain self-fulfilment. Without these freedoms, there cannot be development of individual's personality. It is only through freedom of speech and expression that individual feels his status/importance in the nation. Patriotism follows from this significance only. The socialism in erstwhile Soviet Union and other countries collapsed because people denied freedom of speech and expression felt a sense of alienation from their respective political systems. Freedom of speech means the right to express one's opinion freely without any fear through oral speech or writing or broadcasting. It also means freedom of the press. Explaining the importance of freedom of speech, Patanjali Sastri, C.J. observed in *Ramesh Thappar Vs. State of Madras* case that the "Freedom of the speech and of the press lay at the foundation of all democratic institutions, for without free political discussion no public education, so essential for the proper functioning of the process of popular government is possible. A freedom of such amplitude might involve rights of abuse. But (then) ... it is better to leave a few of its noxious branches to their luxuriant growth than by pruning them away, to injure the vigour of those yielding the proper fruits."

As early as 1950, the Supreme Court held that "There can be little doubt that the imposition of pre-censorship on a journal is a restriction on the liberty of the press which is an essential part of the freedom of speech and expression ...." The Indian press enjoys the power of publication. It includes freedom of circulation. The government cannot ban the circulation of any newspaper. Right to freedom and expression also includes film-making.

However the freedom of speech and expression is not absolute. It is subject to reasonable restrictions under the following heads:

- Security of the State.
- Friendly relations with foreign States.
- Public order.
- Decency or morality.
- Contempt of court.
- Defamation.
- Incitement to an offence.
- Sovereignty and integrity of India.

(b) Freedom of Assembly: Right to assemble is a very important democratic right. The Constitution guarantees right of assembly which includes the right to hold meetings and to take out processions. But such meetings or processions should be (i) unarmed and (ii) peaceful. In the interest of public order or the sovereignty and integrity of the country, this right may be restricted. The government may impose Section 144 in certain areas which makes the assembly of five or more persons unlawful. Section 129 of the Criminal Procedure

Code authorises the police to disperse any unlawful assembly and also any assembly likely to cause a disturbance to public peace. The assemblies may be subjected to regulation also. The route of a procession may also be regulated to regulate traffic and to maintain law and order. It is also required that before holding a meeting at a public place or before taking out a procession, the permission from the appropriate authority be taken.

(c) *Freedom of Association:* In modern society, the individual needs the right to form associations to achieve his objectives. Therefore, the Constitution declares that all the citizens will have the right to form associations or unions. It includes the right to constitute the association or union, also negative right of not joining any association or union. The importance of this right can be understood by the fact that all the political parties and trade unions are formed under this particular freedom. This freedom is also not unlimited. The state may impose reasonable restrictions in the interest of the sovereignty and integrity of India, public order and morality. Similarly the members of armed forces cannot form associations because that might endanger the sovereignty and integrity of India.

(d) *Freedom of Movement:* This right is very important because an all-India feeling can only be generated among the people if they are able to visit the various parts of the country. By visiting different places, the parochial feelings of provincialism also diminish and the individual perspective gets a wider horizon. Freedom of movement means freedom to go anywhere from one state to another and also within the same state. However, freedom of movement can be curtailed in the interest of the general public and for the protection of the interests of Scheduled Tribes. A person may be prevented from entering prohibited places like military establishments to preserve the security of the state. The right to movement in the Scheduled Tribe areas have been restricted to aboriginal tribes of India which have their distinctive culture, language, customs and manners. The entry of outsiders is likely to affect it.

(e) *Freedom of Residence:* The Indian citizens have a right to reside and settle in any part of the country. However, Jammu and Kashmir is an exception because persons of other states cannot settle there. This freedom is to ensure the removal of inter-state barriers. But this freedom is also subject to reasonable restrictions in the interest of the general public or for the protection of the interests of any scheduled tribe. In case of habitual offenders, restriction of residence can be applied. Prostitutes may be required to reside in a particular area only.

(f) *Freedom of Trade and Occupation:* The Constitution of India guarantees to each of its citizens the right to practise any profession, or to carry on any occupation, trade or business. Like other rights, this freedom is also not uncontrolled, but restricted by reasonable restrictions in the interests of the public. Secondly, the state may prescribe professional or technical qualifications necessary for carrying out any profession, trade or business. For a chemist shop, a degree in pharmacy is necessary. Similarly, for a medical profession, a medical degree is a must. Thirdly, the state may itself take up a certain trade or business which would exclude private individuals from such trade or business. The armament industry has been a monopoly of the State in India. No private individual is allowed to carry on such business.

Articles 20, 21 and 22 provides for Personal Freedom of the Indian citizens.

Article 20 says that "No person shall be convicted of any offence except for violation of law in force at the time of the commission of the act charged as an offence, nor be subjected to a penalty greater than that which might have been inflicted under the law in force at the time of the commission of the offence. *Article 20(2)* says that "No person shall be prosecuted and punished for the same offence more than once. *Article 20(3)* says, "No person accused of any offence shall be compelled to be a witness against himself." Thus a person can be convicted only when he has committed an offence under the law which is already in force. The law cannot be imposed upon him with retrospective effect. In other words, if an act is not an offence at the date of commission, no future law can make it an offence. However in case of civil liability a law can be of retrospective effect. For example a penalty under a tax law can be imposed retrospectively.

Article 21 confers on every person the fundamental right to life and personal liberty. It says, "No person shall be deprived of his life or personal liberty except according to procedure established by law." The right to life is not confined to a guarantee against taking away an individual's life but has a wider connotation. The Supreme Court has ruled "that any act which damages or injures or interferes with the use of any limb or faculty of a person either permanently or even temporarily, would be within the inhibition of *Article 21*. "Right to life means to live with human dignity, free from exploitation." The court has also held that right to livelihood is also included in the right to life "because no person can live without the means of living, that is, the means of livelihood." In another case, the Supreme Court upheld the right of people living in hilly areas for a suitable approach road because right to life in *Article 21* embraces not only physical existence of life but also the quality of life and for residents of hilly areas, access to road is access to life itself. "According to Supreme Court, "the life includes all that gives meaning to a man's life including his tradition, culture and heritage and protection of that heritage in its full measure." Right to personal liberty is available against the state only. In case right to personal liberty is threatened by some private individual, the remedy lies under the ordinary law and not under *Article 21*.

A new *Article 21A* was added vide 86th Constitution Amendment Act, 2002, which provides for right to education to the children belonging to the age-group between 6-14 years. *Article 21A* says, "The State shall provide free and compulsory education to all the children of the age of 6-14 years in such a manner as the state may, by law, determine."

Article 22 gives protection to the detained against arbitrary arrest. It says the following:

(i) A person who is arrested can be detained in custody. But he should be told the grounds of such arrest as soon as may be. He has a right to consult and be defended by a lawyer of his choice.

(ii) The person arrested and detained should be produced before the nearest magistrate within 24 hours. This excludes the time necessary to go from the place of arrest to the court of the magistrate. A person cannot be detained beyond 24 hours without the authority of a magistrate.

There are two exceptions to *Article 22*.

(i) If the person arrested and detained is an enemy alien, or

(ii) He is arrested under any law providing for preventive detention.

The person detained under preventive detention can remain in custody for not more than three months. However, in certain circumstances detention may go beyond three months. In such a case, an Advisory Board consisting of High Court judges or the persons who are qualified to become High Court judges, report that there are sufficient grounds for the detention of the detained person. But this report should come before the expiry of three months.

A person can be detained for more than three months without trial and without the report of an Advisory Board if he has been detained under a law made by the Parliament providing for preventive detention. In such cases, the following stipulations have been made:

(i) The Parliament by law shall stipulate the circumstances, and the class or classes of cases in which a person may be detained for more than three months without obtaining the opinion of an Advisory Board.
(ii) The maximum period for which a person may be detained.

A person arrested under preventive detention should be told the reasons of his detention and he should be given the earliest opportunity to make his representation against the preventive detention. However, the authorities may not disclose the facts to the detained person if they feel, that it is against the public interest. It is to be noted that the 44th Constitutional Amendment (1978), reduces the term of three months to two months of detention without the report of the Advisory Board. However, this has not come into force as yet.

It is a fact that preventive detention legislations have been in force right from 1950. When Sardar Patel introduced the first preventive detention bill, he said that he had two sleepless nights before doing the same. This power of preventive detention was highly misused during the 1975-1977 emergency, when a very large number of people, even children, were detained without trial under COFEPOSA and MISA.

In 2002, the Indian Parliament passed the Prevention of Terrorism Act (POTA). However, there were reports of its widespread misuse and it was repealed in 2004.

(iii) Right against Exploitation

Article 23 prohibits traffic in human beings and begars and other similar forms of forced labour. Traffic in human beings means to trade men and women like goods. It includes slavery. In 1976, the Parliament abolished bonded labour system. Trafficking of women and children for immoral purposes is also illegal. *Begar* means to force work from somebody without making any payment or with making inadequate payment. It means making a person work against his will and without paying any remuneration. In the *Asiad Workers Case,* the Supreme Court held that all unwilling labour is forced labour, whether paid or not, and therefore is prohibited. However, the state may impose compulsory services for public purposes but in doing so it cannot discriminate on grounds only of religion, race, caste or class or any of them. Here, public purpose has been given a wider meaning and it means the welfare of the people as envisaged in the Directive Principles of State Policy. Conscription to army and police is not *begar.*

Article 24 prohibits the employment of children below the age of fourteen in hazardous enterprises, factory or mine. This includes construction work. The Child Labour (Prohibition and Regulation) Act of 1986 enumerates various hazardous industries to give effect to *Article 24.*

(iv) Right to Freedom of Religion

The concept of secularism is implied in the provisions relating to right to freedom of religion. *Article 25* gives every person of India right to freedom of conscience and to freely profess, practise and propagate religion. The Sikhs have been given the right to carry *Kirpans.* However, their right is also not absolute. It is subject to public order, morality, health and other provisions of Part III of the Constitution. Further, the state may regulate or restrict any economic, financial, political or other secular activity which may be associated with religious practice. The state may make laws providing for social welfare and reforms. Further, the state may make laws for the purpose of throwing open of the Hindu religious institutions of a public character to all classes and sections of the Hindus. This was done because the Hindu religious practices did not allow a Harijan's entry into a temple.

Article 26 is the extension of *Article 25.* The followers of every religion have the right to:

(a) establish and maintain institutions for religious and charitable purposes
(b) to manage its own affairs in matter of religion.

(c) to own ad acquire moveable and immovable property.
(d) to administer such property in accordance with law.

Article 27 gives freedom from paying any tax, the proceeds of which are to be spent on an any particular religion. *Article 28* prohibits the imparting of religious instructions in any educational institution wholly maintained by State funds. However, in case of such educational institutions, recognised by state, or receiving aid out of state funds, that may impart religious instruction, no person attending such institution, shall be compelled to take religious education or attend religious worship.

(v) Cultural and Educational Rights

The cultural and educational rights are intended to protect the interests of the minorities. *Article 29* states that the minorities shall have the right to preserve their distinct language, script or culture. According to Supreme Court judgements, this is an absolute right. The Court has also held that 'right to conserve the language of the citizens also includes the right to agitate for the protection of the language'. *Article 29 (2)* declares that "No citizen shall be denied admission into any educational institution maintained by the state or receiving aid out of State funds on grounds only of religion, race, caste, language or any of them."

Article 30 gives protection to religious and linguistic minorities. They have the right to establish and administer institutions of their choice. *Article 30 (1-A)* says that in case of any property of an educational institution established and administered by a minority being acquired by the State, the State shall ensure that the amount fixed for such acquired property should be such as would not restrict or abrogate the rights of that minority. *Article 30 (2)* prohibits state from discriminating in granting aid to educational institutions managed by the religious and linguistic minorities.

(vi) Right to Constitutional Remedies

Dr. Ambedkar explained the significance of the fundamental right to Constitutional Remedies thus—"If I was asked which particular Article of the Constitution was the most important, an Article without which this Constitution would be nullified, I would not refer to any other Article except this one. It is the very soul of the Constitution and the very heart of it." This Article guarantees the right to move Supreme Court in case any of the fundamental rights are attacked. It should be noted that the High Courts also share this jurisdiction along with the Supreme Court, which means a citizen is free to approach either the Supreme Court or High Courts for the redressal. The Supreme Court/High Court issues orders or writs for the enforcement of these rights. They are as follows:

(a) Writ of Habeas Corpus: Habeas Corpus is an English Constitutional term which literally means "to have the body." It is a safeguard against unwarranted arrest. While issuing the *writ of Habeas Corpus,* the court orders the detaining authority to produce the detained person and explain to the court the reasons of his confinement. The court examines the grounds of confinement and sets the arrested person free if he is unlawfully detained.

Writ of Habeas Corpus can even be made by a stranger, a social worker. The general rule that a petition for a writ can be made only by the person whose rights have been infringed does not apply in the *writ of Habeas Corpus.* Even a person who has been granted bail is entitled to apply for Habeas Corpus to have the cause for his arrest investigated because the person is granted bail and he is not set free. He remains in the custody of the court through the agencies of the sureties, he furnishes.

(b) Writ of Mandamus: Mandamus literally means a command. It is issued to a person when there is no other adequate legal remedy. It commands the person to whom it is addressed, to perform some public or quasi-legal duty which he has not performed. The application of *Mandamus* can be made only by the aggrieved party. In issuing the *Mandamus,* the Court may not only ask to act according to law or refrain from acting contrary to law, it can also go further, to direct in positive terms. Particularly in cases involving socio-economic justice, the Court has directed the authorities the particular things which are to be done to carry out the law. According to D.D. Basu it includes:

- to restore possession of property to the applicant or to pay him compensations.
- to omit certain words from the licence granted to the applicant.
- to remove the ban against the petitioner in respect to further employment under the government.
- to make refund of tax illegally or unconstitutionally collected from the petitioner.
- to consider the applicant's case on merit.

- to direct the authority to treat the petitioner as eligible for promotion and to determine his rank in the cadre of promotion, where, from the records it was established that the petitioner satisfied the required criteria for promotion.
- to direct an educational institution to admit the petitioners as students.
- to direct a public authority to pay terminal benefits to discharged employees.

Further, the court has also issued *Mandamus* in case of environmental deterioration to implement the Directive Principles of State Policy. Mandamus can be issued to prevent court martial from exceeding their jurisdiction. It can also be issued to quash an act or order of a Police Officer which he has no jurisdiction to issue and which constitutes a misuse of the legal power of the Police.

(c) Writ of Prohibition: The *writ of prohibition* is usually issued by a higher court to a lower court forbidding it to continue proceedings which are in excess of its jurisdiction. This means that the object of the writ is to compel inferior courts to keep themselves within the limits of their jurisdiction.

(d) Writ of Certiorari: The *writ of prohibition* is available at an earlier stage. For the later stage, the *writ of certiorari* is issued to remove a suit from an inferior court to a higher court as the lower court does not possess the adequate jurisdiction and it is continuing with the proceedings. It is to be understood that both the *prohibition* and *certiorari* are intended to stop the inferior courts from usurping the jurisdiction which they do not possess. Normally the application of *certiorari* is to be applied for by the aggrieved party. But this does not apply in cases of public interest litigation.

(e) Writ of Quo Warranto: The *writ of quo warranto* is issued to prevent illegal assumption of any public office. The court examines the legality of the claim of the person who is enjoying a public office and oust him if his claim is illegal. For example, a person is appointed in a public office at the age of 60 and the retirement age to that office is 60 then the court may issue a writ of quo warrant against that person and declare that official position as vacant. Any person can apply for the *writ of quo warranto.*

References

Arora N.D. and S.S. Awasthy, *Political Theory*, 1996, New Delhi, Har-Anand Publications Pvt Ltd..

Austin, Granville, *The Indian Constitution: Cornerstone of a Nation*, 1972, Bombay, Oxford University Press.

Basu, D.D., *Introduction to the Constitution of India*, 1992, New Delhi, Prentice Hall of India Private Limited.

———*Shorter Constitution of India* 1994, New Delhi, Prentice-Hall of India (P) Ltd.

Bhandari M.P., *Basic Structure of the Indian Constitution*, 1993 New Delhi, Deep and Deep Publications.

Jain, M.P., *Indian Constitutional Law*, 1978, Bombay, N.M. Tripathi Private Limited.

Kagzi M.C.J., *The Constitution of India*, 1967, Delhi, Metropolitan Book Co. Private Limited.

Pylee, M.V., *India's Constitution*, 1974, Bombay, Asia Publishing House.

Rao, B. Shiva, *The Framing of India's Constitution*, 1968, New Delhi, The Indian Institute of Public Administration.

Singh, M.P., Shukla, *V.N.*, *Constitution of India*, 1993, Lucknow, Eastern Book Company.

Siwach, J.R., *Dynamics of Indian Government and Politics*, 1990, New Delhi, Sterling Publishers Private Limited.

CHAPTER V

Idea of Justice II—Directive Principles of State Policy

The fundamental rights contained in Part III of the Constitution, by and large, deal with the ideals of political justice. However, the framers of the Constitution knew very well that the ideals of political justice would remain unfulfilled until they were accompanied by adequate social and economic rights. They were also aware of their limitations, as the colonial rule had left India socially and economically backward. A majority of India's population consisted of teeming millions who were deprived of the basic needs of subsistence. Freedom had generated a great deal of expectations among them from the new political leaders of free India, who were now engrossed in the making of the Constitution. The leaders too, were aware of this. Nehru echoed their views when he said, "The service of India means the service of the millions who suffer. It means the ending of poverty and ignorance and disease and inequality of opportunity. The ambition of the greatest man (i.e. Mahatma Gandhi) of our generation has been to wipe every tear from every eye. That may be beyond us, but as long as there are tears and sufferings, so long our work will not be over." When Nehru said that "That may be beyond us" he was referring to the helplessness of the political leadership. Given the vast magnitude of poverty which could not vanish overnight, as they did not possess any magic lamp to do so, they could only be pragmatic—as much as possible. Therefore, they decided to give political and civil rights to the people immediately after the commencement of the Constitution. But they could not ignore the social and economic rights. Here the Irish Constitution came to their rescue as it had enumerated social and economic needs in the directive principles of State Policy which were declared as non-justiciable. The framers of the Indian Constitution decided to include their spirit in the Constitution.

Initially both the fundamental rights and directive principles were included in Part III of the Draft Constitution. Later on, they were bifurcated and Directive Principles of State Policy found their place in Part IV of the Constitution, which were made non-justiciable.

Besides the Irish Constitution, the Government of India Act of 1935 also contained Instruments of Instructions which were non-justiciable in nature and contained welfare provisions. One of them required the Governor of the provinces "to take care that due provisions shall be made for the advancement and social welfare of those classes who on account of the smallness of their number or their lack of educational or material advantages or from any other cause especially rely on our protection."

Features of Directive Principles of State Policy

The following are the features of Directive Principles of State Policy:

(i) Directive Principles of State Policy are Non-Justiciable

One of the articles of directive principles i.e *Article 37* specifically declares: "The provisions contained in this Part shall not be enforceable by any court, ..." This is in contrast to the fundamental rights, which are enforceable by the court of law. This means in case of violation of fundamental rights, the citizen can approach the Supreme Court or High Courts and the court will listen to him and redress his grievances. However, if for example, a citizen does not get employment which has been mentioned as right to work in *Article 41* of the directive principles, he cannot approach the court to get employment from the state.

(ii) The Directive Principles are positive directions to the State to act in a particular manner

Article 37 says that they are "... nevertheless fundamental in the governance of the country and it shall be the duty of the state to apply these principles in making laws." *Articles 37* to *51* contain the obligations of the State towards its citizens. *Article 38* says that the State shall strive for a social order where "political, social and economic justice shall inform all the institutions of the national life." In this sense, they are positive directions to the state. In the same sense, they can be differentiated from the fundamental rights as they are negative in character and compel the state not to act in a particular manner.

(iii) The Directive Principles lay down the various tenets of a welfare state

The concept of a welfare state is a synthesis between total State control of socialism and the blind pursuit of the profits of liberalism. Removal of economic disparities in the society is the most important task of a welfare State. However, it does not mean that the welfare state is concerned only with economic development of the people. It also aims at the removal of social discrimination based on sex, caste, creed, colour and other factors. The total emancipation of the individual from social and economic disparities is the aim. Viewed in this context, the directive principles give right to work and equal wages for equal work to both the sexes, to the people of India; the ownership and control of material resources of the community are to be distributed to achieve common good; the children, men and women are to be free from exploitation; free and compulsory education to children till 14 years of age, etc. M.V. Pylee rightly states, "Taken together, these principles lay down the foundations on which a new democratic India will be built up. They represent the minimum of ambitions and aspirations cherished by the people of India, set as a goal to be realised in a reasonable period of time. Indeed, when the State in India translates these principles into reality, she can justify claim to be a Welfare State."

Directive Principles of State Policy: Contents

Part IV of the Indian Constitution contains *16 Articles* (*Articles 36* to *51*) of directives which are as follows:

Article 38: State to secure a social order for the promotion of welfare of the people:

(a) The State shall strive to promote the welfare of the people by securing and protecting as effectively as it may, a social order in which justice—social, economic and political, shall inform all the institutions of the national life.
(b) The State shall, in particular, strive to minimize the inequalities in income and endeavour to eliminate inequalities in status, facilities and opportunities, not only amongst individuals but also amongst groups of people residing in different areas or engaged in different vocations.

Article 39: Certain principles of policy to be followed by the State—The State shall, in particular, direct its policy towards securing—

(a) that the citizens, men and women equally, have the right to an adequate means of livelihood;
(b) that the ownership and control of the material resources of the community are so distributed as best to serve the common good;
(c) that the operation of the economic system does not result in the concentration of wealth and means of production to the common detriment;
(d) that there is equal pay for equal work for both men and women;
(e) that the health and strength of workers, men and women and the tender age of children are not abused and that citizens are not forced by economic necessity to enter avocations unsuited to their age or strength;
(f) that children are given opportunities and facilities to develop in a healthy manner and in conditions of freedom and dignity and that childhood and youth are protected against exploitation and against moral and material abandonment.

Article 39 (A): Equal justice and free legal aid—The State shall secure that the operation of the legal system promotes justice, on a basis of equal opportunity and shall, in particular, provide free legal aid, by suitable legislation or schemes or in any other way, to ensure that opportunities for securing justice are not denied to any citizen by reason of economic or other disabilities.

Article 40: Organisation of village Panchayats—The State shall take steps to organise village panchayats and endow them with such powers and authority as may be necessary to enable them to function as units of self-government.

Article 41: Right to work, to education and to public assistance in certain cases—The State shall, within the limits of its economic capacity and development make effective provision for securing the right to work, to education and to public assistance in cases of unemployment, old age, sickness and disablement and in other cases of undeserved want.

Article 42: Provision for just and humane conditions of work and maternity relief—The State shall make provisions for securing just and humane conditions of work and for maternity relief.

Article 43: Living wages etc., for workers—The State shall endeavour to secure, by suitable legislation or economic organisation or in any other way, to all workers, agricultural, industrial or otherwise, work, a living wage, conditions of work ensuring a decent standard of life and full enjoyment of leisure and social and cultural opportunities and, in particular, the State shall endeavour to promote cottage industries on an individual or co-operative basis in rural areas.

Article 43 (A): Participation of workers in management of industries—The State shall take steps, by suitable legislation or in any other way, to secure the participation of workers in the management of undertakings, establishment or other organisations, engaged in any industry.

Article 44: Uniform civil code for the citizens—The State shall endeavour to secure for the citizens a uniform civil code throughout the territory of India.

Article 45: Provision for early childhood care and education to children below the age of six years—The state shall endeavour to provide early childhood care and education for all children until they complete the age of six years.

Article 46: Promotion of educational and economic interests of Scheduled Castes, Scheduled Tribes and other weaker sections—The State shall promote with special care the educational and economic interests of the weaker sections of the people and, in particular, of the Scheduled Castes and Scheduled Tribes, and shall protect them from social injustice and all forms of exploitation.

Article 47: Duty of the state to raise the level of nutrition and the standard of living and to improve public health—The State shall regard the raising of the level of nutrition and the standard of living of its people and the improvement of public health as among its primary duties and in particular, the State shall endeavour to bring about prohibition of the consumption, except for medical purposes, of intoxicating drinks and of drugs which are injurious to health.

Article 48: Organisation of agriculture and animal husbandry—The State shall endeavour to organise agriculture and animal husbandry on modern and scientific lines and shall, in particular, take steps for preserving and improving the breeds and prohibiting the slaughter of cows and calves and other milch and draught cattle.

Article 48A: Protection and improvement of environment and safeguarding the forests and wildlife—The State shall endeavour to protect and improve the environment and to safeguard the forests and wildlife of the country.

Article 49: Protection of monuments and places and objects of national importance—It shall be the obligation of the State to protect every monument or place or object of artistic or historic interest (declared by or under law made by Parliament) to be of national importance. from spoilation, disfigurement, destruction, removal, disposal or export, as the case may be.

Article 50: Separation of judiciary from executive—The State shall take steps to separate the judiciary from the executive in the public services of the State.

Article 51: Promotion of international peace and security—The State shall endeavour to—

(a) promote international peace and security;
(b) maintain just and honourable relations between nations;
(c) foster respect for international law, and treaty obligations in the dealings of organised people with one another, and
(d) encourage settlement of international disputes by arbitration.

Directive Principles of State Policy—A Critique

The directive principles of State policy were criticised in the Constituent Assembly itself. A member called them a set of New Year's resolutions, while another said that they were a cheque payable by the bank concerned at its own convenience. It was also pointed out that the Constitution is a legal document and it should not contain moral precepts which cannot be enforced by the Court of law. The other criticism was that they were borrowed from other Constitutions.

In short, the following are the criticisms levelled against the Directive Principles of State policy:

(i) Directive principles do not have legal sanctions. They cannot be enforced by the courts. Therefore they do not matter.
(ii) These principles are moral precepts.
(iii) They are vaguely stated and illogically arranged. The ideologies as extreme as socialism and liberalism, Gandhism and liberal-intellectual traditions have been put in one place. According to N. Srinivasan, "It combines rather incongruously the modern with the old and provisions suggested by reason and science with provisions based purely on sentiment and prejudice."
(iv) Certain provisions of the directive principles are almost impossible to be achieved. For example Panchayati Raj. There are certain historical processes which cannot be reversed. Panchayati Raj was a system of administration in the good old days when there was little or no development in science and technology. The modern times have witnessed a revolution in science and technology with the result the world has become small. The Individual, and not the village, is the unit of administration. Further, the economies have become international and under such circumstances, any step towards Panchayati Raj is bound to be doomed. Similarly, with the provisions regarding prohibition, wherever prohibition has

been implemented, it has been a failure, whether Mumbai, Chennai, Gujarat, Haryana or Andhra Pradesh. In many cases, the State governments had to retract, because the ill-effects of prohibition became obvious. It led to bootlegging and spurious liquor which led to death of people who drank it. Another provision which is difficult to implement is the uniform civil code. There is a great deal of resentment, especially among the Muslims, with regard to the uniform civil code.

(v) There are principles which can not be implemented in any future—near or remote. Social justice is one such example. And then, there are principles which any government, worth the name, should implement. Care of public health for instance. What, one may ask, is the justification of including those principles which can not be implemented; and what is the justification of including principles which any government should implement if it is to be called a government.

Nevertheless, their significance cannot be underrated. They remain fundamental in the governance of the country. As such, they become the yardstick or the measuring rod, according to which the performance of a government can be judged, as they contain the provisions of a welfare State. A government can be said to be successful to the extent it has been able to provide social and economic rights to the people as enshrined in the directive principles of state policy. Dr. Ambedkar rightly explained the significance of directive principles when he said, "... who should be in power is left to be determined by the people, as it must be, if the system is to satisfy the tests of democracy. But whoever, captures power will not be free to do what he likes with it. In the exercise of it, he will have to respect these Instruments of Instructions which are called Directive Principles. He cannot ignore them. He may not have to answer for their breach in a court of law. But he will certainly have to answer for them before the electorate at election time ..." Even the Supreme Court has, over the years, been taking help from 'these directive principles in deciding various cases. For example in *Unni Krishan Vs. State of Andhra Pradesh,* the court took the assistance from *Articles 41* and *45* and held that every child/citizen of this country has a right to free education till 14 years of age. In *Randhir Singh Vs. Union of India,* Supreme Court recognised the principle of 'equal pay for equal work' not only as a fundamental right but also as a constitutional goal capable of enforcement through the fundamental right to constitutional remedies. It has also held that the Minimum Wages Act is equally applicable in the case of casual workers.

Thus, although the directive principles are non-justiciable, they reflect the pious wishes of the framers of the Constitution and they are a very important part of the Constitution.

Directive Principles of State Policy and Fundamental Rights—Inter-Relationship

It may well be said that directive principles are positive commands to the State, while fundamental rights are negative in character, prohibiting the State from doing certain things. We know that fundamental rights are civil and political rights, while directive principles largely contain social and economic rights designed to bring about a welfare State. Lastly, we also know that the fundamental rights are justiciable and enforceable by the courts, while directive principles cannot be enforced by the courts. But these differentiations cannot explain the complexity of the situation relating to the relationship between the two. They need further elaboration especially in the light of conflict that took place between the judiciary and the legislature on their inter-relationship.

Soon after the implementation of the Constitution, the Supreme Court took the view that fundamental rights enjoyed primacy over the directive principles. In *Champakam Dorairajan case* in 1951, the court declared, "The Directive Principles of State Policy have to conform to and run as subsidiary to the chapter of Fundamental Rights" because the latter are enforceable by the court and the former are not. Later on, the Supreme Court attempted to bring about harmony and balance between the two. In another case (*C.B. Boarding and Lodging Vs. State of Mysore*), the Court saw no conflict "on the whole" between the fundamental rights and directive principles. It declared them "complementary and supplementary to each other." Therefore, in *Kameshwar Singh case*, it upheld the abolition of Zamindari for public purposes keeping in view *Article 47* of the Constitution which enjoins upon the State to raise the level of nutrition and the standard of living and to improve public health. The Minimum Wages Act 1948 was declared lawful as it was made to give effect to the directive principles as in *Article 43*. The Supreme Court also declared the ban on cow slaughter keeping *Article 48* of the Constitution in mind.

However, in the *Golaknath case*, the Supreme Court held that fundamental rights were sacrosanct and could not be taken away or abridged so as to implement the directive principles. But in this case also, the Supreme Court said that it cannot appreciate the agreement that all the agrarian reforms ... cannot be brought about without amending the fundamental rights. According to Supreme Court, the fundamental rights and directive principles were an integrated scheme that was elastic enough to respond to the changing needs of the society. Therefore, the Parliament was free to implement directive principles without curtailing the fundamental rights. The Parliament could not amend the Constitution to curtail or abridge the fundamental rights.

But the Parliament felt that the Supreme Court judgements were a stumbling block in bringing about socio-economic revolution in the country. Therefore, the *Golaknath case* judgement in particular, was highly criticised. However, undeterred by the criticisms, the Supreme Court struck down the nationalisation of 14 banks and the Privy Purses Abolition law. The Parliament decided to amend the Constitution. Accordingly, the 25th Amendment sought to give primacy to directive principles over the fundamental rights. But, the Supreme Court nullified the objective of the 25th Amendment and restored the primacy of fundamental rights over the directive principles as it felt that the fundamental rights were the essential features of the basic structure of the Constitution and therefore could hardly be amended. The Parliament again sought to place the primacy of directive principles over fundamental rights, through the 42nd Constitutional Amendment to the Constitution.

The legality of 42nd Constitutional Amendment was also challenged in the Supreme Court, in the *Minerva Mills* case. The issue was the same as to who enjoys the pivotal position, whether fundamental rights or the directive principles. The court again held that the fundamental rights were more important than the directive principles. However it also stood for the harmony and balance between the two. Chief Justice Chandrachud said, "The Indian Constitution is founded on the bedrock of the balance between Part III and IV. The significance of the perception is that Part III and IV together constitute the core of commitment to social revolution and they, together, are the conscience of the Constitution. Part III and IV are like two wheels of a chariot, one no less than the other. They are like twin formulae for achieving the social revolution. To give absolute primacy to one over the other is to disturb the harmony of the Constitution. This harmony and balance between the fundamental rights and directive principles is an essential feature of the basic structure of the Constitution." Thus, now the fundamental rights enjoy primacy over the directive principles but this does not mean that directive principles cannot be implemented. They have to be implemented as they are fundamental in the governance of the country and it is the duty of the State to enforce them. In *Bandhua Mukti Morcha case,* the court held that directive principles cannot be enforced by the court, yet the court can order the State to enforce the law once the legislature has passed it and particularly when the non-enforcement of law leads to denial of a fundamental right. By now the judiciary is increasingly relying on Directive Principles of State Policy to determine the reasonability of restrictions on the fundamental rights.

Directive Principles of State Policy—Their Implementation

The directive principles embody a vast area and perspective. Therefore it is very difficult to discuss their implementation in brief. Given the limitations, we will try to survey the situation since 1950, when the Constitution came into force.

After the implementation of the Constitution, the Indian political system embarked upon the policy of economic revolution with the specific aim of implementing directive principles of State policy. For the purpose of distributing lands to the landless, land reform legislations were passed by different state assemblies. Ceiling on the amount of land that a person may possess was decided and the excess land acquired and distributed among the landless. The Zamindari system was abolished and intermediaries like *jagirdars, imandars* etc. were also done away with. The land reform legislations were given Constitutional protection through the inclusion of IX schedule, the effect of which was that they could not be challenged in the courts on the ground that they violate or abridge the fundamental rights. Besides these legal steps, a social movement—Bhoodan Andolan (land-donation movement) was organised by Vinobha Bhave in which the excess land was solicited voluntarily from the landowners.

The Government of India established a Planning Commission in 1950, to coordinate the schemes for economic development.

By early 1960's it was being felt that sub-divisions and fragmentation of land holdings was assuming alarming proportions in the countryside. This initiated the second round of State intervention in the land-holding pattern in the country. The Government initiated steps for consolidation of agricultural holdings. In 1970's there was a clamour for another far-reaching set of legislation, fixing land ceiling for different kinds of lands in the countryside. Urban land ceilings acts, already in vogue, prohibited ownership of more than a specified size of plot in urban areas. Usually it was restricted to 400 meters.

There has resulted, substantially, a rise in production of foodgrains in the country. While total production during 1950-51 was barely 50 million tons, we are reaping an annual harvest of over 200 million tons today. We had a massive buffer stock of 58 million tons at Food Corporation of India godowns as on January 1, 2002. This has been made possible by more than doubling the gross area irrigated during the 30-year period of 1960 to 1990. Not only that, during this very period, percentage of irrigated area to the cultivated area has risen from 18 per cent to 33 per cent. This very extension of irrigational facilities has made it possible to bring more land under cultivation on the one hand and to have two crops per year on the other.

Now, 91 per cent of the wheat and 75 per cent of rice-growing areas are using high yield varieties of seeds. In case of millets, we have been able to extend the benefits of agricultural research to at least 50 per cent of the area. In Punjab and the adjoining areas, in the mid-sixties, a Green Revolution took place where mechanisation was highly encouraged and agriculture was organised on scientific lines. Consequently, India became self- sufficient in food grain production.

The State took decisive steps for introducing new technology in agriculture. This was in keeping with the Article 48 which directed the State to organise agriculture on modern and scientific lines. This initiative consisted of mechanisation, high-yield variety of seeds, chemical fertiliser and assured irrigation. The National Seed Corporation was set up to supply high yielding variety of seeds. Several agricultural universities and research centres were established in different parts of the country to encourage research in agriculture. Different river valley projects were undertaken to provide not only irrigation to the farmers, but also to generate electricity. Bhakra Nangal in Punjab, Nagarjunasagar Project in Andhra Pradesh, Tungabhadra Project in Andhra Pradesh and Karnataka, Kosi Project in Bihar, Farakka Project in West Bengal, Damodar Valley Project in West Bengal and Bihar are some examples. These efforts have borne fruit.

Besides the Green Revolution, which made India self-sufficient in food grains, we have also witnessed a White Revolution. The Country has nearly 57 per cent of the world's buffalo population and

16 per cent of the cattle population. While in 1950-51, India produced a mere 17 million tonnes of milk with 124 per capita milk availability, in 2001-02 this has increased to 81 million tonnes with a per capita availability of 217 grams.

The industrial structure of the Indian economy was rather lopsided in 1950-51. Since then, the process of economic planning initiated by the government has led to massive diversification of the industrial base of the country. We are today producing a vast range of consumer, intermediate and producer's goods or machinery and equipment, and the share of industrial sector in total national income has increased substantially. It is interesting to know that the public sector, which was virtually non-existent at the time of independence, now contributes almost one fourth of gross domestic product. Not only this, over 40 per cent of gross domestic formation in the country is also directly affected by government. It also provides help to the private sector to raise funds through equity participation and loans extended to it by government—owned financial institutions. Thus we can say that the State is directly building atleast 2/5 of the capital, providing another 2/5th of private sector large-scale companies' capital by way of equity participation on the part of public sector financial institutions. Not only that, of the total capital invested in the large-scale limited companies in our country, some 80 per cent has been borrowed from the public sector financial institutions. In all 88 per cent of the funds involved have been coming from the public sector. The government has used Industries Development and Regulation Act (IDRA) for giving a socially desirable direction and dimension to a pattern of industrial development in the country so that we can have a more equitable regional distribution and spread of industries.

Massive investment in organised industrial sector has led to modernisation of Indian industries and more than doubled the employment therein. It has further led to increase in the volume of trade, transport, banking and finance sectors. Therefore, a large number of employment opportunities have been created.

Small-scale and cottage industries which constituted the backbone of traditional industrial economy of India have received special benevolent attention from the State under the Five Year Plans. Government has provided technical and financial assistance to small industries' corporations, technology centres and small industries services institutes etc. State sponsored and cooperative marketing organisation for these industries have also been set up to ensure remunerative prices for the manufacturers. The Government has been giving 15 per cent price preference to the small scale industries in its own purchases and procurements. On the top of it we have had a system of reservation of several kinds of industries for the small-scale and cottage industries sector. This sector has responded with much enthusiasm to various development schemes of the Government so much so that in 2001-02 some 18.56 million people were employed in small industries. During the same year, the small-scale sector produced output worth 6,45,496 crores of rupees (at current prices). The small-scale industries have also been earning substantial amount of foreign exchange for the country. In the year 2001-02 they earned 13.13 billion US dollars worth of foreign exchange.

For the promotion of cottage industries, several Boards like the All-India Khadi and Village Industries Board, All-India Handicraft Board, All India Handloom Board, Silk Board, Coir Board have been set up to finance the cottage industries and market their goods.

Educational facilities at the time of independence were grossly inadequate. Schools were not known beyond towns. Colleges and Universities were confined to not more than a dozen or so big towns in the country. The government assumed the responsibilities for making primary education universal and compulsory. Steps were initiated to enroll as large a proportion of population in the age group 5-14 in schools, as possible. The Lok Sabha on November, 2001 passed the 93rd Amendment to the Constitution which makes the right to free and compulsory education in the age group of 6-14, a Fundamental Right. It also makes a Fundamental Duty of the parent/guardian to provide opportunities to their children for education. In 2001-02 a very ambitious program called Sarva Shiksha Abhiyan was launched by the Central Government with the following targets; (i) all children in the age group 6-14 to be given education through schools/Education Guarantee Centres/bridge course by 2003; (ii) children of age group 6-14 to complete five year primary education by 2007 and eight years of schooling by 2010; (iii) focus on elementary education of satisfactory quality, with emphasis on education for life; (iv) bridge all gender and social category gaps at the primary stage by 2007 and at the elementary education level by 2010; and (v) universal retention by 2010. The number of secondary and senior secondary schools have increased from 7,416 in 1950-51 to 1,52,049 in 2004-05. There is an impressive growth in universities and technical and professional education. Special efforts have been undertaken to spread literacy among the adults through the National Literacy Mission. As a result there is a significant decline in the infant mortality rate from 146 in 1950-51 to 57.0 per thousand in 2006. The life expectancy at birth has also improved from 37.2 (male) and 36.2 (female) in 1950-51 to 62.3 (male) and 63.9 (female) during the years 2003-04. This has led to increase in literary rates for all sub-groups of population in the country. Now 75.3 per cent of men and 53.7 per cent of women are reported to be able to read and write. Work participation rate of rural and urban men and women has also improved.

For raising the standards of living (*Article 47*), of the rural population in particular, the Community Development Project was launched by the Government of India in 1952. Subsequently, Integrated Rural Development Programme (IRDP), National Rural Employment Programme (NREP), Drought Prone Areas Programme (DPAP), Desert Development Programme (DDP) and other schemes were also launched.

The world's largest employment programme was launched in 2005 which aimed at providing 100 days of guaranteed employment in a financial year to every rural household in 330 districts. The National Rural Employment Guarantee Act was passed. In 2008, it was extended to all the 604 districts of the country with a total budget outlay of Rs. 16000 crore for the year 2008-09.

Undoubtedly, the NREGS is a massive scheme and there have been many problems. The Union Minister for Rural Development pointed out that only 32.26 lakh or 10 per cent households completed 100 days, with 23 per cent in Rajasthan,13 per cent in MP, 7 per cent in UP, 6 per cent in Andhra Pradesh and 6 per cent in Chhattisgarh. There is also the need to ensure transparent and corruption-free implementation of the Scheme. Leakages and diversion of funds have also been reported. Steps have been taken to make payments of wages through bank and post office accounts, and introduction of a Citizen Information Board to display all information for the work taken.(The *Hindu* April 2, 2008)

The Government has made substantial efforts in uplifting the welfare of women and children. For this, the Department of Women and Child Development was established. The women, as per the programme, were empowered through education and awareness with vocational training so that they could contribute to the economic development of the country as equal partners. The department also started the world's largest nutrition programme for children called the Integrated Child Development Scheme (ICDS) to cover 2694 Projects in the country, catering to 138 lakh children and 27 lakh pregnant and nursing mothers.

Medical and public health as another field, has received the attention of the government. As a result of persistent efforts of the state, supply of potable drinking water is made available to urban, and increasingly large number of rural areas. The country has a large chain of primary health centres and hospitals. Special programmes have been launched for eradicating malaria, T.B. leprosy, general diseases, small pox, cancer and AIDS. Immunization Programmes for infant, child and pregnant mothers have also been launched on a national scale. In 1991, over 8 lakh hospital beds were available in the country which also had close to 4 lakh registered doctors. In 2005, a giant step towards achieving a healthy rural India was taken in the form of National Rural Health Mission which was launched by the Prime Minister Dr. Manmohan Singh. The key components of the programme are setting up a district health plan that integrates nutrition, sanitation and safe drinking water; providing an accredited female health worker to each village; developing a village health plan by a local team headed by the health and sanitation committee of the panchayat; and strengthening rural hospitals and making them accountable through Indian public Health Standards. Yet it cannot be said that the entire population is receiving all kinds of medical and public health services. To a great extent, paucity of resources and ever increasing population can be held responsible for it.

Some states in India have launched old-age pension schemes for the senior citizens of the country. People above 65 years of age can avail of old age pension, subject to certain conditions, ranging between Rs 60 to 100 per month in different states. Certain other welfare measures in the form of maternity leave benefits to female employees in organised sectors have been introduced. There are proposals to further liberalise them. An innovative idea of *paternity leave* has also been implemented.

The Government has also made efforts to provide free legal aid to the poor and disadvantaged people. For this National Legal Services Authority (NALSA) has been created. The motto of NALSA is to provide access to justice for all and the services offered by the Authority for the beneficiary groups include free legal aid, free legal advice, cost of litigation, Lok Adalats, legal counselling, conciliation, arbittration with the objective of eliminating stigma, discrimination and inequality from the society. In 2005, NALSA launched the first every National Legal Literacy Mission (2005-2010) to empower the economically and socially disadvantaged citizens by making them legally literate.

Laws have been enacted fixing the working hours and minimum wages of the labourers and to improve their working conditions. Various security schemes have been formulated. Pension may be made of the Minimum Wages Act of 1948, Employees State Insurance Act of 1948, Industrial Disputes (Banking and Insurance Companies) Act of 1949, Industrial, Disputes (Banking Companies) Decision Act of 1955, Apprentices Act of 1961, Personal Injuries (Compensation Insurance) Act of 1963, Maternity Benefits Act of 1967, Contract Labour (Regulation and Abolition) Act of 1970, Bonded Labour Systems (Abolition) Act of 1976, Equal Remuneration Act of 1976. Interstate Migrant Workmen (Regulation of Employment) Condition of Services Act of 1979, etc. Steps have also been taken to eradicate beggary and undeserved wants. To implement *Article 46,* i.e., Promotion of educational and economic interests of Scheduled Castes, Scheduled Tribes and other weaker sections, many schemes have been undertaken. Since 1950, we have had reservations for Scheduled Castes and Scheduled Tribes in legislative bodies, public sector employment and educational institutions. Since late 1980's another significant chunk of people of backward castes and classes (identified under the Mandal Commission) is being brought under the ambit of reservation policies. We have successfully introduced reservation for women in local bodies and in the Panchayati Raj Institutions. Now, this provision is being extended to State legislatures and Parliament as well.

In pursuance of Article 40 of the Constitution village panchayats have been organised. It has been estimated that there are 2.2 lakhs of village panchayats, 45,000 Panchayat Samitis and 357 Zila Parishads in India. Over the years, their powers have been increased. A major landmark in this regard has been the 73rd Constitutional Amendment Act of 1992 which has provided constitutional status to Panchayati Raj Institutions.

However, much is yet to be done. We cannot claim that any one of the directives has been fully accomplished. The teeming millions still live in poverty. There seems to be lack of will and several other factors responsible for the tardy implementation of the directive principles of state policy. In 2001, the Supreme Court and the people of India were shocked to know that 16 states and the two Union territories had not even identified BPL (Below Poverty Line) families under the new Targeted Public Distribution Scheme. Thus, before the apex court's admonition, Delhi had no BPL family, but after the Court's criticism, Delhi Government was claiming to have at least 20 lakh BPL families. While 50 million out of 325 million people were on the brink of starvation, a massive 60 million ton surplus of food grains was rotting in the Food Corporation of India's godowns. It was revealed that against the minimum basic requirement of 75 kg of food per month per family of five, the government was just providing a mere 10 kg through its public distribution system. The rural poor did not have the purchasing power to buy food grains at fair price shops. There was a lot of corruption also as most of the stock meant for BPL families was diverted to the black market. The state governments were not lifting their allocated stocks from the Food Corporation of India and schemes like Mid-day Meal Scheme for poor children, Annapoorna Yojana for poor senior citizens and Food for Work for drought-hit areas were almost on paper only as there were no takers for the schemes. Even the Antyodaya Yojana, a scheme for the poorest, which provided rice at Rupees two per kg. and wheat at Rupees three per kg had seen very poor results. There were no takers for the subsidized scheme for SC/ST/OBC student hostels for the last three years. Further, it was estimated officially that the number of bogus BPL cards in circulation, was a staggering 7.9 million.

The implementation of land reforms show a chaotic scenario. Benami transactions have taken place to escape the land ceiling acts. Free and compulsory education for children till 14 years of age is still a far cry though this was to be achieved within ten years of its implementation i.e. 25th January 1960. In 2002, the NDA Government took a populist step and made free and compulsory education for the children belonging to 6-14 years of age a fundamental right. The women and the children are still subjected to untold oppression and exploitation. 47 per cent of the children in the age group of 0 to 3 years are undernourished, 51 per cent of them suffer from severe or moderate anaemia. Child mortality (0-5 years) is the highest in the world. The *Hindu,* March 13, 2005, p. 14). The women and the children are still subjected to untold oppression and exploitation. Despite the introduction of new technologies in the countryside, a substantial increase in the volume of output of industries, trade and commerce etc, we have not been able to ensure reasonable employment opportunities for most of the able bodied and willing persons. Over three crore graduates at various levels of education are reported to be registered with Employment Exchanges. The number of less educated and uneducated job-seekers could be, larger than that. Government has been initiating, from time to time, various employment generation/employment guarantee schemes, but the schemes that ensure sustained availability of employment opportunities are yet to come up.

However, there is no need to feel despondent. Poverty is not something which can vanish overnight. The Directive Principles of State policy will always remind the leaders and the people of this country about the unfinished tasks.

CHAPTER VI

Nature of the Indian State

The nature of the Indian State in particular, and of states in developing countries in general, is a complex phenomenon. It is because the societies in those developing nations have been indeed, complex. Like other developing nations, India has its own problems and its own peculiar history. Although India is one of the oldest civilizations dating back to 2500 B.C., when the Indus Valley civilization rose and flourished, its society still remains a traditional one, in which the pace of economic development has been extremely low. The colonial rule was largely responsible for this, as a result of which we could not experience a state that had existed in the developed societies, either in the hands of feudal lords in the feudal society or in the hands of the capitalists in the capitalist society. Because of the colonisation, the historical developments which are the characteristic of western states, are just absent in India. The society in India has developed in such a way that neither have class distinctions been sharply divided, nor has the state been monopolised by any particular class.

The emergence of the Indian State took place on 15th August 1947, as a result of a long struggle against the oppressive British rule, which culminated in the partition of the country into two independent states: India and Pakistan.

Nature of the Colonial State

Although the British left the country in 1947, the legacy of their rule still haunts us because the British rule had represented a classic example of imperialism. They came here as traders, later became the rulers, and ultimately subordinated the Indian economy and social structure to their own imperialistic designs. The traditional rural economy was destroyed and the agricultural production became stagnant. The handicrafts, which were popular in the whole world for their finesse and sophistication, were systematically destroyed to make way for the British, mechanised, manufactured goods, rendering the craftsmen jobless and poor. As the industrialisation in Britain grew, India was reduced to a colony supplying raw materials to the British Industries and a readymade market for the British goods. During the last phase of the British rule, a limited amount of industrialisation was encouraged, making India one of the ten industrialised countries in the world. However this industrial development was under the overall colonial framework, keeping in view the British commercial and imperial interests. Further, the whole industrial development was put under the control of the British capital in which the Indian capital acted as a junior partner. The capital industries which constitute industrial structure was not allowed to develop and the Indian market for the British goods remained intact. As a result of all these British efforts, poverty grew in India as it had never done before. The British also organised the Indian administration with the limited purpose of maintenance of law and order and collection of revenues.

The decadent economy, which resulted as a consequence of the British rule, had a devastating impact on Indian society. It became stagnant. The British rule encouraged this stagnancy deliberately because it was in tune with their imperialist designs. In keeping with their overall objectives, the British rule introduced the western system of education to recruit babus in subordinate positions. This educational system also produced the Indian henchmen who were Indian in colour but English in taste and opinion. These Indians admired everything that was western while they hated everything Indian. The spread of western ideas like democracy, equality and liberty also took place as a result of the English educational system. This encouraged liberalism in Indian society in a very limited way. Gradually, an awareness grew against social evils like untouchability, child marriage, purdah system, polygamy and other practices. But on the whole, the Indian society remained backward and decadent.

The socio-economic backwardness was a major challenge before the newly emerged Indian State in 1947. Coupled with this was the social diversity in terms of religion, caste, creed, colour, language, region and other factors. The framers of the Constitution of India had the gigantic task of framing a constitutional structure which was to be acceptable to all and which could provide socio-economic justice to every section of the population. They decided to give India a liberal-democratic Constitution.

India—A Liberal-Democratic State

During the colonial rule, the British introduced representative institutions in India under a system of limited franchise. The Indian political leadership was thus given a training of democratic institutions in a limited manner. The leaders had studied under the English educational system, either in India or England, and had imbibed the western democratic values and culture. Therefore, they had no hesitation in providing democratic structures in India. According to Myron Weiner, there were two components of the British model already existing in the Indian political scene. Firstly, the British created bureaucratic structures (civil service, judiciary, police, army) which gave legitimacy to the role of state authority in maintaining social order. This bureaucratic system was characterised by prescribed procedures and the rule of law. Secondly, the British introduced and progressively expanded the institution of representative government. As a result, the Indians were aware of the working of democracy. Therefore, there were considerable differences over substantive policies, but no dispute regarding procedures like choosing candidates for elections, conduct of elections and norms of conduct of electing officials. Another important factor was the well-organised Congress Party which had sufficiently entrenched itself in the different parts of the country and was committed to democracy.

Thus the Indian State is a liberal-democratic State, with features as under:

(i) There is the provision of universal adult franchise. Every Indian above the age of 18 has the right to vote without any discrimination based on caste, creed, religion and other factors. The sheer size of the Indian electorate makes India the largest democracy of the world.

(ii) There is a Parliament consisting of two houses at the centre and a State Legislature at the State level. Periodic elections take place, generally at the interval of five years.

(iii) There are numerous political parties both at the national as well as the State level, which are committed to the democratic Constitution.

(iv) The elections are conducted by an independent constitutional body called the Election Commission. There have been examples of rigging in elections but, by and large, the elections have been free and fair.

(v) Peaceful transfer of power has taken place from one government to the other. No government in India has refused to quit when defeated.

(vi) We have the parliamentary form of government in which the executive is responsible to the legislature.

(vii) The Indian State is a federal State. There is a division of power between the Union and the States under Schedule VII of the Constitution. We also have the Panchayati Raj system at the grassroot level.

(viii) India is a secular State. There is no official religion of the State and it is debarred from practising any discrimination on religious grounds. The citizens enjoy freedom of conscience. They have a right to profess, practise and propagate their respective religions.

(ix) The Indian Army is apolitical. So far, it has not nurtured any political ambition even during the internal emergency of 1975-77, even when people lose faith in politicians and there is no political stability.

(x) The Indian Constitution provides a detailed chapter on the fundamental rights of the people. Fox Butterfield, the New York Times correspondent, rightly said that except for the brief interlude of emergency in 1975-77, India "has maintained its political freedom; there have been no unchecked Public Security Ministry, no street committees, no network of forced-labour camps, no persecution of whole group of people because they were intellectuals or had relatives who had once been landlords, no destruction of libraries and universities." Even during emergency of 1975-77, Prime Minister Indira Gandhi always maintained that it was under the democratic Constitution. She showed no hesitation in quitting the office when defeated." In voting Mrs. Gandhi out in 1977, Ramesh Thakur says, "Indians showed that while they can put up with much economic injustice, they would not tolerate tyranny." In other words, democracy has gone deep into the soil of the country.

India—A Liberal-Socialist State

However, describing India as a liberal-democratic state would not conform to reality. Structurally, India is a liberal-democratic State, ideologically it is a liberal-socialist State. It may be called a liberal State with a socialist doze or a Socialist State with a liberal doze. The Preamble declares India to be a secular State, and the objective of the State is to provide social, economic and political justice to the people. For the purpose, Part IV of the Constitution provides for the directive principles of State Policy which are non-justiciable but nevertheless fundamental in the governance of the country. We have seen that many of them have been implemented, although not fully. We have adopted a mixed economy which justifies both the liberal as well as the socialist nature of the State. The nationalisation of industries and the emphasis on the public sector as the commanding height of the economy makes it obvious that we are moving towards a socialist direction while the existence of an ever-expanding private sector, and the new emphasis on it as a result of liberalisation of state control, amply shows that the Indian State is moving towards a liberal direction.

India—A Welfare State

G.D.H. Cole defines the welfare state as "a society in which an assured minimum standard of living and opportunity becomes the possession of every citizen." To Kent, a welfare state is a state that provides a wide range of social services. Schlesinger says that "The welfare state is a system wherein government agrees to underwrite certain levels of employment, income, education, medical, social security and housing for all its citizens." The concept of welfare state means the following:

(i) Every citizen is entitled to a minimum standard of living.
(ii) There is a commitment to a policy of economic stability and progress.
(iii) Every citizen is to be provided employment, as a policy.
(iv) Purchasing power of the citizens is to be raised.
(v) Protection against want, sickness and old age.

The modern times have witnessed the concept of welfare state as a universal principle, which has been adopted in developed, as well as developing countries. India is no exception to that. The Preamble, Fundamental Rights and the Directive Principles embody the welfare provisions in the Constitution. After the implementation of the Constitution, the Indian State has taken various steps to uplift the standard of living of the people. The First Five Year Plan was conceived to ensure the growth of a welfare state in India. The Second Five Year Plan declared, "The accent of the socialist pattern is on the attainment of positive goals, the raising of the living standards, the enlargement of opportunities for all, the promotion of enterprise among the disadvantaged classes and the creation of a sense of partnership among all sections of the community." According to the Third Five Year Plan, "The basic object of India's development must necessarily be to provide the masses of the Indian people the opportunity to lead a good life." The Fourth and Fifth Five Year Plans stressed upon the removal of poverty and unemployment. The Sixth Five Year Plan laid stress on improving the quality of life of the people. The objective of the Seventh Five Year Plan was to promote the good of the people. The Eighth Five Year Plan aimed at increasing agricultural, industrial and consumer products, in order to promote the welfare of the people. The same is being expected from the Ninth Five Year Plan.

In this sense the Indian State is a moderniser or liberator of society. The state leads the society in not only providing the minimum economic requirements of food, cloth and shelter, but also aims at the removal of socio-economic disparities. However, Gunnar Myrdal calls India a soft state because it cannot abolish parochial values. This leads to inefficient and ineffective policy performance and a debacle of the development strategy. There is no denying the fact that the Indian State has failed on many fronts. Still 320 million people are living below the poverty line. Corruption has reached the highest echelons of power. Another distinctive problem is sycophancy. A person in power is worshipped like a god or goddess, which ultimately creates cleavages between the people and the leadership. The rise of backward classes or Dalits is another challenge to the Indian State. The failure of the State in providing justice to them and the growing political awareness among the Dalits have resulted in their rise as a major political power that wants immediate solutions. They are not ready to wait. Coupled with this is the near-disintegration of the Congress Party which has not only been a unifying force in India, but also ensured stability to the state. Now with the decline of Congress Party, a vacuum has been created. The coalition experiment at the centre has not provided political stability. One can hope that sooner or later the polarisation of political forces takes place so that this era of coalition politics comes to an end and a stable government is formed.

Nature of the Indian State—The Marxist View

For the communists in India, the independence of India from colonial yoke on 15th August, 1947, was not a great event. It was just a transfer of power from the hands of foreign capitalists to the Indian capitalists. This belief was based on the writings of Marx, Engels, Lenin, Stalin, Mao, Gramski and other Marxist thinkers.

The Marxist view, on the nature of Indian State, is influenced by their general theory on the nature of the state. According to them, the state is a product of class antagonism and it is a class institution. Engels writes, "The state did not exist from all eternity. There have been societies without it, that had no idea of any state or public power," State is a man-made institution. It came into existence when it was needed in the slave-owning society, which was divided into slaves and slave-owners. The slave-owners owned the means of production and exploited the slave. This exploitation crossed the limits, and the slaves revolted. In the struggle between the slaves and slave-owners, the slave-owners created a number of institutions— including the state—to keep slaves under their control and perpetuate their exploitation. Therefore, as Engels says, "It (the state) is simply a product of society at a certain stage of evolution. It is the confession that this society has become hopelessly divided among itself, has entangled itself in irreconciliable contradictions which it is powerless to banish. In order that these contradictions, these classes with conflicting interests, may not annihilate themselves and society in a useless struggle, a power becomes necessary that stands apparently above society and has the function of keeping the conflicts out and maintaining 'order.' And this power ... is the state." After the destruction of the slave-owning society, feudalism came, followed by the modern age of capitalism. But the nature of the state has remained constant. The state serves the interest of the possessing class which lies in exploiting the have-nots. Marx declared, "The executive of the modern state is but a committee for managing the common affairs of the whole bourgeoisie." Engels also said, "Because the state arose from the need to hold class antagonism in check, but because it arose, at the sametime, in the midst of the conflict of these classes, it is, as a rule, the state of the most powerful, economically dominant class, which through the medium of state becomes also the politically dominant class ..." He further argues, "The possessing classes ... keep the working people in a servitude not only by the might of their wealth, by the simple exploitation of labour by capital but also by the power of the state, by the army, the bureaucracy, the courts."

Going by the above analysis, the Marxists declared India to be a capitalist or bourgeois state. It is a state which serves the interests of the capitalist class who are engaged in the exploitation of the workers. The objective of the Indian state, it would naturally follow, is to perpetuate this exploitation and maintain the hegemony of the capitalist class.

According to the Marxists, the freedom struggle was a bourgeois movement. Sanjeev Banerjee says that after the First World War, the bourgeoisie emerged as an all-India class. The national movement itself was not the creation of the bourgeoisie but through the "close political, personal and financial relations with the top Congress leadership, especially with its right wing," it tried to control the national movement. "Nevertheless," again to quote Sanjeev Banerjee, "the national movement was a bourgeois movement in the sense that its leadership and ideology, and the solution it envisaged and fought for objectively, would lead to the dominance of the bourgeoisie class and the capitalist production." However, he also accepts that the bourgeoisie had a complex, and often contradictory, relation with the national movement.

The Communist Party of India also calls the Indian State a national bourgeois state. It believes that as a result of their participation in the anti-imperialist struggle, certain sections of bourgeoisie have been progressive and therefore, the Indian state has been able to take progressive steps. The Communist Party of India (Marxist) describes the Indian state as "an organ of the rule of bourgeoisie and landlords led by the big bourgeoisie who are increasingly collaborating with foreign finance capital in pursuit of the capitalist path of development."

To the Communist Party of India (Marxist-Leninist) the Indian state is semi-colonial and semi-feudal and, according to its theoreticians, the characteristic features of the new government, in the name of independent India, was continuity of the old regime, of the same social and economic order, the same administrative machinery of imperialism, the same bureaucracy and the police."

A.R. Desai finds three kinds of evidence which corroborate the fact that India is a capitalist state. Firstly, the Indian Constitution is a bourgeois Constitution as it recognised right to property as a fundamental right (now a legal right). This means that the gross disparities in income is acceptable. There is no right to work while a property-owner's right to compensation has been recognised as legitimate. Secondly, the planning process, according to which India's development has been taking place, seeks development on the path of capitalist-mixed economy and accepts the class structure based on private ownership as the basis of economic development. The inequality rooted in private ownership of the means of production continues. The planning system ensures the promotion of Indian economy for capitalist interests. Thirdly, the Indian economy operates on the principles of profit and production for the market. We do have a mixed economy but the area of the private sector is very large. The entire agriculture sector, the significance of which cannot be underestimated as India is essentially an agricultural country, is privately owned. The transport industry and consumer based industries are also in the private sector. The recent liberalisation of the Indian economy has further increased the operational areas of the private sector. The various economic and legal measures in the form of tax reliefs, subsidies and loans also save the richs propertied class. Thus, according to Desai, the Indian economic development is the capitalist development in favour of big capitalists, landlords and rich peasantry. The tax structure also supports this view. Taxes are less on private and corporate sectors while the consuming masses pay more taxes. The agriculture has not been taxed at all which benefits the landlords and rich peasants who dominate the agricultural sector.

However, the Marxists also talk of autonomy of the Indian State which means the Indian State is just not totally favouring the capitalists. Thus, Bardhan argues that the Indian State acted "neither at the behest of nor on behalf of the proprietary classes," at the time of independence. As a result of the introduction of universal adult franchise which led to mass participation, the State power cannot be used to promote the interests of the propertied class only. The State has to undertake a variety of socio-economic measures which would uplift the masses in order to gain legitimacy. All the political parties talk about the socio-economic amelioration of the masses to get votes from them and after coming to power they do act in that direction."

Anupam Seth says that there are a multiplicity of modes of production and Indian society is partly capitalistic. Therefore, no class in India has emerged as the dominant class which ensures the autonomy of State. After its establishment, the Indian State has taken various measures to decentralise the wealth and these have been anti-feudal and anti-monopolistic. Land reforms, nationalisation, green revolution, rural development programmes, anti-poverty programmes and the like have been designed to achieve an egalitarian society. Various labour legislations also have been introduced to benefit the labour class. However, a study of Indian economic development reveals that the government policies have resulted in the expansion of the middle class and lower middle class in cities, and the growth of a rural elite in the rural areas. Thus, in India both the feudal as well as the capitalist modes of production are prevalent and live together side by side.

To conclude, one can say that the nature of the Indian State defies any specific and rigid categorisation. This is true of the other states in the developing countries where there is a mixture of social formation and multiplicity of modes of production and class relations. None of the states in developing societies can afford to ignore the liberal-democratic ideas, yet at the same time, they have to take socialist and welfare measures to ameliorate the condition of the masses.

References

Arora N.D. and Awasthy S.S., *Political Theory*, 1996, New Delhi, Har-Anand Publications Pvt Ltd.

Bhambhri C.P., *The Indian-State Fifty Years*, 1997, New Delhi, Shipra Publications.

Raman Sunder (Ed.), *Indian Government and Politics*, New Delhi, Allied Publishers Private Ltd.

Singh M.P. and Himanshu Roy (Ed.), *Indian Political System Structures, Policies, Development*, 1995, New Delhi, Jnanada Prakashan (P&D)

Thakur Ramesh, *The Government and Politics of India*, 1995, London, Macmillan Press Ltd.

Teaching Politics, The Journal of the Delhi University Political Science Association Volume VIII, 16.2, 1982. The Articles by Sanjeeb Mukherjee, Manoranjan Mohanty and Susheela Kaushik.

CHAPTER VII

Social Structure and the Democratic Process in India

The working of any political process is intrinsically related to the social system. This is more particularly with democracy, because democracy involves mass participation and people behave according to social norms and values resulting from centuries of development of society. India has adopted the Anglo-Saxon model of democracy. But that does not mean that we have the same system. Our democracy is greatly influenced by our social structure and that makes Indian democracy a distinct category altogether. However the relationship between the democratic process and the social structure is not one-way. The democratic process has also influenced the social structure. Thus the relationship between the two is highly complex and complicated.

The colonial State in India under the British was highly authoritarian. Though the representative institutions were introduced progressively and gradually, the franchise was limited. Democracy never worked at the grassroot level and it was confined to a very small section of the population. Before the British rule, the country was always subjected to despotic rule. There was no democracy in medieval India. Thus Indian people had no experience of democracy. After independence, a rather limited democracy was expanded and widened to the entire population through representative institutions and adult franchise. As the British rule had made the Indian society stagnant and reactionary it needed immediate social reformation. It was believed that the democratic institutions would bring about the desired social changes in India and it was with this great expectation that the democratic system was inaugurated in India.

Features of Indian Social Structure

1. *The Caste System*

Indian social structure is based upon caste factor, a uniquely Indian invention. The caste system which dates back to the Vedic period, is a system of classification of the people with a hierarchy. Initially, the caste system was based on *varna* which divided people into four categories: (i) Brahmin, (ii) Kshatriya, (iii) Vaishya and (iv) Shudra. Later on, as a result of a long historical process, it came to be identified as *Jati* which was based on birth and a fifth category of people emerged who were 'out-castes,' presumably aboriginals of India, the *Antyaja* or *Harijans* (as called by Gandhi) or Dalit as they now call themselves. Traditionally the first three were called twice born as they are born a second time after initiation rites. They are the high castes. The lower caste was the 'shudras' who were basically artisans, engaged in different kinds of occupations which were clean and non-polluting. The Harijans constituted the lowest in the stratification and were supposed to be engaged in unclean occupations which were polluting. But before we analyse the relationship between caste and the democratic process, two preliminary observations are to be made. Firstly, caste is a very complicated phenomenon. Caste stratification is there. But at the same time, a limited amount of mobility from the lower caste to higher caste is also permitted. Secondly, the caste system is universal in India. It exists in Sikh, Islam, Christianity and all the other religions that are present in India. Thus the caste system is just not a Hindu religious problem but a problem that encompasses the entire Indian society.

Over a long period of time, the caste system developed many evils. The most serious evil was its basis of inequality which dehumanised the lower castes. The democratic process initiated after independence sought to remove this inequality in the name of social justice by providing, firstly, reservation in government jobs and offices and secondly, by declaring abolition of untouchability, the practice of which was made a constitutional and criminal offence. Though the State was debarred from discriminating against its people on the basis of caste, yet the Constitution indirectly gave the caste system, a legal sanction. The Constitution abolished untouchability but not the caste system. In a way, this was the most pragmatic decision of the framers of the Constitution as the caste system has survived throughout history. No doubt the modern age, with its emphasis on the individual as a unit rather than the community, has broken many caste rigidities, yet the system continues and is a fact of Indian political life. It is also to be noted that despite the rigidities involved, the caste system has also been dynamic. It has worked under the system of accommodation and in the process, the lower castes have acquired higher status.

The relationship between the caste and the democratic process can be seen in two ways. It leads to (i) politicisation of caste and the (ii) politics itself becoming caste-ridden. The political parties contest for power and for this they need followers. The caste system is mobilised to achieve this end. However, as all the political parties are engaged in political mobilisation, the castes get ridden by politics. Every party attempts to select a candidate from the dominant caste in a particular area. This creates intra-caste rivalries and in this process the support of other castes who are not dominant in the area becomes critical. This helps the democratic process as the political parties attempt to absorb all the sections of the population in their folds. The caste factor has also prevented the polarisation of political parties on ideological basis. In such a system maintaining discipline within the party is the biggest problem. In fact, all the main parties in India have been characterised by different factions conflicting with each other. This is also the case with the Bhartiya Janata Party (BJP) which is supposed to be a disciplined party. But as its support base widened, it became a mass party and factionalism also crept in.

The democratic process has led to caste wars in India. In U.P. and Bihar it is most evident. In Tamil Nadu the D.M.K. party rose and came to power on the basis of its anti-Brahmin plank.

Initially in India, the higher castes dominated politics and the lower castes supported them to secure benefits. However, with the passage of time lower castes became conscious and decided to capture political power. The entire Dalit politics can be seen in this context. However, the problem with the Dalit politics is that it does not work on the principles of assimilation and accommodation. The consequence can be disastrous to Indian democracy because dalit politics is essentially based on hatred for higher castes. The caste is being organised for capturing political power to get the material benefits that flow from it. The emphasis is on quick results which may not be possible given the limitation of the Indian State. One can only hope that this is a transitional phase and sooner or later the integrative aspects of caste system, which has been a feature of Indian polity, will again acquire ascendancy. This does not mean that the influence of the lower castes will decrease. The rise of lower castes in Indian politics is a fact and is going to stay. But this should not lead to caste hatred. It has also been felt that the socio-economic benefits extended to lower castes have been utilised by the *creamy-layer* i.e. the affluents among the lower castes. This tendency is also to be checked and the benefits must be extended to other sections of lower castes as well. S.N. Talwar rightly says, "There is no justification for continuing the reservation facilities for the public school educated and affluent children of lower-caste IAS personnel."

2. *Multi Religious Society**

Another aspect of Indian society is its multi *religious* character. India is a country of all religions with Hindus constituting the majority. Then we have Muslims, Christians, Sikhs and other religions. The Hindu-Muslim conflict has been the most potent one in history. The legacy of long Islamic rule in India still haunts the Hindu psyche. Then there are conflicts over the places of worship between the two. Muslim rule in India destroyed Hindu temples and converted them to mosques, now a section of Hindus wants to reconvert them into temples. This is what happened in Ayodhya where the Babri Masjid was demolished. There are differences between the two which date back to Islamic rule in India. However, with the arrival of Akbar, a synthesis between the two started taking place and an environment was sought to be created by Akbar where both the communities could live together peacefully. When the Britishers captured the political power, they suspected Muslims because they had replaced them. The Muslims also did not welcome the British. They remained aloof from the English education, while the Hindus were quick to reap the fruits of the new education system. This resulted in the relative backwardness of Muslims. However as a result of the rise of a powerful nationalist movement, the British adopted the policy of 'divide and rule' by which not only the Muslims but even other communities were given special protection against the Hindus. The British Policy of divide and rule culminated in divide and quit in 1947, when two independent nations—India and Pakistan were created on the basis of two-nation theory. Pakistan was created for the Muslims as per this theory.

But the partition could not solve the Hindu-Muslim problem in the Indian polity, as a sizeable number of Muslims remained in India. The Hindus blamed them for the partition.

The democratic process of independent India sought to solve this problem by incorporating the principle of secularism in the Constitution. The Preamble of the Indian Constitution declares India to be a secular State. Further the State has been debarred from discriminating between its people on the basis of religion. There is no State religion in India and right to profess, practise and propagate religion has been guaranteed as a fundamental right.

However the communal riots between the Hindus and Muslims have been frequently taking place in India since 1947, a testimony to the fact that the Indian democratic process, inspite of its secular dimension, has not been able to establish a secular society in India. In

*Also see Chapter XXIII.

1984, Hindu-Sikh riots occurred in northern India. The 1980's also witnessed the emergence of a strong Hindu movement which ultimately led to the demolition of Babri Masjid and communal disturbances in many parts of the country. In 2002, communal disturbances took place in Gujarat on a very big scale. It is a fact that the India's political system has largely failed in combating communalism. The centres of worship have been misused for political purposes and terrorism and whenever the state has acted against such misuse, its action has been criticised.

It has been observed that the democratic process has also been responsible for communalism in India. In order to secure votes, the political parties have fomented and encouraged communalism in India. It is necessary for the survival of this country as one nation that the political parties desist from such practices. Some concrete efforts should be made both at the level of State as well as society to contain communalism. Then only can the credentials of secularism be established in Indian society.

3. *The Linguistic diversity**

Another source of social diversity is the language. India is a country of many languages. For official purposes, the constitution of India vide Eighth Schedule recognizes 22 languages. They are Assamese, Bengali, Bodo, Dogri, Gujarati, Hindi, Kannada, Kashmiri, Konkani, Maithili, Malayalam, Manipuri, Marathi, Nepali, Oriya, Punjabi, Sanskrit, Santhali, Sindhi, Tamil, Telugu and Urdu. But this does not explain the total linguistic phenomenon of India. There are many other languages and every major language has regional and dialectical variations. Sahitya Akademi, for the purpose of literary awards, considers Dogri, Maithili and Rajasthani as separate literary languages. A very small State, Nagaland, has as many as 19 languages spoken. They are Angami, Sema, Lotha, Ao, Rengma, Chakhesang-Chokri/Chakru, Khezha, Sangtam Pochuri, Sangtam, Konyak, Chang, Pham, Yimchungre, Khiemnumgam, Zeliang-Zemi, Liangmei, Kuku-Chiru, Makware and Tikhir.

Language is a medium of communication. It is also a source of employment. If the recruitment to a particular post is through a particular language, then the person not knowing that language is at a disadvantage and person knowing that language has the advantage. Thus language acquires a socio-economic dimension particularly in a country like India where employment opportunities are less.

The Indian Constitution declared Hindi to be the official language of the Union, while the form of numerals to be used was the international

*Also see Chapter XXIII—Language Politics in India.

form of Indian numerals (*Art. 343*). But the constitution also provided for the use of the English language for official purposes of the union for fifteen years from the commencement of the Constitution. Subsequently, it was decided to continue indefinitely. The Constitution also provided for English to be used in (i) Supreme Court and High Courts, (ii) the authoritative texts of bills and amendments in acts, to be moved/passed by the Parliament or State legislatures (*Art. 348*). However, the Constitution also permitted the use of Hindi or any other language in the High Court with the prior consent of the President and authorisation by the Governor of that State. The Constitution also directed the Union to develop Hindi. *Article 351* says. "It shall be the duty of the Union to promote the spread of the Hindi language, to develop it so that it may serve as a medium of expression for all the elements of the composite culture of India and to secure its enrichment by assimilating without interfering with its genius, the forms, style and expressions used in 'Hindustani' and in the other languages of India specified in the Eighth Schedule, and by drawing, wherever necessary or desirable, for its vocabulary, primarily on Sanskrit and secondarily on other languages." The Constitution also stated that any of the languages used in the State and the Union can be used in representations for redressal of grievances (*Art. 350*). Finally facilities for instruction in the mother tongue at the primary stage of education are to be provided by the State (*Art. 350 (A)*).

During the freedom struggle, there was a demand for linguistic reorganisation of the States which was supported by the Congress. However after independence, it resisted this demand on the plea that the primary consideration must be the security, unity and economic prosperity of India and every separatist and disruptive tendency should be rigorously discouraged. But ultimately the leadership had to give in to the popular demand and in 1956, a new political map emerged on the basis of linguistic reorganisation of States in which 14 States and 6 Union Territories were created. This was not the end of the matter. Further the new States of Maharashtra and Gujarat out of Bombay and Punjab and Haryana were carved out of the unified province of Punjab.

The democratic structure has encouraged the various linguistic groups to assert their language. But division of States according to language cannot be done in water-tight compartments. Every State in India has linguistic minorities. In some States, systematic agitations were launched against the linguistic minorities. In Bombay it was against the South Indians labelled as Madrasis and in Assam against

Bengalis and Marwaris in the 1960s. These are some of the examples of such tirades. The linguistic division also led to boundary disputes between Punjab and Haryana, Maharashtra and Karnataka, Karnataka and Kerala etc.. In some cases linguistic minorities have asked for separate Statehood like Telangana in Andhra Pradesh. The different languages have also demanded their due representations in All India Radio and Doordarshan, thus creating enormous problems for both. The Kohima Station of All India Radio has to broadcast in 25 languages.

Hindi or Hindustani is the lingua franca of many northern States and is, thanks to Hindi cinema, television and other governmental efforts, understood in most of the parts of the country.' However, the southern States have always resisted what they called imposition of Hindi and even threatened to secede from the Indian State. The Indian government came out with the three-language formula which meant the study of Hindi, English and the mother-tongue, if it is different from the first two, in the secondary education. In case of Hindi-speaking areas, the study of a modern Indian language was made essential. However the Hindi-speaking States have been reluctant in doing so. The Sarkaria Commission on Centre-State relations has recommended that effective steps should be taken to implement the three language formula in its true spirit uniformly in all States in the interest of unity and integrity of the country.

Selig Harrison had predicted that the linguistic diversity in India would lead to the balkanisation or political division of the country. But this has not happened. To a great extent, the linguistic reorganisation had led to the consolidation of India. It has also led to enrichment of different languages satisfying the literary and information-related needs of the people. At the same time, it has led to chauvinistic and parochial feelings.

4. *Illiteracy**

Another aspect of the Indian social system which is drastically changing as a result of the democratic process, is widespread illiteracy and ignorance. The table of literacy rate amply illustrates this.

*Also see Chapter XXI—Illiteracy.

Literacy Rate in India (Figures in percentage)

	1951	1961	1971	1981	1991	2001
Overall literacy	18.33	28.30	34.45	43.57	52.21	64.8
Male literacy	27.16	40.40	45.96	56.38	64.13	75.3
Female literacy	8.86	15.35	21.97	29.76	39.29	53.7

Source: Economic Survey 2007-2008.

Literacy is a pre-requisite to the sustenance and continuity of the democratic process. From the British, we inherited a highly uneducated society. The eradication of illiteracy was taken as a big challenge by the democratic process in India which organised literacy campaigns at the mass level and ensured the spread of literacy. From just 18.33 per cent overall literacy rate in 1951, we have achieved 64.8 per cent in 50 years. The male literacy has gone up from 27.16 per cent to 75.3 per cent while the female literacy figures have climbed up from a mere 8.86 per cent in 1951, to 53.7 per cent in 2001. Despite the increase in population, the total number of illiterates has come down from 328 million in 1991 to 296 million in 2001. Another interesting fact is that while the female literacy rate has jumped considerally the male-female gap in literacy rate has not shown any remarkable change. It is a marginal change from 18.20 per cent in 1951 to 21.69 in 2001. This also shows the acute gender discrimination in our country.

We have seen in the chapter on Directive Principles of State Policy, one of the directives to the State was to ensure free and compulsory education for children within ten years of the commencement of the Constitution. However this target was not achieved. Nevertheless, primary education is now free in all parts of the country. This has been ensured through a chain of government and government-aided schools in rural as well as urban areas. The private schools of course charge considerable fees from the students. But the government primary schools have been created on a sufficiently large scale and every child has the opportunity to join them. Education at the middle and secondary levels has also been largely free. The students of scheduled castes and tribes are given scholarships. The Government of India and State governments also give scholarships to talented students selected on the basis of merit. In higher education significant developments have taken place.

In 1986, the Government came out with the National Policy on Education which was called the New Education Policy. It laid emphasis on "equality of educational opportunity, social justice in education, and relating education to development." It envisaged universalisation of primary education and adult literacy by 1990. Priority was also given to the qualitative importance of education especially technical and higher education, vocationalisation of secondary education, development of regional languages, strengthening of monitoring and evaluation machinery for effective implementation of plan programmes, "Operation Blackboard" was started to achieve universal primary education. Another programme called "Non-formal education" for the children who were unable to study in formal schools was inaugurated. The Government also formulated a comprehensive programme called National Literacy Mission (NLM), set up in 1988, to impart functional literacy to non-literates in the 15-35 age group by 2005.

However, on the whole, the educational scenario in India has been lopsided. The target of compulsory education is yet to be achieved. The National Literacy Mission has been more a source of propaganda than reality. The British system of education meant for creating *babus* more or less still continues. Further, the expensive private schools create a remarkable separation of the world of rich children from the rest. The students of public schools have better opportunities than those of government schools in starting their career in life. The standards of government schools have fallen. So much so that even the government has opened public schools. The Navodaya Vidyalaya Scheme initiated by the Rajiv Gandhi Government are the elitist schools for the rich people in the rural areas although the objectives of creating such schools were to provide good quality modern education with latest technical facilities, for all-round development of the talented children without any regard to their family and socio-economic conditions. The fact is that education has been a low priority in the government programmes irrespective of all rhetoric attached to it. This is clear from the expenditure incurred by the government on education. India spends around 2.4 per cent of the national income on education compared to 6.5 per cent by Japan, 6.2 per cent by U.S.A.

However it cannot be denied that the democratic process has done substantial work in the spread of literacy. The growing awareness against illiteracy will certainly help in its eradication.

5. *The Gender Problem**

Another aspect of Indian society has been the backward status of women. According to Census, 2001, women account for 495.7 million representing 48.3 per cent of India's total population. Although there have been a number of women freedom fighters and at least one

*Also see Chapter XX—Women Movement in India.

occupied the pivotal office of Prime Minister of India for a considerable time, the women in India, by and large, remain within the four walls of the house, taking care of its inhabitants.

They are the victims of gross discrimination. The 2001 census of India pointed out that for every 1000 Indian males, India has only 933 females. This is alarming, especially in Punjab (874) and Haryana (861) where marriageable boys are not getting brides. Like the male-female gap in literacy rate, here also the situation has changed marginally, but on the negative side, from 946 in 1951 to 933 in 2001.

Sex Ratio 1951-2001

Census year	Sex ratio (females per 1000 males)
1951	946
1961	941
1971	930
1981	934
1991	927
2001	933

Source: India 2008.

Among the selected countries we are at the lowest ebb. While the world average is 986 females per 1000 females, even Pakistan (938) and Bangladesh (953) are better than us. The following table is a mirror of our relative positions.

Sex Ratio of Selected Countries

S. No.	Country	Sex Ratio (females per 1000 males)
1.	China	986
2.	India	933
3.	U.S.A.	1029
4.	Indonesia	1004
5.	Brazil	1025
6.	Pakistan	938
7.	Russian Fed.	1140
8.	Bangladesh	953
9.	Japan	1041
10.	Nigeria	1016

Source: Census of India, 2001.

The democratic process in India created awareness among the women about their pitiful condition. A number of women's welfare organisations came into being which fought the evils of dowry and dowry-related harassments of women and also other problems. In the

Uttarakhand movement in Uttar Pradesh, women played a very significant role. Similarly the anti-arrack movement in Andhra Pradesh and the village Saathins in Rajasthan are the other examples which have been sponsored by the women themselves with remarkable success. The government has also passed a variety of laws which give justice and protection to women. There are a number of welfare schemes for them. The 73rd and 74th Amendments to the Constitution gave women 1/3 representation in the local self government. Now they are enjoying this privilege in Gram Panchayats, Panchayat Samitis and Zila Parishads. Another constitutional Amendment reserving 33 per cent seats in Parliament and State legislatures is in the pipeline. The number of women in various governmental and private offices is increasing tremendously.

However, it will be wrong to state that as a result of all these efforts (both at the governmental and non-governmental level) all the women in India have emancipated. In fact, the contrary is true. Criticising the reservation of women in Parliament and State legislatures, Syed Shahbuddin remarked that it would only help the upper castes (or classes) to push their women in, and gain what they lost on account of implementation of Mandal Commission report. A workshop of elected women panchayat members in Rajasthan revealed that most women were surrogates for male family members and exercised no independent role. In a Panchayat Samiti in Alwar, Rajasthan, the father-in-law of the young woman Pradhan was reported to be regularly presiding over the meetings of the daughter-in-law who sat near him in *Ghunghat* silently and appended her signatures wherever and whenever he so desired. The survey of the working of Rajasthan Panchayati Raj system revealed that when men could not find place in Panchayati Raj institutions, they got their women folk elected and the rule of man continued defeating the basic objective of the amendments. The Government of Rajasthan also found that the women elected in the local self government bodies were unaware of their rights; a good number of them were observing purdah even in the meetings. A training programme worth Rs 2.5 crores was started. Three observations regarding this training programme are significant here: (i) Many women refused to participate because they had to come alone to district headquarters, (ii) Many of them did not attend because of the pressure from their husbands as training programme was meant for not only females but also males and females were not given separate training, and (iii) during the training men got more attention in the programme than women, both qualitatively and quantitatively.

The women suffer gender discrimination in work place also. According to survey made by the National Sample Survey Organisation (NSSO) in 2008, on an average the women (casual worker) in rural areas get Rs. 20 less as wages than the menfolk though both work equal hours. In case of salary (non-casual worker), the difference is of Rs 50. Even being literate makes no difference. A woman with a graduate degree in rural India gets Rs. 170 per day; the man gets Rs. 239 as wages. For a diploma holder, it increases to Rs 212 per day for a woman and Rs 288 for a man. The survey also found similar discrimination in urban areas.

The emancipation of women is not a simple matter. The so-called empowerment of women can take place only when the desire comes from within, which means the women should feel the need of their empowerment. The democratic process can only create awareness and at the most provide facilities which in case of India has been done to a remarkable extent.

6. *Children**

Children are the future of the country. Yet the children of our society have been given a raw deal by the actual working of the democratic process. The Directive Principles of State Policy while gave them the assurance of free and compulsory education till 14 years of age on the one hand, which still is a lofty ideal, on the other hand they also asked the State to ensure "that children are given opportunities and facilities to develop in a healthy manner and in conditions of freedom and dignity and that childhood and youth are protected against exploitation and against moral and material abandonment." (This clause was inserted by the 42nd Constitution Amendment Act of 1976). More than twenty five years have passed since the amendment but the situation remains grim. According to various estimates the number of child labour in India varies from 44 million to 100 million. The children are engaged in carpet, shoe, bidi and match making industries. Besides there are thousands of children who can be found in dhabas, tea stalls, auto-mobile mechanic shops and working in houses as domestic servants. Then, there are scores of "self employed" children doing shoe polishing or selling small items on roads and railway stations, whose childhood is demanding justice from the world's largest democratic process. To help these helpless children the Government of India

*As per the 2001 census, children in the age group of 0-14 years account for 347.54 million (33.84 per cent) of the total population in the country, out of this 169.03 million (48.64 per cent) are females.

started the National Child Labour Project. In 1986, the government passed a Child Labour Act which envisaged a three phase strategy to eliminate child labour. The first stage visualised the inspection of factories to rescue the children and issuing challans to the factory owners. The second stage consisted in enforcing the law by the prosecution of the culprits i.e. the factory owners. The third stage included the rehabilitation and education of the child labourers. However the tardy implementation has defeated the purpose of the Act. Most of the factory-owners in carpet industry in U.P. have shifted to remote rural areas to escape from the Act where the official machinery does not reach. There have been other manipulative tendencies as well. For example, a factory owner is to be prosecuted only when the child is engaged in the factory. But if the child is given raw material to work at home, it does not constitute an offence. Thus bidis are not manufactured in factory but at the home of child-labourer himself. In fact as Gayala Wahab says, "most child labourers work from home."

In 1996, the Supreme Court held that employment of the child labour was a criminal offence. The employment of child labour would invite a fine of Rs 20,000 per child and an additional Rs 5,000 for the education of the child. In fact we find a lot of judicial activism in this field. In certain cases it has fined the culprits. It also led to identification of child labour in Delhi in tea shops, dhabas, mechanic and pan shops. However the problem remains intact and is obvious to everybody. Despite the ban on child labour, the practice still continues. The NSSO survey in 2008 found that boys continued to work in hotels and restaurants for an average salary of Rs 25 a day in urban India. In the manufacturing and service sectors, a girl gets just Rs 10 per day in urban areas while the boys get Rs 30. The children in rural areas get as low as Rs 12 for a day's work. (HT 31 January 2008). The real solution to the problem lies in the economic emancipation of India.

7. The Economic Disparities

Despite all the anti-poverty programmes, 261 million people of India live below poverty line devoid of basic requirements of sustenance. Many die because of hunger. The gulf between the poor and the rich has widened. Undoubtedly the industrial and agrarian revolution has brought prosperity in India. But the distribution process has been faulty. The concentration of wealth has increased in few families. In 1947, some 20 industrial houses controlled the Indian economy, now it has increased to some 70. The number of middle class and lower middle class has increased but at the same time poverty has also increased. The democratic process which started with the lofty ideal of wiping out every tear could not achieve its goal. Various agrarian reforms have been ineffective. The land reforms have not been implemented in the spirit. The landlords with the connivance of the government officers have defeated the purpose of land reforms. In rural areas especially a lot of benami transactions have taken place. The lands have been transferred to fictitious persons, even in the names of pet animals. Although poverty in India is a universal phenomenon, poverty in rural areas is more than that in urban areas. The landless labourers are subjected to many kind of exploitation. Bonded labour and other kinds of forced labour is still working in villages, despite the abolition by the law. The appalling conditions in rural areas have resulted in shifting of rural folk to the urban areas. This has increased the pressure on urban areas creating a lot of socio-economic and legal problems. The cities have become overcrowded and crimes rates have also risen substantially.

8. Regionalism

Another aspect of Indian social problem is regionalism. Like poverty, this is also partly a legacy of British rule. Unfortunately, after the freedom, the democratic process has further strengthened the evils of regionalism. In free India regionalism grew as a result of economic failures of Indian democratic process. As we have seen above, the distribution process of economic development has been faulty. While the urban areas developed, the fruits could not reach the grassroot levels in village. Certain States like Punjab and Haryana developed while States like Bihar and Orrisa remained backward. Within a State also this disparity can be witnessed. This has resulted in regional movements which have not always remained non-violent. The successes of small States like Haryana, H.P. and Goa has strengthened the idea that people living in small States can become prosperous rather than being a part of larger State. Thus every big State in India is witnessing the demand of separate statehood in different regions. In 2001, regionalism achieved a milestone when three new states Chattisgarh, Jharkhand and Uttaranchal were created. While the regional aspirations of the people of these states were satisfied but definitely this is not the end of the road. The Indian political system will have to face this demand again and again because success in one place inspires and encourages regionalism in another area.

9. Corruption and Criminalisation of Politics

Besides the above mentioned problems, we have other social and economic problems which have either come up because of democratic process or democratic process has encouraged them. We would like to mention atleast two of them. The first is corruption. Corruption has reached the highest echelons of power. Even the prime ministers have been accused of corruption. Some even face the charges of forgery. The ministers have been fined by the Supreme Court on corruption charges. Second is the criminalisation of politics. The democratic system requires maximum vote for a candidate to be elected and for this purpose politicians have to rely on everybody who could fetch votes including the criminals. However, the worst part in Indian polity today is that criminals now themselves are the candidates for the legislative seats in Parliament and State legislature. Like the rest of the country, they probably, have also lost faith on the politicians. By their muscle power and resultant terror, they have been able to get elected also. There are many legislators who have cases pending against them of such heinous crimes like murder and rape. In U.P., a criminal contested the election from behind the bars and got elected. As a result violence, during elections, has also increased. All this gives a very pessimistic scenario of Indian democratic process and raises the fundamental question of the survival of democracy in India.

Trends

Neverthless India has no alternative to democracy. Indian diversity in terms of caste, religion, region and other factors has ensured the existence and growth of Indian democracy. Therefore despite the economic disparity and even the failure of the democractic process in satisfying the revolution of rising expectations which took place in 1947, the democratic process will continue. It should be noted that destruction of democracy in India will annihilate India as a country. The solution to the problems lies within and not without the democratic process. Democracy has survived 60 years of independence, that itself is the assurance that it will continue to survive even after. However the introduction of neo-liberalism in the form of liberalisation which is bringing the free market economy is a dangerous trend. Due to the backwardness of Indian economy, India had to force the liberalisation process as a result of international pressure. Now that is a reality and this process cannot be stopped. However the Indian State should continue its battle against poverty to ensure socio-economic justice in

India. It will also help in fighting regionalism and other challenges to India's unity and integrity as a nation. Lastly an iron hand is needed to eliminate corruption from public life. Gandhi said, "corruption will go when the large number of persons given to the unworthy practice realise that the nation does not exist for them but that they do for the nation." He also said that indifference to corruption is criminal. In 1928, he was almost prophetic when he said, "corruption will be out one day, however, much one may try to conceal it; and the public can, as it is its right and duty, in every case of justifiable suspicion, call its servants to strict account, dismiss them, sue them in a law court, or appoint an arbitrator or inspector to scruitinize their conduct, as it likes." To some extent his words are becoming true. As a result of public interest litigations, the corrupt politicians are being taken to task by the courts. Many politicians are declaring their property and assets. The people are becoming aware and even high officers are being caught for accepting bribes. Efforts are also being made to check the criminalisation of politics.

CHAPTER VIII

Federalism in India

What is A Federation?

Modern governments can be divided into two types—the Unitary government and the Federal government. This division is done on the basis of territorial distribution of power. The unitary government is one in which the powers are concentrated in a single organ of central government. There may be local governments but they derive power from the central government. They do not possess any independent authority or power. In the words of Garner, "Unitary Government is that system when the whole power of government is conferred by the Constitution upon a single central organ or organs from which the local governments derive whatever authority or autonomy they may possess." According to Finer, "The unitary State is one in which all authority and powers are logged in a single centre, whose will and agents are legally omnipotent over the whole area." Unitary governments are functioning in England, Italy, Japan and many other countries.

The term federation is derived from the latin word "Foedus" which means treaty or agreement. Thus a State which is the result of a treaty or agreement is a federation. According to Nathan, "Federation is an aggregate of smaller States which while retaining each its separate identity are united together for common purpose in a nation which theoretically at least is indissoluble." Dicey says, "Federalism means the distribution of the force of the States among a number of co-ordinate bodies each originating in and controlled by the Constitution." According to Birch, "A federal system of government is one in which there is a division of powers between one general and several regional authorities, each of which, in its own sphere, is coordinate with the others, and each of which acts directly on the people through its own administrative agencies." Again according to

Dicey, "A federal State is a political contrivance intended to reconcile national unity and power with the maintenance of 'States' rights'." In modern times, federalism started in U.S.A. and now it is functioning in countries like Canada, U.S.A, Switzerland and Australia.

Following are the essential features or pre-requisites of a federation:

(i) *The existence of a dual government.* In a federation we have two sets of government. Firstly the Federal or central or the Union Government and secondly the regional Governments. They are the units of the government. In Switzerland, the regions are called cantons, in Canada, provinces and in USA, States.

(ii) *There is a division of power between the Centre and the States in a federation.* However a study of different federal Constitutions reveals that there is no uniform approach in the division of power. In USA, the power of the National Government has been enumerated in the Constitution and rest of the powers belong to the States. Conversely in Canada, the powers of the provinces have been defined and the centre is authorised to make laws for the "peace, order and good government" of Canada and with respect to subjects not assigned to provinces. This means residuary powers are with the centre. In Australia, the powers of the Centre are defined, there is a Concurrent List in which both the Centre and the States can legislate. However, the State's powers have not been defined, the residuary powers have been vested in the States. Whatever may be the form of distribution of power but this distribution is necessary so that both the governments understand their respective jurisdictions and there is no conflict over it.

(iii) *This division of power is through a Constitution which is written, supreme and rigid.* The Constitution has to be written because the division of power has to be done in a very precise manner. The Constitution is also the supreme law of the land and both the Central Government and the State Governments derive their respective powers from the Constitution, and they function under its supremacy. The Constitution has to be rigid which means that there is a distinction between the constitutional law and ordinary laws. There is a special provision in amending the constitutional law. This is done so that the distribution of power between the central and State governments is not tampered with and ordinarily it is not changed. The American Constitution is the most rigid Constitution.

(iv) *Finally the federal system envisages an independent and impartial judiciary.* The judiciary acts as the guardian and protector of the Constitution. The final interpretation of the Constitution vests with the judiciary. It has to maintain the balance between the centre and

States so that they function within the limits prescribed by the Constitution.

However, it is to be understood that, as Sarkaria Commission on Centre-State Relations in India observed, federalism is not a static institutional concept but a functional arrangement for cooperative action. The Centre and States have not to be engaged in a competition for acquiring more and more powers. It is a system in which both function ensuring stability and peace to the political system called Cooperative Federalism.

Nature of Indian Federation

Now let us consider as to how far the above pre-requisites have been incorporated in the Constitution.

First, Indian Constitution provides for dual polity. We have the Central Government at the Union level and State Governments in the respective States.

Second, the Indian Constitution also provides for the division of power between the Centre and the States. This division of power has been done under Schedule VII of the Constitution, in which three lists have been mentioned. First is the Union List which comes under the jurisdiction of the Union Government and contains 97 items. The second list is called the States List and it includes 66 subjects on which the State Governments have their jurisdiction. The third list is called the Concurrent List which contains 47 items on which both State legislature as well as the Central Parliament have the jurisdiction i.e. both can legislate on these items. However, in case of conflict between the two, the law made by the Union Parliament will prevail. The subjects which have not been mentioned in any of the three lists are with the Central Government. In other words the residuary power rests with the Centre.

Third, this division of power has been done under the Constitution which is written, rigid and supreme. For the purpose of making the Constitution, a Constituent Assembly was convened and after detailed deliberations, the Constitution of India was made. It is the bulkiest Constitution of the world containing 22 Parts, 395 Articles and 12 Schedules. The Constitution is rigid as it differentiates between the Constitutional law and the ordinary law which are passed by the Parliament and the States legislatures. For the purpose of amendment, the provisions of the Constitution fall under three categories and it provides specific procedure for amending all the three categories*

*For amending procedure, see Chapter XVI.

The Constitution is not only written and rigid, it is also supreme. The Constitution is the supreme document from which the power flows. The Union as well as States are required to work under the limits of the Constitution.

Finally, the Indian Constitution provides for an independent judiciary which acts as a guardian of the Constitution. The power of final interpretation of the Constitution rests with the Supreme Court.

Thus the Indian Constitution fulfills all the four essential qualifications of a classical federation. However, right from its inception, the federal nature of the Indian Constitution has always been questioned. According to K.M. Munshi, India is a quasi-federal union vested with several important features of a unitary government. K.C. Wheare says, "The Indian Constitution established a system of Government which is almost quasi-federal, almost devolutionary in character, a unitary State with subsidiary federal features rather than federal States with unitary features." C.N. Joshi also holds the view that "The Union is not strictly a federal polity but a quasi-federal polity with vital and important element of unitariness." A former Chief Justice of India, Gajendragadkar also says that it is not federal in the true sense of the term. It has also been called psudo-federation or "federal in form but unitary in spirit." Now let us study those aspects of the Constitution which are unfederal or unitary. Some of them are as follows:

(i) *Article 1* of the Indian Constitution says, "India, i.e. Bharat, shall be a *Union of States.*" Thus the Indian Constitution does not declare itself as a federation. Instead the term "union" has been used. The dictionary meaning of Union is uniting or being united. Thus the emphasis is on unity while the federation is a system of government in which unity and diversity are both taken into consideration and a balance between the two is sought. While moving the Draft Constitution on November 4, 1948 in the Constituent Assembly Dr. Ambedkar explained why the term "union" instead of federation was used. He said, "The Drafting Committee wanted to make it clear that though India was to be a federation, the federation was not the result of an agreement by the States to join in a federation, and that the federation not being the result of an agreement, no State has a right to secede from it. The federation is a union because it is indestructible. Though the country and the people may be divided into different States for convenience of administration, the country is one integral whole, its people a single people living under a single *imperium* derived from a single source. The Americans had to wage a civil war to establish that the States have no right of secession and that their federation was indestructible. The Drafting Committee thought that it was better to make it clear at the outset rather than to leave it to speculation or to dispute." Thus as B. Shiva Rao points out that the term Union was used as a symbol of the determination of the Constituent Assembly to maintain the unity of the country.

(ii) The Indian Constitution does not guarantee a State of its continued existence. The Parliament may by law form a new State by separating some territory from any State or by uniting two or more State or parts of States or by uniting any territory to a part of any State. It may diminish the area of any State. It may also alter the boundaries of any State and finally it may also change the name of any State. The only restriction is that in doing so, the views of the affected States's legislature will be sought. However, such views are not binding on the Parliament.

(iii) The federal basis of equality of States has also not been met in the Indian Constitution. The State of Jammu and Kashmir enjoys a special status and has more freedom than other States. The amendments introduced in the Indian Constitution under Article 368 donot apply to Jammu and Kashmir.

(iv) The equality of States in a federation is best guaranteed by their equal representation in the upper House of the federal legislature. Thus in United States of America, every State sends two representative, irrespective of their size in terms of area or population to the Senate which is the Upper House of American Congress. However this is not applicable in case of Indian States. They have unequal representation in Rajya Sabha, the following table makes it very clear.

State wise Distribution of Seats in Rajya Sabha

States	No. of Seats
Andhra Pradesh	18
Arunachal Pradesh	1
Assam	7
Bihar	16
Chhattisgarh	5
Delhi	3
Goa	1
Gujarat	11
Haryana	5

States	No. of Seats
Himachal Pradesh	3
Jammu & Kashmir	4
Jharkhand	6
Karnataka	12
Kerala	9
Madhya Pradesh	16
Maharashtra	19
Manipur	1
Meghalaya	1
Mizoram	1
Nagaland	1
Orissa	10
Pondicherry	1
Punjab	7
Rajasthan	10
Sikkim	1
Tamil Nadu	18
Tripura	1
Uttaranchal	3
Uttar Pradesh	34
West Bengal	16

The Table reveals that while the biggest State of UP has the largest representation of 34 seats, smaller States like Manipur, Meghalaya, Mizoram, Nagaland, Sikkim, Goa, Arunachal Pradesh and Tripura send just one representative each to the Rajya Sabha. Besides, the President has been empowered to nominate as many as 12 members in the Rajya Sabha who have special knowledge or practical experience in literature, science, art and social service. This provision of nomination itself is contrary to strict federal practices.

(iv) The division of power between the Centre and the States is not justified from the State's point of view. While the Centre has 97 subjects, the States have only 66 subjects to their jurisdiction. The Concurrent List having 47 subjects gives power to legislate for these items to both Centre as well as the States. However the superiority of the Centre has been guaranteed. In case of conflict between the laws of Centre and the State on the subject mentioned in the Concurrent List, the central law will be applicable.

In fact, there is a pre-dominance of the power of the centre. In case there is a subject which is included in both the Union List as well as the State List, the Union legislature alone is competent to legislate on that subject. Similarly, if there is conflict between the State List and Concurrent List, the union power will prevail. And if there is overlapping between the Union List and Concurrent List, the Union List will prevail. Thus in case of conflict or overlapping among the three lists, it is the Parliament whose law will be the final word. In addition the Centre has residuary powers.

The Constitution also enumerates certain conditions in which the Union Parliament is authorised to make laws on a subject mentioned in the States List. These conditions are as follows:

(i) The Rajya Sabha may pass a resolution supported by not less than two-thirds of the members present and voting declaring that it is necessary or expedient in national interest that Parliament should make law in any matter enumerated in the States List. In such case, the Parliament gets the power to make law on such subject for one year. The Parliament may further increase for another year and this may go on till the Parliament wishes.

(ii) In case of emergency in the country, the Parliament acquires the right to make laws under the subjects mentioned in the State List.

(iii) If the State legislatures of two or more States pass resolutions that the Parliament should make law in any subject mentioned in the State List, then the Parliament can do so. But such law(s) will be applicable to only those States who so desire. Subsequently, other States may also adopt that law by passing resolutions in their legislatures. Such act can be amended or repealed by the Parliament only and not by the State legislature.

(iv) The parliament is empowered to make any law in order to implement any treaty, agreement or convention with foreign countries or any decision made at any international conference or association. This may also enable the Parliament to legislate on the subjects mentioned in States list.

(v) Any law passed by the State legislature can be reserved by the Governor of that State for the consent of the President. The President may veto such a law without giving any reason. Thus, in such case, the President's power of veto is absolute.

(vi) The amending procedure of the Indian Constitution is also unfederal. First, the States cannot initiate the amendment to the Constitution. This power is vested only with the Union Parliament. Second, most of the provision of the Constitution can be amended without any reference to the States. Thus the States have no role in amending most of the provisions of the Constitution. Third, in a few specified cases only, the ratification by one-half of the States is necessary.

(vii) A federal system envisages dual citizenship for its citizens. First they are the citizen of the particular State and then they enjoy the citizenship of the country. This has been provided for in the American Constitution. However, in India we have a single citizenship which is certainly a feature of an unitary Constitution.

(viii) The Governor of the State is appointed by the President of India for five years. But he remains in the office till the pleasure of the President which means he can be dismissed whenever the President wishes. The Constitution pre-supposes dual role for a Governor. (i) He works as the head of the State, and (ii) He is the agent of the Centre in the States. The working of Indian federal system clearly reveal that the Governor has acted more as the agent of the centre than as the head of the State. This is more so when different political parties have been in power in the Union and the States. The centre has used the office of Governor in controlling the States.

(ix) In a federation, Constitution provides for the political structure of the central government and division of power between the federal government and Federating units. Within the limits of division of power, the States are free to make their own Constitutions. But this is not the case with Indian Constitution, which caters to the political structures of the States as well. The States have not been given the freedom to make their own Constitutions. Only exception to this general rule is the State of Jammu and Kashmir which has a separate Constitution.

(x) Another federal principle has been violated in the organisation of judiciary in India. The federal principles envisage a dual system of courts; There are federal courts and State courts. The jurisdiction of the federal court extend to the federal laws while the state courts dispense justice in matter relating to state laws. But in India we have a unified judiciary with the Supreme Court at the apex. The decisions of the High Courts, even in case of State laws relating to state list can be challenged, in the Supreme Court. The civil and criminal laws are codified and applicable to the entire country. To ensure their uniformity, they have been placed in the Concurrent List. Further, the judges of the High Courts are also appointed by the President of India who can be transferred to any other High Court. They can be dismissed through an impeachment process by the Parliament only.

(xi) The uniformity in Indian federation is also visible in the administrative system. We have All India services like Indian Administrative Services or Indian Police Service. The members of the

All India Services are appointed by the Centre through Union Public Service Commission. These officers are appointed in the States and their service rules are governed by the Union Public Service Commission. These officers ensures the uniformity of the administrative system and emphasise the unitary character of Indian political system. The States governments cannot take disciplinary action against them. Besides we have Election Commission whose members are appointed by the President and is responsible for free and fair elections in the entire country. The election machinery is under its direct control. The Parliament has the power to fix the size of constituencies and there is only one general electoral rule for the entire country.

We also have the office of the Comptroller and Auditor General which is managed by the officers of Indian Audit and Account Services, a central service. This office is concerned not only with the accounts and auditing of the Union Government but also those of the States.

(xii) The emergency provisions in the Indian Constitution are the most striking anti-federal features. The Constitution envisages three kinds of emergencies—(a) National Emergency, (b) State Emergency or the President's rule in the State, and (c) Financial Emergency. During the times of national emergency, the Constitution becomes unitary Constitution. The Presidential Rule is imposed on a State where the administrative machinery cannot be carried on in accordance with the Constitution or where the law and order machinery has broken down. In case of financial emergency, which is imposed due to grave financial crisis, the President may direct the States with necessary instructions which are bound to be followed by the States. The President may direct the State to reduce salaries and allowances of persons serving under the State. The direction may also include the reservation of all money bills passed by the State legislatures for the consideration of the President.

(xiii) Even in normal times the Centre has a right to issue directions to the States. Under Article 256, the States are under obligation to exercise their executive powers to ensure the compliance of the laws made by the Parliament and for this purpose the Centre may give necessary directions to the States which are binding on them. Besides the Centre may give directions with regard to (a) the constructions of the means of communication declared to be of national or military importance, and (b) measures to be taken for the protection of railways within the States. Non-compliance of the centre's directive by a State may invite Article 356 i.e. imposition of President's rule.

(xiv) Financially the States have been allocated inadequate resources. This is also one of the most unfederal features of the Indian

Constitution. The distribution of revenues between the Centre and the States gives lesser finances to the States. On the other hand, they have to incur expenditures on education, health, family welfare etc. which donot generate any finances. Therefore, the States have to depend upon the Centre for financial assistance which further weakens the position of States as a federal unit.

(xv) Further the actual operation of Indian political system has been more in the lines of a unitary model. Till 1967, the Indian political system was dominated by the charismatic personality of Jawahar Lal Nehru (who died in 1964) and the Congress Party. Both Union as well as the States were being controlled by the Congress. The Congress high command was a very powerful institution and the State Governments were strictly controlled by it. The States' position were hardly better than municipalities. After 1967, the Congress hegemony came to an end. Practically all the Governments at the centre have misused its power under Article 356 to throttle the democratic institutions in the State for political gains.

The Planning Commission is another form of Central domination over the States. The States who are financially weak had to look forward to Planning Commission for developmental programmes. The Planning Commission is presided over by the Prime Minister and has been termed as "super-cabinet" or a band-master which calls the tune of economic policy of the country. It has been also termed as a steam-roller eroding whatever little autonomy, the States enjoy. It's not only in the financial sphere but also in legislative and executive arena we find that over the years, the Centre has become more and more powerful at the expense of the States.

The study of the above points definitely leads to the conclusion that India is not a federation in the strict sense of the term. It has very strong unitary tendencies and these unitary tendencies have further consolidated as a result of the working of the Indian Constitution during the last 50 years.

Why is the Centre Strong?

Now the question is why the framers of Indian Constitution favoured a strong centre. Most of the federal provisions of the Indian Constitution have been taken from the Government of India Act 1935. Then Congress had opposed the Act on various grounds including that it did not grant sufficient provincial autonomy. Its 1945 election manifesto gave minimum powers to the Central government and states were even given the right to secede from the Indian federation. But later on it was decided to provide for a strong central government under the Indian Constitution. Following are the reasons:

(i) *Partition:* Initially the Constituent Assembly was in favour of a Constitution which would make the State strong and the centre was to be given minimum subjects like foreign affairs, defence and communication. The residuary powers were to be enjoyed by the States. This had been decided to accommodate Muslim League so that the partition could be avoided. As the partition was becoming a reality it was clearly stated in the Constituent Assembly on July 4, 1947, that "The Constitution should be a federal structure with a strong Centre."

After the Partition, the major stumbling bloc (*i.e.* Muslim League) in having a highly centralised State was removed. The Partition was accompanied by communal riots throughout the country and it was felt that only a strong Central government could control them and bring about law and order in the country. K. Santhanam writes, "...the main constitutional results of the Partition of India was that the pendulum swung from one extreme to another extreme. From the idea of minimal federation almost all leaders and, much more than leaders, the followers wanted a maximal federation." The Partition also created a big refugee rehabilitation problem which, it was felt, could be tackled by only a strong Centre.

(ii) *Concern for Unity of the Nation:* The Partition divided India into two countries. There were still disruptive forces in the country which were threatening the unity of the country such as the Princely States, the communist rebellion in Telengana and the Pakistani invasion of Kashmir. The Partition had already created a fear complex in which, as H.V. Patasker explained, "... the result was that the autonomy of the States, or their semi-autonomy came to be looked upon as a matter of national danger." We have already seen that the Constituent Assembly now chose to use the term "union" instead of federation because the dominant feeling was that only a strong central government could ensure the unity of India.

(iii) *Need for Economic Revolution:* The British colonialism had left India poor. Poverty was rampant both in rural as well as urban areas. Indian agricultural growth had stagnated and there was no industrial infrastructure necessary for industrial revolution. The Indian leaders argued that India had to develop very fast in order to meet the requirements of economic revolution. This, they envisaged, through the planned economy, whose basic requirement was a strong central State.

(iv) *Experience from Other Federations:* The framers of the Constitution also studied the actual working of federal constitution in different parts of the world. They found centralising tendencies in every federation, including that of U.S.A. which started as a weak federal State but later on acquired strong central government.

(v) *Lesson from Indian History:* During the framing of Indian Constitution, it was also felt that a study of Indian history revealed the necessity of a strong Central government. Turk invasion took place when India was divided into small States often conflicting with each other. The British conquest of India also took place when there was no strong Central government and India became a slave country. Conversely, under strong Central governments like that of Ashoka, Samudra Gupta and Akbar, India not only could contain foreign aggression but peace and prosperity also flourished in the country. Therefore, the compulsions of Indian history required a strong Central government.

(vi) *The Congress Party:* The Constituent Assembly was dominated by the Congress Party. The Congress has always been a unitarian party. During the making of the Constitution, it was dominated by Nehru, Patel and Rajendra Prasad who wanted a strong Central government. The D.M.K. document submitted to the Sarkaria Commission says, "In their jubiliation over Independence, they thought that Congress and its God-like leaders would rule the country for ever and they never even considered the possibility of other parties coming to power in the units."

Evolution of Indian Federalism (1950-2002)

As we have seen the Indian Constitution is heavily biased against the States and it has established a strong Central Government. This is further reinforced by the actual working of our federation during the last 59 years. These 48 years can be classified as under:

(i) 1950-1967
(ii) 1967-1977
(iii) 1977-1989
(iv) 1989-2009

(i) *The First Phase* (1950-67): The first phase of Indian federalism was marked by the domination of Congress party in the Centre as well as in the States. The Congress party alongwith the charismatic leadership of Nehru further strengthened the centre which already had been made strong by the Constitution. The Chief Ministers and the ministers were chosen by Nehru and the Congress High Command and they could not assert themselves. Even the candidates to the legislature in elections were decided by the High Command. In different States, the

Congress had factions and in many cases they were even encouraged by the Central leadership so that no Chief Minister could become strong. This process of subordination of the State Government to the centre culminated in 1963 when under the Kamraj Plan six Chief Ministers were made to resign.

During this period, three general elections of 1952, 1957 and 1962 were held and Congress was returned to power in almost all the States. In 1952, it won absolute majority in 18 out of 22 States, in rest of the four, it was the single largest party, in 1957 it secured absolute majority in 11 out of 14 States and in 1962, 12 out of 14 States. The party also enjoyed absolute majority in the Parliament as well. In Kerala it saw to it that the Communist government did not remain in power by misusing Article 356. This period also witnessed the food grain crisis and three wars—(a) Indo-Pakistan war of 1948; (b) Indo-China war of 1962; and (c) India-Pakistan war of 1965. These crisis further helped in making the centre strong.

The most important instrument of central domination over the States also came into existence during this period and that is Planning Commission. The Planning Commission was set up for the following purposes:

(a) to make an assessment of material, capital and human resources of the country, including technical personnel, and investigate the possibilities of augmenting such of these resources as are found to be deficient in relation to the nation's requirements;

(b) to formulate a plan for the most effective and balanced utilisation of the country's resources;

(c) on a determination of priorities, to define the stages in which the plan should be carried out and propose the allocation of resources for the due completion of each stage;

(d) to indicate the factors which were tending to retard economic development and determine the conditions which, in view of the current social and political situation, should be established for the successful execution of the plan;

(e) to determine the nature of the machinery which will be necessary for securing the successful implementation of each stage of the plan in all its aspects;

(f) to appraise from time to time the progress achieved in the execution of each stage of the plan and to recommend the adjustments of policy and measures that such appraisal might show to be necessary; and

(g) to make such interim or ancillary recommendations as might be appropriate on a consideration of the prevailing economic conditions, current policies, measures and development programmes, or on an examination of such specific problems as may be referred to it for advice by central or State governments for facilitating the discharge of the duties assigned to it.

The Planning Commission was presided over by the Prime Minister and some of the Ministers were also its members. Experts as members were also included. The commission worked more or less as a cabinet, and in the process the Finance Commission which is a Constitutional body got marginalised. The growing importance of the Planning Commission was objected to by some of the States, especially West Bengal. The Planning Commission was to look after the economic and social services and under these services it was dealing with education, medicine, public health, agriculture, cooperation, social welfare and industrial housing which were all State subjects. The West Bengal government contended that real federation should prevail and the Union government and State governments should be limited to their respective spheres.

Another institution that cropped up during this period was the National Development Council in 1952. This organisation was more democratic in the sense that all the Chief Ministers of States were its members. National Development Council was seen as an experiment on cooperative federation to strengthen and mobilise the efforts and resources of the country to support the planning process and to ensure a balanced and rapid development of various parts of the country. K. Santhanam termed it as a super cabinet of the Indian federation, a Cabinet functioning for the Government of India and the Government of all the States. But the National Development Council also functioned as a medium of the Central government. In one of its meetings, the States surrendered to the centre their sales tax on textile, sugar and tobacco. K. Santhanam observed, "Normally, this would be a major constitutional issue because there were taxes which have been assigned to the States. Under normal federal political conditions, there would have been discussions in every State legislature and in the press as to whether the State should surrender or not." K Santhanam was right because given the Congress dominance in which the Centre-States relationship was mainly the Congress party's internal issue, the States could not assert themselves. K. Santhanam further remarked, "I believe the decision to surrender the taxes ... was taken at a single sitting (of the Council) at which many of the Chief Ministers had not even fully consulted their own cabinets."

Under the provisions of the States Reorganisation Act, Regional Zonal Councils were set up to discuss various issues of mutual interests and to enable the Centre and States to cooperate in evolving uniform policies in social and economic matters. At the same time, it also became clear that these Zonal Councils, as the then Home Minister Pant said, were to attain the emotional integration of the country and to help in arresting active regional consciousness and all divisive trends. These Zonal Councils were advisory bodies and they did try to foster cooperative federalism. Yet they were formed within the system of central domination over the States.

Thus the first phase of Indian federalism is the phase of central domination over the States. We can say that we started with a contradiction. While we had a federal system of government, the governmental system in India worked more on unitary lines. The States even surrendered some of their major powers to the centre.

(ii) *The Second Phase* (1967-1977): This phase saw the emergence of assertion on the part of the States and the Centre reacting to such assertion by demonstrating its effective powers. 1967 is the most important year in the development of Indian federal system. In 1967, the fourth General Elections took place which resulted in the breakdown of Congress monopoly of political power. The charismatic personality of Nehru was not there and Congress lost in as many as nine States significantly. In Parliament also, it could command only a thin majority. After the congress-split, it became a minority government with the support of leftist parties. In several States, the non-congress governments which were essentially coalition governments came into existence. The Congress party attempted to regain the political power by engineering defections and all other means at its disposal including *Article 356.* The Rajasthan case in the classical example of such means where the fourth General Elections, the opposition parties formed a United Front elected its leader and requested the Governor to invite its leader to form the government. The Governor refused and recommended the President to invoke *Article 356*. The President accordingly invoked *Article 356,* but the States Assembly was not dissolved only suspended. The Congress engineered defections in the opposition parties to its side and ultimately was able to muster majority. The President's rule was invoked and a Congress government under Mohan Lal Sukhadia was formed in Rajasthan.

During the period between 1967-71, the Union-State conflict was at its peak. The States under the non-Congress governments asserting their rights and the Union Government's refusal to accept such assertion. A variety of issues cropped up in the area of Centre-States relations, which we shall study later on. But the most important factor during this period was the emergence of regional forces to fill up the vacuum created by weakening of Congress Party.

However, the mid-term elections to the Lok Sabha again changed the political scenario. The Congress Party under the charismatic leadership of Indira Gandhi came back to power in the Centre as well as the States. Mrs. Gandhi used the Congress dominance in making the centre stronger. The Forty-Second Amendment to the Constitution was made which resulted in the increase of powers of the Central government at the expense of the States. The centralisation of authority in the hands of centre was complete with the infamous Emergency of 1975-77.

(iii) *The Third Phase*—1977-89: In 1977, the Congress lost the political power at the centre. The Janata Party, which came into power, had declared in its manifesto that there had been "a high degree of centralisation" and it believed in decentralisation of economic and political power. However, Janata Party's first act was the continuation of Congress manipulative politics when it dismissed the Congress governments in the States by invoking Article 356. The States now reasserted their demand for more autonomy. The States of West Bengal, Tamil Nadu, Punjab and Jammu and Kashmir particularly voiced their demands for more powers. A demand was also made to appoint a parliamentary committee to study the Centre-State relations which was not accepted by the Prime Minister Morarji Desai. The only thing that the Janata government did was scrapping of Article 357(A), through 44th Constitutional Amendment, which had been inserted by the 42nd Constitutional amendment and which enabled the centre to deploy army and para-military force for dealing with any grave situation of law and order in the state.

Mrs. Gandhi came back to power in 1980 and she also got the Janata governments in nine States dismissed through *Article 356*. Subsequently elections took place in these State Assemblies. While Congress came back to power in many States but still in a number of States including Andhra Pradesh, Tamil Nadu, Jammu and Kashmir, Karnataka, and West Bengal, non-Congress governments were formed where regional parties came into power (the CPM government and the Janata government in Karnataka were also more or less regional party governments). There was acceleration of Punjab crisis where Akali Dal was demanding more autonomy. The four Southern States declared the formation of a regional council to buttress the demand for greater State autonomy. All this led to the appointment of Sarkaria Commission to look into the Centre-State relationship.

Mrs. Gandhi's assassination was followed by Rajiv Gandhi's ascendancy to the Indians Prime Ministership. However, he was no different than his mother. Rajiv Gandhi did try to build-up alliances with the regional parties because of political compulsions. Yet he also attempted to centralise powers. He called the conference of District Megistrates for the first time in India in which he could directly communicate with the districts of India ignoring the State governments. Again he did the samething while introducing Panchayati Raj Bill and Jawahar Rozgar Yojna.

(iv) *The Fourth Phase* (1989-2002): There are certain characteristics of this phase: (i) Congress dominance became a thing of the past; (ii) It is the phase of coalition governments at the centre; (iii) The regional parties asserted themselves; (iv) The Central Government became weak.

Barring P.V. Narasimha Rao Government which somehow managed the Congress government, all the other governments that were formed after 1989, have been coalition governments supported by regional parties. V.P. Singh, the Prime Minister of National Front/Janata Dal reactivated the idea of Inter-State Council and set up a secretariat to service it. But shortly he had to go. His successor P.V. Narasimha Rao didnot pursue it. He even abondoned the practice of calling regular meetings of National Development Council. The Sarkaria Commission report which was submitted in 1988, was also ignored.

A landmark in the development of Indian federalism took place in 1996, when the United Front Government with the support of Congress (I) came into power. This was the government of 14 regional parties comprising Janata Dal, Communist Party of India (CPI), Communist Party of India (Marxist) (CPM), Asom Gana Parishad (AGP), Forward Bloc (FB), Revolutionary Socialist Party (RSP), Samajavadi Party (SP), Telugu Desham (TD), Dravida Munnetra Kazhagam (DMK), Tamil Mannila Congress (TMC), Congress-Tiwari, National Conference (NC) and Indian Union Muslim League (IUML). The leader of the United Front H.D. Deve Gowda himself was a regional leader. Even his colleagues with the exception of P. Chidambaram were regional leaders. The Prime Minister was chosen by the leader of Telegu-Deshum (TDP) and Chief Minister of Andhra Pradesh Nara Chandrababu Naidu. After the fall of Deve Gowda Government, again he alongwith Harkishen Singh Surjeet (CPM) played the role of king-maker in installing I.K.Gujral as the Prime Minister.

Infact the novelty of the United Front exercise was that the power shifted from the Centre to the State. The most important thing was that for the first time the Central Government had acknowledged the need to recast Centre-State relations.

The Common Minimum programme which was the basis of the functioning of the United Front Government envisaged "to advance the principles of political, administrative and economic federalism." It also wanted to go beyond the recommendations of Sarkaria Commission because "there has been a new articulation of States's rights and the need for greater powers to the States to meet the aspirations of their respective States. "According to the Programme, the State should have greater say in determining their priorities in developmental programmes, greater freedom to draw their plans within the broad framework of the National Five Year Plans. It also stood for the transfer of most of the centrally-sponsored schemes to the control of State Governments. The document also promised to amend Article 356 to prevent its misuse. It also promised to "reactivate and energise institutions like National Development Council and the Inter-State Council. The regional parties also formed a Federal Front to safeguard the interests of their States.

In the changed political scenario, the regional parties not only dominated at the centre, they were also in power in many States including Assam, Haryana, Bihar, Orissa, Andhra Pradesh, Karnataka and Tamil Nadu. This can also be viewed as a healthy trend towards not only cooperative federalism but also the national unity. The States may become more responsible and responsive. In Andhra Pradesh, the government attempted to raise its own financial resources by cutting the populist programmes like prohibition. The regional parties also emphasised the national unity. The Chief Minister of Tamil Nadu declared that the DMK's first goal was to ensure the survival of the country.

The short span of 412 days of the existence of twelfth Lok Sabha only witnessed the internal bickerings and constant struggle within the coalition led by Shri Atal Behari Vajpayee. The thirteenth Lok Sabha elections brought the National Democratic Alliance led by Vajpayee to power. This coalition seemed to be more matured than earlier coalitions. Vajpayee saw to it that the power did not shift to regional parties. His Government refused to accept Akali Dal, a coalition partner's, demand that the Udham Singh Nagar remain with the UP and not given to the newly-created state of Uttranchal. Similarly, it displayed a remarkable confidence and assertion in dealing with another Alliance Partner, Trinamool Congress which later on quit the NDA on the creation of Hazipur Zone of the Railways. Vajpayee said that he believed in federalism and was totally committed to it. He declared that his government believed that regional parties should have a say in the management of national affairs. The Central

Government also successfully tackled the unprecedented situation created by the Jayalalitha Government in Tamil Nadu by arresting the Union Ministers Murasoli Maran and T.R. Balu alongwith the former Chief Minister of Tamil Nadu Dr. M. Karunanidhi which might have led to a major showdown between the central government and the Tamil nadu Government as all the three affected leaders belonged to DMK, a partner in NDA. The DMK Party also expressed its satisfaction after the release of all the three leaders which was done after the Union Government warned the State Government. T.R. Balu said that the previous Governments had invoked *Article 356* to dismiss State Governments but the NDA Government at the Centre did not want to take any hasty step regarding imposition of Presidents' rule since it was a responsible Government and believed in federation." The Inter-State Council was made active and there was regular interaction with the State Governments. Thus a true of spirit of cooperative federalism seemed to be in vogue.

Tension Areas in Indian Federation

Now let us examine the areas of tension between the Centre and the States. As we have already seen that historically we have two phases so far as the Union-States conflicts are concerned. The first phase, which ended with the Fourth General Elections in 1967, was marked by the domination of Congress Party in Centre as well as the States. During this phase, the Union-State conflicts were internal problems of Congress party and resolved at that level only. The post 1967 political scenario saw the emergence of non-Congress governments in States as well as in the Centre. Now, the internal mechanism of the Congress party could not resolve the conflicts and they not only came to the surface but also became increasingly intensive. Now, let us examine the various issues in which the Union-State conflicts have taken place in India.

(i) *The Role of Governor:* The Governor is appointed by the President of India for five years. But he remains in the office till the pleasure of the President, which means he can be recalled any time. This means his continuation in the office depends on the will of the centre. The Supreme Court has held that the Governor's office is an independent office and neither it is under control nor subordinate to the Government of India. However, a study of governors in the States clearly reveals that most of them have been active politicians before becoming governor and the rest were the bureaucrats. They are appointed on political basis and therefore hardly expected to play a non-partisan role.

It is the governor's partisan role that has been the focal point in Union-State conflicts. The governors have furthered the political interests of ruling party of the Centre in the States. This has been done most notably in the appointment of Chief Ministers, summoning, proroguing and dissolving the State Assemblies and in recommending President's Rule.*

(ii) *Article 356***: Article 356 is the most controversial article of the Constitution. It provides for State emergency or President's rule in State if the President, on receipt of report from the Governor of a State or otherwise, is satisfied that a situation has arisen in which the government of the State cannot be carried on in accordance with the provisions of the Constitution. The duration of such emergency is six months and it can be extended further but in any case, it cannot be more than three years. In the Constituent Assembly, Ambedkar had made it clear that the *Article 356* would be applied as a last resort. He also hoped that ".... such articles will never be called into operation ... and that they would remain a dead letter."

Unfortunately *Article 356* didnot remain a dead letter. It has been misused more than 100 times and is the one of the most contentious issues in Centre-State relations. It has been used as a coercive weapon to remove or not to allow the opposition party to form a government in the States by the Centre. The most blatant misuse of Article 356 took place in Kerala in 1959, when the communist government was removed from power despite enjoying the majority support in the State Assembly. After 1967, the imposition of President's rule in States became a frequent phenomena. In 1967, it was imposed on Rajasthan to prevent non-Congress parties to form the government. Subsequently it was revoked when the Congress, through defections, acquired majority. In 1968, in West Bengal, when the leftist's parties coalition refused to accept the advice of the Governor to call the session of the Assembly and to seek a vote of confidence, the Governor dismissed the ministry and appointed a Congress-led ministry. But without seeking the confidence vote, the President rule was imposed. Similarly in Haryana in 1967 President's Rule was imposed without giving a chance to the ministry to test its majority. No doubt large scale defections were taking place in Haryana but still the ministry appeared to be enjoying a majority. In 1971, in Orissa President's Rule was imposed because the Congress government had lost the majority support and the opposition parties led by Biju Patnaik was not to be

*For details see Discretionary powers of the Governor in Chapter XIII.

*For details see Chapter X—Emergency Powers of the President.

allowed to form ministry. In 1976, the DMK Ministry in Tamil Nadu was dismissed on the charge that it was a corrupt government and *Article 356* was invoked.

In most of the cases, *Article 356* was invoked despite the fact that there was no grave law and order situation and no breakdown of constitutional machinery. In 1977, the Congress lost elections in the Lok Sabha heavily. The Janata Government dismissed the nine Congress led ministries and imposed President's Rule in all the nine States on the plea that those ministries didnot reflect the wishes of the electorate. When Mrs. Gandhi came back to power she did the same thing and President's Rule was imposed on nine States. In 1995, President's Rule was imposed on U.P. thrice consecutively because the United Front Government in Delhi was determined to prevent BJP from assuming office on the basis of its being the single largest part in the new Assembly.

It is interesting to note that all the parties have misused the Article 356. When in power at the centre, they have supported its invocation on different grounds and while in opposition, they have criticised it as an anti-federal and anti-democratic measure.

(iii) *The Maintenance of Law and Order in States:* The maintenance of law and order is a State subject. However, there is a general complaint among the States that the Union Government has been encroaching upon the State's domain. The Union Government has done this through the deployment of para-military forces like Border Security Force (BSF), Central Industrial Faculty Force (CISF) and Central Reserve Police (CRP). In 1968, the CRP was despatched to Kerala without consulting the State Government. Similarly in West Bengal it was deployed. In both the cases, the State Governments objected to it. However, the Central Government asserted its right to deploy para-military forces in the States in case there is any danger to Central Government's Undertakings and property and the State Government is unable to protect them. In 1984, CRP was deployed in Andhra Pradesh which according to the State Government was done for political reasons.

(iv) *Encroachment by the Centre on States List:* Another issue which has been a bone of contention between the Union and the States has been the State List under the Schedule VII of the Constitution. The States have complained that over the years the Central Government has been encroaching upon the State List and snatching their powers. It has been pointed out that the Centre had monopolised the control of industries, trade, commerce and production and distribution of goods which are State Subjects. Even the essential items like sugar, wheat, kerosene, rice etc have been brought under central control which are also used for political purposes. Besides items like Education and Forest which were in State List were brought under Concurrent List in which the Centre has the dominance. Some of the States have also objected to Article 200 which says that Governor can reserve a bill for the assent of the President. In certain cases, the President has refused to give his consent. Infact, the States have questioned the very distribution of power between the Centre and the States. They are now demanding more autonomy in legislative sphere.

(v) *The Financial Aspect:* The financial weakness of States have been a major area of tension between the Centre and States, next only to the role of Governor and the *Article 356*. The Constitution of India has made elaborate arrangement regarding the distribution of financial resources between the Centre and the States which is as follows:

(i) Certain taxes are imposed by the Centre but collected and appropriated by the States.

(ii) Certain taxes are imposed and collected by the centre but are assigned to the States.

(iii) Certain taxes like the income tax are levied and collected by the centre and distributed between the Centre and the States according to the principles laid down by the Finance Commission. Similarly the proceeds of Union excise duty is also shared between the two.

(iv) The Centre may give grants-in-aid to States.

The Constitution also provides for a Finance Commission which is appointed after every five years to make recommendations regarding the division of the proceeds of the taxes which are to be distributed between the Centre and the States, and also allocate the respective shares of States.

However from the States's point of view, this distribution is faulty. The State's resources in raising finances are meagre whereas they have been assigned a wide range of responsibilities of social welfare, education, rural development, public health and industries. On its own the State cannot take up any major project. Infact, they are financially so handicapped that in many cases the States are unable to pay the salaries of their employees. The Centre has also adopted discriminatory attitude based on political reasons in the allocation of grants-in-aid to the States. Centre also grants loans to the States and in doing so it functions as a money-lender. It charges interests from the State for the loans. There also have been cases when centre has obtained loans from international agencies at lower interest and passed them to States on higher interest. The States have to take loans from the centre and over the years there has been an enormous accumulation of outstanding debts of the States to the Centre. The States are now demanding that the centre waive off the loans which the centre is not ready to accept.

The role of Planning Commission is also another controversial matter. Over the years the role of Finance Commission which is a statutory body under the constitution, has decreased and the Planning Commission's role, a commission created by the decision of the Central Government which is a non-statutory body, has increased. The Planning Commission has been accused of political considerations in allocating developmental projects to the States. The poorer States like Bihar have always complained that they were not being given enough funds.

Centre-State Conflict—New Issues

MP in 2008 complained that the Centre was supplying sub-standard imported wheat to the state under the public distribution system. The MP Chief Minister Shivraj Singh Chauhan expressed his apprehension that the imported red wheat could be infested with many alien species of wild grasses as happened in the case of Kharpatwar gajar ghas (carrot grass) which could cause significant damage to the local natural eco-system and bio-diversity and have an adverse impact on the cattle population. They could also damage the common man's health. He also pointed out that the wheat procured from other parts of the country was much better. The CM also complained that the Indian farmers were being paid poor support price. The Union Government was offering Rs. 1000 per quintal of wheat to the farmers during the rabi season while it was paying Rs. 1600 per quintal for imported wheat. He said," If the farmers in the country were offered better support price, there would be no need to import wheat.

The Chief Minister even went on a 24-hours 'fast' in protest against 'deliberate' neglect of the State's demands by the Centre. He pointed out that he could bear any amount of pain inflicted on him 'but not the injustice being perpetuated by the Centre on the people of Madhya Pradesh.' He also pointed out that his struggle would continue till the centre addressed the issues confronting the people of his state. He further pointed out the plan. The next stage would be to launch a signature campaign followed by a 'nyaya-yatra' before embarking on a peaceful struggle for justice. The Chief Minister Shri Chauhan listed ten (questions) grievances against the centre which included reduction of power supply from 350MW to 31 MW to the State from central grid, reduction of supply of low-grade coal to the State, less assistance than even Kerala for building dwelling units for poor (the state has 37 lakh houseless families but funds were given to construct 47,000 dwellings) and that the State was given poor quality 'red wheat' for distribution under the public distribution system.

The Rajasthan CM Vasundhara Raje sought permission to grant as additional quota of reservation to Gujjars under nomadic category and to Rajputs, Brahmins and Vaisyas under economically backward class. She also asked the various groups demanding reservation facilities to approach the Centre to get justice on quota.

The UP CM Mayawati demanded change in the law to provide her the SPG protection as she feared danger to her life. She also demanded exemption and impunity from various authorities including the taxmen. She also demanded Rs. 80,000 crore special package for UP. She alleged that UP was being given a step-motherly treatment. She demanded a Special Area Incentive Package for poorvanchal and bundelkhand. Mayawati also blamed the central government for the price-rise in essential commodities. She said that the hike in petrol and diesel prices by the centre had resulted in increase in transportation cost and as a result the prices of essential commodities like wheat, rice, maida, ghee, mustard oil, medicines etc had gone up. In another occasion, Mayavati attributed the rampant corruption and price-rise to the economic policies pursued by the UPA and NDA governments at the centre. She pointed out that the development of the country had come to a stand-still due to the policies of these governments.

A significant issue which is likely to become a major conflict area between the Centre and the States was the Centre's assessment of poor households in the country. The states like Punjab, Karnataka, West Bengal, Kerala, Bihar, MP, Chhattisgarh, Orissa, and the Union Territory of Daman and Diu contested the poverty figures of the Planning Commission. As per the Planning commission's figure the number of poor people was 26.1 million while the States have estimated this figure to be 42.1 million. This is a crucial issue because on the basis of poverty figures, allocation of subsidized foodgrains is made by the centre under the Targeted Public Distribution Scheme (TPDS) to the states.. As a result of Centre's estimates at least 16 million Below Poverty Line (BPL) families in eight States and one union territory were recognized by the Centre as eligible for the various central schemes including subsidized foodgrains allocation. According to the Bihar Government, the numbers of the poor were 121 lakh families while Centre recognized only 65.23 lakh poor families in

Bihar. Similar variations were found in other cases. In Punjab, the state Government estimation was 14 lakh as against 4.68 lakh as estimated by the Centre. Karnataka had 63 lakh while the centre recognized only 31.29 lakh. The States figures in MP and Orissa were 60 lakh and 57.50 lakh while the Centre's figures were 41.25 lakh and 32.98 lakh respectively. The union Minister for food and Consumer affairs complained in the parliament that as many as 17 States/Union territories had issued ration cards in excess of the poverty estimates of the planning commission for allocation of foodgrains to the TPDS beneficiaries. Before this in January 2008, the Bihar CM Nitish Kumar had termed the NREG Scheme as 'flawed' and sought a meeting of the Union Government with States to remove the weaknesses and if necessary to amend the law.

Another issue came up when the Chief Ministers of five states (MP, Rajasthan, Orissa, Chhattisgarh (BJP-ruled states) and Jharkhand (Congress-ruled state) demanded a re-think in the New Mineral policy. They felt that the new mineral policy favoured foreign direct investment and multi-national mining companies by promoting liberal export of minerals. They also demanded that the rights of the mineral-based states should not be 'usurped' by the union Government. Their joint memorandum submitted to the Prime Minister said," the state's right to select the best applicants (for mining rights) should not be compromised in the name of seamless transition or security of tenure and should not be usurped by the centre under any pretext." Further it pointed out," The Government of India is anxious to promote free export of minerals in order to satisfy multinational mining companies ... If the policy is accepted as it is, it may result in a situation where a few MNC mining companies acquire control over the vast mineral resources." The document also said,: Since minerals are our national wealth, this approach of the government of leaving exploration in private hands is certainly not in the national interest."

The CM of HP alleged discrimination on political grounds by the centre. Shri Prem Kumar Dhumal charged the UPA government at the centre of discriminating against the BJP-led HP Government. He complained the state was not being provided with sufficient development projects and allocation of financial assistance. The State was faced with a huge debt of Rs. 22,930 crore and the state had "not received the much promised financial package promised during the previous congress regime by the Central Government."

He also alleged that the centre was even taking away whatever had been announced and implemented by the previous NDA Government at the Centre including the industrial package. Shri

Dhumal pointed out that his State had been clearly discriminated against in the allocation of IIT and central university which the Prime Minister had promised in 2007. He further protested that while the North-Eastern States were extended special package and financial assistance again and again, "(T)he industrial package (sanctioned by the NDA Government) for the State was valid till 2013 but then it was curtailed by the UPA Government to March 2007 and extended to March 2010 after protests." He demanded its restoration to its original date.

The Central Government's policy with regard to Special Economic Zones (SEZ) was not appreciated by the States. While Bihar CM declared that his State had decided against the setting up of SEZ 'in principle (The Hindu 10 Jan 2008), West Bengal CM Buddhadeb Bhattacharjee criticised the 'mad rush' for SEZs and demanded a clear-cut and uniform policy for setting-up Special Economic Zones with emphasis on two points attracting advanced technologies from foreign countries and promoting exports from India. Buddhadeb saw no virtue in setting up 400 SEZs in the country. He demanded restrictions on setting up SEZs and said that there should be some ceiling on allotting land for such zones and the allotted land should not be put to use for any other purpose. Buddhadeb also demanded that foreign companies should not be allowed to invest in retail trade and the field should be left open for the big Indian companies. At the same time the interests of small traders and businessmen should be protected.

Haryana Chief Minister Bhupinder Singh Hooda demanded that the central government should link the Minimum Price Index (MSP) with the price-index. He also wanted that the MSP should be decided on a regional basis as the cost of production in agriculture had increased manifold. He also demanded that 'frost' should be included under the Natural Calamities Relief Fund.

Gujarat Chief Minister Narendra Modi complained that the central assistance to the state was negligible as compared to the revenue it contributed in form of taxes. He said, "Central assistance to Gujarat is about 2.5 per cent of total tax collection of Rs. 40,000 cr (by the state to the Centre)". Modi said that Congress-led United Progressive Alliance at the Centre went out of its way to help state government in West Bengal but discriminated against Gujarat. He also alleged that the Centre's attitude had been very negative on various state government initiatives on economic development. He also criticised the union Government for not approving the state's Gas Act. Narendra Modi demanded that labour reforms should be made a state subject to augment employment generation. He pointed out that the ground realities were different in Gujarat and they should not be compared with other states in India. He said that Gujarat would stop paying taxes to the Centre and, on its part, would not expect support from the Centre. He even challenged the Union government to book him for sedition.

Centre-State Relations—Constitutional Mechanisms

The founding fathers were aware of possible centre-state disputes as they are very natural in a federal setup where there is division of powers between the two. Therefore they provied mechanisms for their redress. These mechanisms were of two kinds—mechanism for solving centre-state disputes and mechanism for state coordination to foster the spirit of cooperative federalism.

1. *Mechanism for sorting out Centre-state disputes:* The following arrangements have been provided in the Constitution to solve the future Centre-state disputes:

(i) The Supreme Court is empowered to resolve disputes between the Union and the States. (Article 131)

(ii) Parliament can make laws providing for adjudication of any dispute or complaint with respect to the use, distribution or control of the waters of inter state rivers and river valleys. (Article 262)

(iii) Article 280 provides for constitution of a Finance Commission for distribution between the Union and the States of the net proceeds of taxes.

(iv) There is freedom of trade, commerce and intercourse throughout the territory of India and subject to restrictions stipulated in the Constitution and the Parliament can by law impose restriction in public interest. (Article 302). Further the Parliament may create an authority in this regard. (Article 307).

2. *Mechanism for Centre-State Coordination:* The Constitution also provided for certain institutional mechanisms for Centre-State coordination. For the purpose Article 263 provides for the creation of an Inter-State Council. This Inter-State Council was set up in 1990.

Inter-State Council

Article 263 of Indian constitution provides for the creation of an Inter-State Council. The President can create such a body in public interest. He is also empowered to define the nature of the duties to be performed by it and its organization and procedure. The Inter-State council shall have the following duties:

(a) Inquiring into and advising upon disputes which may have arisen between states;

(b) Investigating and discussing subjects in which some or all of the States, or the Union and one or more of the States, have a common interest; or

(c) Making recommendations upon any such subject and in particular, recommendations for the better co-ordination of policy and action with respect to that subject,

The fourth general elections were the watershed in the Union-State relations as they ended the monopoly of congress party over the political power. Different parties came up at the centre as well as the states and a multi party system started working in India. The changed situation demanded a new approach towards Union-State relations. The Administrative Reform Commission (1969), Rajamannar Commission and the Sarkaria Commission recommended the creation of an Inter-State council as provided under Article 263. In 1990, the Inter-State council was formed. The Inter-State Council has a Secretariat and its officers and staff is appointed by the Prime Minister in his capacity as Chairman of the Council.

Composition of the Council—The Prime Minister is the Chairman of the Inter-State Council. He presides over the meetings of the Council. In his absence an Union Minister of cabinet rank nominated by him presides over the meeting The Inter-State Council has the following members;

(a) Prime Minister:

(b) Chief Ministers of all States

(c) Chief Ministers of Union territories having a Legislative Assembly and Administrators of Union territories not having a Legislative Assembly;

(d) Six Ministers of Cabinet rank in the Union Council of Ministers to be nominated by the Prime Minister. (Other Ministers and Ministers of State having independent charge in the Union Government are invited to attend the meeting if the issue relating to a subject under their charge is to be discussed).

Duties of the Inter-State Council—The Council is a recommendatory body and has the following duties:

(a) To investigate and discuss such subjects which are brought before it, in which some or all of the States or the Union and one or more of the States have a common interest;

(b) To make recommendations upon any such subject and in particular recommendations for the better coordination of policy and action with respect to that subject; and

(c) To deliberate upon such other matters of general interest to the States which may be referred by the Chairman to the Council.

5. *Procedure of the Council:* The Inter-State Council order of 1990 also defines the procedure of Inter-State Council. It says that "The Council shall, in the conduct of its business, observe the following procedure, namely:

(a) The Council shall adopt guidelines for identifying and selecting issues to be brought up before it;

(b) The Council shall meet at least thrice every year and at such time and place as the Chairman may appoint in this behalf;

(c) The meetings of the Council shall be held in camera;

(e) Ten members (including the Chairman) shall form the quorum for a meeting of the Council;

(e) All questions which may come up for consideration of the Council at a meeting shall be decided by consensus and the decision of the Chairman as to the consensus shall be final—and

(f) The Council shall, in the conduct of its business, observe such other procedure as it may, with the approval of the Central Government, lay down from time to time.

Besides the Inter-State Council, Central Council of Health, Central Council of Local Self Government, Council for Sales Tax and State Excise Duties (for each of Northern, Eastern, Western and Southern Zones.), Transport Development Council, Central Council for Research in Ayurveda, Unani, Homeopathy, Yoga and Nature cure and Central Family Welfare Councils have been set up under Article 263. Several inter-state consultative bodies have also been set up under executive orders at different times like National Water Resources Council, Mineral Advisory Council and Indian Labour Conference. National Development Council was set up. Five Zonal Councils were set up under the States Reorganization Act, 1956 to deliberate on contentious regional issues. North East Council for the North-East area was set up in 1981.

The Issue of State Autonomy

The over centralisation of power in the hands of the Centre and the emergence of different Party governments at the Centre and the States has led to the demand of State autonomy. The Central Government appointed the Administrative Reforms Commission which gave its report in 1969. The Commission felt that 'No Constitutional amendment is necessary for ensuring proper and harmonious relations between the Centre and the State, in as much as the provisions of the Constitution governing Centre-State relations are adequate for the purpose of meeting any situation or resolving any problems that may arise in the field." Nevertheless it gave many recommendations in regard to the role of Governor, the problem of law and order and the Centre-State financial relationship. But the report was not implemented.

The Tamil Nadu Government appointed Rajamannar Committee in 1969 which gave its report in 1971. The Rajamannar Committee demanded readjustment of VII Schedule and residuary powers to the States. Among the other recommendations of Rajamannar Committee were (i) the repeal of *Article 249* which gives power to the Parliament to legislate on the subjects mentioned in States List in the national interest by two-third majority of the Rajya Sabha, (ii) The Governor's power to reserve any bill passed by the States Legislature for Presidents consent (*Article 200*) and *Article 201* which gives President the power to refuse his assent should also be scrapped.

In December 1977, the West Bengal Government adopted a memorandum called the *West Bengal Memorandum* which made the following important recommendations:

(i) Where ever the word "Union" has been used in the Constitution, it should be substituted by the word "Federation."

(ii) The residuary powers should be given to the States.

(iii) While the State should not transgress the spheres allotted to the Central Government, the Centre should also not interfere in the legislative and executive spheres of the States.

(iv) *Article 249* giving power to Parliament to legislate on a subject in the State List under the plea of national interest should be deleted.

(v) The subjects such as defence, foreign affairs including foreign trade, currency and communications and economic coordination should be with the Centre. The role of Centre should be one of coordination. In planning, fixing of prices, wages etc, the Centre may not only coordinate but also issue directions. But in planning and economic coordination, the Centre will have to conform to the general guidelines formulated by the National Development Council in which the States will have representation along with the Centre.

(vi) The Planning Commission should be made a Constitutional body for which a separate Article be included and the composition of Planning Commission will be determined by the National Development Council. The States must have a say in the manner of operation of Planning Commission.

(vii) The Articles regarding the Finance Commission and the distribution of revenues should be amended to provide for 75 per cent of the total revenues raised by the Centre from all sources for allocation to different States by the Finance Commission. The State must also be accorded more powers for imposing taxes on their own, and to determine the limits of public borrowing in their respective cases. The Centre should not also have the power to put restriction on trade and commerce.

(viii) *Articles 356* and *357* which enable the Parliament to dismiss a State Government or dissolve its Assembly should be deleted. *Article 360* which provides for Financial Emergency should also be deleted.

(ix) *Articles 200* and *201* which empowers the Governor to reserve Bills passed by the State Assembly for President's assent should be removed.

(x) Rajya Sabha should have equal representation from all States except in cases of States which have less than three million of population. The elections to the Rajya Sabha should be done directly by the people.

(xi) All India services like IAS, IPS, etc should be abolished. There should be Union Services and State Services and recruitment should be made by the Union and States respectively in these services. The Central Government should have no jurisdiction over the personnel of the State Services.

(xii) The name and area of a State should not be changed by the Parliament without the specific consent of the State concerned.

(xiii) English should continue to be used for all the official purposes of the Union alongwith Hindi till as long as people of the non-Hindi regions so desire.

In 1978, the Akali Dal came out with a controversial resolution called the *Anandpur Sahib Resolution*. It demanded greater autonomy for the States seeking Centre's authority to be confined to only Defence, Foreign Relation, Communications, Railways and Currency. It also demanded residuary powers for the State.

In the eighties, as the regional parties became very assertive, they put-forth the demand for State autonomy in an organised manner. Their "conclaves" were held at Vijaywada, Delhi and Srinagar which raised the demand for redefining the Centre-States relations.

The agitation for State autonomy led to the creation of Sarkaria Commission by the Central Government to recommend changes in Centre-State relationship. The Commission submitted its report in 1988. While it made the general observation that the Constitution is basically sound and there is no need for drastic changes in the basic character of the Constitution, nevertheless it gave the following recommendations:

1. Ordinarily, the Union should occupy only that much field of a Concurrent subject on which uniformity of policy and action is required in the larger interest of the nation, leaving rest of the details for State action, within the broad frame-work of the policy laid down in the Union law.
2. Whenever, the Union proposes to undertake legislation on a subject belonging to the Concurrent List, the States views must be ascertained through Inter-governmental councils.
3. Parliamentary law passed under clause (1) of *Article 252*, on request of two or more States, should not be perpetual but should be for specific period not exceeding three years.
4. On receipt of a resolution from a State recommending creation or abolition of a Legislative Council, the same will be presented before the Parliament *within a reasonable time.*

Administrative Relations

5. *Articles 256, 257* and *365* are wholesome provisions, designed to secure co-ordination between the Union and the States for effective implementation of Union laws and the national policies indicated therein. Nonetheless, a direction under *Articles 256* and *257* and action under *Article 365*, in event of non-compliance, is a measure of last resort. Before issue of directions to a State and invocation of *Article 365*, utmost caution should be exercised and efforts must be made to settle point of differences by other available means.
6. Federalism is more a functional arrangement for cooperative action than a static institutional concept. Hence, *Article 258*, an effective tool must be used for the purpose—i.e. the power of the Union to confer powers etc. on States in certain cases.

Appointment and Role of Governor

(The Constitution does not provide for transfer of Governors, but they have been treated and transferred like civil servants. Because of frequent transfers, Maharashtra had seen seven Governors between 1980-87 and the Punjab saw six between 1984-88).

7. A person appointed must be eminent, from outside the States, a detached figure and must not have actively participated in politics, a person belonging to minority groups must be given preference. Consultation with Chief Minister is desirable. The Vice-President and/or the Speaker of Lok Sabha may be confidentially or

informally consulted though there is no constitutional obligation to do so.

8. Governor's tenure must not ordinarily be cut short.
9. As a matter of convention, he should be eligible for re-appointment as Governor, Vice President or President but for no other office of profit either under the Union or the States Governments. He and his wife must get reasonable post-retirement benefits irrespective of the duration of Governorship.

Duties and Responsibilities of a Governor

10. Govenor should appoint a Chief Minister who can face the Assembly and must be able to enjoy the confidence of the House. Such a Ministry must not be dismissed.
11. Governor can function independently as Chancellor of the University, if the Act so provides—No obligation to consult the Ministry.
12. Ad hoc and fortnightly reports must be sent, after taking Chief Minister into confidence.
13. Article 163 (Aid and Advice of the Council of Ministers) should be left untouched. Also, discretionary powers be left to the Governor (Article 163)
14. Normally, in discharge of the functions under Article 200, the Governor must abide by the advice of his council of Ministers. Needless reservation of Bills for President's consideration should be avoided; the policy embodied in the Bill cannot be the grounds for reservation. It may be done when, in the opinion of the Governor, the provisions of the Bill are patently unconstitutional, beyond the legislative competence, endanger the sovereignty, integrity and unity of the nation, and/or violates the Fundamental Rights etc.
15. As a matter of statutory convention, reserved Bills must be disposed of by the President within four months period from the date of receipt.
16. The wrong practice of mechanical and repeated re-promulgation of an Ordinance, without caring to get it replaced by an Act of the Legislature must be eshewed.

Emergency Provisions

17. *Article 356* should be used very sparingly, in extreme cases, as a matter of last resort; a warning should be issued to the errant State

in specific terms-alternatives must not ordinarily be dispensed with.

18. It should be provided through an appropriate amendment that notwithstanding anything in clause (2) of *Article 74* of the Consitution, the material facts and grounds on which *Article 356 (1)* is invoked, should be made an integral part of the Proclamation issued under the Article. This will also assure control of the Parliament over exercise of this power by the Union Executive, more effective.
19. The Governor's Report must be a "speaking document" and it should be given wide publicity.

References

Austin Granville, *The Indian Constitution: Cornerstone of a Nation*, 1972, Bombay, Oxford University Press.

Chanda Asok, *Federalism in India, A study of Union-States Relations*, 1965, London, George Allen & Unwin Ltd.

Fadia B.L. and Manaria R.K.: *Sarkaria Commission Report of Centre-State Relations*, 1990, Agra, Sahitya Bhawan.

Fadia B.L., *Indian Government and Politics*, 1996, Agra, Sahitya Bhawan Publications Commission on Centre-State Relations, Government of India, 1988 Part I and II.

Mukarjee, Nirmal and Balveer Arora (Ed.), *Federalism in India: Origins and Development* 1992, New Delhi, Vikas Publishing House Pvt. Ltd.

Raman S. (Ed.), *Indian Government and Politics* (Ed.) New Delhi, Allied Publishers Pvt Ltd.

Rao B. Shiva, *The Framing of India's Constitution*, 1968, New Delhi; The Indian Institute of Public Administration.

Singh Mahendra P., Shukla V.N. *Constitution of India*, 1994, Lucknow, Eastern Book Company.

Siwach J.R., *Indian Government and Politics*, 1990, New Delhi, Sterling Publishers Pvt Ltd.

Thakur Ramesh, *The Government and Politics of India*, 1995, London, MacMillan Press Ltd.

CHAPTER IX

The Parliament of India

The Concept of Parliamentary Democracy

On the basis of relationship between the legislature and executive, we define two kinds of governments—Presidential and Parliamentary. The Presidential form of government is based on separation of legislature and executive while the parliamentary system envisages a close relationship between the two. In brief, the following are the characteristics of a Parliamentary form of government which we have adopted in India.

(i) There are two heads in a Parliamentary system. One, the head of the State, and the other being the head of the government. The head of State enjoys nominal powers. Though all the powers are used in his name but he himself does not exercise them. In England which is the mother of the parliamentary system the maxim is "The king can do no wrong." He cannot do wrong because he himself does not exercise the powers. The powers are really exercised by the head of the government called the Prime Minister. In India, the President is the head of the State, while the Prime Minister is the head of the government.

(ii) The Prime Minister and his Council of Ministers are the members of the legislature. If any of them is not, then he has to become a member within six months of becoming the minister.

(iii) The Prime Minister and the Council of Ministers are collectively, as well as individually, responsible before the Parliament. They have to answer for all the lapses. The Parliament by a no-confidence motion may dismiss a ministry. The ministry remains in power till it enjoys the confidence of the Parliament, or to be specific, the lower House of the Parliament. There are other methods also, through which the Parliament exercises control over the executive—like asking questions and supplementary questions, various kinds of motions, budget, discussions etc.

(iv) The Prime Minister and his cabinet are politically homogeneous. In a coalition government they may be heterogeneous. But whatever the case, the system works under the leadership of the Prime Minister. There is a team spirit and the differences between the Prime Minister and a minister or ministers, or differences among the ministers, are normally a top secret.

Supremacy of the Parliament: In England the Parliament is supreme, there is no limitation. However, in India the powers and functions are defined and Parliament's role is limited within the constraints provided by the Constitution. We have a federal system which itself is a limitation on the powers of the Parliament. The Supreme Court of India has asserted that there are definite limitations on the amending power of the Constitution of the Parliament. It cannot change the basic structure of the Constitution. Thus unlike English Parliament, Indian Parliament is not supreme.'

Composition of Indian Parliament

The Parliament of India is composed of President and the two Houses—Rajya Sabha and Lok Sabha.

Rajya Sabha: The Rajya Sabha or the Council of States is a permanent House. It is also the upper chamber. Rajya Sabha has 250 members out of which 238 are elected from the States and the Union Territories. 12 members are nominated by the President of India, having special knowledge or practical experience in such matters as literature, science, art and social service.

The representatives from the States are elected by the members of the Legislative Assemblies of the respective States on the basis of prepositional representative by means of single transferable vote. The members of the Union Territories are elected as decided by a law of the Parliament. The membership to the Rajya Sabha is not uniform for the States, unlike the federal principle, which gives equal representation to all the States. It is based on population. It is stipulated that for the first five million of its population, the State will get one member per one million. After that for every additional two millions, there will be one member. Thus the bigger States get more representation than the smaller States, like Sikkim and Tripura, who send only one member to the Rajya Sabha.

As the Rajya Sabha is a permanent body, it cannot be dissolved. One-third of its members retire after every two years. The Rajya Sabha is presided over by the Vice-President of India who is its ex-officio chairman.

The qualifications for becoming a member of Rajya Sabha is as follows:

(i) He should be a citizen of India.

(ii) He should make and subscribe to an Oath or affirmation, expressing his true faith and allegiance to the Constitution and for upholding the sovereignty and integrity of India.

(iii) He should not be less than 30 years of age.

(iv) He should possess all other qualifications as laid down by the Parliament in the Representation of the People Act, 1951. A significiant change was made in 2002, in this Act. He should be registered as a voter in any parliamentary constituency. Earlier it was mandatory to be registered in the State from which he was contesting.

Lok Sabha: Lok Sabha or the House of the People is elected by the people of India directly through universal adult franchise. The maximum strength of the Lok Sabha cannot exceed 550, out of which 530 are to be chosen from the territorial constituencies of the States and 20 members from the Union Territories. Two members of Lok Sabha are nominated by the President of India from the members of Anglo-Indian Community. Every citizen of India, of 18 years and above, has the right to vote in the Parliamentary elections, subject to the law made by the Parliament. At present the membership of the Lok Sabha is 545.

Representation of States/Union Territories in the Lok Sabha and Rajya Sabha (2005)

S. No.	States/Union Territories	No. of seats Lok Sabha	No. of Seats Rajya Sabha
1	Andhra Pradesh	42	18
2.	Arunachal Pradesh	2	1
3.	Assam	14	7
4.	Bihar	40	16
5.	Chhattisgarh	11	5
6.	Goa	2	1
7.	Gujarat	26	11
8.	Haryana	10	5
9.	Himachal Pradesh	4	3
10.	Jammu & Kashmir	6	4
11.	Jharkhand	14	6
12.	Karnataka	28	12
13.	Kerala	20	9

S. No.	States/Union Territories	No. of seats Lok Sabha	No. of Seats Rajya Sabha
14.	Madhya Pradesh	29	11
15.	Maharashtra	48	19
16.	Manipur	2	1
17.	Meghalaya	2	1
18.	Mizoram	1	1
19.	Nagaland	1	1
20.	Orissa	21	10
21.	Punjab	13	7
22.	Rajasthan	25	10
23.	Sikkim	1	1
24.	Tamil Nadu	39	18
25.	Tripura	2	1
26.	Uttaranchal	5	3
27.	Uttar Pradesh	80	31
28.	West Bengal	42	16
29.	Delhi	7	3
30.	Dadra & Nagar Haveli	1	-
31.	Daman and Diu	1	-
32.	Andaman & Nicobar Islands	1	-
33.	Lakshadeep	1	-
34.	Pondicherry	1	1
35.	Chandigarh	1	-
	Nominated	2	12
	Total	545	245

Source: Indian 2008, Government of India.

The normal duration of Lok Sabha is five years. However, it can be dissolved by the President of India before the completion of its term. The term of the Lok Sabha may be extended for one year at a time when the emergency is in operation. But it will not exceed six months after the emergency has ceased to operate.

The qualification for becoming a member of Lok Sabha is as follows:

(i) He should be a citizen of India

(ii) He should make and subscribe to an oath or affirmation expressing his true faith and allegiance to the Constitution and for upholding the sovereignty and integrity of India.

(iii) He should be not less than 25 years of age.

(iv) He should be possessing such other qualifications as may be laid down by Parliament. Accordingly the Representation of the People Act 1951 requires that his name should be registered in any Parliamentary constituency.

Disqualifications for Membership of Parliament

The Constitution enumerates the following disqualifications for being chosen as and for being a member of either House of the Parliament:

(a) If the person holds any office of profit under Government of India or any State, other than an office declared by Parliament by law not to disqualify its holder.

(b) If he is of unsound mind and stands so declared by a competent court.

(c) If he is an undischarged solvent.

(d) If he is not a citizen of India, or has voluntarily acquired the citizenship of a foreign State or is under acknowledgment of allegiance or adherence to the foreign State.

(e) If he is so disqualified by or under any law made by Parliament.

(f) If he is disqualified on the grounds of defection.

Summoning and Prorogation of Parliament

The President of India is authorised to summon and prorogue both the Houses of the Parliament. However the Constitution stipulates that six months should not intervene between the last day of the last session and the first day of the next session. This means before the expiry of six months of the last sitting of the Parliament, the President is duty bound to call the session of the Parliament. The President also prorogues the Parliament, which means the end of the session.

Dissolution of the Lok Sabha

The President of India may dissolve the Lok Sabha before its completion of the five year term. Normally, it is done on the basis of advice by the Prime Minister and his Cabinet.

Quorum

The quorum means the minimum number of members required to be present to enable the House for its meeting. In both the Houses, the quorum is one-tenth of the total number of the members of the respective Houses.

Committee System in the Parliament

Modern Parliaments suffer from the paucity of time. There are so many issues which a rise from time to time and the Parliament has to spare time for them. The Parliament has to pass laws. It has to keep the executive accountable to it. With the result, Parliament is always under pressure. Therefore the committee system has developed. The Parliament concentrates on discussions on broad policies and the public issues, while the committees of the Parliament go into the details and in-depth study of the governmental matters. In fact, now- a-days no Parliament can work without an effective committee system and Indian Parliament is no exception to this general rule. According to Subash Kashyap, a Parliamentary Committee may be defined as one that

(i) is appointed or elected by the House or nominated by the Speaker/Chairman;

(ii) works under the supervision of the Speaker/Chairman;

(iii) presents its report to the House or to the Speaker/Chairman; and

(iv) has a secretariat provided by the Lok Sabha/Rajya Sabha Secretariat.

There are two kinds of Parliamentary Committees. (i) Ad-hoc Committees, and (ii) Standing Committees.

(i) Ad-hoc Committees

The Ad-hoc Committees are constituted by the House or the Speaker/Chairman. They are constituted for a specific purpose for consideration and reporting and they cease to operate thereafter, like Joint/Selection Committee on a Bill under consideration in Parliament.

(ii) Standing Committees

The Standing Committees are relatively permanent in nature. They are elected by the House or nominated by the Speaker/Chairman every year or from time to time. According to Subash Kashyap the Standing Committees in each House, and certain Joint Committees may be categories in terms of the nature of their functions as follows:

(a) *Financial Committees:* Committee on estimates of Lok Sabha, Public Accounts Committee and Committee on Public Undertakings.

(b) *House Committees:* These are the committees related to the day-to-day business of the House viz., Committee on Absence of Members from the Sittings of the House, Business Advisory Committee, Committee on Private Members' Bills and Resolutions and Rules Committee.

(c) *Enquiry Committees:* Committee on Petitions and Committee of Privileges.

(d) *Scrutiny Committees:* Committee on Government Assurances Committee on Subordinate Legislation, Committee on Papers Laid on the Table, Committee on the Welfare of Scheduled Castes and Scheduled Tribes.

(e) *Service Committees:* These are the committees concerned with the provision of various services to members viz., General Purposes Committee, House Committee, Library Committee and Joint Committee on Salaries and Allowances of Members of Parliament.

Powers, Functions and Role of Indian Parliament

We have a parliamentary government in which the Parliament enjoys a pivotal position. However, unlike England, our Parliament is not supreme. The powers and functions of the Indian Parliament have been limited by the federal constitution. Even in case of amendment to the Constitution, Supreme Court has held that the Parliament cannot alter the basic features of the Constitution the following are the powers and functions of the Indian Parliament.

(i) Legislative Functions

Basically the Parliament is a law-making body. We have seen in an earlier chapter, that the Constitution has divided power between the Centre and the States according to List system—The Union List, State List and Concurrent List. The Parliament is empowered to make law in the subjects mentioned in the Union List. The items not mentioned in any of three Lists are residuary powers of the Union and therefore fall under the purview of the Parliament. Along with the State legislature, it can make laws on the subjects mentioned in the Concurrent List. But in case of conflict between a law made by the Parliament and a State law on a concurrent subject, the Union law shall prevail. The Constitution also gives supremacy to the Union List. In case there is a conflict or over-lapping between the three lists, it is the Union List which shall prevail. With regard to State Lists, ordinarily the State Legislatures make law, but in certain circumstances, the Union Parliament is empowered to make laws mentioned in the State List. These circumstances are as follows:

(i) If Rajya Sabha, by not less than two-third majority of members present and voting, passes a Resolution declaring a subject mentioned in the State List as having assumed national importance, then the Parliament can legislate on that subject. But such Resolution will remain in force for one year. After the completion of one year, the Rajya Sabha may further pass the same Resolution.

(ii) If there is emergency in the country, the Parliament can make laws with respect to all matters mentioned in the State List.

(iii) If two or more State legislatures pass a resolution that Parliament should make a law on a subject mentioned in the State List, the Parliament acquires the power to make a law on that subject. However such law will be applicable to such States only. The other States may also adopt it by passing a resolution in the respective State legislatures. Such law can be amended or repealed only by the Union Parliament.

(iv) In order to implement any treaty, agreement or conversation with any other country or countries or any decision made at any international conference, association or other body, the Parliament may, if necessary, invade the State List.

Thus the law-making power is very wide. It covers the Union List, Concurrent List and, in certain circumstances, even the State List.

(ii) The Executive Powers of the Parliament

The Parliamentary system of the government envisages a close cooperation between the legislative and executive wings of the government. The executive is responsible towards the legislature for all its omissions and commissions.

The Prime Minister and his Council of Ministers are collectively responsible to the Lok Sabha and not to the Rajya Sabha. By a no-confidence motion, the Lok Sabha can discuss a ministry. However, the no-confidence motion is an extreme motion. There are other ways by which the Parliament exercise control over the executive, they are as follows:

(i) By asking questions and supplementary questions. Members of the Parliament have a right to seek information and elicit facts on a matter of public importance. However certain types of questions are not permitted, such as questions making discourteous reference to foreign countries with whom India has friendly relations, questions seeking information regarding cabinet discussion or advice given to President in relation to any matter. The government can also refuse to answer any question in the name of public or national interest.

(ii) If a member is not satisfied with the answer by the government, he may demand a "half-an-hour Discussion" on the subject.

(iii) The Parliament also exercises control over the executive through various motions. Calling Attention Notices and Adjournment motions are such motions in which some recent matters of urgent public importance can be raised. In such conditions the Parliament Sets aside the normal business and discusses the matter.

(iii) Financial Powers

The Parliament is the repository of the union purse. No money can be spent without its approval. The budget is approved by the Parliament. However the Parliament can discuss the expenditures charged on 'Consolidated Fund of India.' It may increase, but not decrease the amount. The expenditure charged on the Consolidated Fund of India include the emoluments and allowances of President, Vice-President, Deputy Chairman of Rajya Sabha, Speaker and Deputy Speaker of Lok Sabha, judges of Supreme Court and High Courts.

(iv) Electoral Functions

The Parliament participates in election of President of India. It elects the Vice-President. Besides both the Houses elect their presiding officers.

(v) Judicial Functions

The Parliament also performs certain judicial functions. It can impeach the President, Vice-President, Chief Justice and Judges of the Supreme Court and High Courts etc.

*(vi) Amending Power**

The Parliament has the power to amend a major portion of the Constitution. In certain cases, it needs ratification by at least half of the States to amend the Constitution. However Parliament cannot amend the basic features of the Constitution. In the electoral, judicial and constitution amending functions, both the House of the Parliament have equal powers.

(vii) Miscellaneous functions

Besides the above-mentioned functions and powers, the Parliament enjoys many other powers, some of which are as follows:

(i) The Parliament approves the proclamation of emergency. Such approval is granted by both the Houses, with a majority of total number of the House and a majority of not less than two-third members present and voting.

(ii) The Lok Sabha can disapprove the continuation of national emergency (under *Article 352*) by a simple majority. For this purpose, a special sitting may be convened by the President, if one-tenth of the

*For amending power of the Parliament. See Chapter XVI—Amending Process in the Indian Constitution.

Lok Sabha members demand a special session of the House to consider a resolution for the discontinuance of the emergency.

(iii) Parliament may admit or establish new States on such terms and conditions as it thinks fit.

(iv) Parliament may (a) form a new State by separation of territory from any State or by uniting two or more States or parts of States or by uniting any territory to a part of any State; (b) increase and decrease the area of any State; (c) alter the boundaries and the name of any State.

(v) Parliament may regulate the right of citizenship.

(vi) Parliament may extend the functions of Union Public Service Commission.

(vii) Parliament may abolish or create legislative councils of States.

(G) Finally, Parliament has the important function of removing the grievances of the people of India. For this purpose the people of India have a right to present petitions to the Parliament.

Role of the Indian Parliament

The above study of power and functions of the Parliament leads to another question—what exactly is the role of Parliament in the Indian political system? This question is all the more relevant because frequently we talk about the decline of Parliament (which we will discuss in the next section). It is said that Parliament does not perform all the functions that have been assigned to it. Nevertheless, the Parliament is the central focal point of the democratic system. Its role can be summarised as follows:

(i) Representative Role

The Parliament of India is the representative of different sections and regions of the country. It is a body in which the people of India find the articulation of their demands, urges and aspirations. Dr. Subash Kashyap rightly observes, "Parliament represents the changing moods and needs of the people. It is not only a microcosm and mirror of the people, but also a barometer of their mood and pulse." Manohar Joshi, a speaker of the Lok Sabha, aptly said, "Our Parliament has always been receptive to the aspirations of the people and the requirements of the changing times." Since its membership is drawn from the entire country, the various conflicts among the people are voiced and synthesised. Thus the Parliament becomes a forum for conflict-resolution and harmonisation in the Indian Society. This also leads to its national integrative role. Nehru, while congratulating the nation for the successful completion of the Third Lok Sabha General Election process said, "We meet here in that long tradition representing the final and ultimate sovereignty of the people of India ... a country of manifold variety, a great country with a great tradition in the past which is setting out into new fields. It has people who differ in their religions and their customs .... This House had a real task ... of moulding them into a single unity, that is India, that is the people of India, maintaining at the same time their own special features and this House gives them every opportunity to protect them and to cherish these features; yet fully preserving the unity of India. We have had in our general life, and more especially in this House, to face this great question of the people of India maintaining their rich diversity and at the same time their essential unity by which alone they can progress and maintain the real sovereignty of the people, because sovereignty comes not merely from each person asserting his rights but of each person recognising the rights of others and thereby maintaining the common rights of all." The representative character of the Parliament not only reflects India's unity in diversity but also gives legitimacy to the Indian political system.

(ii) Educative Role

When the universal adult franchise was introduced in free India, there were many who believed that given the vast illiteracy among the rural folk and the backwardness of women, it would not work. But the successful completion of the First Lok Sabha election belied such fears. It was discovered that women had participated in greater numbers than men and illiterate villagers were more enthusiastic in exercising their votes than the urban folk. Nehru said, "The elections compelled candidates and their supporters to visit every village. It was a tremendous task of political education. Many people talk superiority of the ignorance of the illiterate voter and even suggest that he is not worthy of the vote. My own experience has been and this has been, supported by many others, that the so-called illiterate votes showed greater civic sense than most of the people of the towns." The electoral process, the working of the Parliament and other aspects of democracy educates the masses to become political and understand and evaluate the performance of political parties and leadership.

(iii) An Outlet Forum

The Parliament provides a forum in which the people's grievances are expressed and their redressal demanded. Every citizen of this country has a right to present a petition to the Parliament. The members of the Parliament, from time to time, also raise the problems of the people. In fact in India, we find that the Parliament has always been sensitive and quick to react whenever problematic situations arose. Whether it is a labour strike, a police firing, a border incident, atrocity in any form on any section of the population or death in custody, the next day we have the echoes and reverberations in Parliament. All kinds of causes, big or small, have their champions in the Parliament. All this puts the government on its toes and hence we get a responsive government.

(iv) A Check on the Executive

The Parliament exercises control over the executive. The Parliamentary system of government envisages the Parliamentary control over the executive. We have described the various methods by which the Parliament keeps the executive in check. Here suffice it to say that no government even if it commands absolute majority in Parliament, can behave in a despotic way. The opposition has a right to criticism and it is the duty of the government to respect the criticism. In the second Lok Sabha, Ashok Mehta described the President's address to Lok Sabha as odourless, colourless and generally inane, Nehru accepted the criticism in a sporting manner and said, "As members of the Government, who are responsible for the President's address that criticism applies to us certainly, I am prepared to say that criticism is partly justified."

(v) Protector of the System

The Parliament's role as the protector of the democratic system is also very vital. Given the Indian diversity, tensions and disruptive tendencies are the natural corollary. However, by providing a forum of expression to them, it helps in containing them. In India there have been political parties and groups who talked about secessionism but later on assimilated into the system in which Parliament had a definite role. The political parties instead of annihilating each other, as they tend to, as Subash Kashyap puts it, "agree to disagree and to accommodate or tolerate each other." 'The Parliament becomes the legitimate arena of power struggle' and it is on the floor of the House that delicate issues are solved. Parliament not only helps in protecting the system, it also ensure its continuity day by day, thus further strengthening the system.

(vi) Recruitment Role

The Parliament plays the recruitment role of the political leadership of the country. Subash Kashyap says, "Parliament is the recruiting and training ground for Ministers." The members of Parliament, while serving as members of different committees, acquire considerable knowledge in various fields and make good ministers. The performance of various members in the Parliament and in various committees help the Prime Minister in selecting ministers. This is also how continuity in leadership is ensured.

(vii) As a Channel of Communication

The Parliament is a channel of communication between the Government and the people. It is through Parliament that Government comes to know about the needs and requirements of the people. People also understand the problems faced by the Government. All this creates an atmosphere in which tolerance and restraint develops within the minds of the people. They understand that India's economic and social problems are gigantic and government cannot be expected to eradicate them by magic. However at the same time the people cannot be expected to be despondent. They keep a vigil and evaluate the performance of the Government and refuse to give mandate in the next election if the performance is not up to the mark. During the emergency of 1975-77, this channel was broken when almost the entire opposition was put behind bars. The people reacted very strongly and not only was the Party-in-Power defeated, even the Prime Minister, for the first time in India, could not win her seat in Lok Sabha. On the whole, the Parliament acting as a communication channel between the people and government creates an atmosphere which eventually strengthens the democratic process.

(viii) Parliament as an Agency of Socio-Economic Development

The modern State is a welfare State and the Parliament plays a very important role in reforming social structures which become outdated. The Parliament is also committed to eradicate social evils in the society. Since the commencement of the Constitution, we find a large number of social reform legislations have been passed by the Parliament. For example, laws providing for special considerations and benefits to Scheduled Castes, Scheduled Tribes and other backward classes. A number of legislations aimed at emancipation of the status of women in India have been enacted by the Parliament. Similarly laws providing for social security, minimum wages, old age pensions etc give protection to the weaker sections of the country.

In 1954, Nehru explained in Lok Sabha what Parliamentary democracy was. He said, "Why have we chosen Parliamentary democracy? Because we think that in the long run it produces the best results .... What are the results we are aiming at? National well-being, and the happiness of the millions and millions of our people." In India we adopted the planned economic development strategy to overcome the poverty of India. The Five Year Plans are tabled before the Parliament and discussed. Similarly the industrial policy and agrarian policy are discussed and debated in Parliament. These debates and discussions definitely influence the administration. The rapid socio-economic development requires the co-ordering of social structures and institutions. It also needs changes in the value systems and attitudes of the people. The Parliament provides such a theatre by evolving a process of consensus in the politics and society. Thus the socio-economic changes take place, without violence, in a peaceful manner.

Decline of Parliament

In the early years of the Indian Parliament, Parliament was very effective. It was manned by people of high standards. The government was more responsive and the members of the opposition also used to devote time for preparing their speeches and taking the government to task. However, as time passed, there has been a general allegation that Indian Parliament has declined. The following reasons are attributed to the decline of Parliament:

(i) There is a change in the complexion of the Parliament. Earlier lawyers, writers, teachers and educationists dominated the Parliament. The First Lok Sabha had as many as 153 lawyers. Thus it was the educated elite who enjoyed ascendancy in the Parliament. Now the Parliament is a mere representative in the sense that agriculturists and members with rural backgrounds are dominating. The growing democratisation of the political process has led to the fall in the quality of debates.

(ii) From 1952 to 1967, the elections to the Parliament were linked with the State Assembly elections. They were held simultaneously. As a result the people identified their local problems in the sphere of State politics and the members of Parliament had a minimal contact with their constituency. Thus, devoid of petty constituency problems they could devote full time in the Parliament's affairs. However, since

1970's, the delinking of Parliamentary and State legislative elections have taken place. Now the members of Parliament have to look after the local constituency problems also. An MP says, "Now the people's interaction with their MP has increased enormously. As a result much of his time is taken up with constituency problems like schools, roads, and drainage and he has less time for parliamentary works. This has led to a decline in the level of debates in the House." Another MP says "Constituents are not interested in what an MP does in Parliament. They want an MP to take care of their interests." The new development in communication media like Subscriber Trunk Dialing (STD facilities) have further increased the availability of MPs to their respective constituencies. Now the members have to make regular visits to their constituencies. A sample study done by A. Surya Prakash revealed that 42 per cent of the MPs felt that the constituents insisted on their presence while Parliament was in session. With the result, as an MP says, "We do not find time to even read parliamentary papers." From this the point of view, the television coverage of debates of Parliament further puts pressure on an MP. Another interesting development in this regard is the allocation of Rs. 1 crore per annum to the members of Parliament for the development of their respective constituencies. Such development only strengthens the idea of an MP with a local perspective against the national one which is required of him. A. Surya Prakash observes, "If MPs are to have enough time in Parliament, they will have to delink themselves from the nitty-gritty of administration at the village and town level. They will have to limit their concerns to large issues and insist that they be heard on matters pertaining to location and operation of mega projects in areas like steel, communications, fertilisers, railways, ports and airports ... and such other matters that fall within the purview of the union government."

(iii) The party system is also responsible for the decline of Parliament. Parliament is effective when its members are free to express themselves and to vote. But this is not so. The members are elected with party support and the party bosses keep a very strict control over them. Every party in the Parliament has a chief whip and several deputy whips. During Parliamentary sessions, whips are issued in which the members are given notice to be present in the House at the time of voting and to vote in a particular manner. According to anti-defection law an MP who violates a party whip is liable to be disqualified from the membership of the House. The members are also not free to speak, it is the Chief Whip of the party that decides who is going to speak and accordingly the list of the speakers in a particular debate is handed over to the presiding officer. A member remarks, "Today MPs have to go to party bosses and cringe before them for speaking opportunities." This was not so in earlier times when the members were much more free to speak.

In a way, the strength of Parliament is also responsible for this decay. In such a large body of 545 members in Lok Sabha and 245 in Rajya Sabha, every member cannot be given freedom to speak every time. There has to be some selective process. However in the first three Parliaments the members still enjoyed greater freedom which is not so today.

(iv) In theory, the Parliament controls the cabinet but in practice it is opposite. It is the cabinet which controls the Parliament. The cabinet has full control over the agenda of the Parliament. It decides the issue of summoning and proroguing the House. The President's address to the Parliament is prepared by the cabinet. An overwhelming majority of the total time of the House is consumed by the government initiated bills. But the Parliament has never enough time for discussion on the bills. The bills are allotted specific time and after that time is completed, the voting takes place. It is immaterial whether sufficient debate has taken place or not. This is called "guillotine." The Budget is also passed by means of "guillotine." Specific days are allotted for the different demands for grants for different ministries and after the allotted time is over, voting takes place. A. Surya Prakash points out that 85 per cent of the annual demand for grants was passed by the Lok Sabha without examination between 1985-89. S.S. Ahluwalia said, "The budgets presented by them are discussed year after year, but the working of the ministries have never been discussed. As a result ... the ministers need not care for Parliament which does not have the time to discuss their working." Further, there is little possibility of private members' bills being passed. The Parliament transacts the Private Member's Business i.e. Private members bill and resolution only on Fridays that too in the last two and a half hours of the sitting.

(v) The decline of Parliament is also seen in the lack of quorum in both the Houses of the Parliament. The members are simply not interested in the sittings of the Parliament unless forced to do so by the issue of a whip. The quorum or the minimum number of members required for the conduct of business is one-tenth of the total membership of each House. However the fact remains that the Parliament legislates without a quorum. The bill for the creation of the National Bank for Agriculture and Rural Development (NABARD) was passed by the Lok Sabha when only 30 MPs were present who voted in favour of the bill. In 1990, the budget was passed by just 20 members present in the Lok Sabha. In 2002 when the Finance Bill was being discussed, the Lok Sabha had to be adjourned for want of quorum. A weekly magazine commented, "When the economic fate of the nation was being discussed, there were not more than 37 MPs in the House." The problem of absenteeism is very acute in the Parliament and nothing has been done, so far, to tackle this problem.

(vi) The conduct of Parliamentary meetings also shows the decline of Parliament. The members are expected to maintain the decorum of the House. There is a certain parliamentary etiquette which should be followed by them. But invariably this does not happen. The Parliament is plagued by interruptions, noises, dharnas and unparliamentary expressions. No member is supposed to speak without the Speaker's permission but very often this is not followed by the opposition and sometimes even by the party-in-power. Once the Rajya Sabha Chairman Dr. Shankar Dayal Sharma was so upset with the ruling Congress (I) members' defiance that he was close to tears and threatened resignation. In 2004, a Rajya Sabha MP Fali Nariman tabled a non-official Bill—Disruption of Proceedings of Parliament (Disentitlement of Allowances) Bill 2004—which provided for non-payment of daily allowance to MPs in case of adjournment of the House. But the Bill could not be taken up for discussion as the Parliament was adjourned a week ahead of schedule. Besides, boycott of Parliamentary meetings is also becoming routine. The opposition believes that it has a right to stall Parliamentary meetings. The Speaker of the Lok Sabha, Somnath Chatterjee, who also has the distinction of being the longest serving member (10 terms and 38 years) of the House was asked why the members were unruly. Somnath Chatterjee who never had job satisfaction gave the following answer:

"I have talked to members and the response of some has indeed surprised me. According to them, it pays to create disturbance. They say that a matter's importance is felt when it is big enough to stop the functioning of Parliament. In other words, you come up with a studied presentation or a valuable intervention following strict parliamentary traditions, it is hardly noticed; but you create disturbance and you are all over the front pages and the television channels."

Thus Somnath Chatterjee held the media responsible for the disturbances in the House. There may be other reasons as well but the Parliament's capabilities definitely suffer. As a result it is unable to pass important legislation. Sometimes a sort of compromise takes place like the Budgets in 1999 and 2004 were passed without any discussion at all.

(vii) There have also been cases where bills were passed, the President gave assent but still the law was not enforced. According to the Constitution, a law passed by the Parliament, which has received the President's assent, is enforced by the President by issuing a notification in the Gazette of India in which the date of commencement of the act is declared. However this is not done in many cases. For example in the case of the Hire Purchase Act of 1972, the notification was issued and withdrawn, again issued and withdrawn. There are other cases when notification was not issued like The Wakf (Amendment) Act, 1984, Prasar Bharati (Broadcasting Corporation of India) Act, 1990 and Delhi Control Act. Similarly new clauses 4 and 7 in *Article 21* of the Constitution which were included vide Constitution (44th Amendment) Act 1978 has not been brought into force. This shows the lack of will on the part of Parliament to assert itself by not taking any significant objection to the treatment meted out to its laws by the executive.

(viii) The growth of delegated legislation has led to the decline of Parliament. Delegated legislation is a universal phenomenon and the Indian Political system is no exception to it. As the Parliament suffers from paucity of time, it has no time to go into the details of an act. Therefore it passes the Act in a brief manner and the details are to be worked out by the executive. Thus the Parliament delegates its authority of making laws to the executive and hence the name, delegated legislation. Delegated legislation, also called subordinate legislation, includes the rules, regulations and order issued by the executive to supplement the Act passed by Parliament. In theory Parliament has a right to control such legislation. However in practice, the Parliament never has the time to do so. The delegated legislation strengthens the power of bureaucracy who actually frame the rules leading to Bureaucratic Raj. Many times the politicians have alleged that bureaucracy does not enforce the laws, especially laws concerning socio-economic objectives. It ensures the implementation of law in a way so as to defeat the basic objectives of the law.

(ix) Then there is corruption. The members of Parliament have been accused to corruption. The industrialists' lobby always tries to get them into their clutches by corrupt practices. The MPs sublet their flats in Delhi, they sell their telephone or gas connection quotas. The Provisional Parliament in 1951, was rocked by the Mudgal case in which an MP, H.G. Mudgal, was accused of corruption. The Parliament, at that time, had reacted sharply and was about to expel him when Mudgal pre-empted Parliament by resigning from the House. But still the Parliament passed the resolution that Mudgal 'deserved expulsion" and his resignation letter constituted a contempt of the House. But later on, the Parliaments have not been as sensitive towards corruption. In 1970's License Scandal rocked the Parliament in which a minister was also alleged to be involved besides two MPs, Tul Mohan Ram and Yogendra Jha, who had forged the signature of 16 MPs. However no action was taken against them. However, in 2005 when 11 MPs were caught on camera taking bribes for asking questions, the Parliament acted swiftly and, 11 days after the sting operation on what was termed 'cash-for-questions scam', the accused MPs were expelled from the membership of the Parliament. Now, corruption has become a cardinal feature of the Indian Political system and even the highest echelons of power are being accused of corrupt practices. The Parliament has remained ineffective in containing corruption. This had led to a general decline in moral standards.

(x) There is a general loss of confidence in the politicians in the country. Their immoral behaviour and lust for power has been exposed. Further there is a general criminal-politician nexus. A member of the United Front Government had to resign because there were serious cases pending against him. There have been MPs with criminal background. This has also compromised the prestige of the Parliament.

(xi) The decline of Parliament can also be seen in the non-fulfilment of promises made by the Executive in the House. Both the Houses of Parliament have committees on Government assurances which monitor the implementation of assurances made by the Ministers in the respective houses. It has been estimated that till the 1980s, the Governments kept all their promises, in the 90s; the rate of assurances was nearly 90 per cent. But in 2007, only 14.36 per cent of assurances were implemented. The Government in Lok Sabha made 1086 assurances out of which only 156 were implemented while in Rajya Sabha out of a total of 918 assurances, only 198 were implemented. It has been pointed out that in 2004 during the NDA Government, the delivery rate in the Lok Sabha was 85.26 percent. The next year the figure rose to 87.50 but in 2006, it went down to 79.75. The decline in the delivery rate of the assurances shows the scant regard the Ministers have towards Parliament.(HT 2April 2008).

Some efforts were made to improve the situation. In 2005, Rajya Sabha adopted the recommendation of the Ethics Committee of the House. In order to make parliamentary debates more informed, bipartisan and disciplined, the committee had recommended that MPs should declare their areas of interest before participating in a debate or discussion. It was decided that Ethics Committee would maintain a register indicating regular and remunerative activities of members, Shareholding of controlling nature, professional engagement and paid consultancy. It was felt that this information would be used to help make House debates more transparent and disciplined. It was decided that the register would be regularly updated and the Committee would ensure strict adherence of the code of conduct for MPs. It would also take punitive action against erring MPs, like withholding the pension.

The decline of Parliament is a serious development which has its negative impact not only on its law-making function and control over executive but in its total working.

Speaker of the Lok Sabha

The Speaker is the presiding officer of the Lok Sabha. In his absence, the Deputy Speaker presides. After the Constitution of a new Lok Sabha, the first task is to elect a Speaker and a Deputy Speaker. In England the Speaker of the House of Common is held in high esteem. His election is unanimous and usually a back bencher occupies the seat. Person with high political ambitions do not opt for the office of Speaker because it is the end of his political career. Once a Speaker, always a speaker is the maxim that goes in the English Parliament. A person who becomes a speaker remains in his office till he desires, the ensuing House of Commons again re-elects him. The major political parties do not field any candidate against the Speaker in the elections. After getting elected he resigns from his political party and acts impartially not only in the House but also out of the House. As a result the Speaker in English Parliamentary tradition holds a high degree of prestige and decorum. However in India, we have not followed English practices.

The election of the Speaker of the First Lok Sabha was not unanimous. The Speaker, G.V. Mavalankar, was opposed by S.S. More. The second Speaker Ananthasayanam was however elected unanimously after the death of Mavalankar. Similarly the Third Lok Sabha elected its Speaker, G.S. Dhillon unanimously. After that there is one case of Neelam Sanjeeva Reddy where the election took place otherwise now it has been an established tradition that the Speaker should be the unanimous choice of the House. The party-in-power decides the Speaker after due consultation with the opposition.

In India, the Speaker does not sever his party affiliation after being elected to the office. The first Speaker G.V. Mavalankar is credited for establishing such a tradition. "He assured that he would remain impartial and above party considerations as Speaker and it is his duty ... to deal with all members and sections of the House with justice and equity." But he also declared that he would remain a member of the Congress Party. Except for the two exceptions, Neelam Sanjeeva Reddy and G.S. Dhillon, who resigned from their parties after becoming Speaker, the rest of the Speakers have followed the tradition set by Mavalankar. The Speakers were actively involved in party affairs outside the Parliament. Consequently, the office of the Speaker has not been untouched by controversies in India. They have been accused of partisan attitude in conducting the proceedings of the House. There have been resolutions of removal against Speakers like Mavalankar, Sardar Hukam Singh, G.S. Dhillon and Balram Jakhar. However no Speaker in the Lok Sabha has been removed by such resolutions till-to-date. But this only shows that the office of the Speaker in India has not assumed that dignity which the English Speaker enjoys. Further, in India the office of the Speaker is not the end of a political career to its incumbent. Speakers have become ministers, governors, High Commissioners and even President. The following are the powers and functions of the Speaker of Lok Sabha:

(i) The basic function of the Speaker is to preside over the sessions of the House when he is present in the House. In his absence the Deputy Speaker takes the Chair. However, the Speaker cannot preside when there is a resolution for his removal under consideration. The Speaker is to preside over impartially and above party considerations.

(ii) His decision in all parliamentary matters is final. As Subash Kashyap puts it, "A request may be made to him for reconsideration, but his decision cannot be challenged, criticised or questioned."

(iii) No member can speak in the Lok Sabha without the Speaker's permission. He also decides in what order members will speak and how long a member should continue to speak. He may ask a member to finish his speech and in case the member does not listen, he may order that the member's speech should not go on record. He may also order a member to withdraw unparliamentary words.

(iv) He permits a member to speak in his mother-tongue if he does not know either English or Hindi.

(v) The members of the House can only address the Speaker while speaking.

(vi) All the bills, reports, motions and resolutions are introduced with the Speaker's permission.

(vii) He puts the motion to vote in the Lok Sabha. In case there is a tie, he is empowered with a casting vote. However he is expected to cast his vote so as to retain his impartiality and independence.

(viii) He determines a bill to be a Money Bill and his decision is final. He also certifies a money bill.

(ix) The Speaker is to conduct the meetings of the House in a orderly manner. Whenever there is pandemonium or indiscipline in the House, he has sufficient disciplinary powers to handle such a situation. He derives his disciplinary powers from the Rules of Procedure of the House and his decisions in the matter of discipline cannot be normally challenged. He may direct any member, guilty of disorderly conduct, to withdraw from the House, and name a member for suspension if the member refuses to listen him and continues to obstruct the proceedings of the House. For the purpose he may order the marshal or marshals of the House to remove the member physically. In case of grave disorder, the Speaker may adjourn the House. The Speaker also rules on points of orders raised by the members and his decision is final.

(x) Speaker is the principal spokesman of the House and represents its collective voice and wisdom. While felicitating Sardar Hukam Singh as Speaker of the Third Lok Sabha, Nehru said, "It is not merely a question of choosing a good and worthy person for this high office, it is something more than that because you represent more than any of us here in the House—the dignity of this House, the combined wisdom of this House, and so much else." The Speaker can instruct the government to place a document before the House.

(xi) In the event of disagreement over a bill between the Lok Sabha and Rajya Sabha, the President calls a joint-sitting of both the Houses and the Speaker presides over the joint-sitting.

(xii) Certain committees of the Lok Sabha as nominated by the Speaker. He is the supreme head of all the Parliamentary committees whether nominated by him or chosen by the House. He issues directions to the Chairman of the committees in all matters relating to their working and procedure to be followed by them. He can remove a member of the committee on the recommendation of its Chairman, if the member is absent from two or more consecutive sittings of the committee. A committee cannot hold a meeting outside Parliament House without the Speakers permission and cannot call officially any State governments to give evidence without his prior approval.

(xiii) The Speaker appoints a committee consisting of three persons for investigating the charges for the removal of Chief Justice and other judges of Supreme Court and High Courts.

(xiv) He disqualifies a member if he defects under the anti-defection act. But his decision is subject to judicial review.

(xv) The Speaker regulates the entry in the House. He may order the vacation of the Visitors' Gallery.

(xvi) The Speaker is the custodian of the rights and privileges of members of the Lok Sabha. Without his permission no member can be arrested in Parliament.

(xvii) The Speaker accepts all resignations sent to him by the members of the Lok Sabha. He also decides about the genuineness of the resignation.

(xviii) He authenticates all the bills passed by the Lok Sabha and sends them to Rajya Sabha or the President as the case may be.

(xix) The Speaker is the head of the Lok Sabha Secretariat. The Secretary-General is appointed by the Speaker from amongst those who have made their mark in the service of Parliament in various capacities. The Secretary-General is always present in the House during its sittings and advises the Speaker. But the Speaker is not bound by his advice.

Thus the Speaker enjoys a very formidable position in the Lok Sabha. Acharya Kriplani rightly pointed out that the Speaker was not only "to guide and regulate the proceedings of the House, he was also 'the guardian of the liberties of the House and through the House, of the liberties of the people." According, to Nehru the Speaker was not only the "guardian, of the rights of the House but also of the freedom of the many millions of our people which was won after hard struggle and many sacrifices." Therefore, he said, "it is right that he should be an honoured position, a free position and should be occupied always by men of outstanding ability and impartiality." Indira Gandhi, while felicitating Sanjeeva Reddy on his election as Speaker, said, "Sir, you have been closely associated with our party but the party fully appreciates the role of the Speaker and realises that the Speaker must not be a political person and that he must sever his political connections. The contest for the Speakership is not unsual or abnormal, but once a Speaker is chosen, he belongs to all sections of the House. His office makes him so. He must naturally win the confidence of all parties and members by his impartiality and fairness in his decisions and rulings. An equal responsibility devolves on the rest of us to help in defending the rights of the Chair and in upholding the highest standards of conduct in this House." When Mavalankar faced the censure motion, Nehru declared, "... so far as this majority party is concerned, I should like to tell them that not one of them is bound by any whip or any direction: let them vote as they like. It is not a party matter. It is a matter for this House ... because this matter affects the Hon'ble Speaker, of course, but it affects the first citizen of this country, that is the Speaker of this House ... when we challenge his bona fides we betray before our countrymen and indeed before the world that we are little men and that is the seriousness of the situation."

Relations between the Rajya Sabha and Lok Sabha

We have seen earlier that the composition of the two Houses of the Parliament differ. The Lok Sabha represents the people of India and is directly elected by them. The Rajya Sabha, from the federal point of view, represents the States and is elected by an electoral college consisting of elected representatives in the State Assemblies. The Lok Sabha has a fixed tenure of five years unless dissolved earlier by the President or extended for one year if Proclamation of emergency is in operation. The Rajya Sabha is a permanent House which cannot be dissolved. The Vice-President of India is the ex-offico Chairman of the Rajya Sabha while the Lok Sabha has to elect its Speaker.

From point of view of the Constitution, the relationship between the Lok Sabha and Rajya Sabha can be viewed from three angles, which are as follows:

(i) There are certain powers and functions in which Lok Sabha is superior to Rajya Sabha.

(ii) In certain spheres Rajya Sabha has been given special powers which it does not share with the Lok Sabha.

(iii) In certain spheres, both the Houses enjoy equal powers.

Spheres, where Lok Sabha is Superior to Rajya Sabha

There are many areas where Lok Sabha enjoys a pivitol position over the Rajya Sabha. These are as follows:

(a) The Prime Minister and his Council of Ministers are collectively responsible to the Lok Sabha and not to Rajya Sabha. By a no-confidence motion the Lok Sabha can dismiss the Union ministry. No-confidence motion cannot be moved in Rajya Sabha.

(b) On financial matters also, the Lok Sabha enjoys the primary position. A Money Bill can be introduced only in Lok Sabha and not in Rajya Sabha. In case of conflict as to whether a bill is a money bill or not, the decision of the Speaker of Lok Sabha is final. Further Rajya Sabha can only delay the passage of a money bill. After being passed by the Lok Sabha, money bill goes to Rajya Sabha and Rajya Sabha has 14 days for such a bill. It may pass it or it may send it back to Lok Sabha along with its recommendations. In case it has been sent back to Lok Sabha with Rajya Sabha's recommendation, the Lok Sabha may consider them and incorporate them in the bill. The Lok Sabha may reject them also. In any case the bill will not go back to Rajya Sabha, it will be directly sent to the President for his assent. The Rajya Sabha cannot reject a money bill. The Budget being a money bill is also introduced in the Lok Sabha. However, the Rajya Sabha only has the power to discuss the public expenditure and demand for grants. They are not submitted for the vote of the Rajya Sabha.

(c) The Lok Sabha also enjoys the power of disapproving the continuation of emergency. If ten per cent of total number of Lok Sabha members give a notice to the Speaker, if the House is in session, and to the President, if the House is not in session, of their intention to move a resolution disapproving the Proclamation of emergency, then the Speaker or the President, as the case may be, will have to summon a special sitting of the Lok Sabha within fourteen days. If in such a sitting a resolution revoking the emergency is passed, then the President will have to revoke it.

Spheres where Rajya Sabha has Special Powers

(a) Rajya Sabha supported by not less than two-third majority of members present and voting may pass a resolution declaring a subject mentioned in the State List to have acquired national interest and therefore it is necessary or expedient in the national interest that Parliament should make a law on that subject. After passage of such a resolution the Parliament acquires the power to make a law on that subject mentioned in the State List for one year. The Rajya Sabha may further extend this to one year at a time by passing another resolution.

(b) The Rajya Sabha may create one or more All India Services (including an all-India judicial service) if it feels that it is necessary or expedient in the national interest. However a resolution to such effect should be passed by the Rajya Sabha with not less than two-third of members present and voting.

(c) The Vice-President of India may be removed from his office by a resolution of the Rajya Sabha passed by a majority of its members and agreed to by the Lok Sabha. Only Rajya Sabha can initiate his removal.

Spheres, where both the Houses Enjoy Equal Powers

(a) In case of non-money bills, Lok Sabha and Rajya Sabha enjoy equal powers. Such a bill can be introduced in either House of the Parliament and has to be passed by both the Houses before being sent to the President for his assent. In case there is a disagreement between the two, the Constitution provides arrangement for the resolution of the disagreement. According to the Constitution there may be a disagreement between the two Houses if, after a bill has been passed by one House and transmitted to the other House and (i) the bill is rejected by other House; or (ii) the Houses have finally disagreed as to the amendments to be made in the Bill; or (iii) more than six months have elapsed from the date of receiving of the Bill by the other House without it being passed by it. In such cases of disagreement, the President calls for the Joint-Session of the two Houses, in which the decision is taken by the a majority of total number of member of both Houses present and voting. It is assumed that since Lok Sabha has a numerical superiority over the Rajya Sabha, the will of the Lok Sabha prevails. But it may not be true given the complexities of the party system.

(b) Both the Houses enjoy equal powers with regard to amendment of the Constitution. A bill seeking an amendment to the Constitution can originate in either of the two Houses and must be passed with a special majority of not less than the total membership of the House and two-third of the members present and voting. There is no provision for a joint-sitting of both the Houses with regard to constitutional Amendment.

(c) Although, the Rajya Sabha cannot pass a no-confidence motion against the Council of Ministers, it definitely enjoys equal powers with Lok Sabha in asking questions and supplementary questions from the ministers. Motions such as calling-attention notices or adjournment motions can also be brought in the Rajya Sabha.

(d) The ratification of emergency is to be done by both the Houses by a majority of total membership and two-third majority of members present and voting.

(e) Both the Houses enjoy equal powers with regard to elections of President and Vice-President.

(f) Similarly, in case of impeachment of President, Chief Justice and Judges of Supreme Court and High Courts, both the Houses enjoy equal powers.

(g) In the matter of selection of ministers, the constitution does not make any distinction between the two Houses. Ministers may be from Lok Sabha as well as Rajya Sabha. Even in case of the Prime Minister, he may belong to Rajya Sabha although a practice has been developed that he should belong to Lok Sabha or upon becoming the Prime Minister he should become a member of Lok Sabha. However the Prime

Minister and his Council of Ministers, irrespective of their membership, are collectively responsible to only the Lok Sabha.

Jawahar Lal Nehru talked about the equality of status of both the Houses. He said, "Under our Constitution, Parliament consists of two Houses, each functioning in the allotted sphere laid down in the Constitution. We derive authority from the Constitution. Sometimes we refer back to the practice and conventions prevailing in the Houses of Parliament of the United Kingdom and even refer erroneously to an Upper House (Rajya Sabha) and a Lower House (Lok Sabha). I do not think that is correct .... Our guide must ... be our Constitution which has clearly specified the functions of the Council of States and the House of the People. To call either of these Houses an Upper House or a Lower House is not correct. Each House has full authority to regulate its own procedure within the limits of the Constitution. Neither House by itself, constitutes Parliament, it is the two Houses together that are the Parliament of India .... That Constitution treats the two Houses equally, except in certain financial matters which are to be the sole purview of the House of the People. In regard to what these are, the Speaker is the final authority."

Conflict between the Two Houses

In 1954, a member of Lok Sabha, N.C. Chatterjee said "that some of the overzealous radicals of the Upper House which is supposed to be a body of Elders, seemed to be behaving irresponsibly like a pack of schoolboys or a pack of urchins." This resulted in a big hue and cry in Rajya Sabha and a privilege motion was brought against Chatterjee. The matter was amicably settled and Chatterjee apologised. In 1961, for the first time a joint sitting of Lok Sabha and Rajya Sabha took place on the "Dowry Prohibition Act, 1960," in which one of two recommendation of the Rajya Sabha were incorporated. In 1963, a member of the Lok Sabha H.V. Kamath said that Rajya Sabha was like the English House of Lords. The Rajya Sabha members strongly objected to it. It also reacted strongly to an attempt made in Lok Sabha to deprive it of the right to discuss the budget before its discussion in the Lok Sabha. In 1970, the Rajya Sabha rejected the Abolition of Privy Purse Bill passed by the Lok Sabha.

In 1978, a joint sitting of both Houses was called on the Banking Service Commission (Repeal) Bill 1977. In 1977 and 1978, the Rajya Sabha rejected the Finance Bills passed by the Lok Sabha. In 1978, the Rajya Sabha rejected of five out of 49 clauses the 45th Constitutional Amendment Act. The Lok Sabha ultimately had to accept the position of the Rajya Sabha. In 1980, the Rajya Sabha amended the motion of thanks to the President's address.

Thus there have been conflicts between the Lok Sabha and Rajya Sabha. However these conflicts were settled or Lok Sabha ignored the Rajya Sabha's view and in some cases the Lok Sabha simply dropped the matter. In any case they did not create a major controversy in the Indian political system in the long run.

Law-Making Process in the Parliament

The law originates in the Parliament in the form of a Bill. There are three types of Bills which come up before the Parliament: (1) Ordinary or Non-Money Bill, (2) Money-Bill, and (3) Constitution Amendment Bill. Here we will discuss the legislative process of ordinary and money bills.

1. *Ordinary Bill:* Every member of the Parliament has a right to introduce an ordinary bill and from this point of view, there are two kinds of ordinary Bills: (i) Government Bill, and (ii) Private Member's Bill. A Government Bill is a Bill moved by a minister and any Bill not moved by a minister is a Private Member's Bill, which means that the Bill has been moved by a private member. A major part of the time of the Parliament is consumed by the Government's Bills while Private Member's Bill has little possibility of being passed. Only on Fridays, the Parliament devotes time to Private Member's Bills. Here we take a Bill which is Government's Bill and see how it is passed.

(A) When the government decides that a particular Bill is to be brought before the Parliament, the Bill-making process starts within the ministry concerned. Legal experts and professionals are consulted and the overall implications of the proposed Bill are studied minutely. After due discussion, from all points of view, the Bill is submitted for the approval of the cabinet. After the approval of the proposed Bill by the Cabinet, the bill is properly drafted. Finally, the Bill is introduced in one of the two Houses. With the introduction of the bill, the First Reading of the Bill starts.

(i) *First Reading:* In the first reading, the Minister who moves the Bill asks for the permission to do so. He says, "Sir, I beg to move for leave to introduce the Bill. Generally the leave is granted by a voice vote and rarely opposed. Then the Minister say, "Sir I introduce the Bill." ... In this stage, no discussion takes place. However, if a motion for leave to introduce the Bill is opposed, the Speaker may allow the member, who opposes the motion, to speak. After this, the Bill is put to vote.

Thus the First Reading of the bill is the stage of introduction. After its introduction, the Bill is published in the Gazette of India. The Speaker may allow the publication of the bill in the Gazette without it being introduced in the House.

(ii) *Second Reading:* The Second Reading of the Bill is the most vital stage. In this stage, the Bill is discussed in detail. The Second Reading consists of two stages. In the first stage the Bill in general is discussed and not the details. The House may decide to (i) straightaway take it into consideration or (ii) refer to a Select Committee of the House or to the Joint Committee of both the Houses or (iii) to circulate it to elicit public opinion.

If the Bill is referred to a Select Committee of the House or the Joint Committee of both the Houses, the concerned committee considers the Bill clause by clause. Amendments can also be moved by the members of the committee. The committee can also consult experts and public bodies who may be interested in the measure. After due consideration, the Committee submits its report to the House. If the Bill has been circulated to elicit public opinion, the same is done through the agencies of the States and Union Territories. After the opinions are elicited, the Bill is ordinarily referred to a Select Committee or Joint Select Committee for consideration. However, the Speaker may allow to move a motion for consideration of the Bill. The Select Committee or Joint Select Committee considers the Bill in the light of opinions elicited and submits its report to the House.

The second stage of the Second Reading starts when the House considers the report of Select Committee or Joint Select Committee. In this stage a detailed discussion of the Bill, clause by clause, is done in the House. The amendments may also be moved. The bill is passed if the majority of the members present and voting favours its passage in the voting. Amendments, if accepted by the same majority, also become part of the Bill.

(iii) *Third Reading:* After the completion of the Second Reading, the Minister may move that the Bill be passed. At this stage, not much discussion takes place. It is confined to arguments either in support of the Bill or for its rejection, without referring the details further than is absolutely necessary. Only verbal, formal and consequential amendments are allowed to be moved at this stage. After the Bill is put to vote. It has to be passed by the simple majority of members, present and voting.

(B) *Bill in the Other House:* After the Bill is passed by one of the two Houses, it goes to other House for consideration. Here again, it has to undergo three Readings. The other House may take either of the following courses:

(a) It may pass it. In that case the bill is sent for President's assent.

(b) It may reject it leading to a deadlock between the two Houses.

(c) It may pass it with amendments. In such case, the Bill is referred back to the first House. The first House may accept the amendments and they are incorporated in the bill and the bill is referred to President for his assent. The bill will not go back to the other House. However, if the first House refuses to accept the amendments, the Bill is sent back to the other House. If the other House still insists on its amendments, this means there is a deadlock.

(d) It may take no action on the bill and if more than six months have elapsed and the House takes no action at all for its consideration, again this means there is a deadlock between the two Houses.

(C) *Joint Sitting of the Parliament:* As per Article 108, a joint sitting can be called by the President if (i) if one House passes a Bill but the other House rejects it or (ii) if the two Houses disagree on the amendment or amendments to be made to a Bill or (iii) if a House does not consider the Bill even after six months since its receipt and (iv) the concerned Bill is not a Money Bill. In case the President has called the joint sitting of the Parliament and in between the Lok Sabha is dissolved, the joint sitting will still take place... since the President notified his intention to summon the Houses to meet therein'. In such a Joint-Sitting, the bill is passed by the majority of total members of both the Houses present and voting.

Such joint sessions are rare and till now, three times joint sittings have been convened over (i) Dowry Prohibition Bill, 1959 on 6th and 9th May 1961, (ii) Banking Service Commission (Repeal) Bill, 1977 on 16 May 1978 and (iii) 'Prevention of Terrorism Bill 2002 on 26 March 2002.

(D) *President's Assent to the Bill:* After being passed by both the Houses separately or in a Joint-Sitting, the Bill is sent to the President for his assent. The President takes one of the following courses upon receiving the Bill:

(a) He may give his assent. In such a case the Bill becomes the law.

(b) He may withhold his assent and in such a case Parliament has no power to over-rule him. This means the death of the Bill.

(c) He may suggest his recommendations to the bill. In such case the bill is referred back to its originating House. However, if both the Houses pass the bill again, with or without the recommendations of the President, the President will have to give his assent.

(d) In 1986, President took a new course when, instead of giving or withholding assent or returning to the Parliament for reconsideration, of the Post Office (Amendment) Bill, 1986 (Popularly known as Postal Bill), he did not take any action. His successors also did not take any action.

2. *Money Bill: Article 110* defines a money Bill. A Bill is a money Bill if it deals with the following matters:

(i) the imposition, abolition, remission, alteration or regulation of any tax.

(ii) the regulation, or borrowing of money by the Government of India.

(iii) the payment of moneys into or withdrawal of moneys from Consolidated or Contingency Funds of India.

(iv) the declaring of any expenditure to be expenditure charged on the Consolidated Fund of India or the increasing of the amount of any such expenditure.

(v) the receipt of money on account of the Consolidated Fund of India or the public account of India or the custody issue of such money or the audit of the accounts of the Union or of a State.

(vi) any matter incidental to any of the matters specified in *Article 110(1)* sub-clauses (a) to (f).

The money bill is also passed by the Parliament by the different phases of three Readings. However there is substantial differences in the legislative process in relation to an ordinary bill. They are as follows:

(a) Money Bill can be introduced, only along with the prior recommendation of the President, in Lok Sabha and not in Rajya Sabha.

(b) The Speaker of the Lok Sabha is the final authority to decide whether a particular Bill is a money Bill or not.

(c) After being passed by the Lok Sabha, the Bill is sent to Rajya Sabha for its recommendations. Rajya Sabha has 14 days from the receipt of the money bill for its consideration.

(d) Rajya Sabha cannot reject the money Bill. It can only make recommendations.

(e) In case the Rajya Sabha makes recommendations, the Lok Sabha may accept or reject those recommendations. The Bill will directly be sent to the President for assent.

(f) If the Rajya Sabha does not return the money Bill within fourteen days, the Bill will be deemed to have been passed by both the Houses after the expiration of fourteen days and sent to the President for his assent. There can be no Joint-Sitting of both Houses on a money bill.

(g) The President cannot withhold his assent to a money Bill passed by the Parliament.

3. *Budget in Parliament:* Every year the Budget is presented before the Lok Sabha. The budget-making is a big exercise which involves the entire economic structure of the country. The Finance Ministry prepares the budget. The Budget is presented in two parts: (a) Railway Budget and (b) General Budget. Railway Budget is presented by the Railway Minister while the General Budget is presented by the Finance Minister. The Budget passes through various stages which are as follows:

(i) *Presentation of the Budget:* The Railway Budget is generally presented in the third week of February, while the General Budget normally on the last working day of February. The General Budget is presented along with the Budget Speech of the Finance Minister, which is divided in two parts A and B. Part A contains "a general economic survey" of the country and Part B deals with "the taxation proposals" for the ensuing financial year. (The financial year starts from 1st April every year to 31st March of the ensuing year). The Budget remains a closely guarded secret till its presentation. After the Budget Speech, the Finance Minister, introduces the Finance Bill which contains the taxation proposal made by the government. The House rises thereafter, and there is no discussion on the day of the presentation of the Budget.

(ii) *Discussion on Budget:* The discussion on Budget is done through two stages: (a) General discussion, and (b) demands for grants for each ministry. In the "General discussion" the general economic policy is discussed and there is no detailed discussion on taxation and expenditures in both the Houses of Parliament. In these discussions, both Houses express their moods regarding the economic policy of the government and a general appraisal of the economic policy is made. Here it should be noted that Rajya Sabha also discusses this. However, it cannot go beyond general discussion.

The "General discussion" is followed by the discussion and voting for demands for grants. Demands for grants for each ministry is discussed in detail. The demands are expenditures to be incurred by the ministry and they are in the nature of requests made by the Executive to Lok Sabha for grant of authority to spend the amount asked for.

In this stage, the various ministries come to a close scrutiny by the Lok Sabha. During this stage, cut motions can be proposed. The cut motions, if passed, may lead to the resignation of the government as it amounts to a vote of censure of the government. The discussion on demands for grants is held alongwith the motion of Guillotine, which means that a time limit is set for various demands and as the time is over, the demand is put to vote irrespective of whether enough and satisfactory discussion has taken place or not. In the last day of the discussion allotted to demands for grants, all the remaining demands even on whom no discussion has taken place are put to vote. With this, the discussion on demands for grants is concluded.

(iii) *Appropriation Bill:* The next stage is the Appropriation Bill which incorporates all the demands for grants voted by Lok Sabha and the expenditures charged on the Consolidated Fund of India. The Bill seeks the legal authority to be given to government to appropriate expenditure from and out of the Consolidated Fund of India. The Bill is introduced, considered and passed in the same manner as any other Bill. However the discussion is restricted to these matters which were not covered on the debate on demands and no amendments are allowed. After the Appropriation Bill is passed by the Lok Sabha, the Speaker Certifies it to be a Money Bill and sends it to the Rajya Sabha. After Rajya Sabha's approval, as per the procedure laid down in the Constitution, the Bill is sent to the President for his assent.

(iv) *Finance Bill:* The Finance Bill contains government proposals for raising revenues. The move for leave to introduce Finance Bill cannot be opposed and it is forthwith put to vote. This Bill has to be considered and passed by the Parliament and assented to by the President within 75 days after it is introduced.

(v) *Vote on Account:* Sometimes the Lok Sabha passes the Vote on Account. Vote on Account is passed normally for two months, when the passage of Budget is delayed for whatever reasons. During an election year it may be passed for three to four months. As a convention, vote on account is treated as a formal matter and passed by Lok Sabha without discussion.

References

Aiyar S.P. and Srinivasan (Ed.), *Studies in Indian Democracy,* 1965, Bombay Allied Publishers.

Basu. D.D., *Introduction to the Constitution of India,* 1995, London, Macmillan Press.

Kashyap Subash C., *Parliament of India, Myths and Realities,* 1988, New Delhi, National Publishing House.

______*History of the Parliament of India,* Vols I, II, III. 1995, New Delhi, Shipra Publications.

______*History of Parliamentary Democracy,* 1991, New Delhi, Shipra Publications.

______*Our Parliament,* 1989, New Delhi National Book Trust.

Malhotra G.C. (Ed.) *Fifty Years of Indian Parliament*, 2002, New Delhi, Lok Sabha Secretariat.

Prakash A. Surya, *What Ails Indian Parliament*, 1995, New Delhi, Indus.

Rao B. Shiva, *The Framing of Indian Constitution*, 1968, New Delhi, The Indian Institute of Public Administration.

Shakdher S.L., *Glimpses of the Working of Parliament*, 1977, New Delhi, Macmillan Book Co. Pvt. Ltd.

Singh MP, *UN Shukla's Constitution of India*, 1994, Lucknow, Eastern Book Company.

CHAPTER X

The President of India

The President of India is the head of the State. The Constitution provides for a Parliamentary form of government in which the President is a titular head, while the actual powers are vested with the Prime Minister and his Council of Ministers. This chapter deals with the election, power, functions and position of the President of India.

Election of President of India

A. The Constitution provides for the following qualifications for the office of the President:

(a) He should be citizen of India.
(b) He should have completed the age of 35 years.
(c) He should be qualified for election as a member of the Lok Sabha.
(d) He should not hold any office of profit under the Union Government or any State Government. However, for this purpose the President, Vice-President, Governor, Union and State Ministers are not the office of profit and as such, they can contest the election to the Office of President.

Besides these qualifications, the President of India issued an ordinance in 1997, according to which the candidature to the Indian presidency should be proposed by 50 members of the electoral college and seconded by another 50. It also provides for security deposit of Rupees 15,000. This has been done to prevent non-serious candidates from contesting the august office of President of India.

The election to the office of President is held in accordance with the system of proportional representation by means of single transferable vote and secret ballot system. The election is a very complicated affair, which can be understood by dividing it in different heads which are as follows:

(i) *The Voters in the Election of President:* The President of India is elected by a Electoral College consisting of elected members of (i) both Houses of the Parliament; and (ii) State Legislative Assemblies. The Constitution says that there should be (a) uniformity in the scale of representation of the different states; and (b) parity between the States as a whole and the Union at the election of the President. This is achieved by a formula given in the Constitution. According to this formula, first of all, the value of one vote of a member of Legislative Assembly of a state is to be ascertained. This is done by the following formula:

$$\text{Value of one vote of an MLA} = \frac{\text{Total Population of the State}}{\text{Total number of elected members of the Legislative Assembly}} \div 1000$$

In calculation, if the remainder figure is 500 or more, it is counted as one and if it is less, it is ignored.

For example, the total population of Andhra Pradesh is 43,502,708 (1971 census), while the total number of elected members in the State Assembly is 294. By applying the above mentioned formula, the situation will be as follows:

$$\frac{43{,}502{,}708}{294} \div 1000 = 147.96 = 148$$

Thus a member of the Andhra State Assembly will be entitled for 148 values of his vote in the election to the President.

With this process we will be able to calculate the total number of values of votes enjoyed by the different State Assemblies of India. Next comes the process of ascertaining the total number of votes which a member of Parliament is entitled to. Again this is done by a formula which is as follows:

$$\frac{\text{Total number of value of votes of all the members of Legislative Assemblies}}{\text{Total number of elected members of both Houses of Parliament}}$$

In calculation, if the remainder figure is 500 or more, it is counted as one and if it is less, it is ignored.

For example in 1992 election, the total number of value of votes assigned to the members of Legislative Assemblies was 5,44,971 and total number of members of both Houses of Parliament were 776 (543 Lok Sabha + 233 Rajya Sabha), the number of value of a vote, each MP enjoyed was:

$$\frac{544971}{776} = 702.282 = 702$$

(iii) As per the above formula, the election to the post of the President takes place in New Delhi and the capitals of different States. The voters cannot divide the value of their votes, which means all the values of vote of a voter will go to a single candidate only. However the voter may indicate his preference by marking 1, 2, 3 (as many candidates as are contesting the election).

(iii) The next step is the calculation of the quota. Quota, or the minimum number of votes necessary for a candidate to be elected to the office of President, is calculated as per the following formula:

$$\frac{\text{Total number of valid votes}}{\text{Number of member to be elected (i.e.1)+1}} + 1$$

(iv) After the calculation of quota, the counting starts. The objective of the counting is to achieve the quota. As soon as the quota is achieved by any candidate in the counting, the candidate is declared elected to the office of President of India. First preference votes are counted first. If any candidate secures the quota, he is declared elected. But if no candidate secures the quota, the candidate who has secured the least number of votes is eliminated and such votes are opened and the second preference votes are counted which are added to the number of votes obtained by the remaining candidates. The process goes on till a candidate secures the required quota.

Till to date, twelve Presidential elections have taken place. Only one President was elected unopposed i.e., N. Sanjeeva Reddy in 1977: ten Presidents were able to secure quota in the counting of first preference votes only; One President i.e. V.V. Giri in 1969, was elected after elimination of all the candidates.

In the thirteenth President's elections, Pratibha Patil with 638,116 votes won over her rival Bhairon Singh Shekhawat who got 331,306 votes. Thus Pratibha Patil became the first female President of India.

Pratibha Patil was supported by the UPA while Bhairon Singh Shekhawat, the Vice-President was supported unofficially by the NDA. Shekhawat filed his nomination as an independent candidate.The details of number of voters and votes for this presidential election are given below:

XIII Presidential Election (2007)

Sr. No.	Name of State	Number of Assembly Seats (elective)	Population (1971 (Census)	Values of vote of Each MLA	Total value of votes for the state
1.	Andhra Pradesh	294	43502708	148	43512
2.	Arunachal Pradesh	60	467511	8	480
3.	Assam	126	14625152	116	14616
4.	Bihar	243	42126236	173	42039
5.	Chhattisgarh	90	11637494	129	11610
6.	Goa	40	795120	20	800
7.	Gujarat	182	26697475	147	26754
8.	Haryana	90	10036808	112	10080
9.	Himachal Pradesh	68	3460434	51	3468
10.	Jammu & Kashmir*	87	6300000	72	6264
11.	Jharkhand	81	14227133	176	14256
12.	Karnataka	224	29299014	131	29344
13.	Kerala	140	21347375	152	21280
14.	Madhya Pradesh	230	30016625	131	30130
15.	Maharashtra	288	50412235	175	50400
16.	Manipur	60	1072753	18	1080
17.	Meghalaya	60	1011699	17	1020
18.	Mizoram	40	332390	8	320
19.	Nagaland	60	516449	9	540
20.	Orissa	147	21944615	149	21903
21.	Punjab	117	13551060	116	13572
22.	Rajasthan	200	25765806	129	25800
23.	Sikkim	32	209843	7	224
24.	Tamilnadu	234	41199168	176	41184
25.	Tripura	60	1556342	26	1560
26.	Uttarakhand	70	4491239	64	4480

(B) *Oath taken by the President:* After being elected to the office of the President, the person concerned has to take an oath in the presence of Chief Justice of India or in his absence the senior-most judge of the Supreme Court available, which is as follows:

"I A.B., do swear in the name of God/solemnly affirm that I will faithfully execute the office of President (or discharge the functions of the President) of India and will be to the best of my ability preserve, protect and defend the Constitution and the law and that I will devote myself to the service and well-being of the people of India."

Thus, in his oath the President undertakes to preserve, protect and defend the Constitution and law and to devote himself to the service and well-being of the people of India.

(C) *Tenure of the President:* The President is elected for five years. But he is eligible to be re-elected to the office. However, in practice only Rajendra Prasad was elected twice to the office of the President and after him no President has served more than one term.

(D) *Removal of the President:* The office of the President becomes vacant due to (i) the resignation of the incumbent President; (ii) the death of the incumbent President; or (iii) as a result of his impeachment by the Parliament.

The President can be removed from his office by impeachment process. The impeachment process can be initiated by either House of the Parliament. For this purpose, atleast fourteen days notice for the resolution to move impeachment is necessary which should be signed by not less than one-fourth of the total members of the House. Such resolution has to be passed by a majority of not less than two-thirds of the total membership of the House. The President can only be impeached on a charge of violation of the Constitution.

After the resolution being passed by the required majority, it goes to the other House. The other House investigates the charge. In this stage only, the President has a right to appear and to be represented. If the other House, after investigating passes a resolution by a majority of not less than two-thirds of the total membership of the House, declaring that charge against the President has been sustained, the President is removed from his office from the date on which such resolution is passed.

Thus, the impeachment process is very rigid as it needs two-third majority of total membership of both the Houses. So far as no President has been removed from office by such process. The office of President has, however, fallen vacant twice due to the death of the incumbents i.e. Dr. Zakir Hussain and Fakhruddin Ali Ahmed. In such case, the Vice-President takes over as the Acting President. The Constitution stipulates that in case of vacancy in the office of President occurring due to his death, resignation or removal, the election to the office must take place within six months and the incumbent will be entitled for full five year term.

Presidents of India 1952-2002

1.	Rajendra Prasad	Jan. 26, 1950	-	May 13, 1962	
2.	S. Radhakrishanan	May 13, 1962	-	May 13, 1967	
3.	Zakir Hussain	May 13, 1967	-	May 3, 1969	
4.	V.V. Giri	May 3, 1969	-	July 20, 1969	(Acting)
5.	Mohammad Hidayatullah	July 20, 1969	-	Aug. 24, 1969	
6.	V.V. Giri	Aug. 24, 1969	-	Aug. 24, 1974	
5.	Fakhruddin Ali Ahmed	Aug. 24, 1974	-	Feb. 11, 1977	
6.	B.D. Jatti	Feb. 11, 1977	-	July 25, 1977	(Acting)
6.	N. Sanjeeva Reddy	July 25, 1977	-	July 25, 1982	
7.	Zail Singh	July 25, 1982	-	July 25, 1987	
8.	R. Venkataraman	July 25, 1987	-	July 25, 1992	

(Conted. on next page)

9.	Shankar Dayal Sharma	July 25, 1992	-	July 25, 1997
10.	K.R. Narayanan	July 25, 1997	-	July 25, 2002
11.	A.P.J. Abdul Kalam	July 25, 2002	-	July 25, 2007
12.	Smt. Pratibha Patil	July 25, 2007	-	July 25, 2012
13.	Pranab Kumar Mukherjee	July 25, 2012	-	Till date

Powers and Functions of the President

The President of India enjoys very wide powers under the Constitution, some of which are as follows:

Executive Powers

(i) The executive power of the Union is vested in the President which are to be exercised either directly or through officers subordinate to him in accordance with the Constitution. The Constitution stipulates that "All executive action of the Government of India shall be expressed to be taken in the name of the President.

(ii) The President is the Supreme Commander of Indian Defence Forces.

(iii) He appoints a variety of officers. The most important appointment is the appointment of the Prime Minister and his Council of Ministers. Besides he appoints the Chief Justices and other judges of Supreme Court and High Courts. The Chairman and members of Union Public Service Commission, Attorney-General of India, the Comptroller and Auditor General of India, Chief Election Commissioner and other members of the Election Commission, Governors in States, Ambassadors and High Commissioner in foreign States, members of Finance Commission and National Commission for Scheduled Castes and Scheduled Tribes and Commission on official language etc.

(iv) The administration of the Union Territories is carried out by the administrator appointed by the President. The President has also a right to make regulations for the peace, progress and good government of the Union Territory of (a) Andaman and Nicobar Islands; (b) Lakshadweep; (c) Dadra and Nagar Haveli; (d) Daman and Diu; (e) Pondicherry.

(v) In the performance of his powers and functions, the President is aided and advised by the Prime Minister and his Council of Ministers. The President may send back an advice to the Council of Ministers for reconsideration. But he is dutybound to act on the advice tendered to him by the Council of Ministers after such reconsideration.

Legislative Powers of the President

The Parliament of India is composed of (i) President and (ii) the two Houses of the Parliament, which means the President is inalienable part of the Parliament. As such he enjoys a wide range of legislative powers some of which are as follows:

(i) The President summons and prorogues the two Houses of the Parliament. Regarding the summoning, the constitutional limitation is that six months interval should not lapse between the last day of the last session and first day of the next session, which means the President has to summon the Parliament within six months i.e. of its prorogation. The President may also dissolve the Lok Sabha.

(ii) After the General Elections, the President addresses the Parliament. Subsequently also, he may address either of the Houses or the joint-sitting of both the Houses. For this purpose he may ask all the members to attend the address.

(iii) The President may send messages to either House of the Parliament with respect to a bill then pending in the Parliament or otherwise.

(iv) The President may nominate two members in Lok Sabha from Anglo-Indian Community if he feels that the community is not adequately represented in the House. He also nominates twelve members in the Rajya Sabha who have excelled in art, literature, science and social service.

(v) If there is a question as to whether a member of the Parliament has become disqualified as per the Article 102(1), the President's decision shall be final. However, before giving such decision, the President will refer the matter to Election Commission for its opinion and act accordingly to such opinion.

(vi) The bills passed by the Parliament becomes law with the approval of the President. There are two kinds of bills and President has different powers regarding the two. In case of a non-money bills to the President (a) may assent to it and thereby the bill becomes the law; (b) he may withhold his assent and this power is absolute which means that is the death of the bill; or (c) he may refer it back to the Parliament for reconsideration alongwith his recommendation. However, if the Parliament again passes the bill, he cannot withhold his assent. Regarding the money bill, the money bill cannot be introduced in the Parliament without his prior approval and upon passage of a money bill, he cannot withhold his assent.

(vii) In case of disagreement over a bill between the two Houses of the Parliament, the President may summon a joint-sitting of the Parliament to resolve the issue.

(viii) Certain bills, besides the money bill, cannot be introduced in the Parliament without his previous recommendation like bill for the formation of new States and alteration of areas, and boundaries or names of existing States under *Article 3* of the constitution.

(ix) In case the Parliament is not in session and a law is needed, the President can promulgate an Ordinance which has the same effect as an Act of Parliament.

Financial Powers

(i) The President presents the Budget in both the Houses of the Parliament before the new financial year begins. In practice this is done by the Finance Minister.

(ii) He may also present a supplementary Budget, if the need arises. In practice, this is also done by the Finance Minister.

(iii) The Contingency Fund of India is at the disposal of the President. For this Fund, the President may make unforeseen expenditure pending authorisation of such expenditure by the Parliament.

Judicial Powers

The President has the power to grant pardons. He may suspend, remit or commute the sentence of any person convicted of any offence. However this is applicable: (i) in all the cases where the punishment or sentence is by a court martial; (ii) in all the cases where the offence in under a law under Central jurisdiction; (iii) in all cases of sentence of death.

Emergency Powers

Now we come to the most controversial powers of the President i.e. Emergency Powers. The Constitution of India provides for three kinds of emergencies which are as follows:

National Emergency: If the President is satisfied that grave emergency exists whereby the security of India or its part is threatened due to (a) war; or (b) external aggression; or (c) armed rebellion, he may declare emergency in the entire country or in a part of the country. The difference between war and external aggression is technical one. From International law point of view, a conflict between two states is a war only when it is specifically declared. Thus Indo-Pak war of 1971, was a war because both sides declared that they were in a state of war against each other. War when not declared constitutes external aggression. Thus Indo-Pak conflicts of 1948 and 1965 and Indo-China war of 1962, were technically not war but external aggression.

Regarding National Emergency following points are to be noted:

(i) The Proclamation of emergency can be issued by the President only when the Union Cabinet advises the President to do so in writing.

(ii) The proclamation of emergency can be issued if there is actual occurrence or a threat of external aggression, war or armed rebellion and if the President is satisfied that there is imminent danger thereof.

(iii) The Proclamation of emergency shall remain in force for thirty days unless otherwise approved by both the Houses of the Parliament. The approval is done through a resolution by a majority of (i) the total membership of the House; and (ii) two-thirds of the members of that House present and voting.

(iv) In case the emergency is declared at a time when Lok Sabha is dissolved or the dissolution of Lok Sabha takes place within thirty days period, and the Rajya Sabha has approved the emergency, the proclamation shall cease to have effect after the reconstitution of the Lok Sabha unless it approves it within thirty days.

(v) The duration of emergency is six months.

(v) One-tenth of the total number of members of Lok Sabha may give a notice in writing to President, if Lok Sabha is not in session or to the Speaker, if Lok Sabha is in session for disapproving emergency. In such case, a special sitting of Lok Sabha will be held and the Lok Sabha by simple majority may disapprove emergency. In such situation, the President will have to revoke emergency.

(vi) The President may issue different Proclamations on different grounds. Thus in 1975, when the emergency due to internal disturbances was proclaimed, the emergency due to war was already existing.

Effects of Emergency: The following are effects of the Proclamation of emergency made under *Article 352.*

(i) The Union Government acquires the power to direct the State Government as to how it is going to exercise its executive power.

(ii) The Parliament acquires the power to make laws in the subjects mentioned in the State List. Thus the Constitution became a unitary Constitution during emergency.

(iii) The President may order amendments in distribution of finances (under the provisions of *Articles 268* to *279*) so that the emergency is tackled properly. However, every such order is to be laid before the two Houses of the Parliament as soon as may be.

(iv) *Article 19* or the right to freedom may be suspended. *Article 32* which deals with right to constitutional remedies if the fundamental rights are violated or abridged, may also be suspended. However, *Article 20* which deals with the protection in respect of conviction for offences and *Article 21* which deals with protection of life and personal liberty cannot be suspended.

(v) The President may also issue ordinance on the subjects mentioned in State List.

(vi) The Parliament also acquires the right to confer powers and impose duties on the Union and its offices and authorities in respect of matters outside the Union List.

National Emergency—Practice: Before we study the practice of emergencies, it is necessary to know that during an emergency originally the Constitution gave very wide powers to the President. The Constitution did not prescribe the time limit for emergency. Thus the emergency could continue so long as the President wished. Even *Articles 20* and *21* could be suspended. The 44th Constitutional Amendment of 1978, made important changes in the provisions of emergency.

The first emergency, due to external aggression was declared on 26th October 1962, as a result of Chinese invasion in Indian territories. The President suspended *Articles 14, 21* and 22 of the Constitution for the persons who were arrested under Defence of India Ordinance, 1962. The proclamation of emergency was revoked on January 10, 1968. When the Indo-Pak war of 1965 broke, the emergency was already continuing, therefore there was no need for a fresh proclamation. The second emergency was proclaimed on December 3, 1971, due to war between India and Pakistan. During this emergency *Articles 14, 19, 21* and *22* were suspended for the persons detained under Defence of India Act and Maintenance of Internal Security Act (MISA). The emergency continued till March 21, 1977. The third emergency was declared on June 25, 1975, on the ground of "internal disturbance." This was done when the second emergency was already continuing. This emergency was also revoked in March 1977.

The first two emergencies did not evoke any controversy and there was not much effect on the social, economic and political life of the country. The Fourth Lok Sabha Elections took place in 1967, when the emergency was already in operation. Only during the actual war times, there were some effects. However the third emergency which was declared on the ground of "internal disturbance" was highly controversial. This was the emergency which found almost the entire opposition behind the bars including such leaders like Jaya Prakash

Narayan and Morarji Desai. It is generally believed that emergency was imposed to thwart the opposition demand of resignation of the Prime Minister in view of the Allahabad High Court judgement which set aside her election to the Lok Sabha on the basis of her employing corrupt methods. The Parliament even passed the 38th Constitutional Amendment Act which made the proclamation of emergency and its continued operation thereafter beyond the purview of the judiciary. Many excesses including the family planning operations and tortures of political prisoners took place during the emergency. However in the election to the Lok Sabha in 1977, the people of India rejected Indira Gandhi and her Congress Party.

The misuse of emergency provisions during the emergency period of 1975-77 resulted in the 44th Constitutional Amendment Act which not only negated the effects of 38th Constitutional Amendment Act i.e. the emergency came within the purview of the judiciary, but also many changes in the emergency provisions were made. Now, emergency could not be imposed on grounds of internal disturbance. The term internal disturbance was omitted and a new term "armed rebellion" was inserted. Besides the President could proclaim emergency only on the written communication from Union Cabinet. The emergency was to be approved by the Parliament with the majority of total membership of both the Houses and two-thirds majority of the members present and voting. The emergency can be revoked by the Lok Sabha in its special sitting called for the purpose with simple majority. Articles 21 and 22 cannot be suspended during the emergency. Thus the emergency provisions are now very rigid and not liable to be misused.

*Emergency in a State under Article 356 or President's Rule**

(A) According to *Article 355* it is the duty of the Centre to ensure that the Government of every State is carried on in accordance with the provisions of the Constitution. In case the Government in a State is not carried on in accordance with the Constitution, it means that there is a breakdown of constitutional machinery in the State under *Article 356*. *Article 356* says that "If the President, on receipt of report from the Governor of a State or otherwise, is satisfied that a situation has arisen in which the government of the State cannot be carried on in accordance with the provisions of this Constitution", President's Rule may be imposed. Following points need consideration with regard to *Article 356*.

*See also Chapter VIII—Tension Areas in Indian Federation.

(a) The President may impose President's Rule on a State in a situation when the government of that State cannot be carried on in accordance of the provisions of the Constitution.

(b) The President may reach such conclusion by himself or on receipt of a report from the Governor.

(c) Such a President's Rule is to be approved by both the Houses of the Parliament. If not approved it will cease to operate after two months. In case the Lok Sabha is dissolved, the Rajya Sabha will approve it and the reconstituted Lok Sabha will have to approve it within thirty days of its first sitting.

(d) The duration of President's Rule is six months. It can be further extended to another term of six months.

(e) After the continued duration of two terms of President's Rule i.e. one year, the Proclamation for the third term can only be passed by the Parliament under following conditions:

(i) If the Proclamation of Emergency is in operation in whole of India or in part of the State at the time of passing such resolution, and

(ii) The Election Commission expresses its inability to hold elections to the Legislative Assembly of the State concerned.

(f) However in any case, the President Rule cannot remain in force for more than three years.

Grounds for invoking Article 356: (i) *Article 355* of the constitution says that "It shall be the duty of the Union to protect every state against external aggression and internal disturbance and to ensure that the government of every state is carried on in accordance with the provisions of this Constitution." The Constitution further says in *Article 356* that in the event of government of the State not being carried out in accordance with the provisions the Constitution President's Rule can be imposed on the State. However, no detailed grounds have been explained by the Constitution according to which the President may reach such a conclusion.

(ii) There is atleast one reason specified in the Constitution for the invocation of President's Rule. The Centre has the power to issue directions to the State: (a) The States are to ensure the compliance to the Acts of Parliaments which are applied in the States. For the purpose the Centre can issue directions; (b) The Centre can also issue directions with regard to the construction of means of communication declared to be of national or military importance; and (c) The Centre can issue directions for the measures to be taken for the protection of railways with in the State.

If the State concerned after being issued directives does not follow them, the President's rule may be imposed. (*Article 365*).

(iii) In the absence of other specific grounds, we find that, in practice, President's Rule has been imposed on political grounds. In practice, the President's Rule has been imposed: (a) because no party was able to provide a stable ministry as in the case of Punjab in 1951, in Pepsu in 1954, in 1956 Travancore-Cochin, in 1961 in Orissa, in 1964 in Kerala, in 1967 in Rajasthan, in 1968, 1995, 1996 in Uttar Pradesh, in 1968 in West Bengal, Bihar and Punjab and in 1969 in Bihar.

(b) In 1966, President's Rule was imposed on Punjab to bifurcate Punjab into two States of Punjab and Haryana.

(c) Defections also provided the cause for President's Rule in Nagaland, in 1967 in Haryana and in 1990 in Karnataka.

(d) The deterioration of law and order was another reason for invocation of *Article 356*. The most famous of such cases is the President's Rule in Kerala in 1959. Despite the fact that the Communist ministry was enjoying the majority support, the President's Rule was imposed. The reason was Congress inspired political movement against the ministry. In 1992, after the demolition of the disputed structure in Ayodhya on December 6, 1992, the BJP Governments in different States were dismissed and President's Rule was imposed because of incidents of riots, arson and killings in the concerned States. In the case of Madhya Pradesh, the Jabalpur High Court declared President's Rule invalid and ordered the restoration of the Government and Assembly in Madhya Pradesh.

(e) The President's Rule has also been imposed on the plea that the State Governments have lost the confidence of the people because the concerned party controlling the State Government lost Lok Sabha elections. In 1977, the President's Rule was imposed on nine States which had Congress ministry on the plea that the Congress lost Lok Sabha elections and these Governments should seek fresh mandate. In 1980 Indira Gandhi took the same plea and Janata-led Governments in States were dismissed and President's Rule was imposed.

(f) Corruption was another reason given for the invocation of President's rule. In 1967, corruption was cited as one of the reasons for President's Rule in Haryana.

In two unprecedented cases, President K.R. Narayanan returned the cabinet's advice for invoking *Article 356* in UP (1997) and Bihar (1998) for reconsideration. In both cases, the cabinet did not advise the President second time to invoke *Article 356* which would have been binding on the President. In case of Uttar Pradesh, Violence and large scale defections in the Assembly were cited as reasons for invoking *Article 356* but the President felt that *Article 356* could not be invoked in such situation. In case of Bihar, frequent breakdown of law and order, crimes and violence, political corruption, maladministration and economic crises were cited as reason for invoking *Article 356* but the President felt that these facts did not constitute the ground for the exercise of power under *Article 356*. In both the cases, the State Government were enjoying majority in the Assembly.

President's Rule is Justiciable: In *S.R. Bommai Vs. Union of India*, the Karnataka High Court has opined that the Court had the power to look into the materials or reasons disclosed for issuing the President's rule and then it might declare President's Rule as invalid.

However the fact remains that *Article 356* is the most abused Article of the Constitution. It also constitute the most important tension area in the Union-States confrontation and the demands have been raised for its total abrogation from the Constitution.

Effects of President's Rule Under Article 356: (i) The State Assembly may either be dissolved or suspended. If the State Assembly is dissolved, fresh elections take place to the State Assembly. If instead it has been suspended, after the invocation of President's Rule, the same Assembly is summoned.

(ii) The law making power of the concerned State Assembly comes in the hands of the Parliament. The Parliament may confer powers on the President for making laws for the State and authorise him further to delegate such power to any other authority.

(iii) The Parliament may authorise the President to make expenditure from the Consolidated Fund of State when the Lok Sabha is not in session.

(iv) The administration comes under the direct rule of the Governor who discharge his responsibility with the help of the advisors appointed by the President. The State Ministry is dismissed.

Financial Emergency

The President is empowered to impose Financial Emergency under *Article 360*, which says that "If the President is satisfied that a situation has arisen whereby the financial stability or credit of India or of any part thereof is threatened, he may by a Proclamation make a declaration to that effect.

The Proclamation declaring Financial Emergency is to be approved by both the Houses of the Parliament. If the Lok Sabha is dissolved, the reconstituted Lok Sabha has to approve it within thirty days. Without the approval of the two Houses, the Financial Emergency can continue for two months.

The Effects of Financial Emergency: (i) Financial Emergency is issued because of grave economic crisis and the President can issue directives to the States necessary to fight such economic crisis. The States will have to observe such canons of financial propriety as specified in the directives, which may include.

(a) Reduction of salaries of all or any class of persons employed by the State

(b) All the Money Bills passed by the State Legislature should be reserved for the President's assent.

(ii) The salaries and allowances of all or any class of persons employed by the centre including the Judges of the Supreme Court and High Courts may be reduced.

Financial Emergency under Article 360 has not been declared so far.

Critical Appraisal of Emergency Provisions

The emergency provision of the Constitution is criticized on the basis of following points:

(i) *Anti-Federal:* The emergency provisions are against the tenets of a classical federation. True every constitution, including the federal one, provides for the extra powers necessary to fight the crisis. However no constitution provides so many details. Dr. Ambedkar accepted this in the Constituent Assembly. He said that our Constitution can both be unitary as well as federal according to the requirements of time and circumstances. "In normal times it is framed to work as a federal system. But in times of war it is so designed as to make it work as though it was a unitary system. No Federation possesses such a power of converting itself into a unitary State. This is one point of difference between the Federation proposed in the Draft Constitution and all other Federations we know of." S.L. Saxena held the view that the President's Rule would reduce the provincial autonomy to a farce. Another important figure in the Constituent Assembly Hridey Nath Kunzru held that even in case of no party getting majority in a State Legislature, the Central intervention could not be justified. If power were given to the Centre to intervene, there was a serious danger that whenever there was dissatisfaction in a State, appeals would be made to the Central Government to come to its rescue and the provincial electorate would be able to transfer its responsibility to the Central Government. Therefore, Kunzru was against the incorporation of *Article 356.*

(ii) *Liable to be Politically Abused:* The emergency provisions can be and has been misused for political reasons. The emergency of 1975-77 was imposed because the Prime Minister's Lok Sabha election was declared as null and void by the Court and she wanted to remain in power. *Article 356* i.e. President's Rule was frequently used to dethrone the State Governments. It was also used to avoid the opposition from forming the Government. If a party in power at the centre found good chances of winning power in the opposition led states, the President's Rule was imposed. This was done by the Janata Government in 1977 and Congress Government in 1980. Therefore there has been a demand to abrogate *Article 356* of the Constitution. In 1996, a shrewd tactics was adopted in the case of President's Rule in UP. It was to be extended for the third time and the Constitution says that President's Rule in a State cannot remain continuous more than a year unless the national emergency is continuing or the Election Commission certifies it inability to hold election to the State Assembly. But this could not apply to UP because there was no emergency and elections to the Assembly had just been completed. To get over the problem first the proclamation of President's Rule was revoked and another proclamation was issued on the night of October 17, 1996. Thus a distinction was made on the basis of time-gap between the two Proclamation. So that the invocation could be justified as a fresh one. In the Constituent Assembly, Dr. Ambedkar has anticipated the possibility of misuse of emergency powers. He said, "I do not altogether deny that there is a possibility of these Articles being abused or employed for political purposes. But that objection applies to every part of the Constitution which gives powers to the Centre to override the Provinces ... the proper thing we ought to expect is that such Articles will never be called into operation and they would remain a dead letter."

(iii) *Anti-Democratic:* The emergency provisions of the Constitution are also anti-democracy. H.V. Kamath echoed this view in the Constituent Assembly when he said, "I fear that by this single chapter, Chapter XI, we are seeking to lay the foundation of a totalitarian State, Police State, a State completely opposed to all the ideals and principles, that we have held aloft during the last few decades, a State where rights and liberties will be in continual jeopardy, a State in which if there be peace, it will be a peace of the grave, and the void of the desert." The Weimer Republic of Germany had similar provisions in its Constitution which were used by Hitler in establishing his dictatorship. In India also, we had a period of 1975-77 when democracy was sacrificed while the Government time and again emphasised that "Emergency is within the Constitution." This emergency saw almost entire opposition, even school boys behind bars.

The abuse of emergency powers led to the 44th Constitutional Amendment but still the loopholes remain. The emergency can continue for one month without the approval of any of the Houses of the Parliament. One month is not a short time for any ambitious President and Prime Minister in derailing the democracy. Further within the stipulated period of one month, the Lok Sabha may be dissolved which mean only Rajya Sabha's approval is necessary for the continuation of emergency in such a situation. It may be difficult to get the required majority support in Rajya Sabha, but it is not a impossible situation. The executive may adopt many means to get such approval. After the dissolution of the Lok Sabha, the Constitution stipulates that within six months fresh election should take place and the new Lok Sabha be convened. But then the executive may adopt other means to ensure its own henchmen's election to Lok Sabha. One may take a lesson from the emergency of 1975-77 when efforts were made to thwart the opposition during election campaigns. Some of the leaders fought election from behind the bars. The press censorship continued during the elections. Before the Forty Fourth Constitutional Amendment, the constitutional provisions regarding emergency helped the ambitious Prime Minister in establishing an anti-democratic regime, the point is despite the 44th constitutional Amendment, the possibility of the repeat of 1975-77 is remote and fanciful but such a fancy cannot be completely ruled out.

However, there is another school of thought which justifies the emergency provisions as necessary. In the Constituent Assembly Dr. Ambedkar and T.T. Krishnamachari were the forceful defenders of the emergency provisions on the basis of their need for national security and unity during the crisis. In case of *Article 356*, it was presumed that it will be used very cautiously.

Prof. M.P. Singh in his work V.N. Shukla's Constitution of India justifies the incorporation of emergency provision thus:

> "The Constitution of India is unique in the respect that it contains a complete scheme for speedy readjustment of the peace time governmental machinery in moment of national peril. These provisions may appear to be hard, particularly in a Constitution which professes to be built upon an edifice of fundamental rights and democracy. But the provisions must be studied in the light of India's past history. India had her inglorious days whenever the Central power grew weak. It is well that Constitution guards against the forces of disintegration. Events may take place threatening the very existence of the State, and if there are no safeguards against such eventualities, the State, together with all that is desired to remain basic and immutable, will be swept away."

The Sarkaria Commission also suggested retaining *Article 356*. It observed, "There has been a growth in sub-nationalism which has tended to strengthen divisive forces and weaken the unity and integrity of the country. Linguistic chauvinism has also added a new dimension in keeping people apart. Dim memories of the historical part are being actively raised to whip up animosities. Unity and integrity of the country is of paramount importance. Unless there is a will and commitment to work for a united country, there are real dangers that regionalism, linguistic chauvinism, communalism, casteism etc may foul the atmosphere to the point where secessionist thoughts start pervading the body politic. It is, therefore, necessary to perceive the overriding powers of the union to enable it to deal with such situations and ensure that the government in the State is carried on in accordance with the provisions of the Constitution. We are firmly of the view that *Article 356* should remain as the ultimate weapon to cope with such extreme situations."

The Standing Committee of Inter State Council in June 1997, proposed a constitutional amendment to *Article 356* which are as follows:

(i) *Article 356* should be retained with adequate safeguards.
(ii) The Centre should take action under *Article 356*, only when the State is warned and served a show cause notice. The State Government would be given a week's time to reply charges.
(iii) The confirmation of imposition of President's Rule should be sought within one month and not two months as present provisions provides for.
(iv) Ten per cent of members of a House (Lok Sabha or Rajya Sabha) may demand for a special session of the House, seeking reinstatement of the dismissed Government.
(v) Only Parliament would decide if the State Assembly should be dissolved or placed under suspension.
(vi) The Presidential Proclamation should include the charges levied against the Centre as well as the reply given by the State.
(vii) Except in extraordinary situations, *Article 356* should be invoked on receiving a report from the Governor.
(viii) Dismissal of any government under *Article 356* should need the approval of Parliament by a two-thirds majority.

Conclusion

Thus the emergency provisions have been justified on the grounds of national security and unity and integrity of the country. However, we have to accept that the emergency provisions have been misused especially Article 356. It may be difficult to remove it altogether because of India's diversity and the need to maintain its unity and integrity but the Constitution may definitely be amended to ensure the use and avoid misuse or abuse of the provisions. The Sarkaria Commission suggested that the material facts and grounds on which *Article 356* is invoked should be made an integral part of the proclamation. This should be accepted because in such case the judiciary will be able to pronounce on the constitutional validity or otherwise of the Proclamation without much difficulty. Lastly, the best safeguard against the misuse is the constant vigil by the people of India.

The Position of Indian President

The actual position of the Indian President is controversial because the Constitution itself does not explain much regarding this. Broadly speaking there have been two views regarding the actual position of the President which are as follows:

(A) President is a nominal Head.
(B) President is not a nominal Head.

President: A Nominal Head

(i) We have a Parliamentary system of government in which the President can only be nominal Head. The actual powers lie with the Prime Minister and his Council of Ministers.

(ii) The Constitution says in *Article 74*, "There shall be a Council of Ministers with the Prime Minister as the head to aid and advise the President who, shall, in the exercise of his functions, act in accordance with such advice." This means that the President has no option but act according to the "aid and advice" of the Council of Ministers. The Constitution further says that the President may ask the Council of Ministers to reconsider its aid and advice but he has to act according to the advice tendered after such reconsideration. This means the President cannot reject the advice of the Council of Ministers, he can only sent it for reconsideration if he does not agree to it. But the President is duty-bound to act according to the advice tendered by the Council of Ministers after reconsideration.

(iii) In all the administrative matters it is the Council of Ministers which takes the decision and it is the Council of Ministers which is collectively responsible to the Lok Sabha. By a no-confidence vote, the Lok Sabha can dismiss a minister. There is no provision in the Constitution which says that the President shall be responsible to the Lok Sabha or Parliament.

(iv) The fact that the Council of Ministers takes the decision is clear from *Article 78* which enumerates the duties of the Prime Minister in relation to President. The Prime Minister is to (a) communicate to the President all decisions of the Council of Ministers relating to the administration of the affairs of the Union and proposals for legislation; (b) furnish such information relating to the administration of the affairs of the Union and proposals for legislation as the President may call for; and (c) if a minister has taken a decision on any matter but which has not been considered by the Council of Ministers, the President may ask the Prime Minister to submit it for the decision of the Council of Ministers.

(v) The President's position can be further clarified by a comparison of constitutional provision relating to President and the Governor of the State. In a State, the Governor is to exercise his functions according to aid and advice of the Chief Minister and his Council of Ministers except in so far he is by or under this Constitution required to exercise his functions or any of them in his discretion. This means that Governor has discretionary powers which are to be exercised independently of the Council of Ministers of the State. In case of Indian President, no discretionary powers have been assigned to him. In other words the President is to exercise all his powers and functions strictly according to the advice of the Council of Ministers.

(vi) Now let us take a hypothetical case. A President rejects or acts against the advice tendered to him by the Council of Ministers after duly exercising his right to send the advice for reconsideration. The Prime Minister and the Council of Ministers will resign. The President will have to find an alternate Prime Minister and Council of Ministers which should have the support of the Lok Sabha. If the outgoing Prime Minister has the support of Lok Sabha, then the President cannot find an alternative. The President can not act without the Council of Ministers. He cannot instal a Prime Minister who does not enjoy the support of Lok Sabha. If he does so, he will be violating the Constitution. Hence the President has no independent position. He is duty-bound to act according to the advice of the Council of Ministers.

(vii) The Lok Sabha controls the purse of the Union. In case of conflict with the Council of Ministers who has the support of the Lok Sabha, the President will find it almost impossible to run the machinery of the government because the Lok Sabha will not approve expenditures incurred by the President.

(viii) The fact that the Constitution provided for President as nominal head can be verified by the debates in the Constituent Assembly. While introducing the Draft Constitution Dr. Ambedkar explained the position of President thus:

"In the Draft Constitution, there is placed at the head of the Indian Union a functionary who is called the President of the Union. The title of this functionary reminds one of the President of the United States. But beyond identity of names there is nothing in common between the forms of government prevalent in America and the form of government proposed under the Draft Constitution. The American form of government is called the Presidential system of government. What the Draft proposes is the parliamentary system. The two are fundamentally different.

Under the Presidential system of America, the President is the Chief head of the Executive. The administration is vested in him. Under the Draft Constitution, the President occupies the same position as the King under the English Constitution. He is the head of the State but not of the Executive. He represents the Nation but does not rule the Nation. He is the symbol of the nation. His place in the administration is that of a ceremonial device on a seal by which the nation's decisions are made known. Under the American Constitution, the President has under him Secretaries in charge of different Departments. In like manner the President of the Indian Union will have under him ministers in charge of different Departments of administration. Here again, there is a fundamental difference between the two. The President of the United States is not bound to accept any advice tendered to him by any of his secretaries. The President of the Indian Union will be generally bound by the advice of his ministers. He can do nothing contrary to their advice nor can he do anything without their advice. The President of the United States can dismiss any Secretary at any time. The President of the Indian Union has no power to do so, so long as his ministers command a majority in Parliament.

The Presidential system of America is based upon the separation of the Executive and the Legislature so that the President and his Secretaries cannot be members of the Congress. The Draft Constitution does not recognise this doctrine. The Ministers under the Indian Union are members of Parliament. Only members of Parliament can become ministers ... they can sit in Parliament, take part in debates and vote in its proceedings. Both systems of government are, of course, democratic and the choice between the two is not very easy. A democratic executive must satisfy two conditions: (1) It must be a stable executive; and (2) it must be a responsible executive. Unfortunately, it has not been possible so far to devise a system which can ensure both in equal degree. You can have a system which can give you more stability but less responsibility or you can have a system which gives you more responsibility but less stability. The American and the Swiss systems give more stability but less responsibility. The British system, on the other hand, gives you more responsibility but less stability. The reason for this is obvious. The American Executive is a non-Parliamentary Executive which means that it is not dependent for its existence upon a majority in the Congress, while the British system is a Parliamentary Executive, the Congress of the United States cannot dismiss the Executive. A Parliamentary government must resign the moment it loses the confidence of a majority of the members of Parliament. Looking at it from the point of view of responsibility, a non-Parliamentary Executive being dependent upon a majority in Parliament becomes more responsible. The Parliamentary system differs from a non-Parliamentary system in as much as the former is more responsible than the latter but they also differ as to the time and agency for assessment of their responsibility. Under the non-Parliamentary system such as the one that exists in the U.S.A., the assessment of responsibility of the Executive is periodic. It takes place once in two years. It is done by the electorate. In England where the Parliamentary system prevails, the assessment of responsibility of the Executive is both daily and periodic. The daily assessment is done by members of Parliament through questions, Resolutions, No-Confidence Motions, Adjournment Motions, and Debates on Addresses. Periodic assessment is done by the electorate at the time of the election which may take place every five years or earlier. The daily assessment of responsibility which is not available under the American system is, it is felt, far more effective than the periodic assessment and far more necessary in a country like India. The Draft Constitution in recommending the Parliamentary system of Executive has preferred more responsibility to more stability."

T.T. Krishnamachari said, "So far as the relationship of the President with the Cabinet is concerned, I must say that we have, so to say, completely copied the system of government that is functioning in Britain today; we have made no deviation from it and the deviations that we have, are only such as are necessary because our Constitution is federal in structure. Dr. Rajendra Prasad also pointed out, "... we have adopted more or less, the position of British monarch for the President .... His position is that of a constitutional President."

(ix) Last but not the least, the operation of Indian political system during the last 50 years suggests that on the whole the Presidents have acted as nominal head. There have been disagreement between the President and the Prime Minister but President has never crossed the limits of Parliamentary system of government.

President is Not a Nominal Head

This has been more or less a legalist view which was more relevant before the 42nd Constitutional Amendment Act. The Constitution had left certain ambiguities regarding the position of President in relation to Prime Minister and his Council of Ministers which were clarified by the 42nd Amendment. The Amendment to the Act provided that the President would act according to the advice tendered by the Council of Ministers. The 44th Constitutional Amendment further provided that he may send an advice for reconsideration but he has to act according to the advice tendered after such reconsideration by the Council of Ministers. But still there are certain arguments which lead one to believe that at least the Constitution did not provide for a nominal head. Some of the arguments are as follows:

Before assuming his office, the President takes an oath to faithfully execute the office of President of India and to preserve, protect and defend the Constitution and the law and that he will devote himself to the service and well being of the people of India. For the purpose of following his oath, he may act independently if he feels that the cabinet advice is contrary to the oath he has undertaken. Further as per the *Article 53* he has to exercise the executive power of the Union either directly or through officers subordinate to him in accordance with the Constitution. This also leaves certain undefined powers with the President.

Conclusion

After looking into both the views we can conclude that the President is a nominal head. He should exercise his powers with the aid and advice of the Prime Minister and his cabinet. As V.V. Giri the former President on his retirement said, "The President has many limitations under the Constitution. If he wants to have a confrontation with the Prime Minister, he should be prepared for a revolution." This however does not mean that the President is a rubber stamp. He has a right to be consulted, to be informed on all matters of the Union and in case the Cabinet's Policy is not fruitful due to any reason or contrary to national interest, he has a right to warn the government. He can also use his power of sending the ministerial advice for reconsideration as President Dr. APJ Abdul Kalam returned the Ordinance on electoral reforms .He sought clarification on the absence of provision relating to guidelines on declaration of previous cases of conviction and assets by a candidate. He also wanted to know why the proposal relating to disqualification of a candidate in case charges were framed against him/her in two or more cases of heinous offences was dropped. But when the cabinet sent the same advice second time, he gave his assent to the ordinance without creating any controversy thus holding the tenets of parliamentary democracy and Indian constitutional system. In 2005, he agreed to sign the Proclamation to impose President's rule in Bihar, but the later events which resulted in judicial censure annoyed him and he became cautious with government's recommendations. Kalam became the first President to return a Bill to Parliament for reconsideration. He returned the controversial office-of-profit Bill for reconsideration to the Parliament which sought to give across the board amnesty to legislators who faced disqualification for holding an office of profit. This act of Kalam became a full-fledged embarrassment for government. But Kalam had sent it back with a message and observations over the need for wide legal and constitutional consultations. He observed that the draft must have a "comprehensive criteria that is fair and reasonable" and be "universally applied" to all states and Union Territories in a clear and "transparent manner. The Parliament reenacted it without any changes and still the President took sometime in giving his assent that too, after Parliament approved setting up of a joint committee to define what constitutes such an office and as the newspaper reports pointed out, after the Prime Minister had an unscheduled meeting with him apparently seeking an earlier assent of the Bill. Dr. APJ Abdul Kalam also returned the file seeking elevation of Justice Jagdish Bhalla to the Kerala High Court. Earlier, he had returned a similar recommendation regarding Justice Vijender Jain's elevation as Chief Justice of Punjab and Haryana High Court.

Before Kalam, President K.R. Narayanan returned the Cabinet's advice for reconsideration in the cases of imposition of President's rule in UP and Bihar in 1997 and 1998 respectively. But in both these cases the cabinet did not insist on its advice. Earlier Dr. Shankar Dayal Sharma rejected the nominations for Rajya Sabha , as suggested by the United Front Government on the ground that they did not fit in the categories given in the Constitution i.e. literature, science, art and social service.

The President's role becomes very important particularly when there is a hung Parliament. In case of a coalition Government, he becomes the centre of focus. And in case the government is in minority, he is not bound by its advice. In case of a hung Parliament, the President's decision becomes decisive. The role of President in India was best summed up by the former President R. Venkataraman who said that he was like an 'emergency light' which automotically came when the normal flow of power was broken and went out after normal working was restored.

References

Basu, D.D., *Introduction to the Constitution of India,* 1992, New Delhi, Prentice Hall of India Pvt. Ltd.

Das, B.C., *The President of India,* 1977, New Delhi, S. Chand & Co. Ltd.

Fadia B.L., *Indian Government and Politics,* 1996, Agra, Sahitya Bhawan Publications.

Pylee M.V., *Constitutional Government in India,* 1968, Bombay, Asia Publishing House.

Patnaik, Raghunath, *Powers of the President and Governors of India,* 1996, New Delhi, Deep & Deep Publications.

Rao, B. Shiva, *The Framing of Indian Constitution,* 1968, New Delhi, The Indian Institute of Public Administration.

Singh, M.P., *V.N. Shukla's Constitution of India,* 1994, Lucknow, Eastern Book Company.

Siwach, J.R., *Dynamics of Indian Government and Politics,* 1990, New Delhi, Sterling Publishers Pvt. Ltd.

Thakur Ramesh, *The Government and Politics of India,* 1995, London, Macmillan Press Ltd.

CHAPTER XI

The Prime Minister of India

Office of the Prime Minister is the most important office in the Indian political system. The entire system is focussed around him. Therefore, many political scientists prefer to call this system as Prime Ministerial instead of Parliamentary or cabinet form of government. However, the Constitution does not explain the real role and position of the Prime Minister as all the executive powers of the Union have been assigned to the President, who is to use them according to aid and advice of the Council of Ministers with Prime Minister as its head. The Constitution only enumerates the duties of the Prime Minister. Therefore to understand the real significance of the office of the Prime Minister one has to see its real working. This chapter deals with the various aspects of the office of Prime Minister.

Appointment of the Prime Minister

Article 74 of the Constitution says "There shall be a Council of Ministers with the Prime Minister at the head to aid and advice the President ..." *Article 75* says that "The Prime Minister shall be appointed by the President and the other Ministers shall be appointed by the President on the advice of the Prime Minister." The same Article further points out that the ministers shall hold office during the pleasure of the President, and the Council of Ministers shall be collectively responsible to the Lok Sabha. The Prime Minister and other Ministers should be the member of either of the two Houses of the Parliament. If not so they should become so within six months.

Now the question arises as to what extent the President can enjoy discretion with regard to appointing the Prime Minister. At the outset, it must be emphasised that President has very little discretion in appointing the Prime Minister. This is especially so when there is a majority party in the Lok Sabha. In such a case, the President has little choice except to appoint the leader of majority party as Prime Minister. Thus Jawahar Lal Nehru, Lal Bahadur Shastri, Mrs. Indira Gandhi, Rajiv Gandhi and Morarji Desai are such examples who had clear majority in Lok Sabha. However, when there is a hung Parliament and no party is able to form the government on its own, then the President can exercise his discretion to select a person who could command majority support in the Lok Sabha. In 1979, Charan Singh was preferred by President Reddy instead of Jagjivan Ram. In such a situation, the parliamentary practice is to invite the leader of single largest party in the House. He may instal him as Prime Minister and ask him to seek the confidence vote of the Lok Sabha.

This was done in case of P.V. Narasimha Rao in 1991 and Atal Bihari Vajpayee in 1996 and 1998. He may not instal the leader of the single largest party as Prime Minister but ask him to explore the possibility of a government with the help of other parties. This was done in 1979, when President Reddy asked Y.B. Chavan, the leader of Congress Parliamentary Party to seek the help of other parties in forming a government. Y.B. Chavan expressed his inability to form an alternative government.

The President may appoint the leader of a party as Prime Minister who has been promised support by other parties. This was the path taken by President Venkataraman in appointing V.P. Singh the leader of Janata Dal/National Front as Prime Minister when the largest single Party (Congress I) decided not to stake claim for forming government and BJP and the Left Parties assured support to V.P. Singh. In 1996, the President appointed Atal Behari Vajpayee as Prime Minister who could not get a vote of confidence from the Lok Sabha. After this, he did not invite P.V. Narasimha Rao although he was the leader of the second largest party. Instead, he informally invited H.D. Deve Gowda to form the government who submitted a list of 190 MPs supporting him and the date of swearing in ceremony was fixed. After President's meeting with H.D. Deve Gowda, P.V. Narasimha Rao called on the President in which the President informed him about the decision, P.V. Narasimha Rao responded by saying that his party had already taken the decision to support H.D. Deve Gowda. After President's meeting with Rao, H.D. Deve Gowda met the President and it was in this meeting that the President handed over the formal letter to Gowda inviting him to form Government.

Thus when the President was assured that Deve Gowda would be able to command majority in the House, he formally invited him and installed him as the Prime Minister. More or less, the same process, was adopted in the appointment of Inder Kumar Gujral (in 1997) and Atal Behari Vajpayee (in 1998 and 1999) as Prime Ministers.

It is clear that the Constitution does not require that a person must prove his majority in Lok Sabha and then only he is to be appointed as Prime Minister. Infact, the normal practice is to appoint a person as Prime Minister and then ask him to win a confidence vote in Lok Sabha. This was done in the cases of Charan Singh in 1979, V.P. Singh in 1989, Chandra Shekhar in 1990, P.V. Narasimha Rao in 1991, Atal Behari Vajpayee in 1996, H.D. Deve Gowda in 1996 and I.K. Gujral in 1997 and again Atal Behari Vajpayee in 1998. Thus in case of hung Parliament when no party has majority, the President's task in appointing Prime Minister becomes difficult. He has to do a lot of exercise in deciding the rival claims and in the process he may also exercise his discretion. But ultimately it is the Lok Sabha which decides who will be the Prime Minister.

There are two practices with regard to the Prime Minister: (i) The person is appointed as Prime Minister after his election as the leader of the majority party/coalition parties/ single largest party. This was done in all cases till now with only one exception of Rajiv Gandhi who was appointed Prime Minister by the President Zail Singh. He was elected as the leader of Congress (I) later on. (ii) The Prime Minister invariably belongs to Lok Sabha and if he is not a member of Lok Sabha, he gets elected to it as soon as possible. Nehru, Shastri, Morarji Desai, Charan Singh, Rajiv Gandhi, Chandra Shekhar, Atal Behari Vajpayee, and I.K. Gujral were Lok Sabha members when installed as Prime Minister. Mrs. Indira Gandhi was the member of Rajya Sabha but soon she became the member of Lok Sabha. P.V. Narasimha Rao and H.D. Deve Gowda were not the members of Parliament when appointed as Prime Minister. P.V. Narasimha Rao became the member of Lok Sabha later on. However, H.D. Deve Gowda chose Rajya Sabha. Thus he has the distinction of being the first Prime Minister who did not belong to Lok Sabha. In 1996, the appointment of H.D. Deve Gowda as Prime Minister was challenged in the Supreme Court on the ground that he was not the member of the Parliament. The Supreme Court ruled that the Constitution permitted a non-member of the Parliament as Prime Minister for a short duration of six months. The example set up by H.D. Deve Gowda was followed by Dr. Manmohan Singh who also belonged to Rajya Sabha.

Tenure of the Prime Minister

There is no fixed term of the Prime Minister of India. According to the Constitution he remains in power so long he enjoys the confidence of the House. Jawaharlal Nehru had the distinction of having the longest-tenure as Prime Minister of India. He remained the Prime Minister for nearly 17 years till his death. Mrs. Indira Gandhi (1966-77 and 1980-84 till her assassination) ruled for roughly 14 years. Rajiv Gandhi and P.V. Narasimha Rao remained Prime Minister for 5 years each after which the Lok Sabha elections were held and they lost the majority support in the ensuing elections. In case of the death of the Prime Minister, the senior-most member of the Cabinet is made Acting Prime Minister as was the case with Gulzari Lal Nanda, who became Acting Prime Minister on two occasions—first after the death of Jawahar Lal Nehru; and secondly after the death of Lal Bahadur Shastri. Following is the table of Prime Ministers of India:

Prime Ministers of India

Prime Minister	**Dates**
Jawahar Lal Nehru	15 Aug. 1947—27 May 1964
Lal Bahadur Shastri	9 June 1964—11 Jan 1966
Indira Gandhi	24 Jan. 1966—24 March 1977
Morarji Desai	24 March 1977—28 July 1979
Charan Singh	28 July 1979—14 Jan 1980
Indira Gandhi	14 Jan 1980—31 Oct. 1984
Rajiv Gandhi	31 Oct. 1984—1 Dec. 1989
V.P. Singh	2 Dec 1989—10 Nov. 1990
Chandra Shekhar	10 Nov. 1990—21 June 1991
P.V. Narasimha Rao	21 June 1990—15 May 1996
Atal Behari Vajpayee	15 May 1996—1 June 1996
H.D. Deve Gowda	1 June 1996—21 April 1997
Inder Kumar Gujral	21 April 1997—19 March 1998
Atal Behari Vajpayee	19 March 1998— 22 May 2004
Dr. Manmohan Singh	22 May 2004 — Till Date

Dismissal of a Prime Minister

Normally no Prime Minister is dismissed by the President. It has not happened in Indian political system till now. Normal practice is that the Prime Minister resigns when he realises that he has lost the confidence of the Lok Sabha. This was done by Morarji Desai and Charan Singh in 1979, Chandra Shekhar in 1991 and Vajpayee in 1996. V.P. Singh and H.D. Deve Gowda resigned after being defeated in Lok Sabha. This also happened in 1999 when subsequent to the withdrawal of support by the AIADMK party to the Vajpayee Government, the President directed the Prime Minister Atal Behari Vajpayee to elicit a vote of confidence from the Lok Sabha which Vajpayee lost by one vote and resigned. But the question is; can the President dismiss a Prime Minister who has the majority support in Lok Sabha. There are three points to be remembered in this regard:

(i) Till now no Prime Minister with a majority support, has been dismissed by the President. Infact, for that matter, no Prime Minister of India has been dismissed.

(ii) It is suggested that the President may dismiss a Prime Minister and his Council of Ministers if he feels that the Ministry does not represent the will of the people. But whenever he does so, the President is taking a grave risk and will create a grave constitutional crisis. In Britain, no government has been dismissed since 1783. However, in 1975 Sir John Kerr, the then Governor General of Australia, dismissed the Prime Minister Whitlem. His action was approved by the people in the ensuing elections but it did create a controversy regarding the role of the head of the State in the Parliamentary form of Government. This also means that a similar kind of situation cannot be ruled out in India.

(iii) In case of utter failure of the Prime Minister and his ministry, the President may be justified in taking such action. There are atleast two instances when the question of dismissal was discussed in Indian polity. (a) After the defeat in Indo-China war of 1962, the opposition demanded that President Radhakrishnan dismiss the Nehru Ministry as it had failed in defending the country. It has been suggested that the President was receptive to such a demand. However he did not dismiss the Prime Minister and his Council of Ministers. (b) In 1987, President Zail Singh claimed that he can dismiss the Prime Minister in certain circumstances, even if he has a majority in the Lok Sabha. The President's Zail Singh relations with the Prime Minister were strained and the President was seriously considering to dismiss the Prime Minister. He even sought the opinions of lawyers on Presidential powers to dismiss the government and order prosecution against the Prime Minister, as was alleged by the then Home Minister Buta Singh. However, later on a rapprochement between Rajiv Gandhi and Zail Singh took place. The Rashtrapati Bhavan issued an unprecedented press note saying that the President had no intention of dismissing the Prime Minister.

Powers and Functions of the Prime Minister

Though the Constitution does not enumerate the powers and functions of the Prime Minister, the Prime Minister in practice enjoys a wide range of powers and functions which are as follows:

(1) *Formation of the Council of Ministers:* The first function of the Prime Minister is to form his Council of Ministers. The Council of Ministers consists of (i) Cabinet Ministers or the members of the cabinet; (ii) Ministers of State; (iii) Deputy Ministers; and (iv) Parliamentary Secretaries. The President appoints all the Ministers on the advice of the Prime Minister. The conventions of the Parliamentary system give the maximum freedom to the Prime Minister in choosing his colleagues

because the Prime Minister has to run the administration which can only be accomplished through team spirit. The Prime Minister should have ministers of his choice, who have no major differences in policy matters with him. However, the freedom to select his colleagues is subjected to Prime Minister's position in his party. For example the first Prime Minister of India, Nehru could not ignore Patel who was very powerful in the Congress Party. He had to include Patel as Deputy Prime Minister and Home Minister and also Patel's supporters in his ministry. After the death of Patel, Nehru became the sole leader of Congress and he ousted Patel's supporters from the ministry and had a ministry which was purely his own creation. Similarly Indira Gandhi, when she became the Prime Minister, had many leaders in her party who were very powerful and she had to include such persons in her ministry whom she didnot like including Morarji Desai who was made the Deputy Prime Minister and Finance Minister. After the 1971 mid-term poll she gained absolute majority and enjoyed maximum freedom in choosing her colleagues.

In a coalition system, the Prime Minister's position is very weak in the formation of Council of Ministers. In the Janata Party Government which was a coalition of different parties, Morarji Desai had many Ministers whom he never knew before. Further, the Ministry consisted of Charan Singh and Jagjivan Ram who were themselves formidable candidates for the Prime Ministership. In case of H.D. Deve Gowda and subsequently I.K. Gujral Ministry, the Ministers were selected not by the Prime Minister but by the leaders of the 14 regional parties who formed the United Front. Same principle was applied in case of coalition governments formed in 1998, 1999, 2004 and 2009.

In the formation of Council of Ministers, the Prime Minister has to keep certain legal considerations in his mind which are as follows:

(a) The total number of ministers, including the Prime Minister cannot exceed fifteen per cent of the total number of members of Lok Sabha. (*Article 75 (1-A)*).

(b) A member of Parliament who is disqualified under the anti-defection act (Tenth Schedule of the Indian Constitution) cannot be made minister. He can only be made minister (1) when his term as member of Parliament would expire or (2) he contests election to Parliament and is declared elected. (*Article 75 (1-B)*).

There are other considerations also which are not legally binding but he has to keep in mind while choosing ministers for his Council of Ministers. They are as follows:

(a) He has to include the important leaders of his party.

(b) All the States should be represented in the Council of Ministers.

(c) The Scheduled Castes, Scheduled Tribes, and women should also be represented.

(2) *Distribution of Portfolios:* After the formation of the Ministry, the Prime Minister allocates different departments among the Ministers. Usually the law ministry is given to a person who has excelled in the field of law. A practice is also developing to allocate finance ministry to an expert on financial matters. However, the Prime Minister enjoys discretion in allocating departments to the ministers. Sometimes he reshuffles the ministry to oust the ministers whom he does not like or who are not upto the mark or to upgrade the deserving ministers or to induct new ministers.

(3) *Giving Life to the Council of Ministers:* The Prime Minister gives life to the Council of Ministers. He presides over its meetings. He is also the presiding officer of the meetings of the cabinet which is a smaller body and takes all the decisions. In case there is a conflict between a minister and the Prime Minister, it is the minister who will have to resign. If a minister resigns, there is no effect on the ministry but if the Prime Minister resigns, it means the resignation of the entire ministry. He may even ask a minister to resign or ask the President to dismiss a minister. In 1998 prime Minister Vajpayee asked Buta Singh to resign as a result of corruption charges being framed against him by the Court. Upon his refusal to resign, the President was asked to dismiss him. The cabinet functions under the leadership of the Prime Minister. The agenda is prepared by him. Though in theory the cabinet's decision may be taken by voting, in practice the cabinet accepts the decisions made by the Prime Minister. The Prime Minister also ensures coordination between the different ministries. He is the arbiter in case of conflict between the two or more ministries. Not only he ensures coordination between different departments, but also has a right to supervision over all the departments. These powers help the Prime Minister to control the ministers, who may be powerful politicians. Nehru insisted that the Prime Minister had to be "more responsible than anyone else for the general trend of policy and for the co-ordination of the work of various government departments." By this insistence, he could even control Sardar Patel who was a very powerful leader in the Congress.

It will not be wrong to say that the ministers swim and sink alongwith the Prime Minister.

(4) *Prime Minister and the Appointments:* One of the important powers of the Prime Minister is the power of patronage. All the major appointments of the Central Government are made by the Prime Minister in the name of the President, which inlcudes Chief Justice and other judges of Supreme Court and High Courts, the Attorney General, the Chiefs of army, navy and airforce, Governors, Ambassadors and High Commissioners, Chairmen and members of various Commissions, the Chief and the members of Election Commission etc.

(5) *Prime Minister as the Link between President and Cabinet:* The cabinet is the supreme decision making body of the Union and the Prime Minister acts as a link between the cabinet and the President. The ministers can meet the President only with the Prime Minister's consent. According to *Article 78,* it is the duty of the Prime Minister to (a) Communicate to the President all decisions of the Council of Ministers relating to the administration of the affairs of the Union and proposals for legislation; (b) furnish such information relating to the administration of the affairs of the Union and proposals for legislation as the President may call for; and (c) if the President so requires, to submit for the consideration of the Council of Ministers any matter on which a decision has been taken by a Minister but which has not been considered by the Council.

(6) *Leader of the Parliament:* The Prime Minister is the leader of the Parliament. As such he advices the President with regard to summoning and proroguing the House. The agenda of the Lok Sabha is prepared by the Speaker with his consultation. All the major policy decisions are made by the Prime Minister in the Parliament. In case a minister makes an error in Lok Sabha, he only can correct it. Similarly if a minister is not able to satisfy the House by his answers, the Prime Minister intervenes. He helps Speaker in maintaining discipline and decorum in the House. He also plays an important role in the formation of various committees of the Parliament. The annual budget and the supplementary budgets, prepared by the Finance Minister are first cleared by the Prime Minister.

The most important power of the Prime Minister with regard to Parliament is to recommend dissolution of Lok Sabha. The President has to accept the advice of Prime Minister who is backed by the majority of Lok Sabha. This is a power by which the Prime Minister controls even the opposition. The members of Lok Sabha normally would like to enjoy the full term of five years. They donot want the dissolution because it means fresh elections in which they may or may not return.

(7) *Chief Spokesman of Foreign Relations:* In international affairs, the Prime Minister is the chief spokesman of the country. In fact the foreign relations have been the key area of the Prime Minister. The tradition was set up by Nehru, the first Prime Minister of India who drafted India's policy of non-alignment. Except in his last days after the Indo-China war of 1962, Nehru retained the foreign ministry under himself. It was only later on that he appointed Sardar Swaran Singh as his

External Affairs Minister. Once when a foreign policy matter caused a rumpus in Parliament, with an angry opposition wanting to know how crucial decisions were taken, Nehru coolly replied, "The Prime Minister decides in consultation with the External Affairs Minister." After Nehru, the tradition continues. All the major international conferences like Commonwealth Heads of Government Meeting (CHOGM) or Non-Alignment Movement (NAM) Conferences or South Asian Association for Regional Cooperation (SAARC) are attended by the Prime Minister personally.

(8) *Chief Spokesman of the Government:* It is not only the foreign affairs, the Prime Minister is actively involved in policy formulation and implementation of other departments as well. Whether it is agrarian policy or industrial policy or a reservation issue, it is the Prime Minister who takes the crucial decisions. The Prime Minister is also the chairman of the Planning Commission, which is entrusted with the enormous task of formulating five year plans for the country. The Planning Commission has been making inroads into the autonomy of States. It has been called the super-cabinet under the leadership of the Prime Minister and the Prime Minister becomes the key person in deciding the priorities in planning and in the allocation of different projects to the States.

(9) *Leader of the Nation:* The Prime Minister is the leader of the nation. He leads the nation in times of war and peace. The people also look towards him for the redressal of grievances. He is praised for the successes of the government and blamed for the failures. Thus Nehru was blamed for the debacle in Indo-China war of 1962, P.V. Narasimha Rao for the demolition of disputed structure in Ayodhya. Shastri was praised for the Indian performance in Indo-Pak war of 1965 and Indira Gandhi was called "Durga" for the success in Indo-Pak war of 1971. The revolution in Communication, the spread of Radio and T.V. provides the Prime Minister an opportunity to talk to the people directly. People may not be knowing a particular minister, but every Indian knows the name of the Prime Minister. Thus, the place of Indian Prime Minister amidst various other ministers is unparalleled. Practically, General Elections turn into elections for choosing a Prime Minister.

(10) *Prime Minister as the Chief Political Executive:* As the Chief Political executive, the Prime Minister plays the role of a manager of Indian polity. He has to control the political conflicts and resolve them within the constitutional system. He is to provide political leadership, identify priorities and take the nation to the path of development and progress. He becomes an all India leader and inspires the people. With his vision and perception of the society and polity, as Harish Khare

points out, "he manipulates and influences the expectations aspirations, anger, resentment and fears in society at large." For this purpose many a times he has to go above party considerations. The best example of this is the role of Nehru during the First General Elections. Nehru refused to postpone the First General Elections on one of his party's colleagues demand that Congress needed some more time to fight the election. He asked the people to vote. He said, "It is right that each of you take an interest in this great democratic process which is taking place on a scale yet unknown to history. It is also important that you take interest as citizens of the Republic of India, the future of which will, no doubt, be affected by these elections. Democracy is based on the active and intelligent interest of the people in their national affairs and in the elections that result in the formation of government." He gave free hand to Election Commission to ensure free and fair elections. Instructions were also issued to ministers not to misuse their official position for party advantage during the elections. When Nehru was told that some corrupt people have been chosen as Congress party candidates, his reply was, "Donot vote for them. I am not infallible and I may have made mistakes but if you know they are corrupt and dishonest don't vote for them." On November 22, 1951, he said in his Radio broadcast to the people, "It is of the utmost importance that all of us, whatever the party to which we belong, should maintain a high level of propriety and decorous behaviour. Our propaganda by speech or in writing should not be personal but should deal with policies and programmes. It should on no account be allowed to degenerate into personal criticism and abuse. The standard we set up now will act as a precedent and govern future elections ..."

"... In a democracy, we have to know how to win and also how to lose with grace. Those who win should not allow this to go to their heads, those who lose should not feel dejected. The manner of winning or losing is even more important than the result. It is better to lose in the right way than to win in the wrong way. Indeed, if success comes through misconceived effort or wrong means, then the value of that success itself is lost."

Nehru also instructed that the government officers should be impartial and neutral. Every party and every candidate must be given a free and equal chance and no special facility be accorded to candidates belonging to the ruling party.

Prime Minister as the Chief Executive ensures that the rules and regulations be applied equally to all; they are observed fairly and scrupulously. He must tackle the various problems of the polity and he just cannot ignore them. Whether it is Punjab or Kashmir problem,

Bofors Scandal or corruption cases or terrorism in North East, people expect him to act and decide. In such cases he has to rise above party interests and take decisions best suited to national interest and ensuring a moral life in politics. Harish Khare rightly says as the Chief Political Executive, the Prime Minister "is the custodian of the nation's constitutional morality and political wisdom."

Prime Minister and President

The experience of Indian political system suggests that the Presidents have been working according to the advice of the Prime Minister and his cabinet. The tradition was laid down by Dr. Rajendra Prasad, the first President and Jawahar Lal Nehru, the first Prime Minister of India. However, Prasad raised very pertinent questions regarding the real position of President of India. He was not prepared to accept that the President's position is just like the British monarch. He asserted his authority many times which was not liked by Nehru who always insisted that President was just a constitutional head. In 1950, Nehru wanted to rush through the Hindu Code Bill. Prasad raised objections to the desirability of such a hasty legislation. As a result Nehru had to postpone the consideration of Hindu Code Bill. He disagreed with Nehru on the Government's proposals to impose ceiling on land holdings, to introduce cooperative farming, and to resort to State Trading in Foodgrains. Prasad also criticised the treaty of 1954 on Tibet with China. He attended the installation ceremony of the deity in Somnath and attended the funeral of Sardar Patel against the advice of the Prime Minister. Nehru ignored Prasad wherever he could. He even started ignoring the President in the matter of appointments of Governors and ambassadors. Prasad reacted angrily and said, "You are laying down bad precedents. A President who didnot like you, could have given you a lot of trouble." H.N. Pandit writes, "There was a feeling of insecurity which haunted Nehru as long as Rajendra Prasad remained at the head of the government. The two men didnot see eye to eye on many questions of national importance, though they never allowed these differences to come out in the open."

After Rajendra Prasad, Dr. Radhakrishnan came to occupy the President's office. It has been pointed out that after 1962 war with China, he wanted to dismiss the Prime Minister. However, he didnot do so. After him we have the Prime Minister's Presidents like Zakir Hussain, V.V. Giri, F.A. Ahmed, and Zail Singh. The Prime Minister's position became very strong. There were disagreements also, yet major controversies did not erupt. During Zail Singh's time, the relations between the President and the Prime Minister became very strained. There was even a time when Zail Singh was considering the dismissal of Rajiv Gandhi. Venkataraman and Dr. Shankar Dayal Sharma, barring few instances had cordial relations with then Prime Ministers. A new chapter was added by K.R. Narayanan when he sent back the cabinet's advise to impose *Article 356* on UP and Bihar. Narayanan openly expressed his reservation on the Vajpayee Government efforts regarding the review of the constitution. After assuming office, President Abdul Kalam wanted to address the members of Parliament. But the cabinet turned it down on the ground that there was no constitutions provisions for it. The Government also didnot appreciate his official visit to riot-hit Gujarat which Kalam choose to visit after becoming President. Kalam also put refugee camps in his schedule. But he did not create any controversy in his Gujarat visit. Kalam also sent back the cabinet's advice to promulgate Poll Ordinance for reconsideration but signed on the dotted lines after cabinet pressed for it. Thus, on the whole, the Presidents have worked only as a constitutional head. But one may agree with the former President R. Venkataraman who stated that the President of India is not an appellate or supervisory authority over the Prime Minister, he is like an emergency lamp which becomes active when power fails and becomes dormant when power is restored.

Relationship between the Prime Minister and his Cabinet

The Prime Minister's position in relation to his cabinet colleagues can be summarised as follows:

(1) The Prime Minister is first among the equals, if he is a weak Prime Minister. This means that in his cabinet there are personalities who are powerful and the Prime Minister cannot ignore them. In the initial years of Nehru and Indira Gandhi, they were first among the equals. The position of Lal Bahadur Shastri also comes under this category. The Prime Minister is weak not only in relation to the cabinet but also his position in his party is weak.

(2) The Prime Minister is a shining moon among the less shining stars when the Prime Minister is very strong. He leads his party and acquires charisma and people vote to his party candidate, thinking they are voting for him. In such a case he overshadows all his colleagues, who have to be his yesmen. Nehru, Indira Gandhi and Rajiv Gandhi are examples of powerful Prime Ministers. In such a case, infact, the entire system can be called as Prime Ministerial system.

Lal Bahadur Shastri set up the Prime Minister's Secretariat which had a group of able and experienced bureaucrats to advise him in particularly with regard to foreign, economic and defence affairs. During Mrs. Indira Gandhi times the Prime Minister's Secretariat grew in size and influence. She relied more on her advisors in the Prime Minister's Secretariat than her cabinet colleagues. She took many decisions without even informing them. She advised President to impose emergency without consulting the cabinet. Morarji Desai renamed Prime Minister's Secretariat as Prime Minister Office (PMO). The PMO under the Prime Minister is the most powerful institution, indeed a superministry. All the major and minor decisions are taken not by the ministers concerned or cabinet but referred to PMO for "guidance and advice." Infact, the PMO functions as an overlord over the Ministry. When we have Prime Ministers like Nehru, Indira Gandhi and Rajiv Gandhi, we have the *Prime Ministerial form of government* which means the following:

(i) The Prime Minister is the leader of the majority party in Lok Sabha. His party wins because of him.
(ii) The General Elections are actually to choose or reject the Prime Minister.
(iii) The Prime Minister has total control over his party.
(iv) The Prime Minister has the full power to select his cabinet according to his discretion. The ministers hold their office at the pleasure of the Prime Minister.
(v) The Prime Minister is the only Channel between the Cabinet and the President.
(vi) The President acts according to the advice of the Prime Minister. Invariably the President is Prime Minister's President.
(vii) He coordinates, supervises and controls the different ministries.
(viii) The office of Prime Minister becomes an institution in itself. All the powers are centralised in PMO. Most orders emanating from the PMO are in fact overruling or approving of decisions of cabinet ministers by officials in the PMO. In such a situation, the Secretary to the Prime Minister becomes very powerful who can overrule and even dominates the Cabinet ministers. The Ministers are helpless; they cannot protest for the fear of being ousted from the ministership.
(ix) There is a over centralisation of authority in the hands of Prime Minister who turns his office, virtually, into a Presidential form of government.
(x) The Prime Minister also dominates the State Politics.
(xi) The system of collective responsibility also suffers. The Prime Minister relies more on his officials than the Cabinet Ministers

who are sidelined and the Prime Minister is directly held responsible for any lapse.

Prime Minister in a Coalition Government

The Prime Minister in a coalition government comes under the third category. The United Front Government led by H.D. Deve Gowda in 1996 and I.K. Gujral in 1997 is a classical example of this category. The Prime Minister is not only weak but also ineffective and inactive. He has no freedom in selecting the members of Council of Minister. In the United Front Governments this was decided by the leaders of the 14 regional parties who constituted the United Front. The Prime Minister himself was selected by them. He does not have mass base. He is not the master of his cabinet. He cannot expand or reshuffle his Council of Ministers on his own. Deve Gowda could not even appoint his Officer on Special Duty (OSD) in his discretion. There was a Steering Committee of the constituents of United Front which was the real or super decision making body and the Prime Minister and his cabinet couldnot make major policy decisions. In such a system the Prime Minister ceases to function as the Chief political executive.

During H.D. Deve Gowda's Prime Ministership, the Election Commission finalised and declared the election Schedule without even informing the Prime Minister. Another feature of this scenario is that the policy decisions-declarations of the Prime Minister are not implemented. The Prime Minister from the ramparts of Red Fort on 15th August 1996 announced the grant of Statehood to Uttarakhand which was not fulfilled. Another interesting occasion was the introduction of women's reservation bill to which the United Front had apparently agreed but in the Parliament one of the very important leaders of the UF embarrassed the Prime Minister by opposing the bill. The Prime Minister chose to remain neutral when the Bihar Chief Minister refused to resign in the Fodder Scam. This lack of initiative on his part irritated even the constituents of the United Front. The CPI, a constituent of the UF, leader A.B. Bardhan said, "It is not enough to say that the Prime Minister is not a policeman or that if he were in Laloo's shoes, he would have quit. He is the head of the government, whose job it is to investigate and punish wrongdoers ... the government is not run on statements of high principles." In short we can say in such a system of United Front coalition, the Prime Minister is not even the first among equals where he is either neutral in major political issues or he is not taken seriously by his own cabinet and the bureaucracy. The BJP led 17 party alliance formed in 1998 proved to be no better. Except for explosion of nuclear devices, the Vajpayee Government had no achievement. The coalition partners were engaged in internal bickerings and the survival of a Government was always at stake. Obviously the position of the Prime Minister was very weak.

In April 1999, the Vajpayee Government was defeated in the vote of confidence and later on the twelfth Lok Sabha was dissolved which had the distinction of having the shortest term of just 412 days (from March 1, 1998 to April 26, 1999). Subsequent to the elections to the thirteenth Lok Sabha, the National Democratic Alliance (NDA) which was a coalition of twenty four parties came into power under the Prime Ministership of Atal Behari Vajpayee. The Alliance was to work under the Common Agenda of Governance which was the program of action for the NDA Government. Prime Minister Vajpayee's position seemed to be very weak where he was reduced to a mere coordinator and conciliator of various constituents of the Alliance. He had no discretion in selecting and dropping his colleagues, belonging to his coalition partners, in his ministry. Prime Minister could do nothing when Power Minister Suresh Prabhu had to resign from the Cabinet because his party (Shiv Sena) Supremo Bal Thackeray 'ordered' him to do so as he had differences with him. Prabhu had the image of an honest and efficient Minister and the Prime Minister liked him but was helpless because the coalition members decide their own representation and not the Prime Minister whose job, under the circumstances, was nothing but to forward the resignation to the President for acceptance. As per the wishes of Shiv Sena Chief, Prabhu was replaced by Anant Geeta who happened to be the State Minister in Finance. Geeta's place went to another Sena MP Anandrao V. Adsul. Vajpayee appointed L.K. Advani, as the Deputy Prime Minister. But then, the very creation of the office of Deputy Prime Ministership showed the weakness of the Prime Minister. It was also alleged that Advani was heading a parallel power structure and the Prime Minister was not taking any decision without consulting Advani. There were also reports of the illness of the Prime Minister. Sonia Gandhi, the leader of the opposition commented that the Vajpayee government had two Chiefs. (*Ek sarkar mein do-do- sardar*) Though Vajpayee could retain Narendra Modi as Chief Minister, he really had a tough time over his retention as many NDA partners were demanding his removal over his allegedly biased role in the Gujarat carnage. There were also differences in the Cabinet over the disinvestment policy and the Cabinet Committee for Disinvestment had to postpone the decision to privatize Hindustan Petroleum Corporation Limited (HPCL) and

Bharat Petroleum Corporation Limited (BPCL) for three months. Though Vajpayee seemed to be better positioned than Gowda and Gujral, the compulsions of the coalition system would always deny him the position which any incumbent to his office would love to have even if he had no problem from his own party.

Similarly the coalition government led by Dr. Manmohan Singh also had the inherent weaknesses. A BJP leader pointed out that UPA Government had a PM (Manmohan Singh), SPM (Super PM—Sonia Gandhi), CPM and UPM (Ultra PM—Laloo Prasad Yadav). In the history of UPA coalition, one can find many instances when UPA chairperson Sonia Gandhi seemed to be more important than the Prime Minister. This can be viewed from the fact that many times she was in the forefront when the UPA government was praised or criticised or addressed for redressal of grievances. Gujarat Chief Minister Narendra Modi termed her as anti-Gujarat person and asked her to supply gas for a power project in the State 'at least' to fulfil her husband's wish. The CPI (M) asked her to direct the Andhra Pradesh Government to stop the regularisation of illegally occupied lands. The leftist constituents of the UPA questioned the FDI policy. They felt that the privatisation policy was not good for the nation particularly when state-owned Banks, oil and other major companies like NTPC were making profits. Under the leftist parties pressure, the Government had to review its earlier decisions and retract them. In November 5, 2004, the Government decided to raise the LPG prices by one-time hike of Rs. 20 and Rs. 5 per month till the entire subsidy of Rs. 158 per cylinder was wiped out. The leftist objected and UPA Left-Coordination Committee met on November 24 and decided to roll back partially the decision. There was open conflict-allegation and counter allegations between the ministers of the two constituents, Laloo Prasad Yadav of RJD and Ram Vilas Paswan of Lok Jan Shakti. There were open differences between the Prime Minister and Railway Minister regarding the role of Election Commission.

A sort of history was repeated when an otherwise competent Union Minister of IT and Communication Dayanidhi Maran (from DMK) had to quit after the DMK's 148 member Administrative Committee in deference to the wishes of DMK supremo Karunanidhi passed a resolution withdrawing him from the Union Cabinet for "violating party discipline" and tarnishing the party's image. Dayanidhi Maran's place was given to A. Raja already a DMK Union Minister of Environment in the Manmohan Singh coalition ministry. Another DMK nominee, Minister of State for Home S Regupathy, was moved to the Environment Ministry. In the entire drama, the Prime Minister

Manmohan Singh was as helpless as Vajpayee was in the case of replacement of Suresh Prabhu by Anant Geeta as per the wishes of Shiv Sena supremo Bal Thackeray.

The rift among the various constituents of the UPA (United People's Alliance) further widened. The BSP of Mayawati withdrew support from the coalition government. The difference between the leftist constituents and the congress also widened with the passage of time. The Indo-US nuclear deal remained under the docks for want of leftist support that have been highly critical of the deal. The phenomenal increase in the prices of petrol, diesel and cooking gas by the central government and the subsequent price rise, soaring inflation rate and in fact the entire economic policy of Manmohan Singh government were very important issues in which the left censored the government in public. The leftist blamed the Manmohan Singh government for inflation. The CPI (M) Polit Bureau in a statement said, "The government had refused to take the measures suggested by the Left such as strengthening and universalizing the public distribution system and banning forward trading in essential commodities. Nor the government was willing to do away with the iniquitous taxation structure and the import parity pricing of the petroleum products. The statement further pointed out, "the government refuses to tax the windfall profits of private refineries such as the Reliance Industries which made a profit of Rs. 10,372 in 2007-08. Even in the US, to whom our rulers look up to, the concept of taxing windfall profits is accepted". The RSP, another constituent of the coalition demanded from Sonia Gandhi, UPA Chairperson and Congress President to seek resignation of Manmohan Singh and the Finance Minister P. Chidambaram as they failed in controlling the price rise. The CPI leader and the general secretary of the All India Trade Union Congress Gurudas Das Gupta termed the Finance minister as inflation personified and declared that the trade unions have called for a general strike across the country on August 20, 2008. The left made it very clear that the Government could not escape its responsibility by simply stating that it was a global inflation. Regarding the Indo-US nuclear deal, the CPI (M) refuted the Prime Minister's claim that the deal in India' s interest as it provides India's growing energy requirements. The CPI (M) pointed out that the nuclear deal' is not about India's energy security. Energy security lies in using indigenous energy resources such as coal and ensuring our future energy supplies from Iran and other countries in west and central Asia'. It further said, "Mythical energy claims are being made in order to promote a bad nuclear deal. Energy is just a cover. The real intent is India-US strategic ties". The party did not appreciate the Government's efforts with regard to the supply of natural gas from Iran. The relation between the left and the congress especially on Indo-nuclear agreement became so tense that the primeminister felt that the left was more critical of him that the opposition BJP. He asked one of the left leaders, "Are you allies or the opposition?"

Role of Prime Minister—Some Observations

The Prime Minister's position depends upon a variety of factors. If he is a votecatcher for his party and is able to lead successfully in elections, he acquires a charisma of his own and becomes very dominant. But if he does not command that charisma, he becomes first among equals. If there is a coalition like the United Front experiments of 1996 and 1997, he is less than the first among the equals. In first two situations, he is the chief political executive of the country, in the third situation he loses that position.

The role of the Prime Minister is highly dependent upon the personality factor. Nehru's position as the powerful Prime Minister emerged due to his personal charisma and his popular appeal which made him the unquestioned leader of the Congress Party after Patel's death. He had a vision of India and as such he became a hope for the masses in their upliftment from social and economic evils. He was also an international visionary. He emerged as a crusader for peace in international conflicts. His role in the international arena further strengthened his position within the country. But the most important aspect of Nehru's personality was his projection as a unifying force in the country. He projected himself as above conflicts, a neutral man who could arbitrate among the conflicting forces. He accommodated the left and the right and had an appeal in all the sections of the population irrespective of caste, communal or other divisive considerations. It was this aspect of his personality which ensured the smooth transition from the British rule to the native rule. When he died in 1964, he left a stable India with a strong democratic system.

After Nehru, took over Shastri who was a weak Prime Minister, and there was the emergence of collective leadership and the politics of consensus. However during the Indo-Pak war of 1965, he showed his excellence as a remarkable statesman and was in the process of acquiring charisma which might have given him the same position as Nehru enjoyed. His death deprived the office of Prime Minister in regaining the glory and charisma of Nehru era. The politics of consensus and collective leadership continued during the initial era of

Mrs. Indira Gandhi. However she witnessed the downfall of Congress dominance and was not the unquestioned leader of the Congress Party. After 1971, particularly after the Indo-Pak war, she became extremely popular and powerful. Not only she led the nation successfully in the war over Bangladesh, in economic front also India became self sufficient in food grains due to Green Revolution. However during her regime, India also witnessed lot of manipulative politics which resulted in the emergency of 1975-77. During emergency many excesses were committed and democracy was derailed. The people of India reacted sharply and her party not only lost the power, she herself lost her seat in the Parliament. The elections of 1977, proved that Indian democracy had matured and people will reject a Prime Minister who crosses the limits. But there is no doubt that during Mrs. Gandhi's regime all powers were concentrated at the Centre and her PMO emerged as a powerful institution as a means of over centralisation. Her ministers were her yesmen. Even in State politics, she was dominating. When she came back to power in 1980, the same tendencies continued to remain dominant in the Indian political system.

Rajiv Gandhi's working as a Prime Minister was the continuity of Indira Gandhi's political style. The Prime Minister and his PMO directed the entire system. He had significant differences with the President and in his presence his party men humiliated the Vice-President in Rajya Sabha. He even made a wrong statement in the Parliament that he was giving all the informations to the President as required by the Constitution. He was also accused of corruption. Rajiv Gandhi started his career as a charismatic personality but soon he lost his charisma and was dethroned by the people.

In 1992, P.V. Narasimha Rao, became the PM of India. He used to remain silent on important issues. However during his tenure, the PMO remained most powerful institution. During his tenure Indian economy also embarked upon a process of liberalisation. After him we had the Prime Ministers H.D. Deve Gowda and I.K. Gujral who did not act like the Chief Political Executive. The problem is that there has been a vacuum in India with regard to national leadership. Chandra Shekhar, V.P. Singh, H.D. Deve Gowda and I.K. Gujral could not become national leaders with a mass following.

With the coalition system gradually gaining maturity, the positions of Vajpayee and Manmohan Singh improved to some extent. But the very nature of their leadership denied them the dominance that a Prime Minister enjoys in the prime ministerial form of government.

The absence of a charismatic leadership and the rise of coalition system of government at the centre have led to the decline of the office of Prime Minister.

References

Fadia, B.L., *Indian Government and Politics,* 1996, Agra, Sahitya Bhawan Publishers.

Kashyap Subash, *History of the Parliament of India* Vol. 2, 1995, New Delhi, Shipra Publications.

Khare Harish, *PM as the Chief Political Executive,* Indian Express, January 29, 1997.

Malhotra G.C. (Ed.), *Fifty Years of Indian Parliament,* 2002, New Delhi, Lok Sabha Secretariat.

Pandit H.N., *The PM's President,* 1974, New Delhi, S. Chand & Co.

Siwach, J.R., *Indian Government and Politics,* 1990, New Delhi, Sterling Publishers Pvt. Ltd.

Thakur Ramesh, *The Government and Politics of India,* 1995, London, MacMillan Press Ltd..

The Week Magazine, July 28, 2002.

CHAPTER XII

The Supreme Court of India

The Supreme Court of India is at the apex of the Indian judiciary. It works under the legal arrangement as provided in the Constitution of India. The Supreme Court is the guardian of the Constitution and as such it has a double role to play in the Indian political system. First, it is the custodian of people's fundamental and other legal rights. This enables the Supreme Court to protect individuals from legislative and executive excesses and thereby protecting, preserving and developing the democratic system becomes its responsibility. Second, it has to maintain correct constitutional balance between the Union and the States. The Constitution has fixed the functions and powers of the Union as well as the States and it is the duty of the Supreme Court to guard the division of powers; the Union should not usurp the powers assigned to States and vice versa. The Supreme Court has a dynamic role which it accomplishes by interpreting and re-interpreting the Constitution. The people of India live under a Constitution, but the Constitution is, what the Supreme Court says.

Organisation of the Supreme Court

Composition

The Supreme Court consists of one Chief Justice and 25 judges. When the Constitution was adopted, it was provided that it should consist of not more than seven judges. The Parliament has the power to raise the number of judges of the Supreme Court. In 1960, it accordingly raised the number of judges to 13, in 1977 to 17 and in 1986 to 25.

Qualifications to become a Judge in Supreme Court

The Constitution provides following qualifications for a person to be eligible to become a judge of the Supreme Court: (i) He/She must be a citizen of India; (ii) He/She should have the experience of at least five years of being a Judge in High Court in India. These five years may be in a single High Court or of two or more High Courts in succession; or (iii) He/She should be an advocate with at least ten years of practice. These ten years should be in succession in a single High Court or two or more High Courts; or (iv) In the opinion of the President, he/she is an eminent jurist. This provision enables the President to get the benefit of the talents of distinguished non-practising lawyers for the Supreme Court.

Appointment of Judges

The Judges of the Supreme Court are appointed by the President by warrant under his hand and seal. Before appointing a person as a judge the President: (i) must always consult the Chief Justice of India; and (ii) he may consult such judges of the Supreme Court and High Courts as he may deem necessary.

In case of Chief Justice of India, the Constitution does not specify the method of appointment. However, a convention has developed according to which the seniormost Judge of the Supreme Court is appointed as Chief Justice. This convention was broken in a few cases. After the retirement of Chief Justice S.M. Sikri in 1973, Justice A.N. Ray was appointed the Chief Justice superseding three Judges—Justices J.M. Shelat, A.N. Grover and K.S. Hegde. All the three justices resigned in protest. Again, when Chief Justice A.N. Ray retired, Justice M.H. Beg was appointed as Chief Justice superseding Justice H.R. Khanna, who also resigned in protest. But the practice of appointing the seniormost Judge as Chief Justice was resumed after the retirement of Chief Justice M.H. Beg when the seniormost Judge, Justice Y.V. Chandrachud was appointed the Chief Justice and the convention has been followed till date.

Tenure

The Chief Justice and other judges of the Supreme Court continue in their offices till the age of 65 years upon which they retire. After retirement they cannot practice in any Court in India.

Removal

The removal of Chief Justice and other judges of Supreme Court can take place in two ways: (i) He/She may resign his office by writing under his hand addressed to the President of India; or (ii) He/She may be removed by impeachment.

A judge of the Supreme Court can be removed by an order of the President on grounds of proven misbehaviour or incapacity. But the President will issue such an order only when the Parliament present him an address. The address is to be passed by both the Houses of the Parliament with a special majority i.e. a majority of total membership of the House and two-thirds majority of members present and voting. Thus the removal of a judge from office is a very difficult process and no judge has been removed till date. The impeachment process was started against Justice V. Ramaswami on charges of financial irregularities committed by him during his tenure as Chief Justice of Punjab and Haryana High Court. However, it could not be passed for want of required majority support. The difficult process of removal of a judge has been included in the Constitution, so as to ensure the security of tenure so that they may be able to act freely, impartially and without any fear.

Oath: The Chief Justice and other judges take an oath or affirmation before the President of India, which is as follows:

"I, A.B. having been appointed Chief Justice (or a Judge) of the Supreme Court of India do swear in the name of God/solemnly affirm that I will bear true faith and allegiance to the Constitution of India as by law established, that I will uphold the sovereignty and integrity of India, that I will duly and faithfully and to the best of my ability, knowledge and judgement perform the duties of my office without fear or favour, affection or ill-will and that I will uphold the Constitution and the laws."

Independence of the Supreme Court

The democratic system demands an independent and impartial judiciary and our Constitution provides for the same. The following conditions in India ensure an independent and impartial Supreme Court:

(i) The judges are appointed by the President of India. However, he does not enjoy absolute discretion here. The judges are appointed after due consultation with the Chief Justice of India. In the case of appointment of Chief Justice, the President must consult such judges of the Supreme Court and High Courts as he may deem necessary. We have the convention of seniormost judge being appointed as the Chief Justice. Whenever it was broken, there was a big protest from all the sections of the people, with the result that now it has come to stay.

(ii) The judges of the Supreme Court enjoy the security of tenure. Their removal on the grounds of proven misbehaviour or incapacity is very difficult.

(iii) During their tenure as Judges of the Supreme Court and after their retirement, the Judges cannot practise in India.
(iv) The Judges also enjoy the security of service conditions. Their salaries have been fixed by the Constitution. Their privileges, rights and allowances cannot be altered to their disadvantage.
(v) The salaries, allowances and pensions of the Judges and the administrative expenses of the Supreme Court are charged on Consolidated Fund of India which are not subject to the vote of the Parliament.
(vi) Only during Financial Emergency, the salaries and allowances of judges can be reduced.
(vii) The Supreme Court has the authority to recruit its own staff and frame rules regarding conditions of service.
(viii) The Constitution debars the Parliament and the State legislatures from discussing the conduct of any judge of the Supreme Court in the discharge of his duties. In such case the Supreme Court can punish the offender as per its contempt power.
(ix) The Supreme Court has to give its judgement in open Court.
(x) In case of majority judgement, a judge can give his dissenting judgement or opinion.

Quorum

In case of a substantial question of a law related to the interpretation of the Constitution and *Article 143* which provides the President's reference (See the powers and functions of Supreme Court in this Chapter), the quorum or minimum number of judges to hear the case is Five. For the rest of the cases, there is no fixed quorum by the Constitution. The Supreme Court, with the approval of the President, makes rules for generally regulating the practice and procedure of the Court. In some cases, there may even be a single-judge bench to hear and deliver judgement.

Seat of the Supreme Court

The seat of the Supreme Court is in Delhi. However, the Supreme Court may sit at any other place. This is to be decided by the Chief Justice of India with the approval of the President.

Powers and Functions of the Supreme Court

The Supreme Court of India has a very wide range of powers or jurisdiction. They are mainly three:

(i) Original Jurisdiction.
(ii) Appellate Jurisdiction.
(iii) Advisory Jurisdiction.

Original Jurisdiction

Original Jurisdiction means the exclusive powers of the Supreme Court. Only Supreme Court can hear and decide disputes (i) between the Union Government and one or more State; (ii) between the Union Government and any State or States on one side and one or more States on the other; (iii) between two or more States. However, Parliament may by law exclude the jurisdiction of Supreme Court in disputes between States with respect to use, distribution or control of waters of any inter-State river or river valley. In such cases different modes of adjudication may be prescribed. Further (a) matters referred to the Finance Commission; and (b) adjustments of certain expenses between the Union and States are also outside the purview of Original Jurisdiction of Supreme Court.

Along with the High Court, the Supreme Court also has the original jurisdiction in case of violation of fundamental rights under *Article 32*. This means a person whose fundamental right has been violated, may approach Supreme Court or High Court.

Appellate Jurisdiction

Under Appellate Jurisdiction of the Supreme Court comes an appeal against any judgement, decree or final order of any High Court in India. Such appeal can be made in either of the two conditions.

(a) with certificate from the High Court.
(b) without certificate from the High Court.

(a) *With Certificate from the High Court:* When the High Court in its decision gives a certificate that the concerned case involves a substantial question of law related to the interpretation of the Constitution, any party in such case may appeal to the Supreme Court on the ground that the case has been wrongly decided.

(b) *Without Certificate from High Court:* Sometimes, the High Court may not grant such a certificate. In such case the Supreme Court, if it feels that the case involves a question of law as to the interpretation of the Constitution, may take up the case.

Three kinds of appeals can be made in the Supreme Court:

(A) Constitutional
(B) Civil
(C) Criminal

(A) *Constitutional Appeals:* The Supreme Court has a final say, so far as the interpretation of the Constitution is concerned. While deciding a case if the High Court certifies that the particular case involves a substantial question of law as to the interpretation of this Constitution, then the Supreme Court can take up such a case for consideration and final verdict. This is a very comprehensive jurisdiction of the Supreme Court which includes civil, criminal or other proceedings of the High Court involving interpretation of the constitution.

(B) *Civil:* Before the 13th Constitutional Amendment only civil cases in which dispute is of atleast Rs 20,000 monetary value could be taken for appeal by the Supreme Court. The 13th Constitutional Amendment has removed the conditions of Rs 20,000, which means that irrespective of the monetary value any civil case can be contested in the Supreme Court against the decision of the High Court. However, there are ten conditions for such an appeal, which should be given in a certificate by the High Court while delivering the judgement:

(i) The case involves a substantial question of law, and (ii) in the opinion of the High Court the said question needs to be decided by the Supreme Court.

(C) *Criminal:* The Supreme Court also has jurisdiction with regard to criminal cases. There are two modes by which the High Court's judgement can be brought before the Supreme Court as an appeal.

(i) With certificate.

(ii) Without certificate.

(i) *With Certificate:* While delivering its judgement, final order or sentence, the High Court may certify that the case involves the interpretation of the Constitution, then the case can be taken by the Supreme Court as an appeal.

(ii) *Without Certificate:* Supreme Court can take up a case as appeal against the judgement, final order or sentence of the High Court in the following conditions:

(a) If the case had come up before the High Court as an appeal in which the accused person had been acquitted and the High Court had reversed the judgement and sentenced the person to death. For example the Sessions Judge acquits a person but the Government makes an appeal against the judgement to the High Court and the High Court sets aside the order of acquittal and sentences the accused to death. Such a case is fit for the Supreme Court to be taken up as an appeal.

(b) If the High Court has withdrawn for trial before itself any case from any Court subordinate to its authority and has in such trial convicted the accused person and sentenced him to death. In such a case an appeal can be made against the decision of the High Court.

Advisory Jurisdiction

Normally the Supreme Court gives its verdict when a dispute comes before it. However, the Constitution also vests the Supreme Court with advisory jurisdiction under *Article 143.* Under *Article 143,* the President can consult the Supreme Court. If the President feels that a question of law or fact has arisen which is of public importance and it is necessary to obtain the opinion of the Supreme Court, he may refer the question to the Supreme Court for consideration. In such case the Supreme Court, after such hearing as it thinks fit, gives its opinion to the President. But the Supreme Court may decline to give its opinion to the President.

There have been many occasions when the President has sought the opinion of the Supreme Court. For example, the cases of Kerala Education Bill, 1957 and the Special Courts Bill 1978. In both the cases, the President asked the Supreme Court whether the bills or any of their provisions would be Constitutionally invalid or not. In 1974, the President asked the Supreme Court that whether it is possible to hold Presidential elections when a State Assembly is dissolved. The Supreme Court advice was in the affirmative. Likewise, an advisory opinion was sought in the context of Keshav Singh Case (1964) and the opinion of the Apex Court was that parliamentary privileges could not override a fundamental right under *Article 21* i.e. right to life and personal liberty. For the first time in Ram Janambhoomi case, the Supreme Court declined to give its advisory opinion. This is very close to U.S. Supreme Court which from the very beginning had refused to give any advisory opinion.

Other Functions

Besides the above, the Supreme Court has the following powers:

(a) *A Court of Record:* The Supreme Court is a Court of record. According to Dr. Ambedkar, "A Court of record is a Court the records of which are admitted to be of evidentiary value and they are not to be questioned when they are produced before any Court." This means that the decisions of the Supreme Court become laws and can be cited in similar cases. In case its verdict is questioned, the Supreme Court has the power to punish the concerned person or persons for contempt of court.

(b) *Special Leave to Appeal:* The Supreme Court can grant special leave to appeal from any judgement, decree, determination, sentence or order in any cause or matter passed or made by any Court or tribunal in India. This means that any decision of any Court or tribunal can be challenged before the Supreme Court and it is in the discretion of the Supreme Court to hear such appeal. However, the Supreme Court cannot grant special leave against the decisions of Military Court or Tribunal.

(c) *Review of its Judgements or Orders:* While the decisions of the Supreme Court cannot be challenged in any Court of law in India, the Supreme Court on its own, can review its earlier judgements. This means that the Supreme Court is not bound by its judgement. In future if a situation arises where there are sufficient reasons to review its earlier verdicts, the Supreme Court may do so. In 1955, while reversing its earlier decision, Supreme Court declared, "There is nothing in the Indian Constitution which prevents the Supreme Court from departing from a previous decision of it, if it is convinced of its error and its baneful effect on the general interests of the public."

(d) *Transfer of Certain Cases from the High Court:* In case, cases of similar nature involving the same questions of law are pending before Supreme Court and one or more High Courts or before two or more High Courts, the Supreme Court can withdraw all such cases to itself and dispose of them. This power of the Supreme Court can be used when (i) the Supreme Court on its own is satisfied; or (ii) on an application from the Attorney General of India; or (iii) by party to any such case.

(e) *Ancillary powers of Supreme Court:* The Constitution authorises the Parliament to confer such supplementary powers on the Supreme Court as may appear necessary to enable it to perform effectively its functions under the Constitution.

Thus the Supreme Court of India has very wide powers and functions. In fact it will not be an exaggeration to say that the Indian Supreme Court is the most powerful Court in the world. Even the U.S. Supreme Court does not enjoy such a wide jurisdiction as the Indian Supreme Court does. The Indian Supreme Court has the power of judicial review and it has further increased its authority by Judicial activism.

Power of Judicial Review

The power of judicial review is the power of the judiciary to review the legislative enactments and executive actions and to declare them null and void if found repugnant to the provisions of the Constitution. Thus the concept of judicial review works in a written Constitution where the powers of different organs of the government are clearly defined and they are expected to work within their respective jurisdiction only. If they transgress their authority, the doctrine of judicial review is applied by the Court to check them and maintain the balance enshrined in the Constitution. According to Gosnell, "By judicial review we mean the authority belonging to the Courts to declare acts of the legislative branch of no effect when, in the opinion of the judges, such acts are inconsistent with the requirements of the Constitution." M.V. Pylee writes, "The essence of judicial review is the competence of a Court of law to declare the Constitutionality or otherwise of a legislative enactment."

The doctrine of judicial review originated in the United States of America where it was declared by the Chief Justice of the Supreme Court, John Marshall in 1803, in Marbury V. Madison case. Marshall said, "It is emphatically, the province and duty of the judicial department, to say what the law is; those who apply the rule to particular cases, must of necessity expound and interpret that rule. If two laws conflict with each other, the Courts must decide on the operation of each. So if a law be in opposition to the Constitution; if both the law and the Constitution, apply to a particular case, so that the Court must either decide that case conforming to law disregarding the Constitution or vice versa. Court must determine which of these conflicting rules govern the case; this is of the very essence of the judicial duty. If then, the Courts are to regard the Constitution and the Constitution is superior to any ordinary act of the Legislature, the Constitution, and not such ordinary act, must govern the case to which they both apply."

The Indian position, with regard to judicial review is closer to that of the American Constitution. In 1950, Justice Mukherjee said, "The Constitution of India is a written Constitution and though it has adopted many of the principles of the Parliamentary system, it has not accepted the English doctrine of the absolute supremacy of the Parliament in matters of legislation. In this respect, it has followed the American Constitution and other systems modelled on it ... In India it is the Constitution that is supreme and Parliament as well as State Legislatures must not only act within the limits of their respective legislative spheres as demarcated in the three lists occurring in the Schedule VII of the Constitution, but Part III of the Constitution guarantees to the citizens certain fundamental rights which the legislative authority can on no account transgress. A statute or law to be valid, must, in all cases be in conformity with the Constitutional requirements and it is for the judiciary to decide whether any enactment is unconstitutional or not."

Prof. M.P. Singh in his work *V.N. Shukla's Constitution of India* says that "Judicial review in India is based on the assumption that the Constitution is the supreme law of the land, and all governmental organs, which owe their origin to the Constitution and derive their powers from its provisions, must function within the framework of the Constitution, and must not do anything which is inconsistent with the provisions of the Constitution."

However, the Indian Constitution does not, in so many words, assign the power of judicial review to the judiciary. It is implicit in *Articles 13, 32* and *226*. *Article 13 (1)* says that "All laws in force in the territory of India immediately before the commencement of this Constitution, in so far as they are inconsistent with the provisions of this Part (Part III i.e. Chapter on Fundamental Rights), shall, to the extent of such inconsistency, be void." *Article 13(2)* clearly prohibits the State from making any law which takes away or abridges the fundamental rights and any law which does so, will be void to that extent. Naturally it is the Court which will decide whether a law is inconsistent with the fundamental rights or not. *Articles 32* and *226* deals with the powers of Supreme Court and High Courts respectively with regard to the protection of fundamental rights by issuing various kind of writs. Further, there are other *Articles 131-136, 143, 145, 246, 251, 254* and *372* from which power of judicial review is also derived. Apart from these Articles, the power of judicial review is derived from the position of Supreme Court as the guardian of the Constitution. As such, it has the final say in the interpretation of the Constitution and by such interpretation, the Supreme Court has extended its power of judicial review to almost all the provisions of the Constitution.

Principles of Judicial Review

Over the years the Supreme Court has developed certain principles with regard to its power of judicial review, which are as follows:

(i) The Court does not, on its own, take up the validity of a law. It hears the Constitutionality of a law only when it is approached by a person.

(ii) The person who approaches the Court must have been affected by the law which he is questioning. This means that the Court will not hear an objection as to the Constitutionality of a law by a person whose rights are not affected by it.

(iii) But in case of "Public Interest Litigation" (PIL) any person or organisation can approach the Court on behalf of person or persons whose rights have been affected but who because of poverty and deprivation are neither aware of their rights nor have the capacity to approach the Court. In such case the Court sets aside the usual formality of filing a writ petition. There have been cases when a telegram or even a letter has been accepted by the Court.

(iv) The validity of a law should be challenged on actual grounds. It should not be hypothetical. The only exception to this is *Article 143* which deals with the advisory jurisdiction of the Supreme Court.

(v) The Court will entertain a challenge to Constitutional validity of a law only when the question involved in the law is substantial.

(vi) The Constitutionality of a law is to be decided in the last resort, which means whenever a law is challenged the Court will examine the material facts and ascertain whether they really attract the provisions of the challenged law. If they do so, then only the constitutional validity of the said law will be examined and decided.

(vii) There shall be a presumption in favour of constitutionality of legislation. This means that the Court takes it for granted that a law passed by the legislature is valid. It is the burden of the person or persons challenging the law to prove that the said law is unconstitutional.

(viii) Normally the Court does not invalidate the entire act. Only such provisions of a law which are unconstitutional are declared so. This is called the doctrine of severability. The invalid parts of a law are severed from the other parts of the law which are not open to challenge and the invalid part or parts are declared invalid. However, the Court can also declare the entire law as invalid.

(ix) The Court does not entertain political controversies normally. It is concerned with legal aspects alone. However, it is the Court that will decide whether an issue is political or not.

(x) The Court is not bound by its earlier decision. It may reverse them.

(xi) Judicial review is the part of basic structure of the Constitution which cannot be taken away even by an constitutional amendment.

Judicial Review: Extent and Limitations

Supreme Court's power of judicial review extends to the (i) laws passed by the Parliament and State legislatures; (ii) the executive action and orders of the Union and the States; (iii) the decisions of public sector organisations and other bodies financed partly or wholly by the government; and (iv) the constitutional amendments. Here it is to be noted that probably the Indian Supreme Court is the only court in the world which exercises the power to determine the constitutional validity of a Constitutional Amendments.

In certain cases, the Constitution clearly puts limitations on the Supreme Court's power of judicial review. For example the Directive Principles of State Policy are non-justiciable. *Article 74* prohibits the Court from inquiring into the question whether any, and if so what, advice was tendered by Ministers to the President ... *Article 77(2)* says that "the validity of an order or instrument" authenticated by the President "shall not be called in question on the ground that it is not an order or instrument made or executed by the President." Similar restrictions have been imposed in case of State executive vide *Articles 163* and *166*. The Court is also prohibited from inquiring into proceedings of the Parliament and State legislatures [*Articles 122(1)* and *212(1)*]. The Presiding Officers of Parliament and State legislatures are also immune from the jurisdiction of any Court [*Articles 122(2)* and *212(2)*]. The validity of any proceedings in Parliament or State legislature cannot be questioned on the ground of any alleged irregularity of procedure [*Articles 122(1)* and *212(1)*] in respect of the exercise of their powers. *Article 329(1) (a)* bars the interference of Court in laws relating to delimitation of constituencies or allotment of seats. *Article 329(b)* excludes the jurisdiction of the Courts to entertain any matter relating to election disputes. Elections can be challenged only in the manner laid down in law made by the appropriate legislature. *Article 105(2)* gives immunity to members of Parliament from Court proceedings for anything said or any vote given in Parliament. In case of anti-defection law incorporated in the Tenth Schedule to the Constitution the Court has no jurisdiction in respect of any matter connected with the disqualification of a member of a House. There are other articles also, purported to be limitations on judicial review. However, in such cases also the Supreme Court has been extending its power of judicial review, by adopting the method of judicial activism.

Working of Judicial Review in Indian Political System

The First Phase

In the initial years of 1950-67, the Supreme Court adopted the attitude of judicial restraint in which the Supreme Court gave a strict and literal interpretation of the Constitution. The nature and scope of judicial review was first examined by the Supreme Court in A.K. Gopalan case where it accepted the principle of Judicial subordination to legislative wisdom. The position of the judiciary was explained by Justice Das in this case, "In India the position is somewhere between the Courts in England and USA." He made the following observations in this case:

(i) The Parliament and State legislatures are supreme in their respective fields.

(ii) However, certain limitations have been imposed on the Parliament and State legislatures.

(iii) The Court will declare a law unconstitutional if these limitations are transgressed. The Court's supremacy is limited to this extent. It cannot go beyond this. Here the Court has no scope to play the role of the American Supreme Court. The American Constitution is based on due process of law where the legislature is subordinate to the judiciary which is not the case with the Indian Constitution.

(iv) The Constitution is Supreme. The Court must take the Constitution as it finds it even if it does not accord with its preconceived notions of what an ideal Constitution should be.

(v) The protection against legislative tyranny lies in a free and intelligent public opinion which must eventually assert itself.

(vi) The Court will not question the wisdom or policy or legislative authority in enacting the particular law, however harsh, unreasonable, archaic or odious the provisions of that law may be.

Chief Justice Kania also said, "It is difficult for any general principles to limit the omnipotence of sovereign legislative powers by judicial interposition, except in so far as the express words of a written Constitution give that authority. It is only in express provisions limiting legislative powers and controlling the temporary will of majority by a permanent and paramount law settled by the deliberate wisdom of the nation that one can find safe and solid grounds for authority of Courts of justice to declare void any legislative enactment. Any assumption of authority beyond this would be to place in the hands of judiciary powers too great and too infinite either for its own security or for the protection of private rights."

This position of judicial restraint in which the power of judicial review was curbed and gave supremacy to the Parliament was repeated in *Champakam Darairajan* and *Shankari Prasad* cases. The Supreme Court also accepted the power of Parliament with regard to amending the Constitution as supreme.

However in Bela Banerjee case the Supreme Court showed its activism by saying that the Parliament can acquire private property only after paying adequate compensation which meant just equivalent of the property acquired. In another cases the Court also ruled that compensation also be paid for any substantial deprivation of property. These rulings of the Supreme Court created a situation in which the Government could not go far in the field of land reforms to which it was committed. It also could not take over the sick mills for the benefits of the workers of those mills without paying full compensation. Therefore to remove the legal hurdles created by the Supreme Court's rulings, the Fourth Amendment Act was incorporated in the Constitution which explicitly declared that—

(a) State will not pay compensation in case of mere deprivation of property. This was to enable the State to take over the management of sick mills.

(b) The amount of compensation fixed by the Parliament can not be questioned in the Court of law on the basis of its inadequacy. In 1958, the Court modified its earlier stand and held that the directive principles of State policy were not superior to the Fundamental Rights of the citizens and the Government should implement the directive principles in a harmonious manner so that the fundamental rights are not taken away or abridged. In other cases also the Supreme Court held the same view but at the same time it exercised judicial restraint by suggesting that the Court will take into account the directive principles of State policy in determining the amendment of fundamental rights and it will try to give effect to both, the directive principles as well as the fundamental rights as per the doctrine of harmonious construction. In the famous Searchlight case the Supreme Court subordinated the freedom of expression and speech to the parliamentary privileges again on the basis of doctrine of harmonious construction.

But in *Keshav Singh* case the Supreme Court created a big controversy and widened its power of judicial review by holding the view that the parliamentary privileges are subjected to the fundamental rights and the Parliament and State legislatures are not supreme in regard to their contempt power. But in *Sajjan case* the Court accepted that the Parliament can amend the Constitution so as to take away the fundamental rights of the citizens.

Thus the first phase of judicial review saw the judicial restraint in which the Supreme Court adhered to the view that 'In interpretion the provisions of our Constitution we must go by the plain words used by the Constitution makers ..." In some cases it tried to assert itself and went beyond the above view. But on the whole it limited itself and exercised judicial restraint.

The Second Phase

The second phase unfolded with the *Golaknath* case which resulted in an open conflict between the judiciary and the legislature. The Parliament asserted its supremacy and the Supreme Court asserted its power of judicial review, which resulted in a series of constitutional amendments in which the Parliament treid to limit the power of judicial review. In the Emergency of 1975-77, the judiciary was made subservient to the legislature and the executive.

In *Golaknath case,* the Supreme Court gave an unprecedented judgement, which was clearly a case of judicial activism. It reversed its earlier judgements and declared that;

(i) The Parliament has no right to take away or abridge the fundamental rights.
(ii) It cannot even do so by the amendment of the Constitution.
(iii) Parliament may convene a Constituent Assembly which can only abridge or abrogate fundamental rights.
(iv) The First Amendment Act, 1951, the Fourth Amendment Act, 1955 and the 17th Amendment Act were invalid because they abridged the fundamental rights.

However, it introduced a new concept of prospective over-ruling which meant that the above mentioned amendments were valid but henceforth the Parliament, from the date of the decision of this judgement, will have no power to amend any of the provisions of the Constitution so as to take away or abridge fundamental rights. Another innovation of the Supreme Court was the idea of Constituent Assembly which the Parliament may convene by making use of residuary power of legislation and which can only abridge or abrogate fundamental rights.

Golaknath case was the first paramount assertion of judicial activism, in which the Supreme Court shed its earlier stand of judicial restraint. Naturally, it created a great controversy and criticism of the Supreme Court. But undeterred by controversy and criticism, the Supreme Court further held the nationalisation of 14 Banks and the President's order derecognising the Princes and abolishing their Privy Purses as unconstitutional. These judgements were criticised by the Parliament and the ruling elite as detrimental to the socio-economic progress of the country. Indira Gandhi, the then Prime Minister said that the Supreme Court was becoming a stumbling block in her efforts to remove poverty. She also talked about a "committed judiciary." The open confrontation between the Parliament and judiciary led to the mid-term poll of 1971, in which Indira Gandhi returned with a thumping majority. The 24th Constitutional Amendment was made to give the Parliament full powers to amend the Constitution including the provisions with regard to fundamental rights. Thus through the 24th Amendment the Parliament got its right to amend the Constitution back. 25th Amendment gave primacy to directive principles of State Policy *vis-a-vis* fundamental rights. Besides 26th and 29th Constitutional Amendment were also made. The 28th Constitutional Amendment Act ended the recognition granted to former rulers of Indian States and their privy purses were abolished. By 29th Constitutional Amendment Act, two Kerala Acts dealing with land reform were included in Ninth Schedule.

All these amendments i.e. 24th, 25th, 26th and 29th were challenged in the Supreme Court in the famous Keshvanand Bharti case which constitutes a watershed in the history judicial review. This is also an excellent example of judicial activism. In its judgement in *Keshvanand Bharti* case the Court held the following:

(i) The Court reversed its judgement given in *Golak Nath* case and declared that the Parliament had the right to amend the Constitution. Accordingly the 24th, 25th, 26th and 29th Constitutional Amendment Act were declared valid. However, a portion of 25th Constitutional Amendment containing the words "no law containing a declaration that it is for giving effect to such a policy" were declared invalid.

(ii) But the Parliament cannot amend or alter the basic structure of the Constitution or as Chief Justice Sikri explained that every provision of the Constitution can be amended provided the basic foundation and structure of the Constitution remains the same.

The Supreme Court by evolving the doctrine of basic structure of the Constitution limited the power of the Parliament to amend the Constitution. It was an innovation which widened the Court's power of judicial review to an unlimited extent. Thus, although the Supreme Court reversed the *Golak Nath* judgement but in fact it extended its jurisdiction even beyond the *Golak Nath* case judgement. In the post-*Keshvananda* scenario, the major parts of the Constitution have come into the ambit of basic structures of the Constitution which the Parliament cannot change.

Judicial Review During Emergency

During emergency, the authority of the judiciary was undermined and was made subservient to the legislature and executive. The reason of imposing the emergency was the decision of Allahabad High Court setting aside the election of Prime Minister Indira Gandhi to the Lok Sabha. The opposition demanded her resignation, instead she imposed emergency and put almost the entire opposition behind bars. The Thirty Ninth Amendment Act was also passed which put Prime Minister's election beyond challenge. The Supreme Court set aside the verdict of Allahabad High Court and declared Indira Gandhi election to Lok Sabha valid. However, it struck down the newly added *Article 329A(4)* which in fact directed the Supreme Court to hold that Indira Gandhi's election to the Lok Sabha was valid. During the emergency, the judges whose judgements were not liked by the executive were transferred or denied promotion or even reverted. Justice Seth of the Gujarat High Court was transferred to Orissa High Court. He challenged his transfer and the Supreme Court held that his transfer was invalid. The judgement was censored and not reported in newspapers. Similarly, the names of 16 judges who were transferred was subjected to censor. The fear psychosis generated by the emergency also effected the working of

Supreme Court in the famous Habeas Corpus case in which the people arrested or detained under preventive detention under MISA (Maintenance of Internal Security Act) could not get relief from the judiciary. The 42nd Constitutional Amendment Act was also passed which put new limitations on the judiciary.

Judicial Review after Emergency or the Third Phase

After the emergency, the 44th Constitutional Act was passed which restored the judiciary's position as it had existed before the emergency. In Minerva Mills case, the Supreme Court declared judicial review as part of the basic structure. In 1978, in *Menaka Gandhi* case, the Supreme Court held that right to travel was part and parcel of personal liberty enshrined in *Article 21* of the Constitution and no one can be deprived of his right to personal liberty except by due procedure established by law and the said procedure must be "reasonable, fair and just."

The 1980's saw the emergence of judicial activism as a powerful factor in Indian polity. The Supreme Court quashed the criminal proceedings against the children languishing in Kanpur Central Jail for more than two years without a trial. In the case of Francis Coralie, a British national who was arrested on a charge of smuggling under the COFEPOSA, was denied the right to meet her child aged 5 years who could meet her only once in a month under the rules. The Supreme Court declared that the restriction of one month in this case was unfair and the child be allowed to meet her mother at least once or twice in a week. In *Faridabad Stone Quarry* case or the *Bandhua Mukti Morcha Vs. Union of India* case, the workers were being denied basic facilities of life. The Supreme Court admitted a writ on the basis of a letter and directed the state (i) to provide the workers with clear and healthy drinking water; (ii) to depute a doctor alongwith a fully equipped medical ambulance once a week to the stone quarries; (iii) to provide facilities of primary education to the children of the workers; and (iv) the stone crushing machines were to be fitted with devices which could contain the dust so that the workers' health was protected. These directions were meant to protect the "basic human dignity of the worker." In the Asiad Project case, the Supreme Court ordered that casual workers be paid the minimum wages as per the Minimum Wages Act. In another case, a writ petition was filed by two professors on the basis of newspaper reports that the condition of abandoned women in a protected home in Agra was extremely obnoxious. The Supreme Court directed the district judge of Agra to investigate and report. On the basis of the judge's report, the Supreme Court gave the State the necessary directions to improve their condition. The list of such public interest litigations is long and the Supreme Court actively indulged in judicial activism. In 1993, the Supreme Court restricted the discretion of the President in appointing judges in Supreme Court and High Courts. It said that the President is bound by the advice of the Chief Justice in the appointment of judges. Thus, now we find that the Supreme Court is no longer exercising judicial restraint. But in fact, it has taken up judicial activism so much so that the year 1996, was hailed as the year of judicial activism.

Judicial Activism

(a) *What is Judicial Activism:* Normally the judiciary adjudicates. However, sometimes, it has to interfere in the legislative and executive fields and that has been called judicial activism. Judicial activism occurs due to non-activity of the other organs of the government and the Court compels them to discharge their duties according to the Constitution. According to H.L. Bhardwaj, former Law Minister, judicial activism "is actually a damage control exercise due to the failure of the Executive to discharge its functions. If the politicians and the bureaucrats do their work properly, there will be no need for the judiciary to intervene." Subash Kashyap says, "what has come to be called hyper activism of the judiciary draws its strength, relevance and legitimacy from the inactivity, incompetence, disregard of law and Constitution, criminal negligence, corruption, greed for power and money, utter indiscipline and lack of character and integrity among the leaders, ministers and administrators." To Nafees Ahmed, judicial activism "is that legal process by which relief is provided to the disadvantaged and aggrieved party."

Judicial activism is not a new phenomenon. It has occured in the past in India and elsewhere also. For example in USA, in 1857, in the Dred Scott case, the American Supreme Court declared slaves as the property of slave owners. This resulted in civil war in America. Again during 1935-36 the American Supreme Court struck down twelve New Deal Statutes aimed at the economic betterment of the society. However, these are the cases of negative judicial activism. Positively the American Supreme Court has declared racial segregation in all its forms unconstitutional and enhanced the Congress power to legislate against racial discrimination. In India also we have the examples of judicial activism in the past such as *Golak Nath case* and *Keshvanand Bharti case.* The present decade has witnessed almost a revolution in judicial activism.

The other extreme of judicial activism is not judicial inactivism but judicial restraint. In judicial restraint the Court follows the policy of judicial subordination to the legislative wisdom. But when the legislature becomes inactive, judicial activism takes over. Both the situations of judicial restraint and judicial activism is the part of judicial decision-making and as such both occur as a part and parcel of Court's power of judicial review. In judicial activism, the Court has devised new ways and tools in dealing with the case. It monitors the development of the case and gives necessary directions to the investigating agency. After the decision, the Supreme Court also sees to it that the decision is implemented for which reports are asked from the concerned authorities about the implementation, quarterly or the duration as fixed by the Court.

In India, judicial activism has taken place through (i) *suo moto* initiative by the Courts, there are instances when the Courts have taken up cases on their own on the basis of newspapers reports. (ii) However, most of the cases of judicial activism have occurred through Public Interest Litigation. In a Public Interest Litigation, any person or group can approach the Supreme Court and High Court for the redressal of grievance/grievances on behalf of the victim or victims who are incapable of approaching the court. Public Interest Litigations are also permitted in cases of public importance like environment and public health issues. Public Interest Litigation has been a novel feature of Indian judicial system which has given relief to millions of poor people. However, there is also a feeling that public interest litigations are being misused. In 1997, the Chief Justice A.M. Ahmadi expressed his concern over the indiscriminate use of PIL in all kinds of cases. He said, "Care has to be taken at all times to ensure that the discretionary jurisdiction is exercised on the basis of well defined and consecrated legal principles, and at no time during the course of the proceedings should an impression be given that the judge has yielded to spasmodic sentiments, or is carried away by emotions of bias." The Court has to ensure that the petitioner, who approaches the Court with PIL, is acting bonafide and not for personal gains, private profit, on political or other oblique considerations. The Court should not allow its process to be abused by politicians and others to delay legitimate administrative action or to gain a political objective. It is interesting to know that most of the scams and corruption cases including the JMM MP's bribery case were unearthed through Public Interest Litigations.

Besides, the Court resorts to judicial activism through the writs other than the PIL and its power of judicial review.

In short judicial activism means the following:

(i) Instead of judicial restraint, the Supreme Court and other lower Courts become activist.

(ii) It occurs mainly when the legislative and executive wing of the government fail to discharge their duties under the Constitution.

(iii) Much of judicial activism has taken place through PIL.

(iv) In judicial activism the Court monitors the development of the case during the trial period and gives necessary directions to investigating agencies.

(v) After the decision, the Court also monitors the implementation of the decision.

(vi) Through judicial activism, the Courts compels the authority to act.

(vii) Sometimes, it also directs the government regarding policies and also how to run the administration.

(viii) Judicial activism is not a new phenomenon. It has occurred earlier also.

(b) *Some Instances of Judicial Activism:* The judicial activism has been a technique to prevent legislative tardiness and executive discretion. Through various cases, like *Menaka Gandhi, Sunil Batra, Bandhua Mukti Morcha, Bihar undertrials, Punjab Police, Bombay Pavement Dwellers, Bihar Care Home, Francis Coralie cases,* it has shown its firm commitment to participatory justice, just standards of procedures, immediate access to justice and preventing arbitrary state action. Now let us see some more examples of judicial activism.

(i) *Health:* The Supreme Court declared in 1995, that health is the basic right of the people. By its decision, the doctors were brought under Consumer Law. In 1996, it decided that the hospitals and doctors, not admitting serious patients would be punished. The Supreme Court also ordered Delhi Government to clean Delhi and make it a "greener, cleaner place to live in." It approved an experimental scheme for distribution of polythene bags for garbage disposal to residents of selected localities. In 1996, Delhi witnessed dengue menace which killed many people. The Delhi High Court expressed its dissatisfaction with the arrangements in the government hospitals. It directed the Centre and the Delhi Government to increase the number of beds and medical staff in their casualty emergency wards of their hospitals so that not more than one patient suffering from dengue fever had to be accomodated in one bed. Earlier the High Court had taken a *suo motto* notice and issued notice to Delhi Government to explain government efforts in combating dengue menace. In another direction, the Delhi High Court, asked the Municipal Corporation of Delhi to take punitive action against private property owners in whose premises stagnant water, breeding medium for dengue mosquitoes, were found.

In 2001, the Supreme Court held that right of access to clean drinking water is fundamental to life and it is the duty of the state to provide drinking water to its citizens. In another case, the Supreme Court observed that smoking in public place was continuing despite the law. It instructed the state to take effective steps to ensure that smoking is prohibited in (a) auditoriums, (b) hospital buildings, (c) health institutions, (d) libraries, (e) court buildings and (f) public offices.

(ii) *Child Labour:* The judicial activism also covered the child labour. In organised sector according to Planning Commission estimates over 17 million children are working. But according to estimates from various non-government sources, the actual number of working children is between 44 to 100 million. Despite the various legislation banning employment of child workers, the system continues. In December 1996, the Supreme Court while disposing of a public interest litigation, directed setting up of a Child Labour Rehabilitation Worker Fund in which employers of child worker were asked to pay a compensation of Rs. 25,000 per child worker. Besides, every offending employer would pay Rs. 20,000 compensation for violating the Child Labour Act of 1986 of the apex court and suggested a number of measures to rehabilitate working children in a phased manner. In 2002, while monitoring the developments which were none the Supreme Court asked the Prime Minister and Finance Minister to finalise the welfare scheme.

(iii) *Environment:* In 1996, the Supreme Court ordered that 'no construction of any type shall be permitted now onwards within a radius of 5 kilometers of the Badhkal Lake and Suraj Kund (in Haryana). All open areas shall be converted into green belts.'

In an another landmark judgement the Supreme Court banned all non-forest activities-including saw mills, veneer or plywood mills and mining in the forest area. At the same time it also protected the workers from retrenchment or removal from service due to the closure order. The Union Parliament in 1980, had passed the Forest Conservation Act according to which all ongoing activities within any forest in any State, without the prior approval, should cease to function. However, this didnot happen. This order of Supreme Court was particularly important for north eastern States where more than 80 per cent of area is covered by the forests but deforestation was continuing at a very high level. The Supreme Court interim order declared, "There shall be a complete ban on the movement of cut-trees and timber from any of the seven north-eastern States to any other State of the country either by rail, road or waterways."

In another unprecedented move, the Supreme Court rescued a park in Delhi from being misused and encroached upon. The park was declared as the best park of the city by the Municipal Corporation of Delhi but now used for marriage and other purposes. The Court gave 60 days to MCD to restore the Park to its original state.

The Andhra Pradesh High Court held that the cremation of the Tamil Nadu Governor at Indira Park and of N.T. Rama Rao at Buddha Purnima Complex was illegal. It directed that further construction be suspended at these places and the areas be used for no other purpose except as parks. It ruled that no cremation can take place unless the said site was registered under the MCH as a burial ground. The Court also awarded exemplary costs against the State Government and the Municipal Corporation of Hyderabad (MCH), which were directed to pay Rs 5,000 to each of the 19 petitioners, who had filed the writ petition per day for every day of the hearing of the case.

In 1996, the Supreme Court ordered the owner of a stone-crushing factory at Jhargram, Midnapore to pay compensation to the next of kin of 16 workers who died of diseases contracted because of poor working conditions. Workers suffering from the diseases were also given compensation. It instructed the State Health Department to immediately send a medical team to the site and arrange for the treatment of the suffering from diseases. The state Government was also directed to inquire into the matter.

The Supreme Court has also initiated strict enforcement of Environmental laws leading to closure of a large number of industries. In Delhi 39,000 industries in residential areas were reallocated. It also monitored the reallocation with the objective to reduce pollution which jeopardized the right to life of citizens. In an another case the Supreme Court ordered that the Ridge area of Delhi, which is a forest area and called the lungs of the capital, where as a result of land grabbing the forest area was fast depleting, should be cleared of all encroachments and greenery restored. It criticised the Union Ministry's Land and Development office for its bad job over the years and passed a series of orders to Union and City governments to enforce the Ridge's status as a notified forest with more accountability. The Court ordered the confiscation of thousands of acres from temples, gurudwaras, school and others. The Ridge Management Board was directed to stand by to take over, securely fence and regreen the land. The supreme court also gave directives to reduce the vehicular pollution in Delhi, and thanks to its efforts, environment in Delhi has improved. The Supreme Court also stopped the mining of Dehradun Valley to stop the environmental degradation. In another case, the Court directed the cleaning of Nainital which it said is a beautiful butterfly but which is turning into an ugly caterpillar.

(iv) *Corruption:* The Judicial activism has been at its peak in exposing corruption. The Supreme Court slapped a fine of Rs 50 lakhs on the former Petroleum Minister Satish Sharma for the illegal and arbitrary allotment of 15 petrol pumps from discretionary quota. It was highly critical of Satish Sharma. It said, "He, in capacity as Minister doled out pumps which is the property of the government and therefore he is a trustee of public property. He has abused his office. We do not find any reason for not allowing an investigation against him." The Court cancelled the allotment of the said 15 petrol pumps. Similarly, former Housing and Urban Development Minister Sheila Kaul was ordered to pay Rs 60 lakhs as exemplary damages for her "arbitrary, malafide and unconstitutional" action in allotting 52 shops and stalls in prime locations in Delhi to her grandsons and close friends in 1995. In this case also, the allotments were cancelled by the Supreme Court.

The Supreme Court also monitored the various cases against the former Prime Minister P.V. Narasimha Rao i.e. Laku Bhai Pathak fraud case, JMM bribe case and others. (Rao was exonerated in all cases later) It also took strong action in Jain Hawala case and other corruption cases and "exercised jurisdiction with courage, creativity and circumspection giving proof of vision, vigilance and practical wisdom."

The Supreme Court also indicated that it intended to adjudicate in detail on a process within the existing legal framework to ensure immunity to Central Bureau of Investigation (CBI) from the influences of powerful personalities. It said, "We have to work out some argument that ensures the independence of this premier investigating agency from individual influences by making a thorough study of models in different parts of the world." The Patna High Court passed severe strictures on CBI Director for interfering in the multi-crore fodder scam investigation and trying to scuttle it, and restrained him from meddling in any manner in the investigation.

In 2003, the Supreme Court directed the CBI to file FIRs against former UP Chief Minister Mayawati and environment Minister Nasimmudin Siddique and six senior bureaucracts in the Rs. 175 crore Taj heritage corridor scandal. It asked the Centre and State Government to start departmental inquiries against the said bureaucracts which was to be completed within four months. In 2005, the Supreme Court ordered the CBI not to prosecute or arrest IAS officer in Haryana who had unearthed teacher's recruitment scam where instead of targeting the culprits, CBI was harassing the upright officer.

(v) *Political Front:* On the political front, the judiciary made the President's Rule under *Article 356* justiciable. In *Sunder Lal Patwa Vs. Union of India* case the Madhya Pradesh High Court declared the President's rule imposed in MP in the aftermath of Babri Masjid demolition as invalid and ordered the restoration of State Assembly and the Government. In *State of Rajasthan Vs. Union of India* the Supreme Court had held that a Proclamation under *Article 356* depended on the subjective satisfaction of the President and the Court would not interfere. However if the satisfaction of the President was malafide based on extraneous or irrelevant considerations or no satisfaction at all, it could interfere. In *S.R. Bommai case* the Court asserted that the question of majority support of the Government should be settled on the floor of the legislative Assembly. In 1996, the reimposition of President's rule in U.P. was declared *ultra vires* by the Allahabad High Court. In a landmark judgement, the Supreme Court ruled that tapping of a citizen's telephone is an invasion on his right to privacy guaranteed under *Articles 21* and *19(1)(a)* of the Constitution. It directed that telephone-tapping order shall be issued by Union Home Minister and Home Secretaries of the State Governments and this order, unless renewed, shall cease to have effect at the end of two months. The Supreme Court also issued notices to Union and State Governments to stop political interference in police administration. In 2002, the Supreme Court directed the Election Commission to ensure from the poll candidates such personal details as pending and previous criminal cases that carry a sentence of two or more years, convictions or acquittals, wealth and income of Self, Spouse and dependents.

Other examples of judicial activism are (i) the Supreme Court order to clear the encroachment along the route to Mirza Ghalib's tomb in Nizammudin, (ii) restoration of Muhammad Zauq's grave in Delhi. It banned the slaughter of buffaloes at the Idgah abattoir and illegal killing of animals in Delhi, and (iii) in a *suo motto* initiative, the Supreme Court made wearing of seat belts in a car for the front seat driver/passenger compulsory and directed the police to enforce it and (iv) the Supreme Court put on hold the disinvestiment of oil PSUs, HPCL and BPCL and asked the government to obtain parliamentary approval for the sale of government's stake in the two companies.

Some other important examples of judicial activism are:

1. In 2006, The Supreme court ordered a 50 per cent ceiling on quotas. The court said, "A numerical benchmark is the surest immunity against charges of discrimination. If the extent of reservation goes beyond the cut-off point of 50 percent, then it results in reverse discrimination." On this basis, the apex court dismissed the Orissa Government petition which challenged the Orissa high Court decision restraining it from providing 66.75 per cent reservation in government jobs
2. The Supreme Court in 2007 ordered colleges across the country to clearly state in their admission prospectus that students indulging in ragging will be expelled. (HT DEC 11 2008)

3. In another important judgment, the Supreme Court brought the Ninth Schedule of the Constitution under the ambit of judicial review. Till then it was regarded sacrosanct and the laws put in the Ninth scheduled could not questioned by the courts.
4. In a landmark judgment in 2008, the Supreme Court upheld the insertion of clause 5 in *Article 15* of the constitution vide 93rd Constitutional Amendment, which gave power to the government to reserve seats in all educational institutions including those that are privately run. It also declared the controversial Central Educational Institutions (Reservation in Admission) Act, 2006 which provided 27% quota for OBCs. It also ruled that the 'creamy layer' among the backwards would not get reservation. The court also directed that a review of the lists of backward classes be made after five years. It also ruled that the caste can be the basis to determine backwardness.

The examples of judicial activism are many. We have given a few examples. But these examples clearly depict the wide range in which the judiciary has directed the government to act.

Why Judicial Activism?

The Judicial activism in present days has arisen mainly due to the failure of the executive and legislatures to act and for this the main culprits have been the politicians. Instead of working for the general welfare of the people, they have been involved in self aggrandisement and corruption. The corruption charges are also levelled against leaders of almost all the important political parties. Besides corruption, there is a Politician-criminal nexus and criminals have become politicians. Chief Justice Ahmedi rightly stated, "The image of the Indian politician today has nose-dived on account of allegations of involvement in financial scandals as also an account of alleged links with the underworld. There is an increasing perception among large sections of the people that the nexus between criminals and politicians has strengthened in recent times." Everyday we hear new scams and corruption cases. In 2002, the petrol pump and gas agency scam rocked the parliament as well as the nation and it was revealed that close kins and relatives of the politicians belonging to the ruling parties as well as opposition (earlier they were ruling) were the beneficiaries of allotment of petrol pump and gas agencies and this had been going on for a long time. Therefore, the people have lost faith in the politicians. The politicians also influenced the governmental machinery including the CBI to scuttle any investigation of the corruption charges. There has been a growing feeling that criminal laws are being applied selectively and the politicians are immune from criminal proceedings. As a result, a vacuum was created in which the governmental machinery seemed to be totally helpless or even connived with the corrupt politicians. The vacuum was filled in by the judiciary. Many scams came out as a result of a Public Interest Litigation filed in the Supreme Court.

There is a feeling that the legislature and executive have failed to deliver the goods. The Indian political system started with Nehru's 'tryst with destiny' speech in which the people were promised that their status will be improved in free India. For this many plans and schemes were launched. But, in total, the result has been far from the people's expectation. Poverty still continues with 320 million people living below the poverty line; child labour, despite the constitutional guarantee that they will have free education upto 14 years of age and a decent living, still exists with a very large number, the atrocities on Scheduled Castes continue, and the police and the bureaucracy work with arrogance and irresponsibility, as they did during the British times. Laws are passed but are seldom properly implemented. In fact the Indian political system is plagued with lawlessness and the government has been a silent witness to it. The demolition of the disputed structure in Ayodhya took place in the presence of paramilitary forces, who did nothing but witness the demolition. In Bihar, the Chief Minister continued to remain in office despite the CBI chargesheet against him in the Fodder case, and later on he quit office only to make his wife Chief Minister. Such a situation has resulted in judicial activism. The then Chief Justice, Ahmedi, rightly said that judicial activism was imposed on the judiciary. He explained that in the initial years, the people were quite satisfied with the policies of the government, for successive governments did attempt to address themselves to issues that touched people's lives. But in recent years as the Parliament became less representative of the people's wishes, the people reacted in two ways. The majority took it as something inevitable, which they could not stop though they felt bad. But fortunately there were a few people, in a minority, who refused to be silent spectators and took up the cause through judiciary, which duly obliged.

The naked violation of basic human rights have been another reason for judicial activism. The prisoners have been behind bars without appropriate authority from the courts for years. In fact, in many cases they have been languishing in jails without trial for more than the period they would have been, if convicted. The atrocities in jails, police custody, mental asylums, women's rescue homes, children's remand homes etc, have been continuing. The legislature did not do anything for the protection of human rights. It was only through the Court interference in *Bandhua Mukti Morcha* case, *Bhagalpur Jail Blinding* case and other cases that justice was delivered by the judiciary. P.B. Sawant rightly remarks, "It can hardly be contended that the Courts should have waited to remedy the situation till the legislature had made suitable changes in the law, procedural or substantial. Taking cognizance of the cases requiring justice and doing justice to the needy is the function of the Court and, in innovating the new procedure, the Courts acted in furtherance of their duty. It would have been a travesty of justice if the Court had thrown its hands up in desperation for want of requisite procedure. The procedure is a handmaid of justice and not *vice versa*."

It is not the question of prisoners but the entire system which has been plagued by ineffectiveness and inactiveness. There were deaths due to dengue in Delhi and the government was doing nothing except suggesting that people themselves were responsible for the spread of dengue mosquitoes. It awakened only when slapped by judicial activism. Similarly, in case of the Bihar Chief Minister accused in Fodder scam, the Union Government was distinguished by its inactiveness and waiting for the Chief Minister to resign on his own. In such cases, judicial activism is the only remedy.

Further, some of the provisions have been misused and abused and there seems to be no remedy. For example, *Article 356* of the Constitution every party has criticised it for its political misuse. But when they came to power, they themselves misused it for their political advantages. As a result, democracy is often denied in the States for the sake of the party or parties-in-power at the Centre. Again the Court had to intervene and consequently *Article 356* has become justiciable.

Judicial Activism—Two Schools of Thought

There are two views regarding judicial activism. One school justifies it as essential in the prevailing conditions and the other criticises it as anti-democratic since the authority of legislature and executive is usurped by the judiciary which is not elected by the people.

Those who support judicial activism say, that the term judicial activism is a misnomer because judiciary is only discharging its constitutional duty of protecting the rights of the people. Nafees Ahmed says, "Earlier judgement and decrees were passed and files were closed and shelved. The present judiciary is following a more pragmatic technique of 'Judgements with Monitoring.' Today not only are judgements pronounced but their result-oriented implementation is also ensured through new tools, methods and techniques. Today government officials are asked to submit their progress reports pertaining to matters subjudice at every stage till the case is finally adjudicated upon."

H.R. Khanna is also of the view that judicial activism is nothing but ensuring the rule of law in the country. There were powerful politicians who were corrupt and thought that the law would not harm them or they were above the law. They indulged in many illegal activities and amassed a lot of wealth as a result. They also hampered the investigations of investigating agencies. The investigation agencies were "subordinate to and under their administrative control. As such they were turning a blind eye to such acts of political corruption and amassing of wealth lest they offend their bosses. The judiciary, in doing so, has removed the shadow of fear and made the investigating officers enforce the rule of law so that none may carry the notion that he is above the law. The judiciary has upheld the basic principle that however high one may be politically or administratively, the law is above him and he cannot avoid the penalties for the infraction of the law.

P.B. Sawant has dealt in detail the criticism of judicial activism and also answered the charges, which are as follows:

(i) The first criticism of judicial activism is that judiciary has encroached upon the jurisdiction of the executive, legislature and other independent and autonomous institutions.
(ii) By judicial activism the judiciary enters an area where it has no expertise and competence to undertake the regulation and management of the affairs.
(iii) The Courts are indulging in activism at the expense of their normal adjudicatory works, and this is one of the reasons for the huge arrears of cases.
(iv) Finally the judiciary may lose the confidence of the people if its directives given in such cases are not complied with.

Sawant's forceful reply to the above charges are as follows:

(i) There are only a few exceptional cases in which the judiciary has really encroached upon the areas of legislature, executive or other agencies. So far as the majority of cases of judicial activism are concerned, they have given directives to the authorities to perform their duties which they were not doing. In some case the judiciary asked the authorities to refrain from doing illegal acts. Thus there is no encroachment. The judiciary is only performing its duty.
(ii) The second criticism also does not hold water because the Court has taken the advice of the experts. Further the Courts have

entered into such fields only when compelled by inaction, and in doing so the Courts have not disturbed the basic framework of governmental organisation. It has only given directions to remove patent illegalities and injustice.

(iii) Judicial activism is not responsible for the huge arrears of cases pending in Courts. The number of cases of judicial activism is negligible in proportion to the total number of cases. Even if it is assumed that judicial activism has affected the disposal of the other cases, Sawant's question is whose interests should weigh more, that of the society at large or a large section of it or of the individual litigants?

(iv) The criticism that the judiciary will lose the people's confidence if its directions are not complied with, is also erroneous. Most of the time the directives are to perform the mandatory duties under the law. It leaves the implementation of the direction to the authorities themselves and only monitors compliance by calling for reports. Further, the judiciary has the power to punish for non-compliance of its directions by invoking its contempt power. Thirdly, experience shows that the authorities have duly complied with the Court's directives.

Sawant further points out that in a democracy, no government will take such measures which may lead to loss of votes in future elections. It is then left to the judiciary which has no vote bank to look to, to compel the authority to perform its obligatory duty for the benefit of the society. In fact many a times the executive, the legislature and others on their own throw the ball in the judiciary's Court and desire direction from them to undertake the measures which they also believe to be in the best interests of society. It is further not correct to say that the people are likely to lose confidence in the Courts because of their "activist" role. The people have instead started looking to the Courts as their only saviours with the executive and the legislature taking an indifferent stance towards their problems.

The fact that the judicial activism is justified in case of legislative and executive inactivity can be deduced from the oath that a judge of the Supreme Court or High Court has to take before entering his office. In his Oath, he pledges to:

(a) bear true faith and allegiance to the Constitution of India,
(b) to uphold the sovereignty and integrity of India,
(c) to duly and faithfully and to the best of ability, knowledge and judgement to perform the duties of his office without fear or favour, affection or ill-will, and
(d) to uphold the Constitution and the laws.

By compelling the authorities to perform their responsibilities, the judges are simply upholding the Constitution and the law. If the authorities do not perform and the Courts also do not compel them to do so, the people will lose faith in the Constitution and may throw it away lock, stock and barrel. By judicial activism, the Courts are maintaining and preserving the Constitution as its guardian.

However, excess of everything is bad and over-activism is also an unhealthy sign. The Courts are to exercise restraint in resorting to judicial activism. The public interest litigation may be misused for populism by individuals and groups and Supreme Court cannot be a party to it. Further there have been cases when the judiciary, in the words of Sawant, "has outstepped its brief." For example the Court's direction to the Parliament to frame Common Civil Code, the Court fixed the percentage of seats for all Indian students for medical course in all universities and the Court's direction to include a player in a cricket team. But such cases have been few. The Supreme Court is also exercising restraint in its activist role. In 1996, it struck down an order of the Himachal Pradesh High Court directing the State Government to construct a particular road, saying such interference would disturb the programme of development chalked out by the State Government. The Court accepted the State Government Counsel's view that, "While it may be true that it is necessary to lay the communication network, but that necessity can be fulfilled only on the basis of the availability of the funds." In an another example where the Supreme Court has exercised caution is that of the reallocation of over 39,000 industries in Delhi's residential areas. The Supreme Court first set the deadline of 31st December 1996, but later on gave the government a free hand in reallocating and waived the time limit. However, it directed the State Government to file quarterly progress reports in this regard. The Court has also tried to check the misue of PIL. In 2004, the Supreme Court upheld a Bombay High Court order imposing a fine of Rs. 25,000 on an advocate who filed a PIL and later used it to blackmail people. One of the Judges observed that PIL should not become 'publicity interest litigation' or 'private interest litigation' or 'paisa income litigation'. In 2005, it dismissed a PIL challenging the inclusion of tainted ministers in the Union cabinet after the Union Government assurance that the matter would be debated in the Parliament. The Supreme Court slapped a fine of Rs. 10,000 on a petitioner for filing a 'Publicity Interest Litigation'. The petitioner wanted 'Sindh' to be replaced by 'Kashmir' in the national anthem.

In fact, the Supreme Court has been continuously warning the high courts to observe restraint. In 2007, a two—member Judge Bench of the

Supreme Court observed, "If the judiciary does not exercise restraint and overstretches its limits, there is bound to be a reaction from politicians and others. The politicians will then step in and curtail the powers, or even the independence of the judiciary." The Bench did not appreciate the Delhi high Court's intervention in cases like nursery admissions, free beds for the poor in the hospital, misuse of ambulances, begging in public, Blueline buses, unauthorized constructions and road accidents. The judges pointed out," Judges must know their limits and must not try to run the government. They must have modesty and humility and not behave like emperors. There is a broad separation of powers under the Constitution and no organ of the state-the legislature, the executive and the judiciary- should encroach into each other's domain." (HT DEC 11 2007) The Supreme Court held that High Court judges, on their own cannot treat anonymous letters and petitions listing allegations against individuals or institutions as public interest litigation and order suo motu investigation. Such letters should be placed before the Chief Justice for his consideration.

In an another case, the Supreme Court rejected the Allahabad high court decision in which the high court asked the State to reconsider its decision to create a new district of Baghpat. The apex court pointed out that the courts should not interfere in matters of policy decision such as creation of a district or State.

In 2008, the Supreme Court dismissed a Public Interest Litigation seeking a direction to the centre as well as the States to enact a road safety act to lay down regulations to prevent road accidents. The apex Court observed, "In our opinion, the prayer made in this petition requires us to give directions of a legislative or executive nature which can only be given by the legislature or the executive." The learned Judges remarked, "PIL has nowadays largely become 'publicity interest litigation', 'private interest litigation' or politics interest litigation' or the latest trend 'paisa income litigation'." The court also observed, "The people must know that.... (T)he problems confronting the nation are so huge that it will be creating an illusion in the minds of the people that judiciary can solve all the problems.... For example, there is a great deal of poverty in this country and poverty is destructive of most of the rights including the right to a dignified life. Can the court issue a general directive that poverty be abolished from the country because it violates *Article 21* of the constitution? Similarly can the court issue a directive that unemployment be abolished by giving everybody a suitable job? Can the court stop price rise which nowadays has become an alarming phenomenon in our country? Can the court issue a directive that corruption be abolished from the country? *Article 21* is not a *'Brahmastra'* to justify every kind of directive." The court felt that remedy to the legislative and executive inaction was not the court but the people "to correct the defects by exercising their franchise properly in the next elections and vote for candidates who will fulfil their expectations." He further cautioned, "When other agencies or wings of the state overstep their constitutional limits, the aggrieved parties can always approach the courts and seek redress against such transgression. If, however, the court itself becomes guilty of such transgression, to which forum would the aggrieved party appeal? As the ancient Romans used to say, "Who will guard the Praetorian guards?" The only check on the courts is its self-restraint." (The *Hindu* 12 April 2008)

The working of judicial activism has justified its existence. In most of the cases, the Courts have acted in a correct manner and restored the law and the Constitution. There have been few exceptions but then mistakes can be committed by the Courts too and the Supreme Court has often realised its mistakes and accordingly changed its earlier decisions. The people of India have also welcomed and supported judicial activism.

Subash Kashyap rightly says "in the ultimate analysis, judgements of the Courts have also to be implemented and given effect only by the administration which functions under the political executive. Judiciary has, in fact to be very cautious to ensure that a situation is not reached where its directives are no more fully respected or obeyed. For, if that happens, the last bastion of democracy will also vanish and people will lose whatever remains of their faith in the polity." Finally one should hope that the recent rise in substantial cases of judicial activism is a temporary phenomenon because ultimately the government has to function in coordination with all its three wings—legislature, executive and judiciary. Each department should discharge its duty duly and according to the Constitution, and when this happens the Courts will also find no reason to interfere in the activities of other departments of the government.

Criticism of Judicial Review

Firstly, the power of judicial review has been criticised on the basis of functional division of power among the three organs of the government that it impairs this division of power. Strictly speaking, the legislature legislates, the executive executes, and the judges adjudicate. By the power of judicial review, especially, when the court take recourse to judicial activism, the division of power is disturbed. The judges not only adjudicate, they also interfere in the working of legislature and executive. It is alleged to be anti-democratic as the legislature and not the judiciary reflect the wishes of the people. The basic policies must be decided by the legislature and not the judges. Secondly, there is the possibility of legislature and executive becoming inactive as they may feel insecure due to the fact that their legislation or action may be declared as null and void by the judiciary. Former Chief Justice of India, Ahmedi, pointed out that while the US Supreme Court had held in 195 years (1790 to 1985) only 135 federal laws and 970 state laws to be wholly or partly constitutional, the Indian Supreme Court in 15 years (1950 to 1975) had held more than 100 Union or State laws to be wholly or partly unconstitutional. Thirdly, the judges belong to a particular class and as such believe in status quo. They may not like revolutionary changes in the society. This criticism was especially labelled against the Supreme Court judges in the Bank Nationalistion case and Privy Purse case. Justice P.N. Bhagwati also accepted this view when he said, "In a country like India where there is so much of poverty, misery and sufferings and a large number of people are constantly oppressed and exploited, it is necessary that the judges should identify themselves with the misery and sufferings of the masses. Otherwise, they will never be able to administer social justice." Fourth, the power of judicial review leads to the conflict between the legislature and executive on the one hand and the judiciary on the other, which has happened in India. The conflict hinders the natural growth of all the three institutions. Fifth, there is a danger of judges becoming populist. They may like to make headlines in the newspapers and in the process their judgement will also be affected. Sixthly, there are dangers of judicial dictatorship. Seventh, the judiciary may also subject itself to political controversies which are unwarranted to the dignity and decorum of the Court. Eighth, the Courts' working has also not been above criticism. The sons, daughters and even grandsons of the judges practice law. It has been pointed out that in Mumbai, children of several judges get into solicitor's firms and these firms regularly represent clients in the Court of those judges. Recruitment of a judge is also from the lawyers. Indira Jaising rightly points out, "By the time a man is 50, he is ready for two things, to become a judge of the High Court and to hand over his lucrative practice to his son who has joined the Bar. There have been serious allegations of improper conduct against the judges whose sons practise in the same court. To mitigate such evils, the transfer of High Court judges was initiated in 1981, which has been only partially implemented. Ninth, the working of judicial review has also created the question of the limits judicial power. By the Supreme Court's ruling, a person who files a case against a judge for something done by him while acting as a judge will mean contempt of court against not only the initiator but also the judges who registered the case or the officer who recorded the information. Both of them will be punished, irrespective of the nature and merit of the complaint. Thus the immunity of judges has been put on the highest pedestal, which is not justified. Tenth, the power of judicial review with regard to constitutional amendments has been criticised. No other Court in the world enjoys such power except the Indian judiciary. M.K. Bhandari gives following reasons for the non-justification of judicial review of constitutional amendments:

(i) This amounts to judicial supremacy which is not warranted by the Constitution because the Parliament may enact a law which is struck down by the judiciary. The Parliament re-enacts the law and again the judiciary may strike it down.
(ii) Ultimately, it is the Court which will decide as to which amendment is permissible. This in fact robs the Parliament of its power of amendment with the Court having the final say. By the doctrine of basic features of the Constitution, which are undefined and untermed, the Courts will be rewriting a new Constitution.
(iii) An amendment of the Constitution derives its validity from the Constitution itself. Irrespective of the subject-matter, the moment a provision becomes validly embodied in the Constitution, it acquires a validity of its own and cannot be challenged.
(iv) The Constitution does not give power to the judiciary to declare a constitutional amendment as void. On the other hand, clause (4) of *Article 13* and (3) of *Article 368* expressly bar the judicial review of constitutional amendment.
(v) The legislators know best the aspirations and needs of the people. So no Supreme Court and no judiciary can stand in judgement over the sovereign will of the Parliament, representing the will of the entire community. The judiciary cannot work as a third house of correction.
(vi) The Courts cannot judge the legality or the constitutionality of the Constitution itself. It is the people through their representative who should have the final say. In *Keshvananda Bharti* case, Justice Dwivedi remarked, "Judicial review of constitutional amendment will blunt the people's vigilance, articulateness, and effectiveness. The Constitution is not for men with a long purse. It is made for the common people." However, the fact remains that judicial review has come to stay in India and it has the people's support.

Conclusion

To sum up, one can say that the Supreme Court has become a powerful institution due to judicial review. The Constitution envisages the Supreme Court to be the custodian of the Constitution and, as such, it acts as the guardian of the federal system and the fundamental rights. The final word regarding the interpretation of the Constitution lies with the Supreme Court. Its power of judicial review has created tensions in the Indian polity. But it has the people's support and that gives the Supreme Court a dominant position in the Indian political system.

References

Advani Poornima, *Indian Judiciary—A Tribute,* 1997, New Delhi Harper Collins Publishers.

Bhandari M.K., *Basic Structure of the Indian Constitution,* 1993, New Delhi, Deep & Deep Publications.

Dudeja, Vijay Lakshmi, *Judicial Review in India,* 1988, New Delhi, Radiant Publishers.

Fadia B.L., *Indian Government and Politics,* 1996, Agra, Sahitya Bhawan Publications.

Ray S.N., *Judicial Review and Fundamental Rights,* 1974, Calcutta, Eastern Law House.

Singh Bakhshish, *The Supreme Court of India as an Instrument of Social Justice,* 1976, New Delhi, Sterling Publishers Pvt. Ltd.

Singh M.P., *V.N. Shukla's Constitution of India,* 1994, Lucknow, Eastern Book Company.

Siwach J.R., *Dynamics of Indian Government and Politics,* 1990, New Delhi, Sterling Publishers.

Politics India, Vol. 1, No. 10, Hon. Editor Subash C. Kashyap, April 1997, Vimot Publishers Pvt. Ltd.

CHAPTER XIII

State Government and their Working

The working of the State Government in India is to be viewed from two standpoints. Firstly, India is a federation in which States are sovereign in their respective fields as per the division of powers between the Union and the States. In a federation, the States have a special constitutional status and enjoy freedom within the limits imposed by the Constitution. However, as we have seen, India is not a classical example of a federation as many unitary provisions have been incorporated in the Constitution. The Constitution has put severe limitations on state autonomy. Further the development of Indian federalism has been more on the unitary pattern than the real federal spirit. The office of the Governor in the State is one of the examples of the unitary pattern. Secondly, in India the same Constitution provides for the political and legal machinery of the States. The Parliamentary form of government has been adopted in States also, which means there are two heads—one, the head of the State i.e. the Governor and the other, the head of the government i.e. the Chief Minister. Under the Parliamentary system of government the Governor should be the nominal head while the Chief Minister, along with his Council of Ministers, is the real functionary. The Chief Minister and his Council of Ministers are collectively and individually responsible to the Legislative Assembly. The Chief Minister and his Council of Ministers remain in office till they enjoy the confidence of the House. However, in practice, the system of Parliamentary democracy has been eroded in the States. The Constitution itself vests enormous discretionary powers with the Governor and the Governors have used them frequently. As a result, the Governor has been more than a nominal head and the Chief Minister less than the real head. These are some of the issues we will examine in this chapter.

The Governor: Appointment and Removal

Appointment

Article 153 of the Constitution says, "There shall be a Governor for each State." However the same person can be appointed as Governor for two or more States. The Governor is appointed by the President by warrant under his hand and seal. He is appointed for five years. But he holds his office till the pleasure of the President, which means the President can recall him any time. Regarding the appointment of the Governor there have been two conventions in India:

(i) The Governor is appointed from outside the State concerned. But there have been instances when this convention was not followed. The appointment of H.C. Mukherjee in Bengal, J.C. Wediyar Bahadur in Mysore in 1956, Ujjal Singh in Punjab in 1966, and Karan Singh in Jammu and Kashmir in 1965, are some examples. The convention of appointing an outsider from the State is to ensure impartiality of the Governor in State Politics.

(ii) The States are consulted by the Centre in the appointment of the Governor. This practice is also not followed in every appointment. In certain cases the State Chief Ministers were not even consulted, for example in case of the appointment of Sri Prakasa in Madras and Kumaraswami Rai in Orissa. In Punjab, Chief Minister Gurnam Singh disapproved the two names proposed by the Centre and suggested a few others, but the Centre did not agree with his names. In Bihar the Chief Minister M.P. Sinha wanted the incumbent Governor M.A. Ayyangar to continue for another term but the Centre appointed a new Governor. The Chief Minister had publicly protested and refused to welcome the new Governor. He described him as an "unwanted and unwelcome Governor."

A study of the persons appointed as Governors clearly reveals that a considerable number of retired politicians have been appointed. Those politicians at the Centre, with whom the Prime Minister is not comfortable, or he wants them to be shifted out of active politics, are also appointed as Governors. In 2008, Shiv Charan Mathur was appointed Governor of Assam as the congress leadership wanted him to be out of the state in view of impending elections in Rajasthan. Even some active politicians have been appointed as Governors, like Arjun Singh in Punjab. After his tenure in Punjab he became the Chief Minister of Madhya Pradesh and continues to remain in active politics. There is a typical example of Harideo Joshi, who relinquished his office of Governor of Assam and the very next day he was sworn in as Chief Minister of Rajasthan. Besides retired bureaucrats and judges and retired army officials have also been made Governors. Such people cannot ensure the impartiality of the office of the Governor. Frequently the Governors have been accused of playing into the hands of party-in-power at the Centre.

Qualifications

The Constitution prescribes the following qualifications for a person to become a Governor:

(i) He must be a citizen of India.
(ii) He must have completed the age of 35.
(iii) The Governor shall not be a member of Parliament or State legislature. In case he is a member of Parliament or any State legislature, he shall be deemed to have vacated his office in that House on the date on which he enters upon his office as Governor.
(iv) He shall not hold any office of profit.

Oath or Affirmation by the Governor

The Governor before entering upon his office takes the following oath or affirmation in the presence of the Chief Justice of the concerned State:

"I, A.B, do swear in the name of God/solemnly affirm that I will faithfully execute the office of the Governor (or discharge the functions of the Governor) of ... (name of the State) and will to the best of my ability preserve, protect and defend the Constitution and the law and that I will devote myself to the service and well-being of the people of ... (name of the State).

Removal of the Governor

Normally, a Governor is appointed for five years. Before this he can be recalled or transferred to another State. He may resign on his own. The Governor continues in his office till his successor takes over from him. But there have been cases when the Governors continued even after the expiry of their term because their successor was not appointed. For example B.N. Chaturvedi continued for three year after the expiry of his five year term. In 1980, Prabhu Das Patwari was recalled from Tamil Nadu. In 1981, the Governor of Rajasthan and Tamil Nadu were dismissed. T.N. Singh of West Bengal resigned in 1982, because the President wanted to withdraw his pleasure. After the Janata Dal and its allies came to power, mass resignations of Governors was sought. Now, it has almost become a practice that with the change of government at the centre, such Governors, as are not liked by the new government, are changed. In 1992, the Nagaland Governor, M.M. Thomas was removed from his office by the President because he dissolved the State Assembly and ordered fresh elections without consulting the Centre. In 2001, Tamil Nadu Governor Fathima Beevi was recalled because she did not keep the Union Government informed of the internal disturbances in the state, duly in which the former Chief Minister Karunanidhi and two Union Ministers were arrested by the Jayalalitha Government. It was alleged that she behaved more like an agent of the ruling party of the state than a representative of the Union Government. The UPA Government removed four State Governors—Vishnu Kant Shastri (UP), Babu Parmanand (Haryana), Kedar Nath Sahani (Goa) and Kailashpati Misra (Gujarat) on the plea that they had RSS background.

Transfer of the Governor

The Constitution does not provide for the transfer of Governors, yet they are transferred. For example G.D. Tapase was transferred to Haryana from U.P. Bhagwat Dayal Sharma was transferred to Madhya Pradesh from Orissa. In 1984, the Governor of Jammu and Kashmir was transferred to Gujarat because he refused to recommend the dismissal of Farooq Abdullah Government, and imposition of President's Rule in the State, as desired by the Centre. A.P. Sharma, the Governor of Punjab was transferred to West Bengal. In 2008, Kerala Governor R.L.Bhatia was shifted to Bihar and the Bihar Governor was sent to Kerala as Governor.

The study of the appointment and removal of Governors shows that, over the years, an environment has been created that compels the Governor to toe the line of the Centre, else he may be removed or transferred. This has made the office of Governor a major tension area in Union-State relations. Frequently demands have been made, ranging from the abolition of the office of the Governor to a proper regulation of his appointment procedure. The Administrative Reforms Commission made the following recommendations:

(i) A person to be appointed as a Governor should be one who has had a long experience in public life and administration and can be trusted to rise above party prejudices and predilections. He should not be eligible for further appointment after the completion of his term.

(ii) The convention of consulting the Chief Minister before appointing a Governor is a healthy one and may continue.

The Sarkaria Commission recommended the following suggestions regarding the appointment and removal of the Governor:

(i) He should be eminent in some walk of life.

(ii) He should be a person outside the State.

(iii) He should be a detached figure and not too intimately connected with the local politics of the state.

(iv) He should be a person who has taken too great a part in politics generally, and particularly in the recent past.

(v) It is desirable that a politician from the ruling party at the Union is not appointed as Governor of a State which is being run by some other party or a combination of other parties.

(vi) In order to ensure effective consultation with the State Chief Minister in the selection of a person to be appointed a Governor, the procedure of consultation should be prescribed in the Constitution itself by suitably amending *Article 155.*

(vii) The Vice-President of India and the Speaker of the Lok Sabha may be consulted by the Prime Minister in selecting a Governor. The consultation should be confidential and informal and should not be a matter of constitutional obligation.

(viii) The Governor's tenure of office of five years in a State should not be disturbed except very rarely and that too, for some extremely compelling reason.

(ix) Save where the President is satisfied that, in the interest of the security of the State, it is not expedient to do so, the Governor whose tenure is proposed to be terminated before the expiry of the normal term of five years, should be informally apprised of the grounds of the proposed action and afforded a reasonable opportunity for showing cause against it. It is desirable that the President (in effect, the Union Council of Ministers) should get the explanation, if any, submitted by the Governor (against his proposed removal from office) examined by an Advisory Group consisting of the Vice- President of India and the Speaker of the Lok Sabha or a retired Chief Justice of India. After receiving the recommendation of this Group, the President may pass such orders in the case as he may deem fit.

(x) When, before expiry of the normal term of five years, a Governor resigns or is appointed Governor in another State, or has his tenure terminated, the Union Government may lay a statement before both Houses of Parliament explaining the circumstances leading to the ending of the tenure. Where a Governor has been given an opportunity to show cause against the premature termination of his tenure, the statement may also include the explanation given by him, in reply.

(xi) As a matter of convention, the Governor should not, on quitting his office, be eligible for any other appointment or office of profit under the Union or a State Government except for a second term as Governor or election as Vice-President or President of India. Such a convention should also require that, after quitting or laying down his office, the Governor shall not return to active partisan politics.

(xii) A Governor should, at the end of his tenure, irrespective of its duration, be provided reasonable post-retirement benefits for himself and for his surviving spouse.

Powers and Functions of the Governor

The Constitution vests with the Governor enormous powers, which may be categorised as follows:

1. Executive Powers
2. Legislative Powers
3. Financial Powers
4. Judicial Powers
5. Discretionary Powers

1. *Executive Powers*

The Governor is the Chief Executive of the State. In the exercise of his functions, he has a Council of Ministers with the Chief Minister at its head to aid and advise him except in where he is to exercise his discretion. The Chief Minister and his Council of Ministers are appointed by the Governor and remain in office during his pleasure. However, the Governor has limited powers in the selection of his Chief Minister and his ministry because, following the Parliamentary form of government norms, they are responsible to the State Assembly and remain in power till they enjoy the confidence of the State Assembly. The Governor also appoints the Advocate General, who is otherwise qualified to be appointed a Judge in the High Court. The Advocate-General also remains in his office during the pleasure of the Governor. The Governor also appoints the members of the State Police Service Commission. The Governor also makes rules for the more convenient transaction of business of the State Government.

All the executive actions of the State are done in the name of the Governor. It is the duty of the Chief Minister (a) to communicate to the Governor all decisions of the Council of Ministers relating to the administration of the affairs of the State and proposals for legislation; (b) to furnish such information relating to the administration of the affairs of the State and proposals for legislation as the Governor may call for; and (c) if the Governor so requires, to submit for the consideration of the Council of Ministers any matter on which a decision has been taken by a Minister but which has not been considered by the Council.

2. *Legislative Powers*

The State legislature is constituted by the Governor and the State Legislative Assembly (in some of the States there is another House called Legislative Council). Thus the Governor is an integral part of the legislature and as such enjoys a variety of powers which are as follows:

(i) The Governor may from time to time summon the House or both the Houses of the State legislature to meet at such time and place as he thinks fit. The only constitutional limitation is that six months should not intervene between the last sitting in one session and the date appointed for its first sitting in the next session.

(ii) The Governor may from time to time prorogue the House or either House and dissolve the State Legislative Assembly.

(iii) The Governor may address the Legislative Assembly or both the Houses or a single House in case of bicameral legislature and for that purpose may require the attendance of members. The Governor addresses the Legislative Assembly or in the States where Legislative Councils also are in existence, both Houses assembled together (a) at the first session after general elections of the new Assembly, and (b) at the commencement of the first session of every year.

(iv) The Governor may send to the House or Houses messages with respect to any Bill then pending in the Legislature or otherwise and House/Houses will consider the matter of the message.

(v) If any question arises as to whether a member of a House has been disqualified under *Article 191(1)*, the question is referred to the Governor and his decision is final. However the Constitution says that before giving such a decision the Governor shall obtain the opinion of the Election Commission and shall act according to such opinion.

(vi) A Bill passed by the State Legislature is presented to the Governor for his assent. The Governor may take one of the following causes:

(a) He may assent the Bill. After his assent the Bill becomes a law.
(b) He may withhold his assent.
(c) He may reserve the Bill for the President's consideration.
(d) He may return the Bill if it is not a Money-Bill to the Legislature for

reconsideration. But after such reconsideration if the Bill is passed again by the Legislature, he cannot withhold his assent.

(e) In case the state legislature is not in session and a law is necessary because of certain circumstances, the Governor may promulgate an Ordinance which has the same force and effect as an Act of the State Legislature. However such an ordinance will cease to have effect at the expiration of six weeks from the reassembly of the State Legislature. The State Legislature by passing a resolution can also disapprove it before the expiry of six weeks. The Governor can also withdraw it any time. However if an Act of the Legislature has been passed which is repugnant to an Act of Parliament, the Governor may issue an ordinance in such case under instructions from the President and such Ordinance shall be deemed to be an Act of the Legislature of the State which has been reserved for the consideration of the President and assented to by him.

(f) The Governor can nominate members of the Anglo-Indian Community to the Legislative Assembly if the said community is not adequately represented. In Legislative Councils, the Governor nominates persons who have special knowledge or practical experience in the fields of literature, science, art, cooperative movement and social service.

3. *Financial Powers*

A Money Bill can be introduced in the Legislative Assembly only on the recommendation of the Governor. No demand for a grant can be made without the recommendation of the Governor. The Budget is also presented with the recommendation of the Governor. The supplementary, additional or excess grants are also laid down in the Legislative Assembly with the recommendation of the Governor. The Governor himself does not present the budget or the supplementary, additional or excess of grants. But it is his duty to present them through the Finance Minister.

4. *Judicial Powers*

The Governor of a State has the power to grant pardon, reprieve, respite or remission of punishment or to suspend, remit or commute the sentence of any person convicted of any offence against any law relating to a matter to which the executive power of the State extends.

5. *Discretionary Powers*

Article 163(1) of the Constitution says that "There shall be a Council of Ministers with the Chief Minister at the head to aid and advise the

Governor in the exercise of his functions, except in so far as he is by or under this Constitution required to exercise his functions or any of them in his discretion." The clause 2 of the same Article further says, "If any question arises whether any matter is or is not a matter as respects which the Governor is by or under this Constitution required to act in his discretion, the decision of the Governor in his discretion shall be final, and the validity of anything done by the Governor shall not be called in question on the ground that he ought or ought not to have acted in his discretion." Thus, the Constitution does not define in, so many words, the discretionary powers of the Governor. In fact, the power to decide his discretion is itself a discretionary power of the Governor. According to Administrative Reforms Commission report, the Governor has the following discretionary powers as Head of the State: (i) appointment of Chief Minister; (ii) dismissal of Ministry; (iii) dissolution of Legislature; (ii) right to advise, warn and suggest; (v) withhold assent from a Bill; (vi) discretionary powers of the Governor of Assam, Nagaland, Arunachal Pradesh, Sikkim, Mizoram, Tripura and Meghalaya.

The discretionary powers of the Governor became an issue after 1967, when the monopoly of power by the Congress Party was broken in the Indian political system and non-Congress governments came into existence in several States. This phenomenon continues and different parties or coalition of parties have come into power in the Centre as well as the States. Now let us study the discretionary powers of Governor in the light of the changed political scenario after 1967.

(a) *Selection of the Chief Minister:* In a situation where there has been a political party, with a clear majority in the State Assembly, the Governor has no discretion in appointing the Chief Minister. He has to install the leader of the majority party as Chief Minister. But in 2001 the Supreme Court held that a person convicted of a criminal offence and sentenced for not less than two years, cannot be appointed as Chief Minister even if he/she was enjoying majority support in the Assembly. Thus the Supreme Court quashed the appointment of Ms. Jayalalitha as chief minister by the Governor Mrs. Fatime Beevi. The Court said, "The governer cannot, in the exercise of his/her discretion do anything that is contrary to the Constitution and the laws." In case of no party enjoying a majority support, the Governor has ample discretion and use of his discretionary power, in such cases, has always created controversies.

In Orissa in 1967, no controversy arose because the Swatantra Party—Jana Congress combined emerged in majority after the General Elections and R.N. Singh Deo, the leader of the combine, was sworn in as Chief Minister of the State by the Governor. But, in the same State in 1973, when the Chief Minister Nandini Satpathi lost the majority support and resigned, Biju Patnaik claimed the majority support. But the Governor refused to give him an opportunity and reported the failure of constitutional machinery in the State to the Centre. Allegations were levelled against the Governor that he was working in Congress Party's interest by not providing Biju Patnaik an opportunity to prove his majority in the State Assembly. It has been pointed out that in case of the single largest party in Legislative Assembly being the same as in the Centre, the Governors have appointed their leader as Chief Minister. However this principle was ignored when a different party enjoyed the single largest party status in the Legislative Assembly, for example in Kerala in 1957 and 1965, West Bengal in 1971, Haryana in 1982 and U.P. in 1995. In case of coalitions also, the Governor acted keeping in view the interests of party-in-power at the Centre. For example in Rajasthan in 1967 the Governor did not install Laxman Singh Gill, the leader of the Samyukta Vidhayak Dal as Chief Minister though he claimed the majority support in the State Assembly.

There have also been cases where a minority government was installed by the Governor. For example in 1984, Bhaskar Rao in A.P. and in 1992, Keshab Chandra Gogoi in Assam and Mrs. Ramachandran in Tamil Nadu in 1988, were installed as Chief Minister, though they did not enjoy majority support in the Assembly. In 2008, the minority government of (the Congress led Meghalaya United Alliance) D. D. Lapang in Meghalaya was installed subsequent to the elections to the Assembly.This was done despite the fact that the rival Meghalaya Progressive Alliance (MPA) had physically presented its 30 MLAs (out of effective strength of 59) before the Governor S.S.Sindhu. But the Governor decided to invite the Congress as it had emerged as the single largest party in the Assembly. In Jharkhand (2005) on a Supreme Court directive the Governor Syed Sibte Razi had to organise a floor test within three days but in Karnataka, Governor TN Chaturvedi gave seven days to Dharmam Singh to prove his majority. When the Governor appoints a person as Chief Minister in a hung legislature, he also gives them time to face the Legislative Assembly. However, the time given has varied depending upon the decision of the particular Governor. In 1979, in Assam the Governor asked the appointed Chief Minister Joginder Nath Hazarika to face the Assembly within a reasonable time. The same Governor gave Keshab Chandra Gogoi six weeks from the date of assuming his office. G.M. Shah and Bhaskar Rao in 1984, in Jammu and Kashmir and A.P. respectively were given one month's time. Mrs. Ramachandran in Tamil Nadu, in 1988, was given three weeks to prove her majority in the Assembly. In UP, in 1997 the Governor Romesh Bhandari gave the Chief Minister Kalyan Singh, (in the words of the Chief Minister), "just two nights and one day" to prove his majority after the withdrawal of support by BSP. Kalyan Singh protested that the time allotted to him was shortest but this made no impact on the Governor. The same Governor, in 1998, gave Jagdambika Pal three days at the first instance but later on extended three more days to prove his majority. In Goa (2005) subsequent to the resignation of four MLAs of the ruling BJP, the Governor gave the CM, Manohar Parrekar, 'barely 24 hours' to prove his majority in the House. The BJP Government was dismissed. In 2008, the minority government of D.D Lapang in Meghalaya was given 10 days to prove its majority. This decision of the Governor S.S. Sindhu was challenged in the Supreme Court and the apex court was requested to reduce the time to 7 days. But the court refused to interfere.

In choosing the Chief Minister, the Sarkaria Commission gave the following recommendations:

(a) The party or combination of parties which commands the widest support in the Legislative Assembly should be called upon to form the government.
(b) If there is a single party having an absolute majority in the Assembly, the leader of the party should automatically be asked to become the Chief Minister.

If there is no such party, the Governor should select a Chief Minister from among the following parties or group of parties by sounding them, in turn, in the order of preference indicated below:

(i) An alliance of parties that was formed prior to the elections.
(ii) The largest single party staking a claim to form the government with the support of others, including independents.
(iii) A post-electoral coalition of parties, with all the partners in the coalition joining government.
(iv) A post-electoral alliance of parties, with some of the parties in the alliance forming a Government and the remaining parties, including "independents" supporting the government from outside.

The Sarkaria Commission also recommended that (i) the Governor should not determine the issue of majority support on his own outside the Assembly but it should be determined on the floor of the Assembly, and (ii) A Chief Minister, unless he is the leader of a party which has absolute majority in the Assembly, should seek a vote of confidence in the Assembly within 30 days of taking over.

(b) *Dismissal of a Chief Minister:* According to normal Parliamentary procedure, a Chief Minister who enjoys the majority support in the Assembly should not be dismissed. However in India, this has not been followed strictly. In 1959, the Communist Government in Kerala was dismissed even as it had the majority support. In 1967, the Ajay Mukherjee Government in West Bengal lost the majority in the Assembly, the Governor insisted upon calling the session of the House immediately and, upon the refusal of Chief Minister to do so, he dismissed the Chief Minister. In 1970, Charan Singh in U.P. was dismissed despite the fact that he claimed majority support and was prepared to face the Assembly. Similarly, in cases of S.S. Barnala (Punjab) in 1987, Farooq Abdullah (Jammu and Kashmir) in 1985, N.T. Rama Rao (AP) in 1984 and Bommai (Karnataka) in 1989, the Chief Ministers were dismissed even when they were ready to face the Assembly. N.T. Rama Rao even went to the extent of parading his 163 supporters before the President after his dismissal as Chief Minister. Still there are cases when the Chief Ministers had lost the majority support due to defections and the Governor neither dismissed them nor insisted on an early summoning of the Assembly to test the majority support. This happened in U.P. when C.B. Gupta, the Chief Minister, lost majority support and there was a demand for an early session of the Assembly to test the majority support, the Governor refused to do so by saying that when somebody "loses majority he should be given some time to find it again." A similar attitude was adopted by the respective Governors in 1967 and 1970 in Bihar, in 1971 in Punjab and Bihar, in 1973 in Orissa and in 1981 and 1982 in Assam. Sometimes, the same Governor has taken different positions in similar situations. For example, Gopala Reddy permitted C.B. Gupta to remain Chief Minister for more than two months in 1969 but in 1970 he was not prepared to wait for three days when the Assembly was scheduled to meet and the Chief Minister Charan Singh was ready to face the Assembly. This time he just dismissed Charan Singh. In 1981, the Anwara Taimur Ministry of Assam was defeated in a cut motion in the State Assembly but still the Governor did not dismiss her. In 1995, Moti Lal Vora, the Governor of UP dismissed the Mulayam Singh Ministry after the withdrawal of support by BSP, though the Chief Minister was prepared to face the Assembly but the opportunity was denied to him. In 1998, Governor Romesh Bhandari of UP dismissed Kalyan Singh Government when the Loktantrik Congress withdrew its support, again, without giving any opportunity to the Chief Minister to prove his majority in the House for which he was prepared. The Governor on his own calculated and decided that Kalyan Singh had lost the majority support. He also installed Jagdambika Pal as Chief Minister and gave him three days to prove his majority in the Assembly. The Governor's actions created a big controversy. Ultimately, the Supreme Court directed a composite floor test for Kalyan Singh and Jagdambika Pal. This was a new invention of the Supreme Court. The composite floor test went in favour of Kalyan Singh. In the same case earlier, the High Court of UP observed that the Governor had exercised his powers in `hot haste' and for `purpose not warranted by law. In its interim order, the Court reinstated Kalyan Singh as Chief Minister and said that a floor test was possible to ascertain whether Kalyan Singh or Jagdambika Pal commanded majority in the Assembly. Relying on the verdict of the Supreme Court in the S.R. Bommai case, the Court said it was of the view unless there were exceptional circumstances which made the floor test impossible, it was not open to the Governor to evade a floor test.

"The Court observed." The very fact that the floor test by Jagadambika Pal having been fixed pre-supposes that floor test is possible and there were no exceptional circumstances rendering it impossible.

"Thus if the floor test was possible in absence of any exceptional circumstances, it was not open to the Governor to evade floor test, though demanded by Kalyan Singh, which fact has not been denied and finds mention in the (Governor's) order itself", the judgement said. Therefore, it was incumbent on the Governor to summon the House for floor test."

Thus there has been no consistency with regard to the discretion of the Governor in dismissing the Chief Minister and his Ministry inviting the criticism that Governors were playing a partisan role. The Sarkaria Commission gave following recommendations with regard to the dismissal of a Chief Minister.

(i) The Governor should not risk determining the issue of majority support on his own outside the Assembly. The majority should be tested on the floor of the Assembly.

(ii) The Governor cannot dismiss his Council of Ministers so long as they continue to command a majority in the Legislative Assembly. Conversely he is bound to dismiss them if they lose the majority but do not resign.

(ii) When the Legislative Assembly is in session, the question of majority should be tested on the floor of the House.

(iv) If the Chief Minister seems to have lost majority, he should not dismiss him "as a matter of constitutional propriety." He should advise the Chief Minister to summon the Assembly as early as possible so that the majority may be tested.

(v) Normally a 30-day period be allowed for the summoning of the Assembly unless there is a very urgent business to be transacted like passing the budget, in which a shorter period may be allowed. In special circumstances, the period may go up to 60 days.

(c) *Summoning and Proroguing the Assembly:* Another area of Governor's discretion which created a lot of controversy is his power to summon and prorogue the Assembly. It is the duty of a Governor to summon the House from time to time. The only constitutional limitation is that more than six months interval should not take place between the last day of the previous session and the first day of the next session. Normally, the State Assembly is summoned on the advice of the Chief Minister and his Council of Ministers. Usually, the Governor does act on the recommendation of the Chief Minister and his Council of Ministers in normal circumstances. But when the Chief Minister seems to have lost the majority support and consequently is reluctant to call the early session of the Assembly, it becomes an abnormal situation and the Governors have behaved in contradictory ways as seen above. But what is important to mention here is that some Governors went out of the way and prorogued the Assembly so that a no-confidence motion could not be passed against the Chief Minister and his Ministry. This was done by K.C. Reddy in MP in 1968, Bhagwan Sahai in Jammu and Kashmir in 1970, B.D. Jatti in Orissa in 1973 and L.P. Singh in Assam in 1981. The last case is more interesting. The Government of Anwara Taimur was defeated on the floor of the House through a cut motion on the Appropriation Bill which meant the Government had lost the confidence of the Assembly. L.P. Singh neither requested Anwara Taimur to resign nor dismissed her. But on the contrary he prorogued the Assembly and issued an Ordinance to authorize expenditure to save the ministry.

The Sarkaria Commission gave the following suggestions for the exercise of Governor's discretion in the matter of summoning and proroguing the State Assembly:

(i) So long as the Council of Ministers enjoys the confidence of the Legislative Assembly, the advice of the Council of Ministers with regard to summoning and proroguing a House of the Legislature and in dissolving the Legislative Assembly, if such advice is not patently unconstitutional, should be binding on the Governor.

(ii) In certain situation, the Governor may exercise his discretion to summon the Assembly only in order to ensure that the system of responsible government in the State works in accordance with the norms envisaged in the Constitution.

(iii) If the Chief Minister does not advise the summoning of the Assembly within the stipulated period of six months, the Governor can use his discretion and summon the Legislative Assembly.

(iv) If the Chief Minister does not summon the Assembly within 30 or 60 days of his taking over and the Governer finds that he no longer enjoys the confidence of the Assembly, he can summon the Assembly for holding the test of majority support.

(d) *Dissolution of the State Assembly:* Another area where the Governor has a discretion is with regard to the dissolution of the State Assembly. Here also the norm of Parliamentary democracy is to exercise this power with the aid and advice of the Chief Minister and the Council of Ministers. However, if a Chief Minister has lost majority in the Assembly, the Governor has a discretion of not accepting such advice and he may try for an alternative government. Thus the advice of Rao Birender Singh in Haryana, Gurnam Singh in Punjab in 1967 and Hitendra Desai in Gujarat in 1971, to dissolve the Assemblies were rejected. But on the other hand, the Assemblies were dissolved in Kerala in 1970, in Punjab, West Bengal and Bihar in 1971, on the recommendation of the respective Chief Ministers. However there has been no uniform approach in the various Governors' approach. For example in 1971, the Chief Minister Hitendra Desai, after being reduced to a minority, advised the Governor to dissolve the Assembly. But the Governor rejected the same on the ground that advice of a Chief Minister who has lost majority support is not binding. In Kerala, the Chief Minister had resigned in the midst of the session of the Assembly in anticipation of his defeat and recommended dissolution of the Assembly, the Governor accepted the advice. Thus in those two cases, the Chief Ministers had lost the majority support and recommended dissolution of the Assembly and Governor took extremely contradictory positions. There is another interesting case of Nagaland in 1992, where the Governor M.M. Thomas was dismissed by the President because the Governor dissolved the State Assembly on the recommendation of the Chief Minister but without consulting the Central Government.

The Sarkaria Commission gave the following recommendations in this regard:

(i) The Governor should accept the advice of dissolution if the Chief Minister enjoys the confidence of the Assembly.

(ii) When a Chief Minister who has either lost or likely to have lost majority support, the Governor should try for an alternative government. He may even summon the Assembly for the purpose.

(iii) If ultimately a viable Ministry fails to emerge, the Governor should consider dissolving the Assembly and arranging for fresh elections after consulting the leaders of the political parties concerned and the Chief Election Commissioner.

(e) *Issuing the Ordinances:* Under the Constitution, the Governor may issue an ordinance relating to the State List when the State Assembly is not in session. This power is also exercised by the Governor on the advice of the Chief Minister and his Council of Ministers. But there have been cases when the Governors have refused to promulgate an ordinance on the advice of the Chief Minister. For example Governor D.C. Pavate refused to issue an Ordinance which would have enabled the legislators to hold certain offices of profit such as Chairman of the Improvement Trust on the basis that it will amount to political corruption. In 1979 G.D. Tapase refused to promulgate an Ordinance nationalising the Private Homeopathic Colleges. Dr. Shankar Dayal Sharma, Governor of AP refused to repromulgate three Ordinances as recommended by N.T. Rama Rao because (i) N.T. Rama Rao was an Interim or Caretaker Chief Minister and an interim government cannot take major policy decisions; and (ii) these ordinances were repromulagated five time in the past one year and it amounted to usurping the power of the Legislature.

Other Discretionary Powers

Besides the above there are other discretionary powers of the Governor which are as follows:

(i) In recommending President's Rule in the State under *Article 356**, the Governor uses his discretionary powers. This power has been highly misused by the Governor in the interest of party-in-power at the Centre, to prevent the opposition party or coalition from forming the government in the State. During the President's Rule, though an advisor is appointed by the President to advise the Governor, he in fact, becomes the real ruler of the State.

(ii) The Governor may reserve a Bill passed by the State Legislature for the consideration of the President. He may also send it back for reconsideration to the State Legislature.

(iii) The Governor has in many cases refused to dismiss the minister on the advice of the Chief Minister, in case of a coalition government.

(iv) In cases of key appointments like Vice-Chancellor and members of State Public Service Commission, the Governor. In 2001, the Governer of Bihar V.C. Pandey refused to accept the State Government panel of lists for the appointment of Vice Chancellors. Instead he

*For details see Chapter VIII—Tension Areas in Indian Federation and Chapter X—Emergency Powers of the President.

appointed commissioner-rank IAS officials as Vice-Chancellors. This, however, was not the first time, earlier also he had done the same, when he thought it was under his power, to refuse the advice of the Chief Minister.

(v) Asking information from the Chief Minister relating to legislative and administrative matters.

(vi) If a Minister has taken a decision but the Council of Ministers has not considered it, the Governor may ask the Chief Minister to submit it for the decision of the Council.

(vii) *Prosecution of the Chief Minister:* Another area where the Governor has a discretion is with regard to prosecution of the Chief Minister. In case of A.R. Antulay, the Chief Minister of Maharashtra, the High Court directed the Governor to decide whether to permit prosecution of the Chief Minister on the basis of facts and independently, on his discretion. The Governor accordingly gave the permission to prosecute A.R. Antulay. Similarly in Tamil Nadu, the Governor gave the permission to prosecute Jaylalitha, the Chief Minister, for corruption charges. In 1997, the Bihar Governor A.R. Kidwai gave permission to CBI to prosecute the Chief Minister Laloo Prasad Yadav on Fodder Corruption case after a long wait.

(viii) In the case of the Governor of Assam, certain administrative matters connected with the tribal areas and settling disputes between the government of Assam and the District Council with respect to mining royalties.

(ix) The Governors of Nagaland, Sikkim, Arunachal Pradesh, Mizoram, Meghalaya and Tripura have also been assigned certain functions which are to be exercised at their discretion.

Position and Role of Governor

The Constitution envisages a dual role for the Governor; (i) as the Constitutional Head of the State, and (ii) as the agent of the Centre.

Governor as the Head of the State

Governor as head of the State works under the parameters of parliamentary democracy which means he is a nominal head and exercises his functions strictly according to the "aid and advice" of the Council of Ministers. Though the administration is carried out in the name of Governor, the real authority is exercised by the Chief Minister and his Council of Ministers which is collectively responsible to the Legislative Assembly. This happened in the Indian political system till 1967. The Congress Party had the monopoly of political power in the

Union as well as the States. Further, this was also the era of Nehru's charismatic personality, in which the Governor as well as the Chief Minister were appointed by Nehru, who dominated both the Government at Centre and States, as well as the Congress Party. Under such circumstances, the Governor had no function to perform except, as Nehru said, "to entertain the people and make them feel pleased." Sarojini Naidu, the Governor of UP felt that she was a bird in a golden cage. To Dr. Pattabhi Sitaramayya, the Governor had only one function—of making fortnightly reports to the President. Naturally an active politician would never aspire to become a Governor. Dr. B.C. Ray, before becoming the Chief Minister of West Bengal, turned down the offer of Governorship and Governors like Rajaji, Sarojini Naidu, K.N. Katju and others took the earliest opportunity to relinquish the post of Governor. In the *Ram Jawaya Kapoor Vs. State of Punjab* in 1955, the Supreme Court held that "the Governor ... occupies the position of the Head of the executive in the State but it is virtually the Council of Ministers in each State that carries on the executive Government. In the Indian Constitution, therefore, we have the same system of Parliamentary executive as in England and the Council of Ministers consisting as it does, of the members of legislature is, like the British Cabinet, "a hyphen which joins, a buckle which fastens the legislative part of the State to the executive part."

The situation changed after the fourth General Elections in 1967, which constitutes a watershed in the development of the Indian federal system. The monopoly of political power by the Congress Party was broken and non-Congress Governments were formed in seven States. This phenomenon continues even today where no one party is capable of forming governments in both the Union and as well as many of the States. This changed scenario redrafted and redefined the position and role of the Governor in State politics. The Governors became actively involved in State politics and invariably they acted in the interests of the party-in-power at the Centre. They also used their discretionary powers for the purpose and thus making the office of the Governor highly controversial with the result that there was a demand to abolish the office of Governor.

The assertion of discretionary powers by the Governor, especially opposite to the interests of party or parties in power in a particular state, and in favour of the interests of the party or parties-in-power in the Centre, has created a new dimension in Indian politics. This has led to frequent conflicts between the Governor and the Chief Minister as in West Bengal after the fourth General Election in 1967 and other states.

Governor as an Agent of the Centre

According to K.M. Munshi, "Governor is the watch-dog of Constitutional propriety and the link which binds the State to the Centre thus securing the Constitutional unity of India." The Governor performs the following functions as the agent of the Centre in the States:

(i) The Union Government is responsible for good governance in the States. In case of Constitutional breakdown of machinery, the Governor may recommend President's Rule or emergency in the State under *Article 356.*

(ii) From time to time, the Governor sends his report regarding the affairs of the State.

(iii) The Centre has the power to issue directives to the States and it is the duty of the Governor to see that such directives are followed by the State Government.

(iv) The Governor of a State can reserve a Bill passed by the State Legislature for the consideration of the President. Certain types of Bills must be reserved by the Governor for President's consideration. For example Bills providing for the compulsory acquisition of property or adversely affecting the powers of the High Court.

Thus, the Governor enjoys a very powerful position in the Indian political system. Unfortunately, his office has been a source of tension between the Centre and the States due to his partisan role. Therefore, it is high time that the adequate amendment to the Constitution be made to ensure a free and fair role on the part of the Governor.

References

Chhabra, Harinder K., *State Politics in India,* 1977, Delhi, Surjeet Publications.

Fadia B.L., *Indian Government and Politics,* 1996, Agra, Sahitya Bhawan Publications.

Gupta D.C., *Indian Government and Politics* 1991, New Delhi, Vikas Publishing House Pvt. Ltd.

Sharan, P., *Government and Politics of India, Recent Developments,* 1986, New Delhi, Metropolitan Book Co. Pvt. Ltd.

Singh M.P., *V.N. Shukla's Constitution of India,* 2001, Lucknow, Eastern Book Company Lucknow.

Siwach, J.R., *Dynamics of Indian Government and Politics,* 1990, New Delhi, Sterling Publishers Private Ltd.

CHAPTER XIV

Panchayati Raj in India

Panchayati Raj is the rural self government system in India. It also means grassroot democracy because people at the grassroot level i.e. the village level are able to participate in the management of their affairs. Panchayati Raj becomes very important in the Indian context where almost 80 per cent of the people live in villages. In such a situation, Panchayati Raj assumes a very effective role in the political education of the rural folk. They are also an important dimension of social policy. As Dr. Gyan Chand observes, "Local authorities are now no longer a training ground for politically immature people; they have to be an integral part of whole system of national self- government and instruments of a national policy conceived in the highest interest of the people."

History of Panchayati Raj in India

The roots of Panchayati Raj in India go back to ancient period where Panchayats enjoyed extensive powers. They had a remarkable autonomy alongwith a fair percentage of the land tax and other revenues collected in their respective areas with the power to utilize them for the local needs. Professor Altekar rightly remarks that the village communities "to a great extent resembled small republics where the voice of the people prevailed." It is because of these village communities that the Indian civilization has distinguished itself in the arena of continuity. While the other civilizations rose, flourished and declined, the Indian civilization is still continuing.

The village communities alongwith village Panchayats continued irrespective of sweeping changes brought about by the rise and downfall of different dynasties in different periods. However it was the British rule in India that destroyed the village community system in order to convert India into a colony which would supply raw materials to the British industries and serve a readymade market for the British industrial goods. The practice of land revenue collection by the village communities was abolished and instead a direct settlement with the Zamindars and individual cultivators was introduced. The British also established a highly centralized system of administration in which the functions performed by village communities were handed over to new judicial and administrative officers appointed by the British Raj.

But the British administration also realised the importance of local self-government in such a vast country like India. Local self governments were developed in big cities like Madras, Bombay and Calcutta. In 1870, Lord Mayo introduced his scheme for the decentralisation of administration in which the development of local self government in villages was given due importance. But the rural committees envisaged under the scheme were largely nominated and the object was to tap local resources of revenue. In 1882, Lord Ripon declared his historic resolution called Ripon's Resolution according to which the local self government in rural areas was ushered in. The objective of local rural bodies was to make local self-government "an instrument of political and proper education. "The Provincial governments were asked to:

(i) maintain and extend throughout the country a network of institutions of local government especially in rural areas.
(ii) introduce a large number of non-official members in these bodies. The number of official members should not be more than 1/3rd of the total membership.
(iii) to exercise control over these bodies from without and not within.

Lord Ripon was hailed as the Father of Local Self-Government in India. He wanted least official control over the local bodies and he also insisted that "where they may still remain indigenous institutions of local government-they should be made use of to the utmost possible extent. Under Ripon's Resolution, the provincial governments introduced Panchayati system in villages especially in Punjab and Madras. In 1907, the Royal Commission on Decentralisation recommended the development of Panchayats as units of local administration. The Commission observed that "the foundation of any strong edifice which shall associate the people with the administration must be the village." The Government of India Acts 1919 and 1935 further gave impetus to local self government. However the effect was only marginal. Besides, the system of reservation was also introduced. For example in Madras seats were reserved for the nominated members, Muslims, Indian Christians, Scheduled Castes, Europeans, Anglo-Indians and Women. B.B. Mishra observes, "The problem of rural development, which were mainly social and economic, thus came to be treated in terms of politics and the elitist game of power."

During the freedom struggle, Mahatma Gandhi stood for the development of Panchayat system in India. He said in 1946, "Independence must begin at the bottom. Thus every village will be a republic or Panchayat having full powers. It follows, therefore, that every village has to be self sustained and capable of managing its affairs even to the extent of defending itself against the whole world."

Panchayati Raj in India

Article 40 of (Part IV) Indian Constitution dealing with the Directive Principles of State Policy stipulates, "The State shall take steps to organise village Panchayats and endow them with such powers and authority as may be necessary to enable them to function as units of self-government." However the leaders in 1950, were not very much enthusiastic about Panchayat Raj in India. To Dr. Ambedkar, "village was a sink of localism, a den of ignorance and narrow-mindedness." Nehru also expressed almost the same view. The Draft Constitution did not even mention it. The inclusion of village Panchayats in the Directive Principles was done, as B.B. Mishra says "after a great deal of wrangling and, there, too, as a thing merely to the desired." Indian Constitution did not create village Panchayats; they were created by the British rule in India. For Nehru, the priority was the economic and industrial development of India which was to be achieved through the parliamentary system and the bureaucracy, the steel frame of Indian Administration.

The Panchayati Raj in India was inaugurated as a consequence of the recommendations of Balwant Rai Mehta Committee set up in 1957, to study the Community Development Programme and National Extension Service launched in 1952 and 1953 respectively. These schemes, despite the high objectives failed because they could not invite rural participation. The Balwant Rai Mehta Committee made the following recommendations:

(i) A three-tier system of Panchayati Raj of Village Panchayats, Panchayat Samities at the intermediate level and Zila Parisads at the District level be established.

(ii) The Village Panchayat was to be in charge of sanitation, provision of water supply for domestic use, lighting of village streets, land management, maintenance of records relating to cattle, relief of distress, maintenance of village roads, culverts, bridges, drains, tanks etc., supervision of primary schools, welfare of backward classes, and maintenance of tax records.

(iii) The Panchayat Samiti was to be constituted through indirect elections from village Panchayats. For this purpose the Panchayats within a block area were to be conveniently grouped together and the Panchas of all the panchayats were to elect among themselves members of the Panchayat Samities. On an average the strength of the Panchayat Samiti was to be elected members, besides representatives of women and, scheduled caste and scheduled tribes, if their population exceeded 5 per cent of the population of the region. The Panchayat Samiti was to have an elected chairman.

(iv) The functions of the Panchayat Samities were to cover the development of agriculture in all its aspects, including the selection of the seeds, their procurement and distribution, the improvement of agricultural practices, provision of local agricultural finance with the assistance of the government and the cooperative banks, minor irrigation works, improvement of local cattle, sheep, goat and poultry, the promotion of local industries, the supply of drinking water, public health and sanitation and medical relief, relief of distress caused by floods, earthquake, scarcity etc, arrangements in connection with local pilgrimages and festivals, construction and repair of roads of local importance (other than the village panchayat roads) management and administrative control of primary schools, fixation of wages under the Minimum Wages Act for non-industrial labour, the welfare of backward classes and the collection and maintenance of statistics. Further, the Panchayat Samiti was to act as the agent of the State Government in executing any special schemes of development or other activities which the State Government might like to delegate to it. The Panchayat Samitis might be given certain other functions like maintenance and development of small forests, the responsibility for the maintenance of watch and ward establishment, excise and other items.

(v) At the highest level were to be Zila Parishads. The members of Zila Parishads were to be elected from the Presidents of the Panchayat Samitis. Besides the members of State legislature and Parliament of the concerned area, district level officers of the medical, public health, agriculture, veterinary, engineering, education, backward classes welfare, public works and other development departments were to be its members. The collector was to be the Chairman of the Zila Parishad.

(vi) The emphasis was on democratic decentralisation which meant "a process whereby the Government divests itself completely of certain duties and responsibilities and transfers them to some other authority." The village Panchayats and Panchayat Samitis were to be the main local bodies for developmental activities.

(vii) The financial resources of Panchayat and Panchayat Samitis were also identified. The main source for village Panchayat would be property or house tax; taxes on markets, bazars, carts, bicycles, boats and pack animals; octroi on terminal tax; income from cattle pounds; fees for registration of animals sold; fees from slaughter houses and grant from the Panchayat Samiti. The Panchayat samiti would give a fixed percentage of land revenue, a cess on land revenue, on primary education, water rate, tax on professions and trades, surcharge on duty on the transfer of immovable property, rents and profits accruing from property such as ferries and fisheries, tolls and leases of roads and bridge, pilgrim tax, tax on entertainment, proceeds, from periodical fairs and markets, a share of the motor vehicle tax, voluntary public contribution and grants from governments.

The recommendations of the Balwant Rai Committee were accepted by the National Development Council in 1959. The Panchayati Raj was first inaugurated in Rajasthan in October 1959, followed by Andhra Pradesh and Tamil Nadu in the same year. Later on, other states also followed suit.

Defects in Panchayati Raj

There are certain defects also in Panchayati Raj system which surfaced very soon since its implementation. According to Ashok Mehta Committee which was appointed by the Janata Government in 1977, the Panchayati Raj in India had three phases—Firstly, the phase of ascendancy (1959-64), the phase of stagnation (1965-69) and finally the phase of decline (1969-77). Despite the Balwant Rai Mehta Committee recommendation of three-tier system of Panchayati Raj, there was wide diversity in terms of structure of the Panchayati Raj. While 12 states (Andhra Pradesh, Assam, Bihar, Gujarat, Haryana, Himachal Pradesh, Maharashtra, Punjab, Rajasthan, Tamil Nadu, and Arunachal Pradesh opted for the recommended three tier system, West Bengal had a four tier system of village Panchayat, Anchal Panchayat,

Anchalik Parishad and Zila Parishad. The state of Madhya Pradesh, Mysore (Karnataka), Orissa and some of the districts of Bihar had two-tier system of village Panchayat and Panchayat Samiti. The states of Jammu and Kashmir, Kerala, Manipur, and Tripura were content with only one-tier system i.e. village Panchayat. Thus there was no uniformity in the structure of Panchayati Raj in India. Even in the function and powers, variations existed in different states.

There was lack of political will also. Despite his initial reluctance, Nehru viewed the three tier system as a model instrument for rural development and during his later times, the Panchayati Raj institutions witnessed the period of ascendency. He created a new Ministry of Community Development in 1956 and in 1957, the administration of the village Panchayat was transferred to the Minister of Community Development. Initially the Minister for Food and Agriculture was responsible for coordinating the work of the new Ministry with that of his Ministry and the new Ministry was to work in full cooperation with the Ministry of Food and Agriculture. In 1958, the control of co-operation was also transferred to the Ministry of Community Development and it was renamed as Ministry of Community Development and Cooperation. But Nehru's successors did not display same enthusiasm as was shown by Nehru. Lal Bahadur Shastri accepted that "he did not share Nehru's faith in the capacity of the people to rule themselves." Indira Gandhi believed in and established a highly centralised polity in which Panchayati Raj Institution (PRIs) were highly neglected. She merged the Ministry of Community Development and cooperation with the Ministry of Food and Agriculture. The centralising tendencies in Indian Political system were not conducive to a healthy development of Panchayati Raj Institutions. The state Governments also lacked political will to implement Panchayati Raj in its true spirit. They already had a grievance of being assigned less power under the constitution. They were reluctant in sharing their powers with the Panchayati Raj Institutions. The bureaucracy also viewed the Panchayati Raj Institution with utmost contempt and suspicion as a potential threat to its dominating position. The 1970's saw the launching of welfare programmes in rural areas without the Panchayati Raj Institution being involved in them. For example Pilot Research Scheme in Growth Centres stated in 1970 and Crash Scheme for Rural Employment in 1971, Small Farmer's Development Agencies (SFDA) and Marginal Farmer's and Agricultural Labour's Development Agencies (MFAL), Tribal Development Agencies (TDA), Drought Prone Area Programme (DPAP), Pilot Intensive Rural Employment Project and Agricultural

Credit and Marketing were such schemes which created separate agencies outside the sphere of Panchayati Raj Institutions. The subjects assigned to Panchayati Raj Institution were also taken away, for example village industries which was the responsibility of Panchayati Raj Institution were assigned to a National Commission as early as in 1953, and these institutions had no role in promoting village industries. Similarly water supply which was Panchayat's subject was given to new water boards or authorities.

It is also to be remembered that there was a variety of perception when the Panchayati Raj was introduced and even after. To the state Government, it was an instrument or an agency to implement Community Development Programmes. In some states fears have been expressed that the Panchayati Raj law may undermine regional identities and thus lead to further centralisation at the state level. To politicians particularly at the grassroot level, it was a local self government. To people like Jaya Prakash Narayan it was Sarvodaya, a new social order to replace the existing exploitative system. During Rajiv Gandhi times, many felt Panchayati Raj Institutions were being viewed as the extension of central Government's powers at the expense of state Government's power. These different perspectives made the Panchayati Raj Institutions a political issue and in the process the PRIs suffered. Technology was also a major factor in the decline of Panchayati Raj. After the severe food shortage in 1966-67, the main plank of Central Government had been to promote new varieties of seeds and other modern concepts to achieve high production. For this purpose Green Revolution was launched under the Central Government's direction. As mentioned above, new schemes were launched which were outside the purview of local self Government and even the State Government. The severe food shortage also led to another development detrimental to Panchayati Raj institutions. The priorities were reshuffled and there was total emphasis on increasing agricultural production only. "In the process," as S.R. Maheshwari says, "a comprehensive concept of rural development got reduced to a mere project for agricultural production."

Lack of adequate financial resources also hampered the effective functioning of Panchayati Raj Institutions. The Panchayats on their own could not take up any programme of rural development. They had no access to capital resources. They were entirely dependent upon the central and State Government funds. It was also seen that the Panchayats would become suddenly operational when they received some grants. After the grants were consumed, they went back to their slumber.

Further, the Sarpanch of the Panchayat arrogated all powers of the Panchayat to himself. He had overshadowed the Panchayat as an institution. The other members of the Panchayat hardly took any interest to ensure its smooth functioning. The Panchayati Raj Institutions also created group rivalries which are the essential consequences of electoral politics and thus vitiated the atmosphere of the villages and hindered the smooth functioning of the system.

Ashok Mehta Committee's Recommendations

The Ashok Mehta Committee emphasised the functional necessity for decentralisation of administration. It recommended the creation of two-tier instead of three-tier system of Panchayati Raj—Zila Parishad and Mandal Panchayats. It did not favour village panchayats. The committee also suggested compulsory power of taxation of Panchayati Raj institutions to mobilise their own resources so that their dependence on funds from Central and State Governments could be reduced. It also advocated open participation of political parties in Panchayati Raj affairs. However the Janata Government soon fell and the new Congress (I) Government shelved the report of Ashok Mehta Committee.

73rd Constitutional Amendment

In 1992, a giant leap forward was achieved when the Seventy Third Constitutional Amendment was enacted, which gave constitutional status to Panchayati Raj Institutions. The amendment had following provisions regarding the Panchayati Raj Institutions.

(i) It made obligatory on the part of all states to provide for the three-tier Panchayati Raj system at the village, Intermediate and District levels. However, the states having a population not exceeding twenty lakhs may not have panchayats at the intermediate level. The 73rd Amendment does not apply in Jammu and Kashmir, Meghalaya, Mizoram, Nagaland and Delhi.

(ii) All the seats in all the three levels are elected directly on the basis of adult franchise. For this purpose each Panchayat area is divided into territorial constituencies in such a manner that the ratio between the population of each constituency and the number of seats allotted to it is the same throughout the Panchayat area.

(iii) The legislature of a state may by law provide representation of the (a) Chairpersons of the Panchayats at the village level, in the Panchayats at intermediate level or where there is no Panchayat at the intermediate level in the Panchayats at District level; (b) of the Chairpersons of the Panchayats at the intermediate level in the

Panchayats at the district level; (c) of concerned members of Lok Sabha and State legislative Assembly in the upper two-levels of the Panchayats; (d) Similarly the concerned member of Rajya Sabha and the Legislative Council of the State may be represented at the upper two-levels.

(iv) The Chairperson of the village Panchayat is elected as per the law made by the state legislature. But the chairpersons of Panchayats at intermediate and district level are elected by their elected members respectively.

(v) The Amendment provides for reservation of seats for Scheduled Castes, Scheduled Tribes and women in all the three tiers of the Panchayats which are:

(a) 33 per cent seats are reserved for women. These reserved seats are allotted by rotation to different constituencies in a Panchayat.
(b) The reservation of seats for Scheduled Castes and Scheduled Tribes is done according to their respective population in the Panchayat area. If their number is not sufficient to qualify for reservation, one seat for the Scheduled Castes or Scheduled Tribes, as the case may be, must be reserved for them.
(c) Out of seats reserved for Scheduled Castes and Scheduled Tribes, thirty per cent seats are reserved for Scheduled Castes and Scheduled Tribes women. When the number of seats is two, one is reserved for Scheduled castes and Scheduled Tribes women as the case may be.
(d) The State legislature may reserve the office of Chairpersons for Scheduled Castes and Scheduled Tribes in some Panchayats.

(vi) The tenure of Panchayats at all levels is fixed for five years. They may be dissolved but within six months of their dissolution the new panchayats are to be elected. In case the dissolution takes place at a time when their remaining period is less than six months, the new Panchayats will enjoy full five years term. In case the dissolution takes place at a time when the remaining period is more, then tenure will be the unexpired duration of the predecessor Panchayat.

(vii) The State Election Commission consisting of a State Election Commissioner, appointed by the Governor holds the election to the Panchayats. The State Election Commissioner can be removed by the same process and conditions as the judge of a High Court. The legislature of State can make rules regarding the elections to the Panchayats.

(viii) The State Legislature has been given power to assign such powers and authority by law as may be necessary to enable them to function as an institution of self-government and such law may contain provisions for the devolution of powers and responsibilities upon Panchayats at the appropriate level with respect to:

(a) the preparation of plans for economic development and social justice;

(b) the implementation of schemes for economic development and social justice including those in relation to the matters listed in the Eleventh Schedule. The Eleventh Schedule lists the following matters to be assigned to Panchayats:

- Agriculture, including agricultural extension
- Land improvement, implementation of land reforms, land consolidation and soil conservation
- Minor irrigation, water management and watershed development
- Animal husbandry, dairying and poultry
- Fisheries
- Social forestry and farm forestry
- Minor forest produce
- Small-scale industries, including food processing industries
- Khadi, village and cottage industries
- Rural housing
- Drinking water
- Fuel and fodder
- Roads, culverts, bridges, ferries, waterways and other means of communication
- Rural electrification, including distribution of electricity
- Non-conventional energy sources
- Poverty alleviation programme
- Education, including primary and secondary schools
- Technical training and vocational education
- Adult and non-formal education
- Libraries
- Cultural activities
- Markets and fairs
- Health and sanitation, including hospitals, primary health centres and dispensaries
- Family welfare
- Women and child development
- Social welfare, including welfare of the handicapped and mentally retarded
- Welfare of the weaker sections, and in particular, of the Scheduled Castes and the Scheduled Tribes
- Public distribution system

- Maintenance of community assets

(ix) The Amendment also provides that the Legislature of a State may, by law,

(a) authorise a Panchayat to levy, collect and appropriate such taxes, duties, tolls and fees in accordance with such procedure and subject to such limits;
(b) assign to a Panchayat such taxes, duties, tolls and fees levied and collected by the State Government for such purposes and subject to such conditions and limits;
(c) provide for making such grants-in-aid to the Panchayats from the Consolidated Fund of the State: and
(d) provide for constitution of such funds and crediting all money received, respectively, by or on behalf of the Pachayats and also for the withdrawal of such money therefrom, as may be specified in the law.

(x) After every five years the Governor of a State is to constitute a Finance Commission to review the financial position of the Panchayats and make recommendations to the Governor as to the principles which should govern

(a) the distribution between the state and the Panchayats of the net proceeds of the taxes, duties, tolls and fees leviable by the State, which may be divided between them under this part and the allocation between the Panchayats at all levels of their respective shares of such proceeds;
(b) the determination of the taxes, duties, tolls and fees which may be assigned to, or appropriated by, the Panchayats.
(c) the grants-in-aid to the Panchayats from the Consolidated Fund of the State;
(d) the measures needed to improve the financial position of the Panchayats:
(e) any other matter referred to the Finance Commission by the Governor in the interests of sound finances of the Panchayats.

(xi) A Gram Sabha may exercise such powers and perform such functions at the village level as the Legislature of a State may, by law provide.

Panchayati Raj—Structure and Functions

Thus we see that the Seventy Third Amendment provides for three- tier system of Panchayati Raj Institutions. These institutions were already existent in many states though their functioning was unsatisfactory. The Seventy-Third Amendment makes it obligatory on all the States to have the three-tier system barring some exceptions. The three levels or tiers of Panchayati system exist at the (a) village (b) intermediate and (c) district levels.

(a) *Panchayati Raj at the Village level*

At the village level, we have the Gram Sabha or the legislature with Gram Panchayat as its executive organ. Gram Sabha which earlier existed as a statutory body before Seventy Third Amendment, has now been provided with a constitutional status. However the membership of the Gram Sabha varies from state to state. In some states all the adult population of the village are its members. In some states it consists of the voters in the area. Thus Gram Sabha is a body of people of the village. Generally the Gram Sabha meets twice a year after the rabi and kharif harvests. The Gram Sabha elects the members of Village Panchayat called panchas and its Chairperson, the Sarpanch and a deputy chairperson, the deputy or Up-Sarpanch. However it has been found that there has been a lack of awareness on the part of villagers about their rights and responsibilities towards the village panchayats. Most of them feel that their duty finishes once they elect the village panchayat. The panchas also do not take adequate interest in the affairs of panchayat. It is the Sarpanch only who functions and is therefore approached by the people. As early as in 1954, the Congress Village Panchayat Committee noted that "Panchayats should be looked at as non-political units. Care has to be taken that in the enthusiasm to provide a democratic set up in the villages, we donot introduce there the evils of western type electioneering." Unfortunately exactly the same has happened in Gram Sabha and elections to village panchayats are held on party basis. The Village Panchayats functions are largely related to (i) civic amenities. (ii) Social work activities and (iii) developmental works. They include construction of public wells, supply of drinking water, maintenance of streets, rural electrification, sanitation, promotion of cottage industries development of agriculture, prevention of fires, promotion of cooperatives, improvement of cattle, help in census operations promotion of social education, control over offensive trades, regulation of shops and buildings, maintenance of panchayat-property, organising voluntary labour, distribution of improved sites, management of public markets, distribution of subsides etc.

In many states, Panchayati Adalats also function at the village level as the modern system of justice is very expensive and time- consuming. It is also inaccessible to the rural areas. The Panchayati Adalats supplement the formal judicial system by reviving and legitimising the traditional system of justice.

(b) *Panchayat at the Intermediate Level*

The second level is Panchayat Samiti which functions at the block level in all the States. It is identified by different names in different states. In Andhra Pradesh, Bihar, Maharashtra, Orissa, Punjab and Rajasthan, it is called Panchayat Samiti while in Assam, Madhya Pradesh, Tamil Nadu, Uttar Pradesh and West Bengal it is termed as Anchalik Panchayat, Janapada Panchayat, Panchayat Union Council, Kshettra Samiti and Anchalik Parishad respectively. The chairperson is also known differently in different states. In Andhra Pradesh, Assam, Gujarat, Madhya Pradesh, Karnataka and West Bengal, he is known as President while in Tamil Nadu, Maharashtra, Orissa and Punjab he is known as Chairman. In Rajasthan he is Pradhan while in Bihar and Uttar Pradesh he is called Pramukh. He can be removed from his office by a no confidence motion of the Panchayat Samiti. There is also a deputy chairperson or up-pradhan. The Panchayat Samiti is to be directly elected as per the Seventy Third Constitutional Amendment. The Panchayat Samiti coordinates and supervises the work of Panchayats. They are also responsible for implementation of various developmental programmes. The functions of Panchayat Samitis include supply of drinking water, drainage, construction of roads, establishment of primary health centres, primary schools and youth organisations and cultural activities, execution of developmental programmes, distribution of improved seeds and fertilizers, conservation of soil, providing credit for agricultural purposes, irrigation facilities, improvement of forest areas, cattle and fodder, development of cottage and small scale industries and opening of cooperatives.

(c) *Panchayat at the District Level*

At the top of Panchayati Raj is Zila Parishad as it is known in Andhra Pradesh, Bihar, Maharashtra, Orissa, Punjab, Rajasthan, Uttar Pradesh and West Bengal. In Gujarat, Madhya Pradesh, and in Tamil Nadu and Karnataka, it is known as District Panchayat, Zila Panchayat and District Development Council respectively. The chairperson is known as "Chairman" in Andhra Pradesh, Madhya Pradesh, Orissa, Punjab and West Bengal while he is "President" in Assam, Gujarat, Maharashtra and Karnataka. In Bihar and Uttar Pradesh he is known as 'Adhyaksha' and in Rajasthan as "Pramukh." He conducts the meetings of Zila Parishad, inspects the lower tiers of Panchayati Raj institutions and submits his report to the Zila Parishad. By a vote of no-confidence he can be removed from his office. As per the Seventy Third Amendment, members of Zila Parishad are elected directly. The Zila Parishad has the overall responsibility of planning and implementation of development programmes. It also coordinates the work of Panchayat Samitis.

The functions of Zila Parishad are to (i) examine and approve the budget of Panchayat Samitis; (ii) issue directions to Panchayat Samities for efficient performance of their duties; (iii) coordinate the development plans made by Panchayat Samitis; (iv) advise the state Government relating to development activities of the district; (v) distribute funds to various Panchayat Samities; (vi) inform the Division Commissioner and the District Collector about irregulavities in Panchayati Raj Institutions; (vii) coordinate the work of various panchayat samitis and (viii) advise the State Government on the allocation of work to be made among the Panchayati Raj Institutions. The Block Development Officer (BDO) is the secretary of the Zila Parishad.

At the centre the ministry of Rural Development monitors the working of Panchayati Raj Institutions in India. At the state level, there is a Department of Rural Development and Panchayati Raj which looks after the Panchayati Raj Institutions. At the district level Collector, Chief Executive officer of Zila Parishad, Additional Collector and Development-cum-Project Directors are associated with Panchayati Raj institutions. At the block level we have Block Development officers and Extension Officers while at the Village Level, the Village Level Worker (VLW) or Gram Sevak play important roles.

The Post-Seventy third Amendment Scenario

By April 1994, all states had enacted legislation as per the requirement of the Seventy Third Amendment to grant power and authority to Panchayats to enable them to function as institution of self governance. The experience has been a mixed one. Madhya Pradesh was the first state to establish the three-tier Panchayati Raj under the Seventy Third Amendment. By the middle of June 1994, the election process for 30,992 Panchayats, 459 Janapada Panchayats and 45 district Panchayats was completed. The State Cabinet decided to establish an organic relationship between the three tier bodies, at the same time ensuring clear division of power. It was decided to convert the district Panchayat into main executive arm with the Janapada Panchayat acting as its extension and the village panchayats to be made the main implementing agencies, responsible for chalking out the action plans.

The Rajasthan Government passed the Panchayati Raj Act, 1995 and elections were held in about 10,000 Gram Panchayats, 237 Panchayat Samitis and 31 Zila Parishads. In Orissa the anti-defection law has been extended to Zila Parishads. In Himachal Pradesh, the Gram Sabhas have been entrusted with the responsibility of selecting the beneficiaries under the various poverty alleviation programmes. Under the Kerala Panchayat Act, the local bodies have been assigned the responsibility of directly managing primary and high schools, hospitals, veterinary hospitals, agricultural farms and Krishi Bhawans at various levels. Rajasthan has launched a significant Programme through which one Panchayat Samiti each from nine districts would locate areas where work relating to potable water and construction of houses and toilets can be undertaken over a period of five years. Tamil Nadu Government has agreed to give more grants by giving 90 per cent of the total receipts from entertainment tax. However in Bihar, Lakshadweep and Pondicherry the elections to the Panchayati Raj bodies were not held partly due to lack of political will and also because of judicial stay orders.

The most important development of Seventy Third Amendment was the reservation of 33 per cent seats for women in the local bodies. There have also been all-women Panchayats in Maharashtra, Madhya Pradesh, West Bengal and Tripura. It has been found that the all-women Panchayats have done remarkably well. Women representatives in tribal areas have also become very active. But this does not mean all has been well. In 1995, a workshop of elected women Panchayat members made an embarrassing revelation-that most women were surrogates for male family members and exercised no powers and functions. Most of these women were illiterate and lived in purdah. They were escorted by the male members who not only took active part in deliberations but also took decisions. In Madhya Pradesh, a woman Backward class Sarpanch of a village Panchayat was stripped naked during an extended Panchayat meeting in the presence of Block Development officer (BDO) when she refused to comply with the demands of her male counterparts. In Alwar, Rajasthan, it was revealed that a young woman pradhan of Panchayat Samiti would sit in ghunghat in the meetings and her father-in-law was regularly presiding over the meeting. It has also been found that the women members did not even attend the meetings of the Panchayats. In some Panchayats, their importance was seen as members who could be used only for fulfilling the required quota without which the meeting could not be held. Once the quota was achieved, they were sidelined. Their functions were duly performed by their husbands. The Bassi Panchayat Samiti in

Rajasthan passed a resolution condemning Bhanwari Devi, an alleged victim of gang rape, for her crusade against the crime which brought "bad" name to the village. When the resolution to the effect was passed many of the women members were not present. They were represented by their husbands and those women members present were guided by their husbands not to oppose the resolution. The Rajasthan Government, after the successful conduct of Panchayati Raj elections, discovered that the women members were not aware of their rights and functions as members or presiding officers of the panchayats. Male members of the Panchayats also faced similar problems. Therefore a training programme was launched for elected women representatives alongwith the males. In many cases the women did not attend the training under pressure from their husbands because there were no separate training programmes for women. However this is too short a period to arrive at any conclusion. One may positively hope that with the passage of time the women will definitely play their due role and their enpowerment will become a reality.

Another aspect of Panchayati Raj has been the caste factor. In U.P. in 1995 the election to Panchayati Raj institutions were held after the Supreme Court set aside the Allahabad High Court's decision declaring the State's Panchayat Act as invalid. However writ petitions were filed against as many as 25 districts where the reservation quota of Scheduled Castes/Scheduled Tribes, other Backward classes (OBC) and women went far above 50 per cent, a limit set up by the Supreme Court for reservation. In Haridwar, the reservation quota was 81.1 per cent followed by Sonbhadra (79.8 per cent), Mainpuri (77.5 per cent), Firozabad (77.5 per cent), Lucknow (77.3 per cent) and Hamirpur (76.6 per cent). It was alleged that the Chief Minister Mulayam Singh Yadav was taking caste politics to the grassroot level. The State Government delimited the Panchayat areas which not only changed the geographical boundaries but also the caste composition of the Gram Sabhas. As a result many upper-caste dominated villages had Pradhans belonging to either OBCs or Scheduled Castes. There was a violent reaction in which a dozen pradhans were killed, a price they were made to pay for becoming the heads of upper-caste dominated villages. The opposition parties had criticised the manner in which elections to the Panchayati Raj bodies was held. They alleged that the Chief Minister Yadav has used the Panchayati Raj not for decentralisation of power, but for its concentration in the fellow-casteists.

Its of unfortunate that corruption has also gone to the grassroots. Funds are not properly utilised. In Andhra Pradesh, there had been reports of auctioning of Panchayat posts. In Mutyalampadu of Guruzala Assembly constituency, the post of sarpanch was allegedly auctioned for Rs. 6.25 lakh to a woman aspirant.

In 1997, the National Institute of Rural Development held a conference on democratic decentralisation in which the chairpersons of Zila Parishads, civil servants associated with rural governance and academics, participated to review the prospects for Panchayati Raj in India. The conference stressed the need for true devolution of power to Panchayati Raj. For this, fiscal autonomy to Panchayati Raj Institutions was also emphasised. For this, it was stated, that we should learn from the Chinese experience where they enjoyed fiscal autonomy. China ensured fiscal autonomy because its local level institutions historically had a bottom-up approach wherein they were required by law to deposit a certain fixed percentage of their revenue mobilisation with the centre and rest they were free to keep for themselves. This gave an incentive to maximise their revenue collection. But in India we have the reverse. The Panchayati Raj Institutions still donot enjoy fiscal autonomy. The Madhya Pradesh State Finance Commission has pointed out in its first report that the Panchayats are being treated as an agency of the State Government when it comes to defining their powers and it appears that the Government has failed to transfer programmes to the Panchayats under the State Panchayati Raj Act as per the spirit of Seventy Third Constitutional Amendment. But there has been reluctance because of other reason also. A massive Rs 15 crore muster roll scam has been unearthed in the Water Resources Department in Madhya Pradesh which is manned by non-professionals. When the huge amounts under various developmental programmes are allocated to Panchayats which are manned by persons without any professional training, there are all the chances that the funds will be misused. The Panchayats have been given control of hand-pumps and they only have a couple of fitters with antiquated tools at their disposal. Therefore it is now increasingly felt that we should go slow in this field and first develop training, expertise, responsibility and infrastructure and then only devolution of fiscal powers be accomplished.

Another aspect of Panchayati Raj Institutions is the salary and allowances to the members. They are given meagre allowances and no salary. They only contest the elections because of the status and prestige associated with the office. But this cannot be a motivating factor for them in the long run. On the contrary this will only breed corruption, a malaise which has already turned into a giant ghost in the Indian politics. The only alternative is to provide them decent wages so that they would not only work efficiently but also honestly. This has been done in other countries and there is no reason why we should not do so in our country.

It is also necessary that the organic link which existed in the three tier Panchayati Raj system prior to 73rd Amendment be restored. The sarpanches of the village Panchayats should be the members of Panchayat Samitis and the presidents of the Panchayat Samities be the members of the Zila Parishads so that the coordination of work is ensured.

But it's also a fact that a silent revolution is taking place in rural India where people are becoming conscious of their rights. In Gujarat, false case of corruption and misuse of office was filed against an upright dalit woman Sarpanch, Shakriben, who was doing a commendable job which led to her removal. But she fought back and with the support of people, she was reinstated. In fact, the women's lot is improving. In Rajasthan, Haryana and many other places they are improving their socio-economic status also by forming self help groups (SHGs) and many of them belong to Below poverty line families.

In 1997 a study was conducted by the Ministry of Rural Areas and Employment which underlined the need to give functional autonomy to Gram Panchayats. It suggested that a system be developed in which they should be able to spend funds without hindrance by the block officials. It also suggested that the contact between the village Sarpanch and the Block officials should be reduced to the minimum. Rather than seeking permission for each technical issue it will be better if a technical manual is prepared giving relevant information on the common types of rural work which can then be used by the Sarpanch of the village Panchayats without the need to refer their problems to the junior engineer or other officials. It suggested special training programmes to train village Sarpanchs and Panchas in understanding muster rolls and measurement books. The Central Government also wants a mechanism evolved by which the people in the villages know about the availability of funds.

Thus it seems that a proper setting is developing in which the devolution of power to the grassroot level may become a reality. However, the path is far from rosy because the reluctance of the State Government to devolve their powers is still there. They already feel that they have been assigned less power by the constitution and do not want to share whatever "little" they have. In fact the Seventy Third Amendment has introduced a three tier polity in India. At the top is the Central Government in the middle, the State Government and at the bottom the Panchayats. The Central Government is reluctant to decentralise its powers so that they can be given to the State Governments and the State Governments in their turn are unwilling to share their powers with the Panchayats.

We can well say that the Panchayati Raj Institutions in India are undergoing a phase of transition. Despite the Seventy Third Amendment, the Panchayati Raj is still a dream. Only time will tell as to what extent the present arrangements will succeed and a real Panchayati Raj established in India. But there is no doubt that a real beginning has been made by the 73rd Constitutional Amendment Act.

References

Arora Ramesh K and Goyal Rajni, *Indian Public Administration, Institutions and Issues*, 1995, New Delhi, Vishwa Prakashan.

Gupta B.B., *Local Government in India*, 1968, Allahabad, Central Book Depot.

Kaushik, Susheela, *Women and Panchayati Raj*, 1993, New Delhi, Har-Anand Publications.

Khanna R.L., *Panchayati Raj in India*, 1972, Ambala, The English Book Depot.

Maheshwari S.R., *Local Government in India*, 1988, Agra Lakshmi Narain Agarwal Educational Publishers.

Mishra B.B., *District Administration and Rural Development*, 1983, Delhi, Oxford University Press.

Puri Dr. K.K. and Barara, *Local Government in India*, 1986, Jalandhar, Bharat Prakashan.

Ramachandran Padma, *Public Administration in India*, New Delhi, National Book Trust.

Singh M.P., *V.N. Shukla's Constitution of India*, 1994, Lucknow, Eastern Book Company.

CHAPTER XV

Nature of Administration—Role in Political and Development Process

The Indian administration system is a legacy of the British Raj in India. The British Government established a system of civil services in India which later came to be known as "the steel frame of the British empire." The steel frame gave strength, support and ruthlessness to the British rule in India.

The establishment of civil service arose out of the Northcote Trevelyan Committee appointed by Lord Gladstone, the then Chancellor of Exchequer to enquire into, and report on, the organisation of a permanent civil service in Great Britain. Interestingly the committee noted that "such a service, was eagerly desired by those who do not wish to face any competition and want to earn their livelihood with little labour and risk." The Committee's report, which was essentially meant for implementation in Britain, could not be accepted due to nepotism and favouritism that existed in Britain. However, the Report formed the basis for establishment of civil service in India. It ended the days of military adventurists who looked upon service in India as an avenue for glory. In its place was the quiet orderly efficiency of the civil services—the steel frame of British Raj in India. The British defined it according to their specific needs. Primarily it was a regulatory administration whose functions were (i) maintenance of law and order in the country ensuring continuance of the British Raj; (ii) collection of revenues. (iii) administration of justice; and (iv) rendering of minimal essential services. The organisation was based on the (i) retention of strategic powers in the hands of the British Civil servants and (ii) subservience of administration to the interests and the needs of British empire. The administration was not subject to popular control. Largely it was an autocratic system catering to the British needs and requirements in India.

Naturally the Indian political leaders were highly critical of the officers of the Indian Civil Service. To Nehru, they were arrogant, overbearing and contemptuous of public opinion. According to him, "They formed a sort of mutual admiration society and were constantly praising each other. Even feeble criticism of their actions was resented by them, so intolerant were they." He was "quite sure that no new order can be built upon, in India so long as the spirit of the Indian Civil Service pervades our administration and our public service." Therefore he wanted to do away with them in free India. However free India decided to keep them. In the Constituent Assembly, when the Indian Civil Service was being characterised as unpatriotic, anti- national and even traitors, Sardar Patel said, "I wish to assure you that I have worked with them during this difficult period. I am speaking with a sense of heavy responsibility and I must confess that in point of patriotism, in point of loyalty, in point of sincerity and in point of ability, you cannot have a substitute. They are as good as ourselves and to speak of them in disparaging terms in this House in public and to criticize them in this manner, is doing a disservice to yourselves and to the country. This is my considered opinion .... I agreed to Partition as a last resort, when we had reached a stage when we could have lost all .... I wish to place it on record in this House that if, during the last two or three years, most of the members of the Services had not behaved patriotically and with loyalty, the Union would have collapsed .... Remove them and I see nothing but a picture of chaos all over the country". One can infer that the "steel frame" helped sustain Indian independence.

Nature of Bureaucracy in India

In modern times, the executive is classified into political and permanent executive. Political executive consists of ministers who are the members of and responsible to the legislature. They take the policy decision in the best interest of the country. Permanent executive are the civil servants who assist and advise the Ministers in policy formulation, on the basis of their expertise, knowledge and experience, and implement the formulated policies. The political executive is temporary in nature as normally after every five years, elections to the legislature takes place and a new political party may come into power. Further, the ministers may be changed or transferred to another department. They may resign also. But the permanent executive is there till the age of their retirement. They are chosen at a young age on the basis of a competitive examination held by the public service commission, and for them it is a career. Such a system has the following characteristics:

(i) Civil Servants consist of a class of officials who are trained, skilled, permanent and paid. They are chosen on the basis of a competitive examination organised by the public service commission.

(ii) Civil Services are hierarchically organised. There is a clear system of superior-subordinate relationship in which the lower level is controlled and supervised by the higher level.

(iii) Civil Servants are politically neutral. Although they exercise their right to vote in elections, they are forbidden from dabbling in political activities. They have to serve the party in power as they are the servants of the state. This ensures a clean, transparent and accountable administration. Policy formulation is the privilege of the ministers. However the civil servants provide them the necessary information and assistance. But once the policy is formulated, it is the duty of civil servants to implement it without any prejudice or reservation. According to H.M. Patel, a retired bureaucrat, "A civil servant in fact has to be committed only to the discharge of his duties as competently, as efficiently and as devotedly as possible. The more objective the civil servant is in the appraisal of the facts and evidence before him, the more capable will he be of discharging his legitimate functions and duties well and adequately. The minister and the government may accept his conclusion or advice, or may not ... His duty, once the decision is made, will be to apply his mind to the ways in which the decision made can be implemented effectively and made a success."

(iv) Anonymity is another characteristic of the civil servant. They work behind the veil and are supposed to remain hidden. It is the Minister who comes into open and is responsible for the civil servant's conduct. Padma Ramachandran rightly says, "The Minister represents the parliament in administration, as well as the administration in the parliament. Hence they must stand by their officials in the parliament, particularly as officials have no forum or opportunity to defend themselves."

(v) The civil servants are not directly accountable to the Parliament. However in a way they are accountable also. There are various parliamentary committees such as the Public Accounts Committee, Estimates Committee, Committee on Subordinate Legislation, Standing Committees, Committee on Public undertaking, Consultative Committees of their respective departments, Joint Parliamentary Committees and Committee of Investigation in which the civil servants appear and have to account for their actions. As Padma Ramachandran says, "Clearly, these are intended to keep the civil servants on their toes all the time as they have to defend government policies and actions."

(vi) The main function of Civil Service is to implement the executive orders and legislative enactments. They are expected to do so impartially, faithfully and with political neutrality. In modern times they play a very important role in law-making in as much as all the government Bills introduced in the parliament are prepared by the civil servants. The ministers have a very poor knowledge of legislative needs and requirements. They also have little time for policy formulation and running their respective departments. The Parliament also suffers from paucity of time and energy in passing various legislative enactments. Hence the role of civil servants achieves greater heights. They not only draft the Bills, they also formulate policies, and run their respective departments. Their increasing role in legislative matters can be seen in sub-ordinate or delegated legislation, in which they make rules and regulations to effectively implement laws passed by the legislature. These rules and regulations or delegated legislation strictly speaking come under the scrutiny of the legislature but in practice legislature seldom finds time. As a result, the modern democratic state has been characterised as Administrative State.

(vii) Finally the bureaucratic system is a rational system. It is characterised by detailed rules and regulations which are impersonal in nature. Basically it is rule of law. As Weber said that bureaucratic administration is "always from a formal technical point of view, the most rational type." The rules are applied to one and all. There is a reliance on written documents, files, records, and the apparatus of modern office management, in which the bureaucrats are trained and made experts.

These are the characteristics of bureaucracy which have developed in most of the western countries and also India. As pointed out earlier,we inherited these features from the British and with little changes, they continue even today. Thus, the bureaucracy in India is the continuation of pre-independence bureaucracy with emphasis on formalism, impersonality, security and also, alleged, lack of initiative.

Union Public Service Commission

For the purpose of recruitment and regulation of public services, *Article 315* of Indian Constitution provides for a Union Public Service Commission at the centre and a Public Service Commission for each state. However two or more states can have one Joint Public Service Commission. The Union Public Service Commission, if requested to do so by the Governor of a State, may, with the approval of the President, agree to serve all or any of the needs of that State. The members of UPSC and State Public Service Commission are appointed by the President and Governor respectively. But one-half of the members of every public service commission up to the date of their respective appointments must have held office for at least ten years under the Government. The members of UPSC and State Public Service Commission retire at the age of sixty five and sixty-two respectively. They are appointed for six years subject to the retirement age. They are not eligible for reappointment to their office. Further the chairman of UPSC is debarred from any appointment under the Union or State Governments after his retirement. The Chairman of the State Public Service Commission may only be appointed as Chairman or member of the UPSC or Chairman of a State Public Service Commission of a State other than where he has already served. Other members of a State Public Service commission may only be appointed as Chairman or member of UPSC or as Chairman of that or any other State Public Service Commission. Similarly a member of UPSC other than the chairman can only be appointed as chairman of UPSC of a State Public Service Commission. These provisions have been made to ensure the impartiality of the Public Service Commission. The service conditions of a member of a Public Service Commission cannot be altered to his disadvantage after his appointment. A member of public service commission can be removed from his office by order of the President on the grounds of misbehaviour after a reference being made to it under *Article 143*. The President may also remove the Chairman or any member if (i) he is adjudged as insolvent; (ii) accepts during his term of office any other paid employment; or (iii) suffers from such infirmity of mind or body, as in the opinion of the President, renders him unfit for continuance in office.

According to the Constitution, the following are the functions of the Public Service Commissions:

(a) The Public Service Commissions conduct examinations for appointments to the civil services. The UPSC, if requested by two or more states to do so, assists in the choosing of candidates with special qualifications.

(b) Normally the UPSC and State Public Service Commission are consulted in all matters relating to methods of recruitment to civil services and for civil posts; on the principles to be followed in making appointments to civil services and posts and in making promotions and transfers from one service to another and on the suitability of candidates for such appointments, promotions or transfers; on disciplinary matters affecting a person serving in a civil capacity; on claims by such a person for payment of costs incurred in defending legal proceedings and for compensation for injuries incurred on duty or on any claim for the award of a pension in respect of injuries sustained by a person on duty and any question as to the amount of any such award. However, the President and the Governor are empowered to make regulation, specifying the matters in which the Commission may not be consulted. In the case of reservation of posts for backward classes, Scheduled Castes and Scheduled Tribes, there is no necessity of consultation with the Commission. The UPSC and State Public Service Commission present, to the President and Governor respectively, annual reports as to the work done by them. These are placed before the legislature along with the memoranda explaining the cases, if any, where the advice of the Commission was not accepted and the reasons thereto. Thus the UPSC and State Public Service Commissions are independent agencies to provide impartial, efficient and upright services in every grade and department of the government at the national and state levels.

Role of Administration after Independence

As we have seen earlier, the civil service in India in the pre-independence era, constituted the steel frame of British administration. It was par excellence, the main support base of British imperialism in India. It consisted of a small administrative aristocracy which was non-technical in nature. Initially the examinations to the civil services were held in Britain and the British Policy was to make it non-Indian in composition. However, after 1922, the examination also began to be held in India, a development highly welcomed by the educated Indians as it became relatively easy for them to enter the civil services. But an anverge Indian always despised the civil services which to him was the main instrument of colonial exploitation. It is also a fact that notwithstanding the Indians who became civil servants, the Indian Civil Service was a class in itself. The Indians who were recruited in the civil services also shared its basic character and values. They were aloof from the masses, while some of them did sympathise with the Indian freedom movement and a few of them resigned to join it, the majority of them served their foreign masters with utmost loyalty. C.P. Bhambhri rightly says that the Indian Civil Service was "a generalist higher service, not used to any task of gigantic nation-building, trained in the tradition of law and order machinery, based on fear and awe and without any institutionalised system of accountability to the people. An irresponsible, unresponsive, autocratic and bureaucratic structure was inherited by the country which operated in the context of a poor and backward agricultural economy." Yet their tasks were enormous. Clive Dewey says, "They collected the revenue, allocated rights in land, relieved famines, improved agriculture, built public works, suppressed revolts, drafted laws, investigated crimes, judged law suits, inspected municipalities, schools, hospitals, cooperatives—the list is endless." But it should not be construed that Britishers were benevolent administrators who had welfare of the people in their hearts. They intervened in times of famines when, hungry people started looting the granaries of the government. They worked for infrastructural and other developments in areas which helped strengthen their empire in India.

After independence, the role of administration underwent a revolutionary change. No longer was it a regulatory machinery to maintain law and order, collect taxes and to safeguard the British imperial interests in India. Now it was supposed to play a stabilising role in the newly-emerged democratic system and its continuance. It was also to play an important role in realisation and protection of national integration. In these aspects, we find that the public services did play a remarkable role and Sardar Patel rightly paid due tributes to them. It was due to political statesmanship of the leadership, combined with the expertise of the bureaucracy that India could surpass the turbulent years followed by the Partition. The phenomenal problems created by the Partition—like the migration of population and rehabilitation of refugees from Pakistan—were handled with utmost courage and determination. As a result in less than a year, peace and tranquility was achieved at remarkable speed. K.K. Katyal rightly states, "The bureaucracy emerged from the post-Partition challenges with its reputation enhanced and with the people reposing faith in its capabilities." The public services played a very important role in tackling the problems arising out of violent armed struggle by the communists in Telangana and the invasion of Kashmir by Pakistan in 1948. After independence, the traditional role of bureaucracy in maintaining law and order acquired renewed emphasis in the wake of the new democratic set up in which strikes, gheraos and Bandhs became the normal political practices, adopted not only by the opposition parties but also by the party-in-power. Further, the princely states were also harmonized in the Indian political system, despite all the fears of balkanization of India. The national leadership also realised it as a necessary source of administrative competence and its potential in nation-building.

But the most important change that took place as a result of independence was the newly acquired role of bureaucracy as an agency of socio-economic development. This was a new perspective where the bureaucracy had little knowledge. Now, they were supposed to incorporate development administration in their ethos, where they had to serve the people or as Shaker P. Mukherjee in 1968 said, "Every civil servant should ask unto himself, when so many of my people are going to sleep with less than one meal during the last twenty four hours and are not sure of the next one; have I given to the society in the shape of service and work as much as I have taken from it." After independence, India became a welfare state and the objective was the establishment of an egalitarian society to provide social, economic and political justice to the people. This was enshrined in the constitution in the Preamble, Fundamental Rights and Directive Principles of State Policy. For the overall development of the country. Five Year Plans were launched so that all round development could take place in a planned way. To eliminate poverty and other related evils in the countryside, the Government of India launched the Community Development Programme in 1952. Later on the Panchayati Raj Institutions were also given emphasis as agencies of rural development. The Seventy Third Amendment to the Constitution gave them a Constitutional status, otherwise establishment of PRIs was only one of the directives to the state under the Directive Principles of State Policy.

However, the developmental strategy of free India was not without loopholes which became apparent as the plans were put into operation. There was a wide gap between the target fixed and their actual implementation. Critics have also pointed out that the targets were such, which could not be fulfilled, within the time frame specified. Rising expectations of the people, accentuated by euphoria of independence could not be translated into concrete programmes which could make a positive difference in the lives of the people. Repeated failures of the governmental policies led to mass discontent.

The bureaucracy was blamed for the tardy development of Indian economy. Indira Gandhi advocated the need of a committed bureaucracy. She said, "The country would be in a rut if it followed the British system in which civil servants were not supposed to be concerned about which political party was in power." Similarly her Planning Minister pleaded for a civil service which is committed not only to the policies and ideas enshrined in the Constitution but also to the policies and programmes of the ruling party which was backed by the majority of the people in the country. He said that the civil servant without such commitment should have no place in the administration. Talking about a socialist State, S.M. Lipset writes. "The socialist State ...

which has as its goal a reintegration of societal values, giving priority to government services, to groups that had been neglected and securing a large measure of governmental control, may fail in its objectives if it leaves administrative power in the hands of men, whose social background and previous training prevent a sympathetic appreciation of the objectives of the new government." However in the Indian context, the problem is that we have adopted a parliamentary democracy with multiparty system as its essential principle and the concept of a committed bureaucracy is fraught with unimaginable dangers. If the bureaucracy is made committed to the programme and policies of the party-in-power what will happen when there is a change and another party comes to power? Should the civil servants shift their loyalty to the new party-in-power overnight? Is it possible? Besides shedding their political neutrality, the bureaucrats may have to provide their expertise to a political party, even help in preparing its election manifesto and then implement it. The result would be the criticism and contempt of administrators by the opposition parties and even political victimisation of them when they came to power. This is not impossible because gone are the days of one-party dominance. Further, in the present political situation which is likely to continue in the absence of one party getting majority, all kinds of coalition congregates of ideologically divergent political parties are formed based on opportunistic politics of somehow getting power, the concept of committed bureaucracy has no place at all and therefore it has been put rightly into cold storage. We agree with B.D. Pande, a former Cabinet Secretary who says, "The word 'commitment' in relation to the civil service ... means ... commitment to the task on hand. And commitment in the wider sense is a commitment to the Constitution of India, for the future welfare of the country .... Commitment to the task on hand and doing it with a great efficiency and greater speed, devoid of any fear or favour is what is asked for .... As far as the political part is concerned, the civil servant is neutral. But it should be emphasized that the neutral civil service has also got to be a positive civil service, and not a civil servant sitting back. The civil service has got to carry out the task allotted with devotion and speed."

Administration in India—The Challenges

But this is not to say that the bureaucracy in India does not suffer from shortcomings. The fact is there are serious ailments which need urgent remedial measures. Some of them are as follows:

(i) Socio-economic background of Civil Service

As stated earlier, the Indian civil service during the British times was elitist in character, a class in itself, completely aloof from the general masses. After independence, its elitist character continued to dominate. It has been pointed out that persons selected in civil services belong to professional middle class of urban areas. Most of them come from English medium Public schools and have been taught in the universities of Delhi, Bombay, Allahabad, Rajasthan, Patna, Jawaharlal Nehru University, Punjab, Lucknow, IIT, all urban based. Socially they either belong to educated upper middle classes or higher castes of rural areas. The reservation for Scheduled Castes and Scheduled Tribes has not affected them much because the candidates selected belong to the creamy class of Scheduled Castes and Scheduled Tribes. Even if they donot belong to the creamy layer, they like to achieve upward class mobility through their entry to the Civil service and tend to ape the behaviour and attitudes of the upper classes. Further their training makes them an elite class and they are not different from other civil servants in their attitudes and behaviour. However, this aspect of civil service is fast changing and bureaucracy is gradually becoming representative of Indian social classes. The UPSC Committee on the system of Examination to the Higher Civil Services or Satish Chandra Committee, appointed to review and evaluate the system of selection to higher civil services which submitted its report in 1989, made following observations with regard to selection in Indian Civil Service:

(a) A fair proportion of successful candidates have come either from villages or small towns.

(b) The poor and deprived sections of Indian population have also entered into higher services. In the 1987, examination there were 66 such candidates.

(c) In 1984-87 about 20 per cent of the general candidates, 55 per cent of the candidates belonging to Scheduled castes and 48 per cent belonging to the Scheduled Tribes were from the low income groups.

(d) It was also observed that during the period 1983-87, between six to 16 per cent candidates belonging to Scheduled Castes came into the merit list by general standards and the list of successful candidates of Scheduled Tribes varied from three to nine per cent.

(e) The number of successful women candidates is also increasing considerably. While in 1951, only four women candidates among the 231 were recommended for higher services, in 1987, their number went up to a staggering 120 out of 817 candidates recommended for IAS and other higher civil services.

However the increasing number of Scheduled Castes, Scheduled Tribes, low income groups and women is yet to reflect in benefits to their respective classes. But there is no denying the fact that social composition of bureaucracy in India is fast changing and is becoming more representative in its character. With effect from 1994, 50 per cent of the seats are being reserved for Scheduled Castes, Scheduled Tribes and Other Backward Classes (OBCs).

(ii) Minister-Civil Servant Relationship

Another major challenge stems from the complexity of minister-civil servant relationship. Unlike the pre-independence period, the civil servants now have to function in circumstances dominated by political considerations. They are guided and controlled by the political consequences of a policy in the democratic framework of the country. Sardar Patel clearly declared, "If you want an efficient all-India service. I advise you to allow the services to open their mouths freely .... Today, my Secretary can write a note opposed to my views. I have given that freedom to all my Secretaries. I have told them, "If you do not give your honest opinion for fear that it will displease your Minister, please you had better go. I will bring another Secretary." The relationship between the bureaucrat and minister is not that of subordination, rather it should be a harmonious relationship with the general purpose of providing efficient administration to the country. However this has not happened in India. The minister wants a bureaucrat who will toe his line and a frank criticism is never appreciated. In fact it has been pointed out that playing musical chairs with the country's key civil servants has become a pastime for their political bosses. In eight years between 1988 to 1996, we had as many as seven cabinet secretaries in Central Government. There has been a Secretary who remained in his job for just 120 days. Similarly during the 49 years of independence, we had 19 secretaries in the Ministry of External affairs and out of 19, 17 had the tenure of less than three years. In such cases the bureaucrats have to play 'yes, minister' so that they could get extension. A former foreign secretary J.N. Dixit says, "Political accountability has become the most important factor in becoming a foreign secretary. The career profile, the work and the intellectual capability all take a back seat." It is now regarded as routine that whenever the Prime Minister is changed, the high level secretaries are also transferred. Rajiv Gandhi set a kind of record when he kicked out the Foreign Secretary P. Venkateswaran, a distinguished officer with 36 years of experience, in a televised press conference. He did not give any reason for the Foreign Secretary's replacement. Naturally Venkateswaran felt humilitated and resigned from the Foreign Services altogether. In 1991, P.V. Narasimha Rao accepted the need to delegate the power to individual cabinet ministers to have a senior civil servant of their choice.

In the states, the situation is much worse. While there have been exceptional Chief Ministers like S.B. Chavan in Maharashtra, who asked his Secretary B.G. Deshmukh' to continue thus "You are the secretary to the Chief Minister and not Naik or Chavan," most of the politicians did not accept this line and they engaged in mass transfers. In 1990, when Mulayam Singh Yadav became the Chief Minister of UP, he asserted that when a new party comes to power and aims to bring about change, large scale transfers are unavoidable and he transferred as many as 326 of 520 IAS officers and 169 of 411 IPS officers. In 2007,within hours of being sworn in as chief minister of UP, Mayawati suspended two senior IAS officers and transferred 79 IPS officers, including 12 of the rank of Inspector. In fact every chief minister in UP has followed Yadav in this regard. These transfers are also made for caste and religious considerations. Therefore we find that there is a division of bureaucracy on political lines who are favoured or punished depending upon who is in power. Even at the district level we find the same phenomenon. The local politicians tend to put pressure on the bureaucrats to act in favour of their men and if the bureaucrats resist their efforts, they are transferred. This has demoralised the bureaucracy very badly. Sometimes they take refuge in the complexities of rules and regulations to stall the development and thus become inactive. There is another extreme, they become eager to comply with the demands of the politicians and sometimes even anticipate their wishes so that they are well secured in their jobs and also get favours from the politicians. In many states this has resulted in bureaucrat-politician nexus in which both are comfortable but it is the administration which suffers. The Administrative Reform Commission in its Report on the Machinery of Government of India and its Procedure of Work lamented that "there is a disinclination among quite a number of Ministers to welcome frank and impartial advice, from the Secretary or his aides, and an inclination to judge him by his willingness to do what they wish him to do. Instances are not wanting of ministers preferring a convenient subordinate to a strong one and thereby making the latter not only ineffective but a sulky and unwilling worker. This has also bred a tendency on the part of an increasing number of civil servants to anticipate the minister's wishes and proffer their advice accordingly. A further development of this unhealthy trend is the emergence of personal affiliations leading to an element of politicization among the civil servants. All these cut at the root of a healthy relationship." Actions of Romesh Bhandari in UP are pointers of the same phenomenon. A former pliable civil servant, willing to please his former masters. The peak of all these unhealthy trends was witnessed during the notorious Emergency of 1975-77, when civil servants became a willing party to the politicians in committing excesses. The Shah Commission appointed to probe into excesses during emergency observed that there was a helplessness among the officers who later on regretted their actions. For many officers "self preservation was at stake" and there was an "imaginary fear of possible and probable consequences for doing the right things" which "have done more havoc than the known consequences that actually may have followed the performance of duties on the right lines by the Government servants". The post-emergency period witnessed the strong indictment of bureaucracy, of its role during emergency which shattered the morale of the civil servants. The greatest height was the arrest of the then Petroleum Secretary B.B. Vohra on the basis of grounds which later turned out to be hollow. The confidence was shaken. The Shah Commission had to give a public assurance that there would not be any vendetta.

The other aspect of politician-bureaucrat relationship is that while policy formulation is the minister's prerogative, implementation of the policy and running day-to-day administration is the sphere of the bureaucrat. However, in India, the disbelief and even hatred of civil servants of the colonial past has continued on the part of politicians. As a result an unfortunate trend has developed. The political bosses also started taking interest in the day-to-day administration. According to K.K. Katyal this resulted in two mutually contradictory consequences. (a) In some cases the bureaucrat, sensing the weakness of the political boss, acquired a dominant say in policy-making. He laid down the policies on his own while the Minister was busy with postings and transfers, yet he (the Minister) remained under the illusion that he was the decision maker. (b) In other cases the bureaucrat became a willing-tool in the hands of politician and acted according to his wishes to promote his career prospects. "It became a partnerships of convenience, with the official working for the Minister's political future and in the process getting handsome rewards."

The National Police Commission, appointed by the Janata Government revealed the misuse of police machinery by the politicians-in-power for political purposes and transfer was used as a weapon against those who refused to be misused. It pointed out that the average period of stay in the same post was just 20 months in the case of Inspectors-General of police, 19 months for Superintendents and 14 months for Inspectors. In some cases the average period of stay for Superintendents was as low as 11 months and for Inspector seven months. This tally does not include transfers for normal administrative reason such as promotions, deputation or retirement. The commission also found the nexus among criminals, police, bureaucrats and politicians. "The nexus between the criminal gangs, police, bureaucracy and politicians has come out clearly in various parts of the country," Further the politicians also have to accommodate the wishes of their supporters in granting favours and concessions and the bureaucrats are compelled to become a pawn in the hands of their political bosses, fulfilling their demands whether regular or irregular. This is particularly visible very widely at the district level. As a result, administration has not been impartial, catering largely to the needs of politicians and their supporters. For the common man it becomes a big leviathan unworthy and incapable of fulfilling his legitimate wishes. K.K. Puri rightly observes, "Political interference and impartial administration cannot co-exist."

There is another dilemma on the part of the bureaucrats. The politicians depend on votes for their survival and they have a limited time at their disposal. During their tenure as ministers, they want to do many things to impress their voters. For this, they seek populist measures and policies which are so far from reality that it becomes difficult for civil servants to implement them. B. Venkatappaiah rightly comments, "unless there are fairly realistic policies and realistic programmes, there would be divergence between the myths' and realities, and the administrators would often be' in dilemma. The dilemma is quite often, not the moral dilemma alone, but a real and factual one." This puts a tremendous amount of burden on the bureaucrat.

(iii) Corruption

Another major problem of Indian administration is the evil of widespread corruption. India has been rated the eighth most corrupt nation. The Central Vigilance Commission has recognized as many as 33 modes of corruption prevalent in India. It is also to be accepted that corruption is not only a worldwide phenomenon but it is very ancient also. Kautilya's Arthasastra says, "Just as it is impossible not to taste the honey or the poison that finds itself at the top of the tongue, so it is impossible for a government servant not to eat up, at least a bit of the king's revenue." The modern state being a welfare state gives abundant opportunities to civil servants for corruption. The Santhanam Committee in 1964 said, "The sudden extension of the economic activities of the Government with a large armoury of regulations, controls, licences and permits provided new and large opportunities for corruption." In India, we have a system of corruption which plagues right from the lower to the highest rung of officials. There is a general feeling that nothing moves without exchange of money. The Government has established Central Vigilance Commission and vigilance organisations in the individual ministries to eradicate corruption. Besides we also have Central Bureau of Investigation (CBI) for the purpose. But there have been cases of corruption in vigilance agencies as well.

The Administrative Reform Commission recommended the institutions of Lokpal at the Centre and Lokayukta at the States, which should be independent and impartial dealing with the acts of injustice, corruption or favouritism. While in some states, Lokayukta have been appointed though their working has been far from satisfactory, at the centre, the institution of Lokpal is still a dream. The Lokayukta of Madhya Pradesh, Justice Faizanuddin, in his annual report to the State Assembly, demanded more powers for Lokayukta to make him an effective tool against corruption. He said if the Lokayukta was not given more powers immediately through a legislative amendment, it would become another glorified institution and corruption, misuse of power, irresponsible actions of bureaucrats and professional dishonesty would continue unchecked. According to him, the major loophole in the Madhya Pradesh Lokayukta Act was that the recommendations of the Lokayukta, in many cases, were scrutinized by political persons whose decisions were not influenced by public interest but other considerations. The persons occupying the office of Lokayukta were senior judicial officers and their recommendations were rejected by such competent authorities whose legal knowledge was limited. He suggested that the existing practice, of 'seeking sanction from the government to prosecute civil or public servants, after the Lokayukta had found prima facie evidence against them, be scrapped. The State Government in Madhya Pradesh had refused to give permission to Lokayukta to prosecute Deputy Chief Minister and Cooperative Minister in a land allotment case. In Bihar the State

Governor took his own time to grant permission to CBI to prosecute the Chief Minister in the Fodder Scam. On the other hand, corruption has been spreading its tentacles to the extent that even the Prime Ministers and chief ministers are being accused of accepting bribes and commissions. Many key civil servants have been accused of corruption, some have been arrested and CBI proceedings against them followed.

In 1996, the Supreme Court directed the Government to initiate disciplinary proceedings against five IAS officers for helping a powerful builder who defrauded the Delhi Development Authority. In Uttar Pradesh, the IAS Association decided to name the three most corrupt officers in the State. A corrupt administration can only give an inefficient and unhealthy administration and unfortunately that has been the state of affairs in Indian administration. The need for eradicating it is too obvious. Given its size and magnitude, a new approach to the entire question is needed, as existing administrative machinery has failed to curtail it. There should be severe punishments which could act as a deterrent in combating corruption. The people's vigilance is also necessary which unfortunately in India is lacking. There is a lack of will on the part of political leadership. The Provisional Parliament in 1951, in the Mudgal case acted very swiftly but after that we do not find such swiftness. Generally, the low salary structure is cited as the reason for corruption. The IAS officers are less paid and therefore not immune to corruption. But we should not derive that the quantum of salary is directly related to honesty or integrity of the person. The prevalence of the culture of speed money has more to do with the unabashed rampant political corruption in the country. This has sent clear signals to the people in high places—that being corrupt and even being caught, does not put one to great disadvantage or problem. Therefore, rather than blaming the salary structure, we must look for the larger issues involved in corruption. Even after independence, we can name scores of civil servants who maintained very high standards of integrity in the same or even lower levels of economic packages.

(iv) Generalist Vs. Specialist Controversy

Another challenge to Indian administration comes from what is termed *"Generalist Vs. Specialist Controversy."* The Indian administrative set up is dominated by the Indian Administrative Services which is termed as 'generalists.' The IAS officers are recruited on the basis of a competitive examination and upon selection, they undergo training for becoming a good administrator. After the training, they are posted in different departments of the government and it is presumed that they can handle any department, even the technical ones. The experts are given secondary position as regards salary and status. This system was best suited in the colonial era, when the functions of bureaucracy were limited. However after independence, the welfare state acquired a variety of functions, which needed technical expertise and knowledge. But the same system continued and dominance of IAS remained, although the leadership felt the need to give prominence to technical experts in handling the technical departments. Talking about farming, Nehru said, "I feel that we do not attach much importance to expertise or technical knowledge and experience of farming. Of course we employ technical officers but we consider them usually of a lesser breed than administrative officers. Technical departments like Agriculture, Animal Husbandary etc. are often headed by administrative officers and not by experts or specialists in these departments. We have inherited this practice from the past. It is not a good practice and I don't know if it exists anywhere else. A minister naturally is not supposed to be an expert. But if the head of a technical department also is not an expert, then we are likely to fail in coming to grips with the problem. We shall continue to think in terms of official memoranda and notes and circulate letters and not have a real understanding of the good earth from which food comes." However he did not effect any change in the bureaucratic system except that he appointed experts as secretaries in the departments of scientific Research, Atomic Energy and Education. Indira Gandhi also once said, "I have no doubt that our present administrative system uses the experts inadequately and indifferently. It gives undue weight to the generalists and persists with criteria of competence developed in times when the range of government decisions were very limited and was unrelated to the demands of economic management and growth. "While delivering her convocation address at the Roorkee University in 1967, she said, "The brightest of our young men choose engineering or medicine. If they happen to go into government, they are very soon overtaken by the general administrator. This must change ..." She also did not do much except appointing specialists in a few departments in the top positions. There has been increasing resentment among the professional groups like engineers, scientists, doctors, economists and university teachers who are demanding equality of pay and status with the IAS. Their associations are even resorting to strikes and other forms of political agitation to end what is termed the IAS hegemony. Even the IPS is now demanding constitutional parity with IAS (HT July 20 2008).

Briefly speaking the specialists want to break the IAS hegemony on the following grounds:

(i) The generalists who are amateurs have neither the orientation nor the capability to handle planning, development and welfare. The objectives of planning and development have remained unfulfilled because the specialists are not given complete freedom to manage their affairs.

(ii) The IAS officers are frequently transferred from one job to another. Today, an IAS may be looking after a district as collector, tomorrow he may be put in charge of Electricity Board and next, he may be controlling a public sector organisation dealing with textile or heavy machinery. He is made to shuttle from one department to another. This does not necessarily make a civil servant an all-rounder, he can surely be called 'Jack of all trades and master of none.' Thus he is not able to grasp the working of one particular department. The concept of the administrative all rounder does not work in the modern environment.

(iii) Because of the above factor, he does not develop any stake in the department. Frequent transfers lead to impersonal, detached and uninvolved attitude among civil servants.

(iv) The generalists are not able to assist their ministers on many a matter, as they are general administrators. To assist the minister on a particular technical subject, they have to consult the specialists. Thus the whole system becomes complicated. The best way is that the minister should be assisted directly by the specialists.

(v) The IAS officers have become an elite class who remain aloof from the people. This feeling of exclusiveness is in direct contradiction with the democratic administration which abhors the concept of special class in any sphere of life.

However the generalists have vehemently resented the attempts of specialists in eroding their authority, prestige and status. They have adovcated following arguments in their support:

(i) The IAS officers by serving various departments acquire the necessary administrative expertise and understanding of social, political and economic conditions. Thus they are specialists in the art of administration.

(ii) It is true that the technical soundness of a project or scheme can be best analysed by an expert or specialist. But this is not enough. The project or scheme has to be understood from other angles also or as K.K. Puri says, it is 'to be examined from various other points of view, its financial and legal implications, administrative feasibility, political justifiability and whether it would be acceptable to Parliament and public.' Ridley says, "Thus the simplest case for the generalist is that the administrative function does not depend on any single form of technical expertise and that the specialist, therefore, has no particular qualification for this sort of job."

(iii) The specialists' outlook is narrow and sectarian. He is over-enthusiastic about his subject and cannot see the things in totality. He lacks perspective, while the generalist has a broad perspective. Therefore the specialist should work under a generalist.

It is to be remembered that the Planning Commission has frequently emphasised the need for change in the administrative set up. In the First Five Year Plan it made it clear that additional trained personnel would be required for economic planning and development. The Administrative Reform Commission in 1969, suggested regrouping of all the present services in which eight cadres with equal status be created and IAS be assigned a specific functional field. But the Government did not accept this proposal. Indira Gandhi, the then Prime Minister said," Our experience is that the generalists and the specialists both tend to be somewhat bureaucratic when they come into the system." However the fact remains that the supremacy of IAS has been successfully challenged by the specialists. The specialists assert that a majority of them (about 80 per cent) had a first class educational career which is not so with the IAS (only about 30 per cent). The resultant strife has led to the weakening of the entire administrative system.

B.D. Pande, a retired ICS officer, has given a very emotional and disheartening picture of Indian Administrative Services in his article 'A rusting steel-frame'. He says, (we quote him extensively) "I start a few years before Independence, from 1938, when I qualified for the Indian Civil Service. At that time the ICS was considered one of the most prestigious civil services in the world and was held in high esteem .... I was posted at Aurangabad, then a sub-division (now a district) of Gaya (in Bihar). Several months were spent in tents. Subsequent postings in various sub-divisions were to places where there was no electricity, no tap water, no telephones. But no one ever grudged this. It was part of the service conditions. We went to where we were ordered to go. No questions were asked. But now a posting to a mofussil station or a somewhat remote area is considered a punishment .... Everyone now wants to be at the national or state capital. "He says that there was a mutual trust between the higher civil services and the national leaders." Because of this mutual trust, the very difficult problems that arose in the wake of partition-the displacement of millions of people, their resettlement, the integration of the princely states, important land reforms such as the abolition of

Zamindari and other issues-were successfully tackled. A new India had taken birth. There was optimism and pride all around.

Fifty years later, all this has evaporated. The wall has not only been broken, but many more have been erected, a barbed wire fencing has been drawn and the civil servants have been emasculated and their spines broken so that they are now reduced to a jelly. Commitment is now asked, not toward the Constitution of the Republic of India but toward individuals, postings are made on that basis. Moreover, momentary and unholy alliances have been formed. From being proud to belong to a service which was acknowledged as one of the best in the world, today one is ashamed to have been one of the original members of the present day successor, Indian Administrative Service, what with several of its members being hauled up in courts for corrupt practices."

B.D. Pande says that in the initial years, during the launching of community development programmes in rural areas, the officers were very enthusiastic in their participation. They would go to the villages and the people were equally enthusiastic. "They came forward to gift land, labour and, where possible, even money for building projects in their village or locality." Unfortunately all this changed "drastically in the 20 years or so" and the officer 'instead of going to the village, now had the villagers approaching him in the usual manner as befits a local potentate to get things done. The experiments of the Fifties had more or less collapsed before the end of the sixties."

Thus the bureaucracy in India has become highly inefficient where there is more emphasis on files, red tapism and delay. There are too many authorities which has made the administration cumbersome and there is a centralisation of decision making power. The situation has gone to such a extreme that in Delhi, the State Governments have to maintain senior liasion officers to chase files in the central ministries. Every state in India has a "Bhawan" in Delhi for the purpose.

Bureaucracy and the Liberalisation

After independence the newly emerged Indian State was characterized by the dominant role in all the spheres of society. It was a welfare state whose objective was to secure political, social and economic justice to all the sections of the Indian population. The Westminister model of parliamentary democracy with universal adult franchise was adopted. In the social field, various evils in society were sought to be eradicated by the State. Untouchability was abolished and social reforms were undertaken. In the economic sphere, the State not only regulated the market, it also emerged as the major employer providing employment opportunities to the people. India adopted the policy of mixed economy, a powerful public sector was created. For Nehru, the public sector undertakings were the temples of modern India. Their objective was to assist in the rapid economic growth and industrialisation of the country. Over the years their number and investments have grown in size and quantity. While in 1951, there were five central public sector undertakings (PSUs) with an investment of Rs 29 crores, now there are as many as 243 enterprises with a total investment of Rs 1,78,628 crores. The private sector was also to play an important role in the mixed economy. However it was highly regulated and controlled economy as far as the private sector was concerned. Rightly it was called the 'licence-quota permit Raj.' However the collapse of the socialist political and economic system in erstwhile Soviet Union and other socialist states led to the emergence of a global economy which meant introducing competitive markets, liberalising foreign trade and opening up the economy for foreign investment. According to Marina Pinto "Liberalisation is the policy of removal of restrictions, trade barriers and protectionist measures to enable the free flow of capital, technology and services. It is generally seen in the context of globalization and privatization." In eighties liberalisation process started taking place in Indian economy. But the severe foreign exchange and fiscal crisis in early 1990's compelled India to take massive loan from IMF and world Bank which as critics point out, dictated India to liberalise its economy. This was done under the leadership of Dr. Manmohan Singh, the Finance Minister in P.V. Narsimha Rao Government. The New Industrial Policy of 1991, stated that "Foreign investment and technology collaboration will be welcomed to obtain higher technology, to increase exports and to expand the production base." The Licence-quota permit Raj has been given a farewell and the economic system has largely become competitive. Even in the public sector, the nine major public sector undertakings or Navratnas—Bharat Heavy Electricals Limited (BHEL), Bharat Petroleum Corporation LImited (BPCL) Hindustan Petroleum Corporation Limited (HPCL), Indian Oil Corporation Limited (IOC), Indian Petrochemicals Corporation Limited (IPCL), National Thermal Power Corporation Limited (NTPC), Oil & National Gas Corporation Limited (ONGC), Steel Authority of India Limited (SAIL) and Videsh Sanchar Nigam Limited (VSNL) have been given considerable financial and functional autonomy. The Government was also planning to include more public sector undertakings in this list. However, this does not mean that the role of the State would recede and it would only concentrate on the maintenance of law and order. The State continues to be a welfare state. It will continue to ameliorate the conditions of the poor and down-trodden. The economic policies are to be realistic. Jagdish Bhagwati, one of the leading economists, says that the first fifty years of independence has been "half a century of foolish policies, which cost her (India) growth and hence a significant opportunity to ameliorate poverty." Now rational policies are to be drafted and implemented with due regard to monitoring of policies in stages. This also means that the generalist administration will either be substituted by the experts or they be given their due place in the administration. The bureaucracy will have to be responsive and transparent and the entire work ethos has to be changed. It also means maximum possible delegation of authority and sufficient decentralized control. Ultimately it may lead to debureaucratization of the administration. The 73rd and 74th Constitutional Amendment providing for local self government is designed to transfer the developmental functions to the local self government. We may be witness to gradual shrinking of the state and its administrative machinery. But this does not mean that the state would recede in the background. It may be a scenario where we have a reoriented, purposive accountable and transparent administration as a friend, philosopher and guide. The essential condition for all this is political will, integrity and honesty at higher levels of politics and the de-criminalisation of politics.

References

Arora Ramesh and Goyal Rajni, *Indian Public Administration, Institutions and issues* 1995, New Delhi, Vishwa Prakashan.

Chaturvedi T.N. (Series Editor), *Development Administration*, 1984, New Delhi, Indian Institute of Public administration.

Gupta D.C., *Indian Government and Politics*, 1996, New Delhi. Vikas Publishing House Private Limited.

Jain R.B. and Bongartz (Ed), *Structural Adjustment Public Policy and Bureaucracy in Developing Societies*, 1994, New Delhi, Har-Anand Publications.

Maheshwari Shriran, *Indian Administration*, 1994, New Delhi, Orient Longman Limited.

Puri K.K., *Public Administration: Indian Spectrum*, 1985, Allahabad, Kitab Mahal. The Hindu, India, Independence Day Supplement, 1997, two articles by K.K. Katyal and B.D. Pande.

Ramachandran Padma, *Public Administration in India*, 1996, New Delhi, National Book Trust.

Tummala Krishna K., *Public Administration in India*, 1996, New Delhi, Allied Publishers Limited.

CHAPTER XVI

Constitutional Amendment—Socio-Political Implications

The Constitution is a legal arrangement which regulates the functions of different organs of the government, and provides and protects the rights of the citizens. It is designed, keeping in view the need and aspirations of the people. Thus, the Constitution is for the people and not the vice versa. It should provide political and social stability to the nation. However, it must also reflect the changing needs and aspirations of the people. In this sense, Constitution becomes a dynamic document. If the Constitution is rigid and refuses to acknowledge the dynamics of social and political changes, it is likely to be overthrown violently, Nehru rightly observed," There should be a certain flexibility. If you make a thing rigid and permanent, you stop a nation's growth, the growth of living vital organic people. Therefore, it has to be flexible." He also added, while replying to the amendments to the objective Resolutions. "We shall frame the Constitution, and I hope it will be a good Constitution, but does anyone in the House imagine that when a free India emerges it will be bound down by anything that even this House might lay down for it? A free India will see the bursting forth of the energy of a mighty nation. What it will do and what it will not, I do not know, but I do know that it will not consent to be bound down by anything. It may be that the Constitution this House may frame may not satisfy India, the free India. The House cannot bind down the next generation or people who will duly succeed us in this task."

The amendment to the Constitution is justified from the view of socio-economic forces which are always subject to change and do not remain static. As and when they change, the Constitution has to adapt itself accordingly otherwise it loses its legitimacy. Dr. Ambedkar succinctly pointed out. "The Assembly has not only refrained from putting a seal of finality and infallibility upon this Constitution but has provided for a facile procedure for amending the Constitution."

Initially, B.N. Rau had suggested that the Union Parliament should be vested with the power to amend the Constitution temporarily for a period of three years as a facile procedure. The Drafting Committee instead suggested this period as five years. B.N. Rau, the Constitutional Advisor remarked on this suggestion: "The process of amending the Constitution during the first few years should be made easier .... In the first place, to mention only one example, the pattern of Indian States is undergoing rapid change and one cannot say with confidence that the Constitution will not have to be continually altered atleast during the initial years, to fit the constantly changing pattern. Other problems too may arise requiring frequent amendment of the Constitution. The Constitution should not, therefore, be too rigid during the first few years. Secondly, we have to remember that the present Constituent Assembly is not based on adult suffrage, the members having been elected by the various Legislatures, which, in their turn, were elected on a very restricted franchise. The Parliament of the new Union of India, on the other hand, will be based on adult franchise. If a Constituent Assembly based on a restricted franchise can by a simple majority frame the Original Constitution, it is illogical to lay down that the Constitution so framed shall not be amended by a Parliament based on adult franchise except by a specially difficult process involving special majorities and in some cases special ratifications." However subsequently this proposal was dropped and Dr. Ambedkar expressed his confidence that "the Indian Federation will not suffer from the faults of rigidity or legalism" as, its distinguishing feature was that it was "a flexible federation."

Amending Process in the Indian Constitution

The amendment to the Indian Constitution cannot take place in a uniform pattern. Different provisions of the Constitution can be amended in different ways. Broadly speaking there are three procedures of amending the Indian Constitution which are as follows:

(i) Amendments by a simple majority,
(ii) Amendments by a special majority of the Parliament, and
(iii) Amendments by the special majority of the Parliament plus ratification by the States.

(i) Amendment by Simple Majority

Some of the provisions of the Constitution can be amended by a simple majority of the Parliament, which are as follows:

(a) Admission of a new state under *Article 2* alongwith the consequential amendment in Schedule I (which defines the territory of a State) and Schedule IV (which deals with the allocation of seats of a State in Rajya Sabha);
(b) Provisions relating to the citizenship of India;
(c) Provisions relating to exercise of executive power by a State or its officers in respect of matter over which Parliament has power to make laws;
(d) Provisions relating to salaries and allowances of Ministers;
(e) Provisions relating to salaries and allowances of the Speaker and Deputy Speaker of the House of People and the Chairman and Deputy Chairman of the Council of States;
(f) Provisions relating to salaries and allowances of members of Parliament;
(g) Provisions relating to number of judges in the Supreme Court;
(h) Provisions relating to privileges, allowances and rights of the judges of Supreme Court;
(i) Provisions relating to appeals to the Supreme Court;
(j) Provisions relating to review of the judgment of the Supreme Court;
(k) Provisions relating to salaries and allowances of the Comptroller and the Auditor General;
(l) Provisions relating to composition of the Legislative Councils in States;
(m) Provisions relating to salaries and allowances of the judges of the High Court;
(n) Provisions relating to continuance of English Language;
(o) Provisions relating to language to be used in the Supreme Court and the High Courts;
(p) Provisions relating to creation of legislature and council of ministers for a Union Territory;
(q) Provisions relating to administration and control of the Scheduled Areas and Scheduled Tribes,
(r) Provisions relating to the administration and control of Tribal Areas; and
(s) The State Legislatures can amend *Article 164 (5)* and *Article 186* which relates to salary and allowances of the Ministers and the Chairman and Deputy Chairman respectively in the States.

It may be pointed out that these are not strict amendments to the Constitution as *Article 368* of the Constitution dealing with the amendment of the Constitution is not invoked. Nevertheless, they are the amendments to the Constitution as the above mentioned provisions stand amended though with a simple majority.

(ii) Amendment by Special Majority

As said earlier, *Article 368* deals with the amendment of the Constitution. Accordingly, the Parliament has a right to amend the major portions of the Constitution.

An amendment to the Constitution is initiated by a Bill which can be introduced in either House of the Parliament. In both the Houses, sitting separately, it must be passed by (i) a majority of total membership of the House, and (ii) a majority of not less than two-thirds of the members of that House, present and voting. After the Bill obtains the required majority and is passed by both the Houses of the Parliament, the Bill is presented to the President for his assent and after his assent, the Constitution shall stand amended. An amendment may specify the date of its commencement or leave it to the President to bring it into effect from such date as he may notify. We have an example of an amendment which has been passed by the Parliament and assented by the President, yet the amended provisions have not come into effect as the President has not notified the date from which it will be effected. The 42nd Amendment added new clauses (4) and (7) in *Article 22* relating to preventive detention which have not been brought to force in the absence of President's notification.

(iii) Special Majority of the Parliament plus ratification by the States

There are certain provisions in the Constitution which require the special majority of both the Houses as referred to above plus ratification by atleast half of the States. The States make this ratification by resolution passed by the State Legislatures.

Amendments in the following provisions require such ratifications:

(a) The election and manner of election of the President (*Articles 54 and 55*);
(b) The extent of executive power of the Union (*Article 73*);
(c) The extent of executive power of a State (*Article 162*);
(d) Provisions dealing with the Supreme Court (Chapter IV of Part V) and High Courts in the States (Chapter V of Part VI);
(e) High Courts for Union Territories (*Article 241*);
(f) Distribution of legislative powers between the Union and the States (Chapter I of Part XI);
(g) The representation of States in Parliament (Fourth Schedule);
(h) Seventh Schedule to the Constitution; and

(i) *Article 368* i.e. the power and procedure of amendment of the Constitution.

Constitutional Amendments and Social Change

The Indian Constitution is not just a political and legal arrangement of a federal and Parliamentary democratic system. It is also a document of social change. The framers of the Constitution were aware of the social and economic evils of Indian society and they wanted to ameliorate the condition of millions of Indians. The Fundamental Rights were given equally to all and various kinds of discrimination were declared as invalid and the State was prohibited from practising discrimination in terms of caste, creed, religion, sex etc. Untouchability was abolished. A Chapter on directive principles of State policy was added to provide socio-economic justice to the people of India. The Preamble to the Constitution also declared the attainment of socio-economic and political justice to be the objective of the Constitution.

To ameliorate the conditions of the rural masses in the wake of prevailing economic inequalities in term of land holdings, the State governments in India went ahead with their programmes of Zamindari abolition and distribution of land among the landless. They passed Land Reform Acts which were challenged in the respective High Courts. The attitude of judiciary was not uniform. Whereas the Allahabad and Nagpur High Courts upheld the validity of the respective Acts abolishing Zamindari, the Patna High Court declared Bihar Land Reform Act, 1950 as Ultra Vires. Appeals in all these cases were filed in the Supreme Court. The necessity of rapid land reforms in the country was felt by the Central Government and the Constitution (First Amendment) Act was made in the Constitution by the Parliament. After the first amendment to the Constitution, it was hoped that there would not be any stumbling bloc in the implementation of land reform programme. However, this hope was belied due to interpretation of the Constitution by the judiciary. Consequently, the Constitution was further amended to overcome the difficulties posed by the judicial interpretation. In total, there have been fourteen amendments which were incorporated in the Constitution to negate the judgements of the Courts and to bring about an egalitarian Socio-economic order in the society. These fourteen amendments are the First, Fourth, Seventeenth, Twenty-Fourth, Twenty-Fifth, Twenty-Sixth, Twenty-Ninth, Thirty-Ninth, Forty, Fourty-Second, Forty-Fourth, Forty-Seven, Sixty-Sixth and Seventy-Eighth Constitutional Amendments Acts.

Congress, while leading the freedom struggle made contradictory promises to different sections of the population, in order to mobilise them in its efforts to gain independence from the British rule. On the one hand, it declared its commitment for rapid land reforms which meant that landless would be given land after independence, on the other, to satisfy the big landlords and Zamindars, it also promised them that their interests would be taken care of in the process of land reforms, which was taken as an assurance by the Zamindars that they would be paid adequate compensation for their land acquired under land reform measures. And this was the major contradiction prevailing during the formation of the Constitution. While there was an urgent need for land reforms, the backward and poverty-stricken Indian economy could not pay the market value of the land to be acquired from the Zamindars. Unfortunately, this contradiction was carried on in the Indian Constitution also. Right to property was made a Fundamental Right via *Article 19(1)(f)* and *Article 31*. *Article 19 (1)(f)* declared that all the citizens shall have the right to "acquire, hold and dispose of property. *Article 31* declared that "No person shall be deprived of his property save by authority of law." It also provided for the acquision of property by law for public purposes. However, such law must provide for compensation for the acquired property. It should either fix the amount of the compensation or specify the principles, according to which the compensation was to be determined and given. *Article 31* also provided that the laws made by the State Legislatures for the acquisition of property be reserved for the President's assent. Thus in case of land reforms, the Zamindar's land could be acquired for public purpose but at the same time the Zamindars were entitled to compensation for the acquired property which the Indian State could not pay. This was the lacuna in the Constitution responsible for the different and contradictory interpretation of right to property by different High Courts. Hence the need to amend the Constitution a number of times.

(i) The Constitution (First) Amendment Act, 1951

The purpose of first Amendment was to overcome the legal hurdles created by the Bihar High Court invalidating the Bihar Land Reforms Act, 1950, which abolished Zamindari system. *Articles 31(A)* and *31(B)* were introduced in the Constitution. *Article 31(A)* declared that no law providing for acquisition of any estate would be invalid on the ground that it is inconsistent with, or takes away or abridges any of the fundamental rights contained in Part III of the Constitution. *Article*

31(B) gave protection to certain specified Acts and Regulation already passed so that they might not be challenged in the Court. For this purpose, Ninth Schedule was included in the Constitution. The Acts and Regulations put under the Ninth Schedule could not be challenged on the ground that they violated the fundamental rights and first Act thus put was the aforesaid Bihar Land Reforms Act, 1950.

(ii) The Constitution (Fourth Amendment) Act, 1955

However, the First Amendment could not clear the ambiguity in the Constitution. Once again the problems arose because of the judiciary's interpretation. These problems were of three types:

(a) There is a concept of power of Eminent Domain of State. It means that the State can regulate a property in public purpose. In this case, the title of the ownership does not change, the State only regulates the property for public purpose. This question arose in *Sholapur Spinning and Weaving Company case* in 1954. The *Sholapur Spinning and Weaving Company Limited* was closed down as a result of neglect and mismanagement of its directors. The Company's lay off affected the production of an essential commodity and also caused unemployment of its workers. The Central Government issued an Ordinance by which the company's management was taken over by the Government for public purpose. Since the State had not acquired ownership title of the company which remained with its shareholders, the Ordinance made it clear that no compensation was to be paid. But the Court held that the State action in Sholapur Mill case amounted to deprivate of property for which no provision had been made for compensation. Therefore, it struck down the *Sholapur Spinning and Weaving (Emergency Provisions) Ordinance, 1950.*

(b) Another problem arose regarding the quantum of compensation. The Supreme Court held in Bela Banerjee case that the compensation must be just and equivalent of what the owner has been deprived of, which meant the real market value of the property to be acquired. The Court also held that the compensation fixed was justiciable.

(c) Finally, the Central Government also desired to extend Constitution protection of Ninth Schedule to seven Acts so that they could be outside judicial review of the Court.

To nullify the effects of Courts decisions in (a) and (b) mentioned above and to include seven Acts in the Ninth Schedule, the Constitution (Fourth Amendment) 1955 was made. It provided that no law shall be called in question in any Court on the ground that the compensation provided by that law was not adequate. Secondly, the

State got the Power of Eminent Domain. *Article 31 (2-A)* declared that, "Where a law does not provide for the transfer of the ownership or right to possession of any property to the State or to a corporation owned or controlled by the State, it shall not be deemed to provide for the compulsory acquisition or requisitioning of property, notwithstanding that it deprives any person of his property."

(iii) The Constitution (Seventeenth) Amendment Act, 1964

However, the Supreme Court in the *Karimbil Kunhikoman Vs. State of Kerala* struck down the Kerala Agrarian Act, 1961, Similarly, *Madras Land Reforms (Fixation of Ceiling on Land) Act, 1961, Rajasthan Tenancy Act, 1955 and Maharashtra Agricultural Lands Act, 1961* were declared invalid. The term 'Estate' used in the Constitution, according to Supreme Court, didnot include land held under ryotwari system and also other lands which figure in various land reform legislations. The Seventeenth Amendment Act was passed to overcome all these problems. The term estate was redefined widely and 44 legislations relating to land reforms were put in Ninth Schedule. But in 1965, the Supreme Court again sought to take back its jurisdiction regarding the compensation in *P. Vajravelu Vs. Spl. Dy. Collector* case. It declared that what had been taken away by the Fourth Amendment was the jurisdiction of the Courts to examine the adequacy of compensation but not the requirement of providing compensation or principles for determining the same. Therefore, the Court could strike down a law as a fraud on the Constitution if the principles for determining compensation were irrelevant to the value of the property at or about the time of acquisition or if the law provided for illusionary compensation. Till now the Supreme Court had exercised judicial restraint as it never challenged the Parliament's power to amend the Constitution even to abridge or abrogate the fundamental rights. But in 1967, the Supreme Court in *Golak Nath* case resorted to judicial activism and gave an unprecedented judgement in which it reversed its earlier decisions and held that Parliament had no power to abridge or abrogate the fundamental rights and Parliament could not do so even by amending the Constitution. Thus, severe restrictions were put in Parliament's power to amend the Constitution. Naturally, the decision of *Golak Nath* case created an uproar in India. But the judiciary remained unaffected with the criticism. In Bank Nationalisation case, it again brought back the question of compensation. The nationalisation of 14 Banks was declared invalid and the Supreme Court held that the Constitution guaranteed right to compensation i.e. the market value of property acquired. Thus the amount of compensation again became justiciable. The Supreme Court also declared the Presidential order abolishing the privy purses and other privileges of the former rulers as invalid. Again the need for amendments to the Constitution arose and the Parliament passed Twenty Forth, Twenty Fifth, Twenty Sixth and Twenty Ninth amendments to counter Supreme Court decisions.

(iv) The Constitution (Twenty Fourth) Amendment Act 1974

This amendment was made to nullify the effects of Supreme Court decision in Golak Nath case. It was made clear that the Parliament had the power to amend the Constitution including fundamental rights.

(v) The Constitution (Twenty Fifth) Amendment Act, 1971

The Twenty Fifth Amendment nullified the effects of *P. Vijaravelu and the Bank Nationalisation decisions* of the Supreme Court. The amendment dropped the word "Compensation" and instead inserted the term "amount" so that there cannot be any question regarding compensation by the Court. The amendment also authorised the Parliament to make laws to give effect to the Directive Principles Specified in Clauses (B) and (C) of *Article 39*. They could not be declared as invalid by the Court on the ground that they abridged or abrogated the fundamental rights guaranteed in *Articles 14, 19 or 31*. For this purpose, a new *Article 31-C* was inserted in the Constitution.

(vi) The Constitution (Twenty Sixth) Amendment Act, 1971

The Twenty Sixth Amendment was made to nullify the effect of Supreme Court's, decision in the *Privy Purse case*. Indira Gandhi described the Privy Purse as an "anachromism." The objects and reasons of the Twenty Sixth Bill declared that "the concept of rulership, with Privy Purses and special privileges unrelated to any current functions and social purposes, was incompatible with an egalitarian social order. Government, therefore, decided to terminate the privy purses and privileges of the Rulers of former Indian States." Accordingly, the twenty sixth Amendment abolished the privy purses and the personal rights, privileges and dignities of the former Indian rulers.

(vii) The Constitution (Twenty Ninth) Amendment Act

By Twenty Ninth Amendment, two land reform acts passed by the Kerala Legislature were included in the Ninth Schedule to bar them from any judicial review. These Acts empowered the State government to take over the land in excess of the ceiling without paying compensation at the market value.

The Twenty Fourth, Twenty Fifth and Twenty Ninth Amendments were challenged in the Supreme Court in the Keshvanand Bharti case. The Supreme Court upheld these amendments as valid but the second part of *Article 31-C* included by the Twenty Fifth Amendment was declared invalid which said that, "no law containing a declaration that it is for giving effect to such policy be called in question in any court on the ground that it does not give effect to such policy." In this case the Supreme Court reversed its judgement given in *Golak Nath case* in 1967. But in fact it went beyond the effects of *Golak Nath case.* On the one hand, it accepted the Parliament's right to amend the Constitution including the Fundamental Rights, on the other, it invented a new doctrine of essential feature of basic structure of the Constitution which could not be amended by the Parliament.

(viii) The Constitution (Thirty Ninth) Amendment Act., 1975 and the Constitution (Fortieth) Amendment Act, 1976

By these two amendments 102 new entries were included in the Ninth Schedule. These were progressive legislations aimed at economic upliftment of the masses. It was felt that if these legislations were allowed to be challenged in the Court, their implementation would be delayed and thus the very purpose of enacting these laws would be frustrated and the national economy would be severely affected.

(ix) The Constitution (Forty-Second) Amendment Act, 1976

The Forty-Second Amendment was a massive exercise in which the entire Constitution was reviewed. It was also aimed at nullifying the decision of *Keshvanand Bharti case.* Through this amendment, all the directive principles were given precedence over fundamental rights. The forty-second Amendment added a few more directive principles i.e. free legal aid, participation of workers in management of industries, protection of environment and protection of forests and wild life in the country. It also sought to assert the supremacy of Parliament in the amendment of the Constitution. The Amendment incorporated the words "Socialist" and "Secular" in the Preamble of the Constitution. It also put severe restrictions on the Court's power of judicial review. For the first time, a Citizen's fundamental duties were also incorporated in the Constitution.

(x) The Constitution (Forty-Fourth) Amendment Act, 1978

The Forty-Second Amendment was highly criticised by the Janata Party. After coming to power, it passed the Forty-Fourth Amendment to undo the major changes introduced in the Constitution by the Forty-Second Amendment. However, the most important change brought about by the Forty-Fourth Amendment is the omission of right to property from the chapter of Fundamental Rights. Instead it was made a legal right under a new *Article 300-A*.

(xi) The Constitution (Forty-Seven) Amendment Act, 1984

By this Amendment, fourteen legislations relating to land reform and Zamindari abolition were given the Constitutional protection of Ninth Schedule.

(xii) The Constitution (Sixty-Sixth) Amendment Act, 1990

The number of entries in the Ninth Schedule was further increased to 257 by this amendment.

(xiii) The Constitution (Seventy-Eight) Amendment Act, 1995

Again, this amendment further added 27 land reform acts in the Ninth Schedule to give them protection from judicial intervention, bringing the total entries in Ninth Schedule to 284. Frequent amendments to put new legislation relating to land reforms show a lack of coherent policy on land reforms on the part of the Government. There has been a lack of political will to implement them also.

A study of above mentioned constitutional amendments clearly reveal that the right to property was a major hindrance in bringing about social change in India, especially in the rural sector, where land reforms were absolutely essential. By incorporating the Ninth Schedule by the First Amendment and subsequently putting many progressive legislations into it, through various Constitutional amendments, the judicial intervention was done away with. In India, the land had been highly monopolized by a few people and was a major cause of poverty in rural sector. Justice Krishna Iyer in 1971, explained the social and economic consequences of agrarian reforms thus:

"The concept of agrarian reform is a complex and dynamic one, promoting wider interests than conventional reorganisation of the land system or distribution of land. It is intended to realise the social function or the land and includes creation of economic units of rural production, establishment of adequate credit system, implementation of modern production techniques, construction of irrigation systems and adequate drainage, making fertilizers available, fungicides, herbicides and other methods of intensifying and increasing agricultural production, providing readily available means of communication and transportation, to facilitate proper marketing of the village produce, putting up of silos, warehouses, etc., to the extent necessary for preserving produce and handling it so as to bring it conveniently within the reach of the consumers when they need it, training of village youth in modern agricultural practices with a view to maximising production and help solve social problems that are found in relation to the life of the agricultural community. The village man, his welfare, is the target.

Further it is thus clear to those who understand developmental dialectic and rural planning that agrarian reform is more humanist than mere land reforms and, scientifically viewed, covers not merely abolition of intermediary tenures, zamindars and the like but restructuring of village life itself taking in its broad embrace the socio-economic regeneration of the rural population. The Indian Constitution is a social instrument with an economic mission and the sense and sweep of its provisions must be gathered by judicial statesmen on that seminal footing."

The ambiguity in right to property led to an unnecessarily prolonged conflict between the judiciary and the legislature. The Forty-Fourth amendment rightly eliminated it as a fundamental right. However, this conflict resulted in the assertion of judicial power to review the legislative and executive actions. The Supreme Court won in this struggle and through its concept of basic structures, it has got the power of final words regarding the interpretation of the Constitution.

Besides, there have been a number of Constitutional Amendments to ameliorate the conditions of Scheduled Caste, Schedule Tribe and other backward classes. The *Article 334,* which provides for the reservation of seats for the Scheduled Castes and the Scheduled Tribes and nomination of representatives of Anglo-Indian Community in Lok Sabha and Legislative Assemblies, has been amended five times i.e. *via* Eighth, Twenty-Third, Forty, Fifty and Sixty Second and Seventy Nine to further extend the reservation for another ten years. The Constitution (Sixty-Fifth Amendment) Act, 1990 provides for the formation of a 'National Commission for Scheduled Castes and Scheduled Tribes consisting of a chairperson, vice-chairperson and five other members who would be appointed by the President by warrant under his hand and seal. The duty of the Commission is to investigate and monitor all matters relating to the safeguards provided for the Scheduled Castes and Scheduled Tribes. The Amendment also empowers the Commission to recommend suitable measures for the welfare and socio-economic development of the Scheduled Castes and Scheduled Tribes. The Constitution (Seventy-Sixth Amendment) Act, 1994 raises the reservation quota of government jobs and seats for admission in educational institutions for socially and educationally backward classes to Sixty nine per cent in Tamil Nadu. This amendment has also been included in Ninth Schedule to negate any chances of judicial intervention or judicial review. The Constitution (Seventy-Seventh Amendment) Act, 1995 enables the State to make any provision for reservation in matters of promotion in government jobs in favour of Scheduled Castes and Scheduled Tribes, if it is of the opinion that they are not adequately represented in the services under the State. The 81st Constitutional Amendment, 2000 was incorporated in the Constitution so as to nullify the effects of a Supreme Court judgement in which the apex Court held that the number of vacancies to be filled up is on the basis of reservations in a year including carried forward reservations should in no case exceed fifty per cent. But then this had already reached to a forty nine and a half per cent. The Act restored the earlier position and now backlog would not be counted in determining the fifty per cent limit in a year.

The 82nd Constitutional Amendment also nullified the Supreme Court judgement which prohibited the relaxations of qualifying marks and standards of evaluation in matters of reservation in promotion. Such relaxations were restored by the 82nd Constitutional Amendment Act, 2002

For the development of tribal areas also, the constitutional amendments have been made. For example the Forty-Ninth Amendment Act of 1984 provides constitutional sanctity to the autonomous District Council in Tripura to ensure rapid and smooth development of tribal areas and self governance of the tribals.

Constitutional Amendments: Political Implications

The 61st Amendment lowered the voting age from 21 to 18 years. The most important changes in the devolution of power were brought about by the 73rd and 74th amendments which gave constitutional status to Panchayati Raj Institutions and urban local bodies. The 73rd amendment made it obligatory on the part of all States to establish three tier system of Panchayats at the village, intermediate and district levels. However, States having a population of less than 20 lakhs are exempted from establishing panchayats at the intermediate level. The seats in the Panchayats are to be filled in by the direct election on the basis of adult franchise. The Scheduled Castes, Scheduled Tribes and women have been given reservation of seats. The women constitute 30 per cent of the total strength. Eleventh Schedule has been included in the Constitution which enumerates the powers and functions of Panchayati Raj Institutions. The 74th amendment provides for Municipal Panchayat, Municipal Council and Municipal Corporation in urban areas.

Through the amending powers, the Central Government has widened its powers. A number of items listed in State List have been shifted to either "Union List" or "Concurrent List." The 42nd Amendment attempted to provide a more centralised State structure. In fact, there has also been misuse of the power. The 38th Amendment was made in 1975, to put the Proclamation of Emergency above the judicial review. This was done to prevent the Court from enquiring into the Emergency imposed on 26th June 1975. The amendment also barred the judicial review of fundamental rights suspended during the emergency. The 39th amendment was made with restrospective effect because Mrs. Gandhi's election to the Lok Sabha was declared invalid by Allahabad High Court and her appeal against the order was pending in the Supreme Court. According to this amendment, the Court could not be approached for the invalidation of the election of the Prime Minister and Speaker to the Lok Sabha. This part was declared invalid by the Supreme Court as it violated the doctrine of basic structure. However, the Court held Mrs. Gandhi's election to Lok Sabha as valid. Her election was declared valid because she amended the Representation of the People Act 1951 through the Representation of the People (Amendment) Act, 1974 (Central Act 58 of 1974) and the Election Laws (Amendment) Act, 1975 (Central Act 40 of 1975) by which those grounds were amended according to which her election had been set aside by the Allahabad High Court. Both these laws were given the constitutional Protection of Ninth Schedule, which means that they could not be challenged in the Court of law. The notorious MISA (The Maintenance of Internal Security Act, 1971) was also given immunity under the Ninth Schedule. (The 44th Amendment restored the earlier position). The 44th Constitutional Amendment also can be seen as an exception which gives constitutional protection from any civil and criminal action to the newspapers for reporting the proceeding of Parliament and State Legislatures unless the publication is proved to have been made with malice. This also applies to Broadcasting Station.

However, this does not apply in case of secret sitting of Parliament or State Assemblies. No new political or civil right has been introduced by any Constitutional Amendment. On the other hand we find restrictions being placed on the rights. For example, the Fifty Second Amendment popularly known as anti-defection law has almost made the elected representatives slaves in the hands of party bosses and if the objective of the amendment was to stop defections then it has been a complete failure. The 42nd Amendment took away the second opportunity of making representation against the proposed penalty by the Civil Servants. It was, therefore, left upon for judiciary to protect, preserve and further develop the rights, as was done in the Menaka Gandhi case in which her passport was impounded and the Government refused to inform her the grounds on which her passport was impounded "in the interests of the general public." The Supreme Court held that the right to travel was a part of right to personal liberty under Article 21 and the person can be deprived of this right only by the "procedure established by law" and the procedure should be fair, just and reasonable. After this case, the Supreme Court has further added new dimensions to Article 21 like right to speedy trial, free legal service, bail, atleast one appeal, capital punishment in the rarest of rare cases etc.

The amending device should not be invoked for each and every purpose. For example, we do not need an amendment for providing reservation of seats to the women. Instead healthy convention should be developed and the Constitution be amended only when it is absolutely necessary and when there is no other remedy left. This is all the more necessary because on the whole the framers of the Constitution did a fine job and it has gained acceptance among different sections and interests of the Indian population; surely, frequent amendments to the Constitution stultifies the sanctity of the constitution and comes in the way of the healthy growth of conventions.

References

Bhandari M.K., *Basic Structure of the Indian Constitution*, 1993, New Delhi, Deep & Deep Publications.

Diwan Paras and Diwan, *Peeyushi, Amending Powers and Constitution Amendments*, 1990, New Delhi, Deep & Deep Publications.

Fadia, B.L., *Indian Government and Politics*, 1996, Agra, Sahitya Bhawan Publications.

Raman Sunder, *Amending Power under the Constitution of India*, 1990, Calcutta, Eastern Law House.

Singh M.P. (Ed.), *V.N. Shukla's Constitution of India*, 1994, Lucknow, Eastern Book Company.

CHAPTER XVII

Party System in India

In India, Jayaprakash Narayan and his friends advocated a Party-less democracy. However, it is difficult to conceive a modern democracy without a well-developed party system considering the sheer size in terms of area and population. The modern state will be unable to provide a stable government without a party system. The introduction of universal adult franchise has made them absolutely necessary or as Sait says that "under a regime of universal suffrage, they are inevitable, like the tides of the ocean."

A political party is a group of people organised to secure political power. To Burke, it is a body of men united for promoting the national interest on some particular principles on which they are all agreed. A political party is organised on the basis of certain principles or programmes which are implemented when the party gets the power to control the government. But this is not the only function of a political party. Political parties provide political education to the masses and make them participate in the political processes. They articulate interests and provide issues before the people. They also play an integrative role by resolving conflicts among the various groups and interests. They accommodate them all and articulate a framework in which peaceful charge becomes possible. Finally, political parties provide opposition to the government in a peaceful and dignified manner which prohibits any coup or a violent change in the government. By opposing the government, they keep a watch over it and make it accountable to the people thereby keeping the flame of democracy alive all the time. It is in these dynamics of government and opposition, within the framework of peaceful competition for political power, that democratic ideals are sustained and allowed to continue.

Features of Party System in India

The party system in India originated in the colonial era in 1885, with the formation of Indian National Congress in Bombay. However, in the initial years, Congress was not a mass organisation. It mainly catered to the interests of the educated class. In the twentieth century, as a result of efforts of extremists like Tilak, and later on Mahatama Gandhi in the militant stage of the national struggle, it became a truly mass organisation reflecting the needs and aspirations of Indian people as a whole. The twentieth century also saw the emergence of Muslim League, another powerful political, albeit, communal, party to protect and safeguard the interests of Muslims. In 1916, Hindu Mahasabha was formed to cater to the needs of Hindus. In 1924, Communist Party was formed. But soon after its formation it was banned by the colonial Government. Therefore it functioned through the Congress Party until 1942, when the ban was lifted as a result of its opposition to the Congress led Quit India Movement and its support to the war efforts of the British Government, it started its operations independently. Congress should be called the mother of all parties in India because most of the parties have their origin in it. The Congress Socialist Party (CSP) was formed in 1934, but it worked within the Congress during the freedom movement. Besides, we also had Justice Party, Akali Dal and DK. Yet the fact remains that during the freedom movement there were only two political parties of significance—the Indian National Congress and Muslim League. After 1947, as a result of the Partition of India, the Muslim League was eclipsed in India but new parties emerged and most of these political organisations were the offsprings of Indian National Congress. Their nature and policies were not at variance from that of the Congress. A significant change took place in 1951, when Bhartiya Jan Sangh was formed which projected programmes and policies which were different from those of the Congress. In 1959, C. Rajagopalachari, the last Governor-General of India and a leading Congress figure, founded Swatantra Party which differed radically from Congress as it opposed the former's Community Development programme, concept of economic planning and socialism. Later on in 1977, both the Bhartiya Jan Sangh and Swatantra Party merged into Janata Party which could not continue for long and split into various parties. The 1990's saw the decline of Congress Party and the emergence of regional parties on the national scene as a force to be reckoned with.

The features of party system in India are:

(i) Initially, the Indian party system was described as 'one party dominant system.' The Indian National Congress was dominating both at the centre as well as the states. The Congress had led the freedom struggle and was supported, for its contribution in achieving the freedom, by the Indian people. There were other political parties as well and in some states, they were able to achieve political power too. But by and large, the Congress Party was dominating the entire scene. This dominance continued till 1967, when its monopoly over political power was broken in a number of states where non-Congress governments were formed. The early 1970's witnessed the re-emergence of one-party dominance which continued till 1977, when Congress lost power in the wake of general discontentment against its policies during the emergency of 1975-77. In 1980, again the Congress Party came into power in the Centre and in many states but the one party dominance era had finished and the multiparty system really came into existence.

(ii) Thus we have a multiple-party system. There are a number of parties operating at national and state levels. In 1951-52 general elections, there were as many as 14 accepted all-India parties and 52 state—recognised parties. In 1957 general elections, we had 4 all-India parties and 19 in State spheres. In 1962, 16 national parties participated in elections. In 1967 and 1971, we had 8 all-India parties. In 1990, we had 11 national parties while as many as 44 recognised state parties plus 251 unrecognized Registered/deemed to be registered political parties. In 1996, we had seven national parties, 39 state (regional) parties and 442 unrecognized registered political parties. The Election Commission has fixed a criteria according to which a party is recognised as national or state party. *A national or all-India party is a party which is able to win a minimum of 4 per cent of voters or more than 3 per cent of seats in atleast four state legislative Assemblies or 4 per cent of votes or 4 per cent of seats in the Lok Sabha.*

There is an interesting study of unrecognised registered parties. Out of 442, 121 of them have prefixes and suffixes like All India or Indian. 44 parties are prefixed or suffixed by words like, Lok, Jan and Janata. "Democratic," "People's," and "Republican" qualify 24 parties. 33 parties are prefixed or suffixed by the word "Congress." Words like "Socialist" or "Samajwadi" can be found in 121 parties. Seven are qualified by the name "communists." Four use the word Ram-Rajya.' There are 80 Republican parties, seven Akali Dals, seven Jharkhand Parties and six Bahujan Parties. It has been pointed out that the multiple-party system leads to instability in the political system as the voters gets confused in the flood of parties. It has also been seen that the bi-party system provides stability to the political system because the voter has to choose one between the two parties.

In India, we had a stable political order mainly because of one party dominance. However, with the decline of Congress, the multiparty system has resulted in instability to the government at the centre. Further, the multiparty system also gives a weak Government because the coalition government has to satisfy the demands of all its constituents. Sometimes the government just becomes inactive and strong decisions are postponed.

However, instability and weak government are not the exclusive features of a multiple party government. In 1967, in Haryana a single majority party Congress Government was formed but instability followed due to mass defections in the Congress. In Madhya Pradesh also, the Congress got majority but soon defections followed. Similarly the P.V. Narasimha Rao Government at the centre displayed inactivity and weakness despite the fact that it was able to achieve majority soon after the elections.

(iii) As we have seen earlier, the number of parties in India have not been stable. Their number has increased and also fallen. As early as 1953, Nehru spoke about the party situation in India thus, "The parties, as they exist in India today, apart from the Congress, may be divided into four groups. There are certain political parties with an economic ideology. There is the communist party with an allied organisation. There are the various communal parties under different names but essentially following a narrow communal ideology, and there are a number of local parties and groups having only a provincial or even narrower appeal." Thus according to Nehru, besides Congress there were four kinds of parties in India in 1953; (i) parties based on economic ideology; (ii) Communist Party; (iii) Communal Parties; and (iv) local parties. During the last fifty years of independence, we also had ad-hoc parties which come into existence for a short while, then they merge with other parties or disappear completely.

(iv) The amorphous growth of parties is also due to the fact that the Indian political parties are not organised on the basis of any political ideology or economic programme. The two major parties-Indian National Congress and Bhartiya Janata Party have little difference so far as their programmes and policies are concerned. The parties have also been personality based. Even the Congress has been such a party. In the initial years, it drew its strength from the charismatic personality of Jawahar Lal Nehru who dominated it. In 1969, the Congress split took place and the Congress (I) was dominated by Mrs. Indira Gandhi. After Mrs. Gandhi, the Congress could survive because of the inherited charisma of Rajiv Gandhi and slowly it became a weak party because of the lack of charismatic personalities like Nehru and Indira Gandhi. P.V. Narasimha Rao could not provide that charisma and the Congress witnessed its downfall. There were people in the Congress who felt that the party could be made stronger once again if someone from Nehru-Gandhi family took over its reins. In 1998, Sonia Gandhi the wife of Rajiv Gandhi, took over as the President of Congress. Except for communist parties and Bhartiya Janata Party, the same situation, more or less, prevails in other parties. A leader of little following starts thinking of floating a political party, the moment he feels dissatisfied or ignored in the parent organisation. Then we also have regional parties which are organised on the basis of language, culture, religion or even caste. The Akali Dal, DMK, BSP are such examples.

(iv) The Indian political parties are plagued with factionalism, which even lead to split in the party. Every party, even the most disciplined party-Bhartiya Janata Party—suffers from factionalism. In Gujarat, it lost power because a factional group led by Vaghela who formed his own party and became the Chief Minister with the Congress (I) support. The Congress Party has also witnessed a number of splits. In Bihar, Laloo Prasad Yadav broke away from Janata Dal and launched his own Rashtriya Janata Dal because his wishes were not fulfilled by the Coalition Government at the Centre which was led by Janata Dal. Similarly, the CPI and CPM have also witnessed splits in the party organisations.

(v) Although the anti-defection law bans defection, defections on a mass scale still occur. In fact, defections are as common as mergers of parties into one group.

(vi) Another important feature of Indian party system is the significant role of regional parties in the national scene. They arose in different states and areas in specific situations and for a long time their interests lay limited to their specific areas of operations. Traditionally, the regional parties operate in a limited geographical area and represent the interest of a particular linguistic, religious, ethnic, cultural or regional group. Their outlook fundamentally differs from that of a national party which has a wider perspective and interest in the entire country. The support base of a regional party is limited to its region and it only seeks to serve the interest of its region. Therefore, there is no inclination to control the power at the centre. The important regional parties are Asom Gana Parishad (Assam), Sikkim Sangram Parishad (Sikkim) Mizo National Front (Mizoram), National Conference (Jammu and Kashmir), Telugu Desam Party (Andhra Pradesh), DMK and TMC (Tamil Nadu), Akali Dal (Punjab), Naga National Council (Nagaland), etc.. Many regional parties have also been ad-hoc parties which came into existence for sometime and later on disintegrated or merged with other parties.

However, after the 1996 elections to Lok Sabha, the situation underwent a major change. Both the national parties-Congress (I) as well as Bhartiya Janata Party could not capture power on their own. The Andhra Pradesh Chief Minister and leader of the Telegu Desam Party, Naidu, announced in Delhi soon after the elections that he would hold confabulations with the other regional parties—the DMK, the TMC, the AGP and Akali Dal to see how the Congress and the BJP could be stopped from capturing power. The result was a 13 party alliance forming a United Front which came to power with Congress support. The regional parties shared power at the centre which changed their perspective and outlook. They made the "Common Approach to Major Policy Matters and a Minimum Programme" document according to which the Central Government was to operate. Political Scientists and leaders have been debating the possible impact of regional parties on the Indian political system but the fact remains that they have come to stay even at the national level and play a very signficant role.

Major Political Parties in India

1. *Indian National Congress or Congress-I*

Indian National Congress was formed in 1885 by a British Civil Servant A.O. Hume with W.C. Banerjee as its first President. It was conceived as a bridge between the English administrators and the common Indian masses. However, in the initial years, the Congress mainly served the interests of the English speaking educated classes in India. It also had a narrow base. However, with the efforts of extremists like Tilak it became an all India organisation. Gandhi turned Congress into a mass movement and a platform for the achievement of freedom. Under Congress leadership, India attained independence. After independence, Gandhi advocated disbanding of Congress as a political organisation and advised it to work as a Lok Sevak Sangh. But his advice was not acceptable to Nehru, Patel and other leaders of the Congress. In November 1947, the All India Congress Committee passed the following resolution in which the new objective of the Congress was declared:

"Political independence having been won, the Congress should address itself to the great task of the establishment of real democracy in the country and a society based on social justice and equality. Such a society must provide every man and woman with equality of opportunity and freedom to work for the unfettered development of his or her personality."

After independence, political and economic reconstruction and nation building was begun by the Congress. A democratic and secular Constitution was formulated and integration of princely states into the Indian Union was achieved. For the economic development of India, Five Year Plans were adopted. Side by side many schemes for the development of rural and other areas were also launched. In foreign affairs, a new foreign policy of non-alignment was inaugurated.

Congress under Nehru became a single party dominant system in which it was ruling at the centre and in most of the states. There was no effective opposition to it which is very essential in the smooth functioning of democracy. Jaya Prakash Narayan once suggested to Nehru that Congress should help to build up opposition. Nehru gave a curt reply "... In India the opposition parties have full opportunity to express opinion and fight elections. There is also freedom for the press to criticise the ruling party. If it was not possible for the opposition to gather strength despite all these opportunities, surely, the Congress could not be held responsible for the weakness of the opposition."

In the 1952 elections, Congress Party could capture as many as 364 seats, while the divided opposition got only 125 seats. In 1967, the party suffered a major electoral defeat at the centre where its majority was highly reduced and it lost power in many states; thus the Congress domination over political power was finished. In 1969, Congress suffered a split but the early seventies saw the re-emergence of Congress era. However this was short-lived and again in 1977, it lost power with Mrs. Indira Gandhi and her many important colleagues losing their seats in Lok Sabha. In 1978, again there was a split in the Congress and the present Congress (I) was born. In 1980, the Congress (I) polled 43 per cent of the votes and won 351 seats out of 539 and it captured power in 15 states. In 1984 elections to Lok Sabha following the assassination of Indira Gandhi, Congress (I) won an unprecedented 396 Lok Sabha seats and 48.1 per cent of the votes and, under the leadership of Rajiv Gandhi, it won in all the states barring Jammu and Kashmir, Andhra Pradesh and Sikkim. But again it was disfavoured by the electorate in 1989, when it could back only 193 seats with 38.21 per cent of popular votes. In 1991 election while its popular votes fell to 37.3 per cent it won 226 votes. In the states it lost heavily. Though it formed a minority government at the centre (later on it achieved majority through dubious means) under the leadership of P.V. Narasimha Rao, in only six states it could form governments. In 1996 elections, again it suffered badly in the Lok Sabha and got only 28.1 per cent votes—a remarkable decline considering that even in the post-emergency 1977 election it had received 34.5 per cent votes and was relegated to second number in Lok Sabha after Bhartiya Janata Party. In States also, the Congress influence had declined manifold. In 1998 it was ruling only three states of Madhya Pradesh, Orissa and Himachal Pradesh. But by 2002, the Congress had consolidated itself and it was ruling as many as 14 states. At the central level, one point definitely goes to its credit: the decline of Congress has not been substituted by any stable replacement, which may be a factor in Congress bouncing back to power. Further, the Congress is the only party which has its tentacles spread in all the parts of India.

Ideologically the party is committeed to secularism, socialism and democracy. The 1999, election manifesto declares Congress commitment to the following beliefs:

(i) Political stability
(ii) Secularism
(iii) Social harmony
(iv) Unity through diversity
(v) Rajniti to lokniti
(vi) Self-reliance.

The Congress manifesto further clarified that the party' has, in its 45 years of governance, by demonstrating its abiding commitment to parliamentary democracy and Sensitive federalism, imparted cohesiveness to the national political stability." It pointed out that only Congress gave a stable political system, while... in just five years, non-Congress governments have given seven Prime Ministers. To Congress, 'stability is not related to government alone but more fundamentally to the stability of ideas, of policies and programmes. But then, for congress, stability is not an end but a means to a stable, harmonious and prosperous nation, based on economic justice, faster growth, more extensive human development and more enduring social harmony. Congress also stands for secularism which means (i) equal respect for all religions which is a private matter of individuals and (ii) a clear separation of religion and politics. The Congress rejects the use of religion for political ends; it cannot be used as an instrument of mobilisation, to whip up passions and sentiments. The Congress is also sensitive to underprivileged and deprived sections and communities and supports reservation for them. The manifesto says 'India is one and many at the same time'. While the oneness has to be, preserved and strengthened, 'the variety has to be recognised, nurtured and given every opportunity for full expression. We have survived because diversity has been allowed to flourish. The Congress also believes in Lokniti. While it wants a strong centre and strong states, it also stands for strong Panchayati Raj Institutions and Nagarpalikas. "Each of these builds on and draws sustenance from each other.' Congress also stands for faster economic growth. It wants 'economic reforms with a human face'. It wants a self reliant India to fight poverty, unemployment and deprivation.

The Congress manifesto also presented a three-pronged agenda-economic, political and social:

Economic

- To increase real investment in agriculture, in rural infrastructure particularly in the backward regions and to revamp the agricultural education, research, extension and credit systems
- To revive the buoyancy in the capital market so that millions of Indians have new and profitable avenues for investing their savings
- To provide special and immediate policy attention and investment focus to employment—intensive economic activities.

Political

- To strengthen local bodies, all rural development funds, over a three year period, will be transferred directly to Zila Parishads and other Panchayat Institutions.
- To set up a Lokpal and bring all political offices, including the Prime Minister and Chief Ministers, under its jurisdiction.
- Initiate moves to amend the Constitution so that one-third of all Seats in the Lok Sabha, the Rajya Sabha and Vidhan Sabhas are reserved for women.
- To enact a Freedom of Information Act to ensure openness in administration
- To amend the Constitution to revive, democratise and professionalise cooperatives.

Social

- To reform India's education system at all levels—schools, colleges, universities.

  To amend the constitution to make free education up to 14 years of age a fundamental right
- Universities to be depoliticised and run on completely professional lines. Tuition fees and maintenance allowances to every scheduled

caste and scheduled tribe student admitted to any University to be guaranteed for a maximum period of six years.

- To launch a time-bound programme to provide potable water and effective sewerage, as also a national movement to promote community hygiene.
- To launch, a new scheme, *Desh ke liye Ek Saal*. Educated youth will be mobilised and paid for their involvement for a year in mission-oriented projects in areas like literacy drives, afforestation schemes and legal rights awareness compaigns.
- To set up a new administrative reforms Commission, key ministries and departments will undergo a major restructuring in terms of structure, functions and procedure.

The Congress, in 1999, promised the following programmes if voted to power:

1. Creation of a hundred lakh jobs a year, at least one member in every family to be provided with a job, for this such laws and regulations to be reviewed and revamped as stand in the way of faster employment generation, the need is to revive economic growth and sustain it in a broad-based manner at 7%-8% per year for a decade and beyond.
2. Reforms in agriculture. Public investment in agriculture to step up, covering irrigation, electrification, godowns, marketing, research and extension.
3. The credit to small and marginal farmers to be doubled in next three years. The rural credit system to be strengthened. All public tubewells to be restored in good working condition in a time-bound programme.
4. The Rural Infrastructure Development Fund to be expanded in which new godowns, storage facilities, cold storage networks and access roads be accorded priority.
5. Greater stress on land reforms: 'the Congress recognises the increasingly acute problem of fragmentation of existing land holdings and the need to consolidate them with, a view to ensure economic viability.'
6. Measures will be taken to increase profitability in agriculture and ensure fair and remunerative prices for their produce.
7. A permanent solution to all inter-disputes will be found and implemented.
8. The eradication of poverty is the most important objective of national development. In rural areas, a sustained 4-5% annual rate

of growth is essential prerequisite for the time bound eradication of rural poverty. All existing anti-poverty programme will be consolidated and rationalised 'to reduce administrative cost and substantially enhance, the funding of anti-poverty and rural development programmes. All central funds for poverty alleviation and rural development will be credited directly to the funds of elected Panchayati Raj institutions ... the Congress will spearhead a massive programme of organising the rural poor for participation in poverty alleviation and rural development programme.

9. The effective devolution of power to Panchayati Raj Institutions: They will be strengthened but will not be allowed to be used against the weaker sections of the society.
10. The cooperatives will be given constitutional protection to function as democratic, autonomous and country assertions,
11. Population control programmes will be given priority.
12. At least 6 % of the nation's GDP will be invested in education, out of which 50 % will be spent on primary education. A time- bound universalisation of elementary education upto the age of 14 will be ensured by 2003. The National Literacy Mission will be consolidated and expanded.
13. Health will be given special consideration and by 2010, the entire nation will reach the quality of life indicators as already reached in some Southern states of the country. The entire country to reach the level of infant mortality as it exists in Kerala by the end of the next decade. An Education Commission on the lines of University Grants Commission well be set up and an University for Health Science be set up in each state to be the implementing arm of the Education Commission.
14. Universal coverage of water supply. A safe water source within a kilometer of each habitation will be provided.
15. Housing schemes will be encouraged and promoted. The Indira Awas Yojna will be expanded and consolidated.
16. Price stability especially with regard to items of consumption for the poor. The Public distribution system to be revamped in the north Indian states.
17. Social Security programmes to be encouraged. The national social Assistance Programme (NSAP) will be fully funded. Special schemes for providing economic security in old age will be launched.
18. A separate statutory National Commission for Scheduled Tribes will be set up.

19. A Commissioner for Minority Educational Institutions will be established and direct affiliation for minority professional institution to central Universities; The corpus of the Maulana Azad Education Foundation will be immediately doubled to spread education and literacy among the minorities. A Central Madrasa Education Board will be established to promote modern and scientific education, along with the traditional curriculum in all Madrasas. The Congress will examine the demand to declare Urdu as an official language in states where there are substantial Urdu-speaking people. The Protection of Places of Worship Act of 1991 will be strictly enforced.
20. Special social security schemes for women working in the unorganised and informal sectors will be launched. Schemes for empowerment of widows will also be launched.
21. Children are to be looked after well. Special programmes for street children.
22. Sports to be encouraged.
23. Fiscal discipline will be established. The fiscal and other barriers in creating a national common market for the entire country will be eliminated in constitution with the state governments.
24. Price stability will be ensured.
25. Many schemes in industrial sector, the Indian manufacturing industry will be revived through new investments and new technologies and for the purpose, a broad based National Manufacturing Competitiveness Council will be set up.
26. The issue of regional autonomy will be given serious and critical consideration.
27. A number of reforms in police, legislative, judiciary and election sectors will be made.
28. The National Security Council will be made a purposeful, forward looking, analysis-based organisation which will represent a wider cross section of intellectual opinion.
29. Relations with neighbouring countries will be improved. The Congress will work towards creating a non-legislative Parliament for South Asia on the lines of European Parliament as a forum for the discussion and issues common to South Asian states. Good friendly relations with Pakistan and China; The consensus on nuclear matters will be restored. (*For details see the Congress Manifesto, 1999*)

2. *Bharatiya Janata Party*

After the split in Janata Party, Bharatiya Janata Party came into existence in February 1980. Largely, it had the members of erstwhile

Jan Sangh who had merged into Janata Party in 1977. In many ways, the BJP is a continuation of Jan Sangh in terms of its policies, programmes and its links with the RSS and the VHP (Vishwa Hindu Parishad), two major pro-Hindu organisations. The BJP is a major force to reckon with in Northern India and, is gradually, spreading in other parts of the country. Its electoral performance is also on the rise. While in 1952 elections to Lok Sabha, Jan Sangh had three seats with 3.1 per cent of total votes, in the Second Lok Sabha four with 5.9 per cent of votes, in Third Lok Sabha 14 seats with 6.44 of votes, in Fourth Lok Sabha the number of seats rose to 35 with 9.4 per cent of votes, in Fifth Lok Sabha its strength declined to 22 with 7.4 per cent of votes. In Eighth Lok Sabha, the BJP suffered a debacle with only two seats and 7.4 per cent of votes. But in the Ninth Lok Sabha it emerged as a major party with 86 seats and 11.4 per cent votes. It was the third largest party. In 1992, as a result of aftermath of destruction of the disputed structure at Ayodhya, its governments in Rajasthan, Madhya Pradesh, Uttar Pradesh, Himachal Pradesh and Gujrat were dismissed. In the Tenth and Eleventh Lok Sabha Elections, the party further improved to 119 seats with 20.8 per cent of votes and 161 seats with 20.29 per cent votes respectively. In the Eleventh Lok Sabha BJP constituted the single largest party. This spectacular rise of BJP alarmed all the parties in the country, compelling them to treat it as politically untouchable so as to keep it out of power. In 1998 and 1999 the BJP alongwith its allies formed the government at the centre. In states also, the BJP has been enjoying power. In 1998, it was a coalition partner in Uttar Pradesh, Haryana, HP and Maharashtra and, on its own, was in power in Rajasthan and Delhi. Its influence is growing in Karnataka, Assam, West Bengal and even in South. However, BJP had to face electoral defeat in 2002 and it was enjoying power only in Gujarat, Himachal Pradesh (Supported by Himachal Vikas Congress, Goa (Supported by independents, Jharkhand (Supported by Janata Dal (United) and Samata Party) and UP (a coalition partner of BSP).

The BJP ideology is based on four concepts of Suraksha (Security), Shuchita (Purity), Swadeshi (Economic Nationalism) and Samrasta (Harmony). It also believes in Hindutva, or Cultural nationalism which will bridge our present to our glorious past and pave the way for an equally glorious future; it will guide the transition from Swarajya to *surajya*. It stands for a "prosperous and strong India" with Hindutva as a "unifying principle which alone can preserve the unity and integrity of our nation." Hindutva which is 'the identity of our ancient nation—Bharatvarsha, the 1996, manifesto says, "It is a collective endeavour to protect and re-energise the soul of India, to take us into the next millennuim as a strong and prosperous nation. Hindutva is also the antidote to the shameful efforts of any section to benefit at the expense of others." BJP wants to construct a magnificent Shri Ram Mandir in Ayodhya "as a tribute to Bharat Mata.' In foreign policy matters, the BJP stands for the promotion of Asian Solidarity, development of South Asian Regional Cooperation and improving relation with neighbours. It wants a stronger dealing with Pakistan. It also wants the illegal migrants especially from Bangla Desh to be sent back. The BJP manifesto of 1996, did not talk about non-alignment. It says that 'The BJP holds that as a departure from the recent past, Indian diplomacy should be conducted in tune with India's position as a strong power and a major player in the world arena. A billion people who do not depend upon anyone for feeding or clothing them are a power which cannot be ignored .... While we believe in partnership with every one, we reject the very thought of patronage by anybody. Back home, the BJP wants to implement the recommedations of Sarkaria Commission. It wants to restore the balance of resources in favour of the states and prevent the misuse of *Article 356*. It is in favour of creation of smaller states like Uttaranchal, Vananchal, Vidharbha and Chattisgarh. It wants to abrogate *Article 370* of the Constitution and favours strong measures to curb terrorism in Jammu and Kashmir and North-East. The BJP has full sympathy with Kashmiri Pandits who are victims of terrrorist violence and displaced from their homes. It has been pleading their cause. BJP has been highly critical of Congress economic policies. It advocates economic growth and employment through Swadeshi.

Some of the programmes of BJP, as envisaged in 1998 election manifesto are as follows:

(i) The BJP will appoint a commission to comprehensively review the Constitution of India, in the light of the experience of the past 50 years and make suitable recommendations.

(ii) A comprehensive electoral reforms to ensure free, fair and fearless elections and to prevent the use of money power and muscle power.

(iii) Judicial reforms for speedy, fair and inexpensive justice.

(iv) Reforms in law and order machinery

(v) Administrative reforms to ensure a responsive and responsible administration.

(vi) To make centre-state relations more harmonious and in keeping with the spirit of a federal policy.

(vii) Panchayati Raj Institutions to be further strengthened and made financially self-reliant.

(viii) To eradicate corruption. A Lokpal will be appointed to enquire into allegations of corruption against anybody holding public office including the Prime Minister; Greater autonomy to CBI so as to prevent investigating agencies from being used to serve the political designs of the ruling party.

(ix) The BJP will enhance public access to information to the maximum extent feasible.

Economic Agenda

(i) BJP believes in Swadeshi or economic nationalism. India must move carefully and gradually towards integration with the global economy suiting its national interests.

(ii) A higher growth rate of GDP of 8 to 9 per cent.

(iii) Emphasis on sectors which offer large potential for employment; including small-scale, artisan based and rural industries, infrastructure, housing (urban and rural), construction, agriculture, waste land development and forestry and labour-intensive production.

(iv) Opting for projects and technologies, wherever choice exist, without reducing productivity, that offer larger employment.

(v) Redesigning the special employment programmes-Integrated Rural Development Programme, Jawahar Rozgar Yojana, Nehru Rozgar Yojana, Scheme for self-employment of the Educated Youth, etc.— to increase their coverage and effectiveness.

(vi) Encouraging the employment of women

(vii) Fully involving the private sector and non-governmental organisations.

(viii) Adopting the institutional approach of cooperative, wherever possible.

(ix) Implementing the special employment programmes through Panchayat institution and

(x) Vocational training

Social Agenda

(i) Ensure house-hold food security commensurate with the national food security so that all families in rural and urban areas get two square meals a day by the year 2003.

(ii) Review and vigorously implement the National Nutrition Policy and the Plan of Action on nutrition so that all goals are achieved by their target dates.

(iii) Revamp and expand the scope of Integrated Child Development Services.

(iv) Use the Public Distribution Scheme (PDS) effectively to help the poorest of the poor.

(v) Housing for all

(vi) Health for all; clean drinking water in all villages and slums, 100 per cent universal immunization of children against preventable diseases. Promotion of cleaniness, sanitation and disease prevention etc.

(vii) Education for all, to increase state spending on education to six per cent and more of our Gross National Product within five years; complete functional literacy in five years and full literacy by the year 2010 etc.

(viii) Employment for women.

(ix) Welfare of Scheduled Castes and Scheduled Tribes.

Foreign Policy

(i) The BJP reject the notion of nuclear apartheid and will actively oppose attempts to impose a hegemonistic nuclear regime by means of CTBT, FMCR and MTCR.

(ii) To give India a role and position into world affairs commensurate with its size and capability.

(iii) Reforms in United Nations and India be made a permanent member of the UN Security Council.

(iv) To re-orient Indian diplomacy to our economic and commercial goals and to ensure that our missions abroad play a more active role in meeting then.

(v) Greater regional cooperation

(vi) Friendship with other countries

(vii) To take active steps to persuade Pakistan to abandon its policy of supporting insurgent and terrorist groups.

(viii) The BJP will re-evaluate the country's nuclear policy and exercise the option to induct nuclear weapons. No compromise with the country's security.

3. *The Janata Dal*

As a result of the merger of Janata Party, Lok Dal (B), Jana Morcha and the Congress (S), Janata Dal was formed in 1988 with V.P. Singh as its President. It fought the Ninth Lok Sabha elections as National Front partner and was able to achieve a remarkable victory by winning 143 seats and 17.8 per cent of total votes. Under the leadership of Janata Dal, the National Front with the outside support from BJP came into power and V.P. Singh (leader of the Janata Dal) became its Prime

Minister. However as a result of withdrawal of BJP support, the National Front Government fell. In Tenth Lok Sabha elections in 1991 Janata Dal's popularity nosedived as it was able to capture only 59 seats with 11.88 per cent of total votes. This further went down to 46 seats and 8.08 per cent of total votes in 1996, Eleventh Lok Sabha Elections. However the Janata Dal alongwith twelve other regional parties formed a United Front and its leader H.D. Deve Gowda became the Prime Minister. After the fall of H.D. Deve Gowda, I.K.Gujral, the Janata Dal leader was made the Prime Minister. The Dal has its support base in U.P., Bihar, Haryana Jammu and Kashmir, Rajasthan, Orissa, Karnataka and Pondicherry. However the Janata Dal has not been able to project itself as a cohesive party. In less than two years, Janata Dal split up and a new party Janata Dal (S) was formed. Later on, Ajit Singh along with his supporters also left the party. In 1997, again a split took place and Laloo Prasad Yadav formed his own Rashtriya Janata Dal (RJD). Janata Dal support base consists of agricultural class. It has been successfully mobilising the dalits and other backward classes. In rural areas AJGAR (Ahir–Jat-Gujjar-Rajput) combination has helped in strengthening the organisation. However rich peasants and big landowners have been the backbone of Janata Dal. Reflecting its support base, the Janata Dal is committed to implement the Mandal Commission report. It stands for the path of democratic, secular, egalitarian, powerful and integrated nation building, "Communal harmony and mutual tolerance for the customs, beliefs and practices of each other must be accepted norms of life." The Janata Dal wants to give the right to work to every Indian citizen.

The 1998 manifesto claimed that the Janata Dal derives its vision from its commitment to Democratic Socialism, based on Freedom, Democracy, Equality, Social Justice and Solidarity. The election manifesto pointed out programmes of Janata Dal, the main features of which are as follows:

(i) A massive programme for utilising all the water available for irrigation purposes. For this purpose all the major rivers of the country will be linked.
(ii) Remunerative prices for agricultural produce
(iii) A compensation scheme for farmers in case of death
(iv) 'Factory on wheels' to help the farmers to get perishable agricultural produce, like fruits and certain types of vegetables, processed and preserved for subsequent sale or export.
(v) Fertilizer subsidy to continue

(vi) Adequate and timely supply of electricity at reasonable prices for agricultural operations, protection of farmers and various schemes for their benefits will be launched.
(vii) The Janata Dal will encourage the unemployed rural youth to start agro-based and food processing units to become self-employed. They will be assisted with capital subsidy through the State Finance Corporations.
(viii) The Panchayati Raj Institutions will be further strengthened.
(ix) Maximise employment generation.
(x) Janata Dal will undertake the re-assessment of the ongoing globalisation and liberalisation for India and take suitable remedial measures to safeguard country's vital interests.
(xi) Public sector reforms to ensure wider participation of representatives of employees in the management and its efficient running. Public sector enterprises to be injected with modern technology, management and functional autonomy.
(xii) Janata Dal will foster self-reliance.
(xiii) Housing for the homeless.
(xiv) Universal literacy to be attained by the year 2010 A.D. Investment in education to be raised by six per cent.
(xv) Special attention to minorities, Scheduled Castes and Scheduled Tribes.
(xvi) Health for all, establishment of a Corpus Fund for medical treatment of the poor.
(xvii) The Janata Dal will promote cooperative federation by involving all state governments in the process of making major national policy decisions as well as in implementing them.
(xviii) Reservation for OBCs and poorer sections among forward castes.
(xix) Empowerment of women. 33% reservation to women in the legislative bodies and 30% reservation in government and private jobs.
(xx) Enactment of Right to Information Act.
(xxi) Friendly relation with India's neighbours, the adoption of Gujral doctrine, to secure a permanent seat for India in the UN Security Council.
(xxii) Drive against corruption.
(xxiii) Creation of smaller states.

4. *Communist Party of India (CPI)*

Communist Party of India was formed in 26 December 1925, as a part of Communist International in Moscow to propagate and spread the communist ideology. It had a galaxy of communist leaders like M.N. Roy (who later denounced communism) Rajni Palme Dutt, S.A. Dange, G.M. Adhikari, Nalini Gupta, Ayodhya Prasad and Shaukat Usmani. However, right from the start, it has been working as a surrogate to the erstwhile Soviet Union, and its policies and programmes changed according to Soviet directives. Thus initially Hitler was dubbed warmonger as he was becoming a formidable threat to the Soviet Union. But after the signing of a pact of non-aggression and neutrality between the Soviet Union and Germany, the same Hitler became a friend of peace and England and France were dubbed as warmongers. Again the CPI had to change its stand when Hitler attacked Soviet Union. The Soviet Union became an ally of England and France. Now for CPI, the people's war (second world war) had begun and England was no longer an imperialist power while Hitler and his allies became warmongers. When Gandhi launched the Quit India Movement in 1942, with a pledge of "Do or die," the CPI decided to support the British war efforts. The British had banned CPI but this was lifted when the CPI decided to extend support to British war efforts in 1942. Before this the CPI was working within the Congress in Congress Socialist Party (CSP). In 1939, all the Communists were expelled from the CSP and in 1945, from the Congress. After independence, the communists declared that India had not achieved real freedom on 15th August 1947 but it was just a transfer of power by the foreign imperialist or bourgeoisie to the native capitalist or bourgeoisie and therefore it waged armed struggle in different parts of the country to win "real freedom and democracy." Consequently, the CPI was banned in certain parts of the country and the armed struggle failed to achieve its objectives. The Soviet leaders advised them to change their tactics and CPI adopted a "Peaceful Approach" strategy. It decided to function as a parliamentary party providing "constitutional opposition" to the Congress Party, As a result, the ban on CPI was lifted in Madras, West Bengal, Travancore-Cochin and Andhra and the communist detenues were released.

The CPI contested the first general Elections. It won 16 seats in the First Lok Sabha with 3.3 per cent votes which was increased in the second Lok Sabha to 27 seats with 8.9 per cent votes. In the Third, Fourth, Fifth, Sixth Lok Sabha elections it captured 29 (9.94 per cent votes), 23 (5.0), 23 (4.7 per cent), and 7 (2.8 per cent) seats respectively. The Eight, Ninth, Tenth and Eleventh Lok Sabha witnessed CPI's representation as 6 (2.7 per cent), 12 (2.6 per cent), 13 (2.46 per cent) and 12 (1.97 per cent) seats respectively. In the first three Lok Sabhas (1952-

57, 1957-62, 1962-67) the CPI was the main opposition group, in the era of single party dominance. After the fourth General Elections, it lost that position. In the State Assemblies, the CPI and its allies captured 181 seats (6.04 per cent of votes in the First General Election. In 1957, it made a history by capturing majority in Kerala State Assembly and formed the first communist Government in India with E.M.S. Namboodripad as Chief Minister. This victory was short-lived as in 31 July 1959, the Namboodripad Ministry resigned as a result of Congress intrigues. The CPI has its pockets of influence in Andhra, Assam, Bihar, Himachal Pradesh, Karnataka, Kerala, Madhya Pradesh, Maharashtra, Manipur, Meghalya, Orissa, Punjab, Rajasthan, Tamil Nadu, Tripura, Uttar Pradesh and West Bengal.

At the lowest level of party organisation, is the cell or branch which can be formed by two or three members of the party in factory, office, workshop or educational institution. Over and above the branch, there are village, town and district committees. At the state level, there is state council. The highest organ of the party is All India Party Congress which elect a General Secretary and the Central Executive of the party. The most important leaders of the party along with the General Secretary form the Central Executive Committee which is the main policy-making organ of the party. The Central Executive Committee is elected by the National Council, while the National Council is elected by the Party Congress, whose delegates are elected by the State Councils.

The objective of the CPI is the attainment of power by the working classes. It stands for abolition of zamindari and confiscation and nationalisation of foreign capital in India. It is opposed to comunalism and caste system

5. *Communist Party of India (Marxist) or CPM*

As a result of split in CPI, the CPM was formed in 1964. This split was an ideological split reflecting the split in international communist movement between the Soviet Union and China. The more "leftists" in CPI like Sundarayya, Jyoti Basu, A.K. Gopalan, Namboodripad, Bhupesh Gupta and Harikishen Surjeet sided with the Chinese while S.A. Dange and his friends remained loyal to Soviet Union. The problem was further accentuated as a result of China's aggression on India. While S.A. Dange and his "rightist" colleagues extended full support to the Indian Government, the leftist refused to condemn China for aggression because they believed that a socialist country can never commit aggression. The Government put a number of communist leftist leaders and workers behind bars. But among the leftists, Jyoti Basu and Namboodripad accepted that China had committed aggression against India. During 1964-66, the CPM was very aggressive and organised demonstrations and bandhs in different parts of the country. However, the CPM soon decided to contest Parliamentary election so that socialism could be realised in a peaceful approach. The CPM also became an independent party in the sense that it refused to become a camp follower of either the Soviets or the Chinese. In fact, it took the view that both the Soviet Union as well as China were "hostile to any organised revolutionary movement" in India. This created a rift within the CPM and a split occurred in 1968, in which the Marxists like Kanu Sanyal and Charu Mazumdar formed another communist organisation— Revolutionary Communist Party, later on Communist Party of India- Marxist-Leninist (CPI-ML).

In the Fourth Lok Sabha Elections, the CPM captured 19 seats with 4.4 per cent of total votes. In the Fifth Lok Sabha it raised its tally to 25 member with 5.1 per cent of total votes. In the Sixth, Seventh, Eighth, and Ninth Lok Sabhas, the CPM captured 22 (4.3 per cent), 36 (6.1 per cent), 22 (5.7 per cent), and 33 (6.5 per cent) respectively. In the Tenth Lok Sabha CPM had 35 (6.16) members and in the Eleventh Lok Sabha it was a United Front partner with 35 seats (6.12 per cent). CPM was in power in West Bengal and Tripura in 1998 and was leading the leftist alliance in Kerala, Besides these states where CPM is highly popular, it also has its support base in Andhra Pradesh, Assam, Bihar, Maharashtra, Orissa and Punjab. Over the years it has become a very cohesive party with a strong cadre based organisation.

The Manifesto of the CPI(M) for the 14th Lok Sabha Elections, 2004 criticised the BJP rule at the centre for pursuing "a combination of communal politics, pro-rich economic policies and craven support to US imperialism." The Manifesto pointed out 'the systematic attacks against non-Hindus and those who do not share the sectarian ideology of Hindutva' particularly in Gujarat, 'economic policies designed to promote the interests of big business and foreign capital leading to erosion of economic sovereignty'. According to the manifesto, the BJP rule had deprived millions of people of their livelihood and transferred wealth to the rich; there were attacks on democratic rights and the rights of the working people were curbed; its pro-American foreign policy was harmful to the country's national interest; and there were unprecedented and brazen levels of corruption. In fact the CPI(M) is fiercely against the BJP and most of the manifesto deals with the severe criticism of various policies pursued by the BJP led NDA Government. Therefore the Manifesto wanted the people to reject BJP as "(A)nother stint of BJP-RSS rule in the name of the NDA would mean facilitating the advance of a Hindutva-based authoritarianism which spells danger for secularism, democracy and social justice. It would mean more reactionary economic policies which would threaten the livelihood of millions. The BJP rule would mean bringing in imperialism and foreign capital in a big way into our economy and society, further eroding national sovereignty and thwarting any semblance of an independent foreign policy."

Some of the important features of the Manifesto were as follows:

- The Ayodhya dispute should be decided by the judicial process. The final judicial verdict should be accepted by all.
- There should be greater powers for the states in the economic and political spheres, institutionalizing the federal system through the Inter-State Council and empowering the National Development Council with sufficient powers.
- Replacing *Article 356* with suitable provisions so that the draconian powers of the Centre to dismiss state governments are curbed.
- Maximum autonomy for the state of Jammu & Kashmir to be provided for within the ambit of *Article 370* of the Constitution; regional autonomy to be provided to Jammu and Ladakh regions.
- An independent and non-aligned foreign policy which defends India from imperialist pressures; initiatives for South-South cooperation and reviving the non-aligned movement on a new basis
- Promote multipolarity in international relations; special attention to improving all-round relations with China; fostering close ties with Russia and special efforts to coordinate relations between India-Russia and China.
- Cancellation of Indo-US military cooperation which links up India with the US global strategy.
- Revert to nuclear policy of using nuclear energy for civilian and peaceful purposes. Provide parliamentary sanction for moratorium on testing. Open talks with Pakistan for de-nuclearised environment in South Asia.
- Promote the policy of no foreign military bases in South Asia.
- Water is a public resource which cannot be privatised.
- Provision of potable drinking water to all villages must be a priority task.
- Housing to be accorded the status of a basic right; housing schemes for urban and rural poor to be stepped up.
- Guarantee right to work as a fundamental right.

- Provide food-for-work programmes to generate employment.
- Scrap freeze in recruitment in the Government sector.
- Grant of pension to working people as a third benefit.
- Network of old-age homes/day care centres to be set up with State support.
- Stringent action against untouchability and atrocities against scheduled castes and scheduled tribes and invoking of the provisions of the Prevention of Atrocities Act for this purpose.
- Ensuring that quotas for reservation for scheduled castes and tribes are filled up.
- Reservation to be extended to dalit Christians.
- Protect land rights of adivasis and restore land illegally alienated from them.
- Ensure the right of access to forests and forest produce; the Forest Act be amended for this purpose. Recording of rights of inhabitants of forest villages.
- No project, industrial or developmental, should be undertaken where displacement of tribal people occurs without a comprehensive and sustainable rehabilitation package. Such a scheme must be put in place before any displacement or work begins.
- Equal rights and opportunities for all citizens, irrespective of religion or caste are essential for a secular-democratic society. The Muslim community and some other minorities suffer from various forms of deprivation and discrimination. Special measures are required to remove their social and economic backwardness.
- Constituting a National Judicial Commission comprising of representatives from judiciary, executive, legislature and bar for appointment, transfer of judges and to ensure judicial accountability.
- There should be a proper balance in the relations between the legislature, judiciary and the executive and the exercise of powers in their respective spheres without encroaching into the legitimate domain of other organs.

Some Regional Parties

(i) Shiromani Akali Dal

Akali Dal in Punjab was formed in 1920, to promote Sikh interests. A section of the Akalis in 1940's had demanded the creation of "Azad Punjab." The Akali Dal was against the Partition and the creation of Pakistan. But it also made it clear that if the country was to be partitioned, the Sikhs should be given a state of their own. In 1946, the Sikh leaders demanded an independent and sovereign Sikh state. After independence the Akali Dal demanded 'Punjabi Suba' as a result of which the united Punjab was trifurcated into Punjab, Haryana and Himachal Pradesh. In 1968, Akali Dal demanded greater autonomy for states. The "Batala Resolution" declared, "The Shiromani Akali Dal demands that the Constitution of India should be on a correct federal basis and the states should have greater autonomy. The Shiromani Akali Dal feels that the Central Government's interference in the internal affairs of the states and the obstacles it places in the proper functioning of the State machinery are detrimental to the unity and integrity of the country. Therefore, whereas this conference demands of the Central Government that necessary changes be brought about in the Constitution, it also appeals to the State Governments to raise their voice to protect and safeguard their rights so that the country may be able to go smoothly on the federal system..."

In 1968 two factions of Akali Dal joined together and political goal of the Panth was defined as, "The order of the Khalsa, as ordained by Guru Gobind Singh and in accordance with his commandments is a sovereign people by birthright and a sovereignty-oriented party suigeneris .... A sovereign people within a free country, to achieve this goal within a free India ... enjoying a constitutional status, is the very foundation of the organisation and constitution of Shrimoni Akali Dal, In 1973, the Akali Dal Working Committee adopted the famous Anandpur Sahib Resolution which demanded that in "Punjab and the other states of the country, Centre's jurisdiction should be limited only to matters relating to the departments of Defence, Foreign Affairs, Post and Telegraph, Railways and Currency. All the remaining departments should be within the jurisdiction of the Punjab and for the management of these, Punjab should have complete autonomy to frame its own constitution. The other demands of Akali Dal include:

Second language status to Punjabi in the adjoining states of Punjab; an end to the forcible eviction of Sikh peasants from the states of UP, Haryana and Rajasthan; allocation of due share to Punjab from the central pool; recruitment to the army on the basis of merit as upto 1974. Restrictions imposed on the basis of population are violative of Article 16 of the Constitution; enactment of the an All India Gurudwara Act on the lines of the Sikh Gurudwara Act, 1925 for proper maintenance of holy shrines and government should not interfere in religious affairs of the Sikhs; Amritsar be granted the status of holy city on the lines of Kurukshetra, Varanasi and Haridwar etc.; Installation of a high-powered transmitter at the Golden Temple, Amritsar for broadcasting the holy Gurubani.

The government accepted certain demands but not all. The Akali Dal has never been a cohesive party, as a result, frequent splits, mergers and then splits have been the chief characteristic of Akali Dal in Punjab. During the agitation for Punjabi Suba, Akali Dali was divided into two factions led by Master Tara Singh and Sant Fateh Singh. While Tara Singh demanded a separate homeland for Sikhs, Sant Fateh Singh opposed this demand. In 1968, two Akali Dal factions merged into one Akali Dal. However, soon Akali Dal was divided into Longowal and Talwandi groups. During the height of militancy in Punjab, the Akali Dal split into half a dozen factions. In 1989, Mann faction which was prominent during militancy won 13 Lok Sabha seats. In 1992, almost all Akali factions boycotted the Assembly elections which brought Congress into power in Punjab. In 1996 Lok Sabha poll, the Akali Dal (Badal group) won eight out of nine seats it contested getting 28.7 per cent votes. The Mann faction of Akali Dal drew a blank but pulled 3.84 per cent votes. The Akali Dal (Badal faction) election manifesto of 1996, contained the following pledges:

(i) More autonomy for states
(ii) Agreements on adjudication of inter-state river waters
(iii) Filling of SYL with earth
(iv) Transfer of Chandigarh and other left-out Punjabi speaking areas into Punjab
(v) Free education to girls upto graduation
(vi) Free power to tubewells
(vii) Pension to all old persons at the age of 60
(viii) Review of Punjab Health systems Corporation
(ix) Federal structure of the Indian Union
(x) Constitution of high level commission by the judges of the Supreme Court for probing into the role of the Congress Party's alleged role on the creation of terrorism and divide and rule policy
(xi) Setting up a human rights commission
(xii) Second language status to Punjabi in other Punjabi speaking states
(xiii) Punishment to the guilty in the anti-Sikh riots in 1984
(xiv) Suitable compensation to the people suffering during the operation Blue Star.
(xv) End of alleged Police Raj
(xvi) Independent working of judiciary
(xvii) Waiving the farmer's irrigation water rent

(xviii) Abolition of the Octroi
(xix) All India Gurudwara Act

In 1967 elections, the Akali Dal emerged as the largest single party in Punjab and formed a coalition government along with Jansangh. But soon the coalition government collapsed. During 1977-79 it had an alliance with Janata Party. The Akali Dal Chief Minister first, Prakash Singh Badal and later on, Talwandi, alleged central discrimination against Punjab. In 1980 elections, it lost power. The Akali Dal backed the short-lived BJP Government at the centre in 1997. Now Akali Dal wants a "broad based confederal" structure in the Indian political system instead of Anandpur Sahib Resolution which demanded a separate Sikh Nation. However the basic support base of Akali Dal remain the Sikhs and even among the Sikhs, the Jat Sikhs and other sections of affluent peasantry. As a result of Twelfth Lok Sabha election in 1998, the Akali Dal captured 8 seats and joined the BJP-led coalition government at the centre. Akali Dal was a constituent of NDA which formed the government after the thirteenth Lok Sabha Elections. But it lost power in Punjab. In 2004 Lok Sabha election Akali Dal bagged 8 seats.

(ii) DMK

DMK or Dravida Munnetra Kazhagam is the inheritor of the earlier Dravida Kazhagam, which was a social or self respecting movement basically, against Hindi, Brahmins and Aryans. DK stood for rationalism, secularism, atheism, widow remarriage, removal of untouchability, emancipation of women, banning of child marriages, imposing prohibition and entry for all to temples and other places of religious worship. Politically it demanded political autonomy and wanted to change the name of Madras to Dravidanadu. E.V. Ramaswamy Naicker was the head of the DK and was affectionately called Periyar (Patriarch). However, because of his autocratic behaviour and especially the marriage of this 72 years old Periyar with a 28 year old party worker led to the split in the party and C.N. Annadurai formed Dravida Munnetra Kazhagam in 1949. DMK articulated the regional politics based on Dravidian ethnicity and Tamil language. There was a time when it demanded Dravidisthan for Dravidians. DMK has been anti Brahmin and it is to be noted that anti-Brahminism is not new to Tamilnadu. As early as in 1909, Madras Non-Brahmin Association was formed which ultimately led to the creation of Justice Party in 1920.

The DMK got its first success in 1959, when it gained control of Madras City Corporation with the help of independents from the

Congress. In 1967, it became a ruling party in Madras with 138 seats out of 233 in the State Assembly. In Lok Sabha it won 25 out of 39 seats allotted to Tamil Nadu. In 1971 elections, the DMK won 184 out 234 seats, while in Lok Sabha also its performance was no less spectacular—23 out of 39 seats. However, in 1972 the party split and M.G. Ramachandran (MGR) formed his Anna DMK. In 1976, he formed All India Anna Dravid Munnetra Kazhagam (AIDMK). DMK lost power in 1997, which was only regained in 1989, when the DMK led alliance wrested 170 out of 232 seats in Tamil Nadu State Assembly Elections. In 1998 Lok Sabha elections, DMK won 5 out of 39 seats from Tamil Nadu and one from Pondicherry

Initially the DMK was based on five principles i.e. social reforms, democracy, propagation of Tamil language and culture among Tamilians, socialism through constitutional means and establishment of sovereign Dravid Nad. The demand for Dravid Nad was the demand of creation of a separate state of Dravidisthan consisting of four Southern States. But with the Chinese aggression and subsequent amendment to the Constitution which made it obligatory for a political party to be loyal to the unity and integrity of the country, this demand, was given up.

DMK demanded greater autonomy for states. In 1969, it appointed a Committee under the Chairmanship of Dr. P.V. Rajmannar, ex-Chief Justice of the Madras High Court to go into the question of Centre-State relationship. DMK was a member of the National Democratic Alliance on the eve of thirteenth Lok Sabha Election, in 1999, and subsequently joined the NDA Government. In 2004, DMK joined the UPA and was able to win 16 seats in Lok Sabha. The party joined the UPA Government and was in power in Tamil Nadu.

(iii) AIADMK

All India Anna Dravida Munnetra Kazhagam was formed by the charismatic film star M.G. Ramachandran in 1972 following a split in DMK. In 1977, as a result of agreement with Congress which gave more seats to AIADMK in State Assembly and less in Lok Sabha, AIADMK captured power in Tamil Nadu. It also got 18 seats in Lok Sabha with 30.5 per cent votes. In 1984, it got 12 seats for 18.4 per cent votes again in alliance with the Congress. In 1987, there was a split in the party with the death of MGR. One group of AIADMK went with his wife Janaki Ramachandaran while the other with his protege co-star Jayalalitha. Both the factions contested the 1989 Assembly elections separately. The AIADMK lost the power to DMK in Tamil

Nadu. However both the groups reunited after the defeat under Jayalalitha and the following 1989, Lok Sabha election saw the Congress—AIADMK combine sweeping the polls. In 1991 State Assembly elections, AIADMK entered into alliance with Congress and the combine swept the polls with AIADMK getting 163 seats and Congress 61 out of a total number of 234 seats. Jayalalitha was sworn in as the Chief Minister of Tamil Nadu. However, the extravagance displayed in the marriage of her foster son and the corruption which became rampant in the state, during her regime and especially, the charges against her, made Jayalalitha very unpopular. In 1996 State Assembly elections, she entered into an alliance with the Congress, however, her party was routed. While for the first time in history, Congress got a single representation in the Assembly, the AIADMK could bag just four seats. But in 2001 Assembly Elections, the AIDMK again came back to power in Tamil Nadu.

The AIADMK stands for "Annaism" and strives for socio-economic reforms. It is pledged to protecting the Tamil Culture and Tamil Language. Releasing the AIADMK election manifesto in 1998, the party General Secretary, Ms. Jayalalitha wanted the BJP to put Ayodhya, Kashi and Mathura issues on the 'backburner or deep freeze' for at least 20 years and concentrate on such national issues like eradication of poverty and unemployment and provision of drinking water and electricity. The party manifesto promised to strive to discover an approach that was 'acceptable to all' regarding a common civil code. The party stands for empowerment of the women. Regarding *Article 370*, the party manifesto committed itself to bringing about a consensus among all the states which seek special privileges or exemptions. The party fought the elections in alliance with the BJP and became a constituent of the BJP led coalition government at the centre. But soon differences arose and AIADMK withdrew its support which led to the downfall of the Vajpayee Government in 1999. In 2004, the Party Could not get even a single seat in Lok Sabha.

(iv) Asom Gana Parishad

Asom Gana Parishad is a regional party in the state of Assam. It owes its existence to the prolonged student agitation against the foreign migration in Assam which resulted in Assam Accord in 1985. In 1985, AGP won 7 seats with 33.4 per cent votes in Lok Sabha. In 1986, it got majority in Assam Assembly and formed its government. However in 1991 State Assembly elections, the party witnessed a humiliating defeat with only 19 seats. It was stated that the voters of Assam had punished the AGP and its President cum Chief Minister P.K. Mahanta because the AGP Government could not control the rampaging United Liberation Front of Asom (ULFA). The defeat of AGP was followed by the formation of Congress Government under Hiteswar Saikia. The debacle of AGP was also due to the vertical split in the AGP and a newparty Natun Asom Gana Parishad (NAGP) came into existence. In 1996, again luck favoured AGP when it won 59 seats in the State Assembly out of 122 seats for which elections were held. Its allies captured 11 seats and thus AGP alongwith its allies formed the coalition Government in Assam under Prafulla Kumar Mahanta The AGP was also a partner in the United Front Government at the Centre. However, in the 1998 Lok Sabha Elections, AGP could not win even a single seat.

The AGP is committed to identifying the illegal migrants from Bangla Desh and their deportation. It also demands more autonomy to the states.

(v) Haryana Vikas Party

The Haryana Vikas Party was launched by Bansi Lal who served Haryana as Chief Minister twice from 1968 to 1975 and June 1986 to June 1987. In 1996, elections Haryana Vikas Party with an alliance with BJP fought Assembly as well as Lok Sabha polls. The HVP manifesto contained the following promises:

(i) Making provision of electricity for 24 hours within two months of coming to power in the State
(ii) Providing more water for drinking and irrigation facilities
(iii) Introducing compulsory prohibition
(iv) Bringing an end to inter-state water dispute
(v) Removing Caste bias
(vi) Bringing cleanliness in State politics
(vii) Appointing Lok Pal for checking corruption
(viii) Restoring law and order situation
(ix) Constructing canals including early construction of SYL canal, Haridwar-Karnal Canal
(x) Utilising flood waters of Yamuna
(xi) Constructing Agra Canal
(xii) Introducing Crop insurance for farmers
(xiii) Granting of easy loans to farmers
(xiv) Charging of electricity rates from the farmers at low rates

(vi) Telugu Desam Party

TDP was formed by the film star turned politician N.T. Rama Rao. The party got a massive mandate in 1983 elections with 202 seats out of 294 seats. In 1985 midterm poll, it retained the same position i.e. 202 seats which was a befitting reply to Congress efforts to topple NTR Government which led to the mid-term polls. However in 1989, it suffered very badly and got just 74 seats and the Congress returned to power. But NTR capitalised on anti-arrack policy which gave him a substantial women's vote and in 1994, he fought back winning 219 seats. Another reason for NTR winning was his promise of availability of rice at the rate of Rs. 2 per Kg. N.T. Rama Rao again became the Chief-Minister. However his marriage to Laxmi Parvati led to family feuds and subsequently division in the TDP. Under the leadership of N. Chandrababu Naidu, the son-in-law of NTR, over 150 MLAs revolted against NTR. NTR resigned and his son-in-law N. Chandrababu Naidu became the Chief Minister in 1995. On January 18, 1996, NTR passed away and in the election that followed N. Chandrababu Naidu gave a crushing defeat to Parvati faction of TDP.

NTR felt that a new party was needed to protect the honour and self respect of the six crore Telugu speaking people. He declared that he was entering politics to serve the suffering masses in Andhra Pradesh. NTR laid emphasis on the pride of Telugu language and tried to unite people under the common platform of language. TDP stands for greater autonomy to the states. It, in 1980's, it initiated a conclave of the non-Congress parties in Vijayawada, which was the first of its kind in post-independence Indian politics. Later on, other conclaves of similar nature followed at New Delhi, Srinagar and Calcutta. These conclaves suggested specific recommendations for the greater autonomy to the states.

The TDP leader Chandrababu Naidu emerged as a key player and even king-maker in the national scene after 1996 Lok Sabha elections.

(vii) Shiv Sena

In Maharashtra, Shiv Sena is a very powerful regional party. It was formed by Bal Thackeray in 1964, to preserve "Maratha Pride." Along with BJP, it formed a coalition government in Maharashtra. Bal Keshav Thackeray is its undisputed leader. 'Kapilacharya' one of its leaders who writes under this pseudonym said, "The Shiv Sena owes its origins to the bitter feelings of frustration taking hold of the rank and file of young Maharashtrians. As a class they feel that in the State of Maharashtra they, who are the sons of the soil and, as such, must get full opportunity to develop their lot in life, but do not get them, even in small measure. They find their interests woefully neglected. Quite naturally it becomes the primary duty to provide adequate opportunities of education, employment, security of food, clothing and housing to the indigenous man." Shiv Sena wants to ensure that the self-respecting, honest and open minded Maratha does not become frustrated, disappointed, destitute in his own homeland. Unless government takes steps to make it possible for the Maratha race to develop its personality and instinct, it will not be able to give its best in the services of the nation." Shiv Sena draws strength from the great national hero, Shivaji who fought against Aurangzeb, the Mughal emperor. The Sena is highly critical of big industrialists and wants to provide justice to the people of Maharasthra. For this purpose Shiv Sena also renders social service.

Shiv Sena has been a militant organisation. It is also a pro-Hindu group. When not in power, it has been resorting to demonstrations, bandhs and strikes. There have been allegations that it has been behind communal riots and killings. It is also alleged that Shiv Sena had a role in the demolition of the disputed structure at Ayodhya.

In 1990, the Shiv Sena won 52 seats in the Maharashtra in alliance with BJP. In 1991, it won four Lok Sabha seats with 9.45 per cent votes. In 1995, BJP Shiv Sena combine captured the power in the state. In the Lok Sabha elections in 1996, Shiv Sena won 15 seats out of 20 which it contested with 16.8 per cent votes. In 1999 Lok Sabha Election, the Shiv Sena fought elections as an NDA ally, captured 15 seats and joined the NDA Government. But in 2004 Lok Sabha election its representation was reduced to 12 seats.

(viii) All Jammu and Kashmir National Conference

The National Conference is a regional party operating in Jammu and Kashmir. It was formed as "Muslim Conference" in 1931 and in 1938, it was renamed All Jammu and Kashmir National Conference. As a Muslim Conference, it waged a struggle against the Maharaja of Jammu and Kashmir and promoted the interests of the Muslims. However in 1938, with the renaming of the organisation, the members of other religions were also welcome in National Conference. Sheikh Abdullah was its undisputed leader. After the merger of Jammu and Kashmir State into the Indian Union, it was because of Sheikh Abdullah and National Conference that the State was given a special status under *Article 370* of the Indian Constitution. In the 1951 election, the National Conference captured all the 75 seats in the State Assembly. In 1953, Sheikh Abdullah was put behind bars because of his anti-national activities and his deputy, Bakshi Ghulam Mohammad, was appointed Prime Minister (as the Chief Minister of Jammu and

Kashmir was then called) of the State. Under the leadership of Bakshi Ghulam Mohammed, the National Conference got the ratification of the accession to India by the Constituent Assembly of Jammu and Kashmir. However Plebiscite Front of Mirza Afzal Beg demanded plebiscite to settle the issue of State's accession to India and posed a serious challenge to the National Conference Government. But the firm hand of Bakshi Ghulam Mohammad tackled the challenge successfully. He also implemented a number of progressive and welfare measures to improve the lot of the people of Jammu and Kashmir. In 1957 State Assembly elections, it secured 68 seats, while remaining six seats went to Harijan Mandal (1) and Praja Parishad (5). In 1957, there was a split in National Conference and another party called Democratic National Conference was launched. However, this new party subsequently merged with the parent body. In 1965, the Congress decided to extend its political activities in the State and the National Conference merged into Congress and Congress became the party in power in the State. In 1966, again the National Conference was revived and in 1972, again it merged with the Congress. In 1975, Sheikh Abdullah became the Chief Minister after the New Delhi Accord in which Sheikh Abdullah accepted the State's accession to Indian Union as final and again the National Conference was revived by him. After Sheikh Abdullah's death, the National Conference Split into two factions-one led by Sheikh Abdullah's son, Dr Farooq Abdullah and the other by G.M. Shah, Sheikh Abdullah's son-in-law. In 1982 State elections, Dr. Farooq Abdullah captured a clear majority. But Dr. Abdullah's Government was dismissed despite the fact that he was ready to face the Assembly within two days and G.M. Shah's faction of National Conference was installed in government with G.M. Shah as the Chief Minister with Congress (I) support. In 1984 elections, Dr. Farooq Abdullah's National Conference swept the Parliamentary elections in Kashmir Valley. In 1987, Congress (I) and National Conference fought together the elections and Dr. Abdullah again became the Chief Minister. Meanwhile the terrorist activities in Kashmir had increased manifold. Dr. Abdullah resigned in January 1990 and State was put under President's rule. In 1996 Lok Sabha elections, the National Conference did not participate, although as Dr. Abdullah declared that it was not a boycott of the elections. The National Conference argued that the prevailing terrorist violence was not conducive to its participation. But, the National Conference demanded the restoration of the pre-1953 status for Jammu and Kashmir. In the subsequent State Assembly Elections, the National

Conference participated in which it got absolute majority and Dr. Farooq Abdullah was installed as the Chief Minister.

(ix) Bahujan Samaj Party (BSP)

BSP banks on Dalit votes. In UP in 1993 polls, it had an alliance with the Samajwadi Party led by Mulayam Singh Yadav but later on BSP withdrew its support. The Mulayam Singh Government fell. BSP formed the Government with the BJP support in June 1995 and Mayawati, the General Secretary of BSP was sworn as Chief Minister of UP. She was the first dalit Chief Minister of the State. But in October 17, 1995, BJP withdrew its unconditional support and Mayawati resigned and President's Rule was imposed. In 1996 Lok Sabha elections, the BSP had 11 members. Its poll percentage went up substantially to about 18 per cent. It has solid Dalit votes plus a chunk of lower caste Muslims and OBCs support. In 2002, it was ruling UP with BJP as its coalition partner. A new light was thrown on the political history of India by Mayawati when she displayed a remarkable maturity and wisdom in getting support from a cross-section of people from different castes and communities as a result of which her party could get majority in the UP Assembly on its own. This was a relief to the state as it ended 16 years of unstable coalition regimes and a party with clear majority got into power. It is difficult to believe that a party whose mantra in the past was Tilak, taraju aur talwar, unko maro juthe char ('Brahmins, traders and the warrior caste should be kicked') now gave the slogan Brahmin shankh bajaega, hathi badhta jaega (Brahmin will blow the bugle and the elephant [BSP's symbol] will make progress). (Mayawati pointed out that the slogan that her party wanted to "boot out" the Brahmins, the Vaishyas and the Kshatriyas was the "creation" of the Congress and the BJP and was intended to create a division between the Dalits and the upper castes. She insisted that the BSP believed in a classless society. This was a new experiment and such experiments at the national as well as state level, if well emulated, can do wonders in eradicating caste conflicts from the Indian polity.

The BSP's support comes from UP where it has substantial following. It also has pockets of influences in MP, HP and Punjab.

References

Ahuja, Gurudas M., *BJP and Indian Politics, Policies and Programmes of the Bharitya Janata Party* 1994, New Delhi Ram Company.

Aggarwal J.C. and Chowdhry N.K., *Elections in India 1952-96,* 1996 Delhi, Shipra Publication.

Chabbra Harinder K., *State Politics in India (A Study of Centre-State Relations),* 1977, Delhi, Surjeet Publications.

Dass H.H. and Choudhry B.C., *Federal and State Politics In India,* 1990, New Delhi, Discovery Publishing House

Fadia, B.L., *Indian Government and Politics.*

Gupta D.C. *Indian Government and Politics 1996,* Delhi, Vikas Publishing House Pvt Ltd.

Kumar Arun, *The Turning Point 1996 Poll Story,* 1997, Delhi, Konark Publishers.

Lal Shiv, *National Parties of India,* 1972 New Delhi, The Election Archives.

Madan N.L. *Congress Party and Social Change,* 1984, Delhi, B.R. Publishing Corporation.

Mishra R.S. *The Congress in Power,* 1976, Delhi Jnanda Prakashan.

Roy Meenu, *India Votes Elections,* 1996, A Critical Analysis, 1996, New Delhi, Deep and Deep Publications.

Siwach J.R. *Indian Government and Politics,* 1990, New Delhi. Sterling Publishers Private Limited.

Zaidi A.M. *The Annual Register of Indian Political Parties 1990 Part one,* 1992, New Delhi Indian Institute of Applied Political Research.

The *Indian Express* supplement 'India at 50'. Facts, figures and Analysis 1947-1997, Published on the 50th Anniversary of Indian Independence.

The *Hindu* Supplement India, Published on the 50th Anniversary of Indian Independence.

Hartmann Horst, *Political Parties in India,* 1977, New Delhi, Meenakshi Prakashan.

CHAPTER XVIII

Pressure Groups in India

The modern society is a pluralistic organisation in which the individuals cannot safeguard their interests in isolation. Therefore, to preserve and promote their interest, they form groups or organisations, that is how the pressure groups have developed in modern times. According to Alan R. Ball, "Pressure groups are organisations which attempt to influence government decisions without seeking to become part of the government." This definition gives one primary characteristic of a pressure group i.e. a pressure group is not interested in capturing political power. It does not become a part of the government or seek power. It only exerts pressure to get a favourable policy decision passed in its favour. There have been cases when a particular pressure group decided to contest elections but that decision was always a tactical one to influence political parties. The pressure groups, usually, rely on a variety of campaigning methods to influence governmental decisions. This may even include demonstration, bandh and strikes. But essentially the pressure group's aim is to pressurise the government through a variety of means to get a favourable decision. This little discussion calls for a need to differentiate between a pressure group and a political party.

While in some cases, the distinction between the presure group and political parties may blur, and there are even some similarities in both, the distinction between the two is based on their respective aims and appeal. A political party is a much larger organisation which desires to broaden its mass base as much as possible. Therefore, the programmes and perspective of the political party is very broad. Political parties cut across various sectional, communal and other interests and try to penetrate everywhere in the political system to seek more and more support. In contrast, the pressure group has a limited membership and is a private organisation of people who have a common interest.

Secondly, a person may be a member of many groups at a time, as he may be having a variety of interests but he cannot be a member of many political parties, at a time. He will have to choose one of the political parties. Thirdly an individual may decide not to become a member of any political party at all. The membership of a presure group is also voluntary but his interest will compel him to become a member of the pressure group. Fourthly, the objective of a political party is to gain power while a pressure group's objective is to achieve particular ends relating to its particular activity. While the groups accentuate the differences by asserting and promoting their particular interest which invariably comes into conflict with the interest of other groups, the political parties normally play an integrative role by assimilating various interest groups and by cutting across economic, social, religious or ethnic interest to broaden thier respective mass base which is the only way of achieving power in modern democracies.

Mainly the pressure groups are the association of private individuals. But there may be public agencies or organisations connected with the state who act as pressure groups. For example the military and civil servant often engage in group tactics. Finally, a variety of terms are used for pressure groups like interest group and political group. However, there have been scholars who differentiate between the interest group and pressure group. According to them, an interest group is an organisation of people having common interests and it only becomes a pressure group when it seeks the favourable governmental policy or decision and exerts pressure on the government for the purpose.

Pressure Groups in India

There is a variety of pressure groups operating in the Indian political system. Following Robert L. Hardgrave, they may be broadly classified as follows:

1. Communal Association.
2. Agrarian Groups
3. Students Organisations
4. Labour Unions
5. Business Groups.
6. Professional groups
7. Women's groups

1. *Communal Association*

The communal association are organised on the sectarion basis of religion, language, caste, ethnicity and tribe. Such organisations are interested in the welfare and promotion of the particular communal group and therefore viewed as a threat to the cause of national integration. In Punjab, we have Akali Dal, which although a political party, works, more or less, as a pressure group to further the cause of the Sikhs. We also have different groups acting as political parties in the North East which demand separate independent states for themselves. Vishwa Hindu Parishad, Rashtriya Swayam Sewak Sangh, Arya Pratinidhi Sabha, Parsi Central Association and Political League and Anglo Indian Association are examples of communal pressure groups. We also have caste-based pressure groups. Harijan Sewak Sangh, Marwari Association, Vaisya Mahasabha, Tyagi Sabha, Jat Sabha, All Indian Kanyakubja Board and other various associations of Scheduled Castes and Scheduled Tribes etc.

2. *Agrarian Groups*

India is a country of villages. But due to peculiar colonial structures created by and for the British imperialist interest, the peasantry in India has been subjected to oppression and grinding poverty. Therefore, it remained highly unorganised. Hence the political parties have come forward to organise the aggrieved peasantry. Particularly the CPI, CPM, CPI(ML) and other communist organisations have taken the lead in this direction, who organised such movements like Tebhaga movement in W. Bengal, Telengana movement in Andhra Pradesh, and Land Grab movement in U.P. and Bihar and Naxalbari movement in West Bengal and Bihar. The main peasant groups like All India Kisan Sammelan, Hind Kisan Panchayat, United Kisan Sabha—all have been dominated by the political parties. However, the fact remains that in rural India the former Zamindars, big landlords and rich farmers who were the main beneficiaries of Green Revolution in post independent India, though not organised, are powerful groups, have nexus with the bureaucracy and other state structures and have been able to withstand various land reform legislations. The failure of land reform movement organised by the state highlight the effectiveness of this unorganised pressure group.

However, as a result of the spread of political consciousness, slowly and gradually, the Indian peasantry is getting organised in pressure groups in different part of the country. They have also resisted the interference of political parties and asserted their independence. For example in Western U.P., Punjab and Haryana, Bharatiya Kisan Union became an important peasant group which demanded more remunerative prices for sugarcane and reduction in electricity and canal water charges. But this group has no symapthy with the agricultural labourers, who still remain unorganised. BKU does not demand fair wages for them. In fact, it has been demanding the scrapping of land ceiling laws and Minimum Wages Act. In Maharashtra, Shetkari Sanghatana under the leadership of Sharad Joshi gave the slogan Bharat vs. India, the country side vs the cities. Like BKU, his movement is also against the domination of urban India over rural India. But unlike BKU, Sharad Joshi has demanded minimum wages of Rs 20 for the agricultural labourers. In Gujrat, Khedyut Samaj has also been playing an important role as a pressure group to highlight the peasantry problems. In Tamil Nadu, R.V. Sangam is led by C.N. Naidu. Thus, though there is no all India orgnaisation of farmers, at the regional level, we do have their strong pressure groups. But all these groups essentially represent the rich farmers and have been able to pressurise the government successfully. They have been vocal in demanding more remunerative prices especially for cash crops like sugarcane, groundnut and tobacco leaf, lowering of electricity and canal water charges, more subsidies and cancellation of loan repayments. In Haryana, the peasants in 1997 organised themselves into Kisan Sangharsh Samiti. They even demanded free electricity for their tube wells and for the purpose they blocked the railway track and even called for bandh. In Mahendragarh, the angry mob led by the BKU activists burnt the railway station, three banks, two petrol pumps, the municipal office and two state Roadways buses besides a police Gypsy and threw a jeep belonging to the Naib Tehsildar's office into a tank in the small town of Kalayat in Kaithal district. The Hindu quoted a senior officer "The banks were the main targets as an attempt was made to burn all records pertaining to loans taken by the farmers." This also shows that rural India is fast dividing into two groups, one consisting of rich farmers who have benefited from governmental policies and are becoming increasingly organised, while the majority of small farmers and agricultural labourers largely remain unorganised and their discontent is expressed in sporadic violence led by communists.

3. *Students Organisations*

During the freedom struggle, the students played a remarkable role but they remained under the influence of party politics. This legacy has continued even today. We have the students organisations closely connected with the political parties. All India Students Federation is affiliated to CPI while National Students Union of India (NSUI) is connected with Congress, the Akhil Bhartya Vidyarthi Parishad (ABVP) is functioning as a wing of BJP. There are other minor students organisations, like the Progressive Democratic Student's Union, Radical Students Union, Lohia Vichar Manch which are affiliated to different parties. The Students took active part in JP agitation in 70's in Gujarat and Bihar. In Assam, the All Assam Students Union (AASU) led the agitation on the question of foreign nationals. In the Bodoland area of Assam, the All Bodo Student's Union (ABSU) led the agitation for Bodoland as a result of which Bodoland Autonomous Council (BAC) was formed under Bodo Accord in 1993. Now the ABSU and its ally Bodoland State Demand Committee (BSDC) is demanding a separate State of Bodoland. There is another faction, People's Democratic Front (PDF) which is closer to Asom Gana Parishad (AGP) and wants only more powers to the Bodoland Autonomous Council. The political affiliation of Student's groups has been an unhealthy trend and has resulted in student's indiscipline. The students groups have successfully resisted increase in fees. They have also demanded cheap transport. In some cases, they have involved themselves in political movements like Telengana and Naxalite movements. They have also opposed the reservation policy of the government without much success. The basic problem with the student's organisation has been lack of direction and perspective and in their absence, the political parties have been able to use them as convenient tools for their political interests. This has resulted in the formulations of unjustified demands like right to use unfair means (in U.P.) and occasionally demanding the scrapping of a question paper which was "hard."

4. *Labour or Trade Unions*

Like the Students Union, the labour or trade union's pressure group politics presents the same scenario. They have been affiliated to political parties. Before Independence, we had leading labour groups—The All India Trade Union Congress (AITUC) and the Indian Federation of Labour (IFL). After independence Indian National Trade Union Congress (INTUC) was established which was affiliated to Congress. The socialists and communists formed the Hind Mazdoor Sangh (HMS). Between the two, the INTUC emerged as a formidable organisation because of its affiliation to Congress Party. The AITUC (All India Trade Union Congress) is affiliated to CPI. The CPM in 1970, founded its own trade union wing as Centre for Indian Trade Unions (CITU). Among these, the CITU has been a militant group. Besides, we also have All India Railwaymen's Federation, the National Federation of Post and Telegraph Employees, the All India Defence Employees Federation, the Confederation of Central Government Employees etc. The government employees become very vocal when the Pay Commissions are appointed. In 1997, after the Fifth Pay Commission report was announced, they formed a Joint Consultative Machinery (JCM) consisting of various employee's unions and compelled the government to accept most of their demands which included 40 per cent wage hike (against the 20 per cent as recommended by the Ninth Pay Commission) for 'C' and 'D' categories of employees, inclusion of 'B' Category non-gazetted employees for payment of bonus, removal of wage eligibility, ceiling on bonus and payment of full arrears in cash. However, the trade union movement in India is not united. Divided on political lines, in every trade organisation, we have multiplicity of Unions. This scenario does not permit them to wage a united struggle. Invariable their presidents have been the politicians who are more interested in the pursuit of their vested interests. Besides, they also have the problem of in adequate finances. The members seldom pay their dues and the Union's activities have been limited to strikes, demonstrations and election work. Therefore, they have not been able to articulate the worker's interests properly. The trade unions have been demanding better conditions of work and more salaries.

5. *Business Groups*

In India, the business groups have been most powerful. Most of the business houses are owned by traditional trading communities like Birlas, Jains, Tatas, Marwaris, Parsis, Vaisyas and Modis. They existed in the colonial era and most of them funded the national movement. After independence, the private sector was increasingly monopolised by a few families like Dalmias, Birlas, Tatas, Goenkas etc. Because of their money power, they have been able to influence governmental policies and decisions. During elections, they provide huge donations to the political parties. Further, they have access to bureaucracy and ministers. As a result, their assets have been growing phenomenally. Many of them have annual growth of 40 per cent. In 1982, the Reliance Textiles achieved a staggering 89.32 per cent growth within a year. In India, the business houses control the newspapers and news agencies. At the apex of business pressure groups is "Federation of Indian Chambers of Commerce and Industries." Then we have Associated Chambers of Commerce, All India Associations of Industries, Bombay; All India Automobile and Ancilliary Industries Association, Bombay;

All India Rubber Industries Association, Bombay; Association of Man-made Fibre Industry, Bombay; Bihar Industries Association, Patna; Faridabad Industries Association, Faridabad; Federation of Gujarat Mills and Industries, Bombay; Federation of Indian Mineral Industries, New Delhi; Madhya Pradesh Organisation of Industries, Bhopal etc. Thus we have a multiplicity of business groups in India. But these business groups are coordinated by four major national federations. The All India Manufacturers Organisation (AIMO) which represents medium sized industries; The Associated Chamber of Commerce and Industry of India (ASSOCHAM) which represents foreign British Capital; the Federation of Indian Chambers of Commerce and Industry (FICCI) which is the largest and most influencial group representing major industrial and trading interests and; the Federation of All India Foodgrain Dealers Association (FAIDA) which represents the grain dealers.

6. *Professional Groups*

The professionals like doctors, engineers, teachers, lawyers have also organised their groups to preserve and promote their interests. A few examples are All India Medical Council, All India Bar Association, various Engineer groups, Delhi University Teachers Association (DUTA) and various civil service associations etc.

7. *Women's Groups*

There are three major women's organisations in India. All India Women's Conference (AIWC), National Federation of Indian Women (NFIW) and the All India Democratic Women's Association (AIDWA). Among the three, the AIWC is the oldest which was formed in 1927. With the help of other women's organisations it was able to get important legislations like Special Marriage Act, the Hindu Marriage Act, Hindu Divorce Act, Interstate Succession Act and Dowry Act. These women's organisations do not have direct affiliation with the political parties. But, still the AIWC has close links with the Congress Party, the NFIW with the CPI and AIDWA with the CPM. All these groups have been fighting for the women's cause. In Shah Bano case they were able to muster public opinion to their side but as the Government submitted to the conservative Muslim demands, they could do little. However, the number of women's groups has been growing. Some of them like Self Employed Women's Association (SEWA) have been very vocal in voicing gender bias and the resultant expectation and opinion of women. They have also formed women's centres in different cities to provide women free legal aid, health care and counselling. As a result of women's pressure groups, 33 per cent reservation in Panchayati Raj Institutions (PRIs) have been introduced and a bill for 33 per cent reservation in Parliament and legislative Assemblies is pending before the Parliament.

The above-mentioned list of pressure groups is not all-comprehensive. In a vast country like India, their numbers cannot be ascertained. Besides these, we have cultural organisations, working both at the national as well as international level, Non-Governmental Organisations (NGOs) which are organised for literacy, environment protection, human rights protection and other social welfare activities.

Features of Pressure Groups in India

The main features of pressure groups in India are as follows:

(i) Most of the pressure groups in India are dominated and controlled by the political parties who use them for their political ends. As such, they become pawn in the dynamics of party system and they are not able to develop their separate identity and personality. The group's political representation takes place through the parties to which they are affiliated, associated or have close links. However the major business groups constitute exceptions as they have developed as autonomous institutions, separate from party connections.

(ii) The fact that party's interest dominate over the group's interest has been understood by many organisations. Therefore, some of them are increasingly disassociating from party politics and have become autonomous. The SEWA (Self Employed Women's Association) and WWF (Working Women's Forum), Bharitya Kisan Union of Mahendra Singh Tikait in UP, Shetkari Sangthana in Maharashtra, Kamagar Aghadi in Bombay and various environmental groups have remained independent of political parties and, therefore, became grassroot movements.

(iii) As a result of political interference in group activities, there is a thin line of demarcation between the pressure groups and political parties. Parties use them for mass mobilisation and pressure groups, on their own, can achieve almost nothing. In some cases, we have political parties acting more as pressure groups. For example, the Akali Dal which fought for and got Punjabi Suba, aims at promotion of Sikh's interests or Jharkhand Mukti Morcha (JMM) which demanded a separate Jharkhand State in Bihar. Every major political party in India has its own youth, student, women and even trade union wing.

(iv) In India, the business groups have largely been organised on the basis of traditional family and kinship structures. As Rajni Kothari points out that unlike most other new nations where the bulk of entrepreneural activities have been performed by the foreigners, "in India, the role of traditional trading and mercantile families in modern business and industry has been prominent." As a result, the family interests dominate the organisation of business which led the noted British-NRI industrialist, Swaraj Paul, to remark that Indian industry suffers from feudalism. Rajni Kothari says that this has prevented its articulation on typically western lines. Similarly, in trade union organisations also, the family, community and caste loyalties have played an important role in their actual operation. They have not been able to develop as a class or a district group as in western countries. Similarly, the political parties also have not taken on a class character in India. This is because "unlike in the west, adult franchise and political mobilisation has taken place simultaneously with other developments, which has meant that all kinds of groups and interests have found entry into the political processes, thus giving to the interest articulation of Indian politics, a diffuse and multi-group character."

(v) The groups and their activities in India are organised, not on social and economic interests, but on the basis of traditional beliefs and structures.

(vi) Finally, Rajni Kothari says, ... it is governmentalization of social and economic structures that provides the dominant framework of articulation in India. Therefore social and economic interests are voiced by political parties and government and not through different groups or organisations. Secondly, trade and business association and even trade unions are not considered legitimate bases for political bargaining. Therefore, they have to operate in and through party and bureaucratic structures. Thirdly, the government itself is bringing about change and modernisation and therefore there is no place for interest groups. They can only influence it through political parties and factions. "This does not mean that there is no place for intermediate structures; on the contrary there is a plethora of such structures. But there have to be more directly political rather than associational in the western sense, (This is why whereas in the West, political demands are often involved in economic strikes and the like, in India, economic demands are ventilated and organised in the form of a political strike or demonstration."

(vii) All this, Rajni Kothari says, involves serious costs. The organised interest groups are recognised only when they are politically organised. This "leads to emphasis on loudness of protest and violent outbursts. For those, who find it difficult to find a political party or faction to champion their cause, the only recourse left is to indulge in street demonstrations and the like." Therefore we find mass movements, rallies, strikes, bandhs, rasta-roko agitations and even violence, are used as instruments by many pressure groups.

Role of Pressure Groups

The basic objective of a pressure group is to exert pressure on the government to accomplish the desired ends. According to Robert Hardgrave, these are the roles of interest groups in India:

1. Interest groups in India are a form of linkage and a means of communication between the mass and the elite. They provide channels of access for expanding participation and their institutionalization is a critical element in the development of a responsive political system, for they are barometers of the political climate by which decision-makers can make and assess policy.
2. The interest groups articulate the interests of its members. In the process, the demands are considered and amendments made to accomodate different views of its members. While the interest group makes demands on society for the benefit of its members, it also serves to restrain them. Interest groups not only act as agents of interest articulation, but they also increase the political consciousness and participation of their membership—democratic achievements, although they may strain the responsive capacity of the system.
3. In India, interst groups have been reservoirs of political leadership. This has been particularly true of trade unions.
4. Further, interest groups are a vehicle for social integration. They bring individuals from ascriptive relationships into new and modern associations for the expression of common interests; they may bridge the gap not only between the mass and the elite but between traditional divisions within the society as a whole. Interest groups may thus serve as agents of both vertical and horizontal integration. Even interest groups that have reinforced existing cleavages in Indian society, such as caste associations, have frequently been catalysts for change, opening the community to increasingly differentiate interests and cross cuttings." The caste

associations in India have become conscious of their role in social change. For instance some of them are now conducting Parichaya Sammelans (introduction meetings) where all the eligible girls and boys meet and are selected for marriage and then mass marriages take place without dowry to do away with the evils of dowry.

Techniques of the Pressure Groups in India

The pressure groups in India follow the following technique to achieve their objectives:

(i) The pressure groups play a very important role during the election with a view to achieving their objectives. They provide funds to the political parties. They also support those candidates who are sympathetic to them and after getting elected, the legislator has to support their demand. Thus it becomes a two way system, in which both are benefitted. Big business houses may not be able to provide man power to the political party, but by providing them enough funds, they ensure that their interests are safeguarded.

(ii) The most important technique is lobbying. The representative of pressure groups contact the members of legislative bodies, ministers and important bureaucrats and influence them so as to get a favourable legislation.

(iii) Pressure groups influence the governmental decisions by providing it with accurate data and information.

(iv) Pressure groups try to influence the government by manipulating public opinion. They do so by speeches, books, pamphlets and the modern media of communication like Press, Radio and T.V.

(v) Sometimes, the Pressure Groups also seek refuge of the courts to undo unfavourable acts of legislature and executive. Of late, the courts in India have been very active and the pressure groups, especially the environment and human rights groups, have forced the executive to act through Public Interest Litigations (PILs).

(vi) They also use corrupt means by bribing the civil servants and politicians. This has become a regular phenomenon of Indian politics.

(vii) Those groups who cannot bribe or adopt any of the above techniques rely on demonstrations, strikes, bandhs and other such methods so that the administration is paralysed and the government is forced to listen to them and act accordingly. Various trade unions, peasant organisations and even professional organisations have adopted this technique which has become an accepted way of Indian political life. The government sometimes accepts and tolerates them, and sometimes suppresses them through the various Acts like Preventive Detention Act or Maintenance of Essential Commodities Act.

The methods and techniques adopted by the Pressure groups have been a matter of great concern and criticism. More particularly, the corruption issue has been dominating Indian Politics. While there is no doubt that corruption is to be curtailed but only pressure groups are not to be blamed for this. In fact, the existence of proper pressure groups is essential to the democratic functioning.

References

Ball Alan R., *Modern Politics And Government,* 1983, London, The Macmillan Press Ltd.

Fadia B.L., *Indian Government and Politics.*

Hardgrave Robert, *India: Government and Politics in a Developing Nation,* 1970, New York, Harcourt, Brace & World Inc.

Pandey V.P., *Issues in Indian Politics,* 1985, Delhi, Durga Publications.

Kothari Rajni, *Politics in India,* 1994, New Delhi, Orient Longman.

CHAPTER XIX

Elections and Participation

Elections are the life and blood of modern democracies. Through elections, the political communication between the government and the governed is channelised. Elections provide an opportunity, to the general masses to get political education. Issues are raised and their pros and cons are discussed and in the process, the electorate learns. Elections are primarily held to decide as to who would govern the country. For this the contestants issue their manifestoes and inform the public about their prospective programmes and agenda if they are elected. The manifesto also assesses the performance of the existing government, the party-in-power would highlight its achievements, while the opposition would display the negative aspects of the existing government. This also results in a government that is responsive and sensitive to the people's urges and aspirations. Election is the only medium available in modern democracies through which a peaceful change in the government is effected or, to use Michael Brecher's words, they are means for the "routinization of political change." The electoral politics leads to increasing political consciousness in which the rich and the poor, old and young, men and women—all use their political right to vote and participate equally in the political process. In fact, there can be no democracy without elections.

Elections in India

During the colonial period, India had a limited experience of election. The Indian Council Act of 1892 provided, for the first time, indirect elections of some non-official members to the council of the Viceroy and provincial Governors, which was further extended by the Government of India Act 1909 in which twenty seven, out of sixty members of the Imperial Legislative Council were to be elected by various indirect means. The constituencies from which they were to be elected were also very large. Separate communal electorates were also provided for the Muslims, which was later on extended to other communities by Government of India Acts of 1919, and 1935 despite the opposition from the Congress Party. In 1917, the British Government declared, that the policy of "His Majesty's Government is that of increasing association of Indians in every branch of the administration and the gradual development of self-governing institutions with a view to the progressive realisation of responsible government in India as an integral part of the British Empire". The Government of India Act 1919 did broaden the franchise considerably but still it was based on restricted franchise. However, women were also given right to vote. Another and the last landmark was the Government of India Act 1935 which extended the dyarchy introduced by Government of India Act 1919 to a significant amount of autonomy to the States. Further, India became a federal state. The federal legislature was constituted which was a bicameral legislature consisting of the Council of States and the House of Assembly. In six of eleven states, bicameral legislature was introduced and in the rest, only one house i.e. Legislative Assembly. The Legislative Assemblies had 1585 seats chosen by some 35 million people, 959 were general seats (including 151 reserved seats for representatives of Scheduled Castes and Scheduled Tribes), 482 were Muslim seats and the rest were reserved for other classes and communal and special groups, i.e. European, Sikhs, Indian Christians and Anglo-Indians and reserved seats for Marathas in certain general constituencies in Bombay.

The Congress had reluctantly accepted the principles of separate electorate. The Nehru Report of 1928 had accepted the joint electorate which, however, was not acceptable to the Muslims. The Congress opposed the Communal Award of 1932 which led to Poona Pact in which joint electorate for the Harijans was accepted. In 1937 S. Satyamurthi (the then Secretary of the Swaraj Party), frankly admitted the position of Congress, "We believe that separate electorates are wholly inconsistent with any concept of democracy or democratic government ... At the same time, the Congress realises that unless and until we can get an agreed settlement with the consent of all communities concerned, it is impossible, it is futile to try to fight the Communal Award." The Congress in 1937, declared that Communal Award was anti-national, anti-democratic and a barrier to Indian freedom and the development of Indian unity, however "a change in or suppression of the communal decision should only be brought about by the mutual agreement of the parties concerned."

The Constituent Assembly which itself was elected on the basis of restricted franchise took two landmark decisions regarding the franchise. Firstly, the principle of separate electorates was done away with. Patel was very clear that the separate electorate had led to the partition of the country and it had no place in free India. Second major decision was to have universal adult franchise. This was a revolutionary decision considering that only 14.6 per cent of population had the experience of right to vote in colonial India. Nehru in his *Discovery of India* wrote, "I am a convinced believer in adult franchise, for men and women; and though I realize the difficulties in the way, I am sure that the objections raised to its adoption in India have no great force and are based on fears of privileged classes and interests." However there were people in India and abroad who were sceptical of the success of universal adult franchise, given the mass illiteracy and other social problems. Fortunately, history proved to be with Nehru and other advocates of universal adult franchise with the successful completion of First General Elections in 1952.

First General Elections (1951-52)

The First General Elections took place in about four months from 25 October 1951 to 21 February 1952. This was because of shortage of election officials and some special problems of geography and climate. As a result, voting schedule was fixed for different places in different dates. There was no national issue or the only issue was support or opposition to Nehru and his Congress Party. For the purpose of superintendence, direction and control, an Election Commission was formed. The 'Provincial Parliament had passed Representation of the People Act 1950 and Representation of the People Act 1951. On 22 November Nehru spoke to the people of India and said, "It is right that each of you take an interest in this great democratic process which is taking place on a scale yet unknown to history. It is also important that you take interest as citizens of the Republic of India, the future of which will no doubt, be affected by these elections. Democracy is based on the active and intelligent interest of the people in their national affairs and in the elections that result in the formation of governments: In the same broadcast, Nehru also pointed out the magnitude of India's first electoral exercise. The country was divided into 3,293 constituencies; 4412 representatives were to be chosen; the number of voters was about 1,76,600,000; each polling booth was to have a presiding officer, five clerks and four policemen; some 56,000 presiding officers, 280,000 clerks and 2,24,000 policemen were to conduct the polls with an estimated cost of approximately one hundred million or ten crores of rupees Nehru also ensured that the elections were held free for which he laid down suitable guidelines:

(i) Every party and every candidate must be given a fair and equal chance. Belonging to the ruling party does not entitle a candidate to any special privileges.
(ii) Officers of the government must function impartially and with the strictest neutrality.
(iii) Ministers must not utilize their official position to further own election prospects in any way. So far as possible, official duties should be separated from electoral work.
(iv) National flag must never be used for party or election purposes in any way.

Nehru also demanded an ideal electoral behaviour from the contesting political parties. He said, "It is of the utmost importance that all of us, whatever the party to which we belong, should maintain a high level of propriety and decorous behaviour. Our propaganda by speech or in writing should not be personal but should deal with policies and programmes. It should on no account be allowed to degenerate into personal criticism and abuse. The standard we set up now will act as a precedent and govern future elections"

The Congress Party got 364 seats out of 479 seats it contested thus capturing more than 70 per cent seats with 44.99 per cent of total votes. The Communist Party of India was the next largest party with 16 seats and 3.30 per cent of total votes. The Socialist Party, Kisan Mazdoor Praja Party (KMPP), and Bhartya Jan Sangh got 12, 9, 3 seats with 10.60 per cent, 5.80 per cent and 3.10 per cent of total votes respectively. The average number of candidates per Lok Sabha seats was 3.8. In states, the Congress won a clear majority in all the twenty two Part A, B and C States except Orissa, PEPSU, Travancore-Cochin and Madras. Later on in PEPSU, Tranvancore-Cochin and a new state of Andhra Pradesh, again elections were held. In PEPSU, Congress won, in Andhra Pradesh Congress and its allies won while in Travancore-Cochin Congress won only 45 seats and it supported the government led by PSP. Thus, the First General Elections ushered in the era of single party dominance in the Indian political system.

The Second General Elections (1957)

The second general elections were held during a period of three months, from 24 February to 14 March 1957. The experience of the first general elections was there, though the electorate had increased by nearly 20,000,000. There were apprehensions, voiced in the newspapers, that the elections would be postponed. But the Election Commission and Nehru were particular about elections being held in India. Nehru said "The elections will be held whatever happens. We are a mature people and can carry on with our constitution and our democratic working and at the same time tackle serious problems. We are not going to run away from the elections." Like the first general elections, there was no significant issue before the public. However, the people of India participated with more enthusiasm than the first general elections. But only 47.54 per cent of the 193 million voters, which was a lower turnout than the first general elections, exercised their right to franchise. Nehru himself was less active in campaigning as he was confident of Congress re-gaining the power. The Congress got 371 out of 489 seats in the Lok Sabha with a little lower percentage of total votes (44.8 per cent) as compared to the first Lok Sabha elections (44.90 per cent). The CPI improved its tally from 16 seats with 3.30 per cent of total votes to 27 seats with 8.9 per cent of total votes. The PSP and BJS got 19 and 4 seats respectively while the other parties and independents bagged 31 and 42 seats respectively. In state legislative Assemblies Congress had reverses but it retained a clear majority in the Assemblies except Kerala and Orissa. The most significant results which attracted world-wide attention was that of Kerala Assembly where CPI alongwith five independents formed the first ever communist government in the world which came to power through parliamentary means. However this government was dismissed in 1959, by the misuse of *Article 356* of the Constitution. The results of second general elections also showed that the Congress' strong position was gradually declining. However it is also true that Indian democracy became stronger. The Election Commission in its report commented, "If the first general elections served to teach the vast number of uneducated voters what the vote means, the second general elections familiarized them with the exercise thereof with discrimination and understanding."

The Third General Elections (1962)

The Third general elections were held amidst deteriorating relations with China and the consequent border clashes on Indo-China borders. However, the elections were held in a peaceful atmosphere between February 16 and February 25, 1962, in a minimum duration of 10 days. During the first two general elections, there were some two-member constituencies which were abolished and they were divided into single member constituencies. In 1957, the total number of single-member constituencies for Lok Sabha was 296 out of which 16 were reserved for Scheduled Tribes. The total number of reserved seats for Scheduled Castes and Scheduled Tribes from two-member constituencies was 76 and 15 respectively. As a result of all the constituencies becoming a single member constituency in 1962, there were 387 general seats and 76 and 31 were reserved for Scheduled Castes and Scheduled Tribes respectively. In State Assemblies in 1957, there were 1827 single member constituencies with reservations for three Scheduled Castes and 104 Scheduled Tribes and 467 two-member constituencies with reservations for 467 Scheduled Castes and 117 Scheduled Tribes. The total number of seats was 3102. In 1962, all this changed with 2428 general constituencies, reservations for 471 Scheduled Castes and 222 Scheduled Tribes with the total number of seats as 3121. Many significant changes in the voting system were also introduced by the Election Commission including the system of identity cards to voters in Calcutta South-west Constituency which however failed and was later given up. The process of slow and gradual decline of Congress could be seen as its membership in Lok Sabha fell to 361 with 44.72 per cent of votes as compared to 1952 and 1957 which was 479 with 44.90 per cent and 371 with 44.8 per cent respectively. The CPI slightly improved its position to 29 seats with 9.94 per cent of total votes. There was a downfall in PSP's position which got 12 seats with 6.44 per cent of total votes. However the rightist elements in Indian politics improved significantly. The newly formed Swatantra Party got 18 seats with 8.19 per cent of total votes and Bhartiya Jan Sangh improved its position from 4 seats with 5.9 per cent votes in 1957 to 14 seats with 6.44 per cent of votes in 1962. The Congress won a clear majority in all the states except Madhya Pradesh.

The Fourth General Elections (1967)

The fourth general elections were held without Nehru who died in 1964. By 1967, the Congress had suffered very badly in terms of its popularity due to Indian reverses in Indo-China war and mounting economic problem especially the food shortages due to bad monsoon. The Indo-Pak conflict of 1965 had not resulted in decisive victory for India. Besides, the law and order situation had become very critical leading to apprehensions that the polls would be postponed. Certain foreign observers also predicted that it would be the last poll in India. Although this prophecy turned out to be false, the one-party dominance of Congress Party was broken. In Lok Sabha, it suffered severe losses and though in terms of total percentage of votes the reverses were not very significant (from 44.72 per cent in 1962 to 40.8 per cent in 1967), in terms of votes, the party could capture only 283 seats as against 361 seats. The CPI also suffered from 29 seats in 1962 to 23 seats in 1967. The newly emerged CPM got 19 seats with 4.4 per cent of total votes in 1962. While the PSP/KMPP and BSSP captured 13 and 23 seats, the rightist parties improved their position considerably. The Swatantra party and Bhartiya Jan Sangh bagged 44 and 35 seats respectively. In centre, the Congress was able to form the ministry as it had majority support (283 out of 520 seats) but in eight states it lost power. Its reverses were significant in Bihar, Kerala, Madras, Punjab and West Bengal. However the electorate had not given a clear verdict in favour of any single political party as it was essentially an anti-congress wave. Hence political instability in many states followed, leading to midterm election in four states of Bihar, Punjab, UP and West Bengal. The results further confirmed the erosion in Congress support base and it was virtually routed. As a result of Congress split in 1969, the party was reduced to a minority government at the centre. It could only function with the CPI and DMK support in the Lok Sabha.

Fifth General Elections (1971)

In 1971 fifth general elections were held, about a year before the scheduled date. Mrs. Indira Gandhi demanded a fresh mandate to implement her secular and socialist policies. The background of this was the Congress split in 1969 and the Supreme Court decisions nullifying the nationalization of 14 Banks and the abolition of privy purses of formers rulers of Indian states. The Congress (O), Swatantra party, Jan Sangh and the SSP formed a "Grand Alliance," while the Congress of Indira Gandhi declared "Garibi Hatao" (abolish poverty) as its objective. There was a lot of violence in the elections. However Mrs. Indira Gandhi secured a sweeping victory with 352 seats and 43.7 per cent of total votes. The CPM emerged next with 25 seats and 5.1 per cent votes. The Congress (O), CPI, PSP/KMPP and SSP captured 16, 23, 2 and 3 seats respectively while the Swatantra party and Bhartiya Jan Sangh 8 and 22 seats respectively. The Congress dominance was coming back which was later confirmed in State Assembly elections of 1972. Because of significant successes in Indo-Pak war of 1971 in which India was not only able to achieve a decisive victory, it could also dismember Pakistan and a new country Bangla Desh was created in

East Pakistan. Congress could win 70 per cent of seats in all the major states. In 1974, a mini general election was held in Gujarat, UP, Orissa, Nagaland and the Union Territory of Pondichery in which the overall mandate was in favour of Congress, yet the fact became clear that the Congress position was again in decay.

Sixth General Elections (1977)

The sixth general elections were held amidst the strong protests against the excesses committed during the internal emergency of 1975-77. There was a strong anti-Congress wave and the emergency had given a opportunity to the opposition to join hands together. Thus the Congress (O), Jan Sangh, Bhartiya Lok Dal and the Socialist Party and Jagjivan Ram's Congress For Democracy (CFD) fought elections together against Indira Gandhi's Congress. The Congress could capture 154 seats with 34.5 per cent of total votes, a severe reverse in which many important leaders of the party including Mrs. Indira Gandhi herself lost their seats. The five party alliance which later merged into one Janata Party, got 295 seats with 41.3 per cent of total votes. The CPI, CPM and other parties got 7, 22 and 52 seats respectively. The 1977 general elections proved that Indian electorate had become mature and would not tolerate weakening of democratic structures. The election to the Lok Sabha were followed by the State Assembly elections in Bihar, Haryana, Himachal Pradesh, MP, Orissa, Punjab, Rajasthan, West Bengal, UP and the Union Territories of Delhi and Pondicherry and Janata Party and its alliance parties came into power, in most of the these states except for Punjab, where (Janata-Akali Dal alliance formed the government) and West Bengal.

Seventh General Elections (1980)

However, the various constituents of Janata Party never forgot their old affiliations and hence the party could never become cohesive. Therefore, the Janata government fell and the first non Congress government experiment at the central level also failed. In 1980, elections were held for Lok Sabha and the people tired of internal bickerings in Janata Party gave a fresh mandate to Mrs. Indira Gandhi and her Congress. The Congress captured 353 seats with 42.7 per cent of total votes. It seemed that the Congress dominance over the political system was coming back which, however, was not true because subsequently in elections in many states, non-congress governments were formed and the Congress monopoly over political power could never come back.

Eighth Lok Sabha Elections (1985)

The eighth general elections were held in 1984 after Mrs. Indira Gandhi was assassinated, which was followed by anti-Sikh riots in north India. The Congress under Rajiv Gandhi appealed to vote for the party as it alone stood between unity and disintegration, between stability and chaos and between self-reliance and economic dependence. However, it was the sympathy wave due to the brutal killing of Mrs. Indira Gandhi on which the Congress capitalized and its performance was startling, almost unparalleled as it surpassed its own records during the Nehru days. The Congress (I) got 415 seats with 48.1 per cent of total votes. The BJP, CPI, Lok Dal were almost relegated to the background with 2, 6, 3 seats respectively. The Telugu Desam Party (TDP) was the second major party after Congress with 30 seats while CPM had to satisfy itself with 22 seats. In 1985, election to eleven State Assemblies of Andhra Pradesh, Bihar, Gujarat, Himachal Pradesh, Karnataka, Maharashtra, MP, Orissa, Rajasthan, Sikkim, UP and the Union Territory of Pondicherry took place in which Congress (I) returned to power in all States except Andhra Pradesh, Karnataka and Sikkim. However the party's performance was not as remarkable as in Lok Sabha elections.

Ninth Lok Sabha Elections (1989)

The ninth Lok Sabha elections witnessed again the anti-Congress wave. Congress (I) fought the elections in alliance with National Conference, AIDMK and Muslim League, while the Janata Dal, Telugu Desam Party, DMK and Asom Gana Parishad (AGP) formed a National Front and it had electoral adjustments with the BJP and CPM. Thus Congress and anti-Congress forces were polarised and in the process. Congress suffered very badly. Although, it was the largest party with 197 seats, the debacle was evident as it held 415 seats in the eighth Lok Sabha. Janata Dal came next with 143 seats while BJP and CPM bagged 86 and 33 seats respectively. Telugu Desam showed a very poor performance as it bagged only 2 seats as against 30 seats in 1984. The National Front with the outside support from BJP and Communists formed the government under V.P. Singh which remained in power for a shortwhile.

Tenth General Elections (1991)

The tenth general elections were held for Lok Sabha and six states of Assam, Haryana, Kerala, Tamil Nadu, UP and West Bengal and Union

Territory of Pondicherry. The tenth general elections were held in two rounds; on 20 May and on 12 and 15 June. The second round was initially scheduled for 23 and 25 May but the assassination of Rajiv Gandhi by a human bomb on 21 May, led to the postponement of polls of the second round which improved the prospects of Congress. There were three issues of Mandir, Mandal and stability in the elections. This was probably the most bloody election ever held in India. Rajiv Gandhi was assassinated. Later, five Lok Sabha candidates and 21 assembly candidates were killed out of which the majority were in Punjab. The militants killed two Lok Sabha candidates and 20 assembly candidates. The militants in Punjab declared the boycott of the polls and atleast 80 persons were killed as a result of their attacks on trains in Ludhiana where the polling ultimately was suspended. In other states also, the atmosphere was far from peaceful. In Meerut (UP), 30 people were killed, one of them was burnt alive. In other places of UP, communal riots broke out and in 21 assembly constituencies, the elections were countermanded. Bihar, Andhra Pradesh, Tamil Nadu West Bengal, Gujarat and Tripura also witnessed a great deal of violence. There were frequent complaints of rigging and booth capturing. In Bihar alone, repolling was ordered in roughly 100 booths and as many as 40 per cent of the polling booths were declared sensitive as against 25 per cent in 1989.

In the Lok Sabha poll of 1991, out of the total electorate of 501, 019, 356 there was a total turnout of 51.13 per cent and out of 511 seats for which elections were held, in 13 seats polling was countermanded. The Congress emerged as the single largest party in the Lok Sabha with 231 seats and 36.50 per cent of total votes. The BJP was the next with 119 seats (20.80 per cent) followed by Janata Dal and CPM with 59 and 35 seats respectively while the other parties got 62 seats. So far the States Assembly elections are concerned Congress (I) came into power in Assam, Haryana and the Union Territory of Pondicherry and Congress dominated United Democratic Front wrested power in Kerala while the UP become the citadel of BJP, the CPM led Left Front retained its hold on West Bengal. In Tamil Nadu, DMK was completely routed and AIDMK became the ruling party. At the national level the Congress Party formed its government under the leadership of Pamulparti Venkata Narasimha Rao.

Eleventh Lok Sabha Elections (1996)

The eleventh general elections were held in 1996, for Lok Sabha and State Assemblies of Assam, Haryana, Kerala, Tamil Nadu, West Bengal,

Mizoram and Union Territory of Pondicherry. Bye-elections were also held simultaneously for State Assembly seats in Andhra Pradesh, Karnataka, Maharashtra, Orissa, Bihar, Nagaland and Meghalaya. There were 591,502,425 electorate for Lok Sabha election with 738,773 polling stations. For the 543 seats, there were a record number of candidates—a staggering 14,274. Delhi had the largest number of candidate per seat with a total of 523 candidates contesting seven seats. In East Delhi Constituency, there were as many as 122 candidates. The polling process was completed in four phases from April 27, 1996 to May 7, 1996 except for the four constituencies of Jammu and Kashmir where polling was held on May 25, and May 30, 1996. The National Conference of Jammu and Kashmir did not contest the Lok Sabha elections.

The Congress had weakened because of scams and scandals. However it declared that it is the only party which can give stability to the country. The BJP was equally optimistic and the party declared, "we will be the single largest party in Parliament and we will form the government. The alternative to Congress and BJP was the Left Front-National Front with CPM, Janata Dal, Samajwadi Party, Tamil Maanila Congress and other regional parties. As a result of elections, the BJP emerged as the single largest party with 161 seats (20.29 per cent of total votes) followed by Congress, 140 seats (28.80 per cent). The Janata Dal captured 46 seats while the CPM and CPI got 32 and 12 seats respectively. A significant aspect of the results was the emergence of regional/state parties in the national scene with as many as 127 seats (21.34 per cent). Atal Behari Vajpayee of BJP was made the Prime Minister for 13 days after which the United Front of 13 parties took over the reins of the Central Government under H.D. Deve Gowda with the outside support of Congress. So far as the States are concerned, in Haryana, Bansi Lal's Haryana Vikas Party BJP alliance got the majority and came into power; in West Bengal, the Left Front of Jyoti Basu retained power with 203 seats; in Assam, the AGP and its allies won a comfortable majority and the AGP President Prafful Kumar Mahanta became the Chief Minister; in Tamil Nadu, DMK won 172 out of 233 seats for which elections were held; in Kerala, the CPM led Left Democratic Front gained the absolute majority; in Pondicherry ,the poll verdict was not clear with DMK led alliance with TMC and CPI won 15 out of 30 seats, the Congress nine, AIADMK three, Janata Dal one, PMK one, and Independent one. The Eleventh General Elections were held amidst the activism of the Election Commission in which the Model Code of Conduct was implemented vigorously. It was also a hi-tech election in which computers, satellites and video-on-wheels were used.

Twelfth Lok Sabha Elections (1998)

The 1998 elections to Lok Sabha were held due to the indecisive mandate in 1996 elections which resulted in a hung Parliament. The Congress (I) had been supporting the United Front Government reluctantly and Jain Commission Report on Rajiv Gandhi Assassination which indicted the DMK Government for its soft attitude towards the Tamil Tigers who were responsible for the brutal killing of Rajiv Gandhi and other people, sealed the fate of United Front Government. The Congress (I) withdrew its support even as the United Front Constituent refused to drop DMK Ministers. The BJP tried to form an alternative government by inducing defections from Congress and other parties but failed. For the first time, more than one hundred fifty members belonging to different parties requested the President not to dissolve the Lok Sabha. However, the President dissolved the Lok Sabha.

There was a significant fall in the number of contesting candidates because the security deposit for general constituency was raised from Rs 500 to Rs 10,000 and for reserved constituency from Rs 250 to Rs 5,000. As a result, there were just 4693 candidates for 540 seats against 13,592 candidates in 1996.

The polling for most of the seats was completed in less than a month i.e. from February 16 to March 7, 1998 in four phases except for five constituencies where elections were held in March 7 (3 constituencies) and June 21 (2 constituencies). The first phase witnessed polling in 222 seats while the second phase was to witness polling in 184 seats. However polling in Coimbatore was postponed due to unprecedented explosions, killing more than 50 people. The third and fourth phase witnessed polling in two and 131 constituencies respectively.

There was a lot of violence in the election especially in Tamil Nadu, Bihar, Assam and UP, in which many people including the candidates lost their lives and many incidents of booth capturing and other large scale poll irregularities were reported especially in Bihar where Election Commission ordered repolling in as many as 2200 polling booths. In all repolling were held in 2920 polling booths spread over 10 states after the first round of poll in February 16, 1998. The polling in the entire Patna constituency was declared null and void. Due to violence, many people including the candidates were killed. There were calls for poll boycott too. In Nagaland, all the non-congres parties boycotted the State Assembly election resulting in the unprecedented unanimous election of 43 congress candidates out of a total of 60 seats.

The activism of the Election Commission also continued and the elections were devoid of any festival mood. The election was itself a big exercise with 605,307,962 voters, 4693 candidates, 8,50,000 polling booths, nearly 2 lakh para-military forces and 13.5 lakhs state police personnel to supervise and ensure a peaceful and free and fair poll. The estimated expenditure; Rs 3,000 crore—Rs 700 crores spent by the Election Commission, Rs 1,700 crores by Union and State Government and approximately Rs 1000 crores by the political parties

The election results again gave a hung Parliament. The BJP was the single largest party and alongwith its 17 allies, it formed the government.

The Election Commission made it mandatory for all the candidates to declare their criminal antecedents in a sworn affidavit in order to weed out the criminals from entering into polls.

Thirteenth Lok Sabha Election

The BJP led coalition government was always runnings on a thin thread of survival. Ultimately it fell due to the withdrawal of support by AIADMK. The Vajpayee government failed to get the vote of confidence. Efforts were made to form alternative government but all in vain. Ultimately, the President on the advice of the cabinet, dissolved the Lok Sabha on April 26, 1999, thus giving the twelfth Lok Sabha a distinction of having the shortest tenure of just 412 days. By this time it had also become clear that elections would again give a hung parliament, as no party on its own was capable enough to woo the voters. On May 15, 1999, the formation of National Democratic Alliance led by Atal Bihari Vajpayee was announced. Telugu Desam Party (TDP) and Trinmool Congress did not formally join the NDA but remained friendly and cooperated with each other. The Congress also entered into electoral alliance with AIADMK, RJD, Rashtriya Lok Dal, Kerala Congress and Muslim League.

Simultaneously, elections to the five Legislative Assemblies of Maharashtra, Andhra Pradesh, Karnataka, Sikkim and Arunachal Pradesh were held. The Election Commission declared five stage elections (September 5, 11, 18 and 25, and Octobers, 1999). These elections were held at the back drop of Kargil war in Kashmir. Thirteenth Lok Sabha elections were issueless as no major issue was contested by the political parties. Among the issues, was the issue of foreign origin of Sonia Gandhi which had also resulted in the division of Congress, and, a section led by Sharad Pawar, P.A. Sangma and Tariq Anwar left it to form the Nationalist Congress Party. Still, the election seemed to be a contest between two personalities—Atal Behari Vajpayee and Sonia Gandhi. The NDA got a comfortable majority and it formed the government under the Prime Ministership of Atal Behari Vajpayee. In Arunachal and Karnataka, the Congress won and formed the government. In Maharashtra it led a coalition government and in Sikkim a regional party Sikkim Democratic Party got 24 seats and formed the government.

It is to be noted that till the Fourth General Elections, the elections to the Lok Sabha and State Assemblies used to be held simultaneously. However, as a result of mid term poll in 1971, this link was broken and now they are held separately.

A study of India's electoral experience from 1952-1998 clearly reveals that the universal adult franchise has been successful in the country and over the period, the Indian electorate has shown its maturity. However, gradually, a clearcut mandate in favour of one party is becoming a thing of the past and coalition politics is becoming a permanent phenomenon at the Centre.

Election Commission of India

In India, the elections are conducted by an independent constitutional organ called the Election Commission. *Article 324* of the Indian Constitution says:

(i) The suprintendence, direction and control of the preparation of the electoral rolls for, and the conduct of, all elections to the Parliament and to the Legislature of every state and of elections to the office of President and Vice-President held under this Constitution shall be vested in a commission (referred to in this Constitution as the Election Commission.)

(ii) The Election Commission shall consist of the Chief Election Commissioner and such number of other Election Commissioners, if any, as the President may, from time to time fix and the appointment of the Chief Election Commissioner and other Election Commissioners shall, subject to the provisions of any law made in that behalf by Parliament, be made by the President.

(iii) When any other Election Commissioner is appointed, the Chief Election Commissioner shall act as the chairman of the Election Commission.

(iv) Before each general elections to the House of the People and to the Legislative Assembly of each state, and before the first general election and thereafter before each biennial election to the Legislative

Council of each State having such council, the President may also appoint after consultation with the Election Commission such Regional Commissioners as he may consider necessary to assist the Election Commission in the performance of the functions conferred on the Commission by clause (1).

(v) Subject to the provisions of any law made by Parliament, the conditions of service and tenure of office of the Election Commissioners and the Regional Commissioners shall be such as the President may by rule determine.

Provided that the Chief Election Commission shall not be removed from his office except in like manner and on like grounds as a Judge of the Supreme Court and the conditions of service of the Chief Election Commissioner shall not be changed to his disadvantage after his appointment. Provided further that any other Election Commissioner or a Regional Commissioner shall not be removed from office except on the recommendation of the Chief Election Commissioner.

(vi) The President or the Governor of a State shall, when so requested by the Election Commission, make available to the Election Commission or to a Regional Commissioner such staff as may be necessary for the discharge of the functions conferred on the Election Commission by clause (1).

The Chief Election Commissioner and other Commissioners are appointed by the President of India for six years from the date on which he/they assumes office and they retire at the age of 65 if they attain this age earlier to the stipulated six years term.

For a long time the Election Commission had been a one-member Commission. In 1989, the President appointed two more members other than the Chief Election Commissioner but after two and a half months he withdrew his notification and the two newly appointed Election Commissioners were removed. On 1st October 1993, the President again appointed two more Election Commissioners M.S. Gill and D.V.G. Krishnamurthy, thus making the Election Commission a three member body which included T.N. Seshan, the Chief Election Commissioner. The President also issued an ordinance which among other things dealt with the transaction of business of Election Commission. It provided that:

(i) The Election Commission may, by unanimous decision, regulate the procedure for transaction of its business as also allocation of its business amongst the Chief Election Commissioner and other Election Commissioners.

(ii) Save as provided in sub-section (1), all business of the Election Commission shall, as far as possible, be transacted unanimously.

(iii) Subject to the Provisions of sub-section (2), if the Chief Election Commissioner and other Election Commissioners differ in opinion on any matter, such matter shall be decided according to the opinion of the majority. Subsequently the ordinance was converted into law by the Indian Parliament.

It was believed that the Government's decision to induct two Election Commissioners was taken because of the strongarm tactics of T.N. Seshan and it was also felt that the Chief Election Commissioner and other Election Commissioners (conditions of Service) Act 1991 favoured the Chief Election Commissioner as against the other Election Commissioners. While the Chief Election Commmissioner was to retire at 65 years, other Election Commissioner were to retire at the age of 62 years, if they happen to attain their respective age of retirements earlier than the normal six years of their duration. The law now has the uniform rule of 65 years for both the Chief Election Commissioner and other Election Commissioners. T.N. Seshan, the Chief Election Commissioners, had resisted the appointment of two Election Commissioners. He even went to the Supreme Court, but the Court declared that "the question whether it is necessary to appoint other Election Commissioners besides the CEC is for the Government to decide and that it is not a justiciable matter." The Chief Election Commissioner and other Election Commissioners are entitled to salary and other facilities, like rent-free accomodation, equivalent to that of a Judge of the Supreme Court.

At the national level, now, we have a Chief Election Commissioner who is assisted by two Election Commissioners, three Deputy Election Officers and Six Secretaries. The Secretariat is divided into eight branches, each headed by an under secretary or officers of equal status. Branches are further divided into thirty sections, consisting of a section officer and a number of Assistants, Upper Division Clerks, Lower Division Clerks and Group 'D' Staff. At the Statelevel, a senior officer of the State Government is appointed as the Chief Electoral Officer (CEO) by the Election Commission in consultation with the State Government. The CEO is subject to the superintendence, direction and control of the Election Commission. The CEO is assisted in the performance of his functions by the Election Department of the State, the strength of which varies from state to state. At the District level, there is a District Election Officer who is an officer of the State Government and is nominated by the Election Commission in consultation with the State Government. District Election Officers are normally the District Magistrates/Collectors or the Executive heads of the Municipal Corporations. The functions of District Election Officer are as follows:

(i) to make provisions of polling stations for Assembly, Parliamentary and council constituencies;
(ii) to appoint staff for election duties during elections.
(iii) to receive the accounts of election expenses of contesting candidates and to submit report on their returns to the Election Commission.
(iv) to provide for safe custody of ballot boxes and election records.

At the bottom, is the polling booth which has a Presiding officer at its head, who is also a government servant. The presiding and other polling officers are appointed by the District Election Officer. In every constituency, Returning officers are appointed by the Election Commission in consultation with the State Government. The Returning officer, who supervises the elections in the constituency, is assisted by one or more Assistant Returning Officers.

Powers and Functions of the Election Commission

The primary function of the Election Commission is to conduct free and fair elections in India. For this purpose, the Election Commission has the following functions:

Delimitation of Constituencies

The first general elections of 1952 were held on the basis of demarcation of constituencies done by the Election Commission. In the first elections, we had two types of constituencies single member and double member constituencies. By the Two member constituencies, (Abolition) Act of 1961, the two Member Constituencies were abolished and they were converted into single member constituencies, which was accompalished by the Election Commission. After the first general elections, the function of delimitation of constituencies was entrusted upon a Delimitation Commission consisting of two serving or retired judges of the Supreme Court and the Chief Election Commissioner who was its ex-officio member. The Election Commission provided the secretarial assistance. The allocation of seats to Lok Sabha in different states and the number of seats in Legislative Assemblies were last demarcated by the Delimitation Commission constituted under the Delimitation Act of 1972. At present there are 543 Lok Sabha constituencies with reservation of 79 and 41 seats for the Scheduled castes and Scheduled tribes respectively. The Forty Second Amendent Act of 1976 provided that the existing arrangements of demarcation of Lok Sabha and State Assemblies seats can be changed only after the publication of first census following the year 2000.

Preparation of Electoral Rolls

The Commission prepare the Electoral Rolls for Parliamentary as well as Assembly elections. Any person can be registered as a voter in a particular constituency provided he fulfills following conditions:

(i) He is a citizen of India
(ii) He is 18 years of age on the January 1, of the year in which the electoral roll is prepared or revised.
(iii) He is ordinarily resident of the Constituency.
(iv) He is not of unsound mind.
(v) He is not disqualified from voting under any law relating to corrupt practices and other offense in connection with election.
(vi) A person can be registered as voter in only one constituency.

Exceptions have been made in certain cases where the voter is not residing in his constituency, but he has the right to be registered in his constituency. Such voters and thier wives, if they reside with them are the following:

(i) The President of India
(ii) Governors of States and Lieutenant Governors of the Union Territories
(iii) Vice-President of India
(iv) Cabinet Ministers of the union and the States
(v) The Deputy Chairman and members of the Planning Commission
(vi) Ministers of State, Deputy Ministers and Parliamentary Secretaries of the Union and the States
(vii) The Speaker of the Union and the States
(viii) The Chairman of any State Legislative Council
(ix) The Deputy Speaker of the Lok Sabha or of State Legislative Assembly
(x) Members of the armed forces of the union or members of force to which the Army Act of 1950 applies
(xi) Members of an armed police force of a state deployed outside the state
(xii) Foreign service personnel and others employed under the Government of India serving outside India

The electoral roll of every constituency contains the name of all persons who have a right to vote in that constituency. The electoral roll is also revised from time to time, generally before a general election and a bye-election in the constituency. There are two methods of revising the electoral rolls—(i) Intensive revision and (ii) Summary revision. The intensive revision is carried out from house to house by the enumerators appointed by the Election Commission and all eligible voters are thus registered. In summary revision, new voters are registered and a supplement to the existing electoral rolls is published. An eligible person can have his name registered in the electoral roll by making an application to the Electoral Registration Officer of the Constituency. But no inclusion in the electoral role can be made after the last date for making nomination for that election.

Recognition of Political Parties

The Election Commission "recognises" the political parties. In India we have a variety of political groups and parties. In the 1996 general elections, the total number of political parties recognised by the Election Commission was 485. Out of 485, seven parties were national parties, 39 were State parties and 314 are recognised and 125 were registered parties. For this purpose, the Election Commission has developed certain yardsticks. As per the Election Commission's norms, there are three kinds of political parties in India, which are as follows:

(a) *Registered unrecognised political party:* A party must be registered with the Election Commission. But a registered political party is not automatically recognised. All Registered parties other than national Parties and state parties are registered Unrecognised Parties.

(b) *Recognised Political Party or State Party:* A party engaged in political activities continuously for five years and having won atleast four per cent of the seats in the last Lok Sabha election or 3.33 per cent of seats in the Assembly election from the state will be called as 'Recognised Political Party'. Otherwise it should have secured atleast six per cent of the total valid votes in the last Lok Sabha or Assembly Elections in the State. Or the total votes polled for the party (excluding votes polled by the party candidates in constituencies where it got less than 1/12th of valid votes) should be atleast four per cent of total valid votes. A party treated as recognised in less than four states enjoys the status of the State party in the states, it is so recognised.

(c) *National Party:* A National Party is one which is treated as a 'Recognised Political Party in atleast four or more states. The seven parties recognised in 1998 as National Parties were Bahujan Samaj Party, BJP, CPI, CPI(M), Indian National Congress and Samata Party. Of these, Samata Party has been deprived of national party status by Election Commission.

Allotment of Symbols to Political Parties

As India has a substantial number of illiterate voters, each candidate and political party is allotted a symbol, which is published alongwith the name of the candidate in the ballot paper in election so that the voter may be able to identify the candidate of his choice by looking at the symbol. The Election Commission recognises the symbol of the candidates and the political parties. There are two types of symbols. Firstly, there are symbols reserved for the recognised political parties at the national and state levels and their respective candidates use them in election. The Election Commission has reserved 'lotus' for BJP 'hand' for Congress (I) 'Chakra' for Janata Dal, 'Flaming torch' for Samata Party, 'ears of corn and sickle' for CPI, Hammer, sickle and star' for CPI(M) in all states and 'elephant' for BSP in all states except Assam, Sikkim and Pondicherry. Secondly, there are free symbols which have been determined by the Election Commission. The free symbols (in 1998, there were 126 free symbols) are given to the candidates of unrecognised parties and independents. The Election Commission also decides the rival claims to an allotted symbol in case of split in a political party. As a result of 1996 elections, the Bahujan Samaj Party (BSP) become qualified to be recognised as national party. The Election Commission agreed to recognise it as a national party provided the BSP gave up its claim to the elephant symbol. This led to a dispute between the BSP and the Election Commission because prior to 1996 elections the BSP was only a "State Party" and the elephant symbol was also granted to other parties i.e., Asom Gana Parishad in Assam, the Sikkim Sangram Parishad in Sikkim and the Pattali Makkal Katchi in Tamil Nadu. Ultimately the Election Commission allotted the "elephant" symbol to BSP in all states except Assam, Sikkim and Tamil Nadu. The Commission accepted the BSP proposal for time to persuade the other three regional parties to give up the "elephant" symbol.

Election Programme

On the recommendation of Election Commission, the President, in case of Lok Sabha elections and the Governor, in case of State Assembly elections, issues notification for the elections. The Election Commissioner then announces the electional programme in which the last date of making nominations, the date of scrutiny of nominations and the last date for the withdrawal of candidatures and the date/dates of the polls are specified. After the nomination papers are recieved by the Returning Officer of the constituency, a formal scrutiny of nomination papers is done by the Returning officer at the time and place decided by him. The scrutiny of nominations is done on the day immediately following the last date for nomination. The Returning Officer examines them and hears objections, if any. He may reject the candidature on any of the following grounds:

(a) The candidate is disqualified under any constitutional provision or Representation of the People Act, 1951.
(b) The nomination papers are incomplete or not submitted in the prescribed manner.
(c) The signature of the candidate or his proposer is not genuine.

Conduct the Election

The most important task of the Election Commission is to conduct the election in a free and peaceful manner. As per the law, atleast 21 days should elapse between the last date of withdrawal of candidature and the polling date, so that the candidates have enough time at their disposal for compaigning. The Election Commission also allots free time to national and state parties on radio and television to address the people. The order of broadcasts is determined by draw of lots. The broadcasts are made after the notification calling for election is issued and concluded 48 hours before the end of the first polling date. The Election Commission has also fixed up a code for such broadcasts which prohibits attack on religion or communities, incitement to violence, criticism of friendly countries, aspersion on the integrity of the President and judiciary, anything affecting the integrity of the nation and anything obscene or defamatory.

The Election Commission has also made a model code of conduct to be followed by all the political parties which is given below:

I. *General Conduct*

(1) No party or candidate shall indulge in any activity which may aggravate existing differences or create annual hatred or cause tension between different castes and communities, religious or linguistic.
(2) Criticism of other political parties, when made, shall be confined to their policies and programme, past record and work. Parties and Candidates shall refrain from criticism of all aspects of private life, not connected with the public activities of the leaders or workers of other parties. Criticism of other parties or their workers based on unverified allegations or distortion shall be avoided.

(3) There shall be no appeal to caste or communal feelings for securing votes. Mosques, Churches, Temples or other places of worship shall not be used as forum for election propaganda.

(4) All parties and candidates shall scrupulously avoid all activities which are "corrupt practices" and offences under the election law, such as bribing of voters, intimidation of voters, impersonation of voters, canvassing within 100 meters of polling stations, holding public meetings during the period of 48 hours ending with the hour fixed for the close of the poll, and the transport and conveyance of voters to and from polling station.

(5) The right of every individual for peaceful and undisturbed home-life shall be respected, however much the political parties or candidates may resent his political opinions or activities. Organising demonstrations or picketing before the houses of individuals by way of protesting against their opinions or activities shall not be resorted to under any circumstances.

(6) No political party or candidate shall permit its or his followers to make use of any individual's land, building, compound wall etc., without his permission for erecting flag-staffs, suspending banners, pasting notices, writing slogans etc.

(7) Political parties and candidates shall ensure that their supporters do not create obstructions in or break up meetings and processions organised by other parties. Workers or sympathisers of one political party shall not create disturbances at public meetings organised by another political party by putting questions orally or in writing or by distributing leaflets of their own party. Processions shall not be taken out by one party along places at which meetings are held by another party. Posters issued by one party shall not be removed by workers of another party.

II. *Meetings*

(1) The party or candidate shall inform the local police authorities of the venue and time any proposed meeting well in time so as to enable the police to make necessary arrangements for controlling traffic and maintaining peace and order.

(2) A Party or candidate shall ascertain in advance if there is any restrictive or prohibitory order in force in the place proposed for the meeting. If such orders exist, they shall be followed strictly. If any exemption is required from such orders, it shall be applied for and obtained well in time.

(3) If permission or license is to be obtained for the use of loudspeakers or any other facility in connection with any proposed meeting, the party or candidate shall apply to the authority concerned well in advance and obtain such permission or license. (4) Organizers of a meeting shall invariably seek the assistance of the police on duty for dealing with persons disturbing a meeting or otherwise attempting to create disorder. Organisers themselves shall not take action against such persons.

III. *Procession*

(1) A Party or candidate organizing a procession shall decide beforehand the time and place of the starting of the procession, the route to be followed and the time and place at which the procession will terminate. There shall ordinarily be no deviation from the programme.

(2) The organizers shall give advance intimation to the local police authorities of the programme so as to enable the latter to make necessary arrangements.

(3) The organisers shall ascertain if any restrictive orders are in force in the localities through which the procession has to pass, and shall comply with the restrictions unless exempted specially by the competent authority. Any traffic regulations or restrictions shall also be carefully adhered to.

(4) The organisers shall take steps in advance to arrange for passage of the procession so that there is no block or hindrance to traffic. If the procession is very long, it shall be organised in segments of suitable lengths, so that at convenient intervals, especially at points where the procession has to pass road junctions, the passage of held up traffic could be allowed by stages thus avoiding heavy traffic congestion.

(5) Processions shall be so regulated as to keep as much to the right of the road as possible and the direction and advice of the police on duty shall be strictly complied with.

(6) If two or more political parties or candidates propose to take processions over the same route or parts thereof at about the same time, the organisers shall establish contact well in advance and decide upon the measures to be taken to see that the processions do not clash or cause hindrance to traffic. The assistance of the local police shall be availed of for arriving at a satisfactory arrangement. For this purpose the parties shall contact the police at the earliest opportunity.

(7) The political parties or candidates shall exercise control to the maximum extent possible in the matter of processionists carrying articles which may be put to misuse by undesirable elements especially in moments of excitement.

(8) The carrying of effigies purporting to represent members of other political parties or their leaders, burning such effigies in public and such other forms demonstration shall not be countenanced by any political party or candidate.

IV. *Polling Day*

All Political parties and candidates shall:

(i) co-operate with the officers on election duty to ensure peaceful and orderly polling and complete freedom to the voters to exercise their franchise without being subjected to any annoyance or obstruction.

(ii) supply to their authorized workers suitable badges or identity cards;

(iii) agree that the identity slip supplied by them to voters shall be on plain (white) paper and shall not contain any symbol, name of the candidate or the name of the party;

(iv) refrain from serving or distributing liquor on polling day and during the twenty-four hours preceding it;

(v) not allow unnecessary crowd to be collected near the camps set up by the political parties and candidates near the polling booths so as to avoid confrontation and tension among workers and sympathizers of the parties and the candidate;

(vi) ensure that the candidate's camps shall be simple. They shall not display any posters, flags, symbols or any other propaganda material. No eatables shall be served or crowd allowed at the camps; and

(vii) co-operate with the authorities in complying with the restrictions to be imposed on the plying of vehicles on the polling day and obtain permits for them which should be displayed prominently on those vehicles.

V. *Polling Booth*

Excepting the voters, no one without a valid pass from the Election Commission shall enter the polling booths.

VI. *Observers*

The Election Commission is appointing Observers. If the candidates or their agents have any specific complaint or problem regarding the conduct of elections they may bring the same to the notice of the Observer.

VII. Party in Power

The party in power whether at the Centre or in the State or States concerned, shall ensure that no cause is given for any complaint that it has used its official position for the purposes of its election campaign and in particular:

(i) (a) The Ministers shall not combine their official visit with electioneering work and shall not also make use of official machinery or personnel during the electioneering work;

(b) Government transport including official air-crafts, vehicles, machinery and personnel shall not be used for furtherance of the interest of the party in power;

(ii) Public places such as maidans etc., for holding election meetings, and use of helipads for air-flights in connection with elections shall not be monopolized by itself. Other parties and candidates shall be allowed the use of such places and facilities on the same terms and conditions on which they are used by the party in power;

(iii) Rest houses, dak bungalows or other Government accommodation shall not be monopolized by the party in power or its candidates and such accommodation shall be allowed to be used by other parties and candidates in a fair manner but no party or candidate shall use or be allowed to use such accommodation (including premises appertaining thereto) as a campaign office or for holding any public meeting for the purposes of election propaganda;

(iv) Issue of advertisement at the cost of public exchequer in the newspapers and other media and the misuse of official mass media during the election period for partisan coverage of political news and publicity regarding achievements with a view to furthering the prospects of the party in power shall be scrupulously avoided.

(v) Ministers and other authorities shall not sanction grants/ payments out of discretionary funds from the time elections are announced by the Commission; and

(vi) From the time elections are announced by Commission, Ministers and other authorities shall not:

(a) announce any financial grants in any form or promises there of; or
(b) (except civil servants) lay foundation stones etc. of projects or schemes of any kind; or
(c) make any promise of construction of roads, provision of drinking water facilities etc.; or
(d) make any ad-hoc appointments in Government, Public Undertakings etc. which may have the effect of influencing the voters in favour of the party in power.

Note: The Commission shall announce the date of any election which shall be a date ordinarily not more than three weeks prior to the date on which the notification is likely to be issued in respect of such elections.

(vii) Ministers of Central or State Government shall not enter any polling station or place of counting except in their capacity as a candidate or voter or authorised agent.

For the purpose of ensuring free and fair poll, the Election Commission has been taking many steps which includes setting up of separate polling stations in colonies inhabited by Harijans and other weaker sections of society and providing sufficient police force to prevent intimidation of voters so that they may exercise their right to vote without fear, appointing observers to look after the elections in constituencies who make frequent rounds in sensitive and vulnerable areas and scrutinize the records of the polling stations. The Commission through its officers, also keeps strict vigil on the law and order situation and it has a right to order re-poll if booth-capturing, rigging, violence and other illegal means are adopted by the candidates. While canvassing is banned within a distance of one hundred meters of the polling station, no public meetings are allowed 48 hours before the commencement of the polling. After polling, counting takes place as per the programme fixed by the Election Commission and the candidate getting the maximum number of votes is declared elected by the Returning officer. After the conclusion of counting all over the country, in case of Lok Sabha or in a State, in case of State Assembly, the Election Commission issues a notification which contains the names of all the persons elected.

Scrutinization of Election Expenses

Before 1966, the election of a candidate could be challenged before the Election Commission for which it used to constitute Elections Tribunals. Since 1966, election petitions are heard by the concerned

High Court whose decisions are subject to appeal in Supreme Court. However, the Election Commission has the power to scrutinize the election expenses incurred by the various candidates. There is a ceiling on expenses to be incurred in Parliamentary as well as State Assembly elections. Every candidate is required to file an account of his election expenses within 45 days of declaration of results. In case of default or if the candidate has incurred more than the prescribed expenses, the Election Commission takes appropriate actions and the candidate elected may be disqualified and his election countermanded.

Thus, the Election Commission handles the entire gigantic task of conducting an election. We can also say that it has achieved a considerable amount of success in holding peaceful, free and fair elections. This is not to say that ideal elections take place in India. There have been cases of rigging, booth capturing, intimidation of voters specially the Harijans and the other weaker sections of the society and misuse of governmental machinery in elections, but on the whole, the elections have been impartial, and this puts India as the real largest democracy of the world.

General Observations about Elections in India

We have seen above that in the period following the independence, the Indian electorate has successfully used its franchise thus establishing the largest democracy in the world. Initially, the Congress Party was able to capture power in both centre as well as the states which brought about the single party dominance in the Indian politics. The Indian electorate over the years has also shown a remarkable degree of maturity. It punished the Congress Party in 1967, for its poor performance in Indo-China War of 1962 and the food crisis. Again in 1977, the Congress Party was punished for the excesses committed during emergency of 1975-77, when even its leader and the Prime Minister Indira Gandhi lost her Lok Sabha seat. Similarly, in 1989 and 1996, Congress Party was punished for its bad performance. However, while the electorate punished the Congress Party, it has not been able to make a decisive choice in favour of a single non-Congress Party. Therefore, a major characteristic of the non-Congress coalition governments formed at the centre has been instability and the consequent political crisis.

Another aspect of elections in India is the voting behaviour of the electorate in which very little study has been done. In the initial years, we find the charismatic personality of Nehru dominating the Indian politics and people were actually voting Nehru, instead of Congress Party. Later on, we witness waves during the election. In 1971, it was Indira wave which brought Indira Gandhi and her party with two third majority in the Lok Sabha. In 1977, we had Janata wave. In 1980, we had Indira wave again. In 1984, there was a sympathy wave due to the assassination of Indira Gandhi. In 1989 we witnessed anti-Rajiv Gandhi wave. In 1991, due to the assassination of Rajiv Gandhi, there was a remarkable swing in favour of Congress Party which brought it, into power, but again in 1996, we saw the anti-Congress wave.

It will be difficult to say that the Indian electorate is totally matured who decides according to the issues or the performance. In a major part of India, the caste factor is very important and the political parties decisions to field a candidate from a particular constituency is determined by the caste factor. The Scheduled castes had been a vote bank for Congress Party for a long time. However, this has been changing and now they do not vote en bloc for one political party. During the last few years, we find the upsurge of Dalit votes which have been crucial in deciding the election results. In 1996, "the three major political formations the Congress, the NF-LF and the BJP agreed that the crucial Dalit vote could make or break their fortunes." The Congress Government even attempted to promulgate an ordinance for the reservation of Dalit Christians. Religion also plays a very important role in the voting behaviour. The Muslims like the Scheduled Castes had been a vote bank for the Congress Party for a long time. But now, we find a mad rush on the part of political parties to get their votes by proclaiming secularism. The Congress lost their support due to the demolition of disputed structure in Ayodhya in 1992. In 1994, they supported Shiv Sena in Maharashtra but were again compelled to lend support to Janata Dal and its allies due to the dismissal of the Minorities Commission and Sri Krishna Commission by the Sena Government. In 1996 elections, various Muslim organisations felt the need of a solid Muslim voting against the BJP. In Uttar Pradesh, they supported Samajwadi Party and BSP, in other places they supported either Congress or Janata Dal to ensure BJP defeat. However, the religion of the majority of India-the Hindus fortunately have not been voting in a strict religious sense. This is the reason why the BJP could not get any political mileage because of demolition of disputed structure at Ayodhaya. Regionalism has been another factor in determining voting behaviour. A major outcome of the 1996 election had been the rise of regional parties at the centre. In 1996 elections, they could capture as many as 127 seats with 21.34 per cent of total votes. Money is also crucial in elections. There is a ceiling on the amount of money to be spent in the Parliamentary and Assembly elections which ranges from Rs 60,000 (in Lakshadweep Parliamentary Constituency) to Rs 4,50,000 (in Andhra Pradesh, Gujarat, Haryana, Karnataka, Kerala, Madhya Pradesh, Maharashtra, Orissa, Punjab, Rajasthan, Tamil Nadu, Uttar Pradesh and West Bengal parliamentary constituencies). However, for the purpose of calculation of expenditure of a individual party candidate, the expenses footed by the political party is excluded as per the 1974 Amendment to the Representation of the People Act. The political party collects funds from companies and business houses and other sources by legal and illegal means. This money is used to influence the voting behaviour. Reports of liquor being distributed in the poor areas and other such practices have been frequent during elections. Last is the role of muscle power which has been a very important feature in rural areas. Earlier, the criminals used to support candidates in elections by intimidating the voters and rigging the elections, In the present decade, they have come out in the open by contesting elections leading to criminalisation of politics. It is easy to guess as to how they get elected.

This also takes us to the need of electoral reforms in India. It has been pointed out that there are many lacunas in Indian electoral system that calls for poll reforms. Some of them are as follows:

(a) Many corrupt practices are adopted during elections. There is a widespread allegation that misuse of governmental machinery is common among the party-in-power.
(b) Money and muscle play a very important role in Indian elections.
(c) The caste and religious factor is most notable.
(d) All the political parties do not have equal opportunity in respect of access to resources. The party-in-power is always in advantageous position than the opposition parties.
(e) There is a multiplicity of parties and candidates, which puts tremendous pressure on the electorate to decide. Since 1952, when the first general elections were held the number of independent candidates have been rising, while the number of such successful candidates are decreasing. In 1952 election, 533 independent candidates contested out of which 38 got elected and 356 lost deposits, while in 1991 elections as many as 5,230 independent candidates contested, out of which only one got elected and as many as 5,203 candidates lost their deposits. This is also clear from the fact that in 1952, average number of contestants per Lok Sabha seat was just 3.8 which rose to 26.3 in 1996. In 1980 Lok Sabha election, one candidate stood from as many as 13 Parliamentary constituencies. However, this problem has been solved to some

extent by increasing the amount of security deposit to Rs 10,000 for general constituency and Rs 5000 for reserved constituency.

(f) There is a wide gap between the votes polled and seats won by a political party. In the 1952 elections, the Congress party received 47.8 per cent of total votes polled and captured 371 seats, in 1984 Lok Sabha elections the percentage of total votes slighty increased to 48.1 per cent but it was able to capture 415 seats. In 1989 elections the percentage of votes polled by the party was 39.5 but it could capture only 197 seats. In 1991 and 1996 the Congress Party got 36.5 per cent and 28.8 votes, while the seats won were 231 and 140 respectively. No party could ever muster 50 per cent of total votes in any elections.

Demands for electoral reforms have been frequently made in Indian political system. In 1974, Jaya Prakash Narayan appointed a committee popularly called as Tarkunde Committee which suggested following electoral reforms:

- The appointment of the Election Commission should be made by the President of India on the advice of a committee comprising of the Prime Minister, the leader of the opposition in the Lok Sabha and the Chief Justice of India.
- The Election Commission should have three members.
- The minimum age for voting should be 18 years.
- The Television and Radio should be made autonomous.
- In the individual constituencies, Voter's Councils should be formed to ensure free and fair elections.

In 1990, Dinesh Goswami Committee under the Chairmanship of the then Law Minister Dinesh Goswami was formed to suggest electoral reforms. The Committee made the following recommendations:

(i) To reduce the multiplicity of parties and candidates in the elections the committee suggested that security deposit be increased and they must secure atleast one-forth as against one-sixth of the valid votes polled, else their security deposit be forfeited.

(ii) The arrangement of the names of candidates in ballot box should be in the following order:
  (a) Candidates of recognised national parties
  (b) Candidates of recognised state parties
  (c) Candidates of registered parties
  (d) Independents

(iii) A person should not be allowed to contest election from more than two constituencies.

(iv) The Committee also suggested various measures to curb the evil of booth capturing which included ordering of repoll or even countermanding the reports from not only the returning officer but also granting the Election Commission the power to appoint investigating agencies, prosecuting agencies and ask for the constitution of special courts.

(v) Photo identity cards should be introduced to eradicate bogus voting or impersonation during elections.

(vi) The model code of conduct should be vigoursly implemented and misuse of governmental machinery and media should be curbed. Announcement of financial grants or laying of foundation stores for projects should be stopped and there should be statutory backing for the purpose.

(vii) Unauthorised expenditure during election, failure to maintain and submit accounts or submission of false accounts, should also be made offences.

(viii) The plying of mechanised vehicles, moving of persons with lethal weapons and fire arms and sale and distribution of liquor should also be banned.

(ix) State assistance to the national and State parties be given in kind and not in cash.

(x) The Chief Election Commissioner should be appointed by the President in consultation with the Leader of the opposition in Lok Sabha and Chief Justice of India. In case, there is no leader of the opposition available, the leader of the largest opposition group in the Lok Sabha should be consulted. The other members of the Election Commission should be appointed by the same group which, however, should also include Chief Election Commissioner. This consultation process should have a statutory backing.

The Election Commission from time to time has been making several recommendations for electoral reforms. As a result, in 1989, two important amendments were introduced in the Representation of Peoples Act 1951 which gave the Election Commission power of Countermanding elections in case of booth capturing and ordering of fresh elections in the concerned polling stations or even the entire constituency in case of large scale booth capturing. The Election Commission used this new power in Amethi, Jammu and Kashmir and Meham Assembly Constituencies in 1989. In Meham, it ordered re-poll in the entire constituency. In 1993, the Election Commission cancelled the bye-elections in Kalka Constituency for Assembly because the Chief Minister of Haryana announced several new schemes and inaugurated new projects in the constituency thereby violating the

Model Code. Similarly, in Tamil Nadu, polls were postponed for three-months for bye-elections as the Chief Minister of Tamil Nadu Ms. Jayalalitha had announced new schemes. In Madhya Pradesh, the bye-elections were postponed because the Governor of Himachal Pradesh had misused the official machinery in favour of his son. The Governor had to resign. In Tripura, the entire general election in 1993 was cancelled in view of misuse of official machinery by the party-in-power. In 1998, the entire election in Patna constituency was cancelled and re-poll ordered. In 1994, the Election Commission issued a notification ordering the political parites to elect their respective office bearers as per their constitutions within four months. In 1996, another notification was issued as a result of which all the political parties elected their office bearers. The Commission's argument was that since the political parties were registered on the basis of their respective constitutions, they must adhere to them. In fact, under the dynamic leadership of T.N. Seshan, the Election Commission initiated many measures to ensure free and fair elections which included video coverage of polling booths to curb booth capturing and other malpractices during polling, the introduction of Photo Identity Cards, voter awareness campaigns, engraving serial number in the ballot box to eradicate its substitution, confiscation of arms and ammunition during the poll period, closure of liquor shops and tabs on anti-social elements and criminals. The activism of the Election Commission led to serious differences between the Commission and the government and even the political parties. The government reacted by making the Election Commission a multi member body. Two Election Commissioners G.V.G. Krishnamurthy and M.S. Gill were appointed, but T.N. Seshan continued to dominate the activities of Election Commission. The 1996 Lok Sabha election dates were fixed by the Election Commission as the Government was late in communicating the dates for elections to the Commission. The Central Government was reluctant in holding Assembly elections in Jammu and Kashmir while the Election Commission was in favour. After the intervention of Supreme Court, the Election Commission's view prevailed and it declared the schedule of elections for Jammu and Kashmir. The Election Commission also took up the issue of voting rights of Kashmir refugees for Lok Sabha elections 1996, with the Government. As a result, the Government passed an ordinance by which 1.5 lakh Kashmiri migrants were able to exercise their franchise. The Election Commission also strictly applied the Model Code of Conduct. Consequently, as Meenu Roy points out. "The election campaign was now without thrills, frills and colour. For a country, which has always considered elections a mega festival, the general elections of 1996 might go down in history as the most quiet and tame affair.... The absence of blaring loudspeakers gave a feeling that elections were not round the corner." With the cameras of the Election Commission haunting the Candidates, they had changed methods of canvassing by laying emphasis on small, street-corner meetings and undertaking door-to-door contacts. The watchful eye of the Election Commission and the fear that the Election Commission observers might report any extravagance, candidates and parties had kept a very low profile and were scared even to fly party flags, banners, put up arches or cut outs." The commission also decided against holding the elections to Lahaul and spiti constituencies (in Himachal Pradesh for the Assembly elections) as they were completely snow bound. In 1997, the Election Commissioner disclosed that 40 MPs in the then Parliament and nearly 700 out of 4072 legislators in State Assemblies had criminal records. The Commission issued a directive that any person convicted by a court under section 8 of the Representative of People Act would be debarred from contesting elections. For the first time in Indian election history, the candidates in the Rajya Sabha elections were required to file an affidavit stating that they did not have a criminal past.

In 2002, the Election Commission refused to conduct elections in Gujarat after the dissolution of the Assembly. The Chief Election Commissioner along with his two colleagues decided to have a personal experience of the riot-hit areas of Gujarat before deciding to go for elections or otherwise. In his tour which was widely witnessed by the people of the entire country through the audio-visual and writing media, he pulled up politicians, and bureaucrats, acting almost like an enquiry officer or chief executive, for Gujarat carnage which left officially 1000 people dead (unofficially the figure was estimated to be twice) and property worth crores destroyed and more than one lakh people rendered homeless. While, for politicians his publicised comment on Gujarat riot was, *'Sab politicians ki badmashi hai'*, (all this is the politician's mischief), he called the collector a joker and enquired "Aren't you ashamed of yourself? "The Election Commission decided that the environment was not conducive to holding elections because (i) displacement of a sizeable section of the population had taken place from riot-affected areas, (ii) revision of the voters list which was necessary would take time, (iii) rehabilitation of riot victims had been inadequate and (iv) the minority community continued to live in fear. It also gave an unprecedented recommendation of imposing Article 356 on the state.

A Bill: The Representation of the People (Second Amendment) Bill, 1996 was moved in the Eleventh Lok Sabha which could not be passed due to lack of support. The Bill, however, had incorporated many recommendations made by Goswami Committee. The salient features of the Bill were as follows:

(i) The Bill proposed to reduce the campaign period from 21 days to 14 days.
(ii) An independent candidate or a candidate not put up by a recognised party must have his name proposed by 10 people from his constituency.
(iii) The security deposit for both the Parliamentary as well as Assembly elections would be Rs 5,000. For Scheduled Caste and Scheduled tribes candidates it will be Rs 2,500/-.
(iv) A candidate could contest maximum from two constituencies simultaneously.
(v) The bye-elections would have to be held within six months after a vacancy has occurred.
(vi) The Bill also proposed disqualification for six years for any candidate convicted of an offence punishable under Section 2 or Section 3 of the Prevention of Insults to National Honour Act, 1971. The said candidate would be disqualified for contesting election for six years.
(vii) The Bill also proposed to eradicate rigging during elections. It enabled the Election Commission to appoint Observers, with powers to direct the Returning Officers to stop counting of votes or stay declaration of results in constituencies where booth capturing or large-scale tampering with ballot papers had occurred.
(viii) The candidates in the ballot paper would not be listed according to the alphabetical order, as was the practice but would be listed in three categories; those from recognised political parties, those from registered parties and other candidates.
(ix) There should be ban on the sale or distribution of liquor in a polling area during the 48 hour period before the conclusion of the poll.
(x) On the death of a candidate, the election in the particular constituency would not be countermanded as was the practice, but only be adjourned.

In 1997, the Election Commission demanded many changes in the existing election law which are as follows:

(i) A candidate should be disqualified from contesting elections for six years after completion of any jail term exceeding six years, even if his appeal is pending in the higher courts. At present the six-year provision applies to only specific offences.

(ii) There should be a three member Election Commission. Besides the Chief Election Commissioner there should be two additional election commissioners.
(iii) In the calculation of a candidate's expenditures in election, his party's expenditure on him should also be included in determining whether the candidate exceeds the permitted ceiling.
(iv) The ceiling on expenditures to be incurred by the candidate should be raised to Rs 15 lakh for Lok Sabha poll and Rs. 6 lakh for an assembly poll.
(v) There should also be flexibility in fixing the ceiling for election expenses. The Election Commission, accordingly, should have the power to suitably amend these limits for smaller or larger constituencies.
(vi) The Election Commission must have adequate powers to punish erring government employees requisitioned for poll duties.
(vii) It should be obligatory on the part of employees of all state governments, state run firms, banks and statutory bodies to make available their employees to the Election Commission for poll-duty requisition.
(viii) There have been major lacunas in the Rajya Sabha election process. A candidate has to be in the voter's list from the state from which he is contesting. For this purpose, the candidates frequently give false declarations of their address and enroll themselves in the electroal roll of the state. The Election Commission has suggested that a candidate be allowed to contest the Rajya Sabha polls from any parliamentary constituency in the country so long as he or she is a valid voter.

Their is no doubt that India needs poll reforms drastically. A few have been implemented like the voting age has been lowered from 21 years to 18 years. Another landmark change has been the increase in the amount of security deposit by the candidate to prevent frivolous contests. In 1998, the security deposit was raised from Rs 500 to Rs 10,000 for general constituencies and Rs 250 to Rs 5,000 for reserved constituencies. The deposit is returned only if the candidate secure at least one sixth of the total votes. But a lot is to be done. We have to eradicate various evils that have unfortunately cropped up like criminalisation of politics, booth capturing, rigging and intimidation of weaker sections and Scheduled Castes and Scheduled Tribes. There is also an urgent requirement of state funding of political parties to reimburse their poll expenses. This is a practice prevalent in many democracies. For example in West Germany, parties polling a minimum percentage of votes are entitled to reimbursement of their election expenses. In France and Canada, a partial reimbursement of poll expenses is ensured. In USA, the state funds the election to office of the President. Fortunately, now a consensus is emerging regarding this and very soon the system of state funding of election will be adopted. It is, however, also true that the State funding will not eliminate the corruption but definitely play an important role in combating it. To reduce the gap between the votes polled and number of candidates elected, there is a need for serious thinking of adopting proportional Representation system of election in which the parties get the representation according to the votes polled. There is also a need of reorgnisation of constituencies. In Delhi itself, while one parliamentary constituency consists of four lakh voters, another constituency has as many as 22 lakh voters. This large difference in terms of population must be done away with. But when all is said and done, the fact remains that Indian elections have been largely free and fair and successfully conducted which gives the country, the proud distinction of being the largest democracy in the world.

References

Bhagat Anjana Kaw, *Elections and Electoral Reforms in India*, 1996, New Delhi, Vikas Publishing House.

Butler David, Ashok Lahiri and Prannay Roy, *India Decides, Elections 1952-1989*, 1989, New Delhi, Living Media Ltd.

Fadia B.L., *Indian Government and Politics*, 1996, Agra, Sahitya Bhawan Publications.

Hausen A.H. and Douglas Janet, *India's Democracy*, 1972, Delhi, Vikas Publishing House.

Indian Express supplement, *India at 50 Facts, Figures and Analysis 1947-1997*.

Kashyap Subash C., *History of Parliamentary Democracy*, 1991, Delhi, Shipra Publications.

Singh Mehendra P., *V.N. Shukla's Constitution of India*, 1994, Lucknow, Eastern Book Company.

Kashyap Subash C., *History of the Parliament of India, Vol I and II*, Delhi, Shipra Publications.

Kothari Rajni, *Politics in India*, 1994, New Delhi, Orient Longman Limited.

Kumar Arun, *The Tenth Round Story of Indian Elections 1991*, 1991, Delhi, Rupa & Co.

Palmer Norman D, *Elections and Political Development*, 1975, New Delhi, Vikas Publishing House Pvt Ltd.

Ray Meenu, *India Votes Elections 1996: A Critical Analysis*, 1996, New Delhi, Deep & Deep Publications.

Thakur Ramesh, *The Government and Politics of India*, 1995, London, Macmillan Press.

Weiner Myron, *India At The Polls The Parliamentary Elections of 1977*, 1978, Washington, American Enterprise Institute for Public Policy Research.

CHAPTER XX

Social Movements in India

Social movements primarily result from the conditions of deprivation and exploitation and they aim at social change. As Wallace points out, they develop out of a deliberate, organised and conscious effort, on the part of members of a society, to construct a more satisfying culture for themselves. On the one hand, while they express the agencies of deprivation and exploitation of existing conditions, on the other, they enumerate a detailed programme of social action to achieve better conditions. The present chapter deals with the following social movements in India;

(i) Peasant movement
(ii) Trade union movements
(iii) Tribal movements
(iv) Women's movements
(v) Dalit movement

Peasant Movements

Causes of the peasant movements can be traced back to tenurial arrangements and land revenue payment systems in the country. The Pre-British system of payment of land revenue was somewhat peasant-friendly. Therefore, there were fewer problems in the countryside. The village communities were organised as economic units which had a very high degree of mutual dependence amongst different households. The most common mode of exchange was barter, which was spread over the yearly cropping cycle and was more of a settlement pattern of mutual obligations. However, beginning with the permanent settlement of Bengal (1783), a new system of land revenue collection was introduced in the countryside. Different clusters of villages were designated as revenue units, and revenue collection rights were auctioned out to the highest bidders. These collection contractors came to be known as Zamindars and the system based on them was called Zamindari system. This change had a two-fold effect on rural India. Now land revenue had to be paid in cash. Earlier, revenue was paid as a share of gross produce. If there was a famine, the revenue liability was very meagre. But the new system did not recognise crop failure as a problem. The Zamindar wanted a certain amount of money in hard cash at the time of his choice. Even when a good harvest was reaped, the farmer had to resort to distress sale to settle the land revenue claim of the Zamindar. The transport system was not very developed. The prices at the harvest time hit rock-bottom. In fact, it was availability of cash with the local trader that determined the agricultural prices at harvest time. The farmers were forced to sell a very large proportion of the entire crop. Some time, they were not left with even the seed stock for the next cropping cycle, and were unable to pay land revenue. Thus, the peasantry sunk into debts from which it could never emerge.

The other effect of this system was breakdown of mutuality in the village community. Now peasants could not meet traditional obligation to other craftsmen and artisans in the village. They, too could not be expected to continue to provide traditional services without any immediate payment. In fact, artisans were forced to buy food grains for cash as traditional payment by farmers, at harvest time, had become a thing of past. So they demanded cash for their services. To meet this demand, a farmer was expected to sell an even larger proportion of his crops left after paying land revenue.

Zamindars did introduce their own hierarchy of officials to effect realisation of revenue. This *bureaucracy* had to impose additional claims on peasantry to ensure its own survival. This led to a highly exploitative revenue-collection regime in the country, which in turn resulted in several types of peasant agitations and struggle, some of which are:

The Tebhaga Movement

On the eve of Indian independence, a powerful movement in Kakdwip, West Bengal was progressing. It was launched in 1946 which demanded 'Tebhaga' principle in the production of crops. i.e., two-third share of the produce to the share-cropping cultivators instead of half, which had been the practice. The landowners used to give their lands to share-cropping cultivators, who were in fact chained to the lands of their masters like serfs or half slaves. They were also subjected to many evil practices like *Dera-bari* which meant enforced borrowing by the share-croppers at the rate of 50 per cent in kind, subject to increase at a compounded rate. Besides they were also compelled to pay for village festivals and other charges like *Nazrana* (occasional presentation to the landlords), *Kayali* (wage of the weightman of share-cropping crops, *khamar chuilani* (charge for preparation of landlord's yards, *Prachi ghera* (charge for making walls around the yard), *Naibiana* (charge for account keeping by landlord's agent), *Dwaroani* (charge for the service of landlord's darwan or guard), *Selami* (annual charge for rented land), Education cess and *Golakamti* (paddy charged for its loss of weight which resulted from its being dried up in the landlord's farm preserved for advance to the share-croppers). There were also the practices of eviction, exactions and ill treatment like physical torture and dishonouring of their womenfolk. Besides the share-croppers, the tenants were also subjected to the exploitation and oppression of the landlords. The Tebhaga movement was led by the Communist Party of India. Besides the demand for tebhaga, the other demands were to abolish Zamindari, right to stock crop in the peasant's place to stop all oppressions, and land to the tiller. The movement became so intensive that the West Bengal Government declared the affected area as disturbed area. As a result of combined oppression of landlords and the police, the tebhaga movement failed. However, according to Krishna Kanta Sarkar, the following were the achievements of the tebhaga movement:

(i) In the harvesting season of 1946-47, the movement was successful and in the next session, it was partly successful.
(ii) It was the movement by which all illegal exactions were done away with for ever.
(iii) *Dera-bari* and eviction ceased
(iv) All sorts of ill-treatment, ranging from physical torture to the dishonouring of women came to be a story of the past.
(v) The movement brought Kakdwip to the attention of the Government. To take the edge out of the Communist movement, the B.C. Ray Ministry provided in its budget for the financial year of 1952-53, a portion of Rs 1,50,000 earmarked for the communist-affected area, which seemed definitely to be the Kakdwip area.
(vi) The tebhaga movement of Kakdwip had undeniably contributed towards the agrarian land-reform laws of the subsequent years.
(vii) Over and above all, what is more significant, was that within a few years, the peasantry of Kakdwip underwent a revolutionary change in their thinking and outlook, in that they were not only

able to shake off their servile and submissive mentality, but also elevated themselves from the 'half free' status of a serf to the status of a citizen."

Telengana Movement

The first major peasant movement in India was the Telengana movement in Hyderabad during 1946 to 1951. Under the Nizam's rule in the State of Hyderabad, the jagirdars, landlords and government officials were exploiting the peasants very badly. The absentee landlordism and an oppresive system of land tenure was prevalent and between 1910 and 1940, land alienation took place and many cultivators had to become tenants-at-will, crop-sharers and landless labourers. They were also subjected to the practice of free and forced labour and exactions. As early as 1930, the Andhra Mahasabha was formed in order to educate the people against the forced labour and other social evils like untouchability. The Andhra Mahasabha also stood for eradicating purdah system, child marriage and taboo on widow remarriage. In 1940s, the Andhra Mahasabha became dominated by the Communists, while the liberals opted for Congress party. After the Indian independence on 15th August 1947, the Nizam of Hyderabad declared his own independence on 27 August 1947. The Congress and the Communists joined together for the accession of Hyderabad into the Indian Union. The Razakars of the Nizam retaliated by large-scale looting, murder, arson and rape. They also incited Muslims against the Hindu. The Communist Party raised the slogan of 'land to the tiller' and land owned by the landlords and rich peasants were confiscated and together with the government—owned land, was distributed among the landless. In 1948, the state of Hyderabad was acceded to Indian Union by a police action by the Indian Government. After the accession, the landlords and rich peasants supported the Congress which had earlier resented the armed struggle of communists to distribute the land among the landless. Now the landlords and rich peasants attempted to get back their lands and communists decided to launch an armed struggle against the Indian Government in order to stop them from doing so. For the purpose, guerilla squads were formed. The Indian Government arrested the communist leaders and the communist uprising was crushed. The armed struggle got converted into individual acts of terrorism and the movement lost the people's support. In October 1951, the Communist Party withdrew the armed struggle and thus the Telengana uprising came to an end. The Communist Party of India learnt a lesson from this and decided to participate in the 1952 General Election, thus realising the futility of armed struggle to achieve the desired objectives. There is another aspect of the Telengana uprising which is very important. Acharya Vinobha Bhave started the Bhoodan movement in 1951 from Telengana, in which the landlords and rich peasants donated their lands to him to be distributed among the landless. Thus the violent struggle gave way to a non-violent method of resolving the disparity in land holdings. The Government also abolished the jagirdari system and land reform legislation was passed in which many landless were given land to cultivate. Thus from the poor landless peasants point of view, the Telengana uprising did not prove to be a futile exercise.

The Naxalite Movement

The Naxalite movement has been the most important peasant movement in post independence India. However, this movement has its roots in the Tebhaga movement. As Partha N. Mukherjee points out, some of the slogans which were used initially by the Naxalites had the historical continuity of Tebhaga like

(i) We want the abolition of Zamindari system
(ii) Land to the tiller
(iii) Tenant eviction will not be tolerated
(iv) 25 per cent interest for borrowed paddy
(v) Go on cultivating without surrendering
(vi) Defeat the Congress

The regions affected by the Naxalite movement were the Police Stations of Phansidewa, Naxalbari and Khoribari which covered an area of about 274 square miles with a population of about 1,50,000. The movement soon spread to a major part of West Bengal and Andhra Pradesh and certain areas of Madhya Pradesh and Bihar. It was spearheaded by the various breakaway groups of CPM, which initially was to wage this struggle. However, with the United Front Government along with the CPM participation in West Bengal as a result of 1967 elections, led to the second split in the Communist movement in India and the breakaway groups of CPM—the Naxalbari-o-Krishak Sangram Sahayak Samiti, the Maoist Communist Centre (MCC), the group led by Charu Mazumdar, Kanu Sanyal and Souren Bose; Amulya Sen and Kanai Chatterjee's 'Chinta' group; and Swadesh Mitra's Surjya Sen group, led the Naxalite uprising. Later on Communist Party of India (Marxist Leninist) was formed which included many of these groups. The movement was directed against the jotedars and plantation workers (owners). However right from the beginning, there were severe differences regarding the strategy and the plan of action. The Charu Mazumdar group was more radical which believed in the Chinese path for the liberation of India and wished to have an agrarian revolution through armed struggle and, for the purpose, building up of a secret party organisation. The Kanu Sanyal group agreed with Charu on many points but felt the necessity of building up mass organisation and mass movement. The Charu group wanted the total appropriation of the lands of the big jotedars, disarming of their lethal weapons, appropriating their pay, cattle and all other such property, establishment of a people's government and annihilation of the jotedars and zamindars through armed revolution. The Kanu Sanyal group wanted to wait and see the result of seizure of land of jotedars by the Naxalites, and then only would think of armed revolt. In 1967, both the groups came to an agreement in which the peasants were asked to (i) seize the lands of the jotedars; (ii) seize the lands of the plantation workers who had purchased land from the poor peasants; (iii) cultivate lands held under (i) and (ii) and retain all the produce from lands appropriated from the jotedars, but share half of the crop produced on the plantation worker's lands, (iv) where the jotedar is engaged in self-cultivation, such lands should not be seized. By 1969, the Naxalite movement became very violent in which frequent murders and dacoities were committed by the Naxalites. It no longer remained a mass movement of peasants and workers, instead, it became a conspiracy where murders were executed by secret guerilla squads with the urban based radical youth taking over the movement. Violence and strikes were directed against the educational institutions, administration and the police. This alienated the common peasant and workers from the movement whereas they were its backbone in 1967. The Government also retaliated ferociously in putting down the movement. The liberation of Bangladesh by India also had a telling impact on CPI-ML followers who preferred to join the Congress. In 1972, Charu Mazumdar died in police custody which created a vacuum in the movement as there was no competent leader to replace him. The Naxal movement now is conspiratorial and has terrorised people in Bihar, Jharkhand, Madhya Pradesh, Chattisgarh, Andhra Pradesh and West Bengal, where they have killed innocent people and policemen.

The land grab movements were also launched in UP and Bihar between 1967 and 1970. This was due to the fact that despite land reform legislation, the disparity in land holdings could not be tackled properly. The landlords and former zamindars resorted to large scale benami transfer of their respective lands. The Planning Commission

Task Force headed by P.S. Appu pointed out that the land reform legislation was poorly implemented and the reasons enumerated were (1) the lack of political will, (2) absence of pressure from below as the poor peasants and agricultural workers are passive, unorganized and inarticulate (3) lukewarm and often apathetic attitude of the bureaucracy (4) absence of up-to-date land records and (5) legal hurdles in the implementation of land reforms. As a result the ceiling of landholdings was never implemented properly. A former Prime Minister, while assuming his office of Prime Ministership, donated 700 acres of his land to the nation in 1991. The fact that he could hold so much land despite the land reform legislations, is a classic example of failure of land reform legislation in India.

Peasant movements have also taken place in Gujarat, Madhya Pradesh, Haryana, Tamil Nadu, Kerala, Punjab, Maharashtra, Nagaland and Mizoram. In Kashtakari Sanghatna agitation in Maharashtra, the women took an active. A fundamental characteristic of these movements has been the leadership of the political parties who organised these movements along with the local Kisan organisations.

However in Maharashtra, Haryana and UP the recent trend has been the rise of rich peasant movements which have kept the political parties at bay. In Haryana, the Bhartiya Kisan Union (BKU) has been spearheading the Kisan movement. The farmers have resorted to agitation in South Haryana comprising Faridabad, Gurgaon, Rewari, Mahendragarh, Bhiwani and Jind. They resented the hike in power tariffs. This led to the conflict between the Haryana Government and the peasants. The Government adopted a carrot and stick policy which resulted in police firing on the farmers that led to some deaths. The farmers refused to pay the electricity bill and even demanded free electricity for their tubewells. The problem is accentuated because of the low level of water in the region. The Bharat Kisan Union did not take the loan waiving announcement by the central government in 2008 kindly. It described the 60000 crore loan waiver as discriminatory and sat on an indefinite dharna at Parliament Street. Union President Balbir Singh Rajewal demanded a total loan waiver on all agricultural loans as they were the result of the Union Government's policies. He said, "The loan waiver does not benefit the farmers of Punjab who sacrificed everything to feed the country and got themselves trapped in a debt trap." He also criticised the Government for banning the entry of private players in wheat purchase and threatened to launch a wheat rok (stop the wheat) agitation in Punjab by boycotting the grain markets (Hindu 14 March 2008). However, the movement is plagued by dissensions and splits which may inhibit the accomplishment of the desired objectives.

Trade Union Movement in India

The Indian Trade Union Movement is highly dominated by the political parties. As per the provisional figures of membership of trade union organisation in India upto 31 December 1989 released by the Chief Labour Commissioner, Bhartiya Mazdoor Sangh (BMS) which is the largest trade union group with 31.17 lakhs member is affliated to the Bhartiya Janata Party, followed by Indian National Trade Union Congress (INTUC) with a 27.06 lakh members which is affliated to Indian National Congress. The Centre of Indian Trade Unions (CITU) with a membership of 17.19 lakhs is a camp-follower of CPM. The Hind Mazdoor Sabha (HMS) was launched in 1949 by the Praja Socialist Party. The All India Trade Union Congress (AITUC) with a membership of 9.24 lakhs at present was the first trade union organisation, launched in 1920 to represent the interests of the working class and to coordinate the activities of various labour organisations in India. Later on AITUC became to be controlled by the Communist Party of India (CPI) and in 1947, Indian National Trade Union Congress controlled by Indian National Congress was formed as a result. The United Trade Union Congress was launched in 1949 by some radicals which now has a membership of 5.40 lakhs. This also shows the fragmented nature of Indian labour union movement. In 1951-52 while there were as many as 4,6233 registered trade unions in India, in 1990 the number swelled to 52,016. Out of these, nearly three-fourths have a membership of less than 500.

The basic function of a trade union is to protect and promote the interests of its members. A trade union is also supposed to keep the larger interests of the country, which in the Indian context means the promotion of national integration. It also helps in the formulation of socio-economic policies of the country. In India, the trade unions have been associated with the nation-building activities. The Government of India frequently consults them in the planning and other developmental activities. For the purpose of representation in national and international conferences and for consultations, the Government of India has recognised 10 trade unions or central organisations of workers. They are Indian National Trade Union Congress (INTUC), Bharat Mazdoor Sangh (BMS), Hind Mazdoor Sabha (HMS), United Trade Union Congress (Lenin Sarani), All India Trade Union Congress (AITUC), Centre of Indian Trade Unions (CITU), National Labour Organisation (NLO), National Front of Indian Trade Union,

United Trade Union Congress (UTUC) and Trade Union Coordination Centre.

In order to protect the interests of their respective members, the trade unions in India have frequently resorted to strikes to solve industrial disputes to their favour. This has also forced the employers to go for retrenchments, dismissals and even lock outs. As a result of lock outs by the employers and strikes by the trade unions, the number of man-days lost is increasing tremendously. In 1951, 31 lakh man-days were lost. In 1979 while 358 lakh man-days were lost due to strikes, 81 lakh man-days were lost due to lock outs. In 1980, a total of 219 lakh man-days were lost due to strikes and lock outs. In fact after the emergency of 1975-77, we find the lock outs have been prominently responsible for man-days lost. In 1985, 65 per cent of man-days lost were due to lock-outs. In 1992 and 1993, lockouts accounted for 52 per cent and 72 per cent of man-days lost respectively. This has been partly because of irresponsible leadership in the trade union and partly because of the privatisation policy of the Indian Government. As early as 1958, a code of discipline was adopted at the Indian Labour Conference which was accepted by the workers unions and the employers organisations. The broad features of this code of Discipline were, as Ishwar C. Dhingra points out, as follows:

(i) The code prohibits strikes and lock outs without prior notice as also intimidation, victimisation and the adoption of 'go-slow' tactics by the workers
(ii) No one-sided action can be taken by either party in any manner.
(iii) All disputes must be settled through the existing machinery set up by the Government for this purpose.
(iv) A common grievance procedure for the settlement of disputes after full investigation has been provided for.
(v) The employers will not increase work load without prior agreement with the worker.
(vi) The employers will provide all facilities for an unfettered growth of trade unions. To this end, they should discourage the use of unfair labour practices like victimisation of the member of the recognised trade unions.
(vii) Prompt action will be taken against the officers whose conduct leads labour to breach of discipline.
(viii) The workers will not indulge in any trade union activity during working hours, nor will they engage in any demonstration or activity, that is not peaceful.
(ix) The workers will implement their part of the awards and settlements promptly and will take action against those office bearers of the trade union who are guilty of violating the code.

(x) The unions will discourage negligence of duty, careless operation, damage to property, disturbance of normal work and insubordination.

Thus the code of discipline was made with the objective of avoiding strikes so that the development process is not affected. Yet the fact remains that the trade unions more have worked as strike committees in the post-independence era. V.V. Giri enumerated three defects in the trade union movement in India. First there is a predominance of small sized trade unions. Secondly, poor finances of the trade unions which is the result of their small size and thirdly, the absence of whole-time paid officers. Some of the major defects of the trade union movement in India are as follows:

(i) In India, the working class who are illiterate and ignorant has largely come from the rural background. They also develop differences in terms of caste, creed, religion and language. Their approach and attitudes still remain traditional. But they continue to possess a poor capacity to pay subscription to the trade unions.

(ii) It has been pointed out that the trade unions in India have used all their energies in organising strikes to get economic concessions and better working conditions from the employers. But they have not gone beyond that. There are no cultural or educational activities of the unions. They have also ignored such beneficial activities like the provision for medical aid and sick relief or assistance to kin and dependants of the workers. In short, the trade unions have been more active during strikes and disputes with the employers, in the absence of which they are totally inactive.

(iii) The trade unions are highly dominated by the political parties who use them for the promotion of their political interests. In the process, workers' welfare often suffers.

(iv) There is a multiplicity of trade unions who are beseiged with political rivalries. Thus, there is no unity in the trade union movement which is so necessary for a strong bargaining power with the employers. The need of the hour is to have one union, one industry.

(v) There is also a need to have a responsible trade union leadership. Strike is an extreme method of resolving disputes and should be used rarely. The workers should also be educated to perform their duties properly. In 1982-83, there was a prolonged strike by the Bombay Textile workers for over 18 months under the leadership of Datta Samanta in which such demands were made which were impossible to be met. Such demands and strikes only make the position of employers strong and weakens the trade union movement. The employers have also felt that labour productivity has not matched the rise in labour wages and therefore the they prefer to close down the establishment than to submit to trade union's demand for the higher wages.

(vi) Given the poor economic conditions of the workers, the bargaining capacity of the trade union is also limited and therefore a long strike leads to failure of the movement. The working class has also imbibed the modern materialistic values. They want to have refrigerators, television, a decent house and other items suited to a modern way of life. As a result, they do not prefer to go on long strikes which affect their life style.

Tribal Movement in India

India has the largest number of tribal people in the world. As per 2001 Census, their number is 84,326,000 and they constitute 8.2 percent of the total population. They have been called (by different authors) aborigines, aborginals, backward Hindus and even submerged humanities. The Indian Constitution accepts them as Scheduled Tribes which is defined as "such tribes or tribal communities or parts of or groups within such tribes or tribal communities as are deemed under *Article 342* to be Scheduled Tribes for the purpose of this Constitution." Initially 212 tribes located in 14 states were recognised as Scheduled Tribes, the number now has swelled to as many as 538. We have primitive tribes which have still resisted any absorption by the mainstream, as in Andamans and Nicobar and certain parts of Bihar and M.P. There are also so-called criminal tribes who have not been able to adjust to modern life and therefore have taken recourse to crimes as a matter of faith. Among the Indian tribes, the Mundas living in Bihar, Jharkhand, MP, Chattisgarh and Orissa are supposed to be the oldest who trace their ancestry to the Indus Valley Civilization. Other numerically important notable tribes are the Gond, Santhal, Bhil, Oraon, Kondh, Bhuiya, Ho, Savara, Kol, Korku, Pathariya and Baiga. The tribals in India are in the various stages of cultural and social development and therefore a particular tribe may be a `Scheduled Tribe' in one state but not included in the list in another state.

During the British period, with the introduction of colonial economy, the tribal areas were increasingly assimilated into the new politico-economic system in which the tribals lost their autonomy which they had been enjoying from time immemorial. As A.R. Desai puts it, "... these tribesmen lost their moorings from their tribal economy, tribal social organisation, tribal religion and tribal cultural life. A large section of this population was reduced to the status of bonded slaves or agrestic serfs of moneylenders, zamindars and contractors who emerged in Indian society as a result of the political and economic policies pursued by the British. Another section was reduced to the category of near—slave labourers working on plantations, in mines, railways, road construction and other enterprises. They were uprooted from their habitat and have been living a wretched existence. A section of these tribes were branded as criminal tribes, where the members could only survive by methods officially described as crimes because of loss of land, occupation and no accessibility to alternative occupation, as a result of the economic and political measures adopted by the British Rulers to enhance their colonial economic exploitation." A section of these tribes were also converted by the Christian missionaries into Christianity both before and after the independence.

The tribals reacted violently against the British policies which dispossessed them from their land and forest products which were a means of their survival. Among the notable tribal revolts during the British period were, the 1772 rebellion of Maler of Rajmahal Hills, 1831 Kol uprising, 1855 Santhal rebellion, 1857 Bhokta uprising and the Ra Movement, 1880 Kach Nagas rebellion, 1900 the Sardari or Mulhi Larai and the Bisra Munda movement. However, after independence, the grievances of the tribals in India continued as the tribal land was taken over by the non-tribals and even government and private enterprises for various developmental projects. For example, in Jharkhand approximately 80 per cent of the tribal land has been lost to building of dams like Koel-Karo project, Suvarna Rekha Project, Damodar Valley Corporation, Steel Authority of India Limited (SAIL) and Heavy Engineering Corporation and private sector enterprises like TISCO and TELCO. Despite the Chota Nagpur Tenancy Act of 1869 which prohibits outsiders from buying tribal land, the land has been transferred from the tribals to non-tribals. The tribals have resisted the non-tribal settlement, sometimes violently. For example, looting and arson by the endangered Jarawa tribe in South Andaman Island on the nontribal settlements of Tirur Villages have been increasing over the past few years. The policy of reservation of forests introduced by the British and later on carried on by the successive Indian Governments deprived the tribal from access to forest resources which was the main source of livelihood during the British period and still remains an important source of livelihood although the tribals have taken to agriculture as their primary source. But at times, when there is not enough cultivation due to drought or other factors, they have to look to the jungle for an alternative source of food. As a result of this deprivation, they become vulnerable to moneylenders and traders, adding to the poverty of tribals. A.R. Desai rightly points out, "The desperate violent and militant struggles which are being launched by the tribal population in various areas are revolts directed against the inhuman conditions to which they have been subjected and which are being perpetuated even after independence." Further, the modern system has led to a feeling of alienation and despair as the traditional systems of tribals have broken down and the tribals feel lost in the process. There is also a feeling among them to search for a new identity. The tribals speaking the same language or having a tradition of common ancestry are coming together. At the same time, internecine conflicts are also not uncommon among them.

In the Constituent Assembly, the tribal leaders expressed their grievances over their treatment in the new set up. Jaipal Singh said, "It is only a matter of political window dressing that today we find six tribal members in the Constituent Assembly." H.S. Saksena also complained that the Constituent Assembly did not properly deliberate on the Scheduled Caste and Scheduled Tribes issue. There was a larger participation when the minority issue was discussed but "Interestingly, however, when the protective framework came to be confined to the S.C. and S.T., participation and interest decrease. Out of a total membership of 324 only 103 members i.e. about 30 per cent participated in the debates of these constitutional provisions. Even out of a these 103, no less than 66 spoke only once or twice. Thus only 37 members spoke on more than two occasions. If we take out the names of the members of the Drafting Committee or the sub-committees on Tribal Areas of Assam, Excluded and Partially Excluded Area (other than Assam), the number would stand reduced to about 30 i.e. about nine per cent of the total membership of this august body." Jaipal Singh speaking about the tribals and the rest of the Indian population said, "...If there is a group of Indian people that has been shabbily treated, it is my people. They have been disgracefully treated, neglected for the last 6000 years. The history of the Indus Valley Civilization, a child of which I am, shows quite clearly that it is the newcomers—most of you, here are intruders as far as I am concerned—it is the newcomers who have driven away my people from the Indus valley to the Jungle.... You cannot teach democracy to the tribal people; you have to learn democratic ways from them .... We want to be treated like every other Indian.... The whole history of my people is one of continuous dispossession by the non-aboriginals of India, punctuated by rebellions and disorder...."

There is no doubt that the Indian tribals continue to be exploited, oppressed and harassed despite the existence of laws to the contrary. This has resulted in violent reactions, as earlier, among the tribes, which has resulted in further violence from the oppressors with help from the police. The forests continue to be cut and land belonging to tribals appropriated by the non-tribals. In Madhya Pradesh, the tribals have formed their own organisation called the Adivasi Mukti Sanghthan which to some extent has been able to tackle such problems as shortage of drinking water, schools and land. But this also angered the vested interests who have formed their own organisation called the Adivasi Samaj Sudhar Shanti Sena which is known to have fabricated police cases against the tribals. The Sanghthan activists are attacked and their homes are being destroyed. There have been cases of death of tribals in police custody and rapes of tribal women. The Adivasi Mukti Sanghthan and the Adivasi Samaj Sudhar Shanti Sena have been involved in violent confrontation, with the police siding the latter. Similarly, the tribes in Tripura have a general complaint that the police belong to the non-tribals, particularly the immigrant Bangali community who have formed their organisation called Amra Bangali with whom tribals continue to have violent clashes.

The tribal unrest has continued unabated in North East India. In Assam, Bodoland activists under the National Democratic Front of Bodoland are demanding a separate Bodoland under the Indian Constitution, while the United Liberation Front of Assam is committed to the 'liberation' of Assam from 'Indian colonialism.' Both the movements have been very violent, putting Assam into a perpetual state of turmoil and instability. In 1993, the Bodoland Autonomous Council (BAC) Act received the President's assent but the dispute arose over the demarcation of BAC areas. Originally 2,600 villages were to be brought under the BAC jurisdiction but out of them only about 1000 villages had a Bodo tribal majority and hence Bodo's fear that they would have just 40 percent representation in the BAC. There have been ethnic clashes between the Bodos and non-Bodos also, with all of them becoming very sensitive about preserving their respective identities. In 1997, 29 people of a non-tribal community were gunned down by the Bodo extremists. In an apparent retaliation, the underground organisation, Bengali Tiger Force (BTF) killed seven Bodo tribals. The ULFA, Bodos and other groups have sophisticated weapons, like AK47 and are experts in handling explosives.

In Nagaland and neighbouring Manipur area, the National Socialist Council of Nagaland (NSCN) is a terrorist organisation which is demanding a Greater Nagaland comprising of certain parts of Manipur, Assam and Arunachal Pradesh and it also includes the Naga inhabited areas of Myanmar. The NSCN is also broken into two groups, NSCN (I.M. or ISSAC-Muirah faction) and NSCN (SS Khaplang faction) and both the groups have been involved in a violent struggle against each other. It has been alleged that NSCN (I-M) faction is running a parallel government in Nagaland and extorting money from traders and others. Every house in Nagaland has to pay Rs. 100/- as House Tax and Ration Tax to NSCN(I-M). In Manipur Kukis and Nagas have been fighting against each other. The Kuki National Front in Manipur has been demanding a separate Kukiland and has carried out many raids on the villages inhabited by the Paite, Zou and Waiphei tribes, which killed atleast 38 tribals in 1977. Over 400 houses, granaries, cowsheds and shops were destroyed in the process and an indefinite curfew was clamped in Churachandpur. The KNF is also in violent conflict with Zoumi Reunification Organisation (ZRO)) of Zoumi stock, who it accused to be in league with NSCN (I-M). It has accused the ZRA of kidnapping and killing several Kukis and had advice the ZRO to reverse relations with the NSCN (I.M.) and unless it does so, the KNF would massacre members of the ZRA. There is another group of Zoumi Revolutionary Army (ZRA), an underground organisation of Paites tribes and some other groups. The Kukis also have a Kuki National Army operating primarily from Myanmar which wants peace on the condition that Paites should declare themselves belonging to the Kuki stock. But the ZRA and ZRO maintain that historically Paites belong to Zoumi stock. In February 1997, the NSCN (I-M) faction met the then Prime Minister Gowda at Zurich for the possible solution of Naga insurgency problem, This meeting created misunderstanding in Manipur that Centre might accept the demand for the creation of Greater Nagaland. As a result of Centre's talks with NSCN (I-M), a ceasefire for three months with effect from August 1, 1997 was declared. On August 13, a section of the press reported, quoting NSCN (I-M) President Issac Chisi Swu that the Centre had 'accepted in principle' the Naga demand to integrate all the Naga-inhabited areas adjoining Nagaland into a single administrative unit. The report turned out to be false with the denial of the Union Home Minister but disturbed Manipur where people thought that Manipur's integrity had been threatened. People's apprehensions were in a way justified also, as the then Chief Minister of Manipur, Rishang Keishing was a Tangkhul Naga and NSCN

(I-M) which demands a Greater Nagaland is also dominated by the Tongkhuls, and in the early 1970's, Keishing had floated a party called 'United Naga Integration Council' which stood for a United Naga State. The situation worsened in 2001 when the Central Government decided to extend the cease-fire with NSCN (I-M) without territorial limits to all Naga-dominated areas in north eastern region. Unfortunately, the Central Government took this decision without consulting the north easten states and negotiations with NSCN (I.M) have always been secret, creating suspicions about the centre's intention. Immediately after the declaration there were protests in Manipur and Assam. In Manipur, the Assembly and many other government fieldings were set on fire, 14 people were killed and curfew reimposed

The worst is that the psyche of the dominant Meitei tribes in Manipur, who believed that Nagas always received favourable treatment and they had been discriminated against, had been hurt. They argued that when Nagaland was carved out of Assam, areas like Dimapur and Rangapara were included in it even though they didn't have much of a Naga population. Assam also protested. The Chief Minister of Assam Tarun Gogoi refused to implement ceasefire in Assam. He accused NSCN (I-M) of being involved in the killing of nine Assam Rifle Personnel and categorically stated, 'We are not concerned about the extension of ceasefire to other parts of the country but so far as Assam is concerned we are not gong to allow them a free run. He also enquired,' 'The government of India has been saying that the ceasefire will have no impact on the territorial integrity of the north eastern states but it has not made it clear whether (Muivah rebel leader of NSCN (I. M.)) has also agreed it." The feeling of insecurity was also felt in Arunachal Pradesh where there are Naga dominated pockets and ceasefire also applied there.

Meanwhile new, violent groups are coming up, for example, the People's Revolutionary Party of Kangleipak (PREPAK) in Manipur. This banned extremist group stands for the expulsion of 'outsiders' from Manipur.

In the 2008 Nagaland Assembly elections, which saw a turnout of 87.79 per cent, the NSCN (I-M), NSCN (Kaplang) and the Nationalist Socialist Council of Nagaland boycotted the polls. While the NSCN (I-M) said that the Naga cause was more important and it would not compromise its principles by participating in the elections held under the 'Indian Constitution', the NSCN (Kaplang) asked all the underground organisations not to involve in the election in any form.

The Naga National Council (NNC) organised a poster campaign against the elections across the state. The poster compaign declared 'no to Indian election' and pointed out 'three Nagas Stand' of "Nagaland for Nagas, Nagaland not for sale and Nagas reject India's interference in our country".

The situation is equally bad in Tripura. The National Liberation Front of Tripura is heading the insurgency and has been ambushing security personnel. Tripura has as many as 19 different tribes and the tribal people constitute 31.05 lakh out of a total of 31.99 state's population. After the Partition, the State saw a large scale population influx from the then East Pakistan now Bangla Desh which reduced the tribal majority in many areas of Tripura.

There is another aspect of tribal problems and unrest in various parts of India; many tribal communities who have not been recognized as Scheduled Tribes, are now increasingly demanding the status of Scheduled Tribe. In Rajasthan and parts of northern India, the Gujjar community raised this demand and their struggle brought a big part of the country to a standstill. In Assam also this problem exists which has led to clashes between tribal communities and between tribal and non-tribal. The Tea Garden Labour (around 20 million in number) and ex-Tea Garden Labour community call themselves Adivasi and demand Scheduled Tribe status. Besides, there are five other OBC communities (Tai-Ahom, Moran, Motok, Chutia and Koch-Rajbongshi) also desire ST status. The first four live in upper Assam while the Koch-Rajbongshi are the residents of western Assam, living along with the Bodos. Their main grievance is they are not recognized as a tribal community though historically they belong to authentic tribal stock. It has been observed that these Adivasis' fight is not so much for their recognition as a tribal community as for the restoration of the tribal identity to which they believe they are entitled. (M.S.Prabhakara). They are the descendants of various central Indian tribal communities whose ancestors were brought to Assam. As per the rule, a Munda in Jharkhand is a tribal but in Assam he is not and if he goes back to Jharkhand, he again gains the ST status. This peculiarity is because the tribal origin is linked to the place of origin. Even in Assam, tribal communities belong to two categories- Hill Tribes and Plain Tribes. While 14 communities are recognized as Hill Tribes who live in the Autonomous districts of Karbi Anglong and North Cachar Hills, 9 tribal communities belong to the rest of Assam supposedly all plain. The location itself is confusing but they lose their tribal identity if they migrate from one area to another. Then there are other communities also who want recognition as Scheduled Tribe. The complexity of the problem from the government's point of view can be easily understood from the fact that the estimated 20 lakh Adivasi population constitute about 60 per cent of the total ST population of the State and the existing ST communities would never accept their inclusion in the ST category as it would affect existing allocations in areas such as reservation of seats in legislative structures, higher education and jobs. Put simply, such identity struggles carry a cost, and a price. (M.S.Prabhakara).

Thus the situation in the North East is highly confusing with the tribals having conflict with the State, outsiders and also among themselves, putting the entire area in turmoil. The situation was no better in Jharkhand area of Bihar where the various political parties had supported the tribals' demand for a separate Jharkhand state. After a long struggle, which many a time, became violent, Jharkhand was made a separate state in 2001.

The national importance of Jharkhand lies in the fact that while the area constitutes 2.5 percent of the national area, it produces 28 percent of the mineral wealth of the country. The area produces the greater part of the country's coal and iron, as a consequence of which Jharkhand has always attracted outsiders, who came and settled down here. In the pre-independence era, these outsiders, protected by the powerful British rulers, exploited the tribals mercilessly which compelled the tribals to revolt. The eminent educationist, and himself a tribal from Jharkhand area, Dr. A.K. Dhan, pointed out to the present writer, "The very first uprisings against the British rulers originated in Jharkhand; for example, in 1785, there was Tilka Manjhi Movement; in 1797, the Munda uprising in 1798-99, the Bhumij Revolt of Manbhum, in 1800, the Chero uprising of Palamau and so on. The present Jharkhand movement is a continuation of these tribal uprisings. The uprisings have been described by historians and sociologists as "cries of despair." After independence, the exploitation of tribals has become more callous, systematized and intense." The Birsa Munda uprising of 1900-04 was mercilessly put down by the British as had been the earlier revolts. In 1928 a tribal organisation, Unnati Samaj, demanded a separate state of Jharkhand from the Simon Commission. In 1936, Adi Mahasabha was founded and in 1948, Jaipal Singh founded the Jharkhand Party. The Jharkhand party finally merged with the Congress and this resulted in the formation of a number of political parties, all demanding the creation of a separate Jharkhand State. Finally in 1995 at the instance of the Central Government, the Jharkhand Area Autonomous Council (JAAC) was constituted.

Jharkhand is the home of some of the major and most ancient tribes of India i.e., the Mundas, Oraons, Kharis, Santhals, Hos etc. These tribes have their own languages and culture. Their original religion is Sarna, which is a form of nature worship. However, a number of them have been converted to Christianity and Hinduism.

The significant feature of Jharkhand movement was that the people of the area belonging to different tribes, as well as the indigenous non-tribals, were united in their demand for a separate state. This was because of exploitation by outsiders. It is important to note in this respect that 70 per cent of the total revenue of the state of Bihar was generated by Jharkhand whereas only 20 per cent of the state revenue was spent here. To give an example, only 5 per cent of the cultivated land was irrigated in Jharkhand as compared to 40 per cent in the rest of the state. Similarly, in matters of electricity, roads and hospitals, Jharkhand was far behind the rest of Bihar. To add to this, was the fact that the bulk of scams in Bihar had taken place in Jharkhand i.e. Forest Scam, Bitumen Scam, Tribal Land scam, Fodder Scam etc.

The Indian constitution provides reservation in government jobs and educational facilities for tribals. The Sixth Schedule contains special provision for the administration of tribal areas in Assam, Meghalaya, Tripura and Mizoram. The governments in different states have launched various welfare measures to ameliorate the conditions of the tribals. To give one example, the Madhya Pradesh Government launched a movement to help the 46 tribes and seven primitive tribes which accounted for 23 per cent of the state population, under which a number of developmental programmes were launched. But this could not satisfy the tribals who were determined to have a separate state. They succeeded when a new state of Chattisgarh was created, out of tribal areas of Madhya Pradesh, in 2001.

There is a need of formulating a comprehensive plan to uplift the condition of the tribals. But there is a primary condition to maintain law and order and create a peaceful atmosphere in the tribals areas which will also lead to creation of real tribal leaders with an effective tribal movement. Only then the real upliftment of the tribals will take shape.

Women's Movement in India*

The women's movement in the entire world, including India, has developed out of the feminist philosophy which speaks of man's

*See also Chapter VII—The Gender Problem.

domination of woman as a curse inflicted on her by a socially-structured-male society. What is actually a natural sex-inequality, is made a social gender inequality and then all sorts of values (if at all they, really, are) are associated with masculinity. The female, feminism believes, is regarded as inferior to the male in all qualities. Physically she is dubbed as weak; intellectually, as a being with less or no wisdom; socially, she has a place lower than man. She is considered ineligible for all public life; her life is confined to the private life of the family—mothering the babies. Even in the family, she is not only second, but is always secondary. All her miseries, the feminists say, are the result of man's atrocities. Because she is physically weaker than man, she is made to lead a subordinate life. Almost half of humanity lives and has, in the past lived, in servitude, dependent always, at one or another, on man: be he a father, brother, husband or son. Until recently, public or political life had been, for her an area out of bounds. This is the situation in most parts of the world to-day for most women. The rise and development of feminism have helped in not only understanding women's woes but also in bettering their conditions—social, economic, familial. Indeed, there have been cases of dowry deaths, brides burning and of Sati, yet women, today, is no more a commodity to be bought and sold at man's whims.

Nature has bestowed certain sexual or biological inequalities and in the context of women's movements, it is to be noted that these movements are not against sexual inequalities. They are against gender discrimination.

Over the years, the women's movements has developed a theory which sees the relationship between the sexes as one of inequality, subordination and oppression and regards this as a problem of political power rather than a fact of nature. What it means is that the feminists regard the distinction between men and women not merely as biological, but also sociological and thereafter political; men and women are made biologically different, but they are seen, regarded and structured socially as different genders. The masculine gender, being physically strong and having made himself as the superior being, exploits woman by considering her an inferior being, a slave, and a commodity.

In India, there have been scores of women's organisations that have been representing the women's cause. Among them, the All India Women's Conference is the oldest one, which was formed in 1927 during the freedom struggle. This does not mean there were no women's groups before 1927. In 1910, Sarla Devi Choudhurani founded the Bharat Stree Mahamandal. She was highly critical of male champions of women's cause. She said, "They are the so-called social reformers. They advertise themselves as champions of the weaker sex; equal opportunities for women, female education and female emancipation are some of their pet subjects of oratory at the annual show. They even make honest efforts at object lessons in the above subjects by persuading educated ladies to come up on their platform and speak for themselves. But woe to the women, if they venture to act for themselves." During this period, there have also been various Mahila Samitis, Women's clubs and Ladies Societies in various cities and towns of India. Gandhi also stood for women's emancipation and incited them to join the national movement which they did and played a commendable role in picketing and demonstrations. The key women's leaders during the freedom struggle were Saroj Nalini Dutt, Sarojini Naidu (who also became the first woman President of Congress), Kamladevi Chattopadhyay and Hansa Mehta who presented the national flag in the constituent Assembly on behalf of the Indian women. It was due to their active role in India's struggle for freedom that the Constitution recognised the equality of man and woman and the State was debarred from making any distinction on account of sex. However much needed to be done to ameliorate the conditon of Indian women and they fought for it through AIWC and other organisations. As a result, the special Marriage Act (1954) the Hindu Marriage Act and Divorce Act (1955), the Adoption Act (1956), Interstate Succession Act (1956) and Dowry Acts were enacted.

AIWC still continues to exist. However, there are two more national organisations of women i.e. National Federation of Indian Women (NFIW) which was formed in 1954 and All India Democratic Women's Association (AIDWA) formed in 1981. These women's organisations also have close political affiliation. While AIWC is sympathetic to Congress, NFIW and AIDWA have close links with CPI and CPM respectively. Besides, we also have Mahila Samitis and organisations with various names who espouse the women's cause. To cite few examples, the Akhil Bhartiya Janvadi Mahila Samiti, Centre for Women's Development Studies, Joint Women's Programme, Mahila Dakshata Samiti, Young Women's Christian Organisation and other women's groups working at State, regional or local level. There are also women's groups like self Employed Women's Association (SEWA) and Working Women's Forum (WWF) who look after the interest of the women in the informal sector, like SEWA in Delhi looks after the Zardosi workers and used- 'lifafa' makers in the Turkman Gate area. The women's organisations have concentrated on many issues from gender injustices being meted out to individual women, victims of rape and police highhandedness, anti-price movements, demands for civic amenities, water supply, anti eve-teasing campaigns to anti- arrack movements. During the struggle for a separate Uttarakhand state, the women under the leadership of Uttarakhand Mahila Manch took active part, along with men, and had to face police atrocities. The Uttarakhand Mahila Manch also mobilised the womenfolk into the Uttarakhand movement, and organised them to launch a campaign against the sale of arrack in the region in order to eliminate male drunkenness. In Andhra Pradesh also, the women went for mass mobilisation against arrack which compelled various political parties to adopt or support a policy of prohibition which was seen as women's burning issues.

However, the women's movement in India has largely remained urban. Women's participation in politics has also been on the decline, while the participation of other groups like farmers and dalits have increased due to their organised movements. While the women's vote in terms of numbers is not much behind that of the men, their representation in legislative bodies have been very poor. The highest representation of women in Lok Sabha was in 1984 and that too only eight per cent. Women's representation in political party's decision-making bodies is very low. In State Assemblies also, the women have a meagre representation. Not surprisingly by the Report of the Committee on the Status of Women in India indicated that the women are alienated from the political system. It noted that the women are increasingly 'losing faith in the political process to change their condition in life' and may opt out of the political system.' Therefore, many political scientists are feeling a need to have an exclusive women's political party which would not only increase their participation in representation but also help change their condition in a very big way. In the present decade, two important steps have been taken to increase women's participation in the political system—Firstly, there has been 33 per cent reservation for women in the Panchayati Raj Institution and Municipalities under the 73rd and 74th Constitution (Amendment) Acts in 1992. Secondly, there is a proposed Bill in Parliament to provide 33 per cent reservation of seats in the legislative bodies. But the experience of women's reservation in Panchayati Raj Institutions is not very encouraging though hailed as the greatest example of women's political empowerment in the world where the women have been either surrogates to their menfolk or there have been many instances of women being victimised for their stands. Even if the proposed Bill for women's reservation in legislatures is passed, in the growing atmosphere of criminals entering politics and becoming members of august bodies, decent people, including the women, may not find it conducive to join politics. In such cases, there is every likelihood that the reserved quota would be filled by the wives and daughters of the powerful male politicians who might have little inclination for women's causes. Such examples are not exceptional in Indian politics with the extreme case of Bihar where the male Chief Minister got his wife appointed as Chief Minister before going to jail on corruption charges, substantiating his claim aptly that he would rule Bihar from the Jail. The fact remains that the political emancipation of women can only take place when it is preceded with social and economic emancipation, plus a healthy development of democratic processes devoid of corruption and criminalisation of politics.

In India, women are subjected to gender discrimination right from birth. Female infanticide is widely prevalent in different parts of the country especially in the South. According to one estimate between 1981 and 1991, more than four million girl children joined the ranks of India's missing women and an estimated 1.2 million lives were snuffed out either through abortion or post-natal murders. The girls are allowed to remain undernourished and, therefore, the female mortality rate is much higher than that of boys. As they grow, they are denied the proper educational facilities, nourishment and medical facilities. They are seen as a burden to the family and if not handled well, likely to bring dishonour to the family for which they are subjected to untold miseries culminating in their murders or 'suicide.' The number of dowry harassments and deaths have been increasing along with India's economic and material development. The gender bias is reflected not only in political and social attitudes but also in police, judiciary, civil services, professional services like scientists, engineers, doctors etc. where they are highly unrepresented. In many places, they are denied job opportunities because the job is unsuited for them and men are better equipped to do the job. There is also a feeling that the right place for women is her kitchen and rearing children and looking after members of the family within the four walls. True, there have many social legislations designed to achieve betterment of women, they remain paper tigers rarely to be followed. Women also have to face sexual harassment on the streets and at the workplace. The position of dalit women is worste because they have to face discrimination on account of caste also.

Yet the women's movement in India is gaining momentum. As a result of their untiring efforts, a National Commission for Women

(NCW) Act was passed in 1990 to look after their problems. Earlier the Rajiv Government prepared the National Perspective Plan for Women (NPP) which listed goals to be achieved by 2000 for women's development. Besides the reservation in PRIs and municipalities and the proposed Bill regarding the reservation in legislative bodies, the important point is that there is growing awareness among the women about their ills and the need for their elimination. Another important aspect is that there have been allegations that the women's movement in India is dominated by the elite women belonging to the upper middle class and middle class but, as Devaki Jain puts it, "The women's movement in India has been noticed for its identification with the masses." It has echoed the demands and grievances of all the women, including the deprived ones, of India. There are instances where the leadership has come from the lower class. To cite an example, Hosaina Begum, a Zardosi worker had been the Vice President of SEWA, Delhi, an organisation of Zardosi workers and used-paper 'envelope (bag)' makers living in the Turkman gate area of Delhi.

The Supreme Court also contributed towards providing a good environment for women to develop. It gave a landmark judgement to prevent sexual harassment of women workers in their place of work. The Supreme Court defined sexual harassment and included in its ambit, unwelcome sexually-determined behaviour, such as physical contact and advances, a demand or requirement for sexual favours, sexually-coloured remarks, showing pornography and any other unwelcome physical verbal or non-verbal conduct of a sexual nature. According to Supreme Court, these acts constitute sexual harassment of a women worker, if committed in a place of work and where the victims apprehends that they are meant to intimidate and cause health and security hazards. Such sexual harassment is discrimination because it is designed to affect appointment and even promotion and also to create an environment which will be inimical to her. The judgement makes it the duty of employers of public and private institutions to prevent acts of sexual harassment and to provide procedures for the resolution, settlement or even prosecution of such acts. To prevent such harassment, the employers of public and private institutions are required to take following steps:

(i) To notify, publish and distribute the sexual harassment notices as defined by the Supreme Court

(ii) The government and public enterprises should include in their mutual behaviour and disciplinary code, provisions to stop sexual harassments and punishment for the offenders.

(iii) The private sector employees are to include the provisions under the Industrial Employment (Regulation Order) Act 1946.

(iv) The women should be provided adequate working conditions in terms of work, holidays, health and sanitation so that they should not feel disadvantaged because of being women.

The Supreme Court directive also includes the prosecution of the accused as per the law and a choice before the victim to get her or the offender transferred. It also directs the employers to set up a complaint committee for the purpose which may include NGOs or other professional counsellors. The Complaint Committee should be presided over by a women and it should be composed of at least half women. The complaints should be settled within a timeframe. If a woman is harassed by some outsider, then the employer or manager should take all necessary and adequate steps to help the victim. These directives are binding and mandatory so long as adequate legislation is not effected.

The women's movements in India have become very strong, despite the fact that it remain scattered and not unified. This is also natural, given the vast size of the country. The empowerment of women will lead to a better rational society and it may be a remedy to India's growing population. However, the women's movement has also resulted in new social conflicts. The women no longer accept the subordinate position in the family and outside. There have been unjustified demands and expectations also. As a result, there have been instances of male harassment by the womenfolk as well. As the law only protects the female and not the male, the latter is always in a vulnerable position. There have been misuse of anti-dowry and other legislation by the womenfolk. It is also a fact that, in many cases, the enemy of woman is no other than another woman. The women's movement has to think all these aspects and others which are not necessarily the result of male domination.

Dalit* Movement in India

Dalit movement is meant to uplift the lower castes within the Hindus. They were formerly called further untouchables. Gandhi called them Harijans, other words used are Scheduled Castes as used in the Indian Constitution, depressed classes and Bahujans. The term "dalit", it has been pointed out, came from Maharashtra where the dalit movement

*The term 'Dalit' was coined by Dr. B.R. Ambedkar. Later on Dalit Panther Movement used it and now it is being used commonly. They constitute more than one-sixth of Indian population, roughly 160 million people.

has been very strong. In Marathi, the term means ground, broken or reduced to pieces generally. Thus dalit means a person who has been deliberately ground or broken to pieces by others. The dalit movement, which has become a force to be reckoned with in the present decade, can be traced to various lower caste movements during the colonial period led by Mahatma Phule, Dr. Ambedkar in Maharashtra, Ramaswamy Naicker in Tamil Nadu and others. Now the dalit movement has become a very powerful movement demanding equality and betterment. Particularly in Maharashtra, the dalits have developed their own literature, theatre and culture which echoes not only the discrimination and oppression, but also a sense of identity and self-confidence.

According to M.S.A. Rao, the protest ideologies of the Backward classes movement in India has revealed four organising Principles. (a) Reinterpretation of myths of origin or of one's own religion (b) rejection of Hinduism and Aryan religion and culture, (c) civil rights and (d) class conflict.

Reinterpretation of myths of origin or one's own religion

Many backward castes such as Ahirs in North India, the Gopas in Bengal, the Gaulis in Maharashtra, the Gollas in Andhra Pradesh and Karnataka, the Konars in Tamil Nadu claimed the descendence from Lord Krishna's famous Kshatriya dynasty of Yadu. They organised themselves into an All India Yadava Association. In Bihar, they donned the sacred thread (symbol of the twice-born reserved for only Brahmins, Kshatriyas and Banias.) This was to claim a high varna status to gain respect, honour and esteem. M.S.A. Rao points out, "This was not a process of imitation but a language of aggression by which sections of the Backward classes challenged the monopoly of the upper castes in terms of access to the rituals and religious services of brahmanical Hinduism from which they had been banned for centuries." The bhangi castes in North India call themselves `Valmiki' claiming their lineage from Valmiki, the author of Ramayana. The modern dalits regard Vyasa, son of a Brahmin sage and a fishergirl, as a fellow-dalit. The dalits in Maharashtra believe that:

(i) "they are and were the creators of culture as Dr. Ambedkar is reported to have said

"The Hindus wanted the Vedas and they sent for Vyasa who was not a caste Hindu.

The Hindus wanted an Epic and they sent for Valmiki who was an untouchable.

The Hindus wanted a Constitution, and they sent for me.

(ii) they were the lords of the earth, the original inhabitants of India and

(iii) that they were and are a militant people, with heroes who used their strength in a self-sacrificial way for their people."

Rejection of Hinduism, Aryan religion and culture

In Kerala till 1935, the Izhavas belonged to the scheduled caste category to be untouched by the clean castes. A great social reformer, Shri Narayan Guru Swamy gave them a new religion of one God, one religion and one caste which transformed their lifestyle and outlook. Thus a parallel religion to Hinduism was formed which gave Izhavas a sense of self respect and esteem.

In Tamil Nadu, the Dravida Kazhagam movement attacked and rejected the Aryan culture and religion and instead idealized the Dravidian culture and religion. To the movement, Ravana was virtuous while Lord Rama was wicked. Ramaswamy Naicker, its leader, revolted against the Brahmanical way of life. In Maharashtra, under the leadership of Dr. Ambedkar, the Mahars rejected Hinduism and adopted Buddhism. According to Dr. Ambedkar, Buddhism was a the most revolutionary and egalitarian religion of India as it arose and grew out of the struggle against the caste system. He emphasised that the Buddha created his Sangha on a model of a casteless society. This conversion reflected the message of new identity, says M.S.A. Rao, that the Mahars now belong to a religion which stands for egalitarian values and hence they are superior to the caste Hindus.

In 2002 a Dalit leader tried to add a new dimension to *Ramjanam Bhumi vs Babri Masjid* dispute. He *claimed that in Ayodhya neither* a Babri Masjid nor a Ram Temple existed but a Buddhist Vihara. The leader said, " Ram is a mystical figure. But Buddha was a living legend. Its a Hindutva conspiracy to deny Buddhists their historical legacy."

Besides these two ideologies of reinterpretation and rejection which are religious in nature, the ideologies of (iii) civil rights and (iv) class conflict have been secular in nature. While the civil rights ideology of the dalit demanded equality in educational, economic and political opportunities based on democracy. The class conflict ideology encouraged them to destroy Hindu caste system, the landlords, capitalists and moneylenders. They have been very militant also, like the Dalit Panthers in Maharashtra.

The Dalit movement originates from the fact that for centuries, the dalits have been subjected to various kinds of social, economic and political exploitation and oppression. They have been treated as less than human and were made untouchable. During the freedom movement, their cause was championed by Gandhi himself who desired to be born as an untouchable in his next birth. After independence, the Indian Constitution—drafted by a committee under the headship of Dr. Ambedkar who has been called the father of the Indian Constitution—provided for social justice and equality. *Article 14* provided for equality before the law and the equal protection of the laws within the Indian territory. *Article 15* prohibited discrimination based on grounds of religion, race, caste, sex or place of birth. *Article 16* gave equality of opportunity in employment under the state and also gave the state the freedom to reserve posts and appointment for any backward class. *Article 17* abolished the practice of untouchability and made its practice a constitutional offence.

But this does not mean that the backward classes were uplifted, in fact only a fundamental step towards it was launched by the constitution. The Dalits remained poor though a considerable number of their people became prosperous as a result of reservation in public employment. But the bulk of them, who primarily live in villages, are still denied civil rights and subjected to oppression and exploitation. In 1989, the Indian Parliament enacted the Scheduled Caste and Scheduled Tribes (Prevention of atrocities) Act which defines 15 types of atrocities that would attract punishment under this law. But there have been reports of this law being misused, particularly in UP.

Dalits are not something unique to Hindu society. They exist in other religions as well, though they are not scheduled caste in the legal sense. For example, the Helas of Ujjain who are Sunni Muslims and work as sweepers and untouchability is practised against them by the Muslims. They are prohibited from entering Idgah for Namaz. The Muslim Dalits include, Jolaha, Nutt, Bakkro, Bhatiyara, Kunjra, Dhunia, Kalal, Dafali Halakhor, Dhobi, Lalbegi, Gorkan, Meeishikar, Check, Rangrej and Dairzi. These castes have been abused by the high caste Muslims'. Dalits are present among Indian Christians also. In 1996, just before the announcement of Lok Sabha elections, the P.V. Narasimha Rao Government tried in vain to extract political mileage by getting an ordinance promulgated by the President giving reservations to the Dalit Christians. According to one estimate, the Dalit Christians account for 70 percent of the total Christian population and of late, the caste-based discrimination against them is coming to the surface However, the National Commission for the Scheduled Caste in 2007 rejected the demand for reservation for Dalit Muslims and Christians on the grounds that untouchability being the main criterion for reservation, is peculiar to the Hindu religion.

However, at the very outset, the Dalit movement is highly fragmented despite the fact that all political parties prefer upliftment of Dalits. In Maharashtra, there is the Republican Party of India which was able to unite ten warring Dalit leaders, Prakash Ambedkar, Ramdas Athavale, Raju Dhale, T.M. Kamble, B.C. Kamble, Shiv Ram Mogha, Jogendra Kawade, Namdeo Dhasal, R.S. Gavai, Ghanshyam Talwakar in 1995. But the unity was shortlived and differences among the dalit leaders became apparent. Even the second wife of Dr. Ambedkar, now in her eighties, and her son Prakash Ambedkar, do not see eye to eye with each other. To Savita 'Mai' Ambedkar (Ambedkar's second wife) Prakash Ambedkar is a headache and because of him, the movement will suffer. She thinks that she has the requisite 'charisma' to lead the dalits. In North India, Bahujan Samaj Party (BSP) led by Kanshi Ram is leading the dalits. As a result, the dalit votes, which had been a traditional vote bank of the Congress, are increasingly switching over to BSP, especially in Uttar Pradesh. The BSP is also widening its support base in Madhya Pradesh and Punjab. But in 1997, there was a split in BSP. In Bihar, Ram Vilas Paswan formed his Dalit Sena which, however has not been able to achieve much success. In Tamil Nadu, the dalits are highly divided into as many as 16 factions. The Devendra Kula Vellalar Federation, Republican Party of India-Shaktidasan faction, Republican Party of India—Dr. Seppan faction, Indian Natives Association, Ambedkar People's Liberation Front, Dalit Action Committee, Ambedkar Indian Democratic Movement, Ambedkar Freedom Panthers, Ambedkar Freedom Tigers, Dalit Youth Brigade, BSP, Tamil Nadu Unit, The Movement for Uprising of the Oppressed, the Confederation of Ambedkar Organisation, SC and ST Federation of Tamil Nadu, The Tamil Nadu Wing of the All India Ambedkar Movement and the Coordination Committee of the Arunthathiyars.

The situation is further complicated by the fact that even within dalits there is a hierarchical order, some are supposed to be lower in caste rank. Then, there is some confusion as to who is a Dalit. Some identify dalits with the list of Scheduled Castes enshrined in the Indian Constitution. This was also the view of Dr. Ambedkar. Kanshi Ram has preferred to use the term Bahujan instead of dalits and his category includes non-Brahmin, non-Kshatriya, non-Vaisya and the religious minorities. The Dalit Panthers of Maharashtra would define dalits "as members of the Scheduled Castes and Scheduled Tribes, neo Buddhists, the working people, the landless and poor peasants, women and all those who are being exploited politically, economically, and in the name of religion." However, Dalit Panthers are dominated by one jati among the Scheduled Castes i.e. Mahars in Maharashtra. This is also true of the Republican Party in Maharashtra which again is dominated by Mahars to which Dr. Ambedkar belonged. The Andhra Dalit Mahasabha is dominated by the Malas. There is an increasing tendency among the Scheduled Castes to launch their own movement. The Dalits welcomed the implementation of Mandal Commission report which extended reservation to other Backward Classes (OBCs) to the tune of 27 per cent. But then there have been violent conflicts between the dalits and OBCs, at least in Tamil Nadu. It is also a fact that the dalit leaders, like all political leaders, are also fast losing credibility among the people. They have also been accused of corruption and political opportunism and being power-hungry.

The Dalit movement in India is becoming increasingly violent to counter violence against the dalits in villages. In 1972, in Maharashtra, Dalit Panthers, a militant group was formed. A similar group was also formed in Gujarat . However, these groups have not remained united and are plagued with internal conflicts. Similarly in North India, the BSP supporters have frequently taken recourse to violence to express their anger against the upper castes. This has led to caste rivalries and conflicts in the Indian political system. In 1987, the Maharashtra Government brought out a volume on Dr. Ambedkar which contained Ambedkars unpublished book, Riddles of Hinduism which was taken as an insult to Hinduism by the Shiv Sena who held a huge demonstration against the publication and demanded a ban on the book. Various dalit groups joined together and organised a counter-demonstration. Later on Shiv Sena performed a purification ceremony of Hutatme Chowk where the dalit demonstration had taken place and which the Shiv Sena claimed had been defiled by the dalits. Ambedkar's abuse of Hindu Gods was countered by a Marathi journal `Sobat' who attacked Mahatma Phule, guru of Dr. Ambedkar and leader of Maharashtra social reform movement during the freedom struggle. In 1978, the Maharashtra Assembly decided to rename the Marathwada University at Aurangabad after Dr. Ambedkar which resulted in large- scale caste riots in Maharashtra. As a result the renaming was suspended. In 1993, a youth belonging to Dalit Panthers immolated himself in support of renaming the University which resulted in demonstration by the various dalit groups to press their demands. Ultimately, the Sharad Pawar Government in 1994 renamed the university. The Shiv Sena called a statewide bandh against the renaming. Bal Thackeray, the Shiv Sena Supremo, charged that the

Ambedkar was an agent of the former Nizam of Hyderabad. In UP, the BSP and BJP entered into an understanding to share power for six months in turn. Accordingly, Mayawati of BSP became the Chief Minister, and started many ambitious' Dalit schemes, mainly to honour Dr. Ambedkar. She further developed the scheme of Ambedkar villages launched by Mulayam Singh Yadav of Samajvadi Party in 1990-91, according to which over 11,000 Ambedkar villages were identified for development, which had more than 50 per cent Harijan population. Mayawati made an amendment according to which villages with 30 per cent Harijan population could be included in the scheme. She also started a unique version of land reforms in which land deeds were distributed to landless Dalits. Under the scheme, the gram sabha land distributed to landless and later disputed would go back to dalits and it was reported by May 31, 1997, 5503 dalits had been returned the land and another 7,249 such disputes had been identified. A few other schemes intended to uplift the dalits' socio-economic conditions were as follows:

(i) Over 100 statues of various sizes of Ambedkar were built in Lucknow, Kanpur, Allahabad and other towns.
(ii) A Rs 100 crore Ambedkar Park in Lucknow was built for which many financial irregularities have come to surface.
(iii) In memory of social reformers like Ambedkar, a gigantic square was being contructed in Lucknow.
(iv) Mayawati declared that twenty five per cent Station House Officers' posts (SHOs) at UP would be reserved for dalit officers.
(v) Another controversial decision was creation of three commissionarates, eight districts and 12 Tehsils which were named after Gautam Buddha and his family, Jyotiba Phule and Shahuji Maharaj.
(vi) Under another scheme, named after Ambedkar, marriage allowances for dalit girls were doubled.

However, Mayawati's actions were not beyond controversies. Besides the criticism that funds were diverted for parks and statutes in a state which is highly backward, with Lucknow, the capital of UP, lacking even basic amenities such as drinking water and drainage, little efforts were made to really rejuvenate the dalits. All the schemes and projects were merely political in nature. It also resulted in anger, among the upper caste population, especially against the schemes that named districts after Dalit leader's names, and the Ambedkar Statues. In some places desecration of Ambedkar statutes took place. This also happened in certain areas of Maharashtra, most horrifying was that of Ghatkopar in Bombay in which the police had to resort to firing and killing 10 persons on the spot and forty three were injured. On July 12, Mumbai Bandh was called by the Republican Party of India which was supported by most of the opposition parties. Bandhs and demonstrations were also held in 35 other towns of Maharashtra. In retaliation to the desecration of Ambedkar statues, the Shivaji statue in Mumbai was disfigured. The trouble also spread to the neighbouring Gujarat where bandhs was sponsored by as many as 26 Dalit organisations on July 16 and where police firing took five lives and left 10 people injured by July 20. Later on more people were killed in various towns of Gujarat. During the bandh, the civic headquarters building in Rajkot was set ablaze, buses of the Ahmedabad Municipal Transport stoned and police had to resort to firing in many places, despite the directives of the Chief Minister Shankar Singh Waghela—whose Rashtriya Janata Party had supported the Dalit organisation protest moves—to exercise restraint.

Thus the Dalit upsurge led to retaliation by the caste groups in India. Arun Shourie wrote a book-Worshipping False Gods, on Ambedkar and the facts which have been erased—in which Dr. Ambedkar has been portrayed as a self-centred unpatriotic, power hungry, anti-national, and a stooge of the British during the freedom struggle. Arun Shourie writes, "There is not one instance, not one single, solitary instance, in which Ambedkar participated in any activity connected with the struggle to free the country." Shourie also refuses to believe that Ambedkar was the father of the Indian Constitution, as he only piloted the draft constitution. According to him, Ambedkar's conversion to Buddhism was also mere opportunism. However, the most vehement attack on Ambedkar was that he collaborated with the British for material gains. One can only comment that this is a very sorry affair in Indian society where Dalit awakening, on the one hand, has become more a political issue than social or economic which in any case will not help the Dalit cause, the caste-Hindu retaliation (both intellectually and on the streets by desecration of Dalit leaders' statues), on the other, will only encourage the cleavages in the society. The obvious fear is that in the process, the real issue will be sidetracked. Partly, Dalit leaders are to be blamed for this sorry state of affairs. Dalit's upliftment cannot take place by building statues and parks in the name of dalit leaders and by renaming Tehsils and districts after them. This, itself, is a case of political opportunism.

Another case of political opportunism could be seen in Andhra Pradesh where the Chief Minister took up the Dalit cause. He led a group of Dalits in Laxmi Bhavani temple in Peddareddypet village of Medak district in 2001. Similarly, in other temples Dalits were allowed entry in a 10 day-campaign. The government boasted of it as a symbolic gesture which would break the social barriers of untouchability. It was also termed as empowerment of Dalits. But after a year it was discovered that;

- Almost all temples, which Dalits entered, were "cleansed" and whitewashed;
- Caste Hindus, in connivance with revenue and police officials, were foisting false cases against the Dalits;
- Many of them were being denied work in the government's food-for-work programme and were forced to migrate to other villages in search of jobs;
- They are barred from entering temples in 110 villages. In remaining villages, Dalits either had their own places of worship or were simply not interested in angering upper castes by asking for worship rights.
- Dalits are not allowed to share the same bus shelters with upper castes in 226 villages; are not allowed haircut by local barbers in 76 villages; are not allowed to cremate their dead on the village land in 74 villages; and are denied access to the drinking water wells and taps in 34 villages.

Thus nothing changed for the Dalits and the Dalits were quietly forgotten after the 10-day campaign.

The need of the hour is to wage a united struggle of Dalits under a united and real (even apolitical) leadership for a radical change for social and economic upliftment of the Dalits. Violence and counter-violence is no answer to a problem which has been in existent from time immemorial. Further, the Dalits must sink their differences and treat themselves as one cohesive unit. For this, discrimination practised within the Dalits against their own folk should be eradicated. There is also a need to forge alliance with other backward classes (OBCs). From this point of view, the clash between the Thevars and the Scheduled Castes in Tamil Nadu which left some 90 people dead in three months, in 1997, was a very unfortunate development. There have been violent clashes among the Dalits in Maharashtra. In Hyderabad the official Ambedkar Jayanti celebrations in 2008 ended abruptly because two Dalit communities of Mala and Madiga fought with each other and the police had to intervene. The caste people will also have to show restraint and corrective measures be used which would instil confidence among the Dalits that there is no opposition to them so far as their social upliftment is concerned. There is also no denying of the fact that Ambedkar was a nationalist. So far as the economic upliftment of the dalits is concerned, it should be taken as part and parcel of overall economic development of India's teeming millions. This is more necessary in the wake of liberalisation and privatisation in which the market forces have been allowed to reign freely and the poverty, unemployment, illiteracy, homelessness and frustration continue to be the cardinal features of the Indian political system.

References

In the preparation of this chapter many newspapers and news magazines have been consulted

Arora N.D. and Awasthy S.S., *Political Theory*, 1996, New Delhi, Har-Anand Publications.

Desai A.R. (Ed.) *Peasant Struggles in India*, 1985, New Delhi, Oxford University Press.

Dhingra I.C. *The Indian Economy Resources, Planning, Development and Problems*, 1995, New Delhi, Sultan Chand and Sons.

Kumar Nita, *Women as Subjects*, 1994, Calcutta Stree in Association with the Book Review Literary Trust, New Delhi.

Misra S.K. and Puri V.K., *Indian Economy—Its Development Experience*, 1995, Bombay, Himalaya Publishing House.

Pandey V.P., *Issues in Indian Politics*, 1985, Delhi, Durga Publications.

Saksena H.S., *Safeguards for the Scheduled Castes and Tribes: Founding Father's views (An Exploration of the Constituent Assembly Debates)*, 1981, New Delhi, Uppal Publishing House

Sengupta Padmini, *The Study of Women of India*, 1974, Delhi, Indian Book Company.

Thapar Ramesh (Ed.), *Tribe Caste and Religion 1981*, New Delhi, Macmillan India ltd.

Rao MSA, (Ed.), *Social Movements in India 1984*, New Delhi, Manohar Publications.

Zelliot Eleanor, *From Untouchable to Dalit*, Essays on the Ambedkar Movement, 1996, New Delhi, Manohar Publications.

Hindustan Times p.11, New Delhi, March 8, 2002 and p. 13, October 1, 2002.

Statesman New Delhi 21 December 2001.

BROKEN PEOPLE, caste violence against India's Untouchable, 1998, USA, Human Rights Watch.

CHAPTER XXI

The Problem of Underdevelopment

The most crucial problem of Indian political system is that its economy is underdeveloped. When we talk of underdevelopment, our yardsticks are the developed economies of western countries. The underdeveloped countries have low per capita income, high infant mortality, low life expectancy, large scale illiteracy and lower industrial and agricultural development. There is agonising poverty and fewer medical and educational facilities. The basic cause of this underdevelopment has been the exploitative colonial rule which also accounts for the relative prosperity in the developed economies. In the Indian context we will study the problem of underdevelopment with reference to:

(i) Poverty
(ii) Illiteracy
(iii) Regional Imbalances, and
(iv) Environmental Degradation

Poverty

According to the Government of India's Economic Survey 2001-02 poverty in India had fallen from '36 percent in 1993-94 to 23 to 26 per cent in 1999-2000 according to alternative estimates. However, India is one of the poorest countries in the world where the measurement of the magnitude of the poverty itself is a severe problem before the political analysts and economists. In general terms, one can define poverty as the denial of minimum basic requirements of food, shelter and clothing. The World Bank defined absolute poor as those having income less than $1 per day per head which according to this estimate puts 525 million Indian people as absolutely poor (see UNDP date in HDR 1999) The Sixth Five Year Plan defined it by calculating a minimum consumption of food in terms of calories and taking into account some essential non-food items like shelter and clothing and thus demarcated a poverty line. Thus, the minimum consumption of food in rural and urban areas were taken to be 2400 calories and 2100 calories per person respectively and some essential non-food items at Rs 65 and Rs 75 per capita per month at 1977-78 prices respectively. Accordingly, the Sixth Five Year Plan estimated the Indian population below the poverty line in 1977-78 to be 38.19 per cent in the urban areas and 50.82 per cent in the rural areas with a total of 48.13 per cent poverty in the rural and urban areas. In 1992, the Central Government claimed that by 1987-88 the poverty in India had been reduced and that there were about 29.9 crores poor Indians, 33.4 crores in rural areas and 20.1 crores in urban areas. The later official estimates of people living below poverty line in 1993-94 could put any Indian into a pleasant situation as the rural poverty had further been reduced to 18.1 per cent; 19.9 in rural areas and 13.2 in urban areas. However, many economists disputed these claims and ironically they turned out to be true. In 1997, the Planning Commission adopted a new formula to fix the number of people below poverty line. According to this new formula, the minimum living standards which defined poverty remained unchanged, they were only upgraded taking into account the decline in the purchasing power of the rupee. This revised the earlier estimates of Indian poverty thus:

Earlier Official Estimates

	1987-88	1993-94
Rural	33.4	19.9
Urban	20.1	13.2
Combined	29.9	18.1

New official estimates based on modified expert group methodology

	1987-88	1993-94	2004-05
Rural	30.09	37.27	28.3
Urban	38.20	32.36	25.7
Combined	38.86	35.97	27.5

Source: The Times of India 12 March, 1997

This revision did not include the hitherto 'non-poor' into poor category as the figures were only updated as per the fall of purchasing power of the rupee. But, it definitely doubled the number of poor persons in India from 162 million to 320 million which meant that a staggering 36 per cent of India's population lived below the poverty line. The notable poorest states in India are Orissa, Bihar, Uttar Pradesh, Madhya Pradesh, Tamil Nadu, West Bengal, Maharashtra and Andhra Pradesh.

The British rule in India has been largely responsible for the poverty in India. After independence, the Indian Government adopted the strategy of rapid economic development to remove the cause of poverty from India. This was the strategy of planned economic development. It was believed that as a result of overall economic development, the employment opportunities would improve and the deprived section would be benefitted. Besides a number of poverty, alleviation programmes were launched in different times. Notable among them were the Integrated Rural Development Programme (IRDP). National Rural Employment Programme (NREP), Rural Landless Employment Programme (RLEGP). Both the NREP and RLEGP were later merged into Jawahar Rozgar Yojna and Employment Assurance Scheme (EAS). These programmes aimed at the upliftment of rural poor. For the upliftment of urban poor, various self-employment schemes were launched for which the funds of the public sector were channelised. Besides the Jawahar Rozgar Yojna, Prime Minister's Rozgar Yojna (PMRY) was launched in 1993-94. In 1995-96, five new programmes of National Social Assistance Programme (NSAP), the Mid-Day Meal Programme, the Rural Group Life Insurance Scheme (RGLIS), the Indira Mahila Yojna (IMY) and the Prime Minister's Integrated Urban Poverty Eradication Programme (PMIUPEP) were introduced.

Another anti-poverty programme called Swarnjayanti Gram Swarojgar Yozna (SGSY) was also launched in the same year by amalgamating earlier programmes like Intergrated Rural Development Programme (IRDP), Development of Women and Children in Rural Areas (DWCRA), Training of Rural Youth for self Employment (TRYSEM), Million wells Scheme (MWS) etc into a single self employment programme. In 2000 Sampoorna Grameen Rozgar Yojana (SGRY) was launched in which Employment Assurance Scheme (EAS) and Jawahar Gram Samridhi Yozna (JGSY) was fully integrated with effect from April 1, 2002.

These efforts have yielded results to some extent as the number of people living below the poverty line has decreased to 25.7 per cent in 2007-08 from 54.9 per cent in 1973-74.

Estimates of Poverty

Year	All India Number (Million)	Poverty Ratio (per cent)	Rural Number (Million)	Poverty Ratio (per cent)	Urban Number (Million)	Poverty Ratio (per cent)
1973-74	321	54.9	261	56.4	60	49.0
1977-78	329	51.3	264	53.1	65	45.2
1983	323	44.5	252	45.7	71	40.8
1987-88	307	38.9	232	39.1	75	38.2
1993-94	320	36.0	244	37.3	76	32.4
1999-2000	260	26.1	193	27.1	67	23.6
2004-05	302	27.5	220	28.3	81	25.7

Source: Planning Commission Economic/Survey 2001-02/2007-08.

The period from 1993-94 to 2004-05 shows that some changes in poverty ratio in rural areas where a decline of nearly four percentage points. However, in urban areas, a much steeper decline of more than seven percent has taken place.

Since 1970s, we find substantial improvement in poverty ratio in the country compared to very high incidence of poverty in 1973-74 when 56.44 people were living below the poverty line. In 2004-05, we observe that barely 27.5 per cent of Indian populace is forced to live below poverty line. Still one must not lose sight of the fact that even these 27.5 per cent poor constitute 302 million human beings. If we have a look at the disaggregated statewise data then quite a few revealing facts emerge. Some of the states have made tremendous progress in settling the problem of poverty. Punjab is one of the most astounding examples where barely 8 per cent people are living in poverty. Contrast this with 46 per cent in Orissa and 40 and near about in Bihar, Chhattisgarh and even West Bengal which has been boasting of commitment to social justice for the last four decades reports a fourth of its population living in poverty. Gujarat and AP have made really rapid strides and have brought down poverty ratio from 46 to 48 per cent to near about 16 per cent. In Rajasthan, incidence of poverty has been halved from over 44 to 22 per cent while even the most progressive states of TN, Karnataka and Maharashtra report poverty ratio of 22.5, 25 and 30.7 per cents in 2004-05. All there figures are higher that the comparative figure for Rajasthan.

However, despite these efforts, poverty is a big challenge before the Indian democracy. It has been argued that the various poverty alleviation programmes have not really benefitted the poor. They remain under-nourished, homeless and starving. In many cases the poverty has led to suicides. The economic development has been retarded because of increasing population. This is despite the fact that colossal amounts have been spent on family planning programmes particularly in Uttar Pradesh, Bihar, Madhya Pradesh and Rajasthan, the states which have contributed to 42 per cent of the population increase in 1980, the family sizes still average over four children, in Uttar Pradesh it is over five. There have also been populist measures, on the part of the politicians for the sake of getting votes from the poor. This has resulted in the loss of credibility of government sponsored programmes. The emphasis on increased production has not benefitted the landless and the various land reform legislations have failed to achieve the desired objectives. Despite the cries of socialistic pattern of society and socialism, the Indian economy has developed on capitalistic path and economic disparities have increased to the disadvantage of the poor. There is also a valid contention that the anti-poverty programmes have been plagued with corruption. Privatisation and liberalisation is further detrimental to the interest of the Indian poor. Under such circumstances, the removal of poverty seems to be a pious wish and politics a means to aggrandise the wishes of the vested interests. The poor, therefore, are increasingly losing interest in the political system which has failed to uplift their conditions. Ultimately, this will have drastic impact on the democratic system and therefore, there is a urgent need of a serious anti-poverty social movement in India to ensure not only the elimination of poverty but also the survival of Indian democracy.

Illiteracy

Another major problem of Indian political system is the widespread illiteracy. In India about 35 percent people are illiterate; 29 per cent drop out at the primary stage A recent study on the state of Indian education pointed out that the gross enrollment rate for class 1 to 5 in the age group 6-11years was about 107% which meant that virtually every child took admission but in the middle category i.e. class 6 to 8 in the age group of 11-14 years , this proportion fell to about 70 per cent; in the class 9 to 12 the proportion dropped to about 40 per cent and in the higher education (18-24 years), it came down to just about 10 per cent. It means that for every ten children in the class I, only one gets the higher education. In fact, India tops in child illiteracy and this is despite the provision of Directive Principle of State Policy under *Article 45* which said 'Provision for free and compulsory education for children- the State shall endeavour to provide within a period of ten years from the commencement of this constitution, for free and compulsory education for all children until they complete the age of fourteen years." This holy directive was never achieved even after more than fifty years but was transformed suddenly into a fundamental right in 2002 vide 86th constitutional amendment which included *Article 21A* which says, "The State shall provide free and compulsory education to all the children of the age of 6-14 years in such a manner as the state, may by law, determine." At the same time a directive was provided in *Article 45* which said, "Provision for early childhood care and education to children below the age of six years- The State shall endeavour to provide early childhood care and education for all children until they complete the age of six years." The 86th constitutional amendment is yet to be notified to become effective.

After the populist exercise in 2002, nothing concrete has been done till date. Some of the features of education in India are as follows:

1. In 1961, about 28 per cent people were literate and now we have about 65 percent literacy rate. It seems to be impressive growth at the outset but unfortunately it leaves over 380 million people which is more than the population of India at the time of Independence. This is further frustrating when we see that in high income countries over 92 per cent of the eligible age group (5-24 years) and in low-income countries, close to 56 percent are studying.
2. While the expenditure on education has increased from 7.92% in 1951-52 to 13.0% in 2006-07 as percentage of all public expenditure, the expenditure as percentage of GDP in not very encouraging. In 1951-52, this was 0.64 and in 2006-07, this figure was 3.6. In 1951-52, the total expenditure on education at all levels was nearly Rs 64.46 crore which increased to Rs 1.33 lakh crore in 2006-07. Obviously, this expenditure is not sufficient for a country with huge populace.
3. Most of the expenditure is spent on salaries of the teachers and little is left for other facilities.
4. In fact low spending on education has in general led to decline in quality of education. It has also created inequity as rich get better education while the majority gets mediocre or poor educational standards.

5. Schools exist without adequate buildings with very little or no teaching materials and without adequate number of qualified teachers. A school in name is provided without the conditions for its effective functioning. Many schools do not even provide basic facilities to students and teachers. The all India percentage for schools with drinking water is 85 per cent. In Assam it is 62 percent. This means that a large number of schools do not even provide drinking water to the students. The toilet facility is also very bad. 58 percent of Indian schools have toilet facilities and the figures for Jharkand, Assam and Chhattisgarh are 25 and 26 and 27 percents respectively. In Chhattisgarh, Jharkhand and Bihar, over 805 schools have no separate toilets for girls. The all India percentage of schools with pucca buildings is 71% while in Orissa and Assam only 22 and 33 percent schools have pucca buildings.
6. The drop out rates among the scheduled caste, scheduled tribes and women are very high. Out of ten in class one, only seven SC students go to the college. The respective figures for ST and women are 5 and 9. 29 per cent children drop out up to class 5, 51% up to class 8 and 62 percent up to class 10. The drop rates among the scheduled castes, scheduled, tribes and women are much higher as it is clear from the table below.

Gross Enrollment Ratio
(% Share of Total 6-24 Age Group)

	All	SC	ST	W
Class 1-5 (6-11 yrs)	107.8	115.3	121.91	104.67
Class 6-8 (11-14 yrs)	69.93	70.17	66.98	65.13
Class 9-12 (14-18 yrs)	39.91	34.68	27.68	35.05
Higher Education (18-24 years)	9.97	6.72	4.86	8.17

Drop-Out Rates (%)
The traditional disadvantages suffered by SC/ST groups are reflected in drop-out rates

	All	SC	ST	W
Up to Class 5	29	3421	42.32	25.42
Up to Class 8	50.84	57.26	65.87	51.28
Up to Class 10	61.92	71.25	78.97	63.88

Selected Education Statistics, MHRD, *The Times of India*, July 6, 2008 Statistics, MHRD.

7. The majority of children in the age group of 6-14 years supplement their parent's earning and are working children. They are not allowed to attend the school by their parents for it means loss of family income.
8. There is a wide gap between the pass percentage at the primary stage and class 12 stages. Till class 10 almost everybody passes. Thus the all India pass percentage till class 4-5 is 95, and till class 7-8, it is 88. Students face their first public examination conducted by different boards in class 10. In class 10 only 64% students pass which slightly increases to 69 in class 12.
9. College education is relatively better. But according to national assessment & Accreditation Council (NAAC), just 9 percent of colleges are of high quality, 66% were of medium quality and 24% were of low quality.
10. The system of distance education is an excellent way of spreading education. However, in the Indira Gandhi national Open University with the enrolment of over 3.2 million students in 2006, only 18% passed and only 2.5 % of the women candidates got through.
11. There cannot be one single alternative schooling model for the working children. Until we are willing to experiment with a variety of choices in alternatives to formal school education, the working child will continue to be an out-of-school child.
12. India has a vast majority of disabled or severely handicapped children belonging to the age group of 4-15 years. Further, there are another 1.7 million mentally handicapped or learning disabled children. There is no significant headway in providing appropriate education for these children.
13. The compulsory education below the age of 14 was never seriously implemented because it was envisaged more as a cost saving mechanism than a desirable objective to be achieved. The investments in the schools have been ineffective.
14. The history of primary education in India is replete with unsuccessful experiments and discarded models of innovation. There is also uniformity in school education. The national curricular framework has led to this uniformity. Infact, the school education should be suited to the local needs.
15. The teachers in the present set up are also helpless and there is no creative academic activity. The text book symbolises the authority under which the teacher must work and they are reduced to mere implementers of state specifications. Therefore, re-establishing text-book preparation as a creative activity and tapping such

potential in the larger society outside the bureaucratic framework is the need of the hour.

16. In the primary schools teaching should be imparted in the mother-tongue and at present 51 languages are used as mediums of instruction. Yet there are millions of children who are forced to learn their primary education in a language other than their mother-tongue.
17. The school teaching continues to be a low-status profession and therefore, teacher training remains a poorly rated academic activity. The training of elementary level teachers in particular, and all the school teachers in general, remain largely untouched by academic grounding in modern child-centred pedagogy. Even the system of evaluation gives greater legitimacy to external examination and continuous comprehensive evaluation has been a matter of rhetoric.

There is no doubt that child literacy in India has been full of rhetoric. The current wave of liberalisation has the inherent potential of ignoring the poverty and also various social development programmes including the Constitution's promise of providing free and compulsory education to all Indian children below 14 years of age. Besides child illiteracy, we also have the problem of adult illiteracy. There have been a number of mass literacy campaigns sponsored by the Government as well as various non-governmental organisations (NGOs), yet adult literacy remains a distant dream. Further, in many cases the females are discriminated against in the opportunities to education.

The aim of literacy is wider than merely providing employment and helping the illiterate to fight against economic exploitation. It is to inculcate rationality in individuals so that they become a responsible and responsive citizen of the Indian democratic experiment which lacks any alternative given the social and regional disparities of this vast country. Education gives them the potential to judge the credibility of the various promises made by the political parties. It also provides them with perspective to evaluate governmental performance. In the absence of a rational measurement which is bestowed only by the education, the illiterates are liable to succumb to not only populist ventures but also to corrupt means so often adopted by Indian political parties. In fact, illiteracy constitutes a scourge to the democratic system and its preservation and, therefore, a serious attempt towards its complete elimination is the need of the hour. However, in Indian context, one should also remember that at times the Indian illiterate population has shown a remarkable maturity in political participation, especially after the infamous emergency of 1975-77 when it rejected the undemocratic working of the political leadership led by Mrs. Indira Gandhi. But this point should not be stretched too far as the same people had been carried away by the slogan of Garibi Hatao (Remove Poverty) earlier in 1971 which eventually turned out to be a populist measure. There is, no doubt, that literacy facilitates the development of an ideal citizen for a healthy democratic setup.

Regional Imbalance

Another aspect of India's underdevelopment is the regional disparities. Stability and prosperity in the country can only be ensured if there is a balanced regional development. The Planning Commission of India rightly noted 'Development of regions and the national economy as a whole have to be viewed as parts of a single process. The progress of the national economy will be reflected in the rate of growth realized by different regions and, in turn, greater development of resources in the regions must contribute towards accelerating the rate of progress of the country as a whole!"

Almost every country in the world suffers from regional imbalances. However, in India it has several distinctive features. Firstly, the possession of natural resources is no indicator of relative prosperity as the states of Bihar and Orissa have rich natural resources but they continue to be highly underdeveloped economies. In contrast Maharashtra is relatively poor in natural resources, yet it is a better off State in India. Thus regional imbalance can be viewed from the fact that certain states in India have developed relatively more than other states. Further, regional imbalances also exist within a state. The hill areas of Uttarakhand (now a seperate state Uttaranchal) in UP and Jharkhand (now a separate state) area of Bihar are backward while the other parts of these states are relatively advanced. Regional disparities can also be viewed from the point of view of rural vs urban areas as the fruits of India's economic development have reached the cities and town while the rural areas have remained inaccessible to them.

Indicators of Regional Imbalance

As Datt and Sundaram point out, the following socio-economic indicators reflect the regional imbalances in the development of 25 states of Indian Union.

(i) *Per capita Incomes:* In the year 1991-92 the national average of per capita income was Rs. 2250 and as many as 19 states had a lower per capita income than the national average. Among them the poorest states were Bihar, Madhya Pradesh, Uttar Pradesh, Orissa, Jammu and Kashmir and Kerala. Their respective positions have also remained unchanged. Only six states registered per capita income higher than the national average. They were Goa, Punjab, Haryana, Maharashtra, Gujarat and Arunachal Pradesh. However, it is to be remembered that in 1970-71, the six states of Punjab, Haryana, Gujarat, Maharashtra, West Bengal and Karnataka were the leading states in per capita incomes but the states of West Bengal and Karnataka suffered due to poor economic growth. The states with higher per capita incomes have witnessed a high degree of agricultural and/or industrial development.

Situation in the year 2005-06 does not indicate any substantial change. Bihar still remain the Poorest so do UP, Orissa and MP. In fact separation of Jharkhand, Uttaranchal and Chhattisgarh from Bihar, UP and MP respectively led to further detuioration in the parent states. Relatively better off segments of parent States have been separated from them. As a result their per capita income appear to be all the more depressed. Among the leading major states, we find that now Haryana is at the top followed by Punjab, Gujarat and HP. Kerala seems to have picked up well. W. Bengal too, is catching up with national average.

(ii) *Percentage of Urban Population to Total Population:* Another indicator of regional imbalance is the widespread disparity in the percentage of urban population to the total population of respective states. Against the national average of 26, Manipur tops the rest with 46 percent followed by Goa (41), Maharashtra (39), Gujarat (34), Tamil Nadu (34), Karnataka (31), Punjab (30), Manipur (28), West Bengal (27), Andhra Pradesh (27) and Kerala (26). This means as many as 14 states had lesser urban population percentage with Himachal Pradesh and Sikkim (both 9 each) and the states of Assam (11), Bihar and Orissa (both 13) slightly fairing better. The states having a higher degree of urbanisation also have a relatively higher per capita income, exceptions apart.

(iii) *Net Irrigated Area as Per cent of Net Area Sown:* The regional imbalance also persist in terms of irrigation facilities enjoyed by different states. This can be seen from the net irrigated area as per cent of net area sown. While Punjab tops the list with 93 followed by Haryana with 73, Maharashtra (11) and Mizoram (12) are at the bottom. As many as 16 states had the lower percentage in this regard than the national average of 33.

(iv) *Percentage of Population Below Poverty Line:* Another indicator of regional imbalance is the percentage of population below poverty line living in different states. In this regard, Orissa has the largest percentage of poor (55.6) closely followed by Bihar (53.4). Along with them Uttar Pradesh (42) and Madhya Pradesh (43.4) are also lowest per capita income states. While they constitute the poorest states in India, we have Punjab and Haryana who have the least number of poor in terms of percentage. Seven states are above the national average of 39.3 per cent of population below poverty line. It is also to be seen that poverty is widespread in India and even the relatively industrialised states of Maharashtra, Tamil Nadu, Gujarat, West Bengal, Andhra Pradesh and Karnataka have a fair amount of poverty with Tamil Nadu at the top (45.1). The states of Maharashtra, Karnataka, West Bengal and Tamil Nadu have a fairly high per capita incomes, yet they also possess a high level of population living below the poverty line. This reflects the highly defective distribution process in the Indian economy.

(v) *Industrialisation:* Before independence West Bengal and Maharashtra were the leading industrialised States. After independence, the states of Andhra Pradesh, Kerala, Karnataka, Punjab and Haryana have achieved a significant industrial growth. In terms of regional location of industries the six states of Maharashtra, Tamil Nadu, Gujarat, West Bengal, Andhra Pradesh and Karnataka have developed faster and together they account for 62.7 as against the all India per centage of 100. This means that the rest of 37.3 per cent industries are located in 19 states. This corroborates the fact that industrial growth in India has been highly imbalanced.

(vi) *Regional Imbalances within a State:* Regional imbalance also exists within a state. The eastern area of Uttar Pradesh is highly backward, while western Uttar Pradesh is flourishing. In West Bengal, 70 per cent of new industrial capacity was located in the Hoogly district. In Maharashtra nearly 86 per cent of registered factories are located in few urban areas and in Punjab, the figure climbs to a staggering 95 per cent. In the united state of Bihar, Jharkhand tribal area was highly neglected though it produces a large amount of natural resources. There is a tendency to establish industries in the urban areas which have the required industrial infrastructure as a result the backward areas have the least chance to develop.

The following table shows the statistics:

Table 1
Select Socio-Economic Indicators for Different States in India

State	Per capita income at 1980-81 prices [1991-92]	Percent of Population below poverty line [1987-88]	Per centage of urban population to total population [1991] population [1985]	Average daily employment of factory workers per lakh [1990-91]	Net irrigated area as per cent of net area sown	Consump-i tion of electricity per capita Kwh [1992-93]	Per Capta State domestic Product of Current Price
1. Goa	4,800	23.4	41	NA	15	663	17,112
2. Punjab	3,869	12.7	30	1,400	93	863	34, 929
3. Haryana	3,455	16.6	25	1,630	73	673	38,832
4. Maharashtra	3,381	40.1	39	1,750	11	524	37,081
5. Arunachal Pradesh	3,012	37.5	12	NA	21	128	23,788
6. Gujarat	2,412	32.3	34	1,890	27	622	34,157
7. Tamil Nadu	2,322	45.1	34	1,400	43	431	29,958
8. Karnataka	2,255	38.1	31	1,340	20	357	27,291
9. Himachal Pradesh	2,074	15.5	9	NA	17	296	33,805
10. West Bengal	2,015	44.0	27	1,510	36	165	25,223
11. Manipur	2,002	32.9	28	NA	46	140	20,326
12. Meghalaya	1,906	34.6	19	NA	23	159	23,420
13. Nagaland	1,900	34.9	17	NA	31	100	NA
14. Assam	1,887	36.8	11	400	21	91	18,598
15. Kerala	1,826	32.1	25	1,080	15	255	30,668
16. Andhra Pradesh	1,788	27.2	27	910	39	365	26,211
17. Rajasthan	1,733	34.6	24	520	24	320	17,863
18. Tripura	1,689	36.8	15	NA	15	84	24,700
19. Jammu & Kashmir	1,687	23.2	24	NA	41	380	NA
20. Madhya Pradesh	1,621	43.4	23	250	22	312	15,647
21. Uttar Pradesh	1,589	42.0	20	420	61	209	13,262
22. Orissa	1,512	55.6	12	400	31	226	17,299
23. Bihar	1,091	53.4	13	600	44	61	7,875
24. Mizoram	NA	32.5	46	NA	12	126	NA
25. Sikkim	3,369*	34.7	9	NA	17	—	26,412
26. Jharkhand							19,066
27. Chattisgarh							20,151
28. Uttaranchal							24,585
All India	2,229	39.3	26	1,050	33	330	25,716

* For 1990-91, NA Not available.

Source: CMIE, Statistics Relating to the Indian Economy. Vol.II (1994), Draft Mid Term Appraisal of the Eighth Five Year Plan (1992-97), Report of the Expert Group on Estimation of Proportion and Number of Poor (1993), Indian Economy by Ruddar Dutt and K.P.M. Sundharam.

The 1990's saw the inauguration of a new phase of economic reforms and opening up of Indian economy to the world market. Unfortunately this had a telling impact on the regional situation in India. The statistics reveal further widening of the regional disparities. For example in 1980-81 in the pre-reform period the difference between the per capita income of Punjab and Bihar was 2.9 which had shot up to 4.7 in the post reform period of 1996-97. Similarly, the annual average growth rate in the pre-reform period of the eight rich states of Punjab, Maharashtra, Haryana, Gujarat, West Bengal, Karnataka, Kerala, Tamil Nadu and Andhra Pradesh was 5.2 per cent which rose to 6.3 per cent in the post-reform period. And while the backward states of Madhya Pradesh,

Table 2

Statewise Net State Domestic Product at Factor Cost

(At 1980-81 Prices)

State	*1980-81*	*(Rs. crores)* *1990-91*	*1997-98**	*2002-03*	*Annual Average Growth Rate* *1980-81 to 1990-91*	*1990-91 to 1997-98*	*1990-91 to 2002-03*
Forward States							
Punjab	4,449	7,505	10,142	37,582	5.3	4.4	3.9
Maharashtra	15,163	27,244	42,932	153,429	6.0	6.7	5.6
Haryana	3,032	5,719	7,545	31,952	6.5	4.0	4.8
Gujarat	6,547	10,839	18,433	75,447	5.2	7.9	6.3
West Bengal	9,594	14,458	22,767	89,792	4.2	6.7	6.8
Karnataka	5,587	9,112	13,683	63,978	5.0	6.0	6.6
Kerala	3,823	5,262	7,782	37,037	3.2	5.8	5.4
Tamil Nadu	7,218	12,423	18,193	81,019	5.6	5.6	5.2
Andhra Pradesh	7,324	11,723	17,936	82,046	4.8	6.3	5.1
Sub-total	**62,737**	**1,04,265**	**1,59,413**	**6,52,272**	**5.2**	**6.3**	**5.6**
(55.0)	**(54.8)**	**(57.8)**					
Backward States							
Madhya Pradesh	7,012	11,107	14,748	43,770	4.7	4.1	0.4
Assam	2,298	3,426	4,302	16,788	4.1	3.3	2.6
Uttar Pradesh	14,012	22,780	27,365	96,011	5.0	2.6	2.1
Rajasthan	4,126	8,473	11,138	44,769	7.4	4.0	3.5
Orissa	3,443	4,345	6,013	21,862	2.3	4.7	4.1
Bihar	6,349	10,253	10,653	34,553	4.9	0.6	–0.7
Sub-total	37,240	60,384	74,219	2,57,753	4.9	3.0	1.7
(38.8)	**(31.7)**	**(26.9)**					
All-India	1,10,340	1,90,218	2,75,895	11,69,793	5.6	5.5	5.4
	(100.0)	(100.0)	(100.0)				

* Provisional

Source: Compiled and Computed from data given in RBI, Handbook of Statistics on Indian Economy (1999) Indian Economy Rudden Dutt and Sunderam 2007 edit.

Assam, UP, Rajasthan, Orissa and Bihar registered a growth rate of 4.9 percent in the pre reform period, the figure fell down to 3 per cent in the post reform period. Among the rich states only Punjab and Haryana witnessed as decline where the growth rate was lower than the national average. But none among the backward states were near the national average. Table 2 clearly reveals this.

It has been pointed out that the rich states have been luckier in terms of investment proposals and financial assistance as more than two-thirds of investment proposals were concentrated in the forward states and same situation prevailed in the disbursal of financial assistance.

Table 3
Investment Proposals and Disbursal of Assistance for Investment

(Percentage Distribution)

-	*Percentage share of Investment Proposals (Aug'91 - Dec' 98)*	*Cumulative share of Financial Assistance Disbursed by All-India Financial Institutions (up 31st March' 97)*	*Cumulative Financial Assistance disbursed by State Financial Corporations (up 31st March 97)*
Forward States			
Punjab	3.4	2.4	3.6
Maharashtra	18.0	21.0	11.5
Haryana	3.6	2.5	4.8
Gujarat	18.7	13.5	9.3
West Bengal	3.3	3.9	2.5
Karnataka	5.6	6.1	15.5
Kerala	1.1	1.7	4.4
Tamil Nadu	7.2	9.0	10.6
Andhra Pradesh	8.3	7.2	7.8
Sub-total	**69.2**	**67.3**	**70.0**
Backward States			
Madhya Pradesh	7.4	5.1	3.2
Assam	0.7	0.5	0.5
Uttar Pradesh	9.4	7.9	11.1
Rajasthan	3.9	4.5	6.1
Orissa	2.2	1.8	3.7
Bihar	1.2	1.4	2.0
Sub-total	24.8	21.2	26.6
All-India	100.0 (7,37,516)	100.0 (3,12,502)	100.0 (20,896)

Note: 1. Figures in brackets indicate totals of Rs crores.
2. Data has been arranged according to our classification of forward and backward states.

Source: N. J. Kurian, *Widening Regional Disparties in India, Economic and Political Weekly*, February 12-18, 2000. *Indian Economy* by Ruddar Dutt and Sunderam

The above table makes it clear that the percentage share of investment proposal was considerably higher in case of forward states (69.2) as against 24.8 for the backward states. This difference also exists in the disbursal of assistance for investment.

The backward states also suffer in terms of quality of life. The selected indicators of human development i.e. life expectancy, Literacy rate, infant mortality rate (IMR) death and birth rates are also higher than the forward states. The following table clearly depicts this situation.

Table 4
Selected Indicators of Human Development for Major States

S. No.	State	Life expectancy at birth (2001-06)		Infant Mortality Rate (per 1000 live births) (2002)			Birth rate (per 1000) 2002*	Death rate (per 1000) 2002*
		Male	Female	Male	Female	Total		
1	2	3	4	5	6	7	8	9
Forward States								
1.	Andhra Pradesh	62.79	65.00	64	60	62	20.7	8.1
2.	Gujarat	63.12	64.10	55	66	60	24.7	7.7
3.	Haryana	64.64	69.30	54	73	62	26.6	7.1
4.	Karnataka	62.43	66.44	56	53	55	22.1	7.2
5.	Kerala	71.67	75.00	9	12	10	16.9	6.4
6.	Maharashtra	66.75	69.76	48	42	45	20.3	7.3
7.	Punjab	69.78	72.00	38	66	51	20.8	7.1
8.	West Bengal	66.08	69.34	53	45	49	20.5	6.7
9.	Tamil Nadu	67.00	69.75	46	43	44	18.5	7.7
Backward States								
1.	Madhya Pradesh	59.19	58.01	81	88	85	30.4	9.8
2.	Orissa	60.05	59.71	95	79	87	23.2	9.8
3.	Assam	58.96	60.87	70	71	70	26.6	9.2
4.	Bihar	65.66	64.79	56	66	61	30.9	7.9
5.	Rajasthan	62.17	62.80	75	80	78	30.6	7.7
6.	Uttar Pradesh	63.54	64.09	76	84	80	31.6	9.7
	India	**63.87**	**66.91**	**62**	**65**	**63**	**25.0**	**8.1**

*Provisional.

Source: Economic Survey, 2004-2005.

Progress of Human Development in India

In Indian States we find very striking contrasts and variations in human development and economic performance:

1. Kerala—high HDI but low income
2. Haryana—low HDI but high income
3. Rajasthan—Fast economic growth but slow HDI
4. Mutual reinforcement of growth and human development-Punjab, Gujarat, Maharasthtra and West Bengal
5. Mutually depressing growth and human development—MP, UP, Orissa and Bihar

In the last group there is an urgent need to break this vicious circle by fostering investment to step up the growth and then taking care of human development. AP had initiated this process during 1990s.

Rajasthan needs to be cautious as this high pace of growth may slow down in a few years. Therefore, there is a need for paying extra attention to strengthening human development process. On the other hand, the state of Kerala must take up programs for acceleration of economic growth so that it can take advantage of its high level of human development.

Causes of Regional Imbalances

1. The process of regional imbalance started with the British period in India when Maharashtra and West Bengal were preferred by the British for development as they possessed the required facilities for manufacturing and trading activities. Only the three metropolitan cities of Calcutta, Bombay and Madras witnessed industrial development leaving the rest of the entire country as neglected and backward. The British policy of land system only benefitted the Zamindars and moneylenders in the rural areas. Dutt and Sundaram say "The absence of effective land reforms allowed the structure in most of rural India to remain inimical to economic growth. The uneven investment during the British period helped some areas become prosperous under the British rule." To a great extent, the British rule in India is responsible for its widespread poverty. By developing a colonial economy, in which India was to remain a supplier of raw materials and act as a readymade market for the British finished goods, the British destroyed the native economy which was quite healthy even from the modern standards.

2. In India the development has largely been concentrated in the urban areas because the physical geography plays an important role in economic growth. Certain areas are just inaccessible like Northern Kashmir, the Hill districts of Himachal Pradesh, Bihar and NEFA. Climate, too plays, an important role in the low economic development of many regions in India as reflected in low agricultural output and absence of large scale industry.

3. Further certain areas develop because of locational advantages. For example, you cannot have a steel plant in Punjab as the basic raw materials of iron and coal are not available in the land of Punjab while a steel plant can be made in Bhilai, Durgapur, Bokaro or Rourkela because the basic raw materials are available there.

4. The private entrepreneurs also prefer to invest in the developed regions rather than going to a backward area. This is because of the absence of infrastructural facilities in backward regions, unlike the already developed regions where there are readymade facilities available. Thus while the developed regions continue to register further growth, the backward areas remain backward.

5. The development strategy in India has also contributed to the regional imbalance. This is despite the fact that the achievement of balanced regional development has consistently been the goal of planning process in India. The Industrial Policy Resolution of 1956 stressed the need to reduce regional disparities by encouraging the location of Public Undertakings in economically backward states. The Second Five Year Plan pointed out that in any comprehensive plan for development, it is axiomatic that the special needs of the less developed areas should receive due attention. A pattern of investment must be devised so as to lead to balanced development. The successive plans also emphasised the need for the removal of regional disparities. For this, the backward areas were identified and schemes launched for their development. However, the Seventh Plan (1985-90) gave a limited reference to the need for regional balance by suggesting that "The pattern of growth envisaged for the Seventh Plan is expected to contribute toward the reduction of interregional disparities in levels of development." Accordingly, the stress was given in the increase of agricultural productivity in the backward regions. The Seventh Plan also envisaged the human resources development through primary education, health care, universalisation of elementary education and elimination of poverty amongst young adults, greater emphasis on minimum needs programmes like water supply, rural roads and rural

electrification and it was expected that with the development of human resources, the regional disparity would be reduced. The Eighth Plan almost ignored the problem of balanced development of states and the Ninth Plan accepted the fact that the economic reforms are increasing the regional imbalance and it would continue to increase. It relies on agriculture and rural activities to reduce regional disparities.

6. Planned economy means a disciplined development of different sectors in a preferred manner. A particular area is preferred at a time and developed because of the paucity of time, energy and finances. After the development, that particular area should help others to develop. Unfortunately in India this has not happened. The developed states do not want to contribute in developing the backward states. Infact they have been guided by their self interests only. The is the reason why a chief Minister of a rich state said that the centre should allocate more funds to a state whose performance of the economy was better.

It is also a fact that the planning mechanism has always favoured the developed states in the allocation of per capita plan outlays which is obvious from the Table 5 (see page 437).

Therefore the regional disparities in India continue to be widening with successive plan allocations. This has also resulted in tension areas between the centre and the states. The states of Bihar, UP, Orissa and Rajasthan have, in particular, frequently complained about the stepmotherly treatment by the centre with regard to allocation of finances to them.

Besides, the central funding in terms of plan outlays and assistance, specific schemes like the Drought Prone Area Programme (DPAP), the Desert Development Programme (DDP), the Hill/Tribal Area Programmes, the North Eastern Council Programmes, the Border Area Programmes, the other Special Area Programmes, the Island Development Authority Programmes have been initiated with central assistance. The Government of India had also been providing special incentives to private investments in backward areas which included subsidies, tax benefits and concessional finances from the public sector financial institutions like Industrial Bank of India (IDBI), the Industrial Finance Corporation of India (IFCI) and the Industrial Credit and Investment Corporation of India (ICICI) and also from the public sector banks. The IDBI has also established several Technical Consultancy Organisations (TCO's) in various parts of the country which provide technical consultancy in the backward areas.

Table 5
Per Capita Plan outlays: First to Eighth Plan

	I Plan 1951-56	*II Plan 1956-61*	*III Plan 1961-66*	*IV Plan 1969-74*	*V Plan 1974-78*	*VI Plan 1980-85*	*VII Plan 1985-90*	*VIII Plan 1992-97*
Haryana	—	—	—	358	481	1,385	1,871	2,838
Punjab	175	146	212	316	531	1,179	1,695	2,951
Gujarat	58	76	108	204	376	1,037	1,485	2,700
Maharashtra	37	57	103	199	372	983	1,434	3,101
Madhya Pradesh	34	48	84	114	254	687	1,146	1,742
Tamil Nadu	28	57	98	134	201	651	1,063	2,427
Karnataka	46	62	100	128	276	614	749	3,138
West Bengal	54	48	80	82	200	600	653	1,144
Andhra Pradesh	33	52	91	98	236	584	841	1,858
Kerala	31	49	101	156	224	578	727	2,378
Rajasthan	39	53	97	120	237	577	718	2,548
Orissa	56	54	120	113	207	536	897	2,123
Uttar Pradesh	25	32	72	132	237	535	803	1,372
Assam	29	57	103	136	190	526	850	2,066
Bihar	25	40	67	85	155	456	626	592
All States	38	51	92	142	262	687	1,026	1,965

Source: Centre for Monitoring Indian Economy, *Basic Statistics Relating to the Indian Economy*, Vol. 2, States and Planning Commission, Ninth Five Year Plan (1992-97) (1989), Indian Economy by Ruddar Dutt and K.P.S. Sundharam.

However, the recent spurt of privatisation and liberalisation has weakened the government's efforts in uplifting the backward areas. For example, earlier the applications for industrial licences for 'no industry' districts were given overriding preferences but now the entire industrial licencing system, with the exception of certain industries related to security and strategic concerns, has been abolished and the benefit of licencing preference to backward areas has lost its significance. With the increasing emphasis on market and competition and the consequent neglect of backward areas, India is poised for further regional disparities. Instead of their removal, they are more likely to be further widened.

Lack of Infrastructural Development

Investment alone cannot determine the level of development in an economy. Economic and social infrastructure can make critical difference in the economic performance of a society. This fact is abundantly clear by a look at the differences of forward and backward states of Indian union. See table

Centre for Monitoring Indian Economy has compiled composite industrial infrastructural developmental index. It has assigned weights to seven components of social-economic infrastructures. These weights are;-

a. Transport 26%
b. Energy consumption 24%
c. Irrigation facilities 20%
d. Banking facilities 12%
e. Communication 6%
f. Education 6%
g. Health 6%

Last column of our table indicates socio-economic infrastructure indices of different States

Table 6: Levels of Infrastructure Development

	Per Capita Power Consumption 1996-97	Registered Vehicles per 100 persons as on 31.3.97	Road Length per 100 kms. of Area of the States	Telecom Lines per 100 persons as on March 31, 1999	% of Irigated Area is gross Cropped Area 1994-95	Social and Economic Infra-structure Index 1999
	(1)	(2)	(3)	(4)	(5)	(6)
Forward States						
Punjab	790	103.2	113.1	5.34	94.8	187.6
Maharashtra	557	57.2	73.1	4.93	15.3	112.8
Haryana	508	64.6	61.0	3.18	77.2	137.5
Gujarat	686	91.5	55.6	3.75	28.9	124.3
West Bengal	197	19.8	69.9	1.86	28.7	111.3
Karnataka	338	56.5	73.0	3.25	23.9	104.9
Kerala	236	46.5	358.2	4.66	13.6	178.7
Tamil Nadu	469	56.9	157.5	3.84	49.5	149.1
Andhra Pradesh	332	42.1	20.7	2.36	39.6	103.3

Backward States						
Madhya Pradesh	368	38.8	47.6	1.38	22.3	76.8
Assam	108	19.9	86.7	0.95	15.0	77.7
Uttar Pradesh	194	22.7	72.7	1.21	62.6	101.2
Rajasthan	295	45.1	38.0	2.11	29.1	75.9
Orissa	447	22.9	134.8	1.05	25.8	81.0
Bihar	145	16.4	50.6	0.58	43.2	81.3
All-India	**338**	**44.0**	**91.7**	**2.55**	**36.5**	**100.0**

Source: Planning Commission, *Ninth Five Year Plan* (1992-2002), CMIE, *Profiles of States*, March 1997 and Tata Services Ltd., *Statistical Outline of India* (1999-2000) and *Eleventh Finance Commission* (2000)

Punjab heads the table with the index of 187 and Rajasthan appears to have index of 75.9 in comparison with all India level of 100. Also notice that states of AP and Karnataka do not have a very high level of infrastructure development. They are almost at the same level as UP. On the other hand, economically not so progressive Kerala is marginally behind Punjab.

Environmental Degradation

The term environment means the aggregate of all the external conditions and influences affecting the life and development of an organism. Environmental degradation has occurred from man's assertion that he is the master of the earth and the earth is for him. As a result in the name of his development, the environment has been totally neglected. Global warming has become a major environmental issue which is giving 'Greenhouse effect.' 'Greenhouse effect' means that in normal conditions, the planet's Ozone layer absorbs part of the harmful ultraviolet solar radiation and facilitates the outgoing infrared radiation (heat) dissipate into the space but the Ozone-layer itself is depleting, as a result, the reduced Ozone layer lets in more dangerous rays to the earth and the build up of water vapour and carbon dioxide prevents heat from escaping, making the earth warmer. The carbon dioxide, methane, nitrous oxide and other gases trap heat in atmosphere as they are transparent to incoming sunlight but absorb infrared radiation earth emits back towards space. Fuel combustion is biggest man-made source of carbon-dioxide and nitrous oxide. Decomposition of organic waste is a major source of methane. The basic reason for such effect is the industrial revolution. It has been estimated that from 1800 to 1994, roughly the age of industrial revolution, the quantity of carbon dioxide rose from 280 parts per million to 358. As a result, global temperature rose between 0.3 and 0.6

degree centigrade. When the temperature rises, the oceans also expand and may have risen 10 to 25 centimeters. It has also been estimated that by 2100, if the gases are emitted at current rates, the global temperature would rise by 1 to 3 degree celsius and the sea levels would increase by 15 to 90 centimeters, which means many islands and lands adjacent to sea would be inundated and permanently lost. This means land area will continuously shrink. It has been estimated that if temperature were to rise by 2.5 degree celsius in the next century, there will be (i) irreversible expansion of deserts leading to large scale desertification; (ii) changes in vegetation leading to increase in carbon dioxide emissions; (iii) more health diseases including heart diseases and more widespread tropical illness; (iv) increased risks of famine; and (v) the lives of 92 million people will be threatened with the oceans rise by 50 cm. It is also predicted that global warming will drastically reduce moisture levels in current fertile zones which will turn them into deserts. In short such is the magnitude of problem caused by the environment degradation and man himself is responsible for such devastating consequences. Following is the list of world class polluters as on 1996.

Table 7
World Class Polluters

Country	Percentage of CO_2 emissions (1996)
USA	22.4%
China	13.4%
Russia	7.1%
Japan	4.9%
India	3.8%
Germany	3.5%
UK	2.4%
Canada	2.0%
Ukraine	1.8%
Italy	1.7%

Source: US Oakridge Nat Lab/Envista/The Asian Age 25 November 1997.

Thus India ranks fifth in the list of world polluters with the United States of America at the top of the list. However, there is no doubt that the developed nations are more responsible than the developing nations like India for the Greenhouse effect. But, there is no point in blaming each other for the environmental degradation as all the countries, some more and some less, have contributed to it. Now let us see the environmental degradation in India.

Like other nations, the environmental degradation in India refers to pollution in land, air and water, the adverse effects of which can be seen on plants, animals and human beings. Now let us take them one by one.

Land

In India the land has been degraded by many factors including deforestation, faulty irrigation and drainage practices, soil erosion by wind and water, inadequate soil conservation measures, steep mountain slopes and overgrazing by livestock. Further, intensive agriculture based on chemical fertilizers and pesticides has diminished the health of soils in many parts of the country. Approximately 175 million hectares of country's area (out of 329 million hectares) is facing the problem of soil erosion and land degradation.

The erosion of soil takes place as a result of surface soil being washed away due to excessive rains and floods. This happened because of indiscriminate felling of trees which do not allow soil, erosion by fixing the soil with their roots, deforestation and conversion of forest into cultivating lands, excessive grazing by cattle and wrong methods of cultivation. India is also losing a large quality of natural fertilizers every year by this soil erosion. To enrich the soil, chemical fertilizers are used and pesticides to kill the insects, both to ensure agricultural productivity. However, they have contributed to soil infertility in Punjab, Haryana and western UP. The remedy lies in the adoption of traditional products like the derivatives of neem, turmeric, tobacco and animal products which the Indian farmers had been using for centuries together. There are natural predators for specific pests and insects like snakes to kill rodents. The chemical pesticides destroy them. Further, snakes are killed for exporting their skins and also for domestic leather industry. This should be stopped immediately. Further, we need an intensive tree planting drive.

In India, the size of the grazing land has declined, only about 13 million hectares of land is classified as the permanent grazing land. The common land of villages used for grazing has been encroached upon, which is either converted into cultivated land or it is used for housing. As a result, there is overgrazing in the rest of the surviving land. It has been estimated that in highly grazed areas, six cms of top soil disappears in one monsoon. The problem is further aggravated by the fact that the cattle population in India is rising very sharply, alongwith the rise in India's population. The effect of over grazing is highly devastating to the soil as it destroys the capacity of regeneration.

Other problems, relating to land, is the water logging and salinization. These problems exist, where there are big irrigation projects. About 35 per cent of India's agricultural land is irrigated. Salinization and waterlogging occur due to seepage from canals, over-irrigation and poor drainage. These problems led to the downfall of Indus valley civilization, a fact demonstrating that they are not new problems to India. Unusual heavy rains and floods in the irrigated area also lead to waterlogging. The problem of waterlogging is a menace in Punjab, Haryana, UP, West Bengal, M.P. and Maharashtra. Salinity means the arrival of salt in the surface as a result of coming up of subsoil water. This salt, in the surface, ruins the crop and makes cultivation impossible. The Indira Gandhi Canal in Rajasthan is facing a severe crisis in this regard. Salinization has very badly affected small farmers in the Green Revolution areas who had to leave their lands. Waterlogging and salinization is also critical in the highly water-retentive black cotton soils of Maharashtra, Madhya Pradesh, Karnataka, Andhra Pradesh and in the deltaic coastal areas. To prevent salinization, the usual practice is to pump out the subsoil water by tube wells. Besides there is also a need to line the canals with concrete to prevent its seepage.

Another aspect of environmental degradation is the widespread deforestation in India. As per the 1995 assessment of forest cover by the Forest Survey of India, about 64 million hectares or 19.5 per cent of India's land area is under forest. But only 39 million hectares or 11.73 per cent of the total land area has a crown cover of 40 per cent and above which means 0.04 hectares forest per person in the country of 950 millions. This is very low. The main causes of deforestation in India have been: (i) conversion of forest land into agricultural land. Between 1951 and 1972, 2.433 million hectares of land was converted for cultivation, (ii) River valley projects, (iii) industries like railways, paper, pulp and polyfibres, (iv) road and communication, (v) overgrazing by livestock and (vi) the requirements of fuel, wood, charcoal and timber by the rural and urban people. Another important killer of forests have been the big dams like Bhakra, Tehri and Sardar Sarovar. These dams submerge not only the forests, they displace thousands of inhabitants and also submerge the cultivated lands, thus increasing the pressure on the remaining forest areas. It has been estimated that within the short span of seven years between 1975 and 1982 the country lost 1.3 million hectares of natural forest every year. The commercial plantation has also contributed to deforestation. As per an FAO analysis, between 1980 and 1990 the natural forest cover declined from 57.23 million hectares to 51.73 while plantation increased from 3.18 to 13.23 million hectares. The plantations are increasing at the expense of natural forests. The commercial exploitation dates from the British period which established total control over the forests. This resulted in a series of tribal uprisings who traditionally were the users of their forests while at the same time protecting them from degradation. The British policy was followed by the free India government and the destruction of the forest continued. As a result, there were popular movements like Chipko movement in Garhwal and silent valley struggle in Kerala in 1970's and later on movement against Sardar Sarovar project in Narmada river and Tehri Dam in Uttaranchal. The Chipko movement succeeded in changing the official strategy regarding forests. The silent valley project which was to construct a hydo-electric Project that would have destroyed part of silent valley was also stopped. The movement against Sardar Sarovar Project and Tehri dam is still continuing.

The uncontrolled mining exploitation has also led to environmental degradation in different parts of the country. The mining activities have degraded the environment in following ways:

(i) Mining involves removal of vegetation in the surface and top soil. This leads to uprooting the trees and soil erosion.
(ii) The mineral dust pollutes the air.
(iii) It means conversion of agricultural land into new cities, railway lines and stockyards.
(iv) Low agricultural productivity as the mining dust settles on land.
(v) After mining, the area is left uncovered which means a permanent loss of the land.
(vi) The underground fire and stockyard fires damages the land. In Bihar, Jharia Coal Mines is suffering from underground fire since 1932 and a number of villages are under its effect. As a result the people have to leave the area and seek settlement elsewhere.
(vii) Mining activities also pollute the underground water.

Thus the cumulative effect of mining activities means the destruction of land, water, forest and air. They have also created many severe health problems.

The unchecked and rapacious exploitation of land has also resulted in the development of wasteland in India. According to the estimates of a non-government organisation (NGO)—the Society for Promotion of Wastelands (SPWD) over 100 million hectares which means almost one-third of India's area constitute wasteland in India. This excludes wasteland in degraded forest areas. In the western districts of Rajasthan, and parts of Gujarat and Haryana where wind erosion from shifting sands of the deserts has affected 13 million hectares of land. Despite the efforts to the contrary, the desert has been expanding at an alarming rate.

Water

In 1995, a World Bank study disclosed that almost all the surface water in India, except those of mountain areas, is unfit for human consumption. The industrial wastes, silt from soil erosion and dissolved minerals are some of the reasons of this pollution which has led to many water-borne diseases like as typhoid, cholera, dysentery, infectious hepatatis and cancer. In agricultural areas, the water is contaminated by various pesticides and fungicides. The ground water has also been contaminated in almost all parts of the country and the TDS (Total Dissolved Solids) level prescribed for drinking water has been exceeded. Besides almost all the rivers in India are highly polluted especially the Ganga, Yamuna, Mahanadi, Krishna, Kaveri and Godavri. This is because the rivers have been convenient dumping grounds of human and industrial wastes. The Ganga which is revered as the most holiest Indian rivers, is butchered by over 60,000 animal carcasses and more than 10,000 human corpses, annually, who are dumped into the river. The city and industrial wastes are pollutiing water and the efforts to stop their dump has proved of no consequences. In Delhi alone, about 70 crore gallons of highly contaminated water is discharged by various industries per day. Further, about 17 drains release about 17000 million litres of sewage water everyday. Besides, the Najafgarh drain adds hazardous substances like chromium, nickel, copper, zinc, lead and cadmium, daily. According to the Central Pollution Control Board, the river water is not fit for bathing even after treatment. There is provision for releasing of contaminated water after proper treatment but violation is more common. The ground water of Delhi is highly polluted and unfit for human use. The piped water supplied by the Municipal Corporation of Delhi is also not safe for drinking.

The water in the seas is also highly contaminated thus contributing to marine pollution which has endangered the marine life. The contaminated water of the rivers flows into seas. The coastal areas also dump huge amounts of sewage and industrial wastes. The enormity of industrial waste flowing into sea can be estimated by just one example of Travancore Titanium Products Ltd, a state owned industry at Thiruvanathapuram, Kerala which discharges 4 million litres of effluent into the sea per day. In Mumbai, 90 per cent of the sewage is allowed to flow into the sea without any treatment. This all has played havoc with the coastal water as wastes donot disperse in the open sea and remain present along the coastal line. The Mumbai coast, now, has degenerated into a zone of heavily sullied lifeless water. The marine pollution has destroyed the marine life, as a result the fisherman communities who depend on the fishes for their livelihood have registered a decrease in catch and consequently a loss in their income.

Besides Marine pollution, mangroves, wetlands and estuaries in India are also facing human onslaught. As a result, many mangroves have been lost permanently. Now they survive in Sunderbans in West Bengal, Andaman and Nicobar Islands and in certain parts of Andhra Pradesh, Tamil Nadu, Orissa, Maharashtra, Gujarat, Goa and Karnataka. India has about 7 per cent of the world's mangroves. The wet lands are being reclaimed due to population pressure. In Calcutta, as a result of the growth of Salt Lake City, the wetlands have been destroyed.

It is to be noted that as a general phenomena, the sea level in India is rising, threatening the Indian coastlines. The following table shows the threatened areas in different states.

Table 8
Sea Level Rise threatening Indian Coast Lines

State	(Area at risk in Square Km.)
Gujarat	1810
West Bengal	1220
Tamil Nadu	670
Orissa	480
Maharashtra	410
Karnataka	290
Goa	180
Kerala	150

Source : JNU (1993)/Business World 22 October 1997.

The reality of the threat can be realised from the fact that India's neighbour Maldives is expected to be submerged in toto.

Air

As a result of industrialisation and development, the air in India is also extremely polluted, especially in metropolitan areas where vehicular pollution is widespread. The Government has specified the limits of emission for different vehicles but again the violation is the general rule. The level of SPM is very high and results in major respiratory diseases allergies, eye-irritation and neurological afflictions.

The following table shows the level of suspended particular matter (SPM) in 10 major cities of India.

Table 9
Level of Suspended Particulate Matter (SPM) in 10 major cities

City SPM	*Level*	*Causes*
Delhi	460	Vehicles, NO2 from power plants
Calcutta	460	Coal-based industries, traffic snarls
Kanpur	350	Vehicle, industries
Mumbai	220	Industrial emissions from suburbs
Jaipur	230	Desert sands, diesel three-wheelers.
Ahmedabad	200	Industry, textile mills
Nagpur	230	Vehicles, industries
Bangalore	190	Two-wheelers. Trees keeps level down
Hyderabad	150	Pollution higher in city's congested areas
Chennai	150	Efficient public transport system checks pollutants.

Source: India Today, December 15, 1996.

Besides, the Industrial units and power stations also contribute their due in the increase in the air pollution. In Delhi, 82 per cent of industrial pollution is caused by three power stations, 4 per cent by two chemical plants and 14 per cent by 400 other large industrial units. Besides, there are numerous unauthorised industrial units which are contaminating the air. The cities also witness a lot of noise pollution.

According to an estimate, 50,000 people in 1995 lost their lives because of diseases related to air pollution. The worst industrial disaster took place in Bhopal, in 1984, in the gas tragedy due to Union Carbide's wilful disregard for safety regulations, which left at least 10,000 people dead and exposed some 300,000 to various visual and respiratory problems as well as an impairment of the body's immune system.

The above discussion is not all-comprehensive as it excludes many other forms of environmental degradation afflicting India. The

Government of India and the State Governments have taken a number of measures to achieve a sustainable development. Briefly speaking, India's national environment policy objectives have been the following:

(i) Conserve and develop a safe, healthy, productive, and aesthetically satisfying environment;
(ii) Upgrade, develop and manage rural and urban settlements to enhance the quality of life;
(iii) Plan development on sound ecological principles with environmental impact assessment and incorporating appropriate environmental safeguards;
(iv) Promote environmental safety technologies, recycling of resources and utilisation of wastes;
(v) Conserve the biotic diversity in the country by creating nature reserves and sanctuaries for specific habitats such as mountains, rain forests, pastures, deserts, wetlands, lakes, beaches, mangroves, estuaries, lagoons and islands;
(vi) Safeguard the environment within the national maritime Exclusive Economic Zone;
(vii) Evolve environmental norms and establish effective mechanisms for monitoring surveillance and collection and dissemination of information;
(viii) Preserve scenic landscapes, as well as historic and cultural monuments and their environs;
(ix) Promote environmental education at all levels and create public awareness;
(x) Encourage research in environmental sciences and technological and social investigations to conserve and improve the environment; and
(xi) Develop adequate manpower, within the country, of ecologists, environmental scientists, planners and managers of the highest quality and recognise their work as an important component of national development.

Accordingly, many programmes to restore the environment has been launched by the Government which includes:

(i) Afforestation drive;
(ii) Social forestry programmes have been launched to provide fuel, wood and small timbers for local use;
(iii) The Government recognised various Forest Protection Committees which were voluntary organisations of local people in forest area to protect forest and the villages guarding the forests were given the exclusive rights for forest products;

(iv) The Central Pollution Control Board has been set up to monitor the extent of pollution;

(v) Ganga, Yamuna and Gomti plans have been launched to cleanse these rivers. Besides Grossly Polluting Industries (GPIs) discharging effluents into water course have been identified. In 1991, the Andhra Pradesh High Court ordered 12 major industrial units in Patancheru to close down until they could devise and implement Pollution Control strategies. The Supreme Court in 1996 directed the shifting of industries to curb pollution in Delhi. The Supreme Court also directed the industries, polluting Ganga, to instal pollution control devices;

(vi) The Eighth Plan (1992-97) provided for action on pollution abatement and conservation of large lakes and reservoirs by repairing the infrastructure and diverting and treating sewage presently flowing into the lakes. 21 lakes have been identified for conservation;

(vii) Strict enforcement of the level of prescribed emission for the different kinds of vehicles. For new cars, the use of catalytic converters with unleaded petrol has been made compulsory;

(viii) In Delhi, Mass Rapid Transport System has been proposed to provide a better transport system to the people;

(ix) Many environmental legislations have been enacted. *Article 51A(g)* of Indian Constitution entrusts upon every citizen a fundamental duty to protect and improve the natural environment including forests, lakes, rivers and wildlife and to have compassion for living beings.' The Air (Prevention and Control of Pollution) Act of 1981 and the water (Prevention and Control of Pollution) Act of 1974 have been passed by the Parliament. In 1986 a more comprehensive legislation called the Environmental (Protection) Act was enacted under which the government can even close down a industrial or manufacturing unit that violates the Act.

Yet a lot needs to be accomplished. A study of environmental degradation will reveal that the laws have failed to achieve the desired objectives. Therefore, there is a greater need for people's awareness and it is only through their concerted and dedicated efforts that the environment in India would be able to improve.

Reference

Bahuguna Sunderlal, Shiva Vandana and Back M.N., *Environmental Crisis and Sustainable Development 1992*, Dehradun, Natraj Publishers.

Datt Ruddar and Sundaram KPM, *Indian Economy*, 1997, New Delhi, S. Chand & Co.

Devi Sarla, *Revive Our Ding Planet*, 1982, Nainital Gyanodya Prakashan.

Nath Kamal, *India's Environment Crisis*, 1995, New Delhi, Environmental Information System (ENVIS) Ministry of Environment and Forests.

Uppal J.S. (Ed.), *India's Economic Problems An Analytical Approach* 1983, New Delhi, Tata McGraw Hill Publishing Company Ltd.

Indian Express India at 50, Facts, Figures and Analysis (1947-1997), 1997, Madurai, Express Publications (Madurai) Ltd.

Parikh Kirits and Sudarshan R., *Human Development and Structural Adjustment*, 1993, Madras, Macmillan.

Times of India, July 6, 2008, *Economic Survey*, 2007-08.

CHAPTER XXII

Strategy of Economic Development in India

India inherited a typical colonial economy in 1947. It had a fairly large industrial sector. It was amongst the ten largest producers of industrial output in the world. Yet, most of the manufactured consumer goods had to be imported. India's industrial sector was, by and large, processing raw materials upto the semi finished stage. These were exported to Britain and finished goods were brought in from there and marketed all over the country. Thus, Indian economy was a source of materials and market for commodities for the British industry. Indian leadership found this type of arrangement very inequitable. They rightly felt that this system would keep India dependent on Britain forever. The common refrain of political dialogue was: without economic independence, the political independence shall remain incomplete.'

We had also inherited a socio-economic system which was not conducive to rapid economic progress. The agricultural most fertile land areas with maximum potential for raising output was under control of zamindars. This system of land revenue collection had been created by British to stabilize extractions from the countryside at minimum costs. However, it had developed into such an exploitative system that not only was the entire surplus from farming activities was expropriated, the farmers were often pushed into perpetual indebtedness as well. So, the farming community, in general, was simply not in a position to make investments and raise productivity.

The social sector of the economy was also highly underdeveloped. The level of literacy was low, facilities for schooling were hardly available in the vast countryside. Similarly, availability of medical facilities was confined, by and large, to same major cities only. Even there, it was totally inadequate. Public health facilities—like supply of potable filtered water and a functioning sewage-disposal system was not available even in the capital of the country.

Added to the above problems was the burden of resettling over one crore citizens who had been displaced from the two wings of the newly-created dominion of Pakistan.

All the above-mentioned factors clearly outlined the enormity of developmental agenda that India had to face. Fortunately, Indian political leadership had been convinced, years before the actual transfer of power, that in free India, the state will take up the major share of responsibility for all-round development. By 1947, experiences of several countries had demonstrated effectiveness of state intervention in enhancing the pace of economic reconstruction and development. Therefore, adopting economic planning as the strategy of economic development, (instead of relying upon the market forces of demand and supply to take care of all allocational problems) was regarded as the automatic choice for independent India. Even captains of Indian industry were quite enthusiastic in their support for this strategy.

What is Economic Planning?

An economic plan is a specific set of economic targets which are to be achieved in a given period of time. These targets may also be called goals of plan. Usually, planners take a stock of current level of achievements of the economy, idetify the areas where specific work needs to be done, assess aspirations of the people and then decide about the goals or specific targets. They also work out the details of what exactly is to be done. They have to specify a timespan over which these definite objectives are to be met. In fact, process of planning is a very detailed exercise. It involves various agencies of the government, right from district administration to the Union. Specific projects are idetified, responsibilities for funding and actual implementation of different stages of projects are assigned and finally, a monitoring process initiated, to ensure time-bound implementation of the scheme. Generally, we say that long term objectives of plans are goals of planning. On the other hand, steps to be taken in the short term to help achieve these goals become objectives of specific plans. These objectives, in their concrete qualitative form are called targets. Consider this example; long term objectives are to ensure high level of prosperity for the general masses. This may be incorporated into a specific plan in the form of objective to raise gross domestic product during the plan by, say, 50 per cent. This alone is not enough. Planners will need to work out, in a comprehensive and consistent manner, specific targets for each sector and sub-sector of the economy which will help achieve the plan target of 50 per cent rise in gross domestic product. These sectoral targets may relate to raising production in, say agriculture. To ensure that, fertilizers production must be raised and additional irrigational facilities may have to be created. Not only that, to ensure that modern technology of farming spreads over larger geographic areas, we may have to extend facilities of institutional finance far and wide, so that farmers in ever-increasing numbers can benefit from it. Rise in farm output necessitates strengthening of network for marketing, transportation and also warehousing of agricultured produce. Somewhere along the line, decisions have to be taken that ensure a fair deal for farmers and also safeguard interests of final consumers. Such decisions have a very important bearing on social justice and regional distribution of economic benefits and welfare as well. Specific crops that attract attention of planned action will, is a way, convey a lot about redistributional priorities built into the planning exercise.

Similarly, setting up of specific industries in different locations, creation of socio-economic facilities in the fields of health and education etc., will all go a long way in allocating social resources for specific users and distributing social product among ever-increasing numbers. Only then, will the overall objective of raising gross domestic product by 50 per cent during the plan be able to contribute towards the attainment of the long-term goal of prosperity for all.

Why Planning?

The economic achievements during pre independence period were not results of any conscious effort or well-thought—out strategy of economic development. Individual businessmen working to maximise their own profits alone had set up industries/factories here and there. But, as pointed out in opening paragraphs, this led to very haphazard and lopsided industrialisation in the country and was grossly inadequate to satisfy aspirations of the Indian masses. Continuing the same pattern of economic growth would not meet the approval of government which wanted economic benefits of independence to be highly visible and available to every citizen. So, it had to chalk out a strategy of economic development and was very fortunate to receive the whole-hearted support of the captains of Indian industry in this endeavour. The industry had itself prepared a blueprint of plan—Bombay plan/Tata Plan which was presented to the government of India. This way, they gave a very significant indication that government must initiate process of planning and private business will play the role assigned to it with full sense of responsibility and partnership.

There were other circumstances too which made it imperative to initiate a process of comprehensive economic planning in the overall context of democratic polity, with motto of "Yojana ki Siddhi—jana jana ki samriddhi" (योजना की सिद्धि–जन-जन की समृद्धि) [Success of plan means prosperity for all]. Those circumstances were as follows:

1. *Lack of Entrepreneurial Development:* Though several big industries had been set up in the country by Indian businessmen over last one hundred years or so, yet anybody who looked at the pattern of management would immediately discover the lack of entrepreneurial talent in the country. The reason was very simple; all the industries had been given away on contract to some British managing agency house or the other. So the so-called Indian industrialists were at best investors only.

2. *Limitations of the Market Mechanism:* Market mechanism can maximise output, but it needs perfect competition in all the markets, perfect knowledge about prices, consumer likings etc., perfect divisibility of the capital and mobility of all the factors of production. Such conditions seldom prevail. Even if price mechanism can help in allocation of existing resources, but does it tell us anything about accumulation of capital or pace of discovery and utilisation? Further, price mechanism does not say anything about equity or economic justice. Market-oriented allocation of resources may not lead to optimisation of long term interests of the economy.

3. *Changes in Decision Making Structure:* Decentralisation may actually result in high rate of wastage. Industrialist or businessmen's actions may be dictated by short term gains and lack of coordination may lead to creation of unduly large excess capacity. Sometimes a regulated monopoly may deliver the goods at a much smaller cost compared to highly competitive industrial structure.

4. *Magnitude of the Effort:* Given the task of all round economic development in the country, massive amounts of investible resources had to be mobilised. However, private businessmen were in no position to mobilise thousands of crores of rupees for the purpose. It may be instructive to note that even in 1980 most of the Indian limited companies did not have a share capital base of even sixty lacs of rupees. So, given the state of development of capital market in the country, the task could not have been entrusted to the private companies.

5. *Infrastructure and Long Gestation Projects:* A strategy of economic development has to include a number of projects which may not be capable of earning private profits even in the long run. Such projects are basically in the field of infrastructure i.e. transport,

communication, power distribution, water supply and sewage disposal, maintenance of roads, construction of bridges, irrigational canals etc. Moreover, many heavy industries take a number of years before they become fully operational. All these projects require massive amounts of capital investment with no possibility of recording any profits in next five to ten years. The private business could not have been expected to ensure proper funding for these lines of activity.

6. *Success of State Intervention in European Countries:* In addition to the achievements—though tarred by highly repressive and authoritarian Stalinist era—of USSR, even non-communist states of Europe had experienced the benefits of state intervention during 1940. First round of such intervention was experienced during the World War II when entire prodution and distribution was subordinated to the War Office dictates. The second round followed immediately after the end of the war. Reconstruction and rehabilitation of war-ravaged western Europe was undertaken by the Marshal Plan administration. This effort at coordinated economic reconstruction was highly successful and presented us with a kind of model to emulate.

7. *Non-Economic Factors in Economic Development:* Sustained growth requires a transformation of not only the economic but the social structure of the country. The problem is not merely one of channeling economic activity within the existing socio-economic framework but one of remoulding the framework itself to enable the progressive accommodation of those fundamental urges which express themselves in the demands for right to work, the right to adequate income, the right to education, and to insurance against old age, sickness and other disabilities. Economic planning is an integral part of a wider process aimed not only at the development of resources in a narrow technical sense, but at the development of human facilities and the building up of an institutional framework.' (Tandon and Tandon, Indian Economy).

Objectives of Planning in India

Directive Principles of State Policy contained in *Articles 38 and 39 (A, B, C)* state that the state shall strive to promote the welfare of the people by securing and protecting as effectively as it may, a social order in which justice, social, economic and political, shall inform all the institutions of national life. Establishment of Planning Commission underlines three principles as special terms of reference; (a) that the citizens, men and women, equally, have the right to an adequate means of livelihood; (b) that the ownership and control of material resources of the country are distributed in a manner that best serves the common of food; (c) that the operation of the economic system does not result in the concentration of wealth and means of production to the detriment of the common people. *Articles 41, 45* and *46* also underline the socio-economic aspects of the state policy:

> *"The State shall, within the limits of its economic capacity and development, make effective provision for securing the right to work, to education and public assistance in cases of unemployment, old age, sickness and disablement, and in other cases of undeserved want" (Article 41)*
>
> *"The State shall endeavour to provide, within a period of ten years from the commencement of this Constitution, free and compulsory education for all children until they complete the age of fourteen years" (Article 45)*
>
> *"The State shall promote with special care the educational and economic interests of the weaker sections of the people, and in particular of the Scheduled Castes and the Scheduled Tribes, and shall protect them from social injustice and all forms of exploitation" (Article 46).*

The First Five year plan had set out broad objectives of planning in India. Each of the subsequent plans had their own chapters on objectives. But, on the whole, common threads do remain visible. The long term goals as set out by first plan were (1) maximum production; (2) full employment; (3) economic equality or social justice along with; (4) self reliance; and (5) modernisation of socio-economic infrastructure.

These objectives were to be achieved in the overall framework of 'democratic socialism' which reaffirmed faith in democratic values for the enrichment of individual and communal/social life, removing poverty and aimed at providing some minimum level of consumer opportunities for all, reducing inequalities of incomes and wealth in the process. All the while, this system would strive to eliminate monopolistic tendencies and ensure equal opportunities for all. Mixed economy model was to be adopted, in which both private initiative and the state would play their respective roles as partners in progress—avoiding pitfalls associated with excessive centralisation of economic activities in the hands of officialdom. In general, it was felt that social gain and not the maximisation of private profits would be the criterion of decision making in the economic affairs of independent India.

Planning Strategy

Indian planners have been making strategic shifts in their approach to economic development from plan to plan. The First Five Year Plan is regarded as a stock taking exercise as well as agriculture-oriented plan. By 1954-55 it was assumed that agricultural sector was responding well to the planning strategy and planners could safely shift their attention to the industrial sector. Second Plan is regarded as the first, rigorously–designed plan in the country. Its principal architect, Professor P.C. Mahalanobis, argued that industrialisation in the country could be sustained only if we develop our own heavy industries base. If we try to develop consumer goods industries in the initial stages, no doubt availability of consumer goods will rise at a very fast pace, but very soon we will run into a kind of stone wall. We will not be able to raise the rate of savings on the one hand and will not be able to sustain on the other, the rate of rise in production of consumer goods, so the society will be forced to resort to import of consumer goods. If it goes in for import of technology for developing its own heavy industries, after a few years time it shall be able to increase the output of consumer goods through domestic efforts, and thus attain the objective of self sufficiency.

This Mahalanobis doctrine continued to guide the economic planners for close to 25 years. However, during 1980's certain new developments necessitated adjustment and refinements in this strategy of planning. By this time the agricultural scene in the country had stabilised. In the industrial sector the licencing policy was being seen as a mill-stone around the neck. Various restrictive measures introduced during late 60's and early 70's, had lost their relevance. Liberalisation in the industrial policy to ensure greater participation of the private sector in economic development had become the cornerstone of the state policy. Private sector had come of age. It had demonstrated its ability to mobilise hundreds of crores of rupees through capital issues. Even mega issues, aiming to lift more than a thousand crores of rupees for a single project, were being contemplated. Naturally, planners could not have been operating in isolation from the emerging realities. So the economic strategy during Seventh and Eighth Plans reflect new trends and the approach to the Ninth Plan puts its seal of affirmation on the strategy of assigning a dominant role to private entrepreneurship.

Investment-oriented planning strategy was found to be inadequate to generate productive employment for the entire labour force.

The Sixth Plan recognised that organised sector would not be able to generate sufficient employment. Therefore, self-employment was considered to be the only alternative available to the unemployed masses. According to the Sixth Plan document the thrust of the policy measures would be to provide training, credit, marketing and general guidance about the various facilities available to the people for starting their own venture.

Besides the direct assault on poverty and unemployment, a policy of progressive liberalisation gathered momentum during the Sixth and Seventh Plan periods. This does not, however, mean a shift away from the broad strategy of investment-oriented growth.

The second alternative strategy of employment-orientation was proposed to be introduced in the aborted Sixth Plan for the period 1978-83. The Eighth Plan has set the goal of employment for all, in a time span of the next ten years. Human development will be the ultimate goal of the Eighth Plan. Achievement of a high growth rate and sustaining it over the decade will be an important goal. Employment generation and poverty alleviation are objectives ultimately related to growth. The Eighth Plan States, "while approaching employment as an objective of the Plan, employment generation and economic growth are to be treated as mutually complementary rather than as a conflicting process." (Tandon and Tandon, Indian Economy)

One important shift in emphasis had been noted during Eighth plan: Private sector investment targets had been fixed at a level higher than public outlays. That represented recognition by the state that private business had come of age. It was now in a position to play more significant, even dominant role in the economic activities. The process of liberalisation had already opened up several areas of infrastructural development to private participation—like power generation, highway construction, telecommunication etc. Ninth plan carried on this process shift further. It states that,

"Our strategy of development must be oriented to enable the private sector to reach its full potential for raising production, creating jobs and raising income levels in the society. A vigorous private sector operating under the discipline of competition and free market, will encourage efficient use of scarce resources and ensure rapid economic growth ... however, it does not mean that state has no role to play-though it must not interfere where market forces can ensure appropriate decision on investment and technology."

The state need not maintain majority stake even in public sector enterprises... may reduce it to 26 percent in most cases. The public investment in infrastructure will be given further push and the private sector will be invited to supplement it wherever possible.

Financial sector reforms, along with further encouragement to foreign investments coupled with extensive industrial modernisation and export growth will also take care of maintaining stability of balance of payments.

The plan also emphasised on the concept of co-operative federalism to devolve greeters resources and responsibilities to Panchayati Raj institutions. It also recognised need to integrate environmental protection with over all developmental process and well being of the people.

Appraisal of Planning Process in India

India has tried to relate its five year plans to long term perspective of development. Allocation of resources and priority decision have broadly been in conformity with long term strategy. This is also reflected in persistence of the goals of rapid economic growth and social justice. Placement of foreign aid in the planning process however shows that the planners attitude towards aid and self reliance has been fluctuating from plan to plan. So much so that it fails to indicate any clear strategy.

The first plan found the external assistance without any strings which compromised country's ability to take independent line in the international affairs, acceptable. The Second Plan, however, realised that massive investment in heavy industries would not be feasible without large dozes of foreign assistance. It was also realised that import of technology was also dependent on possibilities of securing foreign aid. Thus 21 per cent of planned investment was financed by way of aid. Share of external aid as a per cent of planned investment shot up to 36 per cent during the Third Plan. However, this plan period was marked by excessive interference by aid giving agencies in formulation of economic policies, devaluation of rupee in 1966 was one such consequence.

In Fourth Plan, the idea to eliminate the need of foreign aid was promoted. A time frame was sought to be projected. Foreign aid net of debt services was to be reduced to half of the current level by end of the Fourth Plan and eliminated all together by the end of Fifth Plan. However, despite excellent performance of agricultural sector since Green Revolution and general improvement in the overall economic vibrancy it has not been possible to achieve that twenty five years old target even now. Sometimes it is sought to be explained away in terms of Indo-Pak war of 1971 and the consequent massive investment on military hardware. At other points of time, we have been holding rise in oil prices (1973) as the main sector which prevented realisation of the goal of self-reliance. But one unmistakable trend is visible: Sixth, Seventh and Eighth Plans have been marked by substantial decline in the reliance on foreign aid. Role of foreign aid has been whittled down to under 6% during the Eighth Plan. During Eighth Plan, however, significant restructuring, liberalisation and globalisation have taken place in the Indian economy. The state under the new dispensation is no longer the international fakir. The foreign companies are themselves setting up their shops in India either directly or in collaboration with Indian entrepreneurs. This foreign direct investment is moving into the Indian market in accordance with the trends in the profitability ratios in different parts of the world. Thus the need for the planners to depend upon the promises of foreign aid has been obviated to that extent.

There is no doubt that the development strategy has given lot of positive results since independence. While the population has more than doubled, the agriculture production has more than tripled. From 1950-51, the total foodgrains production has increased from 50.8 million tonnes to 216.8 million tonnes in 2006-07. As a result, the large scale famines, which were a frequent phenomenon during the British period, are no longer there. In 1942-43 famine of Bengal as many as three million people had perished. Therefore, Nehru declared that everything else can wait but not agriculture. The initial years saw the import of large scale foodgrains and there was a feeling that India would not be able to feed its growing population. But, fortunately, this did not happen and thanks to Green Revolution, we are self sufficient in foodgrains. We have also witnessed a spectacular progress in the production of cereals, potato, sugarcane, cotton, oil-seeds and horticultural crops. Similar growth has taken place in the production of milk, eggs and fish. The increased food production, building sufficient grain reserves, a public distribution system and promotion of employment generation programmes have enabled India to avoid famines in the last 50 years. The industrial base is much more diversified than what it was in 1947. The volume of industrial production has grown 20 times over. We have sufficient basic industries and for technical personnel we have an edge over many developing countries. The per capita income (in constant prices) has also increased almost thrice. The income of an average Indian which was increasing at about 0.5 per cent per year in the first half of this century, since 1950 it has been growing by almost two per cent a year, in fact, there has been considerable pickup since mid-80s. We have been enjoying a rate of growth of over 5 per cent per annum. The following table gives a brief account of India's development. While the death rate has been cut by two-thirds, life expectancy and birth has doubled and the literacy rate more than tripled.

Table 10

Population	359 million (1950-51)	1122 million (2006-07)
Food grains production	50.8 million (1950-51)	216.8 million tones (2006-07)
Industrial production Index (1993-94 = 100)	7.9 (1950-51)	162.7 247 (2000-01)
Per capita income (at 1993-94 prices)	Rs. 3,687 (1950-51)	Rs. 22,553 (2006-07)
Literacy rate (%)	18.3 (1950-51)	64.8 (2001)
Birth rate (per 1000)	39.9 (1950-51)	23.5 (2005-06)
Death rate (per 1000)	27.4 (1950-51)	7.5 (2005-06)
Life expectancy at birth	32.1 (1950-51)	63.2 (2003-04)
Life expectancy at birth (M)	32.5 (1950-51)	62.3 (2003-04)
LIfe expectancy at birth (F)	31.7 (1950-51)	63.9 (2003-04)

Source: Economic Survey, 2007-08.

But still the development in India evokes disappointment which springs from the fact that 260 millions of teeming Indians live below the poverty line for whom the development strategy, and all talks of India being the largest democracy, is just an illusion. A major problem in this regard has been the widespread disparity between the rhetoric of law and its actual implementation. In law, the Zamindari and other intermediaries were abolished with an overall objective of facilitating land reforms and for the purpose, ceilings were imposed in land ownership. This was a major step because in China, South Korea and Taiwan, land reforms facilitated the rapid, industrial-driven economic growth as it broke agrarian landlordism and removed the obstacles to resource mobilisation for industrial growth. This could have happened in India also. But unfortunately the land reform legislation largely remained on papers were, never given a fair trial and as a result we had to pay. The agonizing rural poverty remains and is a national scourge. Similarly while the income tax rate in India is very high but the collection is very low. The weak law enforcement machinery facilitated the growth of parallel black money economy. A number of times the state came out with attractive voluntary disclosure of income including the VDIS (Voluntary Disclosure Income Scheme) in 1997 but the results have not been very encouraging. The licence-raj in India was introduced to check the concentration of economic power in a few hands. In practice, however, the big industrial houses were able to take advantage of the loopholes of the law and cornered licences. Later on MRTP Act (Monopoly Restriction Trade Practices Act) was formulated which actually failed in spirit and the concentration of economic power in a few hands continued. Over the last decade, liberalisation has virtually demolished whatever controlling authority this commission was originally vested with.

The fact is that agriculture remained neglected in the development strategy, despite Nehru's belief that agriculture and industrialisation are complementary to each other and without proper development of agriculture, industrial progress would be constrained. Under the first five plans, the agriculture and allied services (which contributed anything between 50 to 52 per cent of the national income) were allotted only about 20 per cent of the resources while industries (which contributed between only 18 to 20 per cent of the national income) were allotted between 18 to 24 per cent of the total resources. Charan Singh rightly said that the neglect of agriculture was the 'original sin' of the planners of India's destiny. Further, the emphasis on heavy industries meant the import of machinery and technical know-how from the foreign countries. This resulted in adverse balance of payment problem for India. The surplus from agriculture was also used in the development of infrastructural industry. The planning process was growth-oriented and not employment oriented. As a result the employment problem has become a major one for the Indian economy and has let to social and political unrest in India.

Another flaw in Indian planning is the low rate of exports. According to WTO data, the Indian share in the world trade is just 0.62 per cent. India is the 28th largest importer and 31st largest exporter in the world. There is an alarming increase in the trade deficits of India from Rs. 2,340 crores in the second plan to Rs. 54,200 crores in the Seventh Plan. This has been due to large scale imports of capital goods to develop heavy and basic industry, neglect of agriculture and poor exports. The policy of import substitution and export promotion has not yielded the desired results. This resulted in the shrinkage of foreign reserves leading to the crisis of 1991 when India had to go for massive loans from the World Bank and sweeping changes were made in the Indian economy. The liberalisation of economy took place. But this liberalisation has further worsened the lot of India's poor. The gap between poor and rich has increased.

In retrospect, it will not be wrong to say that the various five year plans have not been a success. The achievements did not correspond with the targets and expectations. The development process did not pay the desired heed to the distribution process and as a result the regional disparities have been widening in India which are now increasingly reflected in social and political unrest. Thus the developmental strategy which was based on planning to tackle the problems of poverty, illiteracy, food deficit, industrial and agrarian backwardness failed in a very big way notwithstanding its achievement which proved far below the rising expectations of Indian people.

References

Datt Ruddar and Sundharam K.P.M., *Indian Economy,* 1997, New Delhi, S.Chand & Co. Ltd.

Tandon B.B. and Tandon K.K., *Indian Economy,* 1997, New Delhi, Tata McGraw-Hill Publishing Company Ltd.

Indian Express, India at 50, Chennai Express Publication (Madurai) Ltd.

The Hindu, India, August 15, 1997.

Economic Survey, 2001-2002, Government of India.

CHAPTER XXIII

National Integration

The British are credited to have achieved Indian unity as they effected the political and administrative unification of this country through modern means of communication. However, to say that India was never one before the British advent in India a belief which is widely spread is a misnomer. The fact is that the whole of India was known at least as early as fourth century B.C. which can be verified from different ancient Indian and foreign accounts notably that of Katyayana, Kautilya and Greek writings. As Dr. Tarachand points out "The ideal of Hindu kingship was nothing short of universal sovereignty, which meant at the least sovereignty of the whole of India " up to the Seas"—the consciousness of the territorial synthesis leads to political synthesis, and itself strengthened by the latter; Like other nationalities, the concept of Indian nationality has developed over a period of time. Initially the nation of Aryavarta was in vogue which included the territories between the Himalayas and the Vindhyas, as evident in Vedic texts. Later on Aryan colonisation extended to Southern India also and the Indian unity found its expression in many religious mantras. A mantra which is even invoked today by a devout Hindu during his bath and worships says, "O ye Ganga, Yamuna, Godavri, Saraswati, Narmada, Sindhu and Kaveri, Come ye and enter into this water of my offering. "The ancient Puranic writings, identified India as the land of seven mountains which encompasses the entire Indian sub-continent. They also talk about seven sacred cities of *Ayodhya, Mathura, Maya or Hardwar, Kashi or Banaras, Kanchi Avanti or Ujjain and Dvaravati or Dwarka.* Ashoka's edicts are found in four corners of the country. Sankaracharya placed four sacred pilgrimage centres—*Badri-Kedarnath* in the north, *Rameshwaram* in the South, *Dwarka* in the West and *Jagannath* in the East." He also established four maths or monasteries in the four corners of India—*Jyotimath* in the north, *Sharda-math* in the west, *Sringeri* in the South and *Goverdhana math* in the East. The places of Shiva worship are scattered through out the four corners of India. Another Hindu God, Vishnu is also worshipped in the entire country. This all shows that in ancient times, the people of this country not only knew India in its geography but also visited the four corners as a religious necessity. This religious sense of unity was accompanied by the politics also. There have been rulers who enjoyed paramount sovereignty over the entire country even in ancient times, which was evident from the notion of a *Chakravarti Raja*. From time immemorial, the ambition of any ambitious king was to rule over the entire country. Chandragupta Maurya also took India as a unit of his governance.

This fundamental unity of India has also been accepted by many foreign observers. According to Vincent A. Smith, the well known authority on early Indian history says, "India, encircled as she is by seas and mountains, is indisputably a geographical unit and as such is rightly designated by one name." He further asserts that the civilisation of India has many features which differentiate it from that of all other regions of the world; while they are common to the whole country or rather continent in a degree sufficient to justify its treatment as a unit in the history of human social and intellectual development. To Sir Herbert Risley, "Beneath the manifold diversity of physical and social type, language, custom and religion which strikes the observer in India there can still be discerned .... a certain underlying uniformity of life from the Himalayas to Cape Comorin." Chisholm says, "There is no part of the world better marked out by Nature as a region by itself than India, exclusive of Burma. It is a region indeed full of contrasts in physical features and in climate,—but the features that divide it as a whole from surrounding regions are too clear to be over-looked."

The Constitution of India calls the country by two names—India and Bharat. However, it must be remembered that the term India was coined by the foreigners. To the outsiders, the country was known by the river Sindu which was changed to Indus by the Greeks to make it easy to pronounce. Even the term Hindu is not an Indian term originally. It was coined by the Persians after Sindhu again due to the same purpose of an easy pronunciation. "The ancient name of this country was Bharatvarsha derived from *Bharat*, a great hero of Indian history." 'Bharat was the leader of a powerful Aryan tribe that played its full part in the original struggles and conflicts by which Aryan policy and culture were being shaped into proper form in the dawn of Indian history. Rig-veda first mentions him and another ancient text

Aitareya Brahmin mention 'his coronation ceremony and subsequent career leading to his overlordship which is duly solemnised by the performance of usual *Asvamedha* sacrifice. *Srimad-Bhagwata* calls him *Adhirat* and *Samrat* i.e. King of kings. After a brilliant career he renounced the world.'

The above discussion is just to make the point that Indian unity has existed from time immemorial, to refute the British claim that they were the framers of Indian unity. A major characteristic of Indian civilization has been the assimilation of various streams of people arriving from outside and settling here. However, Islam which came to India around 1000 B.C. couldnot be assimilated. The Muslim rulers in India adopted the policy of blade and blood to convert the native population into Islam. Therefore most of the followers of Islam in India are converts and though, they changed their religion, they developed primarily within Hindu ethos and environment only. Although Islam does not accept the caste system, the Muslims in India certainly practice it. Same is true about the Indian Christians also. During the British period as a result of their policy of divide and rule, various differences among the Indian people were encouraged in order to strengthen and consolidate the British rule in India.

Communalism: A Big Challenge to National Integration

India is a land of widespread diversities in terms of geography religion, language and other factors. Following is the distribution of population in terms of religion as per 1991 census.

Table 11
Population by Religion

Religion	No. (million)	% distribution
Buddhist	6.4	0.8
Christians	19.6	2.3
Hindus	687.6	82.0
Jains	3.4	0.4
Muslims	101.6	12.1
Sikhs	16.3	1.9

Source: India at 50 Facts, Figure and Analysis 1947-1997, Express Publications (Madurai) Ltd.

Thus 82 per cent of population belongs to Hindu religion followed by the Muslims with 12.1 per cent of population. Jains and Buddhists are closely associated with the Hindus and usually not regarded as a religious minorities. However, certain Buddhists regard Buddhism as a distinct religion from that of Hindu. Another group of Sikhism, an off shoot of Hinduism also regard themselves as a separate religion.

But none of the communities in India can be regarded as homogenous. All of them are divided in terms of caste, an unique ancient institution of India. A variety of people with many diversities in terms of region, language and other factors and also including a significant number of tribal population constitute Hindus. In fact historically speaking Hinduism has been more a way of life than a religion in the strict sense of the term. The Muslims are also not cohesive. The Muslims living in Hindi speaking areas and in Andhra Pradesh generally speak Urdu, in Bengal they speak Bengali and in South-west Malayalam. They are divided among different sects notably Shiya and Sunni. In Kashmir, the Muslims have a special Kashmiri identity and speak Kashmiri rather than Urdu. The Sikhs are also divided into Scheduled Caste and non-Scheduled caste Sikhs, and also between Jat Sikhs and other higher caste Sikhs. The Christians are dispersed in India and speak the local language. In the North-East, the Christians are the tribal converts as also in Bihar. Therefore cultural differences also exist among them. Thus all the religions in India have their own internal divisions which finds expression in inter-religions riots and conflicts. For example, Sunni-Shiya conflicts in Uttar Pradesh and various inter-caste wars in Hindu Society.

As far as the geographical distribution of these religions is concerned Hindus are in majority in most of the states and are scattered in all the parts of the country. Muslims constitute a majority in the state of Jammu and Kashmir but they are widely dispersed. They are in significant number in Uttar Pradesh where the Two-nation theory developed and which culminated in the partition of the country in 1947. Besides, they are a strong minority in Assam, Kerala, West Bengal, Bihar, Karnataka and Andhra Pradesh. The Sikhs are mainly in Punjab. They are also concentrated in Haryana, Rajasthan, Uttar Pradesh and Delhi. Indian Christians are in majority in Nagaland and Meghalaya. They are also in a sizeable number in Kerala, Tamil Nadu and Andhra Pradesh. A number of tribals in Bihar, West Bengal and Madhya Pradesh have also been converted to Christianity.

The existence of these religions in India has resulted in communal struggles and riots, which has become a major challenge to the cause of national integration.

What is Communalism?

Communalism is an ideology of religious fundamentalism. According to Bipin Chandra, "the concept of communalism is based on the belief that religious distinction is the most important and fundamental distinction, and this distinction overrides all other distinctions. Since Hindus, Muslims and Sikhs are different religious entities, their social, economic, cultural and political interests are also dissimilar and divergent. As such the loss of one religious group is the gain of another group and vice-versa. If a particular community seeks to better its social and economic situation, it is doing so at the expense of others." According to Rasheeduddin Khan, communalism is .... "perversion of religion from a moral order to a temporal arrangement of contemporary convenience .... from a strategy of living into tactics of politics .... communalism seeks to conform arbitrary religious tenets, traditions and values to suit exigencies of current political life and tactical interest, Communalism thus is exploitation, naked and subtle of religion and of genuine attachment to a religious community." As such communalism is a divisive force in the society which creates and fosters alienation of one community from the rest of the communities. The aims and objectives of communalism are to foster religious bigotry and present a particular religion against other religion or religions. It means aggrandisement of one religion at the expense of other religions. It means to regard one's religion as the best while the other religions are supposed to be lower. Naturally such an ideology spreads religious hatred and hostility, and, therefore, is regarded as inimical to the healthy development of the society. In India, communalism has led to tensions between different communities and frequent riots notably Hindu-Muslims, Hindu-Sikhs, Hindu-Christians and even Hindu-Buddhists. While Hindu-Muslim conflicts have taken place in Jammu and Kashmir, Uttar Pradesh, Madhya Pradesh, Maharashtra, Andhra Pradesh, Tamil Nadu and other parts of India, Hindu-Sikh riots took place particularly after the assassination of Prime Minister Indira Gandhi in North India. In Bihar, Hindu-Buddhist conflict has taken place. Hindu-Christian conflicts have been concentrated in the State of Kerala.

In modern times, communalism entered into Indian polity during the British period when the colonial rulers adopted a policy of divide and rule to ensure their survival. A British Secretary of State Lord Woods wrote to the Viceroy in India, Lord Bruce Elgin (1862-63), "we have maintained our power in India by playing off one party against another and we must continue to do so. Do all you can, therefore, to prevent all having a common feeling." Similarly, Lord Canning wrote, "As we must rule 150 millions of people by a handful (more or less small) of Englishmen, let us do it in the manner best calculated to leave them divided (as in religion and national feeling they already are) and to inspire them with the greatest possible awe of our power and with the least possible suspicion of our motives." Initially the British encouraged Hindus as against the Muslims as they had replaced the Muslim rulers in India resulting in Muslim animosity towards them. However, with the development of all Indian nationalism, the British became pro-Muslim and encouraged them to develop a communal approach to politics. Later on, as the Indian nationalism entered into the militant stage under the secular leadership of Gandhi, the British policy of divide and rule became very apparent. All the cleavages in the Indian society were used or misused for this purpose. All this resulted in the Muslim's League's demand for Pakistan, as separate homeland for Muslims on the basis of Two-Nation theory which regarded Hindus and Muslims as two separate nations and therefore, entitled for two different states. Ultimately, Partition of the country was affected and Pakistan came into existence in 1947. But the Partition did not solve the communal problem in India as it remained in the body politic like a cancer.

Causes of Communalism in India

The partition of India could not solve the communal problem in India because firstly the partition took place on a wrong notion of two-nation theory. Secondly, the partition left a large Muslim population in India who did not migrate to Pakistan where also a significant number of Hindu minorities remained. Had all the Muslims migrated to Pakistan, probably the communal question would have been solved. But this could not happen because religion alone cannot be a factor in the choice of settling or leaving a particular place of settlement. A man lives in the totality of his environment and many Muslims preferred not to be uprooted from their place of settlement. Their decision was justified also for in Pakistan the migrants from India continued to be discriminated against and are called *Mohajirs*. As far as India is concerned, the Indian Constitution guaranteed the religious minorities their suitable place under the broad secular frame-work. However, despite a secular constitution, communalism continues and communal riots are frequent occurrences in India. Following are the causes of communalism in India.

1. *Historical Legacy*

The past of India, which was full of religious conflicts in the medieval times, comes back to haunt us. Unfortunately the past conflicts inspire the conflicts of the present. The Muslim rulers in India destroyed the Hindu places of worship and imposed taxes like *Jaziya* on Hindus besides forcibly converting Hindus into Muslims. Temples were desecrated and destroyed and in their place mosques were built. This has resulted in conflict over many mosques which the Hindu groups want to destroy or shift. In 1992, the disputed structure of Babri Masjid-Ram Janambhoomi was destroyed by a frenzied mob which led to communal riots in almost the entire India. Besides Ayodhaya, similar disputes are in Kashi and Mathura and many other structures situated in different parts of country which both the Hindus as well as Muslims claim to be their places of worship. After independence the Somnath temple was reconstructed by removing a Muslim graveyard and a chabutara (dais) of Muslim prayer without any resistance from Muslims. Dr. Rajendra Prasad, the President of India had attended the Murti Sthapana ceremony. In order to strengthen its nationalism, every country invokes national heroes which unfortunately in India became highly controversial from communal point of view. Lord Ram and the concept of Ram Rajya alienated Muslims and other communities. This happened during the freedom movement in the present century when religion was used for the purpose of political mobilisation by the extremists and later on by Gandhi. No doubt their secular credentials were above suspicion, yet at the same time a healthy development of all-India nationalism suffered. The British also contributed in a very big way in the growth and development of communalism as per their policy of divide and rule. They encouraged the Muslims to set up their own separate educational institutions and advocated the interests of their community to put a brake on the development of an all-India colonial struggle and nationalism. In the process they could get the Muslim loyalty. Thus M.A.O. College in Aligarh was established in 1875 for making Muslims useful and worthy citizens of the British. The British also partitioned Bengal to curb the rising tide of nationalism in Bengal. As a result of English encouragement Muslim League was founded in 1906. The British Government also provided separate electorate to Muslims under the Minto-Morley Reforms Act of 1909 which was later on extended to Sikhs, Europeans, Anglo-Indians and Christians by the 1919 Act. The British also gave a communal colour to Indian history and accordingly the Indian history was divided into three segments of

Hindus, Muslims and the British. While the fact remains that wars in history were fought between Kings for political reasons, the history was presented as a struggle between Hindus and Muslims during medieval times. Thus the wars between Akbar and Rana Pratap or between Aurangzeb and Shivaji was a political struggle, they were essentially projected as Hindu-Muslim strifes. All this resulted in the Partition of India and communal riots in 1947 in which a large number of people belonging to both the communities were killed and many were transformed into refugees as a result of migration which remains unparalleled in human history. The Partition haunts the Indian psyche even today, especially in the Hindus who blame Muslims for the partition of the country. Even after 55 years of Partition, there are many Hindus who doubt the loyalty of Muslims in India.

2. *Economic Backwardness and Illiteracy among the Muslims*

The Muslims were late in accepting the modern education system which was a major factor in their remaining backward during the British period. After independence, unfortunately, this continued. Although many Muslims adopted the modern education system, their number in relation to their total percentage in India is low. This is the reason of their low representation in various professional and bureaucratic jobs. This economic backwardness inhibits a rational mind and they succumb to various pressures which are mainly designed to foster the vested interests. This is also applicable to economically backward Hindus and other communities. There is no understanding among the poor that religion is no solution to the problems of modern life. It is basically the poor who participate and suffer in the communal riots.

According to Dr. Zaheer Ahmed Sayeed (The Hindu, 16 December 1997) poverty could not be a factor for Muslim backwardness though poverty defies advancement. But then, except for a few rare personalities who can claim inherited advantages, most of the unnamed and unknown Muslim politicians, scientists, bureaucrats and artists have all emerged from humble living conditions to gain their status in Indian society. Persons like Dr. Abdul Kalam (The President of India, popularly known as missile man) Fakhruddin Ali Ahmed, Nasirudeen Shah, Mushirul Hasan, General Zaki and Arif Beg were of humble origin and they developed, what the Muslim community in general lacks, because they had the will to excel in the 'pursuit of excellence.' Since the community lacks this, therefore, as a panacea seeks minority rights enshrined in the Constitution at every step. Commented Dr. Sayeed, "To cry hoarse at each step that the minority rights have been denied to them! True perhaps to an extent but one should remind the Muslim community that a society which keeps vocalising ad nauseum about its rights unaccompanied by an equal intensity of hardwork to be rendered towards their upliftment, does not progress but continues to remain as a subdued citizenry." He noted that such vocalisations was absent among the Christians, the second largest minority community. Dr. Sayeed felt the reason for Muslim backwardness is also the illiteracy widespread among the Muslim men and women, who are more interested in religious education and not in the normal education. Here it behoves the Muslim community to exhibit its strength and reorient its religious heads to the extent that the Muslim at large gets the usual formal education offered in this country. As leaders of the community they should assume the responsibility to push forward the state of formal education of the average Muslim rather than restrict it to the scriptures and in this sense one must accept that they have failed and are responsible for the backwardness of the community at large. Dr. Sayeed believes that Muslims should join other political groups and eschew isolation for '... the cause of Muslim degradation would be served better by his incorporation in the various political groups.' He also wants the Muslims to join BJP because 'whether one likes it or not the BJP with its relatively stable base will assume power sometime. The Muslim polity has to make up its mind whether it wishes to be part of the decision making process at that time.' This does not mean that the Muslims should abandon their scriptures.' Look at the Muslim community in the U.S. It has promoted its young most vigorously in both education and sport but at the same time has retained its identity through weekend classes of scriptural instructions!'

3. *Separatism and Isolationism among the Muslims*

The separatism and isolationism in Indian Muslims led to the Partition of the country. Unfortunately this feeling has continued after the worst turmoils of partition also. Various Muslim organisations like the Jamaat-e-Islami in 1952 advised the Muslims not to participate in the first general election as it would not establish an Islamic State in India. The Muslim League in UP also wants to retain the separate Muslim identity and is opposed to any change in Muslim Personal Law. Besides, we have Jamait-Ul-Ulema, the Dini Talimi, Majlis-e-Mushawarat the Iteahad-al-Musalmeen, the Anjuman-e-Taragoee-Urdu. In 1997, the All India Milli Council demanded reservation for Muslims in Parliament and state legislatures. Dr. M. Manzoor Alam, the convenor of AIMC's Karvan-e-Azadi said that the share of Muslims in power structure was inadequate and therefore, suitable measures would also have to be taken to give them adequate representation in the administrative services and the police and para-military forces. The AIMC demanded that the Muslim-dominated constituencies should be notified on the lines of constituencies reserved for scheduled castes and tribes. It also wanted the establishment of an equal opportunities Commission to examine cases of discrimination against minorities and suggest remedial measures. The AIMC also noted "The role of the Muslim in the Independence struggle has been either deliberately ignored or distorted even though prominent Muslim leaders have participated in the movement since 1757." The Council also exhorted secular forces to stop the move by fascist forces to convert the Indian state and polity into a `strong militant Hindu state' as the dangerous political mobilisation, in the name of cultural nationalism, poses a serious threat to the ideal of a plural democratic India. There have been extremists organisation like Al-Umma who murdered a traffic constable in Coimbatore, Tamil Nadu in 1997 whose only crime was that the traffic police had booked certain members of Al-Umma for traffic violations. The murder resulted in communal riot in Coimbatore. Besides Al-Umma, Islamid Sevak Sangh Jam-Iyyatul Issania, Sunni Tiger Force, Islamic Dawa Mission, People's Democratic Party, Malappuram-based National Democratic Front are some of the South India based Muslim terrorist groups. The Al-Umma was allegedly behind the series of blasts in Coimbatore in 1998 on the eve of the Twelfth Lok Sabha Election that shook the entire country and claimed lot of damages both in terms of lives and property. All the Muslim organisations have been encouraging Islamic fundamentalism, many of them talk about glorious medieval past of 'Muslim rule in India. Moin Shakir has blamed all these organisations as 'communal' on four counts: Firstly, they all believe in separate electorate for the Muslims: secondly they all confuse religion with politics and economics; thirdly, they keep the masses ignorant of the realities of the modern age; and lastly they indulge in unprincipled adventurism.

4. *The Compulsions of Democratic Process*

While democracy is the best form of government among the possible alternatives where the popular sovereignty finds its living expression, it also has certain demerits. The system envisages the enjoyment of political power and patronage on the basis of achievement of maximum number of votes. Therefore all the political parties, as all of them are formed for capturing political power, attempt to have vote bank of their own who would blindly support them. In India, the minorities were the vote bank of the Congress Party for a long time. Many critics have pointed that Congress followed an appeasement policy towards Muslims. In 1984, the Congress Party played the Hindu card which was a deviation from its earlier policy and was able to capture as many as 415 seats with a 48.1 per centage of total votes, a figure which it could not achieve even during Nehru era. In 1989, Rajiv Gandhi started his campaign from Faizabad by promising Ram Rajya. In order to achieve power in Punjab, the Congress Party promoted Bhinderawale to alienate Akali Dal which ultimately led to terrorism in Punjab and the infamous Operation Blue Star in 1984. In 1989, the Congress Party demanded votes in Mizoram Assembly elections in the name of Christianity. However, the Congress party is not only to be blamed for playing a communal card. The Bhartiya Janata Party (BJP) has also been playing the Hindu card. The 1996 election manifesto declared that 'Hindutva, or cultural nationalism,' (which is the BJP's philosophy), 'shall be the rainbow which will bridge our present to our glorious past and pave the way for an equally glorious future; it will guide the transition from Swarajya to Surajya." BJP's philosophy of Hindutava creates suspicion among the minorities particularly the Muslims. A senior BJP leader who is a Muslim, Bakht said, "A Muslim derives his faith from Islam. He is proud of Islam and he has every right to be so. But the moment a Hindu speaks of Hindutva, he is branded as communal why? Why do we want to deny the Hindu the right to be proud of Hindutva? ... Why was India divided? Who demanded the division of the country on the basis of religion? And what was the result of division? Well, creation of an "Islamic" theocratic state and, by the very logic of history, possibility of creation of a Hindu state. But the ethos of the Hindu refused to submit to the logic of history and made this country proud by giving it a secular polity, a secular constitution. The national temper of this country should have been developed on the basis of the magnificence of this ethos. Instead, the Hindu himself has been sought to the placed in the dock. Can there be anything more unfortunate than denigrating the Hindu and then claiming to strengthen the national fabric? What is India without Hindu? "While there is a certain rationale in the BJP advocacy of Hindutva, its emotional impact certainly alienates the Muslims. Another Hindu party, Shiv Sena has at times openly advocated anti-Muslim perspective. Besides, there are other organisations which do not involve in political activities but they do have their strong influence felt in the political system. RSS (Rashtriya Swyam Sewak Sangh) and VHP

(Vishwa Hindu Parishad) have encouraged communalism in India. The Vishwa Hindu Parishad (VHP) stood for the 'liberation' of Ramjanam Bhoomi and after the demolition of Babri Masjid, it wants to further liberate Krishnajanam bhoomi in Mathura and Shiv Mandir in Kashi. The VHP Working President Ashok Singhal threatened that if Muslims do not agree to handover Kashi and Mathura mosques to Hindus, they will suffer the same humiliation that they did during the Babri mosque demolition in Ayodhya. He said that the Hindus have finally learnt to use their muscle power and would not hesitate to use it again. He declared, "The Hindus asserted themselves for the first time during the Ayodhya incident. We want the Kashi and Mathura issues to be settled amicably, but if the Muslim leadership continues to dilly - dally, we may have to use muscle power again." According to Ashok Singhal, the VHP had learnt the art of making minorities understand "in a language they know." VHP is a non-political organisation but it supports BJP in politics. The RSS (Rashtriya Swayam Sewak Sangh) and Hindu Mahasabha are other groups which emphasise Hindu culture—Hindutva, Hindu rashtra and Hindu Bhasha (Hindi). However, there is no denying of the fact that Muslim communalism and minority politics in India has resulted in Hindu revivalism and consequently communalism has spread its tentacles in Indian politics.

5. *Role of Pakistan and other Islamic Countries*

This is another important factor in the consolidation of Muslim alienation and fundamentalism. The relations between India and Pakistan have never been cordial though both of them have a common culture. Pakistan was formulated on the basis of the two-nation theory which stood for an independent homeland for Muslims of Indian sub-continent. There are reasons to believe that the relationship between India and Pakistan are the continuation of relationship between the Congress and Muslim League before the Partition that created two independent states of India and Pakistan. During the freedom struggle, Congress projected itself as a national secular party which represented the entire population including the Muslims—a claim always disputed by the Muslim League who called the Congress as essentially a Hindu party and simultaneously projecting itself as the representative of the entire Muslim community in India. The Congress, on its part, never accepted the Muslim League's position. Some of the leaders of Congress party also had a doubtful secular credentials. Further the Congress had to function in a society where tolerance to each other's faith had not developed to the required secular ethos. After partition, Pakistan tried to establish its image as the leader of Muslims in Indian sub-continent. The Pakistani Press, Radio and Television have always given a distorted account of Hindu-Muslim conflicts in India. Whenever there is a communal flare up, Pakistan would accuse of genocide of Muslims in India with the Indian Government connivance. The Pakistani Press would publish exaggerated account of Muslim killings in the riots. The successive Pakistani leadership talked about the Muslim oppression in India for its own sake and possibly to create fears among the minority Hindu community living in Pakistan so that they migrate to India. Another reason could be that the very foundation of Pakistan i.e. religion is shaky as it could not save it from dismemberment in 1971. But its propaganda influenced the illiterate Muslims living in India who took Pakistan as their well-wishers. Further, Pakistan's intelligence service ISI is known to be fomenting trouble in various parts of the country. It has also trained and provided armaments to various terrorist organisations in India. It has been actively supporting terrorists in Punjab and also Jammu and Kashmir, a state which Pakistan claims to be part of its territory on the basis of defunct two-nation theory i.e. since the majority in Jammu and Kashmir are Muslims, the state belongs to Pakistan. In 1997, a Foreign office spokesman at Islamabad expressed concern over *the arrest of thousands of Muslims'* protesting against the 1992 destruction of Babri Mosque. The spokesman said that Pakistan expected that India would 'fulfil its promise to rebuild the mosque and to prevent extremist elements from carrying out their threats' of destroying other mosques in India. Kuldeep Nayar rightly points out, "Persistent propaganda against India has conditioned the minds of most Pakistanis to such an extent that India is seen as an embodiment of evil." Pakistani national is trained right from his schools to be anti-Indian. Thus according to a class VIII school textbook, the partition of Bengal in 1904 took place because of Kali Puja which was 'a method of slaughtering the Muslims and presenting them at the altar of the Goddess. The Pakistani armed forces magazine, Al Hilal said, "Hindus have not accepted Pakistan, nor ever will they do so. Therefore, we have to fight for the protection of Pakistan as steadfastly as we did for its attainment." In support, the magazine quoted Balraj Madhok, former Jan Sangh leader as having said that if the British could divide the Indian subcontinent, New Delhi can also reestablish its rule over what the country was, before partition. Commented Kuldip Nayar, "Even the lunatic fringe in India has stopped saying this. But the Pakistan Government has not abandoned this line because it adds to its people's feeling of insecurity." In March 1998, the Information Minister of Pakistan Mushahid Hussain visited the Headquarters of Lashkar-e-Taiba (Army of the Pure) which is an extremist organisation in Muridke in Pakistan, formed to train militants and send them to Kashmir for terrorist activites. Hussain praised Markaz Dawa Al Irshad (Centre for Preaching) which trains and maintains Lashkar-e-Taiba. Hussain said that true concept of Jehad (Holy War) was being taught by the Markaz. The Markaz Chief Hafiz Mohammad Saeed declared that after the liberation of Kashmir, his organisation would launch a 'jehad' for the liberation of 20 crore Indian Muslims who, he claimed had been living a second and third grade life. (*The Hindustan Times Evening News*, April 21, 1998).

Besides Pakistan, other Muslim countries especially their group called Organisation of Islamic Conference have no hesitation in interfering in India's internal affairs. In 1997, the Islamic Conference's resolution on Kashmir spoke of self determination. The Iranian Ambassador to India Alireza Sheikhattar defending the OIC resolution said, "Kashmir is considered a Muslim problem. India's point of view is different from that of Pakistan. Other countries may not have the same point of view but there is a consensus that the Kashmir issue is a Muslim community problem." The newspaper report painted out that initially the OIC secretariat had decided to focus only on Palestine issue and keep other issues, including Kashmir, out of the formal resolution. But ultimately Kashmir was included in the resolution due to Pakistani insistence. While the Organisation of Islamic Conference has ignored the Shias and Sunnis conflict in Pakistan or the slaughter of Kurds of Turkey and Iraq, it has always talked about Kashmir or Indian Muslims. An interesting aspect of OIC is that it represents only the 55 states who have clearly declared themselves as Islamic, where any kind of religious conflict or even slaughter of people does not concern the OIC but in countries where the Muslims live and which have not been declared as Islamic like India, China, Russia, Philippines and Bosnia, the problems of native Muslims becomes issues of Islam.

6. *Religious Revivalism*

It is believed that modernisation and development make men more rational, materialistic and less religious. Unfortunately, the Indian experience shows the religious revivalism alongwith modernisation and development. The Muslims, the Hindus, the Sikhs and all other communities are becoming more religious. Various religious occasions are celebrated with more fervour and open demonstration. Religious processions have become very common and all the Temples, Gurudwaras and Mosques use loudspeakers at high volumes to compel people listen to their recitations. While the loudspeakers contribute to the noise pollution, the processions, many a times, have led to communal tensions. In 1997, which had been relatively communal riot free year, religious processions were the cause of communal riots in Patna, Roorkee (Uttaranchal), Hyderabad and Jalgaon district in Maharashtra. The religious revivalism can also be seen in the electronic media where religious serials like Ramayana, Mahabharata etc. are being telecast.

7. *Role of the Government*

Even after fifty years of independence, the Indian Government has not been able to develop a coherent policy to thwart communalism and communal riots in India. No serious study of communal situation have been done by the Government. Adhocism has been the rule. Whenever communal riots have broken, the government comes out of its slumber and various measures like deployment of army and paramilitary forces, imposition of curfew etc. are taken. Some arrests are also made and once the normalcy is restored the government goes back to its slumber and will awaken only when a fresh riot takes place. Very few persons accused of inciting or participating in the communal riots are really convicted. Further, there have been frequent reports of police being partial to one community against the other. Many Muslims believe that they are not provided enough security and relief in the communal riots. While the RSS was being blamed as a communal organisation, in 1965 war with Pakistan, it was assigned civil defence duties by the Indian government which had earlier banned it following the assassination of Mahatma Gandhi.

8. *Socio-economic Causes*

There are many socio-economic dimensions of communalism in India. Firstly is the conversion. The Muslims and Christians have adopted a policy of converting Harijans and tribals into their respective folds. This is done to increase their number. A complaint is often made by a devout Hindu that the Muslim population in India is growing. While in 1947 their population was 5.1 per cent of the total population, in 1991 it increased to 12.1 per cent. The increase of Muslim population in India has been due to conversions, lack of family planning among Muslims and illegal Muslim migrants from Bangladesh. This has created a fear psychosis among the Hindus, particularly in Assam and other north eastern states, that they will be reduced to a minority in their areas. Hindu organisations like RSS started reconverting the converted people back into the Hindu fold which has further complicated the communal scenario.

There have been economic causes behind communal riots. For example, in Moradabad, the Muslim artisans have been involved in the famous brass work which has a good international market but their marketing was traditionally done by the Hindus. Now the Muslims have also come into exports of the brass work and consequently Hindu traders have suffered. This has been the cause of communal riots in Moradabad. Similarly, the 1980-81 riots in Godhra were the result of clash of economic interests between Sindhi and Ganchi petty traders. In 1981, Baroda also witnessed communal riots because the illicit-liquor and bottlegging, which was hitherto controlled by the Muslims, had also been taken up by the Marathi-speaking Scheduled Caste community of Bhois. Thus the anti-social racket of illicit-liquor and bottlegging became a cause of communal riots in Baroda. In Biharsharif also, the reasons of communal riots were to be found in the acquisition of wealth by the Muslims and the consequent economic rivalry with the Hindus.

Secularism

To combat communalism, the Indian constitution declared India to be a secular state, as per the 42nd Constitutional Amendment in the Preamble of the Constitution in 1976. However, even before this formal declaration the, constitution contained many provisions providing for secularism,

(i) *Article 14* prohibits state from denying to any person equality before law or equal protection of law.

(ii) *Article 15(1)* declares that the State shall not discriminate against any citizen on grounds only of *religion, race, caste, sex, place of birth or any of them.* Further section (2) says that 'No citizen shall, on grounds only of religion, race, caste, sex, place of birth or any of them, be subject to any disability, liability, restriction or condition with regard to—

  (a) access to shops, public restaurants, hotels and places of public entertainment; or

  (b) the use of wells, tanks, bathing ghats, roads and places of public resort maintained wholly or partly out of state funds or dedicated to the use of the general public.

(iii) *Article 16* relates to the equality of opportunity to all the citizens of the state in the matter of employment or appointment to any office under the state and among other factors, religion cannot be a ground for ineligibility or discrimination.

(iv) *Article 17* declares abolition of untouchability and its practice in any form is forbidden.

(v) *Article 25* says that 'subject to public order, morality and health and to the other provisions of this part, all persons are equally entitled to freedom of conscience and the right to freely profess, practise and propagate religion.'

(vi) *Article 26* provides every religion a right (a) to establish and maintain institutions for religious and charitable purposes; (b) to manage its own affairs in matters of religion; (c) to own and acquire movable and immovable property; and (d) to administer such property in accordance with the law.

(vii) *Article 27* prohibits the levying of a tax, the proceeds of which are meant specifically for payment of expenses for the promotion or maintenance of any particular religion or religious denomination.

(viii) *Article 28* provides that no religious instruction shall be provided in any educational institution, wholly maintained out of state funds.

(ix) *Article 29(i)* gives the citizens, right to conserve their distinct language, script or culture. *Article 29(2)* says, "No citizen shall be denied admission into any educational institution maintained by the state or receiving aid out of state funds on grounds only of religion, race, caste, language or any of them.

(x) As per *Article 30(1)* all minorities whether based on religion or language have been given right to establish and administer educational institutions of their choice. Further *Article 30(1-A)* provides that in case of compulsory acquisiton of an educational institution established and administered by a minority, 'the state shall ensure that the amount fixed by or determined under the law would not restrict or abrogate the right guaranteed...'. *Article 30(2)* declares that the state shall not, in granting aid to educational institutions, discriminate against any educational institutions on the ground that it is under the management of a minority, whether based on religion or language.

Thus the constitution makers provided for a secular state while specially mentioning the right of minorities to profess and propagate their religion in accordance with the law, without specifically declaring

India as a secular state. This is commendable given the fact that the overwhelming majority of India's population was Hindu, yet, despite the partition which was based on religion, they did not declare India a Hindu state because they wanted all the religions in India to develop and flourish. The inclusion of 'Secular' in the Preamble thus can only be regarded as a mere formality.

Secularism in India—A Few Observations

The secular outlook of the Constitution was further strengthened by its implementation during the last three years. We have three Presidents who were Muslims, i.e., Dr. Zakir Hussain, Fakhruddin Ali Ahmed and Dr. APJ Abdul Kalam. Besides, Muslims have also occupied senior positions including the Vice Presidency, Chief Justice of India, Chief Minister, Governor, Air Force Chief etc. One of the Presidents of India, Giani Zail Singh was a Sikh. Similarly, Parsis and Christians have also occupied senior military and civilian posts. Apart from political and administrative offices, different communities have their respective representatives in art, science, theatre, films and different sports. Thus one can confidentally assert that in the development of any personality in India, religion has not been an inhibiting factor and opportunities are available for all.

2. Alongwith secularism, communal forces have also developed. Besides the Muslim communalism, the Indian political system has also witnessed the rise and consolidation of Sikh and Hindu communalism. They have become a force to reckon with. Yet there has not been any significant erosion of secularism so far as the Constitution and its implementation is concerned. On the other hand, the belief has been strengthened that Indian political system has no other option than a secular polity.

3. While the secular state has interfered in the religious practices of the majority community, i.e., Hinduism, it has restrained itself from doing the same in case of minority's religion. On their part, the minorities have also resisted any change in their religion by the state. Thus the old antiquated Muslim Personal law still thrives in India. Polygamy is allowed despite the fact that it is disallowed in Islamic countries. Similarly, the women among the Muslims continued to be discriminated against and when the Supreme Court stepped in the Shah Bano case to emancipate them, the Muslim organisations made a big hue and cry and compelled the Rajiv Government to annul the decision by a law. The Sikhs have been also allowed to carry kirpan as a religious practice. When the Supreme Court ordered the wearing of

helmets for the pillion drivers in two-wheelers compulsory as a safety measure, the Sikh organisation demanded exception for Sikh women on the ground of religion. The Delhi Government had to submit to their demand and it made exception to the general rule of wearing helmet to all the women as to distinguish Sikh women, from other women, is an impossible task. Accidents and injuries (even death) do not distinguish people on religious basis but a general rule had to be amended in the name of religion. The non-interference in the religion of minorities by the state and the interference in the religion of the majority has led to a feeling of communal jealousy. Another interesting aspect of state interference in Hindu religion was raised during the debates on the Marriage Bill in early 1950's which introduced the provision of divorce for Hindu couples. It was alleged that the state was being favourable to Hindus alone in reformation of the religion. Acharya Kripalani pointed out, "If they (members of the legislature) single out the Hindu community for their reforming zeal, they cannot escape the charge of being communal in the sense that they favour the Hindu community and are indifferent to the good of the Muslim community or the Catholic community in the matter of divorce. Do we want one community to be in advance of other communities in India, simply because it happens to be in the majority? The charge levelled against Hindu communalists is that they want their community to be in a more advantageous position than other communities." It was pointed out during those days that by modifying Hindu personal law and leaving other communities untouched, the state was in fact acting as a communal state rather than a secular state.

4. Religion continues to play a very important role in politics. All the political parties have used religion for the sake of votes. There is some truth in the BJP's allegation that in India the parties who called themselves as secular are 'pseudo secular' and not really secular. Though every party condemns communalism, there have been reports of their indulgence in inciting or participation in communal riots.

5. It is also a fact that the secular state in India functions in a society which is not secular. There is a lack of tolerance and love among different faiths. In fact Gurudwaras, mosques and temples are used for political purposes. On a few occasions, the state had to use force to prevent the religious places from being misused. Operation Blue Star in 1984 in Golden Temple at Amritsar is a classical case. This has further complicated the communal problem in India because the reaction to such acts has been horrible and as a result, the state has to become a soft state culminating in a helpless situation.

Caste in Indian Politics

Another threat to the national integration comes from the unique Indian institution of caste. The caste system is based on Varna which classifies the Indian society into four fold division of Brahmin (scholar-priest), Kshatriya (warrior), Vaishya (business class) and Sudra (peasants and labourers). However, the complexities of caste system cannot be understood by this four fold classification of the people. A better understanding would be from the jati angle. While varna may be all-India in character, the jati has a definite geographical and even linguistic limitation. The jati not only provides the person his social identity and security but it also defines his duty and responsibility. It is this jati system or caste system which makes the Hindu religion a rigid social order which is otherwise very flexible. Another aspect of caste is that although it is a Hindu institution, it permeates in all the other religions in India, thus really making it an all-India phenomenon. It is also important to note that despite various attempts to eradicate the caste system, the system remains and there is no possibility of its eradication. The framers of the Indian Constitution also accepted this fact and they tried to eradicate some of the evils of the caste system. Although the modern liberal ideas have affected the caste system to a great extent but the basic objection to the caste system remains valid i.e. it is based on inequality and has resulted in miseries to the lower caste people. In the political system, it leads to caste politics and caste rivalries and even violence. On its part, the Indian Constitution sought to amend the rigours of caste system by abolishing untouchability and by a preferential treatment to the Scheduled castes in the matter of education, jobs and state assemblies. Later on the reservation was extended to other backward castes which were identified by the Mandal Commission.

During elections, the role of caste becomes very important. The selection of a candidate from a particular constituency is done keeping in view the caste considerations. He should belong to the dominant caste or should be able to get support from a particular caste or castes. A candidate belonging to a caste, which has the majority in the area, has a fair chance of getting elected. People, also generally, tend to support the candidate of their respective caste. As a result, the caste association play a major role during the elections. The political parties are also caste-ridden. Within a political party, alliances are formed on the basis of caste. There have also been cases of one particular caste aligning with one party and another to another party. For example, in Andhra Pradesh, there has been constant struggle between dominant castes of

Kammas and Reddys. Both have been rival to each other. While the Kammas joined the communists, the Reddys supported the Congress. Similarly, in Karnataka Lingayats and Vokkaligas are in conflicts with each other. These conflict also takes place within a party. Bihar has been a classical case of such conflicts, where Brahmins and Kayasthas have been at loggerheads. In South, however, we have three caste groups of (a) Brahmins; (b) non-Brahmins and (c) Scheduled Castes and Scheduled Tribes. But this is not to say that they are organised in one line, within each group there are rivalries and dissensions.

Another aspect of caste scenario in India is the rise of Dalits as a powerful factor. Dalit movement* is meant to rejuvenate the lower caste people within Hinduism who were formerly called untouchables. The rise of dalit power is linked with the decline of Congress party and what is called the Mandalisation of Indian politics. The Congress in her heydays sought to combine all the castes and classes of Indian society for the formidable task of nation-building. It cut across the caste line and never had to take recourse of upper caste vs lower caste politics. However, at the same time, the party at the state level had the support of the local dominant castes like Marathas in Maharashtra, Reddys in Andhra Pradesh, Patidars in Gujarat and Jats in Uttar Pradesh and Haryana. The lower castes alongwith minorities constituted its vote bank. This is, what had been the Congress consensus system that ensured her political hegemony. However, 1990's saw the decline of this system and with the implementation of Mandal report, Dalit politics came into forefront. But it is to be remembered that Dalits are not organised in one group. They cut across the party lines and the Dalit parties such as Bahujan Samaj Party (BSP) or Republican Party of India (RPI) have not been able to function as unified groups. Like in other political parties, factionalism has been rampant and there have been splits. Further, these parties have little to their achievement so far as the emancipation of dalits is concerned. It is also a fact that the Dalit population has increased from 14.7 per cent of the total population in 1961 to 16.3 per cent in 1991 but the difference between their literacy rate and those of non-dalits has remained almost static. The inability of Dalit leadership to provide an effective leadership to Dalit, for their emancipation, has been exposed in a very short time. However, the Dalit rise has further increased the caste conflicts especially in Bihar and Uttar Pradesh, where caste senas are

*For details on Dalit Movement see Dalit Movement in India in Chapter XX.

being formed. In 1998 in Lakshmanpur-Bathe village of Bihar, 61 dalits were massacred by the Ranvir Sena of upper castes and in retaliation the CPI (M-L) killed the upper caste people.

Thus the caste politics in India is a very dangerous trend and is playing havoc with the national unity and integration.

Language Politics in India

Language is the medium of communication among the people. Further, in modern times it is also a means of getting employment. Both the factors make the language a political issue in Indian politics. Particularly in 1950's and 1960's, it rocked the Indian political scene creating a great danger to the national unity and integration. However, with the passage of time and the flexibility of the political leadership towards the language issue, much of the crisis has subsided and one can say with confidence that language issue no longer remains a major problem towards national integration.

The Indian diversity is best characterised by the existence of too many languages and dialects. The 1961 census recorded as many as 1018 different languages. However, still one can find a sort of unification among these diverse languages and dialects as they fall under four broad language families i.e. Indo-Aryan, Dravidian, Tibeto-Chinese and Austro-Asiatic. Out of this, the first two families of Indo-Aryan and Dravidian dominate the Indian linguistic scenario and there has been a constant borrowing from each other. As per the 1961 census, 73.3 per cent of Indian population spoke Indo-Aryan while 24.5 per cent belonged to the Dravidian family. 1.5 and 0.7 per cents people belonged to the Austro-Asiatic and Tibeto-Chinese language families respectively. Therefore, the Indian Constitution listed fourteen languages of India i.e. Assamese, Bengali, Gujrati, Hindi, Kannada, Kashmiri, Malayalam, Marathi, Oriya, Punjabi, Sanskrit, Tamil, Telugu and Urdu. As per the 1961 census 87 per cent of the people gave these fourteen languages as their mother-tongue. Later on Bodo, Dogri, Maithili, Manipuri, Sindhi, Kokani and Nepali were also included in this list, making the number 22. Another aspect of linguistic scenario has been the fact that there always has been a link language understood in the entire country. Firstly, it was Sanskrit followed by Persian and Urdu. The British period saw the introduction of English language which was spoken and understood by the elite while the common man used Hindustani which was a mixture of Hindi and Urdu or the local language and dialect.

During the freedom movement, the Indian National Congress felt the need of linguistic reorganisation of states but after independence, the Congress leadership was against it. Gandhi feared the danger of linguistic balkanisation of India. The Dar Commission appointed in 1948 also opined that "the formation of provinces on exclusively or even mainly linguistic considerations is not in the larger interest of the Indian nation .... In the formation of new provinces, whenever such a work is taken in hand, oneness of language may be one of the factors to be taken into consideration along with others; but it should not be the decisive or even the main factor. If India does not survive, nothing will be gained by solving her linguistic provinces problems alone." The Congress Committee of Jawaharlal Nehru, Sardar Patel and Pattabhi Sitaramayya also rejected the reorganisation of states on linguistic basis stating that language was not only a binding but also a separating force, and the primary consideration was the security, unity and economic prosperity of India for which every separatist and disruptive tendency should be rigorously discouraged. However, this was not accepted by many. Even the Congress Working Committee headed by P.D. Tandon demanded the immediate formation of linguistic states in 1951. In South, a very strong movement for the formation of Andhra Pradesh for the Telugu speaking people developed which also became violent and led to the creation of Andhra Pradesh in 1953. This encouraged the demand for the formation of linguistic states in other areas and as a result in 1956, the political map of India was remade on the basis of linguistic factor. 14 states were created, i.e. Andhra Pradesh, Assam, Bihar, Bombay, Jammu and Kashmir, Kerala, Madhya Pradesh, Madras, Mysore, Orissa, Punjab, Rajasthan, Uttar Pradesh and West Bengal. Besides, there were six Union Territories also which were to be governed by the Central Government. In 1960, Bombay state was divided into Maharashtra and Gujarat after much of violence and agitation. In 1966, bifurcation of Punjab took place into Punjab and Haryana on linguistic basis.

The reorganisation of states on the basis of language created many problems. Firstly, it created the problem of linguistic minorities in almost every state who were considered as outsiders after the linguistic reorganisation and there have been allegations of discrimination against them. In some states 'son of the soil' theory was advocated and the outsiders were asked to leave the state. For instance, Shiv Sena raised the banner of *Maharashtra* for *Maharashtrians* and the South Indians were attacked and humiliated so that they leave the state. Similarly, Lohit Sena was organised in Assam to oust Bengalis. In West Bengal,

Marwaris became the victim of the son of the soil theory. Particularly in Assam, the Assamese people think that they are a national minority. Though in majority, they fear becoming a minority within the state itself due to influx of Bengalis. The problem has further aggravated because of illegal migrants from Bangladesh. In Guwahati and several towns of Assam, the Assamese are in minority. In Bangalore, the Tamils outnumber the Kannada speaking people. In all these places the son of soil theory finds a fertile place to develop. Secondly, the linguistic reorganisation of states encouraged regionalism. As the states were formed only on the basis of language, they also got developed as well as underdeveloped areas. The backward areas complained of discrimination and soon developed into movements demanding separate statehood. The movements for separate statehood in Telangana in Andhra Pradesh, Vidarbha in Maharashtra, Saurashtra in Gujarat, Jharkhand areas in Bihar, Uttarakhand and Bundelkhand in Uttar Pradesh, Gorkhaland in West Bengal and Chattisgarh and Mahakosal in Madhya Pradesh are some of such examples. Thirdly, the linguistic state reorganisation also encouraged the demand for state autonomy. Particularly, the DMK in Tamil Nadu and Akali Dal in Punjab demanded a review of constitutional division of power between States and the Centre for more autonomy to states. Fourthly, it also led to boundary disputes between the states. We have boundary disputes between Arunachal Pradesh and Assam, Punjab and Haryana, Maharashtra and Karnataka, Karnataka and Kerala etc. However, it is also clear that the linguistic reorganisation of states has consolidated the national unity contrary to the apprehensions of Gandhi, Nehru and other leaders. By reorganisation of states on linguistic lines a major grievance of the Indian people was redressed.

Another aspect of language problem was the question of official language in India. After much controversies and discussions, the Constituent Assembly of India opted for Hindi as the official language of Indian Union. However, for a period of fifteen years from the commencement of the Constitution, English was to continue to be used for all the official purposes of the Union. After the expiry of the said fifteen periods, the Parliament was authorised to provide for the use of English language for such purposes as may be specified in the law. It was also provided that the President might also, during the said period of fifteen years, authorise the use of Hindi in addition to English for any of the official purposes of the Union. The Constitution, further, provided for the formation of a Commission to be appointed by the President after five years of the commencement of the Constitution and, thereafter, at the expiration of ten years. The Commission was to make recommendations to the President on

(i) the progressive use of the Hindi language for the official purposes of the Union;
(ii) restrictions on the use of the English language for all or any of the official purposes of the Union;
(iii) the language to be used for all or any of the purposes mentioned in *Article 348;*
(iv) the form of numericals to be used for any one or more specified purposes of the Union;
(v) any other matter referred to the Commission by the President as regards the official language of the Union and the language for communication between the Union and a state or between one state and another and their use. The recommendations of this Commission were to be examined by a Committee consisting of twenty members of the Lok Sabha and ten members of the Rajya Sabha to be elected by the system of proportional representation by means of a single transferable vote. The President after considering the report of such committee would issue directions in accordance with the whole or any part of that report. However, in making such recommendations, the commission is required to give due regard to the industrial, cultural and scientific advancement of India and the just claims and interests of persons belonging to the non-Hindi speaking areas in regard to the public services. Thus, while the Constitution declared Hindi to be official language of India, it also adopted a pragmatic and cautious approach keeping in view the fact that English was dominating the scene and immediate switchover was not possible due to many reasons including the underdeveloped status of Hindi language and the apprehension of non-Hindi speaking people. Article 351 contained the directive to the Central Government for development of Hindi language. It says, *"It shall be the duty of the Union to promote the spread of the Hindi language, to develop it so that it may serve as a medium of expression for all the elements of the composite culture of India and to secure its enrichment by assimilating without interfering with its genius, the forms, style and expressions used in Hindustani and in the other languages of India specified in the Eighth Schedule, and by drawing, wherever necessary as desirable, for its vocabulary, primarily on Sanskrit and secondarily, on other languages."* *Article 348* also made it clear that all the proceedings in the Supreme Court and High Courts, the authoritative texts of bills to be introduced or amendments in legislatures or acts passed by them and all orders, rules, regulations and bye-laws shall be in the English language. However, as per the *Article 348(2),* the

Governor of a state may, with the previous consent of the President, authorise the use of the Hindi language, or any other language used for any official purposes of the state, in proceedings in the High Court having its principal seat in the state provided that nothing in this clause shall apply to any judgement, decree or order passed or made by such High Court. But where the legislature of the state has prescribed any language other than English for the introduction of Bills, passing of Acts, issuing of ordinances or making of rules, regulations and bye-laws, they will be translated into English and published in the official Gazette under the authority of the Governor and will be considered as the authoritative texts in English.

The framers of the Constitution gave due regard to the regional languages. The Constitution provides that:

(a) The Legislature of the State may by law adopt any one or more of the languages in use in the State or Hindi as the official language or languages to be used for all or any of the official purposes of the State. Until the State Legislature provides otherwise by law, English shall continue to be used for those official purposes for which it was being used immediately before the commencement of this Constitution.

(b) For inter-state communication and for communication between the Union and the State, the official language of the Union shall be used for official purposes. However, if two or more States agree to use Hindi for communication between and among them, they can do so.

(c) If the substantial proportion of the population of a State requests the President that a language spoken by them should be recognised as the official language of the State for certain purposes, and if the President is satisfied about the genuineness of their demand, he may direct that such language should be officially recognised throughout that State or a part thereof for the purposes, he may specify.

Further, there are special directives which (i) entitles a person to submit a representation for the redress of any grievance to any officer or authority of the union or a state in any of the languages used in the Union or in the states, as the case may be (*Article 350*); (ii) provide the state with a duty to endeavour to provide adequate facilities for instruction in the mother-tongue at the primary stage of education to children belonging to linguistic minority groups; and the President may issue such directions to any state as he considers necessary or proper for securing the provision of such facilities (*Article 350-A*);

(iii) empower the President to appoint a Special Officer for linguistic minorities who shall investigate and report to him whether the constitutional safeguards provided for the linguistic minorities under the constitution are being observed and the President shall cause all such reports to be laid before each House of Parliament and send them to the government of the States concerned (*Article 350-B*) and (iv) vest with the union with a duty to spread Hindi language (*Article 351*).

The detailed provisions regarding the language show the genius and wisdom of the framers of the Constitution. However, they could not satisfy the diverse elements of India. On the one hand, the Hindi protagonists became chauvinistic and wanted Hindi even to be imposed on the non-Hindi speaking people. Some of them argued for a highly Sanskritised Hindi which was even difficult for a lay Hindi speaker to be understand. On the other hand, the non-Hindi speakers decried and violently opposed the imposition of Hindi on them. This resulted in anti-English riots in Hindi speaking areas and anti-Hindi riots in non-Hindi speaking areas in which anything written in the other language was removed or defaced and many precious lives were lost in agitations. The use of Hindi language was resisted in South, especially in Tamil Nadu. It was also resisted in West Bengal, Punjab and Assam where they insisted on the use of the local regional language. The Central Government's efforts to promote the Hindi language was not liked by the non-Hindi states. The aggressive anti-Hindi stance of non-Hindi states compelled the then Prime Minister Jawahar Lal Nehru to assure time and again the non-Hindi states that Hindi would not be imposed and that the English language would be continued to be used 'as long as people required it.' In 1963, the Official Language Act was passed which provided that (i) despite the Constitutional provision of replacing English by Hindi after 26 January 1965, English would continue to be used for all official purposes of the Union in addition to Hindi (ii) where a state legislature had prescribed any language other than Hindi for use in Acts of the legislature, a Hindi as well an English translation might be published, (iii) whereas the Constitution required all High Courts judgements to be in English language, the Governor with the prior consent of the President may authorise after 1965, the use of Hindi or of the official language of the state for the judgements, orders or decrees of the states High Court, provided that an English translation would also be issued. The Act evoked a strong protest in Southern States, especially in Tamil Nadu and Andhra Pradesh. Ultimately, the Prime Minister Lal Bahadur Shastri had to repeat the Nehru's assurance that English would continue as an alternative language till the people require it. Accordingly, the Official Language Act of 1963 was amended in 1967. However, in 1965 in accordance with the provisions of the Constitution Hindi replaced English as the official language of the Indian Union.

In 1961 the National Integration Council recommended the adoption of three language formula for secondary education all over the country. According to this formula the schools would teach three languages—English, Hindi and any one modern Indian language. The other recommendation were (i) the replacement of English by the regional language as the medium of instruction in universities and (ii) the need to have a link-language to be used in universities throughout India which was to be English at present but ultimately to be replaced by Hindi. This formula was half-heartedly implemented and subsequently given a good-bye.

The Southern States have always resisted any move to impose Hindi on them and time and again various Prime Ministers have assured them that Hindi would not be imposed on them. Thus the problem remained. However, now we find that the linguistic problem no longer remains a big issue in Indian politics. Many reasons can be cited for this change. Firstly, the voice of Hindi chauvinism is no longer there. The Hindi protagonists no longer talk of Hindi imposition on non-Hindi people or fiercely advocate the cause. Secondly Hindi has been spreading in the entire country. It is due to the Hindi films and the spread of electronic media. Infact, instead of Hindi or English, it is Hinglish (a curious and even ridiculous mixture of English and Hindi) which is being promoted by the electronic media and public personalities. Thirdly, the English language is also spreading. It remains a valid visa for the entrance to science and computers and jobs in the flourishing private sector and multi-national companies. Finally, the regional languages are also developing at a face pace. On the whole, these developments have satisfied the various literary segments in India and the language issue has been marginalised for good.

Violence in Indian Politics

The human being is an animal but still there is a line of demarcation between the other animals and man. While other animals do not possess the sophisticated brain as they function on the basis of their instinct, man has the sophisticated brain which ultimately made him the master of the universe. It is out of his sophisticated brain that civilization developed which means the formulation of national rules and regulations which regulate the code of conduct among the people. The logical conclusion is eschewing of violence as the framed rules and regulations provide a way of redressal of grievances. The system does envisage the adoption of violence but only for the defaulters who do not bother to follow the rules and regulations. This is how the man developed civil society. Yet there has been a very thin line between violence and non-violence. History reveals that man has frequently resorted to violence whenever he felt prudent to do so. In this matter he has been worse than the animal. The animals generally resort to violence in self-defence or when they are hungry, while man has crossed all limits. A political observer has rightly observed, "It will perhaps be closer to truth to say that violence will always remain in life, but non-violence alone can generate the necessary moral force to prevent violence from completely overtaking and destroying us."

India is the land of Buddha, Mahavir and Gandhi who preached non-violence as an essential factor in social and political life. Unlike the western civilization which is based on man's incessant greed for more and more materialistic life, the Indian civilization is founded on spiritual basis, although it never eschewed materialism. The Indian mythology believe in the realisation of truth through discussion.

More than anybody else, Gandhi used the technique of non-violence in the realisation of his objectives in social and political sphere. But it is also a fact that all the movements launched by him subsequently turned violent. Indian freedom struggle was not entirely non-violent. There were many who disregarded Gandhian philosophy to achieve freedom through non-violent means. After freedom, the curse of violence remained in Indian social and political life despite the democratic system which envisages a peaceful solution to each and every problem. Rajni Kothari points out, that by and large, Parliamentary government has failed to embody the idea of democracy and this failure principally stems from the fact that under it, there is little scope for popular participation in political processes. This lack of participation leads to a sense of insignificance in the people, especially in those sections which are more politically conscious and they develop a feeling of powerlessness. He further observes, "We have found that the institution of elections is inadequate as a basis of democratic movement, that the theory of representation is misleading and fails to base government on will of the people, that the ethical basis of Parliamentary government in hedonism which renders it incapable of imbibing true spirit of democracy, and that the assumptions of the natural harmony proves inimical to true participation by people in the political process. What we find in reality is that power tends to get concentrated in parliamentary government. The participation of the people in the process of government is kept to a minimum, the power of the people's representatives is equally minimised under the impact of political parties and government - to speak in a language stripped of all constitutional verbiage and legal jargon—is a government by an organised minority." He further says 'that Parliamentary government thus becomes a rule of minority where the individual is just a constitutional fiction. He has, of course, the right to cast his ballot every four or five years. On that right, indeed, hangs the whole system. But apart from that functional link in mechanism, the individual as such has no role to play. And decisions taken at the seat of the power and enforced by its agents come as a fait accompli to the people. Grievances accumulate. A psychological case is slowly built up in the minds of the people who are affected by such decisions. The normal channels provided for removing the accumulated grievances prove to be impotent when serious disagreement is the issue. The stage is set for Direct Action.' According to Kothari, 'the Parliamentary system has its own limitations. It is divided between the governed and the government and governed are not able to influence the government. The democracy gives rise to certain deep rooted expectations but the parliamentary system frustrates these very expectations. The conflict between promise and possibility is latent all the time. In times of strain it comes out in the open. The result is Direct Action.' While this Direct Action may be non-violent but it also can be violent. The communists also believe in the inevitability of violence due to the capitalist mode of production in a liberal democracy. According to them, democracy is a farce because as Lenin points out, "the workers and day labourers in the villages, are in practice debarred from democracy by the sacred right of property and by the bourgeois state apparatus, that is bourgeois officials, bourgeois judges and so on. The present freedom of assembly and press in parliamentary capitalist democracy is false and hypocritical, because in fact it is freedom for the rich to buy and bribe the press, freedom for the rich to befuddle the people with venomous lies of the bourgeoisie press, freedom for the rich to keep their property, the mansions of the landlords, the best buildings etc."

The Indian democratic system started with high hopes in 1950. It was believed that the native government would end all the evils generated by the colonial rulers. The social and economic disparities would be soon eradicated as the foreign rule which created and encouraged these inequalities was no longer there. These hopes were incorporated in the Constitution which advocated the achievement of Justice-Social, economic and political. The development of economy on the basis of Five Year Plans was envisaged for this purpose. However, the economic development and the consequent prosperity did not match the actual realities. The poor have remained poor. In fact the economic disparities have widened. In social field also, the oppression and exploitation of lower castes and classes remain. The atrocities on Harijans or dalits, as they call themselves, continue and there is a general dissatisfaction plaguing the political system. This is further accentuated by the curse of corruption which has reached from the lowest to the highest echelon of government functionaries. The politicians who are supposed to be at the vanguard of the people stand exposed. All this has resulted into a helpless situation for the people who ultimately turn violent.

In the social and political life of India, there have been different kinds of problems which have found expression in violence, some of which are as follows:

Agrarian Violence

In rural India where the majority of Indians live, the agrarian relations are marked by widespread economic disparities and poverty. The aggrieved frequently resort to violence. When the country became free in 1947, the Tebhagha movement in West Bengal was continuing under the leadership of Communist Party of India which believed that 1947 only witnessed a transfer of power from the foreign bourgeoisie to the native bourgeoisie and the real freedom lay in the achievement of socialism in India which India did not attain. For this it resorted to violence. Later on Naxalbari movement developed which led to many killings of zamindars, peasants, political workers and innocent people. The Naxalite movement is still in existence in West Bengal, Bihar, Madhya Pradesh and Andhra Pradesh and violence has become a fact of life. Especially in Bihar it has become so common that the killings do not even make news. Maharashtra, Karnataka and Uttar Pradesh are other states afflicted by the agrarian violence. In 1995-96, there were 202 incidents with 22 deaths and 406 injured in these three states. Most of these agitations can be generally attributed to land disputes, forcible harvesting of crops, non-payment of minimum wages, rivalry among kisan organisations etc.

Caste Violence

Caste based violence has been growing in Indian politics. The Harijans or dalits are discriminated against by the caste Hindus and they are subjected to atrocities and exploitation. The present decade has witnessed the upsurge of dalits who have also started retaliating. Thus we have violence between the Forward Castes and Backward Castes especially in UP, Delhi, Bihar, Maharashtra and Tamil Nadu. Most of these conflicts have been due to atrocities against the Dalits, land disputes, disputes over sharing of crops, payment of minimum wages, molestation and even rapes of dalit women, prevention of dalits from participating in local religious festivals, old enmity arising out of traditional caste feuds and rise of dalits. The State of Bihar alone has many caste armies or senas. Among them the most powerfull is Ranbeer Sena which was responsible for the massacre of many backward caste peoples. Ranbeer Sena is the caste army of Bhumihar, a forward caste and it has been reported that this Sena has 5000 jawans who are professionally trained and the Sena is well equipped with modern sophisticated weapons. Besides the Naxalites, who have many groups, there are Kunwar Sena, Bhumi Sena, Losik Sena, Sunlight Sena, Panchsheel Sena, Mazdoor-Kisan Sangh, Rana Sena, Kudal Sena, Satyendra Sena, Diamond Sena etc. As a result of violence unleashed by these senas, belonging to forward and backward castes, about 18,000 people have been killed since 1971.

Left Extremist Violence

The various left extremist groups have been responsible for terror in many states like Bihar, Andhra Pradesh, West Bengal and Madhya Pradesh. The agrarian structure and the backwardness of these areas are major reasons for the left extremist violence. Among the notable left extremist groups are the Naxalites who have formed different groups like Maoist Communist Centre (MCC), Communist Party of India (Marxist-Leninist), Indian Peoples Front, Liberation Group, Bhartiya Jan Morcha. These Naxal outfits believe in violent class struggle and forcible occupation of land to be distributed among the dalits. Their main targets have been the higher caste landlords. They have a very brutal judicial process in which the alleged offenders are subjected to inhuman brutality and even brutal murder.

Violence Due to Language Problem

As discussed earlier, after independence, language was a major issue. Broadly speaking, this problem cropped up from two standpoints—Firstly the demand for linguistic reorganisation of states and secondly the *English vs Hindi* issue. The Government had to submit to the agitation which was fast turning into violent movement in South as a result of which Andhra Pradesh was created. Later on, in

1956, an extensive reorganisation of states, on the basis of language, was undertaken. But this did not satisfy everybody. The state of Bombay and subsequently Punjab witnessed many agitations and violent clashes and as a result Bombay was bifurcated into Maharashtra and Gujarat in 1960 and Punjab was divided into two separate states of Punjab and Haryana in 1966. Linguistic violence also took place on the issue of English vs Hindi in northern and southern parts of India in 1960's and 1970's. Another aspect of linguistic violence was the son of soil theory advocated in Bombay, Assam, West Bengal and Karnataka where people speaking other than the local language were attacked and terrorised to leave the state. South Indians in Bombay, Marwaris in West Bengal, Bengalis in Assam and Tamils in Karnataka were subjected to violent activities.

Communal Violence

Hindu-Muslim conflicts in north and South India, Hindu-Christian communal riots in Kerala and Hindu-Sikh riots in Punjab, Delhi, UP and certain other parts of north India are the examples of communal violence. In the wake of demolition of disputed structure of Babri Masjid the communal violence took place in different parts of the country. In 2002, comunal violence took place at Godhra. In fact, Hindu-Muslim communal violence has plagued the country both before and after freedom. After the state's intervention in Golden Temple in Amritsar in 1984 which was followed by the assassination of Mrs. Indira Gandhi, anti-Sikh riots took place in Delhi, Uttar Pradesh, Madhya Pradesh and certain other parts of north India. Kerala has witnessed frequent Hindu-Christian riots.

Regionalism

There have been various forms of regionalism in India. There have been areas which have felt neglected in the matter of education and job opportunities, developmental works and allocation of funds and grants from the Government. Such areas have demanded separate statehood. Gorkha National Liberation Front demands a separate statehood of Gorkhaland in Darjeeling. It has also frequently resorted to violence to achieve its goal. Similarly, Bodos in Assam, tribal areas of Jharkhand, hill areas of Uttar Pradesh etc. have on occasion spawned violent movements. In North-Eastern parts, there have been secessionist movements. The states of Nagaland, Mizoram, Manipur, Tripura, Meghalaya and Mizoram have witnessed insurgency, separatist (demand for a separate state) and even secessionist movements. Naga

National Council (NNC), People's Liberation Army (PLA), Mizo National Front (MNF), People's Revolutionary Party of Kanglei Pak (PREPAK), All Tripura Tribal Force (ATTF), United Liberation Front of Assam (ULFA) etc. These groups have organised armed rebellion and resorted to violence. The NSCN demands independent state of Nagaland outside the Indian Constitution and have carried out armed rebellion against the Government. The Revolutionary People's Front (RPF) and its militant wings of PLA and PREPAK is superheading the movement for freedom in Manipur. In Tripura, the call for secession was given by Tripura National Volunteer Force. The ULFA demands an independent state of Assam. All these movements have used sophisticated weapons putting the entire North-East in turmoil. There have also been inter-tribal violent conflicts among various tribes. In Punjab there had been a movement for an independent state of Khalistan which was aided by Pakistan and wealthy Sikhs settled outside India in U.S., Canada and other countries. In Jammu and Kashmir there have been Muslim Organisations who are against Kashmir's accession to India and aided and trained by Pakistan, they have become violent.

Political Violence

Killing of political persons for the achievement of certain goals constitute political violence. The assassinations of Indira Gandhi in 1984, Rajiv Gandhi in 1991 and Beant Singh, the Chief Minister of Punjab are the examples of political violence. There is another aspect of political violence which takes place during elections. The Indian elections are becoming increasingly violent. There are communal violence, caste violence and inter-party violence. In Bihar a number of Senas resort to violence to rig the election to get their caste candidate elected.

Terrorism

The terrorists use the technique of spreading terror by killing innocent people to achieve their goals. The states of Jammu and Kashmir, Punjab, Haryana, Delhi, Uttar Pradesh, the seven states of North-East, Maharashtra and Tamil Nadu are, particularly, the targets of terrorist violence.

On October 1, 2001 the four-man suicide squad blew up an explosive-laden Tata Sumo in front of Assembly building in Jammu and Kashmir in which 29 people were killed and 60 injured. On August 7,2001, again the militants struck at the Jammu railway station killing

10 and wounding 30 people. January 15, 2001 saw the Srinagar airport being attacked, a three hour cross firing with the security forces went on, killing 6 militants and 4 para-military personnel. The terrorists became so dare devil that they even attacked the Indian Parliament-in-session on December 13, 2001.

Violence from the State and the Police

The use of third-degree methods against the suspects, murder and rapes in Police custody, illegal detention and excessive use of violence during agitations have been the characteristics of Indian Police. In Bhagalpur, the Police blinded the suspected criminals and in Delhi, the blind demonstrators were brutally lathicharged. The police in Bihar, Punjab, UP and Jammu and Kashmir have earned notoriety for its brutality. While the maintenance of law and order constitutes the primary duty of the Police, the Government has to frequently deploy the Indian Army and para-military forces like Border Security Force (BSF), Central Reserve Police (CRP) and Central Industrial Security Force (CISF) to aid Police in maintaining law and order. To curb violence in different parts of the country, the Indian state has to frequently resort to counter-violence and in the process, Indian state has also become a violent state. The use of army in operation Blue Star and in putting down other agitations has compromised with its dignity and image which otherwise has a valiant record and has been a matter of great pride for the Indian people. In the insurgent areas, the Indian Army has also reported to have unleashed violence and terror. In Nagaland which relatively has been a peaceful area, even though insurgency continues, the people still remember the stories of torture, rape and plunder by the army. A young doctor in 1998 said, "Though we never saw anything, there is always a shadow of that past hanging over us which we cannot forget. The Indian Army is held with disdain and parents used to tell children that they will send them to the army to frighten them." In December 29, 1994 Mokokchung was the scene of a massacre after an army colonel, commandent of the 16th Maratha Light Infantry was shot down. The army went on a rampage and torched the town killing atleast 14 people and injuring over 200. There have also been complaints against army for excessive use of violence and torture in Jammu and Kashmir, Punjab and other states of North-East.

Thus violence has unfortunately become the part and parcel of Indian political life and it constitute a grave danger to not only the democratic institutions which stand for a peaceful solution to every problem but also to the national unity of the country.

References

Aiyar, S.P. and Srinivasan, R. (Ed.), *Studies in Indian Democracy*, Bombay, Allied Publishers Private Limited.

Bhambhri, C.P., *The Indian State*, 1997, New Delhi Shipra Publications.

Fadia, Dr. B.L., *Indian Government and Politics*, 1997, Agra Sahitya Bhawan Publications.

Gupta, D.C., *Indian Government and Politics*, 1991, New Delhi, Vikas Publishing House Private Limited.

Kothari Rajni, *Politics in India*, 1994, New Delhi, Orient Longman Limited.

Subash C. Kashyap (Ed.), *Perspectives on the Constitution*, 1993, New Delhi, Shipra Publications.

CHAPTER XXIV

Development Process and Foreign Policy

The International political system among the different states operates through their foreign policies. According to Modelski the foreign policy is 'the system of activities evolved by communities for changing the behaviour of other states and for adjusting their own activities to the international environment.' To Hugh Gibson foreign policy is 'a well rounded, comprehensive plan, based on knowledge and experience, for conducting the business of government with the rest of the world. It is aimed at promoting and protecting the interests of the nation." The formulation and continuity of foreign policy is affected by the national interest. In fact the national interest is, as Margantheu says, 'the last word in world politics.' No country can act contrary to national interest. Nehru the architect of India's foreign policy also said in 1947, "whatever policy we may lay down, the art of conducting the foreign affairs of a country lies in finding out what is most advantageous to the country. We may talk about international goodwill and mean what we say. We may talk about peace and freedom and earnestly mean what we say. But in the ultimate analysis, a government functions for the good of the country it governs, and no Government can do anything, which, in the short or long run is manifestly disadvantageous to the country." While it is difficult to define national interest as it may mean different things in different contexts and there may be divergent views and perceptions regarding the national interests, broadly speaking it means (i) the defence of national boundaries; (ii) the consolidation of national integration and unity; (iii) Promotion of economic interests and maintenance of international peace, respect for international law, peaceful settlement of international disputes and strengthening of the system of international organisations. The objective of foreign policy is to promote the national interest of the country. There are determinants of foreign policy also which include the geographical situation, history and traditions, national morale, political organisation, institutions and leadership, military strength, public opinion and economic strength of the country. Keeping these factors in view a careful and rational foreign policy is formulated and implemented.

Main Plank of India's Foreign Policy

Non-Alignment

India became free at a time when the world was divided into two blocs-one headed by the U.S.A. and the other headed by the Soviet Union. This was the picture of a hostile world divided on ideological basis—the US bloc claimed as free world while many called it democratic or capitalist bloc and the Soviet bloc was termed as Socialist or Communist bloc. The division of these two blocs was further strengthened by military alliances. The American bloc adopted the policy of containing communism and thus NATO (North Atlantic Treaty Organisation and SEATO (South East Asian Treaty Organisation) etc were formed. The Soviet bloc retaliated by forming its own military organisation called Warsaw Pact. This division intended to divide the entire world into groups under the slogan 'those not with us are against us! leaving no other alternative to various states but to join one of them. This created what is called cold war in which both sides fought each other with all the means other than the actual war.

It was under these circumstances that India refused to join any bloc and declared its policy of non-alignment. Nehru was confident that the sheer size of India could not make India a stooge of any power bloc. He said, "India is too big a country to be bound down to any country, however big it may be." To Nehru India was the pivot of South, South-East and West Asia, where diverse communities and different races meet. India lies in the heart of the world and all the major sea and air routes of the world pass through it. Nehru described India as the bridge between East and West. Owing to these strategic geographical conditions, India's involvement in either power bloc would not have been a wise proposition. In fact due to its large area and population, Nehru felt that India was to play an active role in international affairs which had to be independent. He declared, "India is going to be and is bound to be a big country that counts in the world affairs."

But Nehru made it clear that non-alignment is not neutrality but a positive approach to world problems. He said, "where freedom is menaced or justice is threatened or where aggression takes place, we cannot and shall not be neutral... Our policy is not neutralist, but one of active endeavour to preserve and, if possible, establish peace on firm foundation." To Nehru the power blocs could only lead to war and destruction. He said, "We propose, as far as possible, to keep away from the power politics of groups, aligned against one another, which have led in the past to world wars and which may again lead to disasters on a very large scale." Nehru believed that India could play an effective role in avoiding another world war, provided it did not align with any group of powers. He observed, "I feel that India can play a big part, and perhaps an effective part, in helping to avoid war. Therefore, it becomes all the more necessary that India should not be lined up with any group of power which for various reasons are full of fear of war and prepared for war."

Disarmament

The power politics of the two blocs led to the race for armament. Armament always leads to war as it is amply clear with two great world wars which were fought in the last century. The loss of men, money and property in any war is unimaginable and the introduction of nuclear weapons has made war most barbarous. It means total wars and total destruction leading to even annihilation of the entire mankind. The cold war after the Second World War intensified the arms race between the opposing blocs, and each bloc began arming its member-states, both with conventional and nuclear weapons, bringing the world closer to the third world war. India was aware of the consequences of the piling of nuclear weapons and the possible nuclear catastrophe. It was convinced that the increase in the number of nuclear states would escalate local as well as global tensions and that the tendency to acquire nuclear weapons would jeopardise the security of every individual state as well as the whole world. Nehru observed, "If and when disaster comes it will affect the world as a whole .... Our first effort should be to prevent that disaster from happening." Therefore India stood against the race for armament and advocated disarmament.

But this did not mean that India would not go to war. India had its own army which was small but efficient and it could be used in the condition of war. In case of world war also India would not remain neutral. It might join any of the blocs keeping in view its national interest. Nehru said, "If there is a big war, there is no particular reason why we should jump into it .... We are not going to join a war if we can help it, and we are going to join the side which is to our interest when the time comes to make the choice." Therefore India did not join the NPT which was discriminatory. India kept the nuclear option open although at the same time it voiced its protest against manufacturing and testing of nuclear weapons. India also refused to sign the Comprehensive Test Ban Treaty (CTBT) in 1996 on the ground that nuclear powers wanted to maintain status quo by not subjecting themselves to a test ban and forcing only non-nuclear powers to sign the treaty. Nehru rightly felt that joining either bloc would compromise with the freedom in foreign relations. When a weak state joins with a powerful state, it loses its independence in the conduct of its foreign policy. We had no option but non-alignment to preserve our freedom.

Anti-Imperialism and Anti-Racialism

Another aspect of India's non-alignment was opposition to imperialism and racism. India itself had been a victim of British imperialism. Anti racism had been a part of its freedom struggle. Anti-imperialism as an integral part of its foreign policy has developed from its experience of the British imperialism. India's anti-imperialism stance was at first in the form of its protest against the British rule in India. Gradually, this anti-British stand took the shape of anti-imperialism in general. India viewed imperialism as exploitation of the weaker nations by the imperialist powers and as an enemy of national freedom. The Indian leaders understood that imperialism leads to exploitation, racial discrimination, inequality, mutual distrust and ultimately to bloody conflicts. They found imperialism and racism antithetical to world peace and gave a sharp anti-colonial and anti-imperialist edge to their foreign policy. In no case India could be an ally of the imperialist countries. India advocated the liquidation of racialism and colonialism in every shape and form. Thus the Interim Government of Nehru recalled the Indian troops sent by the British to suppress the freedom struggles in the Dutch and French colonies. During the Second World War, the Dutch colony of Indonesia came under the occupation of Japan. After the Japanese defeat, the Dutch tried to establish its rule again. India opposed it strongly and cooperated with Indonesia in its efforts to gain independence. India supported the freedom struggles in Asia and African countries such as Indo-China, Malaya, Libya, Algeria Tunisia, Gold Coast (now Ghana), Namibia etc. The racial policy of South Africa came under vigorous criticism by the Indian Government which led to cessation of diplomatic relations with South Africa in 1949. India was instrumental in the application of comprehensive sanctions against the white minority racist regime of South Africa. It was only in 1994 when the apartheid was finally given up and a majority government under Nelson Mandela was duly elected and constituted in South Africa that the Indian Government re-established full diplomatic relations with that country.

Panchsheel

In 1954, India signed an agreement with China in which five principles or Panchsheel were enunciated as a basis of mutual relationships between the two countries. They were:

(i) mutual respect for each other's territorial integrity and sovereignty;
(ii) mutual non-aggression;
(iii) mutual non-interference in each other's internal affairs;
(iv) equality and mutual benefit; and
(v) peaceful co-existence.

Referring to Panchsheel Nehru said, "I imagine that if these principles were adopted in the relation of various countries with each other, a great deal of the trouble of the present day world would probably disappear." Among these five principles, peaceful coexistence needs a little elaboration. During the cold war it was generally believed that there was a consistnent struggle between the ideologies of (capitalism or) democracy and socialism represented respectively by the American bloc and the Soviet bloc and there is no reconciliation between the two and both cannot exist in the same world. This view was never accepted by Nehru who thought that both could co-exist.

Support to the United Nations

India is one of the founder-members of the United Nations organisation. In the interest of World Peace, India used the UN platform. Infact, it was a platform hardly to be ignored, for, unlike its predecessor, the League of Nations, it was universal in character and had a far greater area of operation then the League. To the newly independent countries, in particular, it provided a unique and unprecedented opportunity to play an important role in international politics without being involved in either of the two blocs. The newly independent states actually utilized the United Nations not only to defend their territorial and national sovereignty but also to fight against imperialism and racialism and promote the cause of world peace and security. No wonder then that India attached great significance to the UN in its foreign policy calculation. India has supported several activities of the UN. In 1953 India's Vijay Lakshmi Pandit was elected as the President of the General Assembly of the UN. Several times India has been a non-permanent member of the Security Council. In the collective security and peace keeping operations of the UN, India has always participated whenever called for. In the Korean war, India sent its medical team and participated in the repatriation of the prisoners of war. India was the Chairman of the Neutral Nation's Repatriation Commission (NNRC) for Korea in 1953. In 1954 India chaired the International Commission for Supervision and Control in Indo-China. During 1960-63, peace-keeping operations were organised in Congo by the Indian Independent Brigade. In 1992, an Indian General was heading the United Nations Protection Force in Yugoslavia. India also sought to achieve arms control and disarmament through United Nations. Now India is demanding a permanent seat in the Security Council and India's claim is justified. It was only because of non-aligned nations led by India that the UN did not become a convenient battle ground between the two blocs.

The Gujral Doctrine

Except for Pakistan and China, India has enjoyed good relations with its neighbours. On the whole, India has been soft with its neighbours, helping them in various crisis. Indian Peace Keeping Force (IPKF) was sent to Srilanka as per Rajiv-Jayawardene Agreement in 1987. Nepal has been traditionally enjoying many economic concessions from India. Later on the Indian soft attitude towards its neighbours was expressed in Gujral doctrine. According to this doctrine, India is a big country compared to its neighbours and it is willing to help the smaller neighbours unilaterally. Thus the essence of Gujral doctrine lies in the extension of unilateral concessions to neighbours in the sub-continent. In pursuance of this policy, India concluded an agreement with Bangladesh for sharing of Ganga Waters which enable Bangladesh to draw in lean reason slightly more water as provided in 1977 Agreement. In 1997 India unilaterally announced several concessions to Pakistan tourists, particularly the elder citizens and cultural groups, in regard to visa fees and police reporting.

During the last fifty years, the Indian foreign policy has been characterised by a remarkable continuity. Even the non-Congress governments at the centre including the Janata Party Government with Atal Behari Vajpayee as the foreign Minister in 1977, who partly had serious reservation regarding many issues of Indian foreign policy, did not make any major diversion from it. Over the years, the Non-Alignment Movement (NAM) has also become a force to be reckon with in the international sphere. Following are the principles of NAM.

(i) Respect for the fundamental rights of men and also the aims and principles of the UN Charter.
(ii) Respect for the sovereignty and territorial integrity of all nations.
(iii) Recognition of equality of all races and nationalities-big or small.
(iv) Abstention from intervention and interference in the internal affairs of other countries.
(v) Respect for the right of every country for individual or collective defence in conformity with the UN Charter.
(vi) Abstention from exerting pressure on other countries, abstention from exploiting agreements on collective defence for self-interest on the part of big powers, abstention from acts of threats of aggression and use of force against the territorial integrity or political independence of any country.
(vii) Settlement of all international disputes by peaceful means through conciliation, arbitration, judicial settlements, also through other means as the parties may choose in conformity with the UN Charter.
(viii) Assistance in mutual interest and cooperation and
(ix) Respect for justice and international obligations.

Despite the end of cold war and disintegration of Soviet Union, the Non-alignment policy is still relevant today because of two important reasons. Firstly non-alignment, as J.N. Dixit, a former Secretary says, means retaining the freedom to take decisions related to your interests without external influence to the extent possible' or in other words non-alignment means nation's freedom in the conduct of its foreign and defence policies. Secondly there was the economic basis of non-alignment which is still valid today. Now we shall examine this economic basis of non-alignment policy.

Development Process and Foreign Policy

Colonial rule in India played havoc with its economic system. India was backward in its industrial and agricultural sector. We did not have the capital industries. There was a lack of technical know-how and finances for the economy to take-off. As a result of Partition, India also lost fertile areas which went to Pakistan resulting in food crisis. Nehru rightly believed that the real freedom could only be realised when India became economically self-sufficient. He said, "A country may be marked on the map as independent, but in reality is not independent so long as it is economically dependent upon other countries.... Economic dependence may enable other countries to strangle you, compel you to do what you do not want to do .... For India to be really independent and to really make progress, she must be economically independent."

Nehru proved right because foreign aid was always accompanied with strings. At least two examples from the initial years of Indian independence made it very obvious. Firstly, initially the Indian Government attempted to invite foreign capital to help develop the national economy. In 1948-50 a number of decisions were made by the Indian Government to attract foreign businessmen. But these decisions did not satisfy the foreign businessmen and they demanded a radical revision of taxation system, abolish governmental control in industry and abandon the policy of building large-scale State enterprises. "All this," commented V. Nikhamin, "meant that India had to give up her independent economic policy." The American and British businessmen wanted free trade a market. The Second Five Year Plan (1956-61) which envisaged a considerable growth of heavy industry and expansion of State economy was criticized by them and there was also a threat that the American aid to India would not be forthcoming unless the Indian Government changed its economic policy. Secondly, as V. Nikhamin points out, `In cases when Western monopolies make capital investments in India they think least of all of developing her national economy. In 1951, for example, the Indian Government concluded an agreement with three American firms on the construction of oil refineries with an annual capacity of 3.5 million tons. India had to commit herself not to nationalize these refineries for 25 years and to limit the share of Indian businessman to 25 per cent of the capital, which was a departure from the formerly adopted Act on the regulation of industrial development. Moreover the American monopolies did everything to prevent the development of oil extraction in India proper. On their insistence, the oil for refining had to be imported from abroad, duty free, the purpose being to make India's economy dependent on American oil deliveries. This agreement was highly criticized in India.

One of the major reasons of non-alignment policy was the need for rapid economic development of India. India needed industrial and agricultural revolution, which was to be achieved through mixed economy and its planned development. The Industrial policy Resolution of 1948 and 1956 emphasised the various aspects of India's modern economy; Steel plants and hydro-electric dams, the setting up of heavy industry in the public sector, the application of scientific techniques to agriculture, the development of small scale industries, and our early endeavours to locate petroleum, start petro-chemical industries and develop nuclear energy, the Five Year Plans, the growth of the public sector and its extension to the field of external trade and simultaneous expansion of entrepreneurial skills and private enterprise. India lacked not only technical know-how but also adequate funds. Therefore, there was the need of foreign aid. Nehru wanted foreign aid but without any strings and any compromise with the newly achieved freedom of the country. He said, we would rather delay our development, industrial or otherwise than submit to any economic domination by any country." No aid-giving country would be allowed to interfere in the internal affairs of the country. Said Nehru, "if at any time help from abroad depends upon a variation, however slight, in our policy, we shall relinquish that help completely and prefer starvation and deprivation to taking such help." Nehru was sure that the non-alignment policy had the necessary strength enabling India to extract foreign aid and at the same time maintaining freedom in the foreign affairs. Bandopadhyay rightly pointed out that "the central role played by the state in the process of economic development has created for the Government of India both the opportunity and the obligation to utilise foreign policy for the purpose of economic development. Rationality, in other words demand that Indian foreign policy must be closely integrated."

The diverse needs of India could not be fulfilled by aligning to one power. The United States was ready to provide us with finished goods and food but it was reluctant to give us steel plants or capital industries. The non-alignment policy enabled India to get aids from both the power blocs. Nehru believed that diversification of foreign aid would further strengthen India's position and no power would be able to dominate it. He used to say that we should not put all eggs in one basket.' Dependence on one power for all our needs had the danger of that power withdrawing the aid and we would be nowhere. Sometimes the donor country might threaten to withdraw the aid if we did not act according to their advice and interest. But when there were many baskets, India would always be in comfortable position. Thus the non-alignment policy gave India a powerful bargaining power and enabled it to get aid for all the quarters. An American study published in August 1962, showed clearly that India had received more foreign aid, in sheer money terms from both the US and the SU, than had any other state.

Michael Brecher rightly points out, "India's economic weakness and the basic goal of development alone provided powerful inducements to the policy of non-alignment. The doors must be kept open to all sources of aid, Western and Soviet, if the desired economic revolution is to be achieved..... Non-alignment is deemed essential to the fulfilment of India's economic revolution, for it maintains access to the technical skills and capital of all the great industrial powers." The

Indian emphasis on peace and avoidance of war followed from its developmental needs. Only in an atmosphere of peace, can the development take place. Had there been wars between the two blocs, the foreign aid to India would become scarce.

After independence Nehru successfully attempted to get aid from all countries. He continued the economic relations with the Great Britain, observes J. Bandopadhyay, "To a lesser man than Nehru, the first thought on attainment of freedom would have been to cut off the chains that bound India to the economy of the United kingdom. Indeed some Indian leaders were arguing and thinking in these terms. He continued India's membership of Commonwealth with certain structural changes suiting to India's position as an independent and sovereign country. A formula was evolved according to which Indian Republic would owe no allegiance to the British Crown and India acknowledged the British King as a symbol of free association of its independent members nations and as such the Head of the Commonwealth."

The agreement of 1935 between India and Great Britain continued. "This old agreement particularly its principle `became an important element in our economic relationship with the Commonwealth. In 1962 Great Britain was trying to become a member of European Economic Community. Nehru said in the Commonwealth Conference, "It is only lately that duty-free imports into the United kingdom and preferential arrangements over the Commonwealth as a whole have helped us to build up a sizeable trade in our manufactures, a trade which has proved beneficial not only to ourselves but also to the United Kingdom. "He did not like Great Britain joining the European Economic Community which would mean new tariffs to Indian goods. He said in the same conference, "In order to avoid the barrier erected by the Community, the United Kingdom is seeking to join the Market, but in the case of developing countries like India, whose need to increase exports is manifold, it is proposed to erect a tariff where none existed before." India's membership in the Commonwealth of Nations provided it with technical assistance, educational facilities, trading privileges and military supplies.

The United States of America also came forward to help India. A Development Loan Fund was established in 1957 to provide Indian loans repayable in rupees for procurement of essential capital goods in America. In 1958 the World Bank, on American initiative formed an Aid India Consortium which made heavy commitments to India's Third Five Year Plan. In 1960 the US made the largest single contribution to the Indus Basin Development Fund. India was also supplied wheat under US Public Law 480 which amounted to one-fifth of the total American crop in 1964-65. The US aid focussed on agriculture, rural progress and infrastructure projects such as production of electric power. A thirty years agreement on cooperative development of atomic power plants was signed in 1963 beginning with Tarapur in Bombay. With very few exceptions in the private sector, the US declined to invest in or assist Indian heavy industry. This was done by the Soviet Union.

The Soviet Union gave us the first steel plant in Bhilai for which the US and other western countries were not interested. It was only after the Bhilai Steel Plant that Great Britain gave us the Durgapur Steel plant and West Germany the Rourkela Steel Plant. It is a fact that had there been no Bhilai Steel Plant commissioned by the SU, there would not have been either Durgapur or Rourkela Steel Plants. Later on SU also build up the Bokaro Steel Plant. In the field of oil, the SU help is more remarkable keeping in view the fact that initially the western experts came to India, surveyed its land and found no oil. But the Soviet experts found oil of good quality in abundance in that very region where the western experts could not find the oil. The Indo-Soviet Cooperation had been so gigantic in India's economic sector that can be judged from the fact that in 1976, 30 per cent of India's steel, 35 per cent of its oil, 20 per cent of its electrical power, 65 per cent of heavy electrical equipment and 85 per cent of our heavy machine-making machines were produced in projects set up with Soviet aid. India also had economic cooperation with the Asian, Latin American and African countries.

As a result of its pragmatic foreign policy, Indian economy witnessed a rapid development and by 1967 a noted economist P.S. Loknathan could claim that India was poised for rapid development. "Sufficient overheads have been created, sufficient basic industries have been established and, as for technical personnel, the country has an edge over many other developing countries." In 1967 India was able to secure order for the supply of railway wagons to South Korea in a world tender and it was also venturing out in joint ventures in many developing countries. India has been given the status of a full Dialogue Partner of ASEAN (Association of South East Asian Nations). It has good relations with APEC (Asia Pacific Economic Cooperation). India calls for South-South Cooperation and South Asian Association of Regional Cooperation (SAARC) marked the beginning of regional cooperation in South Asia which was established in 1985. A significant development was the South Asian Preferential Trade Agreement in 1993 which has been described as "an umbrella framework of rules providing for step-by-step liberalisation of trade within the region. It provides for periodic round of trade negotiations for exchange of trade concessions on tariff and related matters." It is expected that soon we will have a South Asia Free Trade Area (SAFTA) by the beginning of 21st century. Another landmark in the South Asian Cooperation has been the formation of South Asian Development Fund (SADF) for regional investment for projects in SAARC countries in 1996. By June 1996, a total of 5 million US dollars was collected as donation for the initial capital of the Fund, with India being the largest donor of US $ 1,605,000. While Pakistan contributed US $ 1,192,500, Bangla Desh and Sri Lanka gave US $ 567,500 each. Japan promised to pay US $ 500,000 to the fund. This fund is to be utilized in large scale manufacturing projects for different South Asian Countries.

The non-alignment policy was thus successful in getting financial and technical assistance, building up a huge industrial apparatus and development of agriculture which ultimately made India self-sufficient in food. There is no doubt that there are serious short-comings in Indian strategy of development which we have discussed elsewhere but it certainly creates the not very remote possibility of India becoming a world economic power in the 21st century. Therefore despite the disintegration of Soviet Union which led to the emergence of United States of America as the single dominating power, the policy of non-alignment is still relevant. Prime Minister P.V. Narasimha Rao, in 1992 in Tokyo, rightly said, "The pursuit of a non-aligned foreign policy is even more relevant today than ever before. Non-alignment basically consists of the espousal of the rights of nations to independence and development, regardless of the bloc phenomenon."

India—A Nuclear Power

A major shift in Indian foreign policy took place in 1998 when the Atal Behari Vajpayee Government decided to use the nucler option and exploded a series of five nucler devices in Pokhran. The Indian Government declared that the tests were conducted due to security considerations. The nuclear explosions drew a world wide condemnation and Pakistan retaliated by seven explosions to get an edge over India despite the US President Clinton's request not to do so and various concessions offered by the US in case it acceeded to US request.

It was a major shift in Indian foreign policy which had exercised self-restraint in conducting nuclear explosions after 1974's Pokharan I. However, so far as BJP is concerned there has been a consistency in its approach towards exercising the nuclear option. Its earlier form, the

Bhartiya Jan Sangh had always demanded that India should manufacture Atom Bomb to meet the external threats from Pakistan and China. It had very graciously and wholeheartedly supported the nuclear test conducted by Indira Gandhi Government in 1974. As Pakistan's secret nuclear weapon programme became more and more open in early 1990, the BJP demanded that the Indian Government exercise its nuclear option to restore the strategic balance in South Asia. The BJP manifestos issued during the Lok Sabha elections always talked about India opting for nuclear weapons. The 1995 election manifesto reiterated its commitment to 're-evaluate the country's nuclear policy and exercise the option to induct nuclear weapons' and 'to give India a role and position in world affairs commensurate with its size and capability.' The 1996 election manifesto also repeated the same position verbatim.

However, it is also a fact that explosion of nuclear devices had been in the minds of Indian policy makers even after the critical reactions to 1974 explosion. It was reported that India tried to explode nuclear devices in 1981 and 1995 but ultimately this was not done under US pressure.

In order to check the nuclear proliferation, there are two significant international treaties which envisage the nuclear monopoly of US., Russia, France, England and China. The first is Nuclear Non-Proliferation Treaty (NPT) of 1970 and secondly the Comprehensive Test Ban Treaty (CTBT) of 1996. The NPT is signed by 165 countries including the five-nuclear power states. India termed it discriminatory saying it allows the five nuclear power states to maintain their hegemony and deny the same to others and has, therefore, consistently opposed to sign it. The CTBT again is a clever move by the nuclear powers, specifically from two considerations. Firstly, when the CTBT talks began in 1994 and the participants agreed to conclude the talks by 1996, China, France and the US rushed to test bombs or announce plans for last-minute testing. The objective was to sign the CTBT and still retain the ability to go on developing fearsome nuclear weapons. Secondly, the US was initially opposed to CTBT but later on it was the main proposer. The reason could be found in the technological developments—the highly sophisticated super computers had arrived. The US can now stimulate high-yield tests in computers and their actual tests are not at all needed. But what about the other four nuclear powers? Obviously, they would not be aggreable to a comprehensive ban test. The US assured them of transfer of stimulation technology and thus their support was achieved. It is to be remembered that this simulation technology was demonstrated by India in its second series of tests. In other words, India has acquired the simulation technology and it does not need to conduct real tests. The CTBT was open for signature on September 24, 1996 and would be in force with effect from September 1996 subject to its ratification by 44 states.

It was because of the fears of definite sanctions being imposed against India that it did not conduct nuclear explosions after the Pokharan-I. It has been reported that the relevant files were pending before the successive Prime Ministers from Rao to Deve Gowda and I.K. Gujral. Everytime the Finance Ministry officials assessed the impact of sanctions and explained that the sanctions would hurt the on-going economic reforms.

After the explosions, Indian Prime Minister proudly declared "we are a nuclear weapon power." Pakistan also declared the same. The nuclear power countries promptly repudiated both the claims on the ground that as per the NPT, only such countries who had conducted explosions before 1967 had the nuclear power status.

Why India chose the nuclear option? There are many answers to this simple question. First, it has been pointed out that the internal contradictions in the BJP led Government were primarily responsible for explosions. Second, as pointed out earlier, the BJP has always stood for India opting for nuclear bombs. For BJP Pokharan II is a matter of national pride and honour. Third, there is consistency in Indian foreign policy so far as nuclear explosions are concerned. Right from Jawahar Lal Nehru, no Indian Prime Minister ever favoured India giving up the nuclear option. After Pokhran I, Indian policy makers only exercised self-restraint. Fourth, the BJP Government was aware of sanctions likely to be imposed in case India became a nuclear power. It opted for it in 1998 because CTBT was to become operative in 1999 and conducting nuclear explosions after that, would have invited far harsher sanctions. Fifth, the geo-political considerations were threatening the security environment of India. India's two neighbours—China and Pakistan have been a security threat. India had a war with China in 1962 which India lost and a considerable Indian area has been under Chinese illegal occupation. China is a nuclear power and entire India is within the range of chinese nuclear weapons. After the explosions, the chinese claimed that India had attacked China in 1962 and 90,000 square kilometer of chinese areas were under Indian occupation. With Pakistan, India had three armed conflicts in 1948, 1965 and 1971, besides the border-skirmishs which takes place every now and then. India and infact, the entire world was aware of Pakistan's secret nuclear weapon programme. Pakistan has been aiding and abetting various terrorist groups in India. These security threats from China and Pakistan had prompted, earlier also, India to go nuclear. Indian nuclear capability would, it was rightly believed, act as a deterent in case of both China as well as Pakistan.

After the explosion, the US government announced the sanctions it imposed against India for conducting nuclear tests which included stoppage of pending investments, new financial commitments and military assistance.

Canada, Sweden, Germany, Japan and Australia also anounced sanctions against India. Russia did not feel happy about the explosions but it did not go alongwith US in imposing sanctions. On the contrary, Russia agreed to sell two nuclear power reactors to be set up in Koodankulam in Tamil Nadu. This was a very significant success from Indian stand-point because with the conclusion of this agreement, the nearly two and a half decades of restrictions imposed by the western countries limiting India's access to atomic energy cooperation came to an end. Under the agreement, the Russians also promised to supply low enriched Uranium, the fuel for the two reactors.

Post Pokharan II saw two major developments. Firstly, the sanctions did not remain for a long time and most of them were gradually withdrawn. Secondly, Indo-US relations have improved in a big way. Infact for this first time India an excellent relation has with the US notwithstanding latter's relation with Pakistan. India was very quick in supporting President Bush's National Missile Defence (NMD) initiative. Certainly the nuclear explosions have not put India to any major disadvantage.

References

Appadorai A., *National Interest and India's Foreign Policy,* 1998, Delhi, Kalinga Publications.

Khanna V.N., *Foreign Policy of India,* 1997, New Delhi, Vikas Publishing House Pvt. Ltd.

Misra K.P. *Studies in Indian Foreign Policy,* 1969, Delhi, Vikas Publications

Nanda B.R., (Ed) *Indian Foreign Policy: The Nehru Years,* 1990, New Delhi, Radiant Publishers.

Rajan M.S., *Recent Essays on India's Foreign Policy,* 1997, Delhi, Kalinga Publications.

Outlook magazine, May 25 and June 29, 1998.

The Week magazine, May 24, 1998.

Index